John Betjeman

Letters

=========

Volume Two: 1951 to 1984

by the same author

John Betjeman Letters
Volume One: 1926 to 1951

JOHN BETJEMAN

Letters

Volume Two: 1951 to 1984

Edited and introduced by
Candida Lycett Green

Methuen

First published in Great Britain in 1995
by Methuen London
an imprint of Reed International Books Ltd
Michelin House, 81 Fulham Road, London SW3 6RB
and Auckland, Melbourne, Singapore and Toronto

A CIP catalogue record for this book
is available at the British Library
ISBN 0 413 66940 8

Typeset by Deltatype, Ellesmere Port, South Wirral
Printed and bound in Great Britain by
Mackays of Chatham Plc

For my mother and father

Contents

Preface

Ten years after my father's death in May 1984, the first volume of a selection of his letters was published. This second volume contains correspondence from the last three decades of his life. As I wrote in the Preface to *Volume One*, when my father died my mother, brother and I received hundreds of letters, not only from friends and acquaintances, but also from people he did not know, telling us what he meant to them. Following the publication of the first volume I once again received a mass of letters, mostly from strangers. 'As you say,' wrote Clement Smith, 'there are many people who never met JB, but who loved him. I am one of them.' David Engleheart, a schoolmaster who had been a pupil of JB's at Heddon Court prep school in 1930 wrote, 'Throughout my teaching life I have tried to impart English to children in your father's way. I read stories to them which he read to us, as well as his poems and prose.'

The years up to 1951 covered my father's life in London and Oxford and at his parents' holiday home in Trebetherick, Cornwall; his marriage to my mother, Penelope Chetwode, and their early years together in Uffington, in Ireland and in Farnborough. In 1951 the family moved house to Wantage in Berkshire and in 1954 my father also began to rent a small flat in London. His life was entering a new phase.

Working on this second volume of letters has been a sadder and harder task. I was able to stand apart from the first one, for the main part of it dealt with a time before I was born or was much aware of what was going on around me. From 1951 onwards I was fully conscious of, and completely involved with, the man who was first my father, then my mentor whom I sought to please above all others, and lastly, together with my husband Rupert, my best friend. For this reason, although I have chosen the letters to represent a little of his life's story, my connecting chapters are less objective than those I wrote for *Volume One*.

As John Betjeman's daughter, I cannot be objective, nor do I want to be. What I have written about his life is what I saw and what I know. My conversations with numerous friends and associates who knew him

well at particular periods of his life have also been of immense help –
people like his secretary Jill Menzies, who worked for him in the early
fifties, or the television director Ken Savidge, who made nearly forty
films with him throughout the sixties. I have also pieced together some
of his achievements and activities in the fields of literature, radio,
television and conservation. Though my chapter introductions may be
judged to cast him in a rosy light, I would not be being true to his
memory if I attempted to paint his portrait in any other way. Some
daughters may be able to judge their fathers from a distance. I can't.

There are two obvious gaps in the correspondence which serve to
distort this volume. My brother Paul, who has lived in America since
1961 and has only returned to England four times since, never keeps
correspondence of any kind (unlike his hoarding sister). Only one letter
written to him by my father survives. The second and more chasm-like
gap is the absence of any letters written by my father to his beloved
Elizabeth Cavendish who became, in effect, his other wife. Ever since I
embarked on editing the letters four years ago, Elizabeth has stuck to
her decision that my father's letters to her should be kept locked in the
Chatsworth archives for fifty years after his death. (My mother, on the
other hand, left all his letters to an American collector of Betjemaniana
who has subsequently made them accessible to the public at Yale
University.)

My father wrote to Elizabeth frequently during the fifties, often
about his family life, but from the sixties onwards, when they were
almost constantly together for over twenty years, his letters were
fewer. I hope that my father's love for both women comes through in
this book because it certainly came across to me during his lifetime. As
his daughter, I found the situation completely without conflict. In my
eyes there was never any competition. When my father was in
Cornwall or in London (which my mother hated and seldom visited
except for exhibitions or lectures) he was with Elizabeth; and when he
was at our home in Wantage and, much later, at Hay-on-Wye, he was
with my mother. In retrospect, and after talking to Elizabeth recently, I
think that he arranged things thus not only so that he could duck any
direct confrontation – great ducker that he was – but to protect me.
Heaven knows how I would have felt had there been a divorce. As
things turned out I was able to love Elizabeth without prejudice. When
my mother died in 1986, two years after my father, Elizabeth was the
first person I rang up.

The second volume has also been harder to compile in practical terms
than the first, partly because at a certain point in the late sixties my

father's handwriting became almost indecipherable even to the most practised transcribers, but overwhelmingly because of the sheer number of letters. They would fill an articulated lorry. From the fifties onwards, as he became more famous, friends and acquaintances began to hang on to their letters from him and so the amount of material I had to choose from was tenfold what it had been for *Volume One*. As to the letters written *to* him during this period, to which I needed to refer for background information, they, too, were legion. I returned to their home in the archives at the University of Victoria in British Columbia where I had spent time working on the first volume two years before. I booked into the same bed-and-breakfast, with its English rose-filled garden and glimpses of the Pacific Ocean, and through enforced solitude except at the kiwi fruit-studded breakfasts with my landlady, was able to concentrate on extracting various essences of my father's life from the thirty thousand or so letters I had not seen during the first round.

Over the ensuing months, various of my long-suffering friends who are knowledgeable in a particular subject were inundated with my questions. One such friend, Michael White, received all unsolved theatrical and film problems, one of which was a line in a letter from my father referring to a dinner with the film director Tony Richardson and 'Yalonde'. Who was Yalonde? Michael asked many of Tony's friends and even rang two people in Los Angeles and I was surprised when he told me his enquiries had reached a dead end. On a second look at the manuscript of the letter it became perfectly obvious that Yalonde was in fact 'a blonde'. My father's handwriting had let me down again.

I have taken almost no editorial liberties, save for translating into ordinary English my father's letters to my mother (and hers to him, when quoting them) from the sort of cockney mixed with Greek code which they regularly employed in correspondence. I have left in a couple of untranslated letters as examples, but their mad spellings were such a personal thing that if anyone else, including myself, reads them for more than a few sentences they serve to irritate and to veil rather than to clarify the closeness which existed between them. My father often wrote entire letters in capitals to make himself legible and these have been typeset conventionally; however, his occasional, often eccentric, use of capitals for emphasis has been retained.

As in *Volume One* many of my father's letters contain funny drawings and these have been included wherever possible. He usually wrote the date in roman numerals but I have made all the dates uniform. He was a stickler for correct spelling and I found hardly any spelling errors, except occasionally in names, which I have corrected. He was also keen on proper punctuation, but since a lot of his letters were dashed off, he sometimes did not have time to read through them. I have inserted the barest minimum where the sense might be misconstrued without it. I have referred to my father throughout as 'JB' for ease; in footnotes I have referred to my mother as 'PB', to my brother as 'PSGB', to Elizabeth Cavendish as 'EC' and to my husband Rupert as 'RLG'. Thumbnail sketches of the friends and acquaintances of JB's who appear often in this volume are given in the Dramatis Personae at the end, rather than a long footnote at their first mention. More often than not they are also mentioned in my introductory chapters and the index will help point towards them. Each chapter sketches the unfolding story of my father's life, but when it comes to references within a particular letter, various bits of information may be repeated as necessary for clarification.

Writing about the last ten years of my father's life was a painful experience, as I recorded his friends dying and his own health deteriorating. When I had to face writing the last chapter and selecting the letters for it, I found myself making any excuse not to begin. Of course I was in floods of tears writing the last paragraph. What woman in my shoes wouldn't have been? I had lived so close to my father for the last four years and suddenly I was reliving the experience of his death.

For a time after finishing the book I felt bereft. I needed him to turn to. He understood better than anyone the point of being alive – how terrible it is a lot of the time and how wonderful at others. Now, later, I can go back to his poetry and recall him with an overwhelming vividness. No father could leave a greater gift to a daughter.

Candida Lycett Green
Compton Beauchamp
April 1995

Acknowledgements

I would like to thank the following individuals and institutions for providing letters (and some articles) and for the immense trouble some of them have taken in finding, sorting and copying them:

All Souls College, Oxford, for letters to John Sparrow; Verily Anderson for a letter to Paul Paget; Lucy Archer for a letter to Raymond Erith; Tim Arlott for a letter to John Arlott; the Athenæum Archives for a letter to the Athenæum; Jill Balcon for letters to C. Day Lewis; Mollie Baring for letters to Desmond Baring; the Estate of Edward Bawden for a letter to Edward Bawden; the Literary Executors of the late Sir Cecil Beaton for letters from Sir Cecil Beaton; Beinecke Rare Book and Manuscript Library, Yale University, for letters to Nicolas Bentley, Bessie Betjemann, Penelope Betjeman, Mr Hubbins, Philip Larkin, James Lees-Milne, Dan MacNabb, Peter W. Mills, Gilbert Nelson, Alan Pryce-Jones, Siegfried Sassoon and letters from PB to JB; Dr G. Kinsman-Barker of the Betjeman Centre for a letter to Mr, Mrs and Miss Prideaux-Brune; Birr Scientific and Heritage Foundation and the Friends of Birr Castle, Ireland, for letters to Anne and Michael Rosse; Bodleian Library, Oxford, for letters to Martyn Skinner and Janet and Reynolds Stone; Special Collections Library, Boston University, for letters to G. B. Stern and Terence de Vere White; British Broadcasting Corporation Archives, Caversham, Reading, for letters to Mary Adams, Television Booking Department BBC, Simon Phipps and Roy Plomley; British Library, London, for letters to Jack Beddington, Candida Lycett Green, Evelyn Waugh and Laura Waugh; British Rail Archives for a letter to Peter Parker; Mrs Bulmer Thomas for a letter to Ivor Bulmer Thomas; Cambridge University Library for a letter to Stanley Morison; Jonathan Cecil for letters to David Cecil; Jan Channel for a letter to Anne Channel; Chatsworth Archives for letters to Nancy Mitford and Pamela Jackson; Vivien Chigwell for letters to Edith and Oliver Garratt; Christ Church, Oxford, for letters to Tom and Ena Driberg; Churchill College, Cambridge, for letters to Cecil Roberts; Alan Clark for a letter from Kenneth Clark; Nest Cleverdon for a letter to Douglas Cleverdon; Collins Archives, Glasgow, for letters to W. A. R. Collins; David Cobb for a letter to the Kilpatrick family; Rosie d'Avigdor Goldsmid for a letter to Henry d'Avigdor Goldsmid; Valerie Eliot for letters to T. S. Eliot; Eton College Library for a letter to Diana Cooper; Faber and Faber for a letter to Charles Monteith; Anne Farquhar for a letter to Edgar Walmsley; Patrick

Garland for a letter to Mr Garland; Beryl Graves for a letter to Robert Graves; Rupert Hart-Davis for a review by William Plomer; Lady Dorothy Heber-Percy for a letter to Robert Heber-Percy; Huntington Library, Pasadena, California, for letters to Kingsley Amis and Patrick Kinross; Peter Patrick Hemphill for a letter to Emily Villiers-Stuart; David Higham Associates for a letter from Tom Driberg; Michael Imison Playwrights Ltd for a letter from Noël Coward; Richard Ingrams for a letter to Malcolm Muggeridge; Trustees of the Edward James Foundation, West Dean, Sussex, for a letter to Edward James; Ginnie James for a letter to Nancy Dennistoun; Mrs V. Johnson for letters to David Johnson; King's College, Cambridge, for letters to Anne, Anthony and George Barnes and E. M. Forster; Deirdre Levi for a review by Cyril Connolly; Lincoln College, Oxford, and Anne Lancaster for letters to and from Osbert and Karen Lancaster; Mary Ling for a letter to Freddie Ling; London Transport Museum for a letter to Maurice and Richard Elliott; Rupert Lycett Green for a letter to Angela Grimthorpe; Magdalen College, Cambridge, for a letter to Francis Turner; Diana Marr-Johnson for a letter from Robin Maugham; McFarlin Library, University of Tulsa, Oklahoma, for letters to Cyril Connolly; McPherson Library, University of Victoria, British Columbia, for letters and carbon copies of letters to Robert Aikman, Sidney Bernstein, Michael Berry, Anthony Blunt, John Edward Bowle, Lionel Brett, Sister Brigitta, Alan Clarkson Rose, Alec Clifton-Taylor, Peter Crookston, H. C. Dear, Lionel Esher, Robert Etty, Ian Fletcher, Denis Forman, Great Eastern Hotel, Miss Hargreaves, H. de Cronin Hastings, Mrs Howells, Canon Jenner, Brian Johnson, Miss Knight, Graham Landon, John D. K. Lloyd, Ralph May, Keith Miller, James Mitchell, Mr Neobard, Mark Ogilvie-Grant, Edmund Penning-Rowsell, Mr Percival, Edward Pickering, Archie Polkinghorne, Peter Quennell, John Summerson, Miss M. L. Tudor, Miss E. Wakeham, Nigel Watt, David Wemyss, Mrs White and Harry Williams; Fionn Morgan for a letter from Ian Fleming; Sally Morris for a letter to Marcus Morris; the Estate of Bryan Moyne for letters to Bryan Moyne; John Murray Publishers' Archives for letters to Edward Ardizzone, Jock Murray and John Foster White, and for an article by Jock Murray; the *Observer* for a letter to David Astor; Helen Osborne and the Estate of John Osborne for letters to and from John Osborne; Patrick Perry for a letter to Mrs Braddell and letters to Lionel Perry; Pierpont Morgan Library, New York, for letters to Siegfried Sassoon; Myfanwy Piper for letters to John Piper; Harry Ransom Humanities Research Center, University of Texas, Austin, for letters to Elizabeth Bowen, Rupert Croft-Cooke and Compton Mackenzie; the BAL Manuscripts and Archives Department, Royal Institute of British Architects, London, for letters to Sir Edward and Prudence Maufe and H. S. Goodhart-Rendel; Martha Robertson for a letter to T. A. Robertson; St John's College, Cambridge, for letters to Cecil Beaton; Bruce Shand for letters to P. Morton Shand; Daniel Skinner for letters from Martyn Skinner; John Smith for extracts from his diary; The Society for the Protection of Ancient Buildings for a letter to Monica Dance; Henry Sotheran and Sons for a letter to Mrs Noonan; Natasha Spender for letters to Stephen Spender; Terence Stamp for a letter to Colonel G. A. L. Chetwynd-Talbot; Gillian Sutro for a letter to John Sutro; David Synnott for a letter to Pierce Synnott; Tate Gallery Archives, London, for letters to Kenneth and Jane Clark; Mary Taylor for a letter to Geoffrey Taylor; Michael Thomas for a letter to Peggy Thomas; Trinity College, Dublin, for a letter to Paul Henry; University of Durham for letters to William Plomer; University of East Anglia for a letter to Joan Zuckerman; University of Hull, for a letter to Rupert Alec-Smith; Hugo Vickers for a letter to Laura Canfield; *Vogue* magazine for a letter to Penelope Gilliatt; Wadham College, Oxford, for a letter from Maurice Bowra; the Muniment Room and Library, Westminster Abbey, for a letter to Edward Carpenter; Margaret Whittick for a letter to Frank Rutherford; Woodrow Wyatt for a letter to the Minister of Housing and Local Government, Whitehall; and Patsy Zeppel for letters to Norman Williams

and the following for their own letters (or extracts):

Maria Aitken, John Aldridge, Noel Annan, David Attenborough, Elsie Avril, Mollie Baring, Ashley Barker, Ralph Bennett, Isaiah Berlin, Michael Bolan, Sophie Bridgewater, Craig Brown, Jemima Brown, Hugh Casson, Jan Channel, Mary Clive, Deirdre Connolly, Patrick Cullinan, Anita Dent, Debo Devonshire, Joan Dyer, Margaret Anne Elton, Duncan Fallowell, Phyllis Foran, Christopher Fry, Patrick Garland, Dorothy Girouard, Mark Girouard, Rosie d'Avigdor Goldsmid, Harman Grisewood, John Guest, John Hadfield, Alice Hardy, Billa Harrod, Rupert Hart-Davis, Bevis Hillier, Laura Hornak, Edward Hornby, Simon Hornby, Barry Humphries, Richard Ingrams, Gerard Irvine, Harry Jarvis, Simon Jenkins, Wayland and Elizabeth Kennet, Joan Kunzer, Pansy Lamb, Audrey Lees, James Lees-Milne, Joan and Paddy Leigh Fermor, Ronald Liddiard, Mary Ling, Hugh Linstead, Constance and Stephen Lycett Green, David Lycett Green, Endellion Lycett Green, Lucy Lycett Green, Imogen Lycett Green, Michael Maclagan, Spike Milligan, Eddie Mirzoeff, Frank Muir, John O'Dea, Charles Osborne (for a piece from his memoirs), Elizabeth Ponsonby, Peter Parker (for his speech), Anthony Powell, Alan Ross, Ken Savidge, Judith Scott, Ronald Searle, Alastair Service, Bruce Shand, Tony Snowdon, the Society of Authors, Gavin Stamp, Jonathan Stedall, Charles Thomson, Henry Thorold, Juliet Townsend, Laurence Udall, Roger Venables, Auberon Waugh, Laurence Whistler, Mary Wilson, Woodrow Wyatt and Patsy Zeppel.

Especial thanks to:

John Bodley and Jane Fever at Faber and Faber; Antonia Bradford of BBC Radio 4; Fiona Clark of the Royal Literary Fund; Susan Evans of Welsh Historical Monuments and Records; Vicki Fielden of Swindon Lending

Library; William Filmer Sankey of the Victorian Society; Vincent Giroud of the Beinecke Library, Yale University; Tom Greeves of the Bedford Park Society; Andrew Griffin of St Bartholomew Hospital Archives; Monica Halpin of Churchill College, Cambridge; Richard Halsey of English Heritage; Warwick Hirst of the State Library of New South Wales; John Jones and Sarah Cooper of Balliol College, Oxford; Bernard Kankas of British Rail; Mark Le Fanu of the Society of Authors; Alan Bell and all the staff of the London Library; Graham Melville of the British Film Institute; Rebecca Morgan of the Landmark Trust; Richard Mortimer of Westminster Abbey; Virginia Murray at Murrays; Chris Petter, Terry Tuey and Terry Humby of the McPherson Library, University of Victoria, British Columbia; Liz Salter and Beverly Harrison of BBC Manchester; Neil Somerville of BBC Archives; Neil Swatton of the Swindon Railway Museum; and Tim Whittaker of the National Trust.

I would also like to thank the following for their time, wisdom and moral support:

Karinna Alexander-Berne, Susie Allison, Mollie Baring, Olivia Bell, Hercules Bellville, David Blaine, Sister Mary Bland, Edward Blishen, Steve Bowyer, Alice Boyd, John Byrne, Maurice Craig, Patrick Cullinan, Mrs Dance, Anita Dent, Pamela Fildes, Reverend John Gaskell, Mark Girouard, Hugh Grafton, Edward Hornby, Simon Hornby, Simon Jenkins, Jim Lees-Milne, Paddy and Joan Leigh-Fermor, Deirdre and Peter Levi, Amabel Lindsay, Jill Menzies, Eddie Mirzoeff, Shirley Nicolson, Victoria Oaksey, Andrew Parker Bowles, Tristram Powell, Joan Price, Roger Pringle, Ted Roberts, Clement Semmler, Bruce Shand, John Smith, Tony Snowdon, Gillian Sutro, Deborah Taylor, Hugo Vickers, Richard and Margot Walker, Mary Wilson, William Witham and Patsy Zeppel

and the following for inordinate kindness:

Gavin Stamp for helping with the architectural letters; Elizabeth Cavendish, Debo Devonshire, Billa Harrod and my brother Paul Betjeman for reading the typescript; Barry Humphries for helping with Australia and more; Chris Holgate for his design; Peregrine St Germans for housing me during the home straight; Alan Bell for helping with transcriptions; Douglas Matthews for compiling the index; Gerard Irvine for ecclesiastical help; John Saumarez Smith for solving mysteries; Michael White for theatrical help; Jean Gordon for helping me in British Columbia; Kenneth Savidge for helping with film letters; Colin Sainsbury for a September's research; Nickie Johnson for her word-processing wizardry; Leonie Brown and Jenny Whittaker for secretarial support; Liza Moylett for looking on the bright side; Colin Leach, Alan Bell, Harry Jarvis, Gavin Stamp and Jonathan Stedall for reading the galleys; Hugh Massingberd for his selflessness; and Mary O'Donovan of Methuen for superb copy-editing and thoughtfulness.

My undying thanks to:

Richard Ingrams for generous help, the ever-patient Geoffrey Strachan, my editor, who steered me gently home, Desmond Elliott for everything and Rupert, my husband, for putting up with me.

Finally, thanks are due to the following for providing photographs of themselves and others (all photographs not credited come from Betjeman family archives):

Joyce Batchelor for 11c; Mollie Baring for 9b; Anthony Barnes for 3a and 9c; Jane Bown for 24; Camera Press Ltd for 10b, 12c, 13b, 15b, 16b and 16c; Lady Elizabeth Cavendish for 5a; the Duchess of Devonshire for 5c; Mark Girouard for 11b; the Hulton Deutsch Collection for 9a, 9d and 10a; Gerard Irvine for 11a; the Reverend Wilfrid Jarvis for 11d; Lady Lancaster for 12b; James Lees-Milne for 12d; Joan Leigh Fermor for 13a; Deirdre Levi for 10c; John Murray (Publishers) Ltd for 12a and 13d; the National Portrait Gallery for 16a; Myfanwy Piper for 14b; David Pryce-Jones for 14c; Anthony Skinner for 15a; Lady Spender for 15c; Jonathan Stedall for 14a, 15d, 18a, 19b, 20b, 22c, 23a, 23b and 23c; Times Newspapers Ltd for 14d; Lady Wilson of Rievaulx for 16d and 18b; and the *Yorkshire Post* for 8.

Grateful thanks are due to the following for permission to quote from copyright material:

Curtis Brown Ltd for Ogden Nash's limerick on page 255, published in a slightly altered version as 'A handsome young rodent named Gratian' in *There's Always Another Windmill* (copyright © 1968 by Ogden Nash); R. S. Thomas for lines from his poem 'Night and Morning' on page 103 (copyright © 1958 by R. S. Thomas); and A. P. Watt Ltd for lines from W. B. Yeats's poem 'Oedipus at Colonus' on page 11 (copyright © Michael Yeats).

Illustrations

Part-title illustrations by JB:

1. The Mead, Wantage, Berkshire.
2. CB's bedroom window at the Mead.
3. Self-portrait for 'Late Flowering Lust'.
4. JB and EC with the Lancasters.
5. PB camping with CB, Marco the dog and CB's pony Dirk.
6. St Enodoc Church, Cornwall.
7. Illustration for 'Overcliffe'.
8. Self-portrait.
9. Careysville, County Waterford.
10. Illustration for 'Our Padre'.

Plate sections photographs:

1a The Mead, Wantage, Berkshire.
1b Group photograph at the Mead, 1952.
1c PB at the Mead, c. 1953.
2a On holiday on the Camroses' yacht *Virginia*, 1951.
2b EC on board the *Virginia*.
3a On holiday in France with the Barneses, c. 1956.
3b Outdoors lunch party at the Mead, 1959.
4a CB in 1951.
4b CB and PSGB at the Mead stables, 1954.
4c PSGB with Willie and Cara Lancaster.
5a EC in the early fifties.
5b Tea break while filming at Fairford, 1956.
5c Speech Day at St Elphin's School, Darley Dale, 1958.
6a A lunch partay with the Barings at Ardington, 1961.
6b PB in Andalusia, Spain, October 1961.
6c JB with CB and Ginny Dennistoun at the Mead, 1962.
7a Moonlight picnic at Knighton Bushes, 1962.

John Betjeman – A Chronology
1951 to 1984

(Book titles are in italic, television film titles in quotation marks)

1944–51   Regular book reviewer for *Daily Herald*.
1946–78   Serves on the Oxford Diocesan Advisory Committee.
1948–63   Serves on the London Diocesan Advisory Committee.
1949–54   Literary adviser/editor to *Time and Tide*.
1951   *The English Scene* (Cambridge University Press).
          Shropshire: A Shell Guide (Faber and Faber) with John Piper.
          Moves to the Mead, Wantage, Berkshire.
1951–59   Weekly book reviews for *Daily Telegraph*.
1952   *First and Last Loves* (John Murray).
1952–62   'Men and Buildings' column for *Daily Telegraph*.
1952–70   Serves on Royal Fine Art Commission.
1954   *Poems in the Porch* (John Murray).
          A Few Late Chrysanthemums (John Murray).
          Rents 43 Cloth Fair, London.
1954–58   Weekly column 'City and Suburban' for *Spectator*.
1954–77   Serves on committee of the Society for the Protection of
          Ancient Buildings.
1955   'Discovering Britain', a series of twenty-six short films
          (Shell).
          Foyle Poetry Prize for *A Few Late Chrysanthemums*.
1956   *The English Town in the Last Hundred Years*.
          'Our National Heritage: Stained Glass at Fairford' (BP/
          Shell).
          Loines Award for poetry.
1957   *English Love Poems* edited with Geoffrey Taylor (Faber and
          Faber).
          'Beauty in Trust' (BP/Shell).
          Poet in Residence at the University of Cincinnati, Ohio,
          USA.
          Honorary Associate, Royal Institute of British Architects.
1958   *Collins Guide to English Parish Churches* (Collins).
          Collected Poems (John Murray).

Duff Cooper Memorial Prize for *Collected Poems*.
Founds the Victorian Society with Anne Rosse.

1958–84 Vice-chairman and committee member of the Victorian
Society.

1959   *Altar and Pew* (John Murray).
Foyle Poetry Prize for *Collected Poems*.
Honorary D. Litt., Reading University.

1960   *Summoned by Bells* (John Murray).
A Hundred Sonnets by Charles Tennyson Turner, selected in
collaboration with Sir Charles Tennyson (Hart-Davis).
'Our National Heritage: Journey into the Weald of Kent'
(BP/Shell).
Queen's Gold Medal for Poetry (for *Collected Poems*).
Commander, Order of the British Empire.
Buys Treen, Trebetherick, Cornwall.

1960–68 'ABC of Churches', a series of twenty-six films (BBC).

1961   Visits Australia (five weeks).

1961–62 Euston Arch demolished.
Collected Poems (with additional poems, John Murray).
A Ring of Bells (John Murray).
'Steam and Stained Glass' (ATV).
'Wales and the West', a series of six films (TWW).
Coal Exchange demolished.

1963   'A Hundred Years Underground' (London Transport).
'Wales and the West', a further series of four films (TWW)

1964   *Cornwall: A Shell Guide* (updated, Faber and Faber).
'Discovering Britain with John Betjeman', a series of five
films (BP/Shell).

1964–7   Regular feature for *Weekend Telegraph*.

1965   *The City of London Churches* (Pitkin Pictorials).
Honorary LL.D, Aberdeen University.

1966   *High and Low* (John Murray).
'Journey to Bethlehem' (BBC).
'Betjeman at Random', a series of four films (BBC).

1967   'The Picture Theatre' (BBC).
'Tale of Canterbury' (Rediffusion).
'Betjeman's London', a series of six films (Rediffusion).
Six Betjeman Songs (Duckworth).

1968   'Contrasts: Tennyson: A Beginning and an End' (BBC).
'Footprints: the Finest Work in England: Isambard
Kingdom Brunel' (BBC).

	Companion of Literature, Royal Society of Literature.
1969	*Victorian and Edwardian London* (Batsford).
	'Bird's Eye View: Beside the Seaside' (BBC).
	'Bird's Eye View: The Englishman's Home' (BBC).
	Knight Bachelor.
	Commissioner of the Royal Commission on Historical Monuments.
1970	*Collected Poems* (enlarged third edition, John Murray).
	Ghastly Good Taste (second edition, Anthony Blond).
	Ten Wren Churches (Editions Alecto).
	'Four with Betjeman: Victorian Architects and Architecture'.
	'Look Stranger: John Betjeman on the Isle of Man'.
	'Railways for Ever'.
1971	*Victorian and Edwardian Oxford* (Batsford).
	'That Well Known Store in Knightsbridge' (BBC).
	'The Isle of Wight' (BBC).
	'Bird's Eye View: A Land for All Seasons' (BBC).
	Honorary Fellow, Royal Institute of British Architects.
	Visits Australia (three months).
1972	*Victorian and Edwardian Brighton* (Batsford).
	London's Historic Railway Stations (John Murray).
	A Pictorial History of English Architecture (John Murray).
	'Betjeman in Australia', a series of four films (BBC/ABC).
	'Thank God it's Sunday', a series of two films (BBC).
	Poet Laureate, 10 October.
	The Mead sold.
1973	'Metroland' (BBC).
	Rents 29 Radnor Walk, London.
1974	*A Nip in the Air* (John Murray).
	Victorian and Edwardian Cornwall (Batsford).
	'A Passion for Churches' (BBC).
1975	Visits Canada for Macdonald Stuart Foundation.
1976	'Summoned by Bells' (BBC).
	'Vicar of this Parish: Betjeman on Kilvert' (BBC).
1977	*Metroland* (Warren).
	Archie and the Strict Baptists, illustrated by Phillida Gili (John Murray).
	'The Queen's Realm' (BBC).
1978	*The Best of Betjeman* (John Murray).
1979	'John Betjeman's Dublin' (BBC).

	'John Betjeman's Belfast' (BBC).
1980	*Church Poems* (John Murray).
	'Nationwide: Southend Pier' (BBC).
	'Betjeman's Britain' (Anglia TV).
	'Late Flowering Love' (Charles Wallace Picture Co).
1981	'Nationwide: St Mary le Strand' (BBC).
1982	*Uncollected Poems* (John Murray).
1983	'Time with Betjeman', a series of seven films (BBC).
1984	Dies, Trebetherick, 19 May.

One:

In a red provincial town

─────

1951 to 1953

At the end of a long-walled garden
    in a red provincial town,
A brick path led to a mulberry –
    scanty grass at its feet.
I lay under blackening branches
    where the mulberry leaves hung down
Sheltering ruby fruit globes
    from a Sunday-tea-time heat.
                    'The Cottage Hospital'

In September 1951 we moved from Farnborough, high up in the
Berkshire Downs, to the market town of Wantage in the vale below.
Our new home, the Mead, had once been a modest seventeenth-
century farmhouse, to which its Victorian owners, who had tile-hung
its southern face, had added a red-brick villa at the eastern end.

The house stood among fields near the middle of the town with a
view towards the church of St Peter and St Paul whose bells chimed the
quarters and played a hymn every third hour. Letcombe Brook
meandered below, just beyond the public footpath which cut through
the bottom field. In the garden there was an ancient, lumpy yew hedge
dividing the vegetables from the lawn, alongside which ran a bed of red
roses bordered by cat mint. A huge walnut tree said to be the oldest in
Berkshire stood at the far end of the lawn and beyond it, from all our
bedroom windows, you could see the downs. At the back of the house
across an orchard there was a small Victorian cowshed where my
mother set up the dairy for her Guernsey cows and two stables in whose
loft my brother and I spent our days playing '78' records on a wind-up
gramophone.

Once again, it was JB who chose the décor and this time he went to
the church furnishers, G. F. Watts and Company, who sold ecclesiastical wallpapers and materials for vestries and altar fronts, many of them
designed by the Victorian architect Bodley. There was a gloomy
Gothic 'Kinnersley' design in terracotta for the hall and a dirty blue
tendrilly design for the drawing room. I was mortified. All I craved

were regency stripes. JB wrote to Alan Pryce-Jones (December 1951), 'The Watts and Co. papers are a terrific success, it's just like living in Nottingham Art Gallery.'[1] JB hung all the pictures at the Mead himself, a series of three-foot-high brass rubbings in Arts and Crafts frames in the dining room, the Temple of Flora down the bedroom passage, my mother's aquatints of India in the spare room, and voluptuous Pre-Raphaelites in the drawing room. JB's library was in the eastern Victorian end. His work table was in the middle of the room, and even with the window shut you could still hear the church bells.

I loved the walk to church with him on Sunday mornings along the footpath beside the brook, across the bridge and up the slight incline between the high red-brick garden walls of Doctor Squires's house and the vicarage. JB enjoyed the incense-laden nine o'clock sung mass the best. We always sat in the same place, halfway up the aisle on the left-hand side, and always behind two Low Church and disapproving ladies who wore hats like hot-water-bottle covers flopping over their grey buns. They never crossed themselves or genuflected during the Creed. We did. They coughed often. Miss Pronger, the local chemist's daughter, remembered sitting next to JB once: 'During the sermon he decided that he was cold and started to put on his overcoat. In an absent-minded manner he thrust his arm down the wrong sleeve. By now he was standing up and, in his mischievous way, he started to laugh. He was lovely. I particularly liked his hats in spite of the fact that they looked as if they had "suffered".'[2] JB often looked up at the roof during services as though he was drinking in the architecture. On the way home again he would pick up litter along the footpath with a spike on the end of his walking-stick. He *hated* litter.

Meanwhile my mother flung herself into Roman Catholic Sunday mornings, befriending several large local Irish families and trying to force a friendship between myself and a certain Sean Connolly whom I loathed. By lunchtime all was ecumenical again and the same old friends kept coming – Maurice Bowra, John Sparrow, John and Myfanwy Piper and Osbert and Karen Lancaster. There was a certain set pattern to life at the Mead. I never remember a Sunday lunch without singing round the piano afterwards and, if we weren't at the Mead, we were at Faringdon with Robert Heber-Percy. John Arlott stayed once a year as regularly as clockwork for the Wantage Cricket Club dinner. Freddie Ling, who was suffering from depression having left the Cowley Fathers, stayed for long stints, as did Cyril Joad who was dying of cancer. We went for two weeks every summer to

Trebetherick and Patrick Kinross stayed with us every Christmas. The 'Miss Butlers', Edmée and Molly, who had been my parents' neighbours in Uffington in the thirties and had lived in Lyme Regis since the war, moved to 'The Knoll' in our road, just two orchards away. They lunched with us most Christmas Days and still called my parents 'Mr and Mrs Betjeman'. They kept up their Edwardian formality until the last.

Bored by the milking and inspired by the brook, my mother planted a dozen willow trees and started a waterfowl farm. She bought a commercial incubator, which was always going wrong, and bred and sold Aylesbury, Peking, Silver Appleyard and Black East Indian ducks as well as Roman and Greyback geese (which sold for four and five guineas apiece). Her writing paper was designed by Reynolds Stone with a wood engraving printed on duck-egg-blue paper. She corresponded with the zoologist Solly Zuckerman about muck mysticism and the special properties of waterfowl mess. I kept a duck called Jemima in my bedroom who lived for twelve years and sometimes followed me into the town. JB preferred the ducks to the focal point of my life, my pony Dirk, which, despite my being ashamed of his poetic name, carried me to victory in every event I entered. At the peak of my career, in the summer of 1952, when my picture was in the local newspaper nearly every week, JB rang the telephone operator one day in order to send a telegram. He was asked to spell his name out, at which the operator said, 'Oh, are you any relation of the little girl who wins all the prizes at the horse shows?'

My brother fared well at Eton during his first few terms but was often embarrassed by parental visits, because of JB's dishevelled appearance. JB was genuinely upset when he learned about this and made considerable and unsuccessful efforts to tidy himself up and look like other parents. He got on extremely well with Paul's housemaster, Oliver Van Oss, and remained friends with him ever afterwards. 'Paul's reports are good, he is an entertaining and independent boy with a clear mind, rather too clear at times,' Van Oss wrote from Eton in 1952. 'He likes things to be definite. He proved a hopeless library fag and was dethroned for casualness, etc. I hope he remembers how hard it is for certain characters to pretend to be valets when he himself is in authority. He has also become rather a good footballer. Very much of a character is Betjie and I value his presence a lot.'[3]

Gradually we all settled into our new life at the Mead. Although I yearned for Farnborough, JB preferred the anonymity of Wantage where, in those early years, he could walk through the town unrecognised. He wrote to his old friend Mr Boswell, the Bookings Manager of the BBC, 'I have returned from Squiredom to a villa and the middle classes from which I sprang. . . . Penelope burnt the waste-paper basket in my library this morning, luckily the books are safe. Jill, my dear secretary, has flu.'4

JB was more than a little in love with Jill Menzies, who had arrived to live with us just before the move from Farnborough. She had written to him, 'I am twenty-two and educated at Milton Mount College, Crawley, Sussex, at St Anne's Society, Oxford where I obtained a second class honours degree in French last summer, and at St Godric's Secretarial College. I can do 100 to 120 words a minute. I find any kind of artistic work interesting and important.'5. JB had arranged to interview her in the offices of *Time and Tide* where he worked on Mondays. Lady Rhondda, JB's formidable editor, had said, 'If she's good-looking, John, take her, because she'll be more confident and hence better at her work.' She had arrived in a navy blue mackintosh wearing a knitted hat. 'When John first saw me,' remembers Jill, 'he said, "Oh *gosh*," and then after a long pause he said, "Are you High?" and I replied, "Middle Stump." He then asked me if I was good at doing up parcels because he needed to send a lot of review books back every week. I said I wasn't – he didn't seem to mind, he took me on.'6

Jill lived as the family. She slept in the old end of the house next to my bedroom and we shared the same bathroom with the brown lino floor. After breakfast JB used to retire to his library and dictate letters to her. 'He'd answer every single letter and some of them from awful people sending hopeless poetry to him,' she remembers. 'It was so good of him because he really didn't need to take quite so much trouble – it took up such a lot of his time. Sometimes I could tell he was *longing* to escape and go on an outing to a church or somewhere and in the afternoon he quite often would. He was the most generous person I've ever met in my life. He was one of those people who, however low he felt, never inflicted it on anyone else; he was always ready to listen to your problems, though. I don't know *when* he ever fitted his poetry in, there were masses of little bits of poetry he used to write, and he left it all over the house – it might just be two lines. I used to make copies of everything I found and if they were in a fairly final form I'd send them to Jock Murray, otherwise I'd keep all the scraps in a drawer.'

JB worried about not writing enough poetry. Between 1951 and 1959 he wrote nearly a thousand book reviews for the *Daily Telegraph*. Sometimes Jill helped him with the reading. 'He really hated the reviewing; he used to absolutely dread it.' Two or three times a month he wrote articles for *Punch* when his friend Malcolm Muggeridge became editor, and he also wrote for any other magazine that offered him enough money, from *Harper's Bazaar* to *Everybody's Weekly*.

JB's old friend John Lehmann wrote to him (15 October 1953), 'I am sure you have heard about the *London Magazine* which I am starting in the New Year as an entirely literary monthly. Poems, stories, critical articles and other prose pieces.'[7] JB sent Lehmann his new poem 'The Song of a Night Club Proprietress'. The *London Magazine* became a platform for many of JB's new poems throughout the next two decades and Alan Ross, its subsequent editor, one of his close friends.

All through the fifties JB was still doing a lot of broadcasting, some for the Home Service and some for the Western Region based in Bristol. But his chief work at home was to try and finish the *Collins Guide to English Parish Churches* which had been under contract since 1944. His collaborator in correlating the lists of churches was Mr Edward Long, a hard-working, pedantic, rather nice man whose patience had been much tried over delays on the book.

'Colonel' Kolkhorst wrote to Jill commiserating about what an awful boss JB must be and offering an Edward Lear-like support in verse: 'I will not flinch, I will not care/If Johnny B shall pull my hair/I will not cry, I will not speak/But turn to him the other cheek./I will not yield to blank despair/Should Johnny kick me down the stair/I will not blush, I will not blench/If Johnny B my heart should wrench.'[8] To JB he wrote, 'You have never been so much at the top of your form or looking so supremely Shakespeare-like, domed forehead, illuminated skin, piercing black eyes (and I am convinced it is Jill's good management). Jill is quite wonderful, as I observed on Sunday. What a delicious light-scented afternoon, thank you so much for the joyous visitation.'[9]

Every Monday JB went to London to work as literary adviser and poetry editor for *Time and Tide*, the weekly magazine which was started in 1920 by Lady Rhondda who managed it for thirty-eight years. It was quite literally her whole life. She was the granddaughter of a coal miner from the Rhondda Valley and the daughter of a colliery owner, the first Viscount Rhondda, whose viscountcy she inherited. As a staunch Liberal she wanted to fill the gap between the *Spectator* and *New Statesman*, but politically *Time and Tide* never cut much ice. On the other hand it had great cachet. Lady Rhondda lived with the high-minded, High Anglican, highly cultivated Theodora Bosanquet (who had been Henry James's secretary) in a flat in Arlington House behind the Ritz Hotel. She always had lunch in the Caprice just next door and at one point had financed its famous restaurateur, Mario. She was

extremely greedy, matriarchal and difficult to work for. She expected
her workforce of fifteen or so to *live* for *Time and Tide* as she did. The
small 'book room' of 34 Bloomsbury Street where JB worked was on
the first floor. It had filthy windows and drifts of dust hovered on the
torn, dark green lino. The room was full to bursting point with books.
To reach it, JB had to walk past the sub-editor Joanna Bourne's
desk. 'Her face would literally light up,' remembers Pamela Fildes
who, together with Margaret Grady, was one of the 'book room' girls.
'He used to arrive bringing with him whoever he'd had to lunch, it
might have been Patrick Kinross, Osbert Lancaster or Paul Bloomfield.
He often lay on the floor and did bicycling exercises. People used to
drop in, because they knew he was there on a Monday and he would
groan with despair sometimes because he was a captive pinned to the
wall. He would *always* give jobs to the hard-up droppers-in like P.
Morton Shand who would say, "Have you got any books to review?"

'He was also the poetry editor and people used to send in reams of
poetry – two dozen or so a week – and he would read them out loud.
Sometimes they were hysterically funny. He'd always answer every
one except the dreadful ones which he returned with a rejection slip.
Quite often he'd ring up somebody like Billa Harrod and say, "What
are you wearing?" and then he'd offer them a book to review. "Would
you do the art criticism for *Tame and Tade?*" he asked Myfanwy Piper,
"for Llady Rhondda is in love with your writing and quite rightly
regards you as a great catch." JB asked Clive Bell, Walter de la Mare
and Siegfried Sassoon to review – in fact he had virtual *carte blanche*.

'The thing about John,' Pamela Fildes continues, 'was that he was
always giving a performance even when he didn't have to. But I knew
there was something deeply marvellous about this performance. He
was completely non-judgemental and at the same time he needed an
immense amount of moral support. He never talked about gossip and I
trusted his insight. I'd never have dreamt of talking to anybody else
about what I'd talked to him about. He was able to be dispassionate. I
never knew about his own sex life, I just thought he was wise and good.
I knew he wouldn't laugh at me, but really listen. I remember being
desperately in love with a boy working in the book room who I knew
had had affairs with boys in the past and, for some reason, although I
didn't know John that well, I felt I could ask him what to do about the
situation. He took me to lunch at the Athenæum and I just knew that
his advice would be wise. He said that it didn't mean anything at all and
that it was perfectly normal and that things would adjust automatically
as the boy got older. He brought me back in a taxi and I remember

saying to him that in a marriage I was looking for a rock and he just sighed and said, "Ah." I felt he needed a rock.'[10]

Although JB may not have realised it at the time, he had already found his rock. In the early summer of 1951 he had been asked to dinner in Lord North Street by Michael Berry, whose father Lord Camrose had founded, and was editor-in-chief of the *Daily Telegraph*. His wife Pamela, or 'Lady Pam' as JB always called her, was the daughter of F. E. Smith and a powerful political hostess. Although she would often entertain the Prime Minister of the day she also had a particular penchant for journalists. JB knew that it was wise to keep in with her. That particular evening he and the other six diners waited for nearly two hours for the last guest to appear and in the end they gave him up for lost and sat down to dinner. Across the table from JB and sitting next to his old Marlburian friend, Anthony Blunt, was a reserved and pretty young woman in her early twenties called Elizabeth Cavendish whom JB had never met before. They did not speak to each other that night, nor did they need to. It only took seconds, during what turned out to be a historic dinner, for JB and Elizabeth to know that they had fallen in love.

The next day it was revealed that the missing dinner guest was Guy Burgess, the civil servant who was in the pay of the KGB and who had fled the country that night. Anthony Blunt was also a KGB agent at the time and must have known all along. Lady Pam rang to tell Elizabeth, adding that she was trying to persuade JB to take a short holiday to Copenhagen on the Camroses' yacht *Virginia*. She said that he was unhappy and that his marriage was going wrong. She then told Elizabeth that he would only agree to come on the yacht if she came too. They both went. 'JB was very flattered,' remembers Jill Menzies. 'Elizabeth was mad about him and he was mad about her. It was a very respectable affair and there was no adultery. Penelope didn't mind about Elizabeth any more than she minded about anyone else, after all, John was always falling in love.'[11] JB received a letter from Colonel Kolkhorst just after he had met Elizabeth saying, 'Is it not about time you gave your heart a rest, for a little while anyway? You have been at it non stop now for I don't know how many donkey's years, it is not good for you. "The trouble about John is," Colonel Dugdale used to say, "that he is always in love." So *do* get a rest and give your poor heart a holiday. It's become a sort of drug, love, and you've become a love fiend.'[12] But JB already had an inkling that Elizabeth was to become the love of his life, his mainstay and his muse.

This did not mean to say that he could not continue to love my mother or that their close friendship, their old ties and friends gathered since the early thirties and their role as parents would ever change. JB wrote in November 1953 to my mother from Elizabeth's brother (the Duke of Devonshire) and sister-in-law's house near Chatsworth, 'Nooni, Nooni, Nuke, her hubby went off for to stay with a Duke. Nibbly, Nobbly, Nibbly, Nob, her husband was clearly a bit of a snob. . . . It is very nice here, the country looks lovely in this golden autumn light. Elizabeth is here after all but sick in bed. I showed her the Lady Rhondda letter and she thinks the only line I can take is objective. She thinks Pamela Fildes may be at the bottom of it. I hope she is not, but if she is it destroys all my confidence in her.'[13]

JB was just about to be sacked by Lady Rhondda. The poetry and books side of *Time and Tide* were, to her, not half as important as the politics and in consequence she never gave him the space he wanted. Things got more and more difficult. Finally she became irrationally furious when he insisted on including a poem by his friend Pansy Lamb. Lady Rhondda thought that she was an invented character, and that it was one of JB's jokes.

JB did not brood. If his job was in jeopardy or his emotional life complicated he side-stepped the issue and filled up his agenda to bursting point. He took Anne Barnes to see the Crazy Gang, and Peter Fleming to the Garrick Club. He lunched with Malcolm Muggeridge and Osbert Lancaster and discussed a series of articles on public schools for *Punch*, beginning with Winchester and Gresham's, to be illustrated with pictures of old boys of distinction. He read poems at the Apollo Society with Peggy Ashcroft, he wrote material for and performed with Joyce Grenfell, he dined with Nancy Astor. He held the poet Frances Cornford's hand before a joint lecture at the Royal Society of Literature, when she was nervous and wanted to discuss things. She wrote, 'Let's meet for tea first before the lecture, I don't know any London teashops. How strongly I disagree about you not being a true poet, of course you are.'[14] He read Hardy's poems at the Eton Poetry Society, he became a member of the council of Bloxham School. He lectured on Victorian architecture at the Museum and Art Gallery in Belfast, and he lectured closer to home – and too near the knuckle – at the Harwell Atomic Research Station, referring to the people who worked there as 'Atomics' and assuming they had no aesthetic judgement. He ended his speech, 'Every age gets the architecture it deserves. . . . Perhaps some Wellsian Utopian is in charge of you. . . . You have the prefab, that human poultry farm with which some civil servant has commanded the vivisection of our downs.'[15]

JB's topographical talks on the radio were becoming ever more popular. After his broadcast on William Morris's house Kelmscott, the private press printer, Sir Sidney Cockerell, wrote in a microscopic calligraphic hand, 'I have just been listening to your enchanting talk on Kelmscott Manor which brought tears to my eyes again and again, so dear has it been to me since I first stayed there with Morris sixty years ago. I have been in bed all this year with heart trouble but I could give you a cup of tea if you ever come to Kew Gardens.'[16]

All this activity did not mean that he had less time for my mother, brother and me. As he had pledged, JB took my mother out once a week, so that they could be alone together, usually to Anne de Winton's country club restaurant in the mill at West Hanney. Anne was the woman about whom W. B. Yeats had written, when she was six years old:

> I heard an old religious man
> But yesternight declare
> That he had found a text to prove
> That only God, my dear,
> Could love you for yourself alone
> And not your yellow hair.[17]

He often took us to the cinema in Oxford, Wantage or Didcot; his love of good films never waned. Paul and I didn't really understand *The Third Man* and I remember him taking great trouble explaining it. He took us to see the Crazy Gang every Christmas holidays without fail and to amateur productions of Gilbert and Sullivan in Reading. But my most vivid memories of those years, before I went to boarding school, are our sketching trips. On any summer afternoon we would drive to villages like Hatford, West Challow or Lyford and try and draw a row of cottages, a barn or a manor house. I envied his proficiency and speed. He praised my drawings, hopeless as they were. But I never forgot the buildings we drew – not a keystone, not a glazing bar.

JB was good at opening doors in other people's minds. The early fifties saw the beginning of the creation of hundreds of conservation and civic societies, formed to protect what the locals thought was worth fighting for. He began to be involved in myriad appeals for buildings under threat and was roped on to many committees. He became a founder member of the William Morris Society, he was on the Hawksmoor Committee, the Historic Churches Preservation Trust, the Council for the Protection of Rural England and the Oxford and London Diocesan Advisory Committees.

In May 1952 he was asked to join the Royal Fine Art Commission, an advisory body for all matters affecting the look of England, from large building developments in London to street lighting or sculpture. It was quite an honour for someone who was considered by many to be a maverick. His friends Stuart Piggott, John Summerson and Christopher Hussey were on the commission already, and no doubt it was they who had suggested him.

The war that JB had been waging since 1950 against concrete lampposts, five years ahead of Ian Nairn's 'Outrage' issue of the *Architectural Review*, lasted for three years, but the Royal Fine Art Commission did nothing to help. JB's letter to *The Times*, in which he wrote, 'I am sure I am not the only one to object to the present craze for erecting lampposts like concrete gibbets with quartz lights dangling off them in old country towns,' engendered the most extraordinarily wide correspondence.[18] People wrote from all over the country: 'Our grateful thanks to you for challenging the sick serpents that now stretch their necks over our country roads.'[19] JB even sent a ten-shilling note to Mr Chisholm, the lorry driver who had been photographed in the local paper inadvertently knocking over a lamppost in Basingstoke. Mr Chisholm wrote back, 'Thank you very much for your generous gift. Although I agree with you that these lamp standards do spoil the countryside, I must point out that it was quite by accident that I knocked this one down.'[20] JB cut out a piece from the *Harrogate Advertiser* of 12 June 1952 which read, 'During the week ending June 14th, six street lamp standards in Harrogate were demolished by vehicles in minor mishaps. This is believed to be a record number.' 'Hurray!' said JB, and sent a congratulatory letter to the editor.

'We accept without murmur the poles and wires with which the Ministry of Fuel and Power has strangled every village,' he wrote in *Light and Lighting*. 'We have put up with the foully hideous concrete lamp standards for which the Borough Engineer and the Ministry of Transport are jointly responsible, each playing off the other so that lorries can overtake one another around dangerous corners at greater speed. We slice off old buildings, fell healthy trees, replace hedges with concrete posts and chain-link fencing, all in the name of safety first which is another phrase for "hurry past".'[21] This campaign was typical of many he was to pursue over the years. He did not give up easily, and became a thorn in the side of local government.

December 1951 saw the publication of the *Shropshire* Shell Guide which JB and John Piper had had such fun compiling in the late forties. 'A highly unconventional choice, worth exactly as much as one is ready to trust to the authors, and they can be trusted,' read the review in the *Listener*. But it was his book *First and Last Loves*, a choice of his prose made by Myfanwy Piper, who had also thought of the title, which made the biggest splash. She wrote to JB (2 August 1952), 'I think the book is a winner and I spent all yesterday re-reading it so I know it is non-repetitive and sustained and the thing that strikes me most is that when there is a build-up to a maze of ideas so that it seems impossible for the writer to extricate himself intelligibly, the solution that follows is not only simple and to the point but all the ideas that built up to it prove to have been essential. You are a great writer, in other words.'[22] JB's friends rallied. Osbert Lancaster wrote in the *Daily Telegraph*, 'The great curse which lay upon almost all those poets who came to maturity in the early thirties was bogus awareness. Socially conscious to the death. . . . In fact Mr Betjeman was the greatest realist of them all.'[23] Friends Mervyn Horder, Christopher Sykes and John Summerson all reviewed it enthusiastically and Cyril Connolly wrote in the *Sunday Times*, 'In another age or another country Mr Betjeman would not be a "failed literary gent", by which I suppose him to mean a scholar and a poet who makes his living as a journalist, but a national celebrity and arbiter of taste. Lovers of good writing would hang on his words, lovers of good building would submit him their plans, he would not be relegated to the limbo of the professional humorist or the clever fellow.'[24] Even a French magazine, *Études Anglaises*, wrote that JB possessed *'un esprit curieux et nostalgique'*.[25]

All through the autumn of 1952 JB's mother Granny Bess lay dying, in a nursing home at number 16 Royal Crescent in Bath. JB and I used to visit her together. She sat swathed in shawls, forlorn and tiny on a window seat. After our last visit she wrote to JB, 'I was so glad to see you and Candida yesterday. It was very kind of you to come. Give Candida my love and tell her the eau de cologne she gave me is sprinkled on my handkerchief and the scent of it wafts across the room. All love, Bess.'[26] I did not visit her in the final throes of her illness when JB stayed in Bath with John Walsham, his childhood friend from Trebetherick who worked in the Admiralty, and his wife Sheila. Bess died with JB beside her in the early evening of 13 December and he returned exhausted to the Walshams' house. He sat down with a glass of whisky and the telephone immediately rang. (Granny Bess had been an inveterate telephoner.) He said to Sheila, 'Oh, my *God*, she's come alive again.'

After her death had sunk in, JB inevitably felt remorse. 'John dear,' wrote Edith Harvey his aunt, 'I don't feel that your remorse is in any way merited, personally I think you have been a jolly good son! Bess was always very proud of you and it must have been a tremendous boost to her to be able to tell everyone that she was your mother.'[27] His cousins Bertie and Freda Widowson sent red roses and Agnes de Paula wrote wistfully to commiserate, 'We do hear you on the wireless sometimes.' Anne Channel wrote from her cottage Tresevens in Rock, which JB nicknamed 'Tresixes', 'I am feeling very sad since I read the news of your mother's death this morning. She was one of the first people here in Cornwall who showed me real hospitality and friendliness.' Granny Bess was buried in the churchyard of St Enodoc, Trebetherick, within sound of the sea. JB's old friend Frederick Etchells FRIBA designed the gravestone in the local black Delabole slate. 'My mother and I had become very inter-dependent over the last few years . . . and I saw her grow dottier and dottier,' JB wrote to Jim Lees-Milne. 'Her death was a slow business but not painful or worried as she made her communion and was anointed.'[28]

In May 1953 Jill Menzies left. JB was devastated. 'I think I was getting too fond of him,' she says. 'I thought it would upset Penelope if I stayed. It had been marvellous working for him, he made me laugh so much; he was so witty, he was like no one else. One evening, just before I left, he took me and his friend Christopher Hollis to the Garrick Club. I had never been anywhere like that before and was very excited. I went upstairs to the ladies' cloakroom to leave my coat; the excitement must have shown as I came downstairs.' Afterwards JB wrote the poem 'A Russell Flint' and sent it to Jill. It later appeared in *High and Low*:

> I could not speak for amazement at your beauty
> As you came down the Garrick stair,
> Grey-green eyes like the turbulent Atlantic
> And floppy schoolgirl hair.
>
> I could see you in a Sussex teashop,
> Dressed in peasant weave and brogues,
> Turning over, as firelight shone on brassware,
> Last year's tea-stained *Vogues* . . .

1. Alan Pryce-Jones's papers, Beinecke Library, Yale University.
2. Miss Pronger, CLG interview (1994).
3. JB's papers, University of Victoria, British Columbia.
4. BBC archives, Caversham, Reading.
5. JB's papers, University of Victoria.
6. Jill Menzies, CLG interview (1994).

7. JB's papers, University of Victoria.
8. Jill Menzies's papers.
9. JB's papers, University of Victoria.
10. Pamela Fildes, CLG interview (1994).
11. Jill Menzies, CLG interview (1994).
12. JB's papers, University of Victoria.
13. PB's papers, Beinecke Library, Yale University.
14. JB's papers, University of Victoria.
15. JB's papers, University of Victoria.
16. JB's papers, University of Victoria.
17. W. B. Yeats, 'Oedipus at Colonus'.
18. Carbon copy, JB's papers, University of Victoria.
19. JB's papers, University of Victoria.
20. JB's papers, University of Victoria.
21. *Light and Lighting* (November 1953).
22. JB's papers, University of Victoria.
23. *Daily Telegraph* (August 1952).
24. *Sunday Times* (14 September 1952).
25. *Études Anglaises* (August 1952).
26. JB's papers, University of Victoria.
27. This letter of commiseration, and two following, all in JB's papers, University of Victoria.
28. James Lees-Milne's papers, Beinecke Library, Yale University.

To Patrick Cullinan   The Mead
                                                            Wantage
All Saints [1 November] 1951   Berkshire

My dear Patrick
Here I am sitting in the ruins of my books. There is a carpet on the floor
and curtains in the window. This is the only room carpeted and
curtained. None of the rest ever will be. I despair. The bath water is
hotter and more plentiful than at Farnborough. The house is undoubtedly much nicer *inside*. I long for you to come and visit. I have written a
very worrying letter to the Colonel full of Spanish and Portuguese.
Come out here in a fortnight when there may be some more carpets and
curtains and a bed for you. Come and stay at Christmas. Oh, I look
forward to your company a lot. I have started to write poetry again –
driven to it by fear of never putting pen to paper. I long to hear about
Italy and the Colonel's behaviour there. He *must* have sweated. Is he
the least known don in Oxford or is Toby [Strutt] less known?
   Love, John B

> P.C. (see *Volume One*), the South African poet, met JB when the latter came to address
> the Poetry Society at Charterhouse. Their friendship developed through their
> correspondence and he came to stay often while he was at Oxford.
>   The 'Colonel' (see *Volume One*) was George A. Kolkhorst, a celebrated Oxford figure,
> much loved by JB.
>   Toby Strutt (see *Volume One*) was a friend of the Colonel's whom everyone else
> thought a bore.

To Rupert Hart-Davis   The Mead
                                                            Wantage
16 November 1951   Berkshire

Dear Rupert,
A neighbour near Newbury, Gerald Phinsy? Finzi? Phinsie? Finzey?
the composer is very concerned about Edmund Blunden who is a great
friend of his. He says B[lunden] has not enough money, lives in great

squalor near Virginia Water, has bad asthma and will soon go to Japan, if he cannot bring himself and his children up more comfortably here. He also says quite rightly that B[lunden] is very proud and would not accept charity and would hate to be discussed as a charitable object. Certainly B[lunden] has to take on all sorts of frightful jobs like reviewing to earn enough to keep his wife and family. I wrote to Harold Macmillan about this in the middle of this year, asking whether Macmillan would provide B[lunden] with any readerships or some salary for his occasional services which would relieve his pocket and not make him think he was accepting charity. H[arold] wrote to say he would look into it. He wrote again to say he would like to discuss it with me when next we met at the Beefsteak. When we did meet there, he did not mention it. Perhaps he had forgotten. I didn't like to remind him in case he had not forgotten. Do you know him or Daniel Macmillan (whom I don't know at all) well enough to ask them whether anything can be done for Blunden of a kind that he will not suspect as charity? Of one thing I am certain, B[lunden] would never complain of his circumstances to anyone. And I don't think G. Finzi (Phinsy, Phinsie, Finzey) is lying.

How good Arthur Calder-Marshall's book is. I was not allowed it for the *Telegraph* though I tried hard. It does not count as fiction it seems. To hell with fiction. Richard Jennings is doing it for *Time and Tide*.

Yours, John Betjeman

Note our new address – a small *warm* Victorian villa in this county town.

R.H.-D. (see *Volume One*), the author, editor and publisher, was a friend of JB's from Oxford days.

JB was an active supporter of the Royal Literary Fund and did much to raise money for the fund and assist ailing authors.

Gerald Finzi (1901–56), the English composer, lived at the village of Ashmansworth. Edmund Blunden (1896–1974) did, in fact, spend the last part of his life in Japan. Arthur Calder-Marshall's autobiography *The Magic of My Youth* had just come out.

To George Barnes   The Mead
                                                               Wantage
6 December 1951   Berkshire

My dear Commander,
My lovely freckled, furry, retroussé-nosed Jill [Menzies] with her slanting grey eyes and pouting lips begs me to tell you how sorry she is

you had that letter. It was addressed to Commander Joel of Betty Joel Ltd and, as you surmised, nothing to do with you. But how nice for you to get another Commander's letter.

I am very much looking forward to your coming with Anne and Little P[rawls] to stay here either all of you at once or in bits. This house is a tremendous success and we both love it. It is warmer and quieter and more practical than Farnborough.

Tell Little P[rawls] it's no good taking views of Cambridge which everyone takes and which make good paintings but not good photographs. Let him look about at *mouldings* and shadows when the sun strikes stone and click his little camera there. Photography is harder in Angleterre. But it needs doing. I'm sorry he is in the Hostel and not the College.

Egdon Heath sounds awful and just as I surmised – the Dorset that is like Bournemouth.

I have made great friends with Compton Mackenzie. He is a very nice, unmalicious and fundamentally modest man for he regards himself as an entertainer and says it is in his blood through the Comptons. He has been reading *Ingoldsby Legends* out loud to me. 'Genius was in the room', to use Anne's phrase re Emlyn Williams, but more so for I thought W[illiams] rather too much *acted* his Dickens, while M[ackenzie] reads [Richard] Barham (*Ingoldsby*) so that it is poetry and really far more mediaeval than William Morris, because more earthy and frightening. My new friend Elizabeth Cavendish is just our kind of girl. She is as bracing and witty and kind and keen on drink as Anne. I long for you to meet her. Tom Moore is a v[ery] good poet. I left a wreath on his grave at Bromham, Wilts[hire]. A cousin of my mother's is Rector there. My mother is permanently in a nursing home with hypochondria. I have therefore had a day a week taken out of my life which I might have devoted to Tottenham. I will devote the days soon to that good subject. We might get the help of the Rev[erend] Martin W. Willson, that excellent W. Reg[ion]: Religious Director of BBC and an old Marlburian.

Love to you all, John B

G.B. (see *Volume One*) was by this time Director of BBC Television. He and his wife Anne lived in a house called 'Prawls' in Tenterden, Kent. Prawls became the generic term for G.B., and their son Anthony was called Little Prawls. He had just gone up to Cambridge.

Jill Menzies was JB's secretary.

The writer E. M. Compton Mackenzie and his wife Faith lived in the nearby village of Denchworth.

Richard Harris Barham (1788–1845) wrote *The Ingoldsby Legends* which were originally
printed in *Bentley's Miscellany* and the *New Monthly Magazine* and collectively in 1840.
JB had met Elizabeth Cavendish (EC) in the early summer of that year.
G.B. was keen to make a programme about Tottenham with JB.

To Kenneth Clark   The Mead
                                                            Wantage
14 December 1951   Berkshire

Dear K[enneth],
I telephoned to Goldilegz [Myfanwy Piper] to find whether you were
in London. She thinks probably, and that you would not mind if this
letter were typed.

It is about concrete lamp standards. As you probably know,
Chippenham, Banbury, Salisbury, Abingdon, Crewkerne, Wantage,
Corsham and Wokingham are ruined by them. Wallingford and
Marlborough are threatened. I can write only of the towns round here
but I imagine it is just the same in every other part of England.

Newbury and Bath provide examples of this new street lighting
which are inoffensive. In both these places brackets are fixed to the
houses and ordinary light pours down which doesn't take from the
colour of building materials.

So far, the only way we have found of preventing more of these
things going up is to get advance information from a friend on the
council. This has happened with Marlborough, and the town *may* be
saved. But that was a lucky chance.

I tried last year with a correspondence in *The Times* to stop these
beastly things. I was sent a brochure of that concrete standard with the
triangular base and the devil's match-box strike on it by a firm named
Standen who advertised on their brochure that the design had been
'approved by the Royal Fine Art Commission'. Before sending the
letter I corresponded with Godfrey Samuel so that the Royal Fine Art
Commission would not be embarrassed by reference to this brochure.
Many letters supporting me appeared, and I received about fifty private
letters in support. *The Times* published one attack on me in personal
terms from a man named Scopes who is the Managing Director of
Standen's though he didn't mention this fact in his letter.

Now I am going to return to the attack with an illustrated article in
the *Daily Telegraph*. I have received letters from Godfrey Samuel
written with civil service caution, which makes me feel that I am an

impetuous journalist seeking publicity for myself. I should like to hand over to you the conduct of this campaign, for it is most important that we should save what is left. But will you take it on? It is asking a lot.

I think the Royal Fine Art Commission should ask the C[ouncil for the] P[reservation of] R[ural] E[ngland] or some other body concerned with the appearance of towns and villages to prepare a list of all the towns still undamaged by concrete standards. Then there should be legislation to stop borough surveyors and the Ministry of Transport from rushing their schemes through the local councils. The lighting of each town should be considered on its own particular merits by the Royal Fine Art Commission, or if that has not the time and the membership to do it, by the local branch of the CPRE and local art and architectural societies.

I have proposed this to Godfrey Samuel and received a damping reply. Could you talk to Lord Crawford about it and possibly someone like David Eccles who seems anxious to help? Together you and they might be able to deal with the Minister of Transport. It is not as though there were no examples of successful lighting which still come up to the Ministry of Transport's new standards. I find Sir Ralph Glyn, our local MP, a useless trimmer who talks only in terms of street accidents and shortages of iron.

Finally I think that flagrant examples of damage as in Salisbury, Chippenham, Corsham and in front of Abingdon Town Hall should be rectified. But that can come second.

I always turn to you as the only hope in these moments of urgency. You did it before with the National Buildings Record. Do, dear K[enneth], oh do, help in this campaign. I wish these semi-civil servants like Godfrey Samuel, Karl Marx and the staff of *The Times* would realise that one is disinterested and not looking for a chair in a university or a seat on a committee.

I enclose some correspondence on the subject for you to look at.

Love to Jane, Alan and the twins. Oh Christmas!

Yours ever, John Betjeman

PS Working on this campaign with me are Paul Methuen and Christopher Hollis but only for local specific danger.

K.C. (see *Volume One*), the great art commentator, was an old friend of JB's.

K.C., who was about to resign from the Royal Fine Art Commission, replied (20 December 1951), 'I really do not know what to do about these beastly lamps. Of course, the Commission ought never to have let itself become associated with them in any way – but that goes for two thirds of what it does. It is really in a completely false position; it should be split up into two bodies: one a council of preservation and the other a far larger and more authoritative body for dealing with new buildings. At present, it does not know whether it ought to be maintaining high standards of taste or making the best of the inevitable bad jobs. Of course, if it only did the former it would chuck out practically everything ever submitted to it and I suppose would end up being dissolved.' In fact, the Royal Fine Art Commission had already approved the lamp standards: 'At present they are committed to making the best of bad jobs . . . When I am off the Commission I will join with you in protesting against individual cases . . . that I fear is about all I can do.'

Godfrey Samuel was head of the Royal Fine Art Commission.

JB's campaign engendered a large correspondence from all over the country.

To Alan Pryce-Jones   The Mead
                                                         Wantage
14 March 1952   Berkshire

My dearest Captain Bog,
I am so thankful to hear that Poppy is better. I guessed you were going through a terrible time, both of you, of strain and anxiety. Eternity is such an awful word, though one often thinks of it in a detached way and therefore wrongly. I will not cease to pray for you both and perhaps we will all meet again on the *Virginia* at Easter if you accept to go. Poor Bog. Poor Poppy. I love you both and once again I am so glad the gloom is lifted.

   Love, JB

   A.P.-J. (see *Volume One*) was one of JB's oldest friends from Oxford.
   His wife Thérèse ('Poppy') had had a brief remission while suffering the first stages of cancer.
   Virginia was the yacht belonging to Lord Camrose, the editor-in-chief of the *Daily Telegraph*, on which JB sailed around Corsica at Easter. Elizabeth Cavendish (EC) was also a guest. Both she and JB had been guests the year before.

To James Lees-Milne   The Mead
                                                         Wantage
26 March 1952   Berkshire

Dear Jim,
I don't know who did Ashdown. It could not be I[nigo] J[ones], it is so unlike him. And I don't think it could be Roger Pratt of Coleshill. The wonderful brick gatepiers which remain at Hamstead Marshall are by a Dutch architect whose name is quarrelled about and speaking from memory it was, I think, Captain William Winde or Wynne who also

designed Combe Abbey for the Cravens. Well, Ashdown is a very foreign looking building and, short of finding papers in the Craven family, I don't see what one can go by except stylistic evidence and this points to Winde or some foreigner. It is like no English house. Its scale is all different. Winde is in the A.P.S. Dictionary. Ask Howard Colvin of St John's College Oxford. He is *the* man on architects as he is compiling a dictionary of those who worked in Great Britain.

How nice to live in Monaco. Give my love to the Monacos. I've never met them. Are you now Monegasque like Daisy Fellowes? P[enelope] sends her love to you both and so do I. P[enelope] is very, very eccentric indeed now and very R[oman] C[atholic] which I am not.

This house is an ugly little thing in a lovely setting of apple trees and meadows by a millstream right in the centre of Wantage. *Rus in urbe* if I may coin a phrase. You must both come down and stay, if you ever leave the Monacos. Do you know the Norways or the Denmarks or the Liechtensteins? Nor do I.

Come between Ascot and Goodwood. It is you who are important, not I. I travel third [class] and am cut by people who count and looked down upon by the new refugee 'scholars' who have killed all we like by their 'research' – i.e. Nikolaus Pevsner that dull pedant from Prussia.

Yours, John B

NORMAN SHAW IS GREATER THAN BERNARD SHAW

J.L.-M. (see *Volume One*), the biographer and architectural writer, first met JB with their mutual friend Robert Byron in the early thirties. He shared JB's passion for architecture.

Sir William Winde (? – 1722) (called 'Wynne' by the architect Colen Campbell) had designed the two other Craven properties, Hamstead Marshall and Combe Abbey.

Ashdown House near Lambourn in Berkshire was built in a remote place on the Downs in *c.* 1665 by William, 1st Earl of Craven, as a refuge from the Plague. He consecrated the house to the unrequited love of his life, Elizabeth, Queen of Bohemia, who died before seeing it.

J.L.-M. had just married Alvilde Chaplin who was living in Monaco while she still had French citizenship.

Daisy Fellowes was a glitzy neighbour who lived at Donnington Grove near Newbury. She was a Singer Sewing Machine heiress, said to be the best dressed woman in the world.

Richard Norman Shaw (1834–1912), architect of New Scotland Yard, was one of JB's favourite architects.

To Siegfried Sassoon   The Mead
                                                         Wantage
19 April 1952   Berkshire

Dear Sassoon,

I'm thrilled, pleased and honoured to have these beautiful *Emblems of Experience* signed by you and presented to me. It is so nice to find you, here in a later volume, an even finer poet than in those earlier volumes which I possess. I have now read through your poems twice, out loud to myself which is the best test. The words roll out full of sound and depth like they do in my beloved Tennyson. And the melancholy in every poem of yours, I welcome so very warmly. It is like the melancholy of Hood, that constant sense of Eternity. Your 'Prayers to Time' seems to me the essence of it. The poems I like best at the moment are 'Old Fashioned Weather' (what a beautiful final stanza), 'A Fallodon Memory' – a portrait that is a Charles Furse picture in its quiet understanding, 'Cleaning the Candelabrum' (a theme that would have been so arch and awful if Austin Dobson had done it and which your melancholy makes into a superb poem) and the poem I like best of all is 'The Messenger'. I understand it particularly because at the moment my mother is dying in a nursing home in Bath with her faculties gradually going, and clinging as hard as she can to the threads of reason and memory left to her. I thank you very deeply for these poems. They are an experience rare today. I do think poetry is looking up (despite the efforts of know-all reviewers who write anonymous attacks on all they understand and only praise the obscure while missing the good in the clear). Andrew Young's *Into Hades* and R. S. Thomas's little volume printed in Newtown Montgomery are in your, and therefore the true, tradition.

I hope I shall one day be allowed to come and see you at Heytesbury and we might make a tour to Upton Lovell and call on Sidney Mavor ('Jenny' Mavor, [Oscar] Wilde's and Alfred Taylor's friend), aged eighty-three, if he is still alive.

I don't blame you a bit for publishing your poems privately and beautifully. That is just what you ought to do. I hope eventually all good poets will. But one needs the cash to do it.

Yours ever gratefully, John Betjeman

S.S. (see *Volume One*), the poet, and JB had become friends through their poetry. He lived at Heytesbury near Warminster in Wiltshire.

Emblems of Experience was a private publication of Sassoon's poetry. The poems mentioned all appeared in the enlarged second edition of his *Collected Poems* published by Faber and Faber in 1961.

Charles Furse (1868–1904) was a great Victorian painter, whose 'Diana of the Uplands' hangs in the Tate.

Sidney 'Jenny' Mavor was the friend of Alfred Taylor and the last boy witness in the Oscar Wilde case still living.

To Paul Henry   The Mead
                                                 Wantage
22 May 1952   Berkshire

Dear Henry,

I am so pleased to hear from you and really honoured that you should have enjoyed the broadcast.

You would find Kelmscott little changed if you were to go there now, and it is not far from here.

I have recently developed a great enthusiasm for the works of [James Abbot McNeill] Whistler whom you knew I believe. I would love one day to see you and hear your impression of Whistler. I have one Whistler etching here, and a nice Cecil Lawson too. I do hope that one day I shall see you, for I have long admired your work.* Do you ever come to England?

Yours sincerely, John Betjeman

*We've met in Ireland, but only in crowds.

P.H. (see *Volume One*) was an Irish artist whom JB had met when serving as Press Attaché in Dublin during the war.

JB's television broadcast on William Morris's home, Kelmscott, for the BBC in a series called *Landscapes with Houses* ended, 'The place is haunting and haunted, for it has been loved as only an old house can be loved.'

There is no evidence to suggest that JB and P.H. ever did meet.

To Evelyn Waugh   The Mead
                                                 Wantage
7 June 1952   Berkshire

Dear Evelyn,

Here you are, ole boy. It's no good. They were just verses turned for the appeal and not meant to be a poem. The drawing is by Henry Rushbury RA.

I have been reading the poems of Alexander Smith (1850s). They are well worth a dekko.

I would very much like to see you. You will soon be, if you are not already, gripped by the beauty of the small Edwardian house such as C. H. B. Quennell and [Charles Annesley] Voysey and [Guy] Dawber and Geoffrey Lucas and Leonard Stokes and Edgar Wood and Baillie Scott used to design. I am not sure that it is not as good as the best Regency. And oh, R. Norman Shaw! There's the man. He was a mighty genius. Bernard Shaw can't hold a candle to him. I like your local architect Sir George Oatley. There is more and more to see and we grow no younger. Love to Laura. P[enelope] is off to a retreat in London for Catechists.

Love, John B

> Across the wet November night
> The church is bright with candlelight
>   And waiting Evensong.
> A single bell with plaintive strokes
> Pleads louder than the stirring oaks
>   The leafless lanes along.
>
> It calls the choirboys from their tea
> And villagers, the two or three,
>   Damp down the kitchen fire,
> Let out the cat, and up the lane
> Go paddling through the gentle rain
>   Of misty Oxfordshire.
>
> How warm the many candles shine
> On SAMUEL DOWBIGGIN's design
>   For this interior neat,
> These high box pews of Georgian days
> Which screen us from the public gaze
>   When we make answer meet;
>
> How gracefully their shadow falls
> On bold pilasters down the walls
>   And on the pulpit high.
> The chandeliers would twinkle gold
> As pre-Tractarian sermons roll'd
>   Doctrinal, sound and dry.
>
> From that west gallery no doubt
> The viol and serpent tooted out
>   The Tallis tune to Ken,

And firmly at the end of prayers
The clerk below the pulpit stairs
    Would thunder out 'Amen'.

But every wand'ring thought will cease
Before the noble altarpiece
    With carven swags array'd,
For there in letters all may read
The Lord's Commandments, Prayer and Creed
    Are decently display'd.

On country mornings sharp and clear
The penitent in faith draw near
    And kneeling here below
Partake the Heavenly Banquet spread
Of Sacramental Wine and Bread
    And JESUS' presence know.

And must that plaintive bell in vain
Plead loud along the dripping lane?
    And must the building fall?
Not while we love the Church and live
And of our charity will give
    Our much, our more, our all.

E.W. (see *Volume One*), the novelist, and JB had long shared interests in architecture and rare books.

St Katherine's Church, Chislehampton, for which JB had written the verses, was built in 1762 and was in urgent need of three thousand pounds to complete its restoration. JB's friends John Piper and John Rothenstein were involved in the appeal. The verses appeared in *A Few Late Chrysanthemums* in 1954.

E.W. and his wife Laura lived at Stinchcombe in Gloucestershire.

Sir George Oatley (1863–1950) practised from Bristol, whose university he had designed among many other civic buildings. He did some restoration work in Gloucestershire near the Waughs' home.

To Patrick Kinross   The Mead
                                           Wantage
11 August 1952   Berkshire

My dear Pa'rick,

I am thankful to hear from you. Capt[ain] Bog [Alan Pryce-Jones] and I heard that tale about someone who had a letter from a friend in Cyprus or Crete or wherever it was you were which said, 'Isn't it sad about

Patrick? But I suppose it was bound to happen sooner or later.' And we thought you were in jug. I actually put you into my prayers. Then we heard that [nothing] had happened. I greatly look forward to seeing you. We are going to Trebetherick (Aunt Elsie [McCorkindale] sends you her love) on 25th of this month until Sept[ember] 8th, then I am back for good. Penelope is going to Rome in the last week in Sept[ember] for a month with Robert Heber-Percy. I shall be alone with my secretary, a beautiful furry-skinned, freckled, slanting blue-eyed, tip-tilted nosed sports girl called Jill Menzies and it would be very nice if you came and stayed so as to keep me from temptation. Though you will not be immune yourself from her schoolgirl appeal. She is away at present. Familiarity with her appearance has inoculated me all right, but I don't like to tempt providence.

Dauntsey's School is not really very good. Farmer Wheeler of Uffington sent his sons there and so do many local farmers. There is a smattering of high-brow theorists' children as well. Sir Stephen Tallents thinks very well of it. I would far sooner recommend Bryanston and could help to get him in there. Also for people of a practical turn there is Oundle where I know the headmaster. What I feel about Dauntsey's is that it is a sort of agricultural Dartington and is rather old-fashioned. But I may be maligning it. Bryanston I know is good.

Please come and stay in the autumn.

Love to Ursula, Pamela and Rosemary and your mother and David Balfour.

Love from JB

P.K. (see *Volume One*) was JB's great friend from Oxford days. He was enquiring about suitable schools for his nephew.

Elsie McCorkindale was not a blood relation but we all called her 'Aunt Elsie'. She lived at Torquil Cottage, Trebetherick.

Sir Stephen Tallents (1884–1958), the Chairman of Group 1 Ltd. and an Hon. ARIBA, was the author of *The Starry Pool and other Tales*.

To Compton Mackenzie
24 August 1952

J. Betjeman
Jokes and Novelties   The Mead   *Short Breezy*
Book Reviews at   Wantage   *Talks on Art,*
Short Notice   Berkshire   *Aeronautics & c*

Author of: Cosy Homes for Moderate Incomes: How I Flew the Channel with
Bleriot: Dirt Track Racing (in blank verse): J. B. Priestley the Man & His
Work: Blueprint for Betterment: Progress in the Fifties: Whither Albania?
Whither Democracy? Whither the Future? The Past – A Retrospect & fifteen
hundred articles in the Vegetarian, Brentford & Chiswick Times,
&c: &c: &c: &c: &:
World copyright reserved: Patent applied for.

Dear Monty,
Many thanks for your kind letters from those clever people. How they
encourage one. The Grimsby Women's Luncheon Club is thirty
guineas for eighty minutes and therefore worth it I think and rather fun
– if they write to you. This is true. So is this: *T[ime and] Tide* is taking up
the Authorship taxation. I will send you their first article. Would you
care to write a letter or a short article on the subject? Love to you all
there in Denchworth. Yours, John B

> C.M. (1883–1972), the writer, who lived locally and had become a great friend, had just
> been knighted. JB had written, 'Come and have a spot of Scotch and splash any time –
> it's Liberty Hall here. The rockery's looking a treat and the rhodies are a sight for sore
> eyes.' There was neither rockery nor rhododendrons at the Mead.

To Cecil Beaton   Bodare
                                                              Trebetherick
                                                              Wadebridge
1 September 1952   Cornwall

Dear Cecil,
How kind of you to write to me the sad news of Sidney Mavor. A quiet
and happy end, I suppose, in a quiet sunny country home in summer in
Wilts. How very far from Solferino's, the Florence and Kettner's. I
wonder if Charlie Parker or Shelley or Woods are alive? It was v[ery]

good of you to go over to Upton L[ovell]. It might be worth seeing the papers he has left behind, if the nephew has any. I shall treasure your graphic record of the visit to Upton.

I am having the last week of my holidays here amid 'bad luck', 'good shot', 'played' ringing over the tamarisks from the tennis courts and fresh young schoolboys and schoolgirls dodging about and ageing schoolmasters plunging into the 'foam bearded Atlantic' and cocktail parties in the villas and a good round of golf in the morning and Penelope typing letters about her farm. We return in the middle of next week to Wantage and I will avail myself, in the autumn, of your kind invitation to come to that beautiful house of yours. I now *believe* I was at Harrow with you and John Summerson, Arthur Bryant, Duff Dunbar, Wyndham Ketton-Cremer, Johnnie Churchill, Villiers David, G. M. Trevelyan, Winston Churchill, Byron, Peel, Turner, Bowen, Galsworthy, Drury, and I wish I could plunge into Ducker and see the windy yard at Bill.

Love from us both, John B

C.B. (see *Volume One*), the photographer, had been a friend since Oxford days. At JB's suggestion, he had been to visit Sidney 'Jenny' Mavor, who lived not far away in Upton Lovell, Wiltshire. When CB arrived Mavor had just died. He wrote (29 August 1952), 'I went yesterday, in great excitement, and under ideal conditions, along the Wylye valley to Upton Newton. Everything at its best. Japanese anemones at every cottage window and all the other things I like – and apparently Harold Nicolson doesn't like – about August. Our goal reached – and a pretty village it is too – we asked a village lady with white hair and a basket of the veritable plums, whereabouts Mr Sydney Mavor lives. A terrible shock to hear her say "Oh, he's dead – at least I think he is, I'll just ask my husband for sure." Her husband in shirtsleeves – and every other fly button buttoned up, came to corroborate the news. "Yes, some weeks ago the old chap (popular in the neighbourhood – a gent) had gone up to the main road to catch a bus. He was at least eighty-three but in fine fettle and would have lasted another twenty years, if he hadn't got over-excited and thinking he'd heard the approach of a bus had run into the street and got knocked over by a motor. Skull cracked. Even so in hospital he refused for some time to die" – and so we've missed the bus too.'

To Tom Driberg   The Mead
                                                   Wantage
25 September 1952   Berkshire

My dear Thomas,
Many thanks for your very scholarly letter, old boy. You are right in every detail. I am very careless, your every sentence is pregnant. I shall never get that superb poem of yours into *Tame and Tade*. I have fussed

about it every week, they are so damned conservative they seem to think politics affect the poetry they publish. I shall have to leave, in fact I will make 'an issue' of it. I have written a v[ery] strong letter to Lady R[hondda]. It is one of the best poems we have had since I have been on *T[ime and] T[ide]*.

Yours with love to you both, John B

T.D. (see *Volume One*), the Labour politician and JB's friend from Oxford days, became JB's textual adviser. His poem 'Cycle with Masks' had been rejected by three literary editors before it came to JB. It was eventually returned and Lady Rhondda wrote to T.D. (24 September 1952), 'John Betjeman has given me your poem of which he thinks highly as does also Theodora Bosanquet to whom I showed it. But I am, I'm afraid, a little worried. Our views – yours and *Time and Tide*'s – are so extremely widely divergent that I cannot feel it to be suitable that you should appear in its columns. It would seem to me really almost as unsuitable as if the Archbishop of Canterbury were to be printed in the *New Statesman*! So I am very regretfully returning it.' T.D. replied (7 October 1952), 'As a socialist who is also a communicant member of the Church of England, I should not myself be troubled by the publication in the *New Statesman* of a contribution by the Archbishop of Canterbury.'

JB always daintified the pronunciation of *Time and Tide* to *Tame and Tade*.

To P. Morton Shand   The Mead
                                                             Wantage
31 October 1952   Berkshire

My dear P. Morton Shand,
I have told Murray's to send you a copy of *First and Last Loves*. You are thanked in its preface, for, you know, you have always known good from bad unerringly, and have taught me how to pick it out. One day, long after you are dead and your bones are lying underneath the shrubs in Norland Square, you will be recognised as the true enemy of Pevsnerism.

The book *First and Last Loves* contains the very essay on Aberdeen which was a wireless talk, which seems to have been bound up with Boumphrey in some other book.

The Mackintosh thesis, for such it can be called, I will send to you. I would have sent it to you before had I not thought almost for certain that you would get it for the *Times Literary Supplement*. It is a singularly ugly book, and a typical 'thesis'. I think Granny [Pevsner] appears on every page. I did think myself of quoting it as an example of the new kind of art history which kills architecture. Moreover it is wrong in

most of its conclusions, and you will remember old Voysey loathed
being connected with Mackintosh and Walton.

Yours Séan Ó Betjeméan

The well known Oirish Nationalist

P.M.S. (see *Volume One*) was JB's architectural guru from his days on the *Architectural Review* in the early thirties.

First and Last Loves published by Jock Murray had just come out – a collection of essays and talks about architecture selected by Myfanwy Piper. John Piper did some special illustrations for it.

Boumphrey was an architectural writer who had worked on the *Architectural Review*.

Charles Rennie Mackintosh and the Modern Movement by Thomas Howarth, published in 1952, is still the standard work on Mackintosh. In a review in the *New Statesman*, John Summerson wrote, 'It is permissible, I think, to doubt whether Mackintosh was really a better or more progressive architect than, say, his contemporary Glaswegian, Sir John Burnet; and to wonder whether our present adulation of him has not more in it of self-justification than of sincere obeisance to greatness.'

P.M.S.'s dislike of Pevsner's writings exacerbated JB's. 'Granny' was a name P.M.S. had given to Pevsner.

At around this time Peter Clarke, who worked for *The Times*, sent JB an eight-verse poem, fanning the anti-Pevsner flame. The first verse went:

> From heart of Mittel Europe
>   I make der little trip
> to show those Englisch dummkopfs
>   some echtdeutsch Scholarship.
> Viel Sehenswurdigkeiten
>   by others have been missed
> but now comes to enlighten
>   der Great Categorist.

To John Piper

9 November 1952

The Mead
Wantage
Berkshire

Dear Mr Piper,
Herewith the Vegetarian Nature Cure
brochure and a letter from the man who
runs it. Now do come. We will laugh
ourselves silly with old Etchell FRIBA.
I will go by motor car. Etchell says it
looks like Guy Dawber from a distance
but when you get near you see it is a
lesser and more recent (*c.*1935) man.
A striking clock was added to the tower in 1935.

Love to Goldilegz, JB

J.P. (see *Volume One*), the artist, was JB's best friend and collaborator.

JB, J.P. and Frederick Etchells (see *Volume One*), the architect, went to Edstone, Stratford-on-Avon, for a nature cure.

Etchells was a close friend of JB and J.P. They often called him 'Etchell' to annoy him.

Sir E. Guy Dawber (1861–1938) was an Edwardian architect who built many houses for the gentry in the Cotswolds.

The original Edstone Hall was pulled down in the twenties and replaced with a thirties Tudor-style house of an irregular shape designed by F. W. B. Yorke.

To John Murray   The Mead
                                                    Wantage
13 November 1952   Berkshire

Dear Jock,

We are starting a magazine here in connection with the Downs Group of churches, to be called the *Country Churchman*, and which will be the parish magazine of twenty parishes in this district. We shall be printing five thousand copies to start with for the first six months, and we want to put on the cover local views. I have said that subject to your approval, the editor of the magazine, who is the Reverend E. J. Rumens, Vicar of Lambourn, Berkshire, can borrow blocks he chooses from the *Berkshire Guide*.

I don't know whether you would be willing to lend the blocks, or whether it would be necessary to have stereos made. The average dimensions of the block will be six inches by six inches for the cover, and smaller for pictures inside. We would need one to two for each issue, one of which I hope would be on the cover.

I do hope you and your uncle and W. L. Farquharson will allow us to do this.

This magazine is a venture of faith. It will never make money, but it will eventually be able to pay humble fees. But not yet. Acknowledgements will of course be made to John Murray if you can grant us this permission.

Yours ever, John B

J.M. (see *Volume One*) was JB's publisher and friend.

The Reverend Rumens lived in the gabled redbrick rectory beside the church at Lambourn and showed films every so often after supper. JB took PB, PSGB and me to see *Kind Hearts and Coronets* there, one of his favourite films.

JB and John Piper had written Murray's *Guide to Berkshire* in 1948, with many photographs by JB.

To Bess Betjemann   Edstone Hall
                                             Stratford-on-Avon
18 November 1952   Warwickshire

Darling Bessie,
I am feeling apprehensive of this 'nature cure' – no smoking, no
drinking and raw cabbage and nuts. But I am told one feels twenty
years younger after it. So when you see me after it, expect a mop of
hair, flushed cheeks and a merry smile.
    God bless you, darling Bessie. Keep brave and calm. Trust in God
and don't worry. I will see you again, and Penelope is coming this
week. I'll write every day.
    Much love from John

> This was JB's last letter to his mother who was in a nursing home in Bath.
>   JB's grandparents added the extra 'n' to their surname during the Victorian craze for
> all things German. JB dropped it again while at Marlborough.
>   JB, John Piper and Frederick Etchells behaved so badly at Edstone during their
> 'nature cure' that they were asked to leave. They were caught red-handed buying
> prohibited food and drink locally.

To Alan Pryce-Jones   The Mead
                                             Wantage
22 December 1952   Berkshire

Dearest Bog,
Ta muchly for yours. It was all less awful than I thought it was going to
be. Prayers and help of friends is invaluable. Kindness and efficiency of
the clergy wonderful – one pardons at once their taste in art and sees
what they are for – so much more useful than doctors. And Bess made
her Communion often over these last few months. Guilt of course
comes on in waves. And you are v[ery] understanding. Prayer drives it
off or at any rate deflects it or sublimates it or something. And death
convinces one of the truth of immortality.
    So glad Poppy is back. Powlie [PSGB] has gone to France to ski in
Les Pyrennes [sic]. Poppy will know how to spell them and pronounce
them. I wish I knew what David P[ryce]-J[ones] looks like. I have no
idea.
    Colds are 'healing crises' they told Etchells and Mr Piper once at the

nature cure resort we went to, and do one good. Do they? Perhaps it is
nice when they stop.
    Love, JB

> JB's mother, Bess Betjemann, died in Bath on 13 December at number 16 Royal
> Crescent. 'Her death was a slow business but not painful or worried,' JB wrote to Patrick
> Kinross.

To Unknown Vicar   The Mead
                                                 Wantage
24 December 1952   Berkshire

Revered and dear Father,
I shall always remember your goodness and kindness to me, your
prayers and those masses during the last days of my mother's life on
earth. I shall always be grateful to you for your consideration and for
coming with me to view her body. I like to think, too, that your
kindness to me will have helped you with the Walshams a bit. I shall
remember you in my prayers and hope you will have a happy
Christmas and an *encouraged* New Year.
    Yours very sincerely, John Betjeman

> JB stayed with John and Sheila Walsham in Bath during his mother's last days. John
> Walsham, who became a naval commander, was working in the Admiralty at the time.
> He had been a childhood friend of JB's from Trebetherick days.

To John Summerson   Written on the
                                           Birkenhead to Folkestone Express
3 January 1953   between Reading and Cinderford

My dear Coolmore,
My many thanks to you for your kind letter. Seeing the dead body of
someone you've known all your life convinces you of the truth of
immortality. The body is so very unlike the spirit which it contained.
So my ma's death, apart from the anxiety while she was dying, the
macabre talk of the nurses – 'There's a smell of death in the room; she's
got that pinched look hasn't she?' said to me in her hearing while she
was supposedly 'unconscious' – was a kind of triumph. And prayers
and sympathy of friends are a great help to lessen the loss.

I too forgot the Diocesan. We might lunch for the next – whenever it is, and I don't know.

Ah, Twickenham and Isleworth! The group at the *latter* is a matter of scale and diverting a trunk road they intend to drive through a v[ery] nice market 'precinct'. Twickenham is safer ground for us. It is a charming riverside village, High Street and all to be destroyed. Nothing of great merit individually, but of surpassing merit *as a whole*. You'll agree, I think. Middlesex for ever.

Yours, JB

> J.S. (see *Volume One*), the architectural historian, was a close friend of JB. He was on the London Diocesan Advisory Committee with JB as well as on the Royal Fine Art Commission (as was Paul Methuen).
>
> In the event, as the *Middlesex Chronicle* (31 May 1984) recorded, JB 'played a large part in preventing old shops in Church Street and houses along Twickenham Embankment from being demolished for redevelopment'.

To William Collins   The Mead
                                                        Wantage
11 April 1953   Berkshire

Dear Collins,

I send herewith the manuscript of the first part of the *Collins Pocket Book of Churches*. It will be followed by the lists which E. T. Long has done and which I haven't got, except those for London, Berkshire, Buckinghamshire, Oxon, and the Isle of Man which I have done myself.

I am very anxious that my text should be seen by an Anglican priest who knows about church history and architecture, in order that any erroneous statements may be excised. The object of my text is to show the continuity of the history of our church as expressed in building and fittings, from Saxon times until today. That is why I have divided it into two halves, old churches and the newer churches, and I have kept off the Reformation as much as I could. The man I have in mind to look at the text is the Rev[eren]d B. F. L. Clarke, of Knowle Hill Vicarage, Reading, Berkshire. He is a scholar and wrote that book on *Nineteenth Century Church Builders* which was published by the SPCK.

If you think the text acceptable and worth having corrected, I should be grateful if you would send it on to him, and perhaps you would give him a fee, which can come out of my earnings, if there are any.

When E. T. Long's lists are in – and I imagine either you or he has them – you will have the complete book, and I then look forward to selecting the pictures, and knowing how much space I am going to have for them, how many to be in colour and how many plain, and I suppose I shall have the pleasure of talking about make-up to Delgado.

Yours ever, Jan Trebetjeman
The Celebrated Cornish Nationalist

W. 'Billy' C. (see *Volume One*) was head of the publishing firm of the same name.
JB had been initially approached by Collins in 1944 to write a guide to parish churches. The book *Collins Guide to English Parish Churches* did not appear until 1958.

To Anita Dent   The Mead
                                                                  Wantage
15 April 1953   Berkshire

My dear Anita (If I may presume to use your Christian name),
Yes, it is true that very dear delightful Jill Menzies leaves me in June.

But I have halved my reviewing which I hate as I have come into a tiny income which enables me to give some of it up. I will still need a secretary, but not a resident one.

I am going to live in London for two days a week and sometimes three with a friend, Lord Kinross at 4 Warwick Avenue, Paddington (by the canal) from when Jill leaves me.

Please answer these questions.

1) How much do you want a week?

2) Do you mind remaining in London?

3) Would you be prepared to be shared between me and someone else who needs a secretary (I would find him if need be and it might be Kinross) as I don't expect to be able to afford to pay a full-time secretary.

For your information I pay Jill three pounds, ten shillings a week and she gets her keep.

Yours, John Betjeman

A.D. had applied for the job as part-time secretary. She was the daughter of Major Leonard Dent, a friend of JB's and John Piper's who was an avid collector of Rowlandson and a local dignitary who lived near Reading.
JB had inherited a small nest-egg from his mother.
She accepted three pounds, ten shillings per week.
In the event P.K. didn't have enough work to merit sharing A.D.

To John Summerson   The Mead
                                                       Wantage
23 April 1953   Berkshire

Dear Coolmore,
You know the London Diocesan Advisory Committee at its last
meeting was calmly going to allow St Etheldreda's, Fulham, by
Skipwith, the only decent church in that dreary borough, to be
demolished and a new church to be built somewhere near with the
money from the War Damage Commission. You are right in saying
how important it is to go to these committee meetings. But I can't be at
the next one when the discussion about St Etheldreda's is going to be
opened again. Do please go if you can, and put in a word on behalf of
the church. You probably remember it, that tall, middle Scott-style
building in Fulham Palace Road. A surveyor's report, written from the
point of view of demolishing rather than preservation, has inspired the
Committee to allow the building to be destroyed. I suggest that another
surveyor be got to prepare a report with the idea of reconstruction, and
to make an estimate which can be compared with the cost of a whole
new church. I have got to give a vote of thanks in Reading for the
C[ouncil for the] P[reservation of] R[ural] E[ngland] on that day, so I
can't go to the meeting. For God's sake, come to the rescue of the house
of God.
    Yours, Nikolaus Pevsner (pp W. R. Lethaby)

        JB served on the London DAC from 1948 to 1963.
          J.S. replied (24 April 1953), 'Very well, I will go on Tuesday and try to help with St
        Etheldreda's. I remember it as a pleasant building and it is really shocking to pull it down
        and then build a dreadful new building.' Nevertheless the church (1896–97), by
        Skipwith, was pulled down and a new one built (1955–58) by Guy Biscoe.
          W. R. Lethaby, Norman Shaw's pupil, was seen by Pevsner as a pioneer of
        modernism. He was one of JB's favourite Victorian architects.

To Patrick Kinross   The Mead
                                                       Wantage
27 April 1953   Berkshire

Dear Pa'rick,
I enclose a ten-shilling [note] for the 'tammy' most gratefully received.
It suits her a treat and she is delighted.

You must imagine the face as freckled, pink and covered with golden fur, the eyes tiger-like and grey, the nose tip-tilted, and sultry lips and darkish hair and a tall hiking figure and high Scottish cheekbones.

I greatly look forward to renting a room from you and I think we can count Osbert and Karen [Lancaster] in for the autumn. O[sbert] says commuting *is* possible for summer months, but won't be in the winter.

My lovely Jill leaves me in June either to marry her young man who comes from Nyasaland or to become a schoolteacher. Will you need a secretary in London? I will and we *might* find one we could share. I shall be there Mon[day]s and Tues[days] for certain, except on [the] second Mon[day] of [the] month when I shall be there Tues[day] and Wed[ne]s[day].

Love to the Baroness. Oh, you are lucky to be in beautiful Ann Street. Love to Dorothy and Phillip Trotter.

Love JB

When in London JB lodged with P.K. in his house in Warwick Avenue, Little Venice. (While at university and afterwards he had often shared P.K.'s house in London in Yeoman's Row.)

JB always referred to P.K.'s mother as 'the Baroness'.

To Edmund Penning-Rowsell   The Mead
                                                               Wantage
29 April 1953   Berkshire

Dear Eddie,
The [19]49 Romaneche Thorins is excellent. I only broached the first
bottle last week. I would like to buy a half dozen of your Chambertin
[19]37 if you can spare it, or if not a half dozen, three.

   I am very amused by the excitement that has been caused by the
voting. I have voted for Douglas McClean, and was delighted with the
memorandum about the candidates that arrived.

   I think really in Brummagem [Birmingham] that the Art Gallery is
superb on nineteenth-century stuff. I also admire Pugin's R[oman]
C[atholic] cathedral of St Chad's, which I hope you saw, and the
beautiful eighteenth-century transparency by Eginton in that classical
church which stands in the middle of the square somewhere north of
Snow Hill station.

   I am very pleased to think that Miss Gere at once recognised the
beauty of Margaret Wintringham. [William] Morris would have been
nuts about her, and I can see her weaving a tapestry for him while he
went on writing his epics. She would look very nice dressed in Morris
curtains and carrying a wooden bucket into which her sad eyes could
drop tears.
   Yours, JB

> E.P.-R. worked for Batsford's, the publishers, and was also an expert on wine. He
> advised JB on what to buy and made him a member of the Wine Society, whose
> committee was just being reorganised. JB bought the Chambertin for seventeen shillings
> and sixpence a bottle direct from E.P.-R., who had overstocked his cellar.
>   Miss Gere was the daughter of the artist Charles Gere, who had worked with Morris.
>   E.P.-R. was married to Margaret (née Wintringham, see *Volume One*) for whom JB
> had a great affection.

To Miss M. L. Tudor   The Mead
                                                               Wantage
22 May 1953   Berkshire

Dear Miss Tudor,
It was so kind of you to see us the day before yesterday.
   I have given much thought to the future of 'A la Ronde', and I am

quite sure that the first thing you should do is to have it valued by an estate agent. It is not worth having it surveyed; that is an expensive business, and anyhow if there is any suggestion of selling the place, the purchaser will make a survey.

What you have to reckon about 'A la Ronde' is this. Its value as a summer holiday house might be considerable to someone who was fond of shell work and liked Georgian decoration, and who was rich enough to turn it into a private paradise of their own. This would ensure its preservation. But such a person would be unlikely to want to show the house to visitors as it is rather small for when they would be in residence. Again such a person might be willing to show it when they are not in residence and get a little income that way. It was for this purpose that I brought Lady Anne Tree down to see the house, since she is an expert on shell work and has done beautiful restoration on her own shell room at Mereworth in Kent.

If you can't find a purchaser, you might leave it to the Georgian Group. But whether you find a purchaser or not, I am sure you should have it valued by a London agent. I suggest someone like Lofts and Warner, 41 Berkeley Square, London w1, because a big London agent will not only know local land values but will also appreciate its interest as a Georgian collection, and will know possibilities of finding a purchaser interested in Georgian work.

I don't think you will find that it is worth twenty thousand pounds. I should have thought more like six thousand or five thousand, because beauty is not something people are willing to pay money for. They think in terms of heat, light, shelter, and it is on that valuation that you will have to base your ideas.

I am so sorry for you having to take people round and go up all those stairs and get so little return, and I do hope that some solution may be found. I am sure that the valuation is the first practical step. Let me know what comes of it.

Yours sincerely, John Betjeman

'A la Ronde', above Exmouth in Devon, with seaward and Powderham Castle views, is a fantasy house built in 1798. It is sixteen-sided with tiny rooms radiating from an octagon, lit above from a lantern. One room is decorated entirely in feathers, and others are filled with shells, pictures, and *objets* all collected by the two Miss Parminters who created the house. JB took PSGB and me there in the summer of 1953. In the end, M.L.T. didn't sell the house. After her death, 'A la Ronde' passed through the female line to Mrs Tudor-Perkins who eventually sold it to the National Trust in the eighties.

To Evelyn Waugh   The Mead
                                                          Wantage
24 May 1953   Berkshire

Dear Evelyn,
Ta muchly, ole man, for your very generous present of this superb
edition of *Love Among the Ruins*. It could not have come at a more
appropriate moment, for only last Sunday I visited Stevenage New
Town in the rainy afternoon. It was exactly like your book. Three miles
of Lionel Brett-style prefabs interrupted by Hugh Casson blocks of
flats and two shopping arcades and concrete roads and lampposts
throughout and no trees, only muddy Hertfordshire inclines. I saw
through the vast, unprivate ground floor window of a house, a
grey-faced woman washing up. My goodness, it was terrifying. And
kiddies' scooters lying out in the rain on the streets and a big vita-glass
school on stilts. The inhabitants have been driven out of Tottenham to
live in it.
    Love Among the Ruins is like all your books, NO EXAGGERATION.
    Ta muchly, ole man, once more for so splendid and beautifully
illustrated a work.
    Yours, John B

> *Love Among the Ruins: A Romance of the New Future* was published in 1953.
> Lionel Brett and Hugh Casson were contemporary architects.

To Patrick Kinross   The Mead
                                                          Wantage
21 August 1953   Berkshire

My dear Pa'rick,
When I asked the Dowager Duchess at Hardwick whether she had ever
used Chiswick House she said, 'Only for breakfasts. But people don't
have them now. We went there by a barouche. In those days *everyone*
had a villa – there was Syon, Osterley and the Buccleuchs had that
place at Richmond.' When I asked whether she used Compton Place,
Eastbourne she said, '*Always* at Whitsun.'
    Off to Aunt Elsie [McCorkindale], Torquil Cottage, Trebetherick,

Wadebridge, Cornwall until Sept[ember] 6th and then with you on Sept[ember] 8th, Mead on Sept[ember] 7th.
Love, JB

> The Dowager Duchess of Devonshire, EC's grandmother, was then living at Hardwick Hall.
> Chiswick House on London's outskirts was built in 1728 for Lord Burlington and had always belonged to the Devonshire family. (It is now in the guardianship of English Heritage.) The Devonshires still own property in Eastbourne.

To Alec Clifton-Taylor   *Time and Tide*
                                                           34 Bloomsbury Street
September 1953   London WCI

Dear Clifton-Taylor,
I am so sorry I have been long in answering your letter, and I am sorry too that I was not there when you called at *Time and Tide*. I understand your distress and I also think you put the case for Pevsner admirably in your letter – or rather not the case for Pevsner but for the sort of thing Pevsner's guides ought to be and are not. I quite agree with you that there is room both for the personal approach and for the catalogue. But if you are writing the latter it is essential that you should be accurate. You and I know really exactly how Pevsner has compiled most of his guides. He has employed a series of *studentium* who have gone round getting things out of directories and sometimes using their own eyes, but not, I suspect, often; he has made full use often without acknowledgement of Goodhart-Rendel's card index in the R[oyal] I[nstitute of] B[ritish] A[rchitects]; and has visited some of the more *important* monuments in the country himself; and the result is that a thing like the guides to *Nott[ingham]s[hire]*, *Durham*, *Devon* and *Cornwall* are something that are neither complete as a catalogue nor distinctive as a personal approach. This I don't think is a matter of opinion but a matter of fact, and that is why I maintain that we cannot continue to praise Pevsner. I very much hope I shall see you soon, for you are, as I have said before, a wonder reviewer.

> A.C.-T., the architectural writer, was a professional acquaintance of JB's who later became a friend.
> JB had written an ungenerous review, picking up minor errors, of Pevsner's *County Durham* in the *Times Literary Supplement* which was edited by Alan Pryce-Jones. A.C.-T. wrote (18 July 1953) a long letter in defence of Pevsner: 'I don't blame you for

disagreeing: clearly they [Pevsner's *Guides*] are not for you. But I do feel grieved that you won't let me tell the readers of *Time and Tide* that I think there is room for both (my simile of the food and wine expresses what I feel exactly). When you first approached me about writing for *T[ime] and T[ide]*, you said that the pay was very bad but that one could at least say what one liked. Aren't you now going back on this? . . . I should like to go on reviewing for you: I greatly appreciate the too-generous things you say about my humble efforts. But I do also feel rather wretched about this business.'

In 1957 JB reviewed Pevsner's *Northumberland*, part of the Buildings of England Series, in the *Daily Telegraph:* 'Doctor Pevsner has continued his steadily improving catalogue of the buildings of England . . . . It is impossible to read Dr Pevsner in a sitting. His work is a reference book and as such it is useful.'

To Janet and Reynolds Stone   The Mead
                                                                 Wantage
9 September 1953   Berkshire

Dear Janet and Reynolds,
We had a very comfortable journey back and tea at Milton Abbas and we looked at the Abbey and then drove around Bryanston and reached home by eight.

In the train yesterday I met Monty [Compton Mackenzie] and Chrissie, and M[onty] was in terrific form, full of a visit to Aberdeen University he had made with Gilbert Harding. The latter was sitting behind a lady with a bare-back dress at a student's play and he had had too much to drink and kept dropping off to sleep and falling forward. His moustache touched her bare back so many times that eventually she had to leave the theatre.

Your house is supremely beautiful and I told Monty all about it. He listened quite a lot. Ta ever so, old things, for ever so jolly a time in so lovely a place.

Love from John B

R.S., the engraver, and his wife J.S. (see *Volume One*) lived at Litton Cheney in Dorset where JB and the family often stayed or visited on the way to and from Cornwall.

Gilbert Harding (1907–60), the outspoken broadcaster and former schoolmaster, began his career with the BBC in 1940. He became famous for being Chairman of the *Brains Trust*, Question Master of *Twenty Questions* and Quiz Master of the *Round Britain Quiz*. JB appeared on television with him often in programmes like *What's My Line?* and *Who Said That?* They got on like a house on fire.

To Patrick Kinross   The Mead
                                                        Wantage
9 October 1953   Berkshire

Dear Pa'rick,
Would you like to dine with me at the Grocers' Co[mpany] on
Nov[ember] 25th at 6.45 for 7.15 – Evening Dress with Decorations?
Major Dent will be there, but no one else you know. I am a very
unimportant Grocer so you will not get a good *placement*, my dear. But
if you've never been to this Victorian assembly, you will find it v[ery]
strange.

What happened about poor old Rupert C[roft]-C[ooke]? I thought of
him all yesterday and the day before. Oh, now I see today's *D[aily]
Telegraph*. To hell with these dreadful laws. He won't win his appeal.
No appeal ever does get through. I wish I could somehow help him.
Prayer I suppose is the only thing.

Yours, Anette O'Brien Saunders

> Major Dent was on the Court of the Grocers' Company, one of the old City of London
> guilds.
>   Rupert Croft-Cooke, the writer, was a friend of both PB and JB. He wrote *Bosie* in
> 1963 and *The Unrecorded Life of Oscar Wilde* in 1972. He went to prison for a longish term
> after getting himself into a 'spot of bother' with a sailor. His term caused a furore among
> the liberal-minded of the day.

To John Murray   The Mead
                                                        Wantage
12 October 1953   Berkshire

My dear Jock,
I have spent a morning looking through my verses. Of the thirty you
have set up to which you can add two which are not set up – 'Remorse'
which I sent to you and one on Willesden Church and in blank verse
soon to come (both poems gloomy) – sixteen are concerned with death
and self-pity and might be arranged under the title 'gloomy', nine are
medium and the remaining seven are light verse and don't pretend to be
anything else.

I think therefore they should be arranged under three sections:
'Gloom', 'Medium/Jocund', 'Light/Blithe', and not in the rather
haphazard order arranged in the galleys.

I see no need for a preface except a sentence of thankfulness on my part for the unexpected popularity of my verse which can appear above the list of acknowledgements. I might also add that I expect soon to be unfashionable and forgotten.

As to title, Goldilegz [Myfanwy Piper] thought of *A Few Late Chrysanthemums* and I like that very much. The most honest title would be *Gloom, Lust and Self-pity* or we might be purely topographical and call it *Baker Street and Other Poems* or we might call it *Neither Jocund Nor Blithe* or we might call it *Grandsire Doubles* or again *Cemetery Verses* or *Necropolis* – this last has a good 'twenties' ring about it.

I think we should omit 'In Overcliffe' and 'Easter 1948' – the first is not good enough and the latter is too personal.

Love from Ewan Quetjeman

> The poems were eventually divided into the suggested sections entitled 'Light', 'Gloom' and 'Medium'. The acknowledgements were short and thanked 'Mr John Sparrow for some sensitive and wise corrections to several of the poems'.
>
> 'Easter, 1948' was not published until 1994 when it appeared in *Volume One* of JB's letters. It was about PB's conversion to Catholicism. 'In Overcliffe' was not published in any collection of JB's poetry:

> In *Overcliffe*, it was in *Overcliffe*
>   That Peter shyly showed me first his trains
> Perched on that turf and thymy clover cliff
>   While down below the seaweed stank like drains
> A warm and blustering sou'wester shook
> The bellows hanging in the inglenook
> Red velveteen I wore, red velveteen
>   Mummy's magenta lipstick on my lips
> My hair was all fluff'd out, fluff'd out with 'Drene'
>   I smiled a little and I swung my hips
> But he said nothing as he held the door
> Except 'The rest are out till half-past four.'

> Ewan Quetjeman was JB's Manx pseudonym.

To George Barnes   The Mead
                                                                     Wantage
29 October 1953   Berkshire

My dear Commander,
Penelope and I laughed so much when we saw *The Times* this morning that I brought up my breakfast with [the] coughing fit induced by my delighted laughter. Well I *am* pleased. But not surprised. I look forward to you showing me the letter of congratulations which B. E. Nicholls

sends you. I am writing separately to Lady Barnes and her son Little Prawlz. Did you learn to kneel on the Studio floor? You are now higher than Paget and well on your way to being Seely. Don't answer this except with the printed slip you have had done for replies to letters like this.

Love from Sir Kenneth, Sir Hugh and Sir Reginald Barnes

> G.B. had just been knighted for services to broadcasting.
> B. E. Nicholls was G.B.'s *bête noir* at the BBC.
> 'The Partners', as JB called Seely and Paget, were architects to St Paul's Cathedral with a flourishing and distinguished practice. John Seely became Lord Mottistone and Paul Paget was not titled.

To Evelyn Waugh   The Mead
                                                    Wantage
26 December 1953   Berkshire

Dear Evelyn,

Oh no, old boy. There was never a pipe from the tap to the basin such as you envisaged. The tap was probably cold, the mouth hot. Patrick's water closet was a genuine part of the works of the wash stand. You'll have to call in an old-fashioned plumber to discover its use. I look forward to seeing it working and in its new setting. I like to think of it at Stinkers [Stinchcombe]. It will be very happy there and safe from the V[ictoria] and A[lbert Museum].

Awful about Hasleden, isn't it? I went to an exhibition of his work at Aldeburgh this year. He was v[ery] deaf and cared for by a horse-maniac daughter. He could only communicate by being written to on a slate.

Penelope reads you every night in bed instead of the Knox translation of the N[ew] T[estament].

Cheerioh ole man and a Happy N[ew] Y[ear]. Love, John B

> JB had given E.W. a wash-stand by William Burges, probably made for Lord Bute in 1875. 'The Betjeman Benefaction' as E.W. called it, arrived at Piers Court, E.W.'s house in Stinchcombe, Gloucestershire, minus an imagined serpentine bronze pipe which was supposed to have led from the dragon's mouth to the basin. He had a big row with Pickfords about it, before discovering that it never had one in the first place. A similar incident later appeared in E. W.'s novel *The Ordeal of Gilbert Pinfold*.
> 'Sad about Hasleden's death, I thought he would see us out,' E.W. wrote (29 December 1953). W. K. Hasleden (1872–1953) did humorous drawings for *Punch* and the *Daily Mirror*.

Two:

I'll walk the streets of London

1954 to 1956

Oh when my love, my darling,
  You've left me here alone,
I'll walk the streets of London
  Which once seemed all our own.
  'The Cockney Amorist'

As the willow trees down by Letcombe Brook grew taller, so my mother's enthusiasm for her waterfowl farm dwindled. Beverley, the girl she employed to help collect the eggs, suffered from *petit mal*, a mild form of epilepsy, and two or three times a week would stand and sway gently, moaning slightly, with her eyes turned to the sky. If she was holding a basket of eggs, my mother would recite consecutive Hail Marys until she stopped. Mercifully she never did drop a basket but her wages were scarcely paid for by the revenue from the farm, so gradually the goose and duck population dropped and my mother took up a new venture instead.

The Martins, who owned a bookshop with a small teashop attached in Newbury Street, just off Wantage's red-brick Market Square, were about to go out of business and approached JB for financial assistance. He agreed to help out. The bookshop soon folded but my mother offered to run the teashop. She called it 'King Alfred's Kitchen', and had painted on its sign, 'Burnt cakes a speciality'. 'No sooner did I start work in the little upstairs kitchen,' she remembered, 'than the floor gave way (no doubt beneath my weight) and we had to close for a fortnight while all the timbers were renewed. Then we started work in earnest. I employed Mrs King, a professional waitress and a former Lyons' "Nippy".' As my mother was an exceptional cook, the teashop soon became a favourite haunt of local gentlefolk, but on the installation of a Gaggia coffee machine (inspired by her latest trip to Italy) from which were served some of the first espressos in the whole of Berkshire, a different clientele began to wander into the 'caff', as she and JB used to call it. Teddy boys in suede shoes arrived on scooters and in buses from Newbury and Oxford. My mother didn't mind, but they only bought one espresso and then monopolised the seats all morning.

She started doing lunches in the hopes of attracting other types of customer. Owing to her staunch moral values, she was so insistent that she couldn't make too much profit that she used to charge three shillings and sixpence for a four-course lunch, actually losing money in the process. JB complained about the funds he had to keep pouring into the 'caff'.

In defiance, and in order to save money by not having a car, my mother bought a Vespa (again because of her love affair with Italy) but finding it too slow, she soon upgraded to a Norton 500cc motor bike. I had to wear a riding hat while travelling pillion and once fell off on the way to Swindon. But far worse, I had to undergo the embarrassment of being picked up at my posh new boarding school, St Mary's Wantage, by my mother on the Norton wearing a yellow circular macintosh. JB refused to ride on the back of the Norton.

One summer's day in 1956 after a good lunch he walked past the Utility Vehicle Centre in Great Portland Street which dealt in second-hand estate cars. In the front showroom, surrounded by red rope, was the only new car in the place – a Peugeot 203 estate car. 'What a pretty car,' said JB to the salesman, Martin Bailey. 'I do like it.' It was grey and very modern looking. JB didn't have the money to buy it. He got Martin Bailey to drive him to the offices of his agent David Higham and persuaded the latter to advance him the money. The Peugeot was the first and last smart car we ever owned. My mother was *furious* at the waste of money, but couldn't deny the car's usefulness for the weekly collection of dustbins full of pig swill from Great Shefford, with which she fed our multitude of free-range chickens.

As time went by, our return journeys from Sunday communion gathered newly made clerical friends and neighbours such as the Reverend Hugh Pickles and sometimes his friend the Reverend Harry Jarvis, who had been born in Wantage and often returned there. One morning I remember getting back to the Mead at about eleven o'clock, and finding the doors locked and arrows painted on card pointing towards the lawn. There, sitting beside the goldfish pond, was JB's teddy bear Archie holding an empty whisky bottle, surrounded by several other empty spirit bottles. My mother didn't approve of JB drinking at the best of times but this was a particularly bad morning because he had got quite drunk the night before at dinner with Robert Heber-Percy at Faringdon. 'There are such good arguments for teetotalism that I cannot attempt to counteract them. Some of the people I like best, including my wife, are teetotal,' wrote JB in the *Compleat Imbiber* later that month. 'I think if you are a strong character you can enjoy the sensation of not having a drink. But suppose you are a weak character? Suppose you need a prop, like me, to your self-assurance, and need stimulants to strengthen it?'[1]

JB formed a great attachment to Wantage. He fought for its shop fronts through the Council for the Preservation of Rural England, he wrote the introduction to the booklet about the Wantage tramcar and took great interest in its route which wound from Wantage Road Station to Wantage. But it wasn't long before he became beleaguered by gentle, well-meaning ladies. 'Oh Mr Betjeman, I *wonder* if you would be *very* kind and open the church bazaar?' The Wantage Sisters asked him to become a governor of St Mary's School. I got glowing reports from Miss Wimpress, the art teacher, and Miss Phillips, the history teacher, both of whom were desperately in love with JB and worshipped him from afar, but bad reports from everyone else. The French mistress was amazed by the French poems Paul and I had been taught to recite from an early age by JB, who had composed them. He told us that these were old French nursery rhymes:

> *Dans le petit jardin*
> *Avec pommes de terre*
> *Marche Monsieur Chardin*
> *Le révolutionnaire.*

and:

> *Ici nous sommes*
> *Dans la même vieux groove*
> *Jean-Paul Sartre*
> *Et Pierre-Jean Jouve.*

As a school governor, JB insisted that for breakfast and tea the margarine be changed for butter, and I was allowed to give up maths and be a vegetarian. I wrote to my parents, 'The food is very nice now and the custard is in a jug on the table, so you don't *have* to have it.'[2]

My brother was reaching the end of his time at Eton. He had become champion of gym, and was in the gym VIII. He could do handsprings and somersaults in the air without a springboard – a fact I bragged about all over school. Oliver Van Oss wrote to JB in the Lent term of 1955, 'Paul has an alert and critical mind. . . . I mean that he gets the answers right, but he seems desperately anxious to leave next half. He is vividly aware that both his parents are unusual and gifted people, with strongly individual personalities. This makes him watchful and wary even in religious matters. He very much wants to be himself and not JB's son. It may be an argument against Oxford, I don't know, he is obviously devoted to his home – but I mention it as it may provide a clue which you can follow up more easily than I can.'[3] It was definitely harder for Paul to accept my parents' idiosyncrasies than it was for me. Alan Pryce-Jones's son David remembers JB coming down to Eton often and taking them both out to tea. 'I always felt mortified for Paul. John used to treat him in a childish way in front of me and I remember Paul curling up with embarrassment. But I also knew he was the kindest man in the world. When my mother died of cancer, John came straight down to Eton the same day and spent a long time talking to me and comforting me.'[4] JB often behaved in exactly the same way to me as he did to Paul – but I took it to be the joke it was. I just told him to shut up. I don't think it was possible for my brother to do so.

On the other hand, Paul revered JB in lots of ways. He was impressed by his juggling. He used to do it with three false tomatoes which he had bought from a butcher's shop where they were used for display among the raw chops and steaks. He was *brilliant* at it. He was good at several conjuring tricks, particularly those involving cards, and passed this enthusiasm on to my brother, to whom he gave an extremely elaborate and expensive conjuring set one Christmas. JB also passed on his love of good wine and exotic food to Paul. He once took us to the Swan just outside Newbury after we'd been to look at the nearby Strawberry Hill Gothic house, Sandleford Priory. He insisted that we both try oysters, his favourite food in the world – he could eat a dozen at any time of the day or night. Although Paul loved his, I distinctly remember swallowing this completely revolting thing which came straight up again. I have never touched one since.

But what we enjoyed most during the holidays was being allowed to accompany him on location film work. In 1954 Independent Television began and, with it, the birth of hundreds of film companies. Because of JB's long experience, not least in making propaganda films during the war, he was inundated with requests to commentate and be involved with topographical films. In 1955 he made twenty-six short films for his friend Jack Beddington, the advertising director of Shell, in a series called *Discovering Britain*. JB wrote to John Piper (16 July 1955), 'I don't think I've enjoyed anything so much since our Shell and Murray Guide days. Of course the secret is keeping the camera on the move, whether looking at a flower, or a box pew or a painted ceiling. The man who does it all, Peter Mills, is a fast motor maniac, mad on engines, but he is just the chap for these films and as funny as you and I are in the same way, and the one thing to avoid is a series of "Dixon Scotts" which is what they show on film in BBC TV and then, of course, one has to do a lot of detail or it does not show on a hideous TV screen and one cannot have too many verticals as they bend at the top and bottom.'[5]

Paul and I went with him on location to Stourhead, Avebury, Great Coxwell Tithe Barn, Clifton Suspension Bridge and Crofton Beam Engine House. 'If I have a mission at all,' JB said, ' – and I am speaking quite seriously about television – it is to show people things which are beautiful so that they will very soon realise what is ugly. I really do want to help people to use their eyes as they go through life. Why, when you look *at* things, instead of just looking through them, life starts absolutely crackling with interest and excitement. Look at that trick of sunlight coming through the bare trees and across the gold hands on the church clock; look at the variety of shade in those bricks; the light and shadow in the graveyard – look at that ivy and that purposeful old lady trying to force her way into St Bartholomew's through the north door which is clearly shut.'[6]

During this time JB also made dozens of programmes in a series called *The Faith in the West*, often entailing specially written verse, for the religious broadcasting section of the BBC in Bristol. He was away from Wantage more and more, and decided that he needed to have a work room in London. Patrick Kinross, his old friend from Oxford, offered him one in his house in Warwick Avenue. JB was used to sharing with Patrick. In the late twenties and early thirties 'the Yeo' in Yeoman's Row, Patrick's earlier house, had been his second home during all his university days and after. He felt quite at home with Patrick. Anita Dent, his new secretary, the daughter of John Piper's and JB's friend Major Dent, worked for him three days a week. She remembers his room at Patrick's being referred to as 'the Holy Church', and being crammed full with books for review.[7] During his time in Warwick Avenue JB became a fringe member of what he called 'the Paddington Set', over which the hostess Diana Cooper presided and which included Patrick, the composer Lennox Berkeley and his wife Freda, and the painter Adrian Daintrey.

JB's social life burgeoned, but then I never remember a time when it didn't. He was one of those people who lit up rooms, not because he was famous, but simply because he had an extra electricity about him – he imbued everyone around him with enthusiasm, and made every-thing fresh – as though he was seeing it for the first time. He seldom said 'no' to invitations. He went to a barbecue given by his friend John Sutro in January 1954 for Texan airmen at Denham Studios at which there was square dancing. He lunched with Michael Balcon at Ealing

Studios. He saw Evelyn Waugh, William Plomer and Jack James his old friend from Marlborough who was now Deputy Master of the Mint. He brought Anthony West on holiday with us to Trebetherick and we stayed with Bertie Abdy, the art collector and dealer, at Newton Ferrers on the return journey and I fell for his son Valentine. 'It was wonderful to see you,' wrote Bertie (5 September 1954). 'Doesn't it show how old I am – I can remember how bad Ingres was and how I was ridiculed in the newspaper for buying *Ingénue* by Renoir for five thousand pounds.'[8]

Throughout his life JB kept in touch with all his old friends. W. H. Auden, who was living in America, sent him a photograph of himself in a deckchair by the sea. Underneath he had written, 'To Clemency from Mrs Fairclough.' It wasn't difficult to make JB laugh. Sam Gurney wrote to him about Church politics in Compton Beauchamp, Alan Pryce-Jones wrote about gossip and 'Cracky' William Wicklow supplied miscellaneous news from Ireland on an almost weekly basis. They commiserated about their much-loved friend the Colonel being ill. The Reverend Colin Stephenson had just written from Oxford (30 January 1955), 'I saw the Colonel this week having been up twice and each time he was asleep. I came away very unhappy because he is in a ward and of course watched all the time and is convinced they are trying to murder him which of course makes him violent. He says they are trying to make him wet his bed and don't wash him properly and I must say he did seem a bit unkempt but then it is possible he won't let them touch him. He does not appear to have any treatment other than dope.'[9] Nor did JB lose touch with 'Freckly' Jill Menzies. He would take her out to lunch and then on an architectural trip. 'Thank you for giving me such a nice time, I'm sorry I was so depressing,' she wrote (October 1955). 'Anyhow I do want to see you again, you needn't think I don't really. You understand things like Croydon as no one else would and I should miss you very much if we did stop seeing each other.'[10]

In the end, the room JB was using at Warwick Avenue wasn't quite large enough. He needed a place of his own. Through his friend George Barnes he had met Lord Mottistone, who owned a tiny house above a shop in the City which he suggested JB should rent. In August 1954 he moved to 43 Cloth Fair up a side alley next to St Bartholomew the Great, within sound of its booming bells and the dawn rumblings of the nearby Smithfield Meat Market. His rent was two hundred pounds a year. William Morris came too; his willow pattern wallpaper graced the narrow stairway, which led to the red 'Bird and Anemone' in the sitting room where a sketch of Belfast by Sir Charles Nicholson hung above the fireplace. The window overlooked St Bart's graveyard. There was a tiny kitchen next door, and upstairs a bathroom and bedroom.

John Mottistone and his companion, Paul Paget, were partners in the architectural firm Seely and Paget and architects to St Paul's Cathedral. They lived in 45 Cloth Fair next to JB in one of the only Elizabethan houses to survive the Great Fire of London. It was sumptuously comfortable inside and had a bathroom which contained two baths side by side. John Mottistone was a stylish and innovative character. In 1955 JB and I went to stay at Mottistone Magna, his home on the Isle of Wight, where the touches of discreet modernity and close-fitting tartan carpets made an indelible impression on me.

Cloth Fair saw the beginning of JB's independence but for the next twenty years he seldom missed a weekend at home in Wantage unless it was for reasons of work. And at the Mead, as always, there were money problems. My mother appeared to need twelve hundred a year to run the house. JB said that was exorbitant. 'The Caff' was losing money and a small Caterpillar tractor my mother had bought to pull harrows over the fields had run away with her up a tree and been uninsured. JB was always difficult about money – extremely generous in some respects but when asked for cash to pay household bills he was the opposite. My mother decided to take in paying guests, not without some pleasure, because she loved talking to people. First there was a young Indian man, a Parsee, called Kaiky. He worked at Harwell and Paul remembers him as being an excellent buffer at meals between JB and our mother. He was followed by an old lady called Mrs Bruce to whom my mother talked about Roman Catholicism and then there were two American débutantes, one of whom my brother fancied, whom my mother took all round Oxford.

Meanwhile JB was writing to his accountant, Mr Masterson, 'Perfectly honestly, I think you could say that the sum of £435 for entertaining and travelling expenses is ridiculously low. I have to take taxis if I am to fulfil all my engagements and they amount to not less than twelve shillings daily, that is to say forty-eight shillings a week. Underground and bus fares amount to say three shillings and sixpence a week, then there are fares to different parts of the country giving lectures or connected with wireless or the Royal Fine Art Commission which could hardly fail to amount to three pounds a month. This is fares only. There is also the matter of entertainment. My work, which in 1956 was the same as now, is concerned with keeping in touch with new buildings, the fate of old buildings; writers and artists about whom I write for a living involve me in belonging to clubs and constantly going out to meals, or staying nights in hotels in provincial towns. Out of the eight meals that I have in London, it probably means that four of them I pay for and four of them I would be the guest at these meals. I would certainly usually drink wine and I think you ought to reckon that my entertainment expenses in London per week amount to eight pounds.'[11] Despite his extensive entertaining, JB was also working hell for leather.

He got eight pounds a week for a column in the *Spectator*, 'City and Suburban'. This gave him a platform for his views on virtually anything he felt strongly about. People began to write to him out of the blue about conservation and he found himself getting into longer and longer correspondences. He published a regular casualty list of threatened buildings in the *Spectator*, together with the names of the demolishers. For instance, he listed, 'Belhus, Averley, Essex, a rambling enlarged manor house. . . . The Essex County Council are the demolishers.' He battled against certain lines of pylons. He waged a war against the Bishop of Ripon in the autumn of 1954 and wrote to Michael Rosse (3 December 1954) referring to the Bishop as 'the Vandal Bishop. . . . He is also going to destroy a Bodley church (St Edward's), the only church in Holbeck, Leeds.'[12] He tried to stop an atomic power station at Bradwell in Essex and wrote to *The Times*, 'When your correspondent, Mr Cox, says, "Progress is a sad thing in some respects but the good of the majority must always come first", is he only thinking of more electric heaters and television sets or is he thinking of England?'[13] He got abusive letters from town clerks. He dined with Sir John Cockroft, head of all the atomic installations in England, in an endeavour to persuade him to consult a lot of aesthetes like John Piper and himself, instead of administrators, when choosing sites for his atomic stations.

He wote to the secretary of the Council for the Care of Churches about the threatened Coal Exchange (17 March 1956), 'Darling Miss Scott, Indeed we must keep up the fight but I am told that [Anthony] Eden wants to show himself as a strong man here at any rate, even if he can't in Cyprus. If we do save it, you and I might go away to the South of France together.'[14] Despite waging serious conservation battles his *Spectator* pieces were often light-hearted – as in June 1955, 'One of the most glorious things about the railway strike has been the virtual silencing of station announcers. Those cultural accents which pronounce all names as "Margit, Ramsgit, Chipnem, Glorster, Cheltnem, etc.", were gradually doing away with local pronunciations.'

When Geoffrey Faber offered JB one hundred pounds to edit an anthology of English love poems, he replied that he would only do it with Geoffrey Taylor, his old and valued friend in Ireland, who had taken over his job as poetry editor at *Time and Tide*. JB wrote to Geoffrey (23 November 1955), 'I think you should have much more than half what Fabers offer for all the work you are going to do. . . . Do you think we are allowed to include homosexual verse?'[15] Geoffrey replied, 'The easiest way would be to go through the various Oxford books (I have them all), copy out the famous bits and have the whole thing done by Christmas – no fun for anyone. As it is, by about March we'll have something good and fairly original anyway; and I at least will have read so much love that I'll probably never love again.'[16] To JB's devastation, Geoffrey Taylor died of a heart attack, completely unexpectedly, in July. One of his last conscious acts was to approve the preface which appears in *English Love Poems*, published in 1957.

JB's collection of poems, *A Few Late Chrysanthemums*, which came out in 1955 was well received by the critics. Malcolm Muggeridge chose it as his book of the year and Evelyn Waugh eulogised him in the *Sunday Times* while Cyril Connolly was on holiday. Perhaps for the first time he was being taken more seriously as a poet. His contemporaries, all nearing their mid-century, knew that it was now or never, as did JB. Sometimes his own reviews of other writers' work in the *Telegraph* brought rewarding letters. Robin Maugham wrote, 'I must write to let you know how much your review of *Behind the Mirror* meant to me. It came out at a moment when I felt really depressed and it just made all the difference – to me and needless to say to the book. I am awfully glad you liked it. And I shall now go ahead and write another one.'[17]

JB continued to write poems and sent two to the *New Yorker*, with whom he had a contract. His poem 'Edward James' was returned as 'not suitable' but 'The Cockney Amorist' was accepted – a poem which he had written for and about Elizabeth Cavendish. It told of their happiness together, but insinuated that she had left him. JB had written to Jack Beddington (2 January 1954) around the time of its composition, 'I am ill from a broken heart at present and the pleasures of life seem very far away.'[18] Elizabeth did not want to break up my parents' marriage and tried her utmost to give him up. She behaved with honour; and for the rest of JB's life, both she and my mother continued to do so.

In the *Spectator* of 31 August 1956 JB wrote, 'This week I had my fiftieth birthday. I had felt it coming on for some time. Standing nude in the bathroom two months ago, I suddenly realised I could not see my toes any more because my stomach was in the way. I started reviewing my past life, first through a magnifying mist of self pity – never quite made the grade, not taken seriously by the *Times Literary Supplement*, Penguin Books, the Courtauld, the Warburg, the *Listener*, the University Appointments Board, the Museums Association, the Library Association, the Institute of Sanitary Engineers. I thought of the many people at school with me who were now knights and politicians. I wanted to cry.'

1. JB 'Unwise and Wise Drinking', *Compleat Imbiber* (1956).
2. JB's papers, University of Victoria, British Columbia.
3. JB's papers, University of Victoria.
4. David Pryce-Jones, CLG interview (1994).
5. John Piper's papers.
6. JB, interview in *Illustrated London News* (1955).
7. Anita McFarlane, CLG interview (1993).
8. JB's papers, University of Victoria.
9. JB's papers, University of Victoria.
10. JB's papers, University of Victoria.
11. Carbon copy, JB's papers, University of Victoria.
12. Michael Rosse's papers, Birr Castle, County Offaly.
13. Carbon copy, JB's papers, University of Victoria.
14. Judith Scott's papers.
15. Geoffrey Taylor's papers.
16. JB's papers, University of Victoria.
17. JB's papers, University of Victoria.
18. Jack Beddington's papers, British Library.

To John Foster-White   The Mead
                                                           Wantage
14 January 1954   Berkshire

Dear Foster-White,
In [the] second stanza of 'Middlesex' which *Punch* could not print because of advertising, you should have as well that letter to you which was the birth of the poem:

> Well cut WINDSMOOR flapping lightly
> JACQMAR scarf of mauve and green
> Hiding hair which Friday-nightly
> Delicately drowned in DRENE
> Fair Elaine the bobby-soxer
> Fresh complexioned with INNOXA
> Gains the garden – father's hobby –
> Hangs her WINDSMOOR in the lobby
> Settles down to sandwich supper and
> The television screen.

I am entranced with your account of the Rodings. I went to Berners R[oding] last year. What a sad tale it is. As a youth I stayed at Shellow Bowells and worshipped in the church.

I will want your help on my church book. I shall be in London during the first days of the week, despite no *T[ime] and T[ide]* and there is no reason why we should not meet. Love to those extraordinary publishers. Remind me to tell you about the late Colonel Harding and the Seely Service Co. Ltd.

Yours, John Betjeman

J.F.-W. (see *Volume One*) was editorial director of the publishers Macdonalds.
  The whole of 'Middlesex' subsequently appeared in *A Few Late Chrysanthemums*.
  The Rodings are a group of villages in Essex. Shellow Bowells is about a mile south of Berners Roding.
  The church book was the *Collins Guide to English Parish Churches*, co-edited with Edward Long. It had been under contract since 1944.
  Seely Service Co. Ltd were publishers.

To Frederick Ling   The Mead
                                                       Wantage
3 March 1954   Berkshire

Dear Freddie,
How very nice to hear from you in that cultivated backward-sloping
writing. I think lovely freckly Jill will marry Nyasa in the end, and she
said to me the last time I saw her that what she liked about Nyasa was
that he was not in love with the idea of being married and looking about
for a woman, but in love with her, and that flattered and pleased her
and made her feel safe. How very nice that you are going Low Church.
You won't have to go to Confession any more. I spend my life trying to
make money. I would very much like to see you. Powlie [PSGB] is very
well and mad about aeroplanes and Wibz [CB] is very happy at St
Mary's and, I think, greatly improved. Penelope is off her head and
very active. There is a new kind of golf ball called 'Spalding Top Flight'
and the ones with black dots look exactly like her.
    Love from JB

> F.L. (see *Volume One*) was a Cowley father, a beloved friend of JB who had also been his
> confessor. He had recently decided to leave the order.
>   Jill Menzies, JB's secretary, had typed out a lot of F.L.'s diaries for him at the Mead
> where he had stayed for long stretches in a state of varying degrees of nervous
> breakdown.
>   Jill did marry Kenneth Storer, 'Nyasa' or 'Nyasaland' as JB called him, and
> eventually went to live in Africa.
>   F.L. married in 1956. He died two years later.

To John Piper   The Mead
                                                       Wantage
11 April 1954   Berkshire

Dear Mr Piper,
    I've done one Beddi-rhyme, so far. Here it is.

>   Here's to the Exercise, rhythmical ringing,
>   The ropes with their sallies fly upwards and down
>   From treble to tenor the ten bells are flinging
>   Their soul-calling cadences over the town.
>   It's my pleasure in life in the belfry to stand
>   And ring for three hours with the bellringers' band.

Think of some more subjects you'd like to draw. It's as easy as pie writing these verses. Penelope thought of 'church-going'. Do you approve? Alter as you like.

Love, John B

Jack Beddington, 'Beddioleman' (see *Volume One*), the Director of Shell-Mex publicity, had commissioned JB to write a series of short verses to go with illustrations called *The Pleasures of Life*, to be used for advertising. This first was on bellringing. 'I could write little quatrains under pictures,' JB wrote to Beddington (2 February 1954).

J.P. collaborated on the project. On 12 April JB sent this verse written down from memory to Beddioleman, in a slightly different form. 'Shoot' appeared instead of 'fly' and 'ring through a peal' instead of 'ring for three hours'.

The rhyme 'Surfing' followed shortly afterwards.

To Penelope Betjeman   The Mead
                                          Wantage
12 April 1954   Berkshire

Darling Plymouth,
Yew are very ijjus.

Oo are these three people? They seem to gnaow each oother. Ronnie S[haw]-K[ennedy] is going to America tomorrow so that rules him out for Low Sunday. Please tell Powlie he has a golf lesson with H. C. Rule on Wednesday at 12.00 at Frilford. Oi owp yew are quoite well. Oi loove yew.

Yorz trewely, Tewpie

PB and JB's peculiar language which they used in writing to one another included words like 'ijjus' meaning hideous and 'owp' for hope. This is one of the two letters where I have left the spelling unchanged. The rest I have transposed into conventional English.

Ronnie Shaw-Kennedy was a friend of PB who regularly came to stay at the Mead.

H. C. Rule was the professional at Frilford Heath Golf Course, where JB often played, sometimes with PSGB but more usually on his own while I trailed behind looking for balls in the rough. Doris Rule, his widow, who worked in the shop there remembered, 'I used to really enjoy it when Mr Betjeman came in – he was always the same, always the very old golf clubs. He used to buy secondhand balls and I remember once offering him some with the two black dots on – he said, "Oh, Mrs Rule, I couldn't ever hit those balls, they remind me of my wife too much." '

To Cecil Beaton   The Mead
                                                               Wantage
17 May 1954   Berkshire

Dear Cecil,
Alas! I shall be away on June 25th, and I should so much have liked to
come to the Foyle's banquet on your book's behalf.

Just let this idea simmer round in your mind. Could we not do a
beautiful book together of the interiors of English theatres, particularly
those rich late-Victorian baroque places to be found in the provinces,
and earlier ones like the Theatre Royal, Bristol and the Theatre Royal,
Worcester, and that superb theatre at Newcastle. A great many of these
theatres have been, like the Swindon Empire, subjected to hideous
modernisation in the twenties and thirties, but others survive and they
should be recorded. I once proposed the idea of this for you and me to
Collins who were very keen on it.

    Yours, John Betjeman

> C.B. replied (30 June 1954), 'Nothing would give me more pleasure. I see so little
> of you, your company delights me and it would be a gorgeous opportunity to see
> you. I don't think the theatres would be very good material for photography, do you?
> – but I trust you're thinking of drawings.'
>   In the event they were both too busy to continue with the idea.

To Stanley Morison   The Mead
                                                             Wantage
18 May 1954   Berkshire

Dear and GREAT TYPOGRAPHER,
Sir Ninian Comper is ninety on June 10th. A dinner for him is being
organised on June 14th in the Athenæum Club, Pall Mall, which he will
attend. The cost, including wine, will be about thirty shillings, and
about thirty of his admirers and friends are being asked. It will be a
great honour if you can come. I enclose a list of those I am approaching
and if there are any others whose names you think I should include, will
you add them to this stamped postcard with your reply.

    Yours ever, Séan Ó Betjeméan

> S.M. (see *Volume One*), the celebrated editor and typographer, was one of the guests at
> the dinner. The others included the Reverend W.R. Corbould, the Duke of Wellington,

To John Piper   The Mead
                                                                   Wantage
22 May 1954   Berkshire
5th Sunday after Easter

Dear Mr Piper,
The more I think of that window, the more the beauty of its colour and
the strength of its great figure – particularly the hands and arms – haunt
me. It is your masterpiece to date.

The Major telephoned to me yesterday to ask me what I thought of it.
My dear, he was *most* enthusiastic. He thought [that] you as artiste,
Reyntiens as executant and interpreter in glass, and Nuttgens with his
experience, were an ideal combination. He was full of enthusiasm for
the design and for the raspberries and for the colour. So I don't think we
need worry about him. He thinks it best that it should be displayed to
the Grocers somewhere in London. He wonders if you could get it
displayed at the R[oyal] C[ollege of] A[rt] Schools in South
Ken[sington] as they would impress the Grocers. I said I would ask
you. Failing that the V[ictoria] and A[lbert Museum]. Or, I suggest,
the B[ritish M[useum] if Tom Kendrick can fix it. He does not think
there is anywhere in Grocers' Hall big enough and light enough
behind, to do it justice.

The *Little Guide to Bed[ford]s[hire]* is excellent, particularly the
architectural preface. The county is full of treasures.

Love to Goldilegz, JB

J.P. had just finished his stained glass window 'The Three Kings' for Oundle School
chapel. It had been commissioned by Major Dent who was a Trustee of the Sanderson
Memorial Fund administered by the Grocers' Company, which paid for it. As a friend of
JB's he had asked him if he would approach J.P. It was the first stained glass window
commission Piper had had and a turning point in his life. It marked the beginning of his
collaboration with Patrick Reyntiens, who made the windows in the studio of the
glassmaker Joseph Nuttgens. In the end it was exhibited in the Grocers' Hall, London.

To Alan Pryce-Jones   The Mead
                                                        Wantage
25 May 1954   Berkshire

  I love the bog villa and also the people
  Whose elegant brogues have the gravel to crunch on
  As sedately the bells from St Cyprian's steeple
  Will summon them northward to share the bog luncheon.

  But alas! alas! I must take my sedanca
  To WANTAGE tomorrow to rest in its stables
  So perhaps you will find me a peeress and banker
  And another occasion for flaunting my sables.

  A.P.-J. ('Captain Bog') had invited JB to a lunch party at his house in St John's Wood,
  north London.
     St Cyprian's, Clarence Gate, Marylebone (1902–3) was a church by the architect
  Ninian Comper and a favourite of JB's and A.P.-J.'s.

To Frank Rutherford   The Mead
                                                        Wantage
25 May 1954   Berkshire

Dear Mr Rutherford,
I am most flattered and intrigued by your letter. You are of course quite
right; a lot of the verses were written with tunes in my head, and
certainly the dactylic group has 'Bonnie Dundee' as a basis, though
probably 'Fête Champêtre' comes from some [Thomas] Moore
melody. 'Senex' was not written with any tune in my head. I don't
think 'Henley on Thames' had anything behind it either. I think 'The
Irish Unionist's Farewell' was composed to the tune of Clementine,
and you will find that 'Flight from Bootle' also goes to that tune. I have
an idea that 'I Love Your Brown Curls' probably comes from Moore,
though I cannot remember which. You will find that 'Spring Morning
in North Oxford' goes quite well to Annie Laurie, to which it was
composed. I did not realise how well Moore's 'Oh Banquet Not' went
to 'Sudden Illness at the Bus-stop'. You are quite right about 'As
History's Muse' for 'The Exile' and 'Myfanwy'. As to the other poems
you mention, I am not at the moment conscious of their being
composed to special airs, but tunes which are ringing through my head

constantly are 'Hyfrydol', 'Tea for Two', 'The Day Thou Gavest Lord is Ended', 'Now the Day is Over', 'Over the Sea to Skye', 'Tom Bowling', 'Iste Confessor' and a good many tunes from *Hymns Ancient and Modern* and the *Methodist Hymnal*.

Yours sincerely, John Betjeman

F.R. was the librarian of the Literary and Philosophical Society of Newcastle-upon-Tyne in the fifties and had met JB when he gave a lecture to the Society in 1948.

To Nicolas Bentley

25 May 1954

The Mead
Wantage
Berkshire

Dear Nicolas,
I will sign the book and I have written a letter to the secretary. I am having to resign from the Garrick owing to poverty and because of the resignation of my friend, Major L. M. E. Dent, which has so altered the character of the club that it is not the same place to me. I expect you know him. He joined in 1918 and was put up by Weedon Grossmith and only came in once, and that was with me about two years ago when he was mistaken for a guest when he sat at the centre table.

Yours ever, John B

N.B. (see *Volume One*), the publisher, artist and author and fellow member of the Garrick, was an old friend of JB's who had long wanted to collaborate with him by illustrating his poetry.

Weedon Grossmith was the illustrator and (with his brother George) the author of *The Diary of a Nobody*.

To Patrick Kinross
29 June 1954

4 Warwick Avenue
London w2

My dear Pa'rick,
We often think about you here. We haven't moved. We often think of you suddenly arriving in from abroad just as though you had never been away at all. We miss you a lot, Anita [Dent] and I, and we often laugh thinking of how you would cope with situations that arise. A dear little kiddy from the slum house next door threw a brick through the window when it was playing at thieves with its sub-normal

companions. But the gardener has mended the pane.

I should learn to split my life into two, though I have tried not to ever since I have been married. But what with the wireless and *Punch* and the *Telegraph* I have so much to do in London that I think I will have to take a flat in London and furnish it with half my books from home – i.e. architectural books. The Holy Church would be too small a room. There would not be room here without altering the character of the house and moving in a lot of my furniture and I think I will have to be on my own if I am to work in London and use Wantage for recreation. I've heard of a very cheap flat in the City in Cloth Fair (Seely and Paget, my dear) which may serve the purpose. Three guineas a week all in but I would have to put in a bed, chairs, table and bookshelves. That means if I do get it, that I would move there in Aug[ust] or early Sept[ember]. So I'd better give in a reluctant notice to your house which has been very nice and increasingly funny.

The amenity opposite is finished and a lovely gents blocks Lennox's view but not ours. No kiddiz unaccompanied are allowed in to the amenity and it is full of refugees. Penelope asked the Wemysses to stay my dear without realising from the time they came to the time they went how very grand they were. I've never been through so much embarrassment. To make it worse she asked other people who didn't fit in. She also had a daughter of Lord Halifax staying who was a neighbour of the Weymsses but didn't know them. I have had a sore throat from anxiety ever since. As it is unlikely this letter will reach you as Anita's letters don't reach you, I won't write any more.

Love, JB

> The architects John Seely and Paul Paget, JB's future landlords at Cloth Fair, lived together as a couple.
> 'The Holy Church' was JB's room in Warwick Avenue.·
> My schoolfriend Elizabeth Charteris's parents, the Earl and Countess of Wemys, had come to stay for St Mary's Parents' Day. They lived in a gigantic house, Gosford, in Scotland.

To Roy Plomley   The Mead
                                                     Wantage
St Swithin's Day [15 July] 1954   Berkshire

Dear Roy,
Miss Howson the stained glass artist lives in your road. Oh yes. I'd love to, old top. But I've done it once already, the very same thing, for Miss

[illegible] Wilshin. And don't forget, I'M NOT MUSICAL so thought I would sing 'Tea for Two' – it's the kind of thing I like.

    Yours, John B

> JB took part in R.P. the radio broadcaster's programme *Desert Island Discs* on 8 October 1954. On this occasion, as well as versions of 'Jesu, Joy of Man's Desiring' and 'Rock of Ages' JB chose ' "Padstow Hobby Horse, May Day Ceremony" (villagers with drum)', 'When Are You Going to Lead Me to the Altar, Walter?' by Randolph Sutton, 'My Heart Stood Still', a recording of bells and a record of railway sound effects. (As his desert island luxury, he proposed the lower half of the west window of Fairford Church in Gloucestershire.)

To G. B. Stern

                                                      The Mead
                                                      Wantage

22 August 1954   Berkshire

Dear Peter,

What a sweet and understanding review of my verse in the *Sphere*. You are a generous and encouraging critic. It is far the most discerning review I have read. I *am* lucky in getting the attention of writers like you, dear Peter, whom I admire. I'm told by Jock [Murray] that the poems are selling quite well, about three thousand so far, I think. Not bad for poetry.

    I've been away in France and we are now off to Cornwall. In France I went to Bordeaux and drank Claret and to Cognac and drank Cognac and I saw about seventy churches.

    Love from us both and my love, John B

> The author Gladys Bertha Stern (known to her friends as 'Peter') (1890–1973), lived in the nearby village of Blewbury, Berkshire. She was a formidable, rather manly widow who normally dressed in black and had a large collection of heavy walking sticks. JB sent her some illustrated lines:

What dreadful things go on inside that school?
   Satchels and caps and bicycles and boys,
This is the chapel – that, the swimming pool
   But from the boot room, what's that whimpering noise?

To Nigel Watt   The Mead
                                                   Wantage
25 August 1954   Berkshire

Dear Mr Watt,
I have heard from Mr Prosser, the founder of the Railway Development
Association, one of whose vice-presidents I am, and he says that he
thinks it is a good idea that I should be president of your Society, since
the aims of the Railway Development Association and your own are
similar. But since hearing from him, I have discussed the matter with
my friend Lord Kinross, in whose house I have been staying while in
London, and who has had an invitation from you to be president. We
both think that the most practical arrangement and the best will be the
one which is going to be most useful toward furthering the objects of
the two societies. As we know one another, it seems most sensible that
Lord Kinross should be your president and that I should also be a vice-
president of the London Area of the Railway Development Association, a position which has been offered to me. In this way Lord Kinross
and I will be able to make common cause when some brutal decision is
made by British Railways. Lord Kinross is an excellent conversa-
tionalist and a wonderfully lucid and vigorous writer, but he asks me to
tell you he is no good at making speeches from public platforms. He
becomes terrified and tongue-tied. If you want the sort of president
who can make public speeches and who is full of knowledge about
railways and in sympathy with our aims, he and I both suggest you
might care to approach our friend Sir Arthur Elton Bt, of 10 Eldon
Grove, NW3. Anyhow, let me know what your Society thinks of the
suggestions.

    One point, the title of your Society. Ought the word Unremunera-
tive to come out? Doesn't it rather suggest that branchlines always will
be unremunerative?

    Yours sincerely, John Betjeman

> N.W.'s newly formed group was called the Society for the Reinvigoration of
> Unremunerative Branch Lines in the UK.
>   They did remove the word 'Unremunerative' and continued as a campaigning body
> until the late fifties.

To Alan Clarkson Rose   The Mead
                                                          Wantage
13 October 1954   Berkshire

Dear splendid actor and producer,
There could be no higher sphere than writing for *Twinkle* but I don't
believe I am enough in touch with the great art of the public to produce
the sort of things you would want. But if an opportunity arises, I will
try and do something about you and variety in general in my *Spectator*
column one day.

    I am so glad *Twinkle* did well at the Chelsea Palace, and I will try and
go and look at it again when next you are there.

    Yours sincerely, John Betjeman

Alan Clarkson Rose,
the well-known
pantomime dame.

JB kept up a long correspondence with A.C.R. and never missed seeing the annual
production of *Twinkle*, a touring revue. He never wrote any revue material for the show,
but wrote an open letter which was used in the programme:

    Variety is a peculiarly English form of entertainment. It has become one of the great
    arts of England and I have followed it all my life, from the days of Marie Lloyd. Its
    mixture of humour and pathos, with skill and dancing; its art of timing and knowing
    what jokes to put where and how soon to follow up with the next one, are all the result
    of hard work and experience, as is all the great art in *Twinkle*, which I always enjoy;
    you keep variety ALIVE, and long you may do so, because television can never establish
    that intimacy between audience and performers, which you so ably created in
    Twinkle.

To Television Booking Department, BBC   The Mead
                                                  Wantage
2 November 1954   Berkshire

Dear Sirs,
I return my contract for Cardiff Castle to you unsigned. I shall be
grateful if you will make out a cheque for the full amount you were
going to pay me to the Rev[erend] Canon A. F. Hood, at 1 Wesley
Street, London w1, and will you tell him that it is to go to the fund for
St Mary Aldermary. I am asking you to do this as a protest against the
disproportion of your television fees. If I take part in that delightful
programme, *Where on Earth?*, there is virtually no rehearsing and I am
given a good meal free, and even if I am asked to appear on the *Christian
Forum* in the Isle of Wight there is still virtually no rehearsing and I am
offered eighteen guineas. Yet I had to make two visits to Cardiff in
connection with the televising of the Castle, spend three nights in the
city and rehearse almost the whole of Sunday. Between the final
rehearsal at 6.15 and the programme at ten o'clock, I was offered not
even a cup of tea, and only through the kindness of one of the local
officials not appearing in the programme, did I manage to get a glass of
beer at a club. Therefore I feel that either the standard of fees for things
like *Where on Earth?* should be lower, or else that the fee for the extra
work and specialist knowledge required over Cardiff should be higher.
    Yours sincerely, JB

To Miss Balch   The Mead
                                                  Wantage
9 November 1954   Berkshire

Dear Miss Balch,
I am pleased and honoured to be a vice-president of the Young Farmers'
Club, though I should think no vice-president of any Young Farmers'
Club knows less about farming than I do.
    Your sincerely, John Betjeman

Miss Balch was the secretary of the Wantage branch of the Young Farmers' Club.

To Compton Mackenzie

December 1954

The Mead
Wantage
Berkshire

Dear Monty,

Macdonalds have asked me to write a preface to the reprint of *The Altar Steps*. This is a great honour for me. I have re-read the book with tremendous pleasure. I should not think there exists anywhere so luxuriant and authentic a chronicle of the gay days of the Anglo-Catholic movement. It is most extraordinary how you conjure up the atmosphere of keen clergy houses, ascetic-looking pioneers, sybaritic laymen, pompous bishops and Protestant persecution. I wish Macdonalds had published all three books in one volume.

Meanwhile, do you think there would be any objection, after all these years, to revealing the real name of some of the main characters?

1. Who is Mark's father, James Lidderdeal?
2. And what is the real name of his church in Nottingdale?
3. Is Nancepean Cury or Gunwalloe?
4. Is Mark's grandfather a real person?
5. Did the wreck incident happen?
6. Did Haverton House really exist, if so, in what town was it?
7. Who was Ogilvie?
8. Where was Mead Cantorum?
9. What was the real name and date of the Pomeroy affair?
10. Who was Lord Danvers?
11. Who was Mr Dorward?
12. What place had you in mind for Wych on the Wold?
13. Is St Osman's Hall St Edmund's Hall? Who was its principal?
14. Who was Father Rowleys of Chatsey? Was it Dolling?
15. The Silchester College Mission is the Winchester College Mission. Am I right?
16. Who was the old Bishop of Winchester? Who was his horrible successor?
17. Where was Malford Abbey? And who was Father Burrowes?
18. Did anything like the Order of St George exist?
19. Who was Sir Charles Horner?
20. Who was the Bishop of Warwick?
21. Who was Arnold Shuter? And where was St Luke's Galton?

Write on one side of the paper only and put your name at the top right-hand corner. The examiners will give marks for neatness and legibility. Do not attempt more questions than you can answer. Time limit, an hour and a half.

Goodness I wish I could see you more. I do miss you.

Yours, JB

C.M. replied, 'I *am* so glad you are doing *The Altar Steps*. . . . Father Rowley is, of course, Dolling of St Agatha's, Landport, Winchester College Mission. James Lidderdale is a complete invention. The Mission Church is a mixture of a little Mission attached to St Michael and All Angels in Nottingdale and another Mission Chapel in Fulham. Nancepean is a mixture of Cury and Gunwalloe, and is actually a valley between the two. Mark's grandfather is mythical and so is the wreck. Haverton House is also mythical. Ogilvie an invention. Also Mead Cantorum. The Pomeroy affair is a changed version of what really did happen in 1898. Dorward is a partial portrait of Sandys Wason. Wych is mythical. Principal of St Edmund's Hall is mythical. Davidson was the Bishop of Winchester who put Dolling out, but it is not in the least a portrait. His predecessor is mythical. The Order of St George was the order of St Paul started by one Father Hopkins as a Mission for Merchant Sailors. Some of the monks are portraits but not all. Sir Charles Horner is founded on Sir Hubert Miller of Froyle. Bishop of Warwick and Shuter are both mythical.'

The Mackenzies had moved from the nearby village of Denchworth to Edinburgh.

To John Murray   The Mead
                                                    Wantage
31 December 1954   Berkshire

My dear Jock,

I must first write to thank you for the handsome present of that bottle of bubbly, old boy. You are a kind old publisher. We drank it as an *apéritif* with John Edward Bowle and his mother, Powlie, Patrick Balfour, Archbishop and Gervase Mathew before Boxing Day luncheon.

I was most surprised at the chorus of praises in the Sunday papers. It looked as though I had fixed it.

If you are reprinting, please look at the space between stanzas. I have not a copy of the book here but from what I remember, the spaces between stanzas are most unnecessarily unequal in very many places.

Love to you all from

A Few Late Chrysanthemums had come out before Christmas.
JB always depicted my brother with an egg-shaped head, and me with a flat one.

To Siegfried Sassoon

The Mead
Wantage
5 January 1955   Berkshire

Dear Sassoon,
I must most warmly thank you for your beautiful, moving book of
poems. Oh, you are good. Your modesty and retiringness add to the
charm. But really these latest poems are better than ever. They are
about the very same things that bother me. Never a day goes by
without my thinking of my death and the lonely journey into eternity –
will it be a journey or will it be blank nothingness? Almost anything, I
think, would be better than extinction. I like 'Another Spring' best of
all – no, I think I prefer 'The Trial' and 'The Darkness' and 'Retreat
from Eternity'. Oh, I don't know, all of them are so deeply felt, so
carefully worked out and so without one wasted word, that they *must* be
immortal so far as this earth is concerned. I am more pleased to have
them than I can say. I quoted one to a Methodist printer called Gibbs
who used to be a Rugby International. He wanted to use some lines of it
with some primroses he sends out to people every year. I expect he will
write to you. Sorry to give you the trouble of replying, if he does.

I often wonder whether the Incarnation is true or not. *If* it is, then all
is much better. But why should it be? Only those lichened churches
you mention tell me it may be a few good old women and persecuted
vicars in country places and hollow-eyed missionaries in towns.

How splendid that your son is going to King's. The best college in the best university and a home of civilisation still and that chapel and Boris Ord's music for inspiration.

Yours, John Betjeman

S.S.'s book of twenty-four poems, *The Tasking*, was printed privately for him by his friend and bibliographer Geoffrey Keynes in 1954 at the University Press, Cambridge.

To Ralph May   43 Cloth Fair
26 January 1955   London EC1

Dear Ralph,

I really have not the time to write another great long script for you, but I think that what you say in your letter provides an idea for an opening. We must at some stage in the film show the difference between English bellringing and continental, and that could well come at the beginning of the descriptions of the actual ringing. I think a very interesting beginning to the film would be a visit to Mears and Stainbank Bell Foundry in Whitechapel and pictures of a bell being cast, which I may say will look like any other of those films where flames flash over a black screen and noises like typewriters and tins crash in the background, with some old worthy explaining the process of making a bell, and then we might look at a fully cast bell, where again this old boy through his walrus moustache, could give the names of the different parts of the bell. Then we could have a sequence of the purposes for which bells are used, and possibly not only church bells. A row of bells in a country house with the names of all the bedrooms; a dinner bell at school, a school bell; a wedding with the bells of St Margaret's and a lot of fashionable people coming out; a stable clock; bells ringing for a church service. And then on to the more intimate life of the belfry, and the handbell ringers coming round to ring in somebody's house, and then on to a peal being rung in compliment to some aged ringer, and from there to the script which I have sent to you.

Other things that could be mentioned and that are of a certain amount of interest, though possibly not much visual interest, are things like the making of bell ropes and sallies, and the hanging of bells in church towers – a very complicated business. There is a firm called White in Appleton, near Cumnor, Oxfordshire, which specialises in this work, and the White brothers might provide you with some interesting material. But certainly it is very interesting how un-consciously throughout all our days bells are ringing for different purposes, marking the passages of time, both of the day itself and of events in our lives.

I am not prepared to do any more for the moment, and I think you will have to get someone who is more of an expert on the subject than I am.

Yours sincerely, John Betjeman

> R.M. was a director of Anvil Films Ltd and had asked JB to lengthen a treatment he had written for a film on bellringing. R.M. decided to go ahead with the project and asked JB to write a commentary when the film was shot and edited. There is, however, no record at Anvil Films and Recording Group Ltd that the film was ever made.

To Graham Landon   43 Cloth Fair
29 March 1955   London EC1

Dear Mr Landon,
I am enchanted with Mr Larkin's words about me. Just what I hoped one day to hear even though it may not be true. And just the right quotations. It is odd that he should appreciate my own favourite about Baker Street Station.

I have written to Murray's for three copies of *Chrysanth[emum]s* and will send them on next week when I return here from my home in Wantage.

Yours sincerely, John Betjeman

> G.L., in an effort to rescue the student literary magazine *Q* of Queen's College Belfast, asked his drinking friend Philip Larkin to write a book review. Larkin's 'Beyond a Joke: The Poetry of John Betjeman' praised *A Few Late Chrysanthemums* and attracted much attention.
> Larkin and JB had yet to meet.

To Evelyn Waugh   The Mead
                                                       Wantage
6 May 1955   Berkshire

My dear Evelyn,
Da Costa was never beaten by me. I was never in a position to beat a boy as I was neither a house captain nor a prefect.

If I knew the date of the Head Girl's visits to S[t Mary's] Ascot, of course I'll come *provided you can do so too*. Mid week e.g. a Thursday suits me but does it suit you?

Did you ever see my former secretary Jill Menzies? Slanting green eyes, freckles, turned-up nose, sulky lips and athletic figure and interested in art. Fur all over her face of a light silver colour.

I would LOVE THE *Archi[tectural] Rev[iew]* of that date. You are too generous. The *Archie* was very good in those days.

I long to come to Stinkers [Stinchcombe] again.

Yours, John B

E.W. had written (3 May 1955), 'Charles Da Costa, a very nice Jamaican Jew with whom I stayed in that island, boasted: a) that Cyril Connolly was his tutor b) that you flogged him at Marlborough. . . . Do you possess, do you want, the *Architectural Review*, bound, 1895–1905 (circa)? I am offered it and would give it to you if acceptable.'

E.W.'s daughter Teresa was Head Girl of St Mary's Ascot. E.W. wrote to Maurice Bowra (14 July 1955), 'Betjeman very kindly came to entertain the girls at St Mary's Ascot. Goodness he gave them a good time in real ENSA [Entertainments National Services Association] style.'

To George Barnes   43 Cloth Fair
19 May 1955   London EC1

My dear Commander,

If there's a possibility – and I shan't know till the week before – I'll come on Trinity Sunday. But it is a very remote possibility as these commercial three-minute films I'm doing take up all good weather. They are RAVISHING by the way. We've done Fairfield and Mereworth in your county and three minutes is just the right length. Television is mostly too long. These are just right for visual delight.

Anyhow, I'll look in if I can't get there. I couldn't get there Saturday morning anyhow as I have to address a protest meeting about the Oxford Canal in Oxford Town Hall (Henry T. Hare) on Friday night.

The Bishop would be very unusual if he didn't celebrate facing east. Only the Pope and Father McLaughlin of St Thomas's Regent Street face west when celebrating. Father Spratt at All Soul's Langham Place takes the 'North End'. I don't think you'll be accused of pope-ing for showing the eastward position. It is usual in England for H[igh] C[hurch]. Henry of Exeter faced east. So, I suspect, did his secretary.

Thank Anne for her letter. 'The Mistress' and I would love to come. Very good about Little P[rawls] liking USA and it liking him. Darling Little P[rawls].

Cheerioh for now.

Love, JB

JB made twenty-six short films called *Discovering Britain* for Random Films as part of a Shell/BP publicity campaign, under Jack Beddington's wing.

G.B. had written (18 May 1955), 'On Trinity Saturday we go to Exeter for the 9.00 a.m. rehearsal of the televising of the Bishop's Trinity Ordination which takes place next day at 10.00 a.m. in connection with the St Boniface celebrations. This is the first Ordination service ever to be televised and the Bishop has decided after much turmoil to celebrate facing east, but there will be a camera to the south-east of the altar so that the viewer will see parts of the celebration face on. (Had the Bishop decided to use the nave altar, he would have followed his normal procedure of celebrating at this service facing west.)'

To Penelope Betjeman   In the train

22 June 1955

Moi darlin Plymmi,
Oi ated leavin yew all blotched and
pouffie with Ay Fever and oi very
mooch owp yew is naow feelin a little
bit better. Oi av thort of yew all thie
time and ow mooch oi wished yew ad
been with us on our filmic expidishes.

Woodhall Spa was an Edwardian paradise in heaped-up cushions of
azaleas and rhodies and many silver birches in Lincs. In its way it really
was rather beautiful, sort of early Mrs Woad [Lady Chetwode] taste
and all of a piece and a *frightfully* good hotel. Oi saw Manchester Town
Hall and Heaton Hall Manchester the day before yesterday and Burton
Agnes and Patrington and Brocklesby yesterday. My, what riches
there are on this island! Even if we could afford it, I doubt if it would be
worth going to Cincinnati. I have not yet seen my letters as I fell in with
a very interesting Govt Inspector of Arshytekture in the train and we
stopped off at Peterborough to go and see a very subtly beautiful
eighteenth-century village near that city. It was well worth it. I will tell
you about it.

Much love moi own darlin
ijjus ayfevery oogli
sweet precious pointed-eaded
eccentric noonyish
Own loovin
Nibbly Plymmi
from Yorz trewely, Tewpie

Woodhall Spa in Lincolnshire was built in 1891 as a resort, but was never a great success
as such. It has one of the best golf courses in the county. The Golf Hotel is large and
half-timbered.
    JB always referred to PB's maiden name of Chetwode as 'Woad'.

To Evelyn Waugh   The Mead
                                                    Wantage
2 July 1955   Berkshire

My dear Evelyn,
I came back the night before last from a filming tour in the North of
England and East Anglia to find your new novel awaiting me and
inscribed by you. I think that bore Peter Green must have been given it
by the *Telegraph*, he is the man who alternates with me. I do hope not. If
by good luck Freddie B[irkenhead] has been given it that will be
splendid. But poor Mr Green is a useless critic and I can't think why
they employ him. Perhaps he is a relation to the Camroses by marriage
like I am.

    I've already started your novel now with that glorious cloud lifted of
having done my fortnight's reviews this week. Oh, how well you write.

The first two chapters, all I have so far read, could not be bettered even by you. I am writing now before finishing the book, so that you'll know I have received it and am enjoying it. Compared with the novels I have to review, it is so good that I forget it is a novel. I am now going to read it when I have taken this to the post.

Of course what one forgets is that you are a very meticulous scholar. That is why you never write badly.

Well, ta for the book, ole man, and here's hoping to see you soon. Can you think of any object near Stinkers which would make a good two-and-a-half-minute film for commercial television? *Discovering Britain* which I am doing for Shell-Mex and BP? Something with detail in it and which looks well as you move along with slow tracking shots and something which it won't matter people looking at – an aqueduct, a grotto, a pump room, a beam engine, a ruin false or genuine. So far I have done Clifton Susp[ension] Bridge, Stourhead Temples and Grotto, and Avebury, Mereworth, Fairfield Church (box pews), Patington Church (Stately Dec[orated]), Burton Agnes, Brocklesby Mausoleum, West Wycombe Mausoleum and caves and gold ball, Beam Engine 1796 on Kennet-and-Avon Canal and still working, and an Essex water mill.

Love, John B

E.W.'s new novel was *Officers and Gentlemen*. The reviewers slammed it and E.W.'s reaction was simply, 'Fuck them.'

JB's relationship with the Camrose family was through PB. Her brother Roger had married Patricia Berry, daughter of the first Lord Camrose, the editor-in-chief of the *Daily Telegraph*. JB was constantly aware that his job with the *Telegraph* was because of this and in consequence gave into all the social demands Lady Pamela Berry (wife of Michael, the subsequent editor) made of him.

To Anthony Powell   43 Cloth Fair
6 July 1955   London EC1

Dear Tony,

You must help me about these plays of Terence Greenidge. He sends me letters and rings me up pleading for a review, and the truth is they are completely unreadable to me – the plays I mean – and I can't see how I can possibly review them. I can't understand the characters or the themes, and I have tried several times to read them, and got stuck even in the first scene, let alone the first act. I have written the enclosed letter to Terence explaining my limitations, or at least I will send him the enclosed letter by this post. And I've told him on the telephone that I have left it in your hands to decide whether to send the plays to the dramatic critic or to me. Well, it's no good sending them to me.

Yours, JB

A.P. (see *Volume One*), the novelist, had been at Oxford with JB and was literary editor of *Punch* (1953–8).

A.P. remembered, 'Greenidge was a friend of Evelyn Waugh's – he wrote these crazy books and plays and rang and appeared at *Punch* morning, noon and night.'

JB wrote to Greenidge, 'I think it must be so many years of novel reviewing that has thus blunted my perception. I can't follow one character all through, and am always mixing him up with others and missing the subtleties of stage-craftsmanship and the arrangements of exits and entrances which a reviewer of plays, to be adequate, should be able to grasp naturally.'

To William Wicklow   The Mead
                                                        Wantage
9 July 1955   Berkshire

My dear Crax,

I was very interested and relieved to have your letter. Your experience at the doors of death is in many ways consoling, but it does not lessen the terrors of eternity *after death*, if there is personal survival. The act of dying I dread, but not so much as what waits me beyond. And if nothing waits me beyond why aren't I at this moment in bed with someone attractive?

I saw the Colonel [Kolkhorst] the week before last. He was quite himself again with the usual complaints about cash but not obsessive. One was also able to play jokes on him again, a great relief. His loony-bin doctor thinking the Colonel is a drug addict, has pleased the Colonel a lot and may keep him off them.

I am very concerned that you are now *permanently ill*. I do not at all like the idea of your predeceasing the Colonel and me and the Mosquito [Patrick Kinross] and the Widow [John Lloyd]. The last had visited the Colonel and said a thing or two in her sharp way. Will you have permanently to remain at the Pembroke Private Hospital with those two phones ringing all day? If so I will come over and see you as I very much like visiting the sick.

There has been a big row here about whether there would be a nave altar in the parish church. Etchell, who has reluctantly accepted the job of architect to the church and has prepared a report on the church, 'refuses to be drawn into the controversy'. The Mosquito was so attracted by my ex-secretary Jill Menzies (turned-up nose, freckles, wide blue eyes, high cheek bones, sulky lips and a boyish figure and very literary and artistic) that he said, 'If I lived in the same town as that girl for a fortnight I'd go normal.' The average Englishman's idea of religion was described by Austin Farrer of Trinity Oxford in a sermon as 'like an advertisement I saw on Folly Bridge:

FOR LADIES
FOR UPLIFT
FOR GENERAL SUPPORT.'

Penelope has hay fever and is very like the hayricks she is making.

Love, JB

> W.W. (see *Volume One*) was JB's beloved friend. Formerly called Clonmore, he had
> become Earl of Wicklow on his father's death in 1949. He trained to be a Church of
> England priest at Oxford but later converted to Catholicism.
>   The nave altar idea at Wantage was turned down.

To Mrs White   43 Cloth Fair
13 July 1955   London EC1

Dear Mrs White,
I hear from my friends the Cobwebs at Chagford, telegraphic address 'Nannie', that you wrote to me and never had an answer. I am sorry. If you could provide me with any kind of regular income, howsoever small, from the *New Yorker*, I would write almost anything you wanted. That's what I need – security. But I don't expect you could supply me with such a job with me writing in London, and I might not be good enough for you and then we would be sunk.
   Yours, John Betjeman

> Mrs W. had been staying at the Easton Court Hotel, Chagford, Devon, a great haunt of
> the literary set, which was run by the Cobbs (also known as the 'Cobwebs').

'Mr and Mrs E.B. White of the *New Yorker*,' wrote Carolyn Cobb to JB (10 July 1955), 'have just spent eight days with us. As you know, they pay big prices. Mrs White told me very sadly that she had always been interested in your work, that she had written to you asking for some material and that you had not even answered her.' This was the beginning of JB's relationship with the *New Yorker*, for whom he began to write book reviews on an irregular basis.

To Penelope Betjeman   Hotel Alpenhof
19 August 1955   Garmisch

My darling Plymmi,
We went yesterday from here on a tour of mad queer King Ludwig II of Bavaria's castles and palaces. Linderhof, of which I enclose a postcard, seemed to me rich beyond dreaming. The atmosphere was exactly like being at Gerald [Berners]'s and I see where the resemblance lies. It was all very beautiful indeed. Lapis lazuli, peacocks' feathers made of jewels and *not* overdone. Then we went to the Wagner castle he built for himself of which I've sent a p[ost]c[ard] to Powlie. It was bigger than Burges but not so good as his work – an imitation really. But the view over the Swinlaken was the most beautiful in the world. Michael T[ree] has done a very good drawing of it. When I get to Venice, to which we go today, we are going on sketching expeditions. It will be very good for my eyes as I find my sight is getting worse and worse for reading.

This hotel at this modern Nazi place is very good indeed. In the evenings we dance at night spots and sleep like logs in the open air. I very much want to return to Bavaria. I find myself very much at home here.

I don't think you will be involved in the IRA activities.

Lots of love from yorz trewely, Tewpie

From 16 to 29 August, together with EC and her sister and brother-in-law Anne and Michael Tree, JB was making a tour through Germany, Austria and the Alps, ending in Venice. During the trip JB wrote 'In the Public Gardens' about EC:

In the Public Gardens,
   To the airs of Strauss,
Eingang we're in love again
   When *ausgang* we were *aus*.

The waltz was played, the songs were sung,
   The night resolved our fears;
From bunchy boughs the lime trees hung
   Their gold electroliers.

Among the loud Americans
Zwei Engländer were we,
You so white and frail and pale
And me so deeply me;

I bought for you a dark-red rose,
I saw your grey-green eyes,
As high above the floodlights,
The true moon sailed the skies.

In the Public Gardens,
Ended things begin;
Ausgang we were out of love
Und eingang we are in.

Gerald Berners's house at Faringdon (see *Volume One*) was decorated in an exotic and unusual style.
PB had taken PSGB and me to stay with Maureen Dufferin at Clandeboye in Northern Ireland.

To Anthony Barnes   43 Cloth Fair
20 September 1955   London EC1

My dear L[ittle] Prawlz,
I was very pleased to have your interesting letter about New York and its wise advice about Cinci[nnati], which I have just had confirmed by my old friend Anthony West. As to Venice, I was there a week, two days of which were occupied by having a frightful sore throat, caused by bathing in the Adriatic or eating scampi. But I was able to decide what I liked best about it. What I liked best, and it was what Freckley Jill also liked best, was its eastern quality. I liked St Mark's and Torcello and those chimneys with waste-paper baskets on top. And I think the Venetian Gothic looks so like Strawberry Hill, because it is not structural but decorative. Only a twist here and there would turn most of the Venetian Gothic into oriental. Also I think those striped poles to which the gondolas are moored are eastern looking. When one comes to Palladio then one is in real architecture and for me the most exciting Classic buildings were the Redentore and the outside of the Salute.

But really what I liked best was the painting, and in this order. The Carpaccios in the St George church, the Tintoretto Crucifixion, the Giorgione exhibition, particularly the first room, the Cima in Madonna del Orto, and of course the Academia pictures.

Coming back to England and looking at galleries is rather a let-down after one has been to Venice. I found what was the most useful thing was an essay by Pater which Penelope had lent to me called 'The School of Giorgione'. It had the secret of the appeal of Venice when it said that the Venetians were not concerned with theories about art, but about how most attractively to cover surfaces. I lived a rich life under the aegis of Ronnie Tree, but punctuated by intensive sightseeing in dim parts. I think the entrance to the Arsenale is one of the nicest bits of architecture.

Love and kisses, Iain MacBetjeman

> A.B. was the son of JB's old friends, George and Anne Barnes.
> JB was debating about going to Cincinnati University as a visiting professor of poetry.
> JB's friend Anthony West, the illegitimate son of H. G. Wells and Rebecca West, was by now living in New York.

To Penelope Betjeman   43 Cloth Fair
16th Sunday after Trinity   London EC1
25 September 1955

Darling Plymmi,
I keep thinking of your little red beret and that curious red blouse with patterns by Mrs Payne and your little brown angry eyes looking so pathetically up as Powlie got so rude in the Dolphin and I miss you terribly. The bells of St Paul's are ringing over the beautifully quiet Sunday city. I hope you are having a nice time and that this will reach you before you leave Venice. My TV film of Avebury has had very nice notices in different parts of the *Sunday T[imes]* and *Observer*, the latter to my great surprise. The Inland Waterways dinner which I attended in the Zoo last night was a great success. But I wish this flat were as peaceful all the week as it is on a Sunday. It really is heaven today with the bells and the trees and the peace. I suppose the French railway strike is off and you got to Grenoble okay.

Cheerioh for the present. Love to P[owlie].

Very trewely yorzs, Tewpie

> Mrs Payne was a dressmaker who lived in Ham Road, Wantage.
> PB had gone on a tour of Italy and then on to visit PSGB in Grenoble where he was studying French.

To Michael Rosse   43 Cloth Fair
25 September 1955   London EC1

Dear Michael,
Of course I will join the Irish Peers Association. My bank is the very
same one at which it banks, a nice dim bank, like the peers. I hope
Crofton, Roden, Lisle, Langford, Ashtown, Ashbrook, Ventry,
Waterpark, Charlemont and Kingston are joining, as well as the
better-known peers. Aylmer is in British Columbia and Massy is
running a grocer's shop in Leicester. Any help I can be of to the
Association I would like to be. I think you should extend it to Irish
baronets. Do you remember when a Sir Somebody Aylmer, a cousin of
the peer, found that his footman was an Irish baronet too, called Echlin,
and advertised for a baronet as second footman and got one called Sir
Thomas Moore O'Connell, the descendant of a Lord Mayor of Cork
and who was selling small coals in that city? As someone said, 'We have
often heard Cork called the Venice of Ireland, but have never heard
Venice called the Cork of Italy' – it sounds like the Widow [John]
Lloyd. It was a joy to hear from you and I am sparing you my
handwriting because it is so illegible now, on account of journalism,
although I am aware that it is rude to type letters. Please forgive me.
Love to Anne. We'll get her a medal.
    Seán Ó'B

> M.R. (the Earl of Rosse) had been a friend since Oxford days.
>   JB long remained an associate member of the Irish Peers Association; the subscription
> was ten shillings a year. It was set up as a means of ensuring that the views of the Irish
> Peers were represented in the House of Lords, as is their right under law.

To Penelope Betjeman   43 Cloth Fair
14 October 1955   London EC1

My darling Plymmi,
I was ever so pleased to have your p[ost]c[ard] from San Marino. Shall
we return there? Are the San Marinese less noisy than the Italians? Are
there any villages in the republic?
    I quite forgot to tell you that I went to MUCKLESTONE and OAKLEY on
my Staff[ord]s[hire] tour. They are both in Staffs. You are a Staffs tart.
M[ucklestone] was a very pretty village on a hillside facing west, and

mild Welsh hills the other side of a dullish hunting non-industrial valley. The tomb of Meadows the agent is at the gate. Mr and Mrs Woad Senior on the other side of the path – flat tombs. The church pretty outside, pale pink stone. Inside dark, nave on north aisle well lit with greenish-Kempe-ish glass in memory of Woads. A big box pew at e[ast] end of n[orth] aisle with wood tablets round, earliest mid-eighteenth cent[ury].

Oakley is in very flat country. Two lodges like that at Woad doubled. Plenty of timbers, a long drive through rather Alderley-Edge-ish scenery with occasional brackish ponds to a 1760 house – but tarted up in 1900-ish idea of 1760 with plate glass. Chas Peace and I did not dare go in. Schoolgirls looked out of windows at us. But it was very dull – rather like Kingston Lisle inside, not the hall I mean, but the drawing room part, only of course school-y and less hideous than K[ingston] L[isle].

I hope you and the P[owlie] are quite well. Very truly yours and oh how I long to see my ijjus Plymmi again, Tewpie

DESIGN FOR CRESTING OF A CHANCEL SCREEN
by Augustus Welby Pugin

Though the Chetwode family had owned the Manor of Chetwode in Buckinghamshire from the fifteenth century, they also owned the Oakley Hall estate in Staffordshire where PB's parents spent sojourns when they were first married. PB had never visited it as it was let all through her father's career in the army, and it was sold in 1920.

G. E. Kempe was a Victorian stained glass artist of some distinction.

D.B. ('Charles') Peace, a friend of JB's, was the Staffordshire county planning officer and lived in Leek.

To George Barnes   43 Cloth Fair
November 1955   London EC1

My dear Commander,
I do congratulate you – Wedgwood and Administration, pottery and
poesy, dons and attractive students. You are very wise. Though it will
mean no more jobs for me on the BBC as I was only employed because I
knew you, I *still* rejoice for you and Anne and Little P[rawls]. And
you'll get decent holidays. I love Stoke-on-Trent, and Charles Peace
(D. B. Peace) the Staff[ord]s[hire] County Planning Officer and his
wife will tell you all the things to see in that excellent district. To hell
with McGivern. You've made the grade, ole man.
    Love from John B

> G.B. had just accepted the post of Principal of the University College of North
> Staffordshire at Keele.

To Penelope Gilliatt   43 Cloth Fair
10 January 1956   London EC1

Dear Editress,
I write poems with great difficulty, very slowly, crossing out and re-
crossing out. They take me weeks. Twenty lines might take me a
month. On the other hand it is a nice subject and I shall have a try, if
you don't mind not depending on me.
    Yours sincerely, John Betjeman

> P.G. was the editor of *Vogue* and had asked JB to write a poem on autumn for a planned
> feature on the seasons. She offered fifteen pounds. JB wrote 'In Willesden Churchyard'
> and P.G. wrote (6 March 1956), 'I like your poem very much. . . . We are hoping to
> make a special feature of it all on its own.' The poem came out in *High and Low* in 1966.

To John Guest   43 Cloth Fair
28 March 1956   London EC1

Dear John,
Mrs J. M. Peace is the wife of the County Planning Officer of Stafford.
She read out some short stories and then some bits of that Journal to me

after a tremendous lot of persuasion when I was staying up there some months ago. She is the mother of two girls, and was brought up Congregational. I said this was the first work by an articulate Congregationalist that I had heard. I must say parts of it I found absolutely thrilling. I imagine that the rest of the Journal is [sections] 1 to 20, and I have never seen that. I said that I would try and get the book published, though I can see that you could not possibly publish all of what she has written. It strikes me that if parts of 1 to 20 are as good as parts of sections 21 to 26, this would be a most wonderful record of what life in a provincial town today is like. A sort of modern Flora Thompson.

As to what she is like. She is rather a nice-looking woman, with blue eyes, greying hair, fresh pink cheeks and boundless energy. She draws very well and learned under Eric Ravilious. Her husband, Mr D. B. Peace, is the reason how I met her, for he has done the Staffordshire churches in my book for Collins and done them extremely well. I hope you are as interested by the book as I am. Surely here there is a real writer and one doesn't often appear out of the outskirts of provincial towns?

Yours, John B

> J.G. was literary adviser to Longmans, the publishers, and on the council of the Royal Society of Literature. 'The Journal was remarkable,' remembers J.G. 'Unfortunately it was extremely long. It was the sort of thing that might well be discovered in *years* to come, and seen then as a fascinating piece of social history. But, in 1956, it presented difficulties as a publishing proposition – its inordinate length being not the least. Most regretfully we had to decline it.'

To Candida Betjeman   Christ's College
9 May 1956   Cambridge

Darling Wibz,
It was very nice to hear your voice on the telephone yesterday. I wish you were here with me. It is far more beautiful than Oxford. The Senate House in which I am writing this is richly ornamented inside with Queen Anne panelling and plasterwork and from the window I can see King's College Chapel, my favourite building in the world. Oh, how I wish you and I were looking round Cambridge together. I shall miss you very much when I come home to Wantage. I love you very much although I sometimes get so angry and irritable and dotty.

I hope you've got off German and will have a happy term and go on being so brilliant that you are top of everything and win scholarships. Lots and lots of love from Mad Dadz.

JB was in Cambridge to give the prestigious Rede Lecture.

To Geoffrey Taylor   43 Cloth Fair
23 May 1956   London ECI

Dear Geoffrey,
I have today sent off the enclosed preface and told Fabers that they must await your approval of it. The anthology and list of poets are with Fabers.

I am so sad to hear of your having had a heart attack. It is a most unexpected thing in one so lithe and spare and calm as you. I will put you into my prayers, the only practical step that one can take, and have earnest hopes of your speedy recovery.

I should have written before to tell you how deeply I enjoyed Mrs Alexander's poems which you sent me. The first three stanzas of 'Sorry on the Sea' are, I think, the best of all. There's one poet whom we have not included, and whom I am going to read with our anthology in view, and that is Arthur Hugh Clough.

Love to Mary. I hope that afternoon in Dublin did not bring on your heart trouble.

Love, John B

G.T. (see *Volume One*), had written to JB (21 November 1955), 'Fabers have written offering us two hundred pounds for the Love Anthology (plus ultimate royalties). I have written accepting for myself. . . . What I suggest is that we should have one hundred pounds each; and that I should do the initial reading and typing and send the results to you; then you should look at it, add or subtract, and write a short introduction. I want to do the preliminary stuff myself, because I want to do it my own way – the long way of reading the poets without consulting existing anthologies. My view being that there are probably as good fish in the forest as ever got into an anthology.'

JB had been to visit G.T. in Ireland for a week in April to finalise the selection. To JB's desolation, for their affinity over poetry and shared laughter was so great, G.T. died in July.

English Love Poems was not published until 1957.

To G. B. Stern   The Mead
                                                                    Wantage
8 June 1956   Berkshire

Dear Peter,
Drinks I could manage on [the] 17th but not dinner, as the Youth Club
is coming in here at eight o'clock for a cultivated lecture from me and as
it has been put off once I can't do it a second time. How very kind of you
to leave me your fish-knives. Of course I'll use them because I AM
MIDDLE CLASS AND PROUD OF IT but I like using the language of the
upper class. I'm fed up with it becoming so well known, this 'U-
business', the whole point of it was that it was a secret. So it would have
remained if it had been confined to my verses which were hidden away
in *Time and Tide* and which vanity made me reprint. But it isn't *all* my
fault. Nancy [Mitford] did it far more competently than I, but with too
much publicity. Leave her some of your fish-knives on those conditions
and I'll proudly take the others.
    Yours, John B

>   Nancy Mitford's book *Noblesse Oblige* had just come out, containing essays by her and
>   Alan Ross on 'U' and 'Non-U' – vocabulary used or not used by the upper class. (Alan
>   Ross was an English professor, not to be confused with JB's friend of the same name who
>   was editor of the *London Magazine* from 1961. They both lived near Brighton.)
>   JB's verse 'How to Get On in Society', which began 'Phone for the fish-knives,
>   Norman', was first published in *Time and Tide* in December 1951 as a competition and
>   was also included in *A Few Late Chrysanthemums*. JB never thought of this verse as
>   anything more than a journalistic joke.

To Anne Barnes   The Mead
                                                                    Wantage
21 June 1956   Berkshire

My dear Anne,
By a strange coincidence worthy of inclusion in Mr Pooter's diary,
someone from Stone-in-Oxney wrote to me on the day after you did.
She must be rather nice. I enclose her letter.
    Ta for the nice things you say *re* the Rede Lecture. God knows how it
went down. I've suggested Gerard Irvine for Dean of Kings to Noel
Annan. He *might* be just what they want. Clever and very holy
underneath.

I am fascinated by your remarks *re* [the] USA. I expect the suburbs
are lovely. I go there (Cinci[nnati]) for March next year and am
absolutely dreading it as I saw a film called *Storm Centre* which
obviously was just like suburban USA, very priggish and good and
humourless and intense and psychological, and public libraries taken
very seriously.

I *bet* you are sad at leaving Prangs [Prawls]. The house has a soul I'm
sure and suffers too. I do understand you. I've never, fortunately, in
our married life been so long in one house that I felt agony at leaving it
but Candida was agonised at leaving Farnborough and I, as a child, was
agonised at leaving West Hill Highgate for Chelsea and still regard
Cornwall as home and have to see it every year.

Prangs must have become all those places to you. There is no cure for
the agony but work and that I suppose you will have plenty of when
fitting up North Staff[ordshire]. One consolation I can give you for
certain and that is that people in the Trent Valley are the nicest in
England and the toofer the roofer, the naicer.

I've talked with Eliz[abeth] and we suggest Monday July 9th for
dining with you, Commander, Little P[rawls] and his bride. Okay?
Ask the Commander. Earlier is not possible.

When at Stoke you will love my Repton friends the Lynam
Thomases – both heavy drinkers and he the headmaster, she an ex-
nurse and very pretty.

Much love, John B

> A.B. (see *Volume One*) was married to JB's great friend George B.
> JB refers to *Diary of a Nobody* by G. and W. Grossmith (1892).
> Noel Annan was Provost of King's College, Cambridge (1956–66).
> Gerard Irvine did not become Dean.
> Prawls near Stone-in-Oxney in Kent was the Barneses' cherished home where JB had
> often stayed during the forties and early fifties.
> Anthony Barnes had just married Susan Dempsey.

To Ronald Searle   The Mead
                                                          Wantage
13 July 1956   Berkshire

Dear Ronnie,
I have gone Vorticist which is why I am writing like this and on the
corner. I have just forged a letter to Etchells from another Vorticist. I
am enchanted with your drawing and very honoured to have it. I can

see the charm of Loughborough. You do draw beautifully. I wish we could get Langdon out of *Punch*, his drawings are so hideous. I wish I could talk to you about art in *Punch*. You and old Ernest H. [Shepard] and Leslie [Illingworth] are the ones, and I *think* old Russell B[rockbank] has got a strange talent which needs bringing out more.

Yours, John B

R.S., the humorous artist, had met JB through *Punch* magazine to which they both contributed.

To Candida Betjeman   43 Cloth Fair
14 July 1956   London EC1

Darling Wibz what could be better
Than your delightful rhyming letter
And so I now take up my pen
To write one back to you again*.
I hoped to go while you and all
Were riding around the Roman Wall
Off to the Shetlands to explore
Each unknown isle and stormbeat shore.
But oh alas I hoped in vain
There is no seat upon the 'plane.
The Powlie now should be at sea
With motor bike for company
Jazz records and a gramophone.
What will he look like? I must own
That when I see his crewcut hair
I'll want to laugh and stare and stare.

When you return to home from school
Where I am sitting as a rule
Inside my smelly lib'ry smoking
Reading and writing, drinking, joking
You will not find me for that day
I must be many miles away
In Cardiff but I shall return
On Saturday. I long to learn
How you got on at school and hear
If you have now dried up the tear
Which started from your moist brown eye,
Because you had to say goodbye

To girls you doted on. I know
How sad these partings are and so
My poor dear Wibz I sympathise
But life's all partings. Dry your eyes
And smile a bit to welcome me
Your loving bald and old MD.

*Pronounced by the upper classes 'agen'.

PB had taken PSGB and me on a riding tour of the Cheviots in Northumberland under
the leadership of Kay Elliot.
   MD stood for 'Mad Dadz' which JB sometimes signed himself.

To Laurence Whistler   Coolgrena
                                                Trebetherick
                                                Wadebridge
13 August 1956   Cornwall

Dear Whistler,
Your most welcome and delightfully unexpected present arrived here,
where I am having a holiday with my family as the guest of your old
private school chum Patrick Lawrence, my friend and neighbour in
Berkshire. He sends you his affections. His Cornish address is Stoptide
Lodge, Rock, Wadebridge, Cornwall.
   I always find I like poetry most when I am in Cornwall and can feel
and think and see again. That is why your book comes just at the right
moment. You have a beautiful gift of expressing melancholy. I think I
remember 'Hotel Bedroom' appearing in a magazine or paper somewhere. It is very moving. But the poem of Lyme Regis I like best of all.
'Shoes cockle up on the mussel-bound sill.' Oh, that's splendid. 'A
Sedation at Day Break' seems to me a launching-out into new and
thrilling seas. I'm no good, though you are so kind about my verse. My
springs are running dry. But yours are flowing up stronger. Write on!
Write on! and thank you so much.
   Yours, John Betjeman

   L.W., the glass engraver, writer and younger brother of Rex Whistler, had sent JB his
book of verse *The View from This Window* which had just come out.

Three:

Half a century nearer Hell

1956 to 1958

The bear who sits above my bed
  More agèd now he is to see,
His woollen eyes have thinner thread,
  But still he seems to say to me,
In double-doom notes, like a knell:
'You're half a century nearer Hell.'

'Archibald'

'Fifty. Not much longer for this world, every day more precious. I
must begin cleaning up this earthly house so as to leave things tidy for
my wife and children,' JB wrote in the *Spectator*.[1]

In September 1956, JB chose to give the annual speech of the Society
for the Protection of Ancient Buildings in one of his favourite ones, the
Coal Exchange in the City of London. Plans were steadily escalating to
demolish it. 'As you are all converted, there is no need for me to say to
you why you like the building. Goodness knows why one likes one
building and not another! . . . I see so many distinguished people here
who, I know, can answer these questions. I see that great man, John
Summerson; I won't mention names any more, but I can see Mortimer
Wheeler, Marshall Sisson and people who really do know, so I am
nervous of speaking. . . . I do not know about proportion. . . . It is one
of those subtle things that you do not notice until you see it wrongly
done. . . . The relation of one building to another in a street and in a
village has something to do with proportion. The relation of this
building to its street is considerably better than the relation of, let us
say, some of those white cliffs that have arisen in this city next to St
Paul's Cathedral. . . . I wonder what Morris would have said if he had
known the SPAB was ever going to meet in a building put up in 1847! I
think he would have said, "It's all right if it's a good building." We
know how Morris tests one. . . . This surprisingly light, airy,
fantastic, imaginative interior is what he would have liked. It seems to
me rather like the City itself, this building: a bold front and a good brain
inside. . . . Let us not write the Victorians off as no good.'[2]

Having long been skirmishing, at this stage in his life JB now embarked on a full-scale war on behalf of good Victorian buildings, hitherto unregarded. Enormous battles were waiting on the horizon and he was already discussing the formation of the Victorian Society with Anne Rosse. They eventually co-founded it in 1958, with JB as vice-president. When all else had failed, JB became a last resort, a last hope, the supreme fighter for the most diverse people. They wrote to him about tree-felling in Huddersfield, shopping precincts in Croydon, traffic detours in Richmond. He was used relentlessly by his friends, like L. T. Rolt, the canal buff, who deluged him with anti-pylon propaganda. Martyn Skinner, the poet, asked him to stop the building of a tall block in Henley. The MP, Nigel Birch, wrote to him about the desecration of Hyde Park. Brian Batsford, the publisher, complained about unacceptable development in Sutton Courtenay. The geographer, Edward Gilbert, wrote about the new Western Bypass skirting Wytham Woods and Godstow. JB replied (16 October 1957), 'My heaven! I was driving to Northampton from Wantage the other day and went round by Wytham and Godstow in the lovely autumn sunshine. It seemed to me amazing at the time that so unspoilt a stretch of country should be allowed to remain and one really cannot be surprised at the action of the council. I will write about it in the *Spectator*.'[3] Indeed he did, but the bypass was built in any case. He campaigned against barrows being ploughed up on the Berkshire Downs. He wrote to the Prime Minister, Harold Macmillan (27 August 1957), 'Here at last is the letter I promised to write to you ages ago about the [plans to modernize the] Albert Bridge. Please, please, try and do something about it.'[4] He campaigned to save Christ Church, Acton Square in Salford; he joined in with the MP Woodrow Wyatt to save the Nash Terraces in Regent's Park.

Worthy as it all sounds, JB never bored his friends with any of his causes. He fired his ammunition at unfortunate planners and developers and above all he kept a light heart. Jim Lees-Milne, who was on many committees with him, shared his passion for good architecture. They had by this time known each other for nearly thirty years and together were on the committee of the Society for the Protection of Ancient Buildings and many others. 'We had the greatest giggles – we were always giggling both in meetings and out of them. . . . One of our favourite things to do was to visit the Geological Museum in Jermyn Street. There was never anyone around and only one custodian. All the exhibits, which were very dim and dull, were covered in dust – odd bits of stone and bone. One day I remember we put in an old hazelnut and another day a pebble from Green Park, as new exhibits. We wrote out cards with complicated inscriptions in Latin which we would slip in beside. Then we would visit the museum a week or two later to see if our things were still there. They always were. Then sometimes we used to go round the city looking at architecture on summer evenings – but it was always the laughter I remembered; those meetings which could have been so dreary, one always looked forward to if John was there.'[5]

JB had a knack of making things enjoyable; he even enjoyed appearing on television, which for most people is a nerve-racking experience. 'The truth is,' he used to say, 'that it's no more trouble to go on one of these conversation-piece programmes than it is to go out to dinner. It's even less troublesome than some dinner parties I have known.' Despite the fact that many of his peers, even Evelyn Waugh, thought that if you went on television it meant you couldn't have any real integrity, JB appeared more and more. He was constantly on panel games and inveigled surprised friends to take part as well – Andrew Wordsworth, who taught at Bryanston School, wrote (12 January 1957), 'Thank you so much for having me with you on the telly, I loved the whole set-up.'[6] His friend Kenneth Clark had been asked by Associated Television to make some programmes on architecture and had asked JB to debate modern architecture with Hugh Casson. JB replied (23 September 1957), 'The trouble is that I like good modern, e.g. the Pimlico Estate and that at Brixton and even features of the one near here. Hugh Casson and I see very much eye to eye and I think that we would make quite an interesting programme between us but not in the form of a pro- and anti-modern debate.'[7]

Apart from his religious programmes on the radio, JB also contributed regularly to the BBC Television religious programme on Sunday evenings. Michael Reddington, his producer, wrote (3 August 1957), 'The programme really does seem to have been a success. So many people have told me how they enjoy it and by the reports in the press we seem to have achieved our object and proved that "nuns are human and ordinary people".'[8] JB also appeared on a discussion about life after death and then wrote to Michael Reddington about a suggested programme on morals (19 June 1957), 'I feel an awful hypocrite in these programmes because my own life is so reprehensible and all the good they may do will be negated. . . . I think you should get somebody of a more blameless life than me and I shall not mind.'[9]

'The Colonel', who had made a miraculous recovery from his illness, was still writing weekly to JB: 'I have lost everything nearly – including

my libido (*entirely*) – now I realise what a difference *it* makes,' he wrote
(3 July 1957).[10] In that month JB sent news of the Colonel to his
cherished secretary from the old days of the British Council and the
Oxford Preservation Trust, Diana Peel (then Craig), who had worked
for him in the forties: 'Having been off his head he is now sane again.'
He also reported on his own family: 'Candida is fourteen and at St
Mary's, Wantage, and very keen on clothes. Powlie is in the army and
just about to go to Northern Ireland. Penelope is in Wantage and
exactly the same. I am fatter, balder, sadder and more depraved.'[11]

Paul wrote to JB from his National Service posting in Germany (June
1957), 'We get up at five every morning. An armoured car is fun to
drive at first as it is very powerful and can go over terrifically rough
country and when new can do eighty m.p.h. in either forward or
reverse, though of course ours are very old in fact, some of them saw
service in the desert in 1942! They are made by Daimler so the engines
are very good. The one I drive is called Blue Peter.'[12] Paul inherited
JB's and his grandfather Ernest's love of fast and beautifully made cars.
After his National Service he went on to Trinity College, Oxford to
read geography, much to the delight of JB's friend the geographer
Edward Gilbert. He played in a band and eventually earned enough
money, when added to what Granny Bess had left him, to buy a vintage
Rolls-Royce. Inevitably, my mother was furious, my father delighted.

Life at the Mead trundled on in the same routine. There were
lunches with David and Rachel Cecil in Charlbury Road, Oxford, and
walks afterwards through North Oxford. (I remember David not being
able to walk straight because he talked so much and kept colliding with
everybody.) Before lunch on Sundays at home, JB often played the
game of taking any slim volume of poetry from anywhere in his library
and reading out a verse or even a whole poem and making everybody
guess who wrote it. John Sparrow sometimes could, but it usually
worked best the other way round. JB nearly *always* guessed right.
Sometimes we had lunch outside in a little sunken garden which my
mother had made beautiful with crowded polyanthus and tulips in the
spring – her favourite time of year – and sweet williams in summer. If it
was cold JB used to get thick coats and rugs for everyone, or if it was too
hot he would bring out myriad different hats, now and then wearing
two or three on top of each other himself. Bryan and Elisabeth
Guinness used to come from Biddesden and Maurice Bowra would ogle
my schoolfriend Sarah Fox-Pitt.

JB wrote to his friend Edward Hornby, 'I realise how important all
our companies are to each other. Michael [Hornby] came last night to

us at Wantage and he and the Pipers and Karen Lancaster and Heck and Guy Knight and the Barings and the children sang popular hits of the twenties until one a.m.'[13] Hester (Heck) Knight recalled, 'The happiest evenings I ever spent were at the Mead when we sang or used to read poetry together after one of Penelope's excellent suppers. I remember the excitement of it, and how John would say, "Do you know this?" and then the whole poem would come alive. And I particularly remember one morning years ago when there was a train strike on, and I gave John a lift to London in my car. He had with him a copy of R. S. Thomas's latest little volume, and all the way he read extracts from it, finishing with one called "Night and Morning" which begins, "One night of tempest I arose and went/Along the Menai shore, on dreaming bent." It is very short, and we learnt it by heart on the drive, and now whenever I see a seashore I remember it, and I remember that sunny morning driving in to London on the old road, and John's voice, and the marvellous feeling of having been transported into a different world thanks to his guidance.'[14]

My holiday life at Wantage revolved around the Baring family who lived in the nearby village of Ardington. I had stayed with them during the move from Farnborough. Anne, or 'Arne' as JB always called her, was my best friend, and her parents, Mollie and Desmond, became inextricably close to mine. Mollie remembers, 'Dessie was a church warden at Ardington and John first met him over some diocesan decision about the clock, I think in 1949. Before the meeting I said to Dessie, "You know John Betjeman is a poet, now don't go and talk to him about racing or hunting." The rapport was instant – wasn't it strange – they had nothing in common but felt utterly relaxed in each other's company. John used to call Dessie's office "the betting room" and he used to say, "What won the four-thirty, Dessie – at Newton Abbot?" when in fact it would be Derby day. He loved the camaraderie of the racing people. He got on like a house on fire with all our racing friends – George Todd, George Beeby and Sam Long, "the Augur", who wrote for the *Sporting Life*. He loved my parents too – my father had known Marie Lloyd and Vesta Tilley – and I remember him doing the charleston with my mother on Christmas night – they were both as high as kites. Of course John discovered early on how fond Dessie and I were of drink – but we hardly ever got drunk. We drank very, very good claret and Penelope used to get furious.'[15]

I don't know why Mollie thought it odd that my parents felt so at home with them. You didn't need to *adjust* at the Barings – it was a relaxed and happy home and JB's favourite port of call on the way back from Didcot station in the evenings. He could always be sure of a laugh.

When my parents went to America for almost a month in March 1957, it was the first time in my life that I felt completely abandoned. JB did it for the money. He was to give a series of lectures at the University of Cincinnati under the auspices of the George Elliston Poetry Foundation. He told me before he went that it would be rather like going to live in Reading. He stopped off in New York on the way to meet the journalist Brendan Gill of the *New Yorker*. The magazine treated JB as their very own eccentric English poet. They had booked a room for him at the Algonquin. Gill wrote, 'He has been persuaded to play the role of Poet in Residence for several weeks. ("I don't much like the young. Whatever shall I say to them? If only they were eighty-five!") Poets are an endearing lot, attracting the protective instinct as a magnet does pins and Mr Betjeman is no exception. . . . He sat sipping a bourbon on the rocks and bubbling over with delight at the American scene: "My first visit you know," he said. "I ordered a bourbon because I understand it's the authentic American drink. I mean to be thoroughly American during my stay at Cinci – I hope it isn't disrespectful of me to call Cinci Cinci so soon. The drive in from the airport this morning was an exaltation. The Woolworth building looks enchanting, all that Gothic work so high in the air so close to eternity! I can't imagine what Cinci will be like. A city of hills. . . . I feel *very brave*." '16

When JB and my mother (who had gone by boat, having refused to fly) finally got to 'Cinci', JB described, 'March in the Middle West when the land was brown and dry and robins as big as pheasants hopped about on the porch swings and the sun sank early behind Lutheran steeples in the land of Uncle Tom's Cabin.'17 He soon searched out good things to look at like the Taft Museum, and enthused over the gas lights in Mount Storm Park saying they were the most beautiful gas lights in the world. This made headlines in the *Cincinnati Times Star*. He charmed the local literary ladies by flashing the red lining in his suit during his lectures. He played games like Consequences with his workshop students, making each one write a rhyming couplet, folding it over each time and then undoing the paper and reading it all out as one. As parting gifts he gave them all a copy of his poems which he had paid for himself. Not surprisingly, my mother hated the American way of entertaining for she didn't drink and was bored by interminable dinner parties – reminiscent of her Dublin days – but she did discover the joys of hunting with the Cammargo pack of hounds and wrote an article about it in *Country Life* on her return to England.

Once back, JB wrote congratulating me on my School Certificate results: 'It must be because of having a flat head. The simply hideous bracelet I enclose I bought in Princes Arcade in Piccadilly. I was too frightened of the saleswoman not to buy it. I do apologise. But you can give it away.'[18] Although I was only just fifteen, my parents put up no resistance when I begged to leave school. I spent a lot of that summer with JB. We went to stay in Norfolk with my godmother, Sylvia Combe: 'It was fun staying at Burnham Thorpe,' he wrote (1 August 1958), 'Norfolk was looking its best with the sun on corn, flint, brown bricks, red tiles, willows, elms and marshes.'[19] It was not fun when one afternoon JB and I decided to go sailing at Blakeney. He wanted to demonstrate his prowess at the sport, which his father had taught him on the Broads when he was a boy. We hired a small dinghy and after three hours had failed to get it out of the harbour. Instead we bumped into one boat after another while affronted sailors yelled at us. We got so embarrassed that we both bent down and pretended there was something wrong at the bottom of the boat. In the end, we had to ask somebody's help to tow us back from where we had drifted uncontrollably. It was only twenty yards away from our starting point. I seldom remember a more embarrassing experience.

We packed a lot into that summer. We went to stay with the Waughs at Combe Florey on the way to Cornwall in what JB called 'Tony Powell country'. We visited the architect Albert Richardson at his red-brick eighteenth-century house in Ampthill, and the art historian David Talbot Rice and his Russian wife, 'Tamara and Tamara and Tamara', in their Cotswold manor. We regularly scoured an antique shop in Bampton in whose premises was a winding lane filled from floor to ceiling with china bric-à-brac. I could not understand how any piece could be extricated without everything else falling over, but the owner knew how and JB bought me a white Sèvres vase, with flowers all over it. He took me to a hidden subterranean garden grotto covered in shells and fossils in a back street of Ware. He took me to see the Stanley Spencers at Cookham and round the Birmingham and Manchester Art Galleries. He gave me a book on Van Gogh and wrote in it, 'Van Gogh's life may well be like yours. When you say that about your wanting to work fast and get a drawing done quickly I exactly understand you. That is the artist's trouble, whether he is writer, painter or musician, the thing *has* to be put down before the inspiration or mood goes and it so often happens that the technique cannot convey the feeling.'[20]

But best of all, in the spring of 1958 he took me on a three-week tour

of the Scottish islands. We sailed in an enormous Swedish liner, hired
by the National Trust for Scotland, to Iona, Canna, St Kilda, North
Rhona, Foula, Muckle Flugga, Fair Isle and May Island. Seton
Gordon, the naturalist, gave talks about birds. We were all sick one
day, along with some of the crew, on the way to St Kilda in the roughest
sea imaginable. It was worth it though; St Kilda was a magic place and
JB and I went off on our own all day and sketched. He loved the
Scottish islands more than I can express, and at Skara Brae on the
Orkneys, as though in celebration, there hung before us, about six feet
off the ground, a bright green mist for about a minute which then faded
to nothing in the morning light.

In May I went to stay with a family in France, which I hated. JB
wrote, 'It's very typical here at the Mead. Mummy is telephoning to
Sheila Birkenhead. Angela Wakeford is here substituting for Mrs
Hughes at the Caff. Marco [my Pekingese] is asleep in the scullery and I
miss you very much. I went into your room and it looked just as though
you were there. It was harvest festival this morning and it went on for
hours and hours. That irritating lady in front of us brought in a lot of
children who crowded out the pews and a family came into where I was
sitting and squashed me out and I had to sit beside that pair of little old
women who cough gently every other minute. Glory to God in the
highest! I had to concentrate a lot to keep charity and God in my heart.
Powlie is now at Trinity College, Oxford. Mummy and Angela went to
his rooms today which are panelled Georgian and looking down the
gardens to those gates that won't be opened until a Stuart ascends the
throne. He has joined the Jazz Club and the French Club. I am going to
see him on Monday evening at the Diocesan dinner which is in
Trinity.'[21]

One June day JB and I went to Sally Weaver's wedding together (I
can't remember why my mother couldn't come). Sally had been my
first and best friend at Uffington – we were exact contemporaries:

> In summer wind the elm leaves sing,
>   And sharp's the shade they're shedding,
> And loud and soft the church bells ring
>   For Sally Weaver's wedding.
>
> With chasing light the meadows fill,
>   The greenness growing greener,
> As racing over White Horse Hill
>   Come bluer skies and cleaner.

The chalk-white walls, the steaming thatch
　　In rain-washed air are clearing,
And waves of sunshine run to catch
　　The bride for her appearing.

Inside the church in every pew
　　Sit old friends, older grown now;
Their children whom our children knew
　　Have children of their own now.

The babies wail, the organ plays,
　　Now thunderous, now lighter;
The brighter day of Sally's days
　　Grows every moment brighter.

And all the souls of Uffington,
　　The dead among the living,
Seem witnessing the rite begun
　　Of taking and of giving.

The flying clouds! The flying years!
　　This church of centuries seven!
How new its weathered stone appears
　　When vows are made in Heaven![22]

JB had a little too much to drink at the reception in the village hall. On our way back to Wantage in the half-light of evening, we were driving along the Icknield Way between Kingston Lisle and Sparsholt, under an avenue of tall beeches like a cathedral aisle. I was at the wheel, and JB suddenly shouted, 'Stop, stop, stop!' Aghast, I stopped the car and asked, 'What's the matter?' He said, 'Just wait and I'll get out and open the gate.' I said, 'What gate?' There was clearly no gate. He said, 'Yes, there is. Across the road.' I told him to shut up and drove on. *Had* there been a toll-gate there? *Had* he seen a ghost? If he had it was not his first, nor perhaps his last. He told me that on one wet evening in the forties, when driving his mother from Lincolnshire to London, he noticed a curious sensation of the supernatural. He stopped the car and on her advice looked at the map to see where they were, as she had noticed it too. They both smelt gunpowder on the air. It turned out they were at Naseby, the scene of the famous battle.

　　JB had written to Elizabeth every day from Cincinnati and once he was back in London she was always by his side. 'Isn't Feeble wonderful?' he wrote to George Barnes. (JB called Elizabeth 'Feeble' and various other words implying weakness of frame. He told me it was because she was so willowy, he thought she might fall over.) Her

mother's house at Edensor in Derbyshire was like another home and his
continual visits became a pleasurable routine. Moor View, which had
been built between the wars in a cosy Arts and Crafts style for the head
gardener at Chatsworth, stood at the top of the village. Sheltered by a
beech hedge, you could look down on to the church spire and across the
park to the moor beyond. JB attended speech day at St Elphin's in
Darleydale, where Elizabeth's niece, Emma Cavendish, was a pupil.
He was the speaker and Deborah Devonshire, Emma's mother,
remembered, 'He delighted the whole school by starting off, after an
exciting pause when everyone tried to guess what was coming, "How
nice you all look!" I glanced over his shoulder and saw he had written
that down. A lesson in a good start. They all settled happily in their
seats and paid attention from then on.'[23]

43 Cloth Fair began to be a Mecca – a place of pilgrimage. Few of JB's
friends and acquaintances worked in the City and it was an expedition
to visit him and to lunch at Coltman's restaurant in Aldersgate. JB had
passed on his love of the Underground to me and I always arrived from
Paddington by the Circle Line to Aldersgate station (now Barbican)
which was out in the open air – rose bay willowherb sprouted from the
walls and it was just a short walk to his house.

On Thursdays JB disappeared and I never thought to ask why, but
years later I discovered it was something he never talked about to
anyone. Soon after he had moved to Cloth Fair and started attending
the church of St Bartholomew the Great, he asked the chaplain, Mr
Bush, who was rather evangelical (JB much enjoyed calling him 'Father
Bush' though not to his face), if he might do hospital visiting. He was
then introduced to Sister Mary Bland, a legendary ward sister who
worked at Bart's for more than thirty years. ('She was madly loved by
everyone,' remembers a colleague, 'and was also a Christian.') Mary
Bland recalled, 'John used to come and have coffee in my room every
Thursday morning and then go round and visit the patients in my
ward. He was able to make all the patients laugh – he was a wonderful
mimic. He much enjoyed the names we all had for the sisters, nobody
ever knew their real names, I was in fact called Sister Percival Pott
which was the name of my ward and John was intrigued by this. He
named the sister who was in charge of all the cleaning ladies, "Sister
Floors" and the sister in charge of the skin department in the
outpatients, "Sister Skins". He would say, "Please can I go and see
Sister Skins." I think because of his horror of death it helped him to see
dying patients. He continued visiting for over a dozen years. He always
used to come with Elizabeth to the Nurses' Guild wine and cheese

parties. I think he was genuinely proud and moved to be associated with St Bartholomew's which is, after all, one of the greatest hospitals in the world. It was founded in 1123 and has survived, on exactly the same spot, the Fire, the Plague, Cromwell but not, perhaps, John Major's Tory government.'[24]

Hugh Dunn was a cancer patient in Percival Pott ward. His widow remembers, 'Your father certainly cheered up his days by his visits when they discussed London before and after the war. Mr Betjeman was at the time a very busy man but he still found time to visit us, and attend Hugh's funeral at Mortlake Crematorium.'[25] Whether his visits to terminal cancer patients deepened JB's gloom or not is difficult to tell. He sent a poem to the *London Magazine* which he had written in December 1956 about dying:

> Now from his remoteness in a stillness unaccountable
> He drags himself to earth again to say goodbye to me
> His final generosity when almost insurmountable
> The barriers and mountains he has crossed again must be.[26]

When JB's secretary Anita Dent announced that she was leaving to get married, Tory Dennistoun, the daughter of the racehorse trainer Ginger who trained at Letcombe Regis and was a great friend of the family, wrote to JB (11 May 1958), 'I have full secretarial training and have just given up my job with the rector of Stepney after nine months as my father wanted me to help him with the horses. I am pretty hot on ecclesiastical affairs.'[27] 'I was surprised and thrilled to get the job – four days a week for seven pounds,' she recalled. 'John was a lovely employer and I was *hopeless*. Sometimes he would sigh and gaze wistfully at a photograph on the mantelpiece of a pretty girl, saying, "Oh, for Freckly Jill" – his perfect secretary. But at other times, when not besieged by demanding letters asking him to open fêtes or advise on literary careers, he would read aloud from Kipling or try out bits of his "epic" on me which he was working on at the time. Occasionally he'd take me to lunch at Coltman's where there was sawdust on the floor and we would sit on bentwood chairs and drink champagne from pewter tankards, and afterwards visit City churches. Archie, propped up on the top of a bookcase, looked over us all the time and probably saw me forget to turn off the Stenorette tape machine one night. I always suspected it was the cause of the fire which nearly destroyed the house, but John never blamed me.'[28]

JB and Tory had to move out while Cloth Fair was resurrected. He wrote to me (26 November 1958), 'Through the kindness of Tony

Armstrong-Jones, the photographer, who has just gone to the USA for a month, I have been lent a room in Rotherhithe while 43 is being repaired after the fire. It is so nice I never want to leave it and I long to take you to see it. I sleep there at nights and am writing this now in it with the sound of a spring tide lapping against the walls under my window. It is a large room and hangs over the Thames.'[29]

By the late fifties JB's literary career was running like clockwork. John Hadfield included his work in the *Saturday Book*; Eddie Penning-Rowsell, who was then working for the Hulton Press, edited a selection of his poems which came out in the *Pocket Poets* series. Heywood Hill, the famous Mayfair bookseller, was being approached about selling JB's manuscripts. The *New Yorker* sent him one-hundred-dollar cheques for poems. He wrote to Jim Lees-Milne (27 July 1957), 'They (Collins) want my church book m[anu]s[cript] by August 1st. They've waited fourteen years. Unless I work on it with my clergyman friend this Saturday and Sunday, there is no chance of getting the final m[anu]s[cript] to them.'[30] He wrote to Mark Bonham Carter, his editor at Collins, 'All the manuscripts of the book are now with you, Yours ever, Larry Olivier.'[31]

In January 1958 JB agreed to write an architectural column in the *Daily Telegraph* once a month, instead of his weekly one in the *Spectator* which was becoming quite a strain. I remember him lamenting to me about having to think about what would make a good paragraph. He had become tired of the constant complaints about his articles that they printed in the *Spectator* and he wanted to get on with his long autobiographical poem. A monthly column wouldn't interrupt his thoughts so much.

JB wrote to my mother (18 November 1958), 'I am getting on well with the epic. I think I will call it "Summoned by Bells". I have finished the Marlborough chapter. Today I am going to start on Oxford.'[32] He had written to Jock Murray (17 March 1958), having sent him the section on Highgate Junior School, 'If you really think it would ever make a book I should like it produced in large type on large paper with illustrations. . . . Stephen Spender wanted to see a copy and I have sent him one but I told him that even if he thinks it good enough to publish [in *Encounter*], you wanted it first as a book.'[33]

On 3 January 1958 Freddie Birkenhead, who was to edit JB's *Collected Poems* and write a preface thereto, wrote to JB, 'I am so much looking forward to editing your poems but have not so far heard from Murrays.' He later wrote (1 June 1958), 'I can't read one word of your bloody artistic writing and therefore cannot riposte. Please send me the poem about being sacked. I am having a hideous time trying to cooperate with Randolph (Churchill) on the Amalgamated Press. It is turning my few remaining locks grey.'[34] JB's *Collected Poems* came out in December 1958 and was a smash hit. The British press went wild and the news travelled across the Atlantic. The *Chicago Sunday Tribune* read, 'No book will offer more rewarding wit and sentiment.'

A piece appeared in the *New York Times* about the furore JB's *Collected Poems* had caused in London. The jubilant publisher Jock Murray was quoted as saying, 'Reviews have been magnificent, JB has been given the Duff Cooper Award which was presented by Princess Margaret. Sales are now stabilising at just below a thousand a day. It is now third on the best-seller list in London. What ho! I never remember such a dance since we published Byron's *Childe Harold* in 1812.'[35]

 1. *Spectator* (31 August 1956).
 2. Society for the Preservation of Ancient Buildings archives.
 3. Edward Gilbert's papers, Bodleian Library, Oxford.
 4. Carbon copy, JB's papers, University of Victoria, British Columbia.
 5. James Lees-Milne, CLG interview (1994).
 6. JB's papers, University of Victoria.
 7. Kenneth Clark's papers, Tate Gallery, London.
 8. JB's papers, University of Victoria.
 9. Carbon copy, JB's papers, University of Victoria.
10. JB's papers, University of Victoria.
11. Diana Peel's papers.
12. JB's papers, University of Victoria.
13. Edward Hornby's papers.
14. Hester Knight, letter to CLG (May 1984).
15. Mollie Baring, CLG interview (1994).
16. 'Poet on Stopover', *New Yorker* (March 1957).
17. CLG's papers, British Library.
18. CLG's papers, British Library.
19. Sylvia Combe's papers.
20. CLG's papers, British Library.
21. CLG's papers, British Library.
22. 'Village Wedding', *New Yorker* (11 July 1959).
23. Deborah Devonshire, letter to CLG (1994).
24. Sister Mary Bland, CLG interview (1994).
25. Mrs Dunn, letter to CLG (1994).
26. From 'Inevitable', *Collected Poems* (John Murray, 1958).
27. JB's papers, University of Victoria.
28. Victoria Oaksey, CLG interview (1994).
29. CLG's papers, British Library.
30. James Lees-Milne's papers, Beinecke Library, Yale University.
31. Collins's archives, Glasgow.
32. PB's papers, Beinecke Library.

33. John Murray's papers, Murray archives.
34. JB's papers, University of Victoria.
35. John Murray's papers, Murray archives.

To H. C. Dear   43 Cloth Fair
19 September 1956   London EC1

Dear Sir,
I write a column in the *Spectator* every week called 'City and Suburban',
and would like to be able to say something to allay people's fears about
new Woolworth's buildings appearing in old towns. For instance, the
proposed new Woolworth's shops in Guildford, on the site of the Lyon
Hotel in Buckingham, a listed eighteenth-century building, and in
Wantage on a site of an old shop in the Market Square. I understand
that your firm no longer now insists on a large acreage of plate glass, and
then a brick façade above, but that you pursue the enlightened policy of
adapting your shops to the scale and texture of the towns where they are
to be built.
     If I could have some sort of official confirmation of this, I would be
very glad to publish it when I write my column next Monday.
     Yours sincerely, John Betjeman

> H.C.D., a director of F. W. Woolworth's, replied (24 September 1956), 'As you know,
> our plans have to be passed by the local planning authorities and it is always our
> endeavour to erect buildings that are a credit to the town in which they are situated.'

To George Barnes   43 Cloth Fair
25 September 1956   London EC1

My dear Commander,
Anne has written proposing November 3rd for a visit to Staffordshire.
That would suit me very well, though I have to be at Marlborough on
Friday, so couldn't get up until the actual Saturday. It is very kind of
you to write. Dear, feeble Elizabeth and I did eighteen holes on a
Municipal Putting course in Fulham Palace Gardens before she went
away with her Little Friend. Perhaps I had better say your Little
Friend. Since then, no news, but photographs of her very dimly in the
background, a recognisable elbow or leg here and there, thinner and
taller than anybody else, and far, far weaker.

As to books on Staffordshire, I have always found the best general books are those *Cambridge Geography* series of the counties which are remaindered now, but could obviously be got somewhere with your influence in the Cambridge Press. And after that, *Kelly's Directory*. My friend, D. B. Peace, 23 Newport Road, Stafford, did a map of Staff[ord]s[hire] I believe showing the buildings of interest. The kind of Norman Shaw architecture which Anne mentions is very often by a most talented Stoke-on-Trent architect called Charles Lynam, who was the father of Skipper and Hum, and a local antiquarian. Then, if you have never read it, you must read this which I enclose, which describes Leek in Staffs, quite one of the best towns anywhere, and the Norman Shaw church with [William Richard] Lethaby fittings and Hamilton Jackson's paintings is finer than its counterpart in Ilkley. As for a secondhand *Kelly*, I haven't got one of Staffs, but can always get them, Foyle's or Heffer's, or even buy one off an hotel who are generally only too pleased to sell the old directory when they have got a new one. D. B. Peace has done a very good list of Staffordshire churches for my book. But as the copy is about to go to Burberry and I have not got a spare one, I cannot let you have it yet.

I very much admire your writing paper. Love to Anne. Love, JB

EC was lady-in-waiting to Princess Margaret. Because EC was tall, JB often referred to Princess Margaret as 'Little Friend' or 'LF'. G.B. thought Princess Margaret beautiful, clever and funny and had taken a great shine to her.

Charles Cotterill 'Skipper' Lynam and A. E. 'Hum' Lynam (see *Volume One*) were respectively headmaster and senior master at the Dragon School, Oxford. Their father Charles Lynam was a Norman Shaw fan, ahead of his time, who had designed the Dragon school buildings.

W. R. Lethaby was Norman Shaw's trusted assistant.

To Alan Pryce-Jones   43 Cloth Fair
9 October 1956   London EC1

Dearest Bog,

The most beautiful rococo Gothic church in England is Shobdon, Herefordshire, which was erected about 1780 by a Lord Bateman. You may have seen it. It is the frontispiece to Marcus Whiffin's book which I reviewed so unfavourably in your little paper. It has suddenly been found that it has death-watch beetle, and nine thousand pounds is needed to restore it. There is no village and this building must be saved.

The only relict of the Batemans is Lady Bateman, Hotel de Paris, Monte Carlo, who is, according to Anne Fleming, colossally rich. Anne thinks she would be open to an approach from someone of rank and intellect, and I am enclosing Anne's postcard to me. Do you think we could have a talk about this before approaching her through the lady mentioned?

Love and kisses, JB

A.P.-J. was editing the *Times Literary Supplement* at the time.

Shobdon originally had a twelfth-century church which was pulled down by Lord Bateman. Parts of it were re-erected on a hill beside the site which still anguishes antiquarians. The church built in its stead is 'a confection of Strawberry Hill Gothic' – painted grey and white inside. There are red velvet pads on the pews.

Anne Fleming (née Charteris) had married Ian Fleming, the author of the James Bond books, in 1952. JB was a close friend of hers, through her brother Hugo Charteris, novelist and playwright.

To William Plomer

Wantage and
43 Cloth Fair
London EC1
Mon[day] to Thurs[day]
Kindly note for your next visit

9 November 1956

to London from Rossida's.

My dear William,
What a heavenly present from Rossida's. That Sussex coast is gloriously suggested and the Foats are exactly like my friends the Penning-Rowsells (C[ommunist] P[arty] members) whose three un-christened children long for religion. Mrs P[enning]-R[owsell] is a sister of the late Tom Wintringham and has strong choirboy appeal for me, and they both are wrong-headed, kindness itself, and observe New Year instead of Christmas. What is so very nice about your story is that the Foats come out of it as 'prigs of a feather' and as you say, much more like Christians of the 'are you saved?' type, than they suspected. And they are not at all like Dick Double Crossman or Wykehamists generally, are they? I think it would be very nice if you wrote some more stories about people in definite categories. Those racing people with the thatched roof and the sun-loggia, for instance, or people who are immensely rich and live on the Wentworth Estate like my cousins the d'Ambrumenils (Rugbeians) – oh it is this glorious categorising which is the oil of fiction's wheels. I should think the church she and

Andrew went to was Sarum Use high, they mostly are in Chichester diocese, and take their cue from the late Duncan Jones 'Family Communion nine a.m.' or 'Sung Eucharist eleven a.m.' 'Take a cup o' tay and a rale Cornish pasty up to Rossida's' (Eden Philpotts).
    Love, John B

> W.P. (see *Volume One*) the poet, had met JB in the thirties through their mutual friend Gerald Berners and through the Society of Authors. W. P. (a Rugbeian) lived at a house called Rossida near Rustington, Sussex. He had sent JB a present of *Winter's Tales*, an anthology of short stories. W. P.'s story, 'A Friend of her Father's', which included the Foats, particularly appealed to JB. It was an amusing piece of Christian propaganda.
>   Margaret Penning-Rowsell, whom JB always referred to by her maiden name of Wintringham (see *Volume One*), had been his *grande amour* in the late forties.
>   Richard Crossman (1907–74), the Labour politician, was at Oxford with JB where he got a double first.
>   JB usually referred to the d'Ambrumenils as the 'Damp Umbrellas'.

To H. S. Goodhart-Rendel   43 Cloth Fair
11 December 1956   London EC1

Dear Goodhart-Rendel,
Oh, how I enjoyed myself. Coming back on the train I changed at Wimbledon so as to be able to alight at Holborn Viaduct. On the journey these lines occurred to me:

> Above the roof tops, the world, and sin,
> What curious *flèches* by Fellowes Prynne
> In the meaner districts – less class, more guts –
> What stalwart lancets by Messrs Cutts
> Half timbered houses in Grange and Park
> Ring seaside Perp-style by Somers Clarke
> Down the blazing high road the traffic pours
> Past W. Habershon's fast-locked doors
> A Protestant answer with prim Dec looks
> To a soaring, mission church by Mr Brooks
> And the parish church, once old, now not
> Is Arthur Blomfield being middle Scott.

I enjoy the private language of nineteenth-century church architects more than any language in the world – Gaelic, French, German, Greek or Latin. You *were* kind to me.
    Yours ever, John Betjeman

H.S.G.-R. (see *Volume One*), the musician and architect, was both a mentor to and cherished friend of JB's.

All Saints, Rosendale Road by G. H. Fellowes Prynne (1855–1927) is prominent on the railway from West Dulwich to Herne Hill.

J. E. K. Cutts (1847–1938) and his brother J. P. C. Cutts (1854–1935) did dreary, pedestrian churches, all more or less alike.

Somers Clarke (1841–1926), with his occasional partner J. T. Micklethwaite, did refined, spacious Late Victorian Anglo-Catholic churches, rather like Bodley's.

William Habershon (1818–91) did boring Low Church Gothic churches.

The Ascension by James Brooks (1825–1901) at Lavender Hill soars above the houses by the railway near Clapham Junction.

Sir Arthur Blomfield (1829–99) got on because his father was Bishop Blomfield of London.

Middle Scott is mad George Gilbert Scott junior (1839–97), Goodhart-Rendel's hero, and JB's.

To G. B. Stern 43 Cloth Fair
December 1956 London EC1

 Caprice

I sat only two tables off from the one I was sacked at
  Just three years ago
And here was another meringue, like the one which I hacked at
  When pride was brought low
And the coffee arrived, the place which she had to use tact at
  For striking the blow.

'I am making some changes next week in our organisation,
  And, though I admire
Your work for me John, yet the need to increase circulation
  Means you must retire
An outlook more *global* than yours is the qualification
  I really require.'

Oh sickness of sudden betrayal! Oh purblind Creator!
  Oh friendship denied!
I stood on the pavement and wondered which loss was the greater,
  The cash or the pride?
Explanations to make to subordinates, bills to pay later
  Churned up my inside.

I fell on my feet. But what of those others, worse treated,
  Your memory's ghosts,

In gloomy bed-sitters in Fulham, ill fed and unheated,
    Applying for posts?
Do they haunt their successors and you, as you sit there repleted
    With entrées and roasts?

Lady Rhondda sitting next to the writer, JB, who copied
this out for Peter Stern (1956).

This poem describes JB being sacked by Lady Rhondda from his post as literary editor of
Time and Tide in 1953, over lunch at the Caprice restaurant.

To Penelope Betjeman   Edensor House
                                                 Bakewell
1957   Derbyshire

My darling Plymmie,
I am very well. I hope you are. I am getting a lot of work done and even
writing poetry. The North Country suits me as it is so nonconformist.
You expect to meet Moses on 'the Heights of Abraham' above the thin
dissenting steeples of Matlock Bath and everyone is honest and rude
and has high tea and keeps himself to himself. It is a completely foreign
county, oop in Derbyshire. It is quite as foreign as Italy and much
odder. I am coming back to London on Monday. I have two articles to
write for the *D[aily] T[elegraph]* before then and so I am rather pressed. I
am so grateful to you for sending my letters. You are a dear little thing
and I do *love* you Plymmi. I think of you buzzing about in the Caff and
all those kiddiz trailing after you to the stables. How is Marco?
    Yorz trewely, Tewpie

        JB was staying with EC's brother and sister-in-law, Andrew and Deborah Devonshire,
    who did not move to Chatsworth until 1959.
        Marco Polo was my Pekingese dog.

To Mr Neobard   43 Cloth Fair
1 January 1957   London EC1

Dear Mr Neobard,
I am very concerned about the Maidenhead Chestnuts. I saw them in
the autumn. Have they gone? A man called Kennedy first drew my
attention to them and told me later that the C[ouncil for the]
P[reservation of] R[ural] E[ngland] local member, whom I told him by
letter to consult, had said I was 'just a journalist looking for copy'. Who
can he be? I ask you, because he must be at your end of the county. If
you can give me his name, I shall be grateful, for I don't intend to let
this matter drop. It is very important that there should be 'solidarity' in
the CPRE and people should not make remarks like that to outsiders
about fellow members. Unless I get an apology in writing, I shall resign
from the CPRE and if my solicitors think there is a case for libel, I shall
take an action. I think I could produce some formidable witnesses to my
integrity. Do let me know who the villain was, if you can.
    Yours sincerely, John Betjeman

Mr Neobard worked for the Council for the Preservation of Rural England.

To Penelope Betjeman   43 Cloth Fair
9 January 1957   London EC1

Darling Plymmi,
I have been thinking that probably why I love you more than anyone
else in the world is because we are married in eternity and really cash,
sex, kiddiz, good and bad fortune, fame and failure are all of less
importance and just worldly irritants. Nooni nooni. Have got two tiny
rooms for Wibz and me at top of Metropolis [Hotel]. If you'd like to
come too let me know. Will meet Wibz off that train ex Oxford (12.27
p.m.) at Brighton 3.25 on Friday.
    Powlie wrote in such a flap because he had lost his cheque book and
wanted me to get one for him and some cash from his account at Brown
Shipley.
    Much love from yorz trewely, Tewpie

Before talking to the Brighton Regency Society, JB took me on a tour of the town. We went to the Pavilion and to his favourite church of St Bartholomew where Max Miller, his music-hall hero, sometimes attended Sunday services. We also visited Gilbert Harding.

To Lionel Brett   The Mead
                                                                     Wantage
25 January 1957   Berkshire

Dear Lionel,
I must seek your help, advice and, if possible, support over this Civic Trust to which I have committed myself in a part-time capacity. I was so excited to think that here was some cash at last for helping the work of amenity societies that I leaped at it. Then when I began to turn the idea over in my mind I realised a broader and less tangible approach than just doling out cash to amenity societies was needed. I mean if you gave cash to the Blackheath Society and not to the London Society the latter would be jealous. So I decided, in consultation with Mr Piper, that what was needed was to make people use their eyes and not just think all new things were ugly and all old ones lovely and all suburbs hideous, but make them see the good from the shoddy whatever its date, the pretentious from the genuine, the accidentally attractive e.g. some allotments and some railway stations and signals from the frankly awful – e.g. artistic advertisement stations. And then I thought how? I think that the best approach is to foster local pride and work locally. For instance one might take Abingdon. One's friends there would be 'The Friends of Abingdon' which exists. One would see the local Education Officer and give prizes for drawings and photographs often taken by schoolchildren. One would arrange an exhibition of these concurrently with an exhibition (with prizes and an outside judge) for drawings of Abingdon by local artists and architects amateur and professional and photographs by the local photographic society. The Mayor would open it. Abingdon is a good start as it has, as well as the ancient, a really decent modern estate for the Atomics. One might also have an illustrated section of eyesores. One might have a lecture by John Summerson or you or Sir Albert [Richardson] (to choose from a rich variety of personalities) on the town. Thus people would begin to look at their streets and houses. This has been done before by some local societies and must have been done by the R[oyal] I[nstitute of] B[ritish] A[rchitects] and Amenity societies. But with the Civic Trust financing and paying lecturers and organisers a decent fee for the use of their

time, we really might do things to save us from future despoliation. I'm
sure that public opinion is easier to educate (for it has a lot of snobbery
in it which can be exploited for 'Georgian' and soon for 'Victorian')
than cocksure Borough Engineers. And thus I would like, after trying a
start with Abingdon which is near enough for me to know who is who
in the town, to move on to neglected towns which are unaware of their
beauties – e.g. Maidstone, Colchester, and, for all I know, Burslem and
Hanley and Dewsbury and Port Sunlight and Birkenhead. Such work
would have to be done through the RIBA and the amenity societies.
Your father is now, I believe, away in the USA or somewhere so I can't
consult him yet. But what do you think of it from the RIBA's point of
view? This is all a letter of thanks to you as I believe you got Mr P[iper]
and me made Hon[orary] Associates.

Yours, John B

> L.B., who later became Lord Esher, was a contemporary of JB's and John Piper's who
> lived near the latter at Watlington in Oxfordshire and was a consultant architect on many
> large town schemes including Abingdon.
> The Civic Trust was a privately funded trust started by Duncan Sandys, a former
> Minister of Housing and Local Government, to foster an interest in good architecture
> and town planning, particularly by encouraging the growth of independent local
> amenity societies and providing expert advice for them. Its first director was Colonel
> Kenneth Post and its first secretary was Michael Middleton.

To Mollie Baring   43 Cloth Fair
25 February 1957   London EC1

Dearest Mollie,
Wot a jolli tame Ay had at your spiffing grate countree house. Ay *deed*
enjoy mayself and ay layked yor hubbie mowst orfly. Ay am just off to
the Stites on location at Cincinnati with Mr Betjeman's wafe. So long
and ta ever so for the jolli tame.

Love from Diana Dors
PS Love to yor little dorter Arne.

> M.B. (née Warner), married to Desmond, was a neighbour and close friend of the
> family. The Barings lived at Ardington House near Wantage, where I had been lodged
> during the move from Farnborough. Their daughter Anne (whom JB always called
> 'Arne', mimicking my pronunciation and also because he had always had a soft spot for
> Dr Arne who wrote 'Rule Britannia') was my best friend, and their sons Peter and Nigel
> friends of PSGB's.

To Candida Betjeman   Vernon Manor Hotel
                                               400 Oak Street
                                               Cincinnati 19
12 March 1957   Ohio

Darling Wibz,
Mummy has bought you a very pretty pink dress here and the other day
I saw in a delicatessen store the following things for sale – broiled
octopus, English liquorice allsorts, rattlesnake meat, fried Japanese
grasshoppers, fried Mexican worms. I get very tired here, nobody stops
talking, the wireless is on everywhere even in the hotel elevators, and
sometimes two different programmes in the same room. I can make
little contact with the students I have to teach as I have so little in
common with them. We are foreigners here. The English are either
much liked or not liked at all. The city is a collection of different
frictions – Jewish v[ersus] Christian, Negro v[ersus] White, R[oman]
C[atholic] v[ersus] Protestant, North v[ersus] South (for Cincinnati is
on the Mason-Dixon line which divides the old southern states who
practised slavery from the ascetic, hard-working, rather egalitarian and
self-righteous North). And oh my goodness it *is* ugly though the Arts
Museum is good. The nearest main road to this hotel is appropriately
called 'Reading Road'. Most roads and towns look like the approach to
Didcot from Wallingford and big towns are like the Great West Road.
The suburbs in Treeclad Hill alone are pretty.

I long to see you and Wantage again – my goodness, I do. Don't
forget Mummy and me. We think of you a lot and envy you *even* at
school. It could not be worse than here.

Tons and tons of love from MD.

JB and PB had gone to live in Cincinnati, USA, for a month. JB gave a series of lectures
at the university under the auspices of the George Elliston Poetry Foundation.

To Anita Dent

Department of English
McMiken College
University of Cinci
Cincinnati 21

12 March 1957
(nineteen more days)

My dear Anita,
This place is HELL, an unrelieved hell, worse than P[enelope] and I thought it was going to be. The kindness and goodness of everyone somehow is no compensation for the ugliness, the central heating, the bright and gaudy cars and hotel bars, the canned music etc. The students are like high school children and they think they are very modern. They are. I have nothing in common with them and could never make contact. My first public lecture went down all right because I have an English accent which amuses them. This place is far more foreign even than France and I feel tired all the time. I long for the noise below you in Cloth Fair.

Please look out for obituaries in *The Times* and tell me if anyone I know like Comper dies – architects, writers, artists and clergymen. Have little time here as I can never get away from the continuous programme of entertainment. Oh God! Oh Cincinnati!

How are your marital affairs? I think of you and them and hope all goes well with you. I believe you will find a solution.

I write to Feebleness [EC] every day and she writes very sweet letters to me. She says she is seeing you. Give her my deep love. Goodness I do *long* to be back. The *New Yorker* offered P[enelope] and me a free fortnight more at the end of our stay, in NY, but I refused. Not a day longer than I need will I stay here. NY is not US. This Middle West is.
    Love, John B

> During JB's time in Cincinnati the *New Yorker* published a piece on him in its 'Talk of the Town' column.
> A.D. had always told JB about her love affairs. She married later that year and JB proposed the toast at her wedding.

To David Johnson   43 Cloth Fair
17 April 1957   London EC1

Dear David,
I hope to be able to come to see you tomorrow (Thursday) afternoon.

That knight has moved along to yet another bottle of sherry. You can
see some more on the right waiting for their corks to be drawn. Those
on the left are empty. A man with a pork pie hat on has been sketching
the next house to me here (it is the only pre-fire house left in the City)
for two days. You or I could have sketched it [in] less than two hours. I
wonder why he takes so long.

   I will telephone to your mother tomorrow, about the time of my
arrival. I hope Richard's measles are better. This repulsive biro pen
gives my hands the measles. I must go and wash them.

   Love from John Betjeman

> D.J., who was twelve years old, was one of the patients in the Percival Pott Ward at St
> Bartholomew's Hospital where JB used to visit, every Thursday, for over a dozen years.
> D.J. was undergoing treatment for bone cancer. He died in July 1957. JB continued to
> visit and write to D.J.'s family for many years afterwards.

To David Johnson   43 Cloth Fair
25 April 1957   London EC1

My dear David,
As I cannot come to see you all at the Vale this week, I am writing a
letter to you instead and please will you thank Richard for his letter
telling me of the trick you played on him. I am very amused by it. I am
writing this coming down in the train from Doncaster. There are not
enough seats on it and I am very uncomfortable squashed between
businessmen with pipes who are travelling at their firm's expense.

   This reads the same backwards and it is the longest sentence of its
kind to do so which I know of – LIVE DIRT UP A SIDETRACK CARTED IS A

PUTRID EVIL. The Secretary of the Royal Fine Art Commission who is travelling with me and to whom I showed this sentence said did I know what Napoleon said when he was defeated? I expect you do. It was ABLE WAS I ERE I SAW ELBA. The skill of that one is that the words themselves fit. He also asked me what was the first remark made by a man to a woman. And when I said I didn't know, he told me it was MADAM I'M ADAM.

And now I must stop writing all this rubbish because it is wasting your time and you may be finishing that poem or writing another or painting a picture. Give my love to Richard and your father and mother and the tropical fish and the museum in your bedroom. I hope that tortoise does not make a noise at night singing or crawling about.

Love from John Betjeman

The Johnsons lived in the Vale, North London.

To John Aldridge   43 Cloth Fair
14 May 1957   London EC1

My dear boy,
What a treat to hear from you. I met your sister the other day and she was very nice. When I think of you I think of poor old Norman Cameron now dead, Gabriel Toyne disappeared, Gilbert Armitage and Eric Shroeder and all the time I have seen your pictures growing in beauty on the walls of exhibitions and on the walls of people's houses. I will go and look at Floral Hall* at once and see what is wrong and where I can do anything. *I have no influence.*

I think that Raymond Erith is the best architect now living and his drawings alone are well worth going to see. I am very interested that you know him. I have never met anyone who knew him and have only admired him from his drawings in the Academy. I have always recommended him and told people to go to him.

Yours ever old top, and forgive typewriting – I am in bed with a cold.

(Signed) Iain MacBetjeman

*Covent Garden; they are busy pulling it down. John [Piper] and I saw it when driving round there a week ago.

> J.A. (1906–83) was a painter and illustrator. He had been a member of the Seven and Five Society in the early thirties which included Ivor Hitchens, David Jones, Ben Nicholson and John Piper. JB, an exact contemporary, had known him from Oxford days. He lived in Essex near the architect, Raymond Erith (1904–73). Erith, who built in a restrained Palladian manner using perfect proportions, was not a copyist: he created his own inimitable style. His most famous buildings include the Library and Wolfson buildings at Lady Margaret Hall, Oxford.
>
> Norman Cameron, the poet, Gilbert Armitage and Eric Shroeder were all at Oxford. Gabriel Toyne, a great friend of J.A.'s, was a handsome Oxford contemporary and an amateur poet who married the actress Margaret Rawlings in 1927. The marriage did not last long. M. Rawlings remembers, 'He went off to some island where he died.' This was Majorca where he became a member of the Robert Graves circle.
>
> The Floral Hall in Covent Garden had recently been damaged by fire.

To Candida Betjeman   On the Great Western
24 May 1957   Plymouth to Paddington

Darling Wibz,

The train is going very fast [so] I am trying to write as clearly as I can. I stayed in M[oun]t Edgcumbe last night, a leafy peninsula in Plymouth Sound. Lord M[oun]t Edgcumbe's house was burned down in the war and he and his old wife live in the stables with their grandchildren. The old people are very good and saintly and nice and funny. Lord Mt Edgcumbe was an Electrical Engineer. I think it surprised him to come into this estate. He is a first cousin of Mrs Bassett and v[ery] fond of her and Joy Bassett. You go to the house and huge park dotted with temples, grottos and ilex trees and palms, by a steam ferry. There is much fine Georgian in Plymouth well worth seeing.

I look forward to seeing you tomorrow (Saturday). I go to London for telly on Sunday. No peace when the Devil drives. I sometimes think I am sold to the Devil. I hope you never are. It is most uncomfortable. No peace is left and you feel you are wasting the joy of being alive.

Tons of love from MD.

> JB had just spoken to the Old Plymouth Society as part of a campaign to save the Barbican, an area of Plymouth on the quayside.

To Anne Rosse 43 Cloth Fair
30 July 1957 London EC1

Dear Anne,

Yes – October 28th to November 2nd will be all right for me, except that I have to speak at the Chenil Galleries on the 29th, on behalf of Holy Trinity Sloane Street at, I suppose, about 6.30. Then, on the 30th October I have to address the National Association of Almshouses at three p.m. Otherwise I am free, except on Saturday night. When would you like me to come and at what time? I should suggest really that we ought to meet for drinks and without the accompaniment of food, which stops thought. What do you think?

The key man to all this, you know, is Goodhart-Rendel. One of the greatest men on earth, and with Michael conducting a meeting we really shall get something done. I will do all the work I can whatever you may say about my being busy and important – I am the former but not the latter – but the saving of Victorian Architecture is most important. We have got to be discriminating in what we decide to say and we must use flattery, and so I entirely agree with your letter.

Love, Iain MacBetjeman

A. R. (née Messel), previously married to Ronald Armstrong-Jones, was now married to JB's great friend Michael Rosse. Her grandparents, Marion and Linley Sambourne, had bought, decorated and furnished 18 Stafford Terrace in London in 1874 and brought up A.R.'s mother Maud (afterwards Messell) and Uncle Roy, to whom it was left on their death. Being a bachelor, he did not change a thing in the house and by the time that it came into A.R.'s care (she did not inherit it until 1960) it was still exactly as it always had been. She and Michael R. used it as a London pied-à-terre and often entertained JB there who loved it. Despite many of her friends deeming this Victorian time-piece hideous and depressing, A.R. understood its value and determined to safeguard it. Michael and JB had been founders of the Georgian Group in the thirties, so why not a Victorian Society?

JB had written (17 July 1957), 'The sort of people we need are John Brandon-Jones, President of the Architectural Association, H. S. Goodhart-Rendel, John Summerson, John Piper, D. B. Peace, County Planning Officer for Staffordshire, Professor-Doctor Pevsner, J. M. Richards, R. Furneaux Jordan, the Rev[erend] B. F. L. Clarke, Christopher Hussey, Hugh Casson, Peter Clarke (Secretary of *The Times*), Tom Greeves, Sir Thomas Kendrick, Director of the British Museum, K. Clark, Lord Crawford, Lord Mottistone, P. Morton Shand, Ian McCallum of the *Architectural Review*. I am sure this list is all too short but it is a beginning. There is one further point. I think the group should include Edwardian architecture, some of which is very fine like the RAC, the Ritz and the work of Lutyens. I dare say it will be best to launch the Group in September or October. I am sure Lord Rosse ought to be the chairman, he is the best chairman I have ever known.' A drinks party was held at Stafford Terrace on 5 November (Michael R.'s cocktails were famous and were *always* followed by champagne).

On 28 February 1958, the Victorian Society was founded. Lord Esher was the first chairman and JB and A.R. its two vice-chairmen. The first committee consisted of Hugh Casson, Gay Christiansen, Peter Clarke, Peter Ferriday, Peter Floud, William Gaunt, Mark Girouard, H. S. Goodhart-Rendel, Ian Grant, Rupert Gunnis, John Brandon-Jones, Christopher Hussey, Ivor Idris, Canon C. B. Mortlock, Nikolaus Pevsner, Jim Richards and Carew Wallace. They started under the wing of the Society for the Protection of Ancient Buildings in their premises in Great Ormond Street and are now in Bedford Park. Their stated aim read, 'The Victorian Society has been formed to make sure that the best Victorian buildings and their contents do not disappear before their merits are more generally appreciated.'

To John Foster-White   43 Cloth Fair
7 August 1957   London EC1

Dear Cork and Orrery,
Indeed, you could not have come to a better man for advice about Cornwall. Bodmin is not a good town despite its railway station, for it is thundered through by lorries and is little more than one street.

Truro is rather worth staying in because of the cathedral and a good deal of Georgian, but it is not much of a centre – at least, it is not for me because my heart is not in those warm tree-shaded creeks of South Cornwall, but among the cliffs and slate and moors of the north coast.

I think I would advise Padstow as a good place to stay. It is a beautiful railway journey from Wadebridge and there is the ferry across to Rock and my own Trebetherick. Avoid Newquay, and walk along the cliffs from Padstow to Stepper Point and look down the chasm of Butter Hole, and fear will set your knees a-trembling. Padstow is not exactly on the sea, and it is on the Southern Railway. The most unimportant town in Cornwall, where nobody ever stays, and which has a certain charm, is Callington and the most beautiful is Launceston. The decayed port of Calstock near Callington is well worth seeing, and by far the most beautiful church in Cornwall is Blisland, off Bodmin Moor. You must see that.

Yours, Ian Trebetjeman
Congratulations on being a Director of the Mystery firm. You deserve to be.

    JB had met the publisher J.F.-W. (see *Volume One*) many years before. He often called
    him by the names of Irish peers, for no apparent reason.

To John Lloyd   43 Cloth Fair
27 August 1957   London EC1

Dear Widow,
It is a rockingly funny poem, and it will be very nice to see you at
Wantage. I have had an extremely amusing letter from Crax ['Cracky'
William Wicklow] about the Colonel. He says he has been to see him,
and that he found he 'now has a new worry – not that he does not sleep,
but that he sleeps all through the night and sleeps on in the morning!
Many people would be only too glad to do this, but he doesn't think it is
healthy. He is also afflicted by the death of the late Mr Donner. As he
had not seen the latter for some years, and he was ninety-one years old,
it can scarcely be looked upon as a tragedy or a shock.'
    Penelope is going to Italy until 26th September, I think it is – alone
on a tour of pictures and churches. She is very extraordinary. If you
come, therefore, come for the last weekend in September. Forgive the
phrase 'weekend'.
    What extraordinary writing you have.
    Yours, JB

> JB had met J.L. at one of Colonel Kolkhorst's Sunday morning parties in Oxford in the
> late twenties. JB had nicknamed him after a shaving soap called 'the Widow Lloyd's'.
> J.L. had written 'An alternative song for the Pirates of Penzance' in eighteen rhyming
> couplets which began:
>
> > I am the very model of a perfect Betjemanian,
> > I know all the London Churches, from RC to Sandemanian,
> > I know that Neo-Gothick is the only truly cultural
> > And my appetite for Butterfield is positively vultural.
> > I've a suitable derision for folk-weave and for pottery
> > And a corresponding passion both for Streetery and Scottery.
>
> Mr Donner was the Finnish Ambassador at St James's and the father of Patrick
> Donner, a friend of the Colonel's.
>   The term 'weekend' was deemed non-U.

To Penelope Betjeman   White Horses
                                                                 Trebetherick
13 September 1957   Cornwall

Darling Plymmi,
I was very happy to have such a lovely letter and such pretty cards from
you today and so was Wibz who has written to you also. A strong wind

and bright sun for several days has meant the sea here is at its most glorious, huge fields of yeasty soup and waves like mountains and terrific surfing. Yesterday we all walked to the Rumps and there were six seals looking like Archie (who is v[ery] happy here in the home of Methodism) playing about in the boiling sea. Lynam [Thomas] and Peggy Thomas are most saintly people, ideal hosts. We all wash up and make our beds, but here where one is grateful to God all day for the beauty of nature and where one is less plagued by telephones and letters, such chores are possible – especially when there are ten people to help as there are here.

I asked the Head [Lynam Thomas] (who has just left for a conference at Oxford) about the mud gorge. He says they are carved by wash from the mountains.

I am v[ery] excited about your snaps. I should not worry too much about writing anything at present. Your snaps will recall all things for you, if you want to write. I am so glad that you are happy with your own company and not too disappointed about Sylvia's not coming. I have done three fresh watercolours.

By great luck I've had a book for review by Arthur Calder-Marshall, an old Communist chum of mine, who writes scripts for films. He was asked to write a film story about an Admiral Woods who after winning the DSO at Jutland became a C[hurch] of E[ngland] priest at a Seamen's mission in Whitechapel. Having received, according to a newspaper cutting Arthur was given, 'no earthly command' at the Battle of Jutland. When he investigated the story, he found that the Admiral was a very humble, ordinary man with an unswerving faith who did not really mind whether people went to church or not, he just loved everybody – like you do and I don't. He found the story about 'no earthly command' was distorted into untruth by the newspaper report, but that F[athe]r Woods was a saint. And by the time he had finished the book, Arthur C[alder]-M[arshall] found that he was, against his will, a Christian. It really is a marvellous book, very well written and absolutely thrilling to read.

This has been the happiest holiday I have ever spent here. Everyone goes to H[oly] C[ommunion] and that makes a difference and Wibz is catered for by little people on the cliffs.

Tonight I am going to the house of a clergyman who lives near, whose son went by motor car from Winchester to Delhi through Persia and Afghanistan. He has photographs in colour such as you have. I'm told they are very good. They would certainly be better than those of Bill and Gladys. I bet yours will be lovely.

Edward Hornby comes today. We leave on Sunday – only one more day, oh dear.

I hope you have a happy time in Florence. It will probably be a summary in painting of all you have seen.

I will be at 43 C[loth] F[air] from Mon[day] to Fri[day] next week or at any rate till Thursday. Will I see you on your way through London? Let me know or else we will meet on Fri[day] at Wantage.

Tons of love. Take care of the Broadwoods.

Very truly yours, Tewpie

> While PB was in Italy, JB and I stayed with Lynam Thomas, the headmaster of Repton, and his wife Peggy who owned a house on the cliff at Trebetherick facing the Atlantic called 'White Horses'.
>
> Arthur Calder-Marshall had worked in the films division of the Ministry of Information with JB during the war. His biography *No Earthly Command* had just come out.
>
> Edward Hornby stayed at White Horses every year. His brother Anthony was JB's stockbroker, his eldest brother Michael JB's neighbour in Berkshire.
>
> JB referred to PB's legs as 'the Broadwoods'.

To Malcolm Muggeridge   43 Cloth Fair
25 September 1957   London EC1

Dear Malcolm,

I should have written ages ago to you to thank you for being so kind an editor to so sparse a contributor as I am. I also wanted to write to say how sorry I am you've given up being editor – not that I blame you. But without you how will [Chris]topher [Hollis] and Tony [Powell] and I be able to get along? You were a marvellous editor – not just in introducing new talent such as me (your greatest failure) but in keeping

us together, giving us life and JOKES. Oh dear, back to old A. P. H[erbert] and the cricketers down the other end. Oh hell. But God bless you, dear Malcolm, for being such a true friend to
    Yours, John B

> M.M. (1903–90), the journalist, had been the deputy editor of the *Daily Telegraph* before becoming editor of *Punch* (1953–7) which he was now leaving. JB and he had met when they had both worked on the *Evening Standard* in the early thirties.
>   When M.M. left the *Daily Telegraph* JB, who was at the time reviewing novels for them, wrote (8 December 1952), 'I don't feel like writing articles without your encouragement.'
>   JB wrote articles and short stories for *Punch* throughout M.M.'s editorship.

To Sidney Bernstein   43 Cloth Fair
3 October 1957   London EC1

Dear Sidney,
You could not have given me a nicer present. Only last night I went for the second time this week to the Met[ropolitan] to see Randolph Sutton and Hetty King and Billy Danvers, who have long been heroes of mine and who, I think, have genius. It was interesting to see old G. H. Elliott too. I wrote a paragraph about them for Peterborough in the *Daily Telegraph*.

Last night I bought six stalls; in future I shall be able to go free to what has always been my spiritual home when not in church – namely, Music-hall.

Would you have the courage to employ Michael Tree, Mereworth Castle, Kent? He is very rich but I think he is a wonderful artist, and Lucian Freud said he was the most exceptional student of his year at the Slade. He has been to the Met[ropolitan] with me in the past.

I think the old place ought to be done in oil. I like your redecoration for it looks as though it had always looked like that, which is the real test.
    Yours, John B

> S.B., the chairman of Granada Television, had sent JB a free pass to the Metropolitan Theatre, Edgware Road. He had written (30 September 1957) telling JB that the Empress Brixton, the Chelsea Palace and the Metropolitan were now under Granada management. He was anxious to get the newly restored Metropolitan sketched and painted. 'Who is the modern Sickert?' he asked JB.

To Deborah Devonshire   The Mead
                                                          Wantage
11 October 1957   Berkshire

Dear Debo,
I wish I could have come. I would love to have done for two reasons:
    (1) seeing you and Andrew and, possibly, Emma
    (2) helping the Rev[erend] the Vicar who seems to me a thundering
good preacher and shy and good.
But alas, on the two dates proposed I am bespoke – on the first in
Northants to address the CPRE there and on the second to open a sale
of work at my own parish church in the City of London. This is very
sad. I've written to the Rev[erend] the Vicar and told him the sad news.
Poor Feeble Elizabeth has had a bad throat. Before she got ill she went
to a party of Bart's nurses in a functional flat. I saw her there. She
looked quite different from everyone else sitting on a divan.

Love to Andrew.
Love and regrets, John B

D.D. had first met JB in the early thirties when her sister Pamela Mitford (later Jackson)
worked at Biddesden as Bryan Guinness's farm manager. D.D. had asked JB to open a
Christmas Fayre.
    Andrew is her husband and Emma her daughter.
    JB's own parish church was St Bartholomew the Great.

To Michael Berry   43 Cloth Fair
16 October 1957   London EC1

Dear Michael,
I am, as you know and sometimes remind me, your Architectural
Correspondent. Since I have been writing in the *Spectator* once a week I
have become the recipient almost daily of letters complaining of
vandalisms by local councils, demolitions of old buildings, high-
handed actions by planning ministries.

More recently Ian Nairn of the *Architectural Review* has established a
bureau at the Architectural Press for receiving these complaints,
requests that are additional to those I receive, and has more work than
he can manage.

Architectural news need not I think be all that 'hot'. It could be
confined to a weekly or fortnightly feature reporting on new buildings
and on vandalisms and demolitions. It should have an illustration
which unfortunately I cannot put in the *Spectator*. I think there is no
doubt of an increasing interest in architecture among the public and this
may be partly due to television.

Would you consider my doing a feature in the *Telegraph*, whether on
a news page or not it doesn't matter, in an agreed amount of space. If
you would consider this I would give up the *Spectator* and concentrate
on it. I have a strong feeling that it ought to be done. I don't think that
we will ever break through the national habit of writing letters to *The
Times* on threats, but I think we could be even more effective ourselves
by having a regular feature on the subject not in form of letters but an
informed regular article.

Yours, John B

M.B., the son of Lord Camrose and a great friend of JB, had become the chairman and
editor-in-chief of the *Daily Telegraph*. His sister Patricia was married to PB's brother
Roger Chetwode, and JB therefore still assumed that he held on to his own job through
nepotism.

JB began his monthly 'Arshytektoral' column in the *Daily Telegraph* at the beginning of
1958, for the same fee as the weekly column in the *Spectator*.

To Candida Betjeman   Gosford House
                                                  Longniddry
26 October 1957   East Lothian

Darling Wibz,
Here I am where you have been before. My bedroom is blueish green
and in the same wing and on the same floor as the library. There is a
very nice affectionate dog called Butterscottish. It belongs to Buffy
[Elizabeth Charteris] to whom I must write. I hope Powlie is over his
influenza and that you have not had it. I like being in Scotland so much
that I wish I lived here. It is as foreign a country as France but with baps
and bannocks instead of omelettes and strong tea instead of wine.

I am off to see Monty [Compton] Mackenzie; we are contemplating a
book called *The Age of Vandalism* which will consist of a hundred years of
protests against the destruction of beautiful buildings and stretches of
country with photographs of what was destroyed and what has taken its
place. I hope you are being as clever as ever and combing your hair and
wearing those extraordinary blue cloaks you all wear in the winter.

Mummy is very active about the Caff, it seems, and to good effect. A
lot of people in Scotland are called Archie, pronounced Airchee.

Tons of love, darling Wibz, from MD.

> JB was staying with David and Mavis Wemyss at Gosford House, near Edinburgh, a
> Robert Adam mansion with huge Victorian wings, the south one of which has huge
> marble halls. The Earl of Wemyss was chairman of the council of the National Trust of
> Scotland. JB was in Scotland to give a lecture at the University of Edinburgh.
> *The Age of Vandalism* became too large a task to undertake.

To Sister Brigitta   43 Cloth Mead
4 February 1958   London EC1

Dear Sister Brigitta,
You asked me to write to Colin Stephenson about bringing in the
subject of sex into his Lenten addresses, and I found this easier to do by
conversation than by a letter so I went to see him on Saturday. He told
me that I could tell you that he thought too much stress on sex might be
harmful, that it had gone on in schools for centuries and repression had
never worked as it drove it underground and might make some girls
morbid and really damage them in later life. Much the best way was to

gain the confidence of the elder girls and use their influence. But of course you know all this.

One thing on reflection greatly disturbed me in that shattering interview I had with you (and may I say that Mrs Betjeman was even more shattered than me), and that was that you told me the chaplain had said to you he was greatly disturbed by the sex in the school, because of what he had heard in the girls' confessions. I do not think that even in the most general terms a priest should make such a breach of confidence. Once at Lancing a boy was expelled shortly after he had been to confession and it took years before they could get anyone to go to confession again. It would be really terrible for the faith of the school if what you said to me became known outside the community. I hope you don't mind my saying this.

I wish I had taken the opportunity you offered me on the telephone one day before the beginning of the term to discuss Candida's future with you. I hope I may have another opportunity some time this term. Perhaps I can telephone to you to make an appointment. My trouble is that like you I am constantly occupied but alas in the world. Tomorrow I am going in for a long pre-arranged retreat to Nashdom. By the way, the lines of the poetry you handed to me are from Andrew Marvell's 'To His [Coy] Mistress' which is, I dare say, in the library. It is unimproved by modern words introduced by Candida.

Yours truly, John Betjeman

> Sister B. was the new headmistress of St Mary's School, Wantage, which I attended and of which JB was a governor. She had summoned JB and PB to see her as a matter of utmost importance over my behaviour. I had copied out four lines, which I considered to be highly *risqué*, from Andrew Marvell's 'To His Coy Mistress' which I had found in the library during prep.
>
> > Had we but world enough, and time,
> > This coyness, Lady, were no crime. . .
> >
> > . . . My vegetable love should grow
> > Vaster than empires, and more slow.
>
> I had substituted the words 'D-cup bras' for 'empires' and passed the lines across to a friend sitting opposite me. Her explosion of laughter caused the piece of paper they were written on to be confiscated and shown to Sister B. who, not knowing her Marvell, took the lines to be an invitation to lesbian frolics. She was at the time cross-questioning the whole school on the question of masturbation. JB wrote to the head of the Order of St Mary's Convent expressing his dismay at the fact that the school chaplain had betrayed the girls.
>
> Colin Stephenson was Vicar of St Mary Magdalen Oxford at the time and a well known personality and friend of the 'Colonel', JB and 'Billa' Harrod.

1a The older end of the Mead, Wantage, showing the dormer windows and tile hanging added by its Victorian owners.

1b A lunch party at the Mead, 1952: (*left to right*) PSGB, Garth Bennett (with Marco Polo), Robert Heber-Percy, Andrew Crowden, 'Freckly' Jill Menzies, JB.

1c PB with Marco Polo and Jemima at the Mead, *c.* 1953.

2a On a Danish beach, while touring on the Camroses' yacht *Virginia*, summer 1951. (*Left to right*) Pamela Berry, JB, Poppy Pryce-Jones, Michael Berry, Alan Pryce-Jones.

2b EC on board the *Virginia*.

3a On holiday in France, c. 1952.
(*Left to right*) EC, Anne Barnes, George Barnes, JB.

3b Lunch at the Mead, 1955.
(*Left to right*) Kaiky the Parsee PG, L.P. Hartley, Elisabeth Moyne, JB (in Harrow straw hat), Karen Lancaster, Osbert Lancaster, Brian Moyne.

4a A gloomy CB in 1951.
JB kept this picture on his
dressing table all his life.

4b The Mead stables, 1954.
PSGB on Tulira, the mare
we brought from Ireland
after the war, and CB in a
milkmaid's hat which PB
insisted I wear to help her
make the butter.

4c PSGB (*far right*) with Willie and Cara Lancaster in their garden at
Henley, before going back to Eton, 1951.

5a JB always carried this photograph of EC, taken in the early fifties, in his wallet.

5b The crew's graveyard tea break, while filming *Our National Heritage: Stained Glass at Fairford*, 1956. CB (*seated*), JB (*in boater*), PSGB (*far right*).

5c Speech Day at St Elphin's School, Darley Dale, 1958. JB with the head-mistress Miss Stopford (*on his left*) and Deborah Devonshire (*in white coat*).

6a A lunch party with the Barings at Ardington, 1961. (*Left to right*) PSGB, Desmond Baring, Mollie Baring, Anne Baring, Nigel Baring, JB and Rover.

6b PB during her journey through Andalusia, Spain, October 1961.

6c JB with CB (*left*) and Ginny Dennistoun, whose looks he greatly admired, at the Mead, 1962.

7a Moonlight picnic at Knighton Bushes near the Uffington White Horse, 1962. (*Left to right*) Jock Murray, Nicole Hornby, JB, Tory Oaksey, Charlie Hornby.

7b JB performing Vachell Lindsay's 'The Congo' at the same picnic.

7c CB and RLG's wedding, May 1963. (*Back row, left to right*) William Bulwer Long, Angela Grimthorpe, RLG, CLG, the Reverend Schaufelberger, JB, PB, PSGB; (*front row*) Daniel Beckett, Elizabeth Loudon, Isobella Lambton, Dreamy Cunliffe Owen, Henrietta Churchill, James Fife.

8 JB arriving at Leeds station, December 1963, to open an exhibition on the church architect Temple Moore. With him is his friend Kenneth Young, editor of the *Yorkshire Post*.

To Candida Betjeman   43 Cloth Mead
Ash Wednesday   London EC1
19 February 1958

My darling Wibz,

My millipede is very well. Miss Evans calls her 'Leonora'. I think I told you that Richard Freeman discovered she was a female by her legs. Those on the seventh segment of a millipede are shorter in the male. In the female they are all the same.

I have had a very funny time this week judging a competition in Holborn Town Hall with a lot of Borough Engineers on the best *international* sign for public lavatories. Some of the entries were most extraordinary – cisterns with arrows coming out of them, sections of water closets pointing the way and little stylised conveniences which looked like those houses for telling the weather where one man comes out and another goes in.

I hope things are better with you. Not a word from Powlie. I much look forward to seeing you this weekend.

There were about sixty at the 7.40 mass today at St Bartholomew-the-Less and [there] had already been two earlier masses. Things are looking up.

Don't you think the Arthur Hughes illustrations – wood engravings – in that book *Sing Song* which I gave to you are rather good?

I'M SO SORRY MY WRITING IS SO BAD. AT THE END OF THE DAY WHICH THIS IS MY HAND GETS TREMBLY.

Tons of love, my darling Wibz, from MD.

> JB, who had always loved insects, had been given a millipede by Maxwell Knight whom he had met on the television panel game, *Animal, Vegetable and Mineral*. He called it Leo thinking it to be male. He loved the way it moved, its legs looking like waves in the sea. Miss Evans was JB's cleaning lady at Cloth Fair.

To Deborah Devonshire   43 Cloth Mead
15 April 1958   London EC1

My dear Debo,
No words of mine can express the joy of Lismore and my visit there – no
words can properly convey thanks, nor could even a bunch of orchids.
Andrew [Devonshire] polished elegant and missing nothing and Crax
[William Wicklow] tightish, enormous, and with a flower in his

buttonhole and also missing nothing made a splendid contrast in the
airport bar. I wonder what Andrew and he said to each other after
Feeble and I left. Crax said to me as we left for the aeroplane, 'What a
nice man!' Two double Powers [whisky] with Crax before lunch and
vin rosé at the luncheon gave a hangover which I still have.

   The visit to Keele was uproariously funny and we all had the giggles
on our return just as though we were kiddiz. Little Friend [Princess
Margaret] was on her best form. Have you ever heard Hiawatha? The
words are dotty enough anyhow.

> Never had our fine tobacco
> Tasted pleasanter and sweeter
> Said the handsome old Nokomis
> O Wa Wa my little owlet!

and that sort of thing – but when it is sung with the London Symphony
Orchestra, the chorus of five hundred and Flash Harry [Malcolm

Sargent] conducting, it is funnier than ever – such a resounding flourish about such tripe. Love to Emma and Peregrine. I do miss their pleasant company. My goodness they *are* nice – really good and kind and thoughtful. Love to Andrew, that great man, that prince among men and love to you dear, kind and beautiful Debo. And love to Lucian [Freud] and his kiddiz dream world and to Old Fury [Bridget Parsons] whom I love so and love to Anne [Tree] – oh no, she will have gone.

I have not yet had a proof from the old Protestant printer. I expect Irish Customs will hold it up as dirty readin' matter.

Love and renewed thanks from John

> JB had written to me from Lismore (9 February 1958), 'Today I went by train to the salmon fishing on the River Blackwater at Careysville. Daffodils in bloom along the waterside, buds just starting in the chestnuts, sycamores, swans flying upstream and all bitterly cold, though beautiful. Lucian Freud drew a salmon in water-colour but he draws so slowly that he had only got as far as the eye when it went bad.'
>
> JB, EC and Princess Margaret had attended a performance at the University College of North Staffordshire where George Barnes was Principal. Princess Margaret had recently become Chancellor of the university.
>
> 'Old Fury' was Bridget Parsons, Michael Rosse's sister.
>
> The proof referred to was for the poem 'Ireland's Own' or 'The Burial of Thomas Moore' which JB had dedicated to D.D.'s children Peregrine Hartington and Emma and Sophia Cavendish. He had had the poem printed out like a Victorian music-hall sheet (ten copies on green paper for the Devonshire family and ten on mauve paper for his friends) and printed by Browne, the printer at Lismore. JB referred to him as the Protestant printer. He had rickety old premises and JB was very fond of him.
>
> The poem was eventually published in *High and Low* (1966).
>
> Lucian Freud, Anne Tree and Ann Fleming were also staying.

To William Collins   43 Cloth Fair
23 April 1958   London EC1

Dear Billy,

I have been reading through the proofs of my introduction and am anxious for your advice and help. This book started in such a different way from how it has concluded that Part One of the introduction seems to me redundant, since the descriptions of the churches themselves are much longer than was originally proposed under the E. T. Long scheme. Also I think my prose is far too lush and as a wise critic remarked to whom I showed the proofs, reads like Kirkland Bridge, if you recollect those absurd advertisements in *The Times* Personal Column about church restoration.

Mark [Bonham Carter] said that he did not think an index was needed and I gather that its format has been worked out with no index.

However, I think this is essential, both for the names of architects and the names of places. The architectural index will tell you all churches by Street, Pearson, Lutyens, Norman Shaw and other great men. The place index will tell you whether the church is mentioned or not. People do not recollect what county a parish is in. I would therefore like in the next six days, occupied by my cruise in Scotland, to reduce very considerably Part One and to include it in the introduction, explaining how the book came to be written and how it is to be used. This should then leave plenty of room for an index and would satisfy me personally very much.

I have had a wonderful idea for a cover. Osbert Lancaster gave me lately a large water-colour of an unrestored church which I am asking my secretary to take down to you tomorrow, Thursday afternoon. As you will see it is dark at the top and light at the bottom and could be cut on either side, probably on the left, to bring it into the proportion of the book jacket. I would suggest that if this drawing were reproduced in colour and the title were done in white letters over the black part and any additional information in black, or some other dark type, on the white pavement, you would have a most attractive cover, symbolising incidentally the spirit of the book which is to list churches which have escaped 'restoration' by the Victorians. This water-colour is of an unrestored parish church, I do not know which, nor will anyone else.

Yours, John Betjeman

> JB's *English Parish Churches* came out later that year. E. T. Long had provided the list of churches after John Piper and JB had laid down the list of conditions which reduced the sixteen thousand parish churches in England by a process of elimination to just over four thousand. Indexes of architects, artists and places were included.
>
> In John Guest's Editor's Note to *The Best of Betjeman* (1978) the latter writes, 'I make no apology for including in Part Two what may appear to be a rather big selection from one source, the introduction to *English Parish Churches*. This essay is half the length of the book itself and is of great importance to the body of Sir John's prose writing.'

To John Summerson   The Mead
                                                              Wantage
3 May 1958   Berkshire

My dear Coolmore,
I arrived from a tour of the ORKNEYS (St Magnus worth the journey alone – pink sandstone with Butterfield stripes only genuine, high-pinched proportions, stone vaulted cruciform and aisled and pleasantly

Edinburgh 1920-ish art nouveau-ly restored by Presbyterians), FAIR
ISLE (no trees: no architecture: cliffs and crofts and puffins and
weirs[?]), RONA (deserted – and my God, what a sea!), ST KILDA (like
Oxford Street because the RAF was building a radar station for
Duncan Sandys and Colonel Post on the highest of its three mountains
and had buggered up the crescent-shaped deserted gloomy marshy
village at the sunless base of the huge hills, with huts and lorries),
RHUM (a 1906 castle, one hundred trees and one hundred square miles
of bare deer forest and no one allowed on but naturalists), IONA (Ian
Lindsay and earlier and very holy in its Presby[terian] Way), STAFFA (a
flop after Mendelssohn Daniel and Turner), ARDROSSAN (*c.* 1827 in red
sandstone) and GLASGOW (the Grosvenor is having its Art Nouveau
taken out by a London architect called Leslie Norton), this afternoon to
find your GLORIOUS LETTER re Spalding. My dear boy, the bird-
watching lairds on the voyage, who included to my surprise E. Clive
Rouse, had never heard of me. But what an evening for you! How like
life. High praise of Pevsner in Capt[ain] Bog's Weekly [*Times Literary
Supplement*] this week. See you soon.

Bung ho ole man, Iain MacBetjeman

> JB and I had gone on the Scottish National Trust cruise in a Swedish liner. Seton
> Gordon, the octogenarian *piobaireachd* (bagpiping) correspondent for *The Times*, and a
> writer on Scottish history and culture, had given lectures on the birds and the flowers.
>
> Duncan Sandys founded the Civic Trust in 1957 and was, at the time, Minister of
> Defence (1957–9).
>
> Colonel Kenneth Post worked with Sandys at the MOD (1957–9) and became the first
> director of the Civic Trust.
>
> E. Clive Rouse was an architect and antiquary.

To Candida Betjeman   43 Cloth Fair
19 June 1958   London EC1

Darling Wibz,
I enclose the Seton Gordon photographs of our
Scottish cruise. I go to Salisbury tomorrow
(Saturday) with a telly producer for the inside
of the day. On Tuesday I interviewed Eden
Phillpotts, the Devon novelist, poet and
playwright. He is ninety-five and
is writing the last chapter of a
new novel. He looks like this

and wears 1890 clothes, has gas only in his house so that the BBC had to bring their cables over miles of fields. He has written two hundred and fifty works and over a hundred novels. His last visit to London was in 1916 and he did not even go up in the twenties to see his play *The Farmer's Wife* which ran for several years. Except that he has cataract in his eyes, he is in good health and his brain is quite clear. He was a close friend of Thomas Hardy and told me a lot about him. He said that Hardy thought that if he had had the choice of whether to emerge on this earth for the short space between the oblivion from which we come and to which we go, he would have preferred not to make the experiment. No wonder Hardy is so gloomy!

Longing to see you. Much and much and much love, MD.

JB was making a film for the National Trust called *Beauty in Trust*, sponsored by BP. Eden Phillpotts, who lived in Exeter, died in 1960 aged ninety-eight.

To Martyn Skinner   J. Betjeman & Co. Writers
                                 Poems promptly executed
6 July 1958   (printed by Elphicks, Biggleswade)

SKINNER! the quill which hesitates to thank
For such a gift as yours, is recreant.
And if this poor acknowledgement is late
Blame not the writer but the GPO
Notoriously slow, in this our isle,
To deal with parcels that are registered
Though nothing that the GPO could pay
Would compensate me, had I not received
Your welcome offering on Saturday.

Long years ago when fresh from MAGDALEN
I thought to ape the lit'rary recluse
And live among my books – oh then how few –
Whiles' being a Pedagogue at *Heddon Court*
Cockfosters, Barnet, Herts (demolished now
In favour of the usual new estate) –
I turned with pleasure to the Reverend band
Whose work you sent to me. 'Twas COWPER's work
Which fired me first to save my meagre means
And, at a time of half term holiday
To buy a ticket down to *Brighton*. Thence
To take the bus and tread the winding lane

Between the chalky slopes toward the church
Where our mild parson once had taught his flock
And wandering within those antique walls
I met & talked with Mr TATTERSALL
A HURDIS addict who by now must lie
In that same courtyard underneath the downs
Beside his mild addiction. Hot July
Hung in the elm-trees; yellow saxifrage
Starred the adjacent downland, one & six
Purchased a pamphlet & for many years
'Twas all I had to tell me of the bard
Until I bought *The Village Curate* bound
In walnut coloured leather printed for
LONGMAN, HURST, REES, ORME, BROWN etcetera
And swiftly did the poet's cheerful lines
Take me in thought to his fair parsonage
And out to hen runs, into farmer's yards
And village fairs and SUSSEX jollities
Long before BELLOC and the *Ditchling* folk
Trampled with heavier feet the grassy sward.
But never, never, in my wildest dreams
Did I expect to find from his own press
The poet's finest poem, Grangerised
By such a pen as that of etcher NIBBS
Whose book of SUSSEX churches I possess
SKINNER! the quill which hesitates to thank
For that & for your fair inscription
Is recreant indeed. And if 'tis late
Blame not John Betjeman.

M.S. (1906–93, see *Volume One*), the poet, had been a freshman at Oxford at the same time as JB, but was not a particular friend of his. The son of the Chairman of Barkers Stores in Kensington, he had been a drop-out during his university days and sought country solitude rather than JB's social whirl.

M.S. had already published, to some acclaim, *Letters to Malaya* in three volumes (his contribution to the war effort), during the forties. Meantime he farmed at Ipsden in Oxfordshire, winning a prize for his malting barley. He *loved* a correspondence and struck one up with JB, writing him over sixty letters from the late fifties onwards. JB sometimes replied in blank verse, or verse, for example his poem 'Lines Written to Martyn Skinner Before his Departure from Oxfordshire in Search of Quiet' (1961) published in *High and Low*. M.S. had just sent JB a copy of *The Village Curate and other Poems* (1788) by James Hurdis. Hurdis (1763–1801) was a Magdalen man and professor of poetry at Oxford. He had lived at Berkhamsted where M.S. was brought up. With the book M.S. wrote:

> Betjeman! lover of the local scene
> And local poet (often in past days
> The parson too) – this copy of a book

> Locally printed at its author's press!
> (Lucky the poet with a private press!) . . .
> This copy, relic of a happier time,
> Seems meant for thee, and so to thee 'tis sent
> By one who used to know the *Buckle Inn*
> And bathe at Seaford when he was a boy . . .

To Candida Betjeman   43 Cloth Fair
17 July 1958   London EC1

Drene dear,

Barry's dad had a seizure while doing his kiddie crossing at Wembley this week and remained stationary holding up his sign in the road for over an hour and a half. When he came to he found that the police had diverted the traffic down side roads. He was able to claim overtime for the extra half hour on top of the usual hour he has for the job.

Shirley and Barry and I went to a good show in town and the woman in front objected to the noise Shirl made with her choc papers. Some people are *too* fussy and la di da.

Well cheerioh, ole girl. See you soon and so long. Love, Max

> JB and I had a long correspondence in 1958 between the two fictitious characters Drene and Max Factor ('Drene' was a popular shampoo, 'Max Factor' a brand of make-up). A lot of it involved 'Barry's dad', who had a job as lollipop man at Wembley Park Secondary Modern where he held up traffic for a quarter of an hour at a time. JB always hated being held up in a car and got very impatient. He had the idea that 'kiddie crossers' (as he called them) were thwarted power maniacs who had failed to get into the police force and enjoyed holding up the traffic for the sake of it. JB had written (12 July 1958), 'Barry's dad is going to the kiddi-crossers' conference at Harrogate this autumn which will be fun as it is all paid for out of the rates.' Other characters in our fictitious world included Tony Curtis and Helena Rubinstein.

To James Lees-Milne   43 Cloth Fair
22 July 1958   London EC1

Dear Jim,

Oh, the guilt I've got. I did not enter it in my diary and so I went as arranged weeks ago to Cardiff instead of putting off Cardiff which would have been pleasanter and less tiring for I should have seen you. So not only have I seemingly insulted an old friend by being away a second time, but I've done myself out of the pleasure of giving myself guilt – a rare paradox in life.

As to the poems, I have read them, with pleasure and interest and emotion and care. I should have thought there was no doubt that the *stuff* of poetry is there – I mean what you see and feel is individually expressed and memorable and sincere and really you and not some ghastly word-patterner trying to show off his erudition. There is one stanza in 'The Return' which is proof to me you are a poet. It is the one beginning 'And then? . . .' and ending 'silk ears of young dogs'. That is observed, private thought made public and easy for all to understand and copying nobody. BUT I don't think any of them read out loud well. I have tried that. For instance 'The Dream' may look as though it keeps the rules of rhyme, but though it does, the rhymes are purely intellectual. You can't use rhythms or rhyme like that. A line should end as you speak. A really natural poem should need no punctuation; it should punctuate itself by the natural cadence of its words. When you write, get some metre or poem of quite simple stanzas which appeals to you and deliberately parody it at first and then go off into what you want to say keeping the parody of the metre in mind. Sonnets are not good practice for this. They are too complicated – look at Smart's 'Song to David' or even Gray's *Elegy* or Watts's hymns. As I'm sure there is poetry there, I hope you don't mind my suggesting these ways of releasing it. After all you are a damn good writer and you like poetry and so *of course* you can write it.

See you soon ole man. Cheerioh, John B

> J.L.-M. did write a few more poems after this, but gave up soon afterwards. 'I knew I wasn't a poet,' he said (1994). 'It makes me squirm with embarrassment to think I sent my poems to John, but this letter displays his inordinate kindness.'

To John Murray

Moor View
Edensor
Bakewell
16 August 1958   Derbyshire

My dear Jock,
The proofs have been sent under separate cover.

(1) I enclose a specimen I forgot to include of how the stanzas of 'Indoor Game Near Newbury' should be set – i.e. internal rhyming lines indented in pairs or triplets as they appear.

(2) I'm not so sure that I'm right about inverted commas as I've suggested on p[roof] c[opy] of the galleys. I leave it to you. In some

poems they look awful but in blank verse they look okay.

(3) I think Michael [Tree] is right. I think the dust wrapper *should* wed in with the binding more. The lettering on the dust wrapper, if it is Cursive, will help.

Osbert and K[aren] and E[lizabeth] all very well and energetic, especially the first mentioned.

Yours, John B

There was trouble with the designs of the dust wrapper for *Collected Poems* which came out at the end of that year. 'If you have any respect for my aesthetic judgement,' JB wrote to J.M. (1 September 1958), 'let me see the dark green against the cream. . . . From the work your artist produced I do not feel at all confident. . . . I prefer the idea of red. Michael T has an eye for colour which amounts to genius.' Osbert Lancaster was involved in the design as well. The dust wrapper ended up in a dark reddish-brown colour.

To Peggy Thomas   43 Cloth Fair
26 September 1958   London EC1

Dearest Peggy,

I can hardly believe, in fact I cannot believe, that this day last week Candida and I walked through the mist to the Rumps and saw a seal and that in the evening we went to Pendogget for that Old Harrovian fare and now I am in the heart of London pitying myself so much that I am sweating with self-pity and poor Candida is in Paris trailing round after culture with Paul and Penelope. I keep recalling your remark that Trebetherick is like an unsuccessful love affair, always having to be broken up because of outside hostile circumstances. And perhaps if we really live there for ever, as we long to do, we'll get like Miss Collins, though at the moment I envy the very apples that rot on her garden path and the puniest slug that slides over her threshold. Perhaps we could all set up at Bodmin Road station by arrangement with the Great Western – you in the refreshment room because of drink, Lynam in the signal box because of administrative ability, me in the booking office because I'm literary, Edward [Hornby] to do the lamps and odd jobs because he's so clever with his hands, Douglas to look after the down platform as head porter and Ted as outside boy, pushing trolleys to Bodmin and greeting motor cars on arrival. We won't have a station master, as we'll be one glorious Soviet. Joan [Kunzer] will run the Bodmin branch.

I always enjoy Cornwall more than anything that happens to me in the year and this year I can say that I enjoyed myself more than ever.

My! how we laughed! How marvellous you and Lynam are as hosts,
how good Joan and Edward [Mott] and Douglas [Eaves] as company.
Dear, sweet Peggy, I can never thank you enough for your kindness
and Lynam's kindness to
   Yours, Chris Guiney[?]
   pp Jan Trebetjeman

> P.T. was married to Lynam T., headmaster of Repton School, in whose holiday house,
> White Horses at Trebetherick, we often stayed.
>   Miss Collins was a fearsome and eccentric spinster who lived in Trebetherick.
>   Edward Hornby was a regular guest at White Horses.
>   Joan Kunzer (née Larkworthy) was JB's earliest girl chum. He had met her at
> Trebetherick when he was four years old.
>   Edward Mott was a contemporary of P.T.'s son Michael.
>   Douglas Eaves had been in Lynam T.'s house at Rugby (before the latter became
> headmaster of Repton) and had gone on to be a schoolmaster at the Dragon School.

To Candida Betjeman   43 Cloth Fair
22 October 1958   London EC1

Darling Wibz,
I was very pleased to have your enthralling, revealing, well written and
heartfelt letter. I absolutely sympathise with your attitude. Let's
discuss it at length when you return for the Christmas hols. Oh, I do
understand. Poor Wibz.

If one is a creative person, as you are, the sort of education which is
designed to instill knowledge is useless unless you can see some point
behind it. I know nothing about French educational methods. They
sound different from St Mary's – but perhaps they produce more good
by bringing about reaction of a good positive sort. Also you are clever
enough to beat the French educational system at its own game by
passing its exams, as you will and being as good as the best of them there
– despite the disadvantage of being Anglo-Irish as you are! I'm sure you
will one day find what particular thing it is you want to specialise in –
drawing, acting, producing, designing buildings, dresses or interiors.
Meanwhile keep your enthusiasms fresh as they are now. They are
vital. And this sort of schooling won't kill them. By putting obstacles in
the way, it will only increase them – for genius is *helped* by having
obstacles to overcome. Also it is good to be thorough and at least this
education sounds to be that. But, my goodness, I *am* thinking for you
and praying for you and I do love you. I hope the Pagèses are nice.

Old Katie Acklam died at Chippenham and I go to the funeral
tomorrow. She gave you some little trinket. She was one of the only
saints I met so that her death is not sad but a triumph for her. It's odd
how unimportant people like her impress one so much more than the
great and famous.

Tons of love, MD

I had been sent to stay with a French family called Pagès, who made the liqueur
Vervaine and lived in Le Puy-en-Velay in France. I went to the local school and
complained about the rigidity of the French methods of teaching.
    Katie Acklam, whom JB often visited, was a cousin whose private room in Frogwell
Hospital in Chippenham he had long been paying for.

To P. Morton Shand   43 Cloth Fair
28 October 1958   London EC1

My dear P. Morton Shand,
Your gloomy letter gave me great pleasure. You express thoughts I
hardly dared put down myself but feel I like to think almost as deeply as
you.

The Victorian Society is necessary of course but it is very hard to get
it working on an effective footing, if I may use a rather nice term which
all we administration boys like to employ. I am surprised and delighted
to find that far the best members of the Victorian Society are young
men with a burning passion for saving Norman Shaw and those sort of
people. I think we suffered a great deal when 'Gloagery' was on its
upgrade. I also think that far more people than we know object to the
shapeless boxes that are rising in London.

I hope Sybil [Shand] is better from her accident and will look
forward to seeing her when you come back to Norland Square.

Yours ever, John B

JB had written to P.M.S. about the formation of the Victorian Society. He had replied
(21 October 1958), 'And what an imposing list of names you have assembled in support
of it, including *even* super-Professor Nikolaus Pevsner! But you see, with the possible
exception of Goodhart-Rendel . . . none of these eminent authorities, and not even you
yourself, lived in, or *knew*, the Victorian Age. I did, and the horror of it abides with me
to this day. So you see that although I have naturally a considerable admiration for
Morris, Lethaby, Philip Webb and Norman Shaw as architects and designers, . . . the
only reason I could wish to see Victorian buildings being preserved (other than those of
the men I've named) is to prevent their sites being occupied by the unspeakable box-
frame crudities now being erected everywhere, with universal admiration, as
enlightened examples of "contemporary modern idiom" and "original cladding".'

John Gloag was an architectural writer of a purist kind who took himself seriously and had no time for Victorian architecture. JB had written a rhyme in the early thirties which went:

> John Gloag
> Is quite in Vogue
> If any *man*
> Can be called the Vogue
> Gloag can.

Sybil S. had slipped while picking wild tulips in Provence and had to stay in a hospital in Lyons for several weeks.

To John Murray

25 December 1958

The Mead
Wantage
Berkshire

My dear Jock,

I've never seen anything quite so swish as that red velvet edition in its Morocco box except that which was in the long royal fingers on that terrifying occasion. No man ever had a kinder or more considerate publisher than you. All I've had from Collins is a bill for twenty-one pounds against some extra copies I ordered of *Parish Churches*. How different is *Mr Murray* who sends delicious wine as well as the books, and in which we drank your health at lunch today. Of course next year there will be the reaction and I shall suffer contempt, neglect and frustration. But I can now always look back to a really thrilling moment of triumph and shall never forget your and everybody's generosity. God bless you old boy. Everyone here sends love as does

Your diffident author, John B

The red velvet edition of *Collected Poems* in its Morocco box was limited to only three: one for JB, one for the Queen and one for J.M. The cost of binding them up was thirty pounds each.

Four:

June and lavender, bring me hope

====

1958 to 1960

F   OL   JB

Carla William

Burst, good June, with a rush this morning,
Bindweed weave me an emerald rope
Sun, shine bright on the blossoming trellises,
June and lavender, bring me hope.

'South London Sketch, 1844'

On his return from Rotherhithe to a refurbished 43 Cloth Fair, JB's shambling figure once more became a familiar sight around Smithfield meat market and Aldersgate. His suits were hopelessly out of shape through heavy books being constantly shoved in their pockets; he always carried a fish basket into which he stuffed more books. He wore a brown felt hat and occasionally the most revolting semi-transparent grey plastic mac which used to embarrass me as a style-conscious teenager. Occasionally he would bicycle gingerly about the City, but never as far as the West End.

On returning to Cloth Fair JB decided to employ male instead of female secretaries. Perhaps he thought they would not be constantly leaving to get married, as Tory had just done. Through his friend Freddy Hood, who had taken it upon himself to find suitable posts for members of the clergy who had been in a 'bit of trouble', he proceeded to employ several in the early sixties. Freckly Jill, his ex-secretary, wrote from Mzuzu in Nyasaland, 'It will be lovely to see you again (if you will see me again). I do good works out here, the African Red Cross sewing party which is hell. . . . Your clergyman sounds nice, hope he has remained nice.'[1]

Harry Jarvis, who had been chaplain at Summerfields School, Oxford, arrived in 1959. He recalls, 'You never had to say anything twice to John, he was with you straight away. His friendship meant an enormous amount to me; he was never shocked and never, at that particular time, judgemental. He made me laugh the whole time: he was so *spontaneous*. I had to do almost everything. Make the bed, make the tea, open the champagne at midday, answer endless letters, answer the telephone – ceaselessly. I eventually learnt to say "no" on his behalf, whenever it was somebody he did not want to talk to, and quite often when he felt like it we would go for a walk looking at buildings nearby in the City. I remember once straying into the Prudential Building and climbing up to a top room and from there climbing on to the window ledge in order that John could show me a view of St Paul's Cathedral. It was fast becoming obscured by office blocks, but you could still see St Martin's spire framed against St Paul's dome. I don't know how he found that room in the first place – it was an office.'[2] Harry, who had been brought up in Wantage and first met JB at a cricket club dinner in the late forties, became very important to him. 'He sometimes used me as a confessor, formally in church, proper confessions in Wantage. At that time clergy were allowed to use extra hands: it was not very regular but just from time to time. He used me much more as a confessor out of the confessional, so to speak. We talked a great deal.'

JB wrote to Harry from Wantage (19 August 1960), 'As the calm mentor of my life and the only person who knows its twisted strands, please remember in your prayers Phoeble (Elizabeth) and me and Penelope and Paul and Candida. I must not make Phoeble unhappy as I do with my ties here. How can I hurt least? It is all very fraught, I know that.'[3] Harry recalled, 'I do not think that at any stage he wanted to leave Elizabeth; he never wanted to leave either of them in fact. Sometimes I think that he thoroughly enjoyed dealing with guilt, to some extent anyway. He was happy some of the time but he went through long periods of being very, very unhappy and consumed with guilt. It was definitely a case of loving two women, I know he loved them both. I did not advise him what to do, he had a very deep love for Penelope but he just could not live with her which made for an impossible situation. They were incompatible in a way.'

By the end of the decade, JB's spirits were low. Although he had sailed through a golden glow for a month or two after his *Collected Poems* came out, he underwent huge personal sadnessess which kept knocking him backwards. The staunch friends, who had so influenced his life, began to fall away. First the Colonel died, switching out a bright light in his life, then George Barnes, his comforting and avuncular friend who had given him such confidence in his work for the BBC. Harry Williams, the chaplain of Trinity College, Cambridge, helped him enormously at the time to bear the pain of George's slow death from cancer.

Jack Beddington, who had been the driving force behind all JB's *Shell Guides*, died soon after, as did H. S. Goodhart-Rendel and P. Morton Shand, all major figures in JB's life – the 'grown-ups' he looked up to.

Comper's partner John Bicknell wrote to him (12 January 1960) about taking Comper, who was by now dying, to Westminster Abbey 'to see again his great windows and warriors' chapel; and also to the afternoon party on the occasion of the retirement of the Dean'.[4] JB wrote gloomily to Evelyn Waugh (22 April 1960), '[Ninian] Comper is ill and he has lost his memory.'[5] Comper died later that year.

Being awarded the CBE and the Queen's Gold Medal for Poetry in 1960 did little to alleviate the sorrow of losing so many revered friends. On the face of it, JB kept cheerful and on receiving a letter of congratulations from Arthur Bryant wrote back that if he had been made a Peer, he would have been chosen to sign himself 'St Pancras', after his favourite station. His social life in London became ever more demanding. Rex Harrison wrote asking him if he could record *Collected Poems* (nothing came of it). Benjamin Bonas, his Marlburian pal, staged an Old Boys get-together: 'It is going to be Black Tie,' he wrote (22 April 1960). 'I am afraid it will be a nuisance for you but I look so much nicer in a dinner jacket than ordinary clothes; so far [Louis] MacNeice and John Edward [Bowle] have accepted; [Anthony] Blunt unfortunately has refused because he is busy with Poussins in Paris.'[6] When Cecil Beaton made a list of people he envied for the *Daily Express* it included the Queen, Prince Philip, Graham Sutherland, Barbara Hepworth, Noel Coward and JB, whom he identified with the rising generation. JB wrote back thanking him: 'Young people are all on our side, or a lot of them are. Our enemies are the town clerks and the borough surveyors of the 1930s Cocoa generation, the Espresso Coffee generation is far more helpful.'[7]

England was about to witness the greatest devastation of its buildings since the war. Property developers were finding it all too easy to ride roughshod across towns and villages. In a long poignant letter just before he died, P. Morton Shand, who had fled to France, wrote, 'London is now such a nightmare of hideous and shoddy Americanised buildings . . . that it has reduced me to a state of mental debility in which I can scarcely credit what my eyes have to confront. . . . I have frightful nightmares, and no wonder, for I am haunted by a gnawing sense of guilt in having, in however minor and obscure a degree, helped to bring about, anyhow encourage and praise, the embryo searchings that have now materialized into a monster neither of us could have foreseen; Contemporary Architecture (the piling-up of gigantic children's toy bricks in utterly dehumanised and meaningless forms); Art and all that, it is no longer funny, it is frightening.'[8]

On a second Scottish islands cruise in 1959 JB met John Smith, another stalwart campaigner and the founder of the Landmark Trust, who observed in his diary, '6 May [19]59: John Betjeman is one of the party, and while we were sorting ourselves out on board he said, for the benefit of anyone who cared to listen, "My daughter Candida couldn't come, so I've brought Elizabeth Cavendish instead." ' His diary continued, '12 May [19]59: We anchored off Mingulay, at the extreme southern end of the Outer Hebrides. . . . On landing, John B rolled up his trousers and, in his grey pork-pie hat and carrying his straw fishmonger's bag, started to paddle in the crystal water, making this remote spot, uninhabited since 1911, feel like Margate. . . . Meeting him, and getting to know him a little, has been a tremendous bonus. There is a real poet inside his prosaic exterior; he makes you see things as you never saw them before. Also he is wonderful company, high-spirited, inventive, and very funny. . . . The other day [when] we landed at some deserted spot now given over to the birds, he said to our eager naturalist companions, "I'm only interested in what Man has done." '[9]

All through 1959, when he had a moment, JB worked on his 'Epic'. After a good stint at Moor View in the autumn of 1959, he wrote to me in November, 'I have written thirty-three letters today which is why this one is so dull. I have written a lot more of my verse autobiography but it is not yet finished, I find that my life pattern is like yours. The nest (home and day school), disturbing the nest (public school and Oxford), flight (the world and literature). . . . I have been working in the Derbyshire Dales – great folding limestone rocks, little black cottages, ivy and tinkling water falls. It is lovely beyond words. I shall not finish my autobiography this side of Christmas which is annoying.'[10] He did another stint at White Horses in Trebetherick in February 1960 within sight of his favourite beach, Greenaway, when the sea was rough and the waves huge. 'I've *finished* the Epic,' he wrote to my mother (10 February 1960). 'Now I will have to spend several weeks revising it and cutting out the dead wood of which there is a lot and rendering some of the blank verse in lyric form, as there might be too much blank verse. I have no confidence in the thing. I doubt if it will even be a *succès d'estime*.'[11]

Summoned by Bells first appeared in the *New Yorker* in September 1960. It was read by Benjamin Bonas who wrote to JB (13 September), 'It brought me right back to Oxford, back to Marlborough – "I walked with strangers down the hill to school." How long is it since I thought about that dreadful walk. Back to childhood, "When firelight shone on green linoleum." . . . What a poet, what an enchanter to make one, nearing sixty, remember so completely, forgetting the years between.'[12] *Summoned by Bells* was published in England in November to a mixed reception.

Meanwhile back at Wantage, the future of King Alfred's Kitchen was in jeopardy after the whole structure had been declared insecure by a building inspector. '*Nil desperandum*, things might be much worse,' wrote JB to my mother. 'The joys of cooking when you really did not feel like it were wearing thin.'[13] Cracky William Wicklow wrote from Dublin (5 December 1960), 'We both know what it is to have wives who have "activities", at times ruinous for the husband.'[14] JB enjoyed Wantage life perhaps because he could distance himself from it. He wrote to Harry Jarvis about the new vicar John Schaufelberger (6 September 1960), 'He is full of jokes, calls everyone "my dear", likes embroidering and I think cats or maybe dogs, lives with his old mother, is dark haired and forty-four and thank God is *very High*. I hope that Our Lady will come back into prominence and life and a little vulgarity.'[15] Schaufelberger had a boyfriend called Harry, and soon they became an accepted couple in the town. They were known as 'Hinge and Bracket', were very happy and certainly filled the church.

My mother sold a piece of buhl furniture which she had inherited from her parents to make a tennis court above the vegetable garden. She thought it would enhance the social lives of my brother and myself. Instead my brother ceaselessly played the saxophone in the loft and I only wanted to go to the Regal cinema in Wantage, the Regent in Newbury or the Rialto in Didcot. It was my father who used the court the most – 'Come over now, darling,' he begged Mollie Baring, 'I've got all these vicars and I don't know what to do with them; we'll have to play tennis.' Because Harry Jarvis was younger than he was, JB always made him play in his cassock to put him at a disadvantage – 'It really *was* vicarage tennis,' remembers Mollie, 'we were all *so* bad and lobbed everything.'[16]

With St Mary's Wantage and sojourns in France and Italy behind me, the last summer of the old decade and the first of the new saw the Mead full of my brother's and my friends, who were often the children of my parents' friends – the Harrods, Powells, Waughs, Clives, Lancasters and Pipers – but many others besides. If they seemed like eager university students, they often alarmed my father. He felt vulnerable among them. He thought he would be found out to be the fraud he believed he was. But when he got to know young people of whom he was frightened, the rewards were often great. David Dimbleby remembers, 'Years ago on one of your picnics on the downs your father asked me what I was going to do when I left Oxford. I said I was in a muddle – and he advised me to go into a monastery for a week for some quiet to work it out. I didn't, but the idea stayed with me – of finding moments of calm in a crisis. But it was his curiosity about what I was doing that really struck me, and taking trouble to think about it. I am sure you have been told of countless examples of that private kindness. It came through in his writing.'[17]

Those evening picnics on the Downs were part of the pattern of our lives in summer. Our favourite place was Knighton Bushes, which my parents had discovered years before, when they lived at Uffington. Friends would ride on horses and in carts, but JB always went by car and always performed his star turn beside the camp fire. This was a recitation of Vachell Lindsay's 'The Congo', gradually working up into a crescendo and beating the rhythm with a stick on a cake-tin top, or sometimes using two saucepan lids as cymbals:

> Pounded on the table
> Beat an empty barrel with the handle of a broom,
> Hard as they were able
> Boom, Boom, BOOM.

'Halcyon days,' recalled my friend Hercules Bellville, 'when you could take *any* poetry book from his library shelf and read out the obscurest of lines and he would unerringly name the writer. He was always so patient with us adolescents.'[18]

JB was genuinely frightened of what he called 'smart' people, 'the Porkers' of his poems, I think because he felt he couldn't win their hearts. I seldom saw him fail to charm anyone, but there *were* local Berkshire people who didn't see the point of him at all. His fear and paranoia of them was quite irrational. As a result of my faintly unconventional upbringing I *longed*, for a brief period, for that 'smartness' my parents lacked. I wanted them to take me to Newbury Races, own a black Labrador and a Landrover and for my mother to wear a headscarf. At about that time, a clever social entrepreneur called Angus Menzies [pronounced Minghies] started a shop called the General Trading Company. It epitomised my dreams, until JB recited in a posh voice:

> Headscarved debs who work
>   For Angus Menzies,
> I'd *love* to, but you see,
>   Mummy says the thing is . . .

My obsession with headscarves didn't last long.

In the New Year of 1960 I was sent to Italy. 'Last night we drove back in thick fog wondering where you were in the train,' JB wrote to me (8 January). 'I have had hundreds of letters lately. I open them without looking. Paul has been helping me open some. This morning he is sad. He tells me you have broken up with MT [Paul's friend with whom I had been in love] – a quarrel or permanent? Time will tell. The one thing to do is to bear no ill will. That empty feeling that comes when one is cut off soon fills. I beg you, however, consider well and give not your heart away until you are quite sure. Sudden clicks must go on for a year before they can be certain of being the real love for life. My whole life has been changed by the discovery of *Valentine* and *Roxy*.'[19]

1. JB's papers, University of Victoria, British Columbia.
2. Harry Jarvis, CLG interview (1994).
3. Harry Jarvis's papers.
4. JB's papers, University of Victoria.
5. Evelyn Waugh's papers, British Library.
6. JB's papers, University of Victoria.
7. Cecil Beaton's papers, St John's College, Cambridge.
8. JB's papers, University of Victoria.
9. John Smith's papers.
10. CLG's papers, Beinecke Library, Yale University.
11. PB's papers, Beinecke Library, Yale University.
12. JB's papers, University of Victoria.
13. PB's papers, Beinecke Library.
14. JB's papers, University of Victoria.
15. Harry Jarvis's papers.
16. Mollie Baring, CLG interview, 1992.
17. David Dimbleby, letter to CLG (June 1994).
18. Hercules Bellville, letter to CLG (June 1994).
19. CLG's papers, Beinecke Library.

To Bryan Moyne

28 December 1958

The Mead
Wantage
Berkshire

My dear Bryan,
How nice of you to write to me about my temporary success at poetry.
I set no store by it. The slump in me will start in a month or two. But
I can say, in the depths of it, that I have at least had my day. And your
boom will arrive. Only wait.
    We are all well and send you all our love.
    John B

> JB and B.M. (see *Volume One*) had never lost touch since becoming such close friends at
> Oxford. We often went to lunch at Biddesden, his home in Wiltshire. PB and he shared a
> common love of Arab horses.
>   JB's *Collected Poems* had received rave reviews. By 1961 it had sold one hundred
> thousand copies.

To David Cecil

31 December 1958

The Mead
Wantage
Berkshire

Dear David,
Our letters crossed, mentally at least, for I was just going to write to
you to say how much I have been enjoying *Modern Verse 1900–50*. What
happened to you about it, as Anne Tree, that wise and wonderful girl,
said to me, is just what she said will happen to me (as I know already
without having to be told). The critics are all over one for a year then all
dead against for another two years, however good you may be. And
there's no doubt that *Modern Verse* is v[ery] good. You could hardly have
found a more representative selection. In fact because it is so
representative the Americans show up well to English critics because
that is a good selection too and it is so different, as US poetry is different
from ours. In the nineteenth century it was a copy of us. Now it is

something on its own. I can't say I'm mad about it. But it is the difference between the *New Yorker* and the good days of *Punch* or it is as different as Blunden from Robert Frost – we are more literary and local. I don't think your selection could have been better or more balanced. And you must have been hard put to it to select from Masefield. You chose far the best. Perhaps your most brilliant selection is that from Bridges – the exactly right proportion of the best lyrics and the 'Testament of Beauty'. What a marvellous poet Uncle Tom Eliot is. I loved re-reading him. I can't think of any omissions, unless it be Newbolt, some of whom I would have liked in favour of less de la Mare. De la Mare has never quite come off with me. It is rather like an Edwardian colour plate illustrated by Arthur Rackham – very good in its way, but his ghosts are not Hood's ghosts nor Ingoldsby's nor Monty James's. That is my only criticism of a book in which I am proud to be included, proud indeed and a bloody good selection. Oh no, it's absolutely *the* modern anthology and I shall use no other. Glad you like the Church book – the *second* edition with the hundreds of needed corrections and additions will be the one worth having of my church books.* Any you like to send welcomed by

   Yours gratefully, JB

*If it materialises.

> D.C., the writer, who had long been a fellow of New College, Oxford, was a close friend of JB and PB's. He had met JB through Maurice Bowra in the late twenties. He and the American poet Allen Tate were asked to compile an anthology of English and American verse. D.C. was unhappy about it and did not include much *avant-garde* poetry as he didn't like it – the book had bad reviews.

To Evelyn Waugh   The Mead
                                                     Wantage
[1958?]   Berkshire

My dear Evelyn,
I stayed last Sunday with John Osborne, a man I like very much and who (rightly) thinks you are the finest living writer in English. He told me how he wanted to put right with you a terrible error he felt he had made. He told me he wanted to make a film of *Pinfold* and that he dictated a draft letter to you which he was then going to copy out in his own hand. He went away for the middle of the week, when he returned he found his secretary had posted the letter and had, to make matters

worse, signed it, 'Dictated by J. Osborne and signed in his absence' – about the worst thing that could have happened. I said, 'What sort of a reply did you get?' He said, 'Very civil,' and gave the sad and understandable reasons for your not wanting *Pinfold* filmed yet. Well, now I've told you.

Penelope is off on a riding tour of Radnorshire and Montgomery and will call on the Widow [John Lloyd] who is once more Mayor of Montgomery.

Best wishes to Laura and Somerset. Best wishes to you. I have just been talking to old Patrick Balfour.

Yours, John B

JB had recently become a friend of the playwright John Osborne and been to stay at his mill house in Sussex which sported plush white close-fitting carpets everywhere.

To Mr, Mrs and Miss Prideaux-Brune   43 Cloth Fair
Undated [1959]   London EC1

Dear Mr and Mrs Prideaux-Brune and Miss W. Prideaux-Brune,
It was very kind of you to invite my friends and Jumbo and me to your house to luncheon yesterday. Speaking for them all, as I listened to their talk on the way back, I can say they thoroughly enjoyed themselves. Though they are not Strict and Particular Baptists as I am, but I was able to have a very serious discussion with Ted and I should be very pleased to meet him and his friends again and perhaps return the hospitality in London they so kindly showed to me in Cornwall. I am sorry to say that Jumbo drank too much before luncheon and displayed the frivolous side of his character to your elephants when he sat among them. I have found him very talkative and above himself since.

You may not know that I am the only bear member of the Society of Antiquaries and am entitled to put FSA after my name. I was interested to read the *Country Life* account of your house which I borrowed from Mr Betjeman [and] though I am only interested in bronze age burial mounds myself, I would like to suggest you should all visit Kilkhampton Church where you will find the carving of the Grenville Monuments by M. Cheke, a Cornish pupil of Grinling Gibbons, who did much work at Stowe [House] and which you may find bears a resemblance to the carving in your Reading Room. Mr Cheke's mortal remains, too long post-bronze age to interest me, lie in Kilkhampton Churchyard.

In concluding on this serious note, I am not unmindful of the kindness you showed to me and my less worthy companions Jumbo and Mr B[etjeman] and Lady E[lizabeth].

Yours very sincerely,
Archibald Ormsby-Gore FSA.

> While on holiday in Trebetherick, JB had taken Archie and Jumbo to lunch at Prideaux Place, the Elizabethan house overlooking the Camel Estuary at Padstow in Cornwall, at the special request of Miss P.-B. and as the guest of her parents whose family had always lived at the house. Miss P.-B. had read about them, and wanted to meet her family's large collection of bears and elephants, two of which sat at the table with Archie and Jumbo during lunch, while the rest were ranged around the shelves in the morning room.
>
> The Grenville Monuments, which Pevsner describes as being of 'indifferent quality', are in the magnificent lofty granite Church of St James, Kilkhampton, Cornwall. The P.-B.s had recently uncovered a marvellous carved ceiling at Prideaux Place.

To Mary Ling   The Mead
                                                  Wantage
4 January 1959   Berkshire

Dear Mary,
I was so sad when I read of Freddie's death that I had to write at once and call you by your Christian name which I hope you won't mind. I wanted someone to share the loss with, and though yours is greater, for you were the good wife he so badly needed and so thankfully found, I hope you will let one of his many friends say how sorry he feels and I will remember you both in my prayers regularly. I first knew Freddie when he was at St Stephen's House and I was an undergraduate at Oxford. Then at Cowley he was my confessor and conducted private retreats for me and the austerity of Cowley was made bearable by the anticipation of the delicious giggles we would have together when retreat was over. He came to stay with my wife and me at Uffington and Farnborough and he prepared my son Paul for confirmation – a preparation which 'took', for now aged twenty-one and an under-

graduate, he still keeps up his duties and was very sad to hear of the death of the friend of his early years. Freddie was one of the only *really* saintly and unworldly men that I ever met. I often used to say to people, 'The sort of man they ought to make a bishop is a saint like Freddie Ling.' Well, he's all right now and better than a bishop and he'll be there to meet us and he's still working for us. I'm sure of that. But the loss is horrible. It must be a great one for you. But it must also be a consolation to know you made the last years of his short life so happy. Please be sure of my prayers and affection. It is a privilege to have known Freddie, to have laughed and prayed with him. I hope we'll one day be able to meet and talk about him.

Yours ever, John Betjeman

Freddie Ling had died of kidney failure on 1 January.

M.L. sent Freddie's Greek Testament to JB in March. 'I am so pleased,' wrote JB (13 March 1959), 'I'm sure we'll see Freddie again. I often feel him near me in my prayers. He is a v[ery] good touchstone – "What would Freddie have done in this or that event?" and then one knows and it is clear and right. I miss him a lot.'

To Candida Betjeman   The Lawn Tennis Association
                                                   River Plate House
                                                   Finsbury Circus
28 January 1959   London EC2

Darling Wibz,

Very glad to have your entertaining letter re ski-ing and Le Puy. As you can see from the above, I am now in the sporting world too. I am in truth spending a few days at Edensor and have heard from Mummy that the Caff is doing v[ery] well, that Marco is recovering fast and his splint comes off this week, and that she is going to build up by the Pragnall's. I don't like that part. But perhaps she will abandon the idea later. I am leaving it to her to decide. She tries to be there more than you, or the P[owlie] or I and she must decide.

Last week I went to Cambridge to do a turn at the Arts Theatre with Joyce Grenfell and I hired a car to drive back to Edensor. It was a lovely crisp frosty night with the moon lighting miles of fen and church towers and willows. Then suddenly outside Nottingham the car landed into a dense fog and I had to walk directing the very nit-witted driver for miles – about six miles. In the centre of Nottingham where we could not even see whether there were houses or shops because you could not even see the width of the pavement let alone the width of the road, we were stranded at three a.m. with everything dead still. Together we set out to find a police station. In a few yards I found an hotel and luckily the night porter was awake and we got beds. It was intensely cold and there were no shillings to put in the electric fire meter. My bedroom was cream-and-coffee-coloured with naked electric bulbs. At breakfast next day there was marmalade on the butter, crumbs in the marmalade and the same knife for kippers as well as for one's toast.

I am delighted but not surprised that you won a prize for drawing or rather were top out of sixty-eight. You are an artist all right. It remains to be seen whether it will take the form of words or pencil and brush with you. All artists suffer. So don't worry if you suffer. It is your heritage. Perhaps you'll reach such a stage of detachment that you will welcome suffering. I have not done that yet! Back on Monday to 43 C[loth] F[air] and Wantage.

> Where the TV masts are thickest
> Where the lorries pass the quickest
> Up the bypass and over the Brent
> That's the way to the Duchess of Kent.

Tons of love from MD

> JB was using this writing paper as a joke.
> PB sold the field where she used to grow kale, north-east of the Mead, for building.
> JB had often worked with and written material for the comedienne Joyce Grenfell.
> JB had fallen head over heels for the Duchess of Kent whom he had only seen from a distance, and in photographs in the press.

To Cecil Roberts   The Mead
                                                     Wantage
13 February 1959   Berkshire

Dear Cecil,
I loved your letter. Nassau! By jove. And to think that our late vicar Roscow Sheddon here was its Bishop. The Cathedral ought to be nice

and High. Perhaps the millionaires will missionise England from there via the church in Nassau. We all need money here for saving old churches.

I have become Ella Wheeler Wilcox overnight. But set no store by it. I now have two of your volumes – and nice they are too – *Through Eyes of Youth* and *Twenty-six Poems* and look forward to your seventieth birthday number.

I dare not drop journalism until my son (now at Oxford and with two years and a bit to go) and daughter (in France and aged sixteen and pretty and clever) are off my hands. Then, by jove, I will. I'm now fifty-two. Can I last the course? I must. Penelope has a small income and so have I, enough to live on, just – but only just.

I must say you do write a good letter. You really ought not to give up writing, even if it has to be in prose for a bit. Your power to interest and hold attention is something marvellous. Last week Freya Stark came here and told me that when she was ill in Persia in some remote place, the only two books in her place of being ill were two of your novels and she read and re-read them and they kept her going. Had I known I was going to hear from you, I would have asked her which they were. She implied that they saved her sanity. I liked very much your 'In A Garden' poem. Keep it up. God bless you. And thank you for writing.

Yours with love, John B

C.R. (1892–1976), the author, and native of Nottingham, had been very successful in the 1920s with his first novel *Scissors*. From then on his decline was gradual but his output prolific. In the late fifties he began to prepare for a literary revival, entertaining biographers and befriending literary figures such as JB, whom he had met at the Athenæum. He was full of lively gossip, likeable and had a hotel life, almost always at the Grand Hotel in Rome.

To Miss Knight   43 Cloth Fair
26 February 1959   London EC1

Dear Miss Knight,
I am sorry you have had so much trouble to get me. I delayed agreeing a fee until I knew how much work was involved. This is now completed. It involved reciting four of my poems, visiting different parts of London one afternoon with Ken Russell, spending a morning at Aldersgate here, being filmed and speaking an introduction into the microphone. Spending an afternoon at King's Cross and Vauxhall Park, being filmed and speaking. Spending a morning going to Hatfield

and being filmed there. Going to Ealing to record. And going on
another afternoon to Vauxhall Park and Finchley. As a self-employed
person my time is my chief expense. Do you really think forty guineas
is enough for what represents a good half-week's work? I do not wish to
be demanding and embarrass the promoters of what I think is an
interesting experiment. But if there is any money to spare I wouldn't
say no to some of it.

  Yours sincerely, John Betjeman

> Miss K. worked in the accounts department of the BBC.
>   JB finally agreed on fifty guineas for his part in the *Monitor* programme for BBC
> Television which was called *A Poet in London*.

To Edgar Walmsley   The Mead
                                                        Wantage
21 March 1959   Berkshire

Dear Sir,
I am proud to be asked to commend the appeal for repairs to St Peter's
spire, Wallingford. It is a stately landmark from many reaches of the
Thames, a worthy welcome to this historic town as one crosses the
bridge from Oxfordshire and a reminder that Wallingford was once a
town of many churches and of great strategic importance. The spire
itself is elegant and unique, the work of a famous Georgian architect,
Sir Robert Taylor, in 1777, and one of the few eighteenth-century
Gothic spires in the country. It is original, light and well-proportioned,
designed as a deliberate contrast with the more solid masonry of the
tower below it. In England where skyline is so important because of our
usually grey climate, a spire like this is a treasure to be preserved at all
costs.

  Yours sincerely, John Betjeman

> Canon E.W. was the priest in charge of St Peter's. This letter is typical of the sort JB
> often wrote to help churches all over the country, and E.W. used it in his brochure for an
> appeal of £1,500.

To Deborah Devonshire

1 May 1959
LABOUR DAY

The Mead
Wantage
Berkshire

My dearest Debo,
I find it hard to believe that this time last week Feeble [EC] and I were sitting in a bar in Mallow eating our sandwiches and drinking Guinness after testing the mineral water in Mallow Spa, an 1840s building near the gasworks. Those glorious days of Lismore were some of the best and most fruitful I have ever spent in my life as I was able to write verse, talk rubbish to Feeble and you and the kiddiz, play with Andrew and admire the castle and cathedral. The phrase 'play with Andrew' is Feeble's. She said one morning I was to go upstairs and write poetry and 'not go playing about with Andrew' until after I had written it.

We had a delicious journey to Dublin. Feeble spent a lot of it asleep in a corner seat, her long white jewelled fingers lying similarly on her knees. She is much too big to fit easily into Irish railway carriages. I can never thank you enough for your kindness to me. I feel really set up and ready to face anything. Oh, that elegant Cathedral of St Carthage, Lismore.
    Love, John B

> JB and EC had stayed at Lismore Castle from 18 to 26 April.

To Miss E. Wakeham
19 May 1959

43 Cloth Fair
London EC1

Dear Miss Wakeham,
Any old thing you like to do, with any old thing by me, is acceptable to me. You have *carte blanche*; I trust you and your dear little copyright department implicitly as a source of unexpected income to
    Yours sincerely, John Betjeman

> Miss E.W. worked in the copyright department of the BBC.

To Candida Betjeman   The Mead
                                                        Wantage
5 June 1959   Berkshire

Darling Wibz,
This is marvellous news of your helping in the festival at Spoleto. Jenny
[Crosse] Nicholson is a very good writer indeed. She once wrote a piece
in, I think, the *Spectator* on Max Beerbohm which moved me to tears.
Her father Robert Graves is, with Tom Eliot, the best living English
poet. You are *right in the swim*. Peter Mills told me that *Gigi* was the best
English film this year. He knows.

Here I am as usual, at my desk in the library writing 'no' to people
who ask me to lecture – 'I fear we cannot offer more than a token fee of
three guineas, but can assure you of a small but enthusiastic audience.'
It may not be easy to get four seats for *West Side Story*. I'll do my best for
a matinée after July 15th.

Nigel [Baring] stayed at 43 C[loth] F[air] on pre-Derby night and
gave me the first and second which I backed! But only ten shillings each
way and I shared it out with the one-armed waiter 'Harry' at
Coltman's.

You sound very happy. So does Powlie. He and I and Mummy had a
lovely evening last week at the Rose Revived, Newbridge on the Isis.
We dined and then went in a punt (P[owlie] punting) through those
sunset-sodden meadows of the upper Thames piping with blackbirds
and cuckoos and full of Matthew Arnold and William Morris. If you
had been there it would have been complete.

Buffy [Charteris], as I told you, made an excellent Maid of Honour
to her Mum.

Oh, Social Life open wide thy Sun and shine on Harpy Wibz!
Tons and tons of love, MD

> I was in Rome learning about architecture.
>   Jenny Nicholson, granddaughter of the painter Sir William Nicholson (who kept her
> mother's name) was helping to run the first year of the Spoleto Festival and asked me to
> be her assistant.
>   Peter Mills was a television film director who had worked with JB.

To Anne Channel   The Mead
                                                        Wantage
11 July 1959   Berkshire

Dear Anne,
Treen of all houses I should like best. It was sweet of you to let me
know. I will write by this post to Mrs Moorhead. You are a good friend
to me. I come down with Paul and Candida to the Thomases
Sept[ember] 7th to 21st and they are the most precious and happy days
of the year.
    I shall be interested to hear what happens to Trenain.
    Love, John B

> JB had met the glamorous A.C. (see *Volume One*) in the 1920s. Thrice married, by this
> time she lived at Tresevens (which JB called Tresixes) in Rock. Back in 1951, he had
> asked her to keep an eye out for a house that he might buy. He bought Treen, a modest
> Trebetherick-style house in Daymer Lane in December 1959.
>   Trenain, a nearby farmhouse, was bought by David Astor, editor of the *Observer*.

To Compton Mackenzie   The Mead
                                                        Wantage
12 July 1959   Berkshire

Dear Monty,
I have never known you in better form, never laughed and enjoyed
myself so much in your company – and that is saying a lot for every visit
to you is like treble whiskys – as I did this time. I always wish I had a
tape recorder with me. Jamie Stormonth Darling told me as we were
walking from the Albyn Rooms [Restaurant] to the air terminal that it
was the best lunch he had had for years. All this was a necessary
prelude and fortification for the unexampled agony I had after my
septic wisdom tooth was taken out in Queen's Gate. I have not known
such torture since school days. And the climax was like a bad dream
come true for I had, last Friday, to address CONVOCATION of the Royal
College of Art, South Ken[sington] only a few yards off from the
nursing home. At breakfast I felt so sick I could not move but just
sweated. I called in a doctor who drugged me so that I could walk and I
was taken to the assembly hall where Augustus John, dressed like a
Druid in robes, John Piper also robed, James Law, Colin Anderson,

Robin Darwin and all the nobs of the art world and five hundred students agog for a 'rag' and one thousand parents and trumpeters and an orchestra and then I had to speak. I TALKED INCOHERENT ROT. There was very modified applause at the end and at the excellent lunch afterwards at which I was in such pain I could not enjoy it, people very kindly did not refer to my speech. In fact they refrained in rather a marked manner. Oh, I *do* look back on Edinburgh as to the sunlight of another and happier world and God bless you and Chrissie for your kindness to

Yours ever, John B

JB had lunched with C.M. in Edinburgh.
  J. Stormonth Darling eventually became director of the National Trust for Scotland.

To John Hadfield   The Mead
                                                          Wantage
29 July 1959   Berkshire

Dear Hadfield,
Eddie [Hulton] told me I was to send my manuscript (kindly sent by Eddie's secretary) of *Church Poetry* to you before July 31st. None of us realised at the time that I was going to have a further relapse as a result of this poisoning from my wisdom tooth. I have however while in bed read quantities of poetry with the Anthology in mind and have collected so far what you see on the enclosed two sheets. I would add to it: 'The Vicar' by Praed which I enclose, though I have not collated this text with my own edition of Praed.

I have also to look through nineteenth-century poetry now and am wondering whether we ought not to end with Philip Larkin's poem called 'In Church' or 'Visiting a Church' or something like that, of which I have not a copy here. The only other living writer I would wish to include would be about a dozen lines from Blunden, which again are up in London.

There may of course be something by Andrew Young and R. S. Thomas. But I shan't mind if we omit the living.

I had hoped to find some church poetry earlier than the seventeenth century. But this I could not do because poetry then was religious in the sense that it did not describe the buildings in which ceremonies occurred but took them for granted. Even in the seventeenth century the building and its use are wedded, as may be seen in George Herbert.

It was not until the eighteenth century became romantic about Gothic and the Regency concerned with characters of priests and their stipends, and the Victorians concerned with the ceremonies of the Church, that what might be definitely called church poetry came into existence. I have omitted deliberately all poetry which is not concerned with the Church of England, as if I moved off into the sects there would be another quality in the book.

I am enclosing for you typescripts of those poems which are not easily available. Those which are, are on my lists and the references to where they can be found are given. Will you of your great kindness tell me roughly how many more pages I am required to fill, supposing there be two pages of introduction (though this could be reduced to one). As I say I have not yet had time fully to investigate the nineteenth century, and I want to put in some comic verse such as 'The Anglican's Alphabet'. I hope that what I have sent you is not too much work. Did I feel better, I would do it myself. In about a week I should be much better.

Yours sincerely, John Betjeman

J.H., who had been director of the National Book League, and now worked for the publisher Edward Hulton, was in charge of *Altar and Pew*, an anthology of church poetry, which JB edited and which came out later that year in the *Pocket Poets* series. The volume, 'confined to descriptions of churches, their priests and people', included Philip Larkin's 'Church Going', Browning's 'Easter Day', John Meade Jackson's 'After Trinity', Hardy's 'Afternoon Service at Mellstock', and 'The Vicar' by Praed.

To George Barnes   The Mead
                                                                  Wantage
5 August 1959   Berkshire

My dear Commander,
I am deeply touched that from a sick bed and in the space between pains you should write to me.

Like you, I've spent my life avoiding pain, mental and, particularly, physical. I only know tooth pains and have faint memories of my only other operation. I know enough however to know how awful pain is, I sometimes think it is the only thing which will reconcile me to dying – to get out of pain. But Anne is quite right. It either is or is not. And when it is not how wonderfully happy one is, even with a cream wall and beige dado which I expect you have at Nathan House. I cannot see that pain serves any purpose except to give one joy and thankfulness for not having it. And as all things on this earth have to be partly in shadow or one couldn't see them, I suppose there has to be pain. I don't think doctors do enough about pain. I remember [Cyril] Joad telling me that when he was ill. They don't seem to realise what it is. They get case-hardened otherwise matrons wouldn't use that word 'not so comfortable' for screaming agony. But the Matron *did* tell me when I telephoned that you were going to get all right. That is something, even if you have to go through a few more tunnels of torture on the way. Keep going for Anne's sake and L[ittle] F[riend]'s and that of your chums and Little P[rawls] and Mrs Little P[rawls] and the kiddi [Brendan] my godson and for poor Feeble's sake – who is only seaweed and drifts as though always drugged.

I've had a letter from a cousin of old Mrs Stirling who is ninety-four and lives in Battersea House which contains:

1) The best and biggest collection of de Morgan's pottery. Mrs S[tirling] is his daughter.

2) Pictures by her sister Evelyn de Morgan.

3) Jacobean furniture v[ery] fine.

4) *Objets d'art*.

Battersea Council have turned down the offer of the house. The Nat[ional] Trust can't afford to keep it up with all the endowment she can afford. What is to happen? Would your college take it on – the collection I mean – for its Pottery and Pre-Raph[aelite] interest? Perhaps this seems remote to you now under the influence of lovely morphia.

Today on my way back from Linc[oln]s[hire] I stopped for three hours at Rugby and can safely say that Butterfield's nave and chancel of the parish church is one of the great wonders of architecture for scale, mystery, subtle colourings (mauves and greys). It is better even than Rugby Chapel.

I go to E[lizabeth]'s cottage at Edensor with Osbert and Kareen [Lancaster] on Monday and will make a point of coming into Manchester to see you and giving a drink or two to Anne.

Meanwhile remember you are buoyed up by the prayers of the faithful Anglo nuns, and the prayers are like angels' wings holding you up and of course you are in a state of grace. If you think fucking puts you out of Grace, you're bloody well wrong. You can't have done any for some weeks! Have H[oly] C[ommunion] and remember it helps *body* as well as soul.

Love, John B

G.B. had been admitted to the Christie Hospital in Manchester where he was being treated for cancer. He wrote, 'Your letter did me no end of good. I must climb out of this well. There's no exit at the bottom.'

C. E. M. Joad, the philosopher and *Brains Trust* contributor, and friend of JB's, died of cancer in 1953.

Old Battersea House was bought by the rich American, Malcolm Forbes, the head of a large publishing organisation. (It remains the property of the Forbes Corporation and is used by them for residential purposes.)

To Osbert and Karen Lancaster   Moor View
                                                           Edensor
                                                           Bakewell
13 August 1959   Derbyshire

Dearest Osbert and Kareen,
We miss you here at Moor View a lot though I left Wantage on Monday in torrential rain with floods which continued to Brackley where I entered a dim empty Great Central train to Chesterfield. There was no rain here. The water situation is no joke and even poor feeble Elizabeth smells a little. There is no water here at all. Brown water from the fields is poured into the lavatory and cold clean water is brought up in a churn for drinking and washing. Without a doubt two is the utmost the house can take in this state. Feeble and I are reading *Richard Feverel*. It's marvellous. Jim Lees-Milne came in last night from the Peacock where he is staying and read with us. I keep thinking how you and K. would love it. Mrs Fountain seems unperturbed. Debo and Andrew [Devonshire] have gone to Bolton. What is v[ery] ironic is that there is plenty of water at Chatsworth though the fountain has been turned off out of respect for public opinion. Today it is damp and rained a little at breakfast time. They *say* that it needs two weeks of rain before the taps work.

Love from John B
We'll send you a wire if the water does come on.

O.L. (see *Volume One*), the artist and cartoonist, was one of JB's oldest friends – they had met at Oxford. O.L. and his wife Karen (who JB always referred to as 'Kareen') lived in Henley-on-Thames and had two children, Cara and William.

The novel *The Ordeal of Richard Feverel* by George Meredith (1828–1909) was published in 1859.

To Rupert Hart-Davis   PUBLIC SERVICES TO DEAD POETS LTD
                                Cloth Fair
20 August 1959   London EC1

My dear Rupert,
The Sonnets of Charles Tennyson Turner (1808–79), the elder brother
of the Bard [Alfred Lord Tennyson], are so surprisingly beautiful that
they ought to be republished in selected form. Macmillans produced
the collected volume of three hundred and forty-seven of them in 1898.
These were too many. They vary in quality but the best, of which Sir
Charles Tennyson and I would make a selection, could be reduced to a
hundred. Will you consider this? Have a look at 'The Brilliant Day',
'Harvest Home', 'Our New Church Clock', 'Wind on the Corn' and
see if you don't agree. I will send you the Macmillan volume if you can't
get it. With an etching or wood engraving of Grasby? and the long view
over the marsh from the wolds, this would make a handsome book to
delight all lovers of poetry and of clear, unregarded, wide-skied
Linc[oln]s[hire].
    Yours ever, John B

> JB had always worshipped Alfred Tennyson, loved Lincolnshire as a result and was
> active in the Tennyson Society.
>   R.H.-D. agreed to publish a selected volume edited by Sir Charles and JB which was
> called *A Hundred Sonnets of Charles Tennyson Turner*. It came out in 1960. Fifteen hundred
> copies were printed and JB and Charles Tennyson received twenty-five pounds advance
> each. 'I am afraid this seems a very small reward for all your trouble,' wrote R.H.-D. to
> Charles Tennyson (3 February 1960), 'but I am afraid the book will be hard enough to
> sell at fifteen shillings.'

To Michael Maclagan   The Mead
                                               Wantage
8 September 1959   Berkshire
Polling Day

My dear Michael,
It was most kind of you to take all that trouble over the son of my friend
Jack James. The Master of the Mint will be touched and pleased and
now it is up to Harrow to do its best for the boy. His history masters,
Jack tells me, regard him as exceptional so the scholarship idea is a good
one.

Why do I think Harrow the best school in England? To avoid talking to you too much while we discuss the heating at Uffington and the tablet for Pusey on Monday, I will write my reasons now:

(1) It is rich and slack.

(2) Being near London its masters can get away from each other.

(3) In lecturing at schools, I have always found Harrovians the most awake and sensitive audiences.

(4) For its size it has produced more *varied* distinguished men than any other school. Churchill, Cecil Beaton, Wyndham Ketton Cremer, Victor Pasmore, Lord Alexander, Arnold Lunn, G. M. Trevelyan, Terence Rattigan, Dornford Yates, John Summerson, Villiers David, Lord Somervell – not to mention all the great Harrovians of the past, Byron, Peel, Trollope.

(5) I like the songs.

(6) I love Metroland.

(7) You get a room to yourself.

Yours gratefully, John B

> M.M., a fellow of Trinity College, Oxford (1939–79) and chairman of the Oxford Diocesan Advisory Committee for twenty years, remarked, 'We were very lucky to have JB and John Piper on the committee at the same time.'
> Michael James, son of Jack James, did get a place at Harrow.

To John Summerson   On the G[reat] W[estern] R[ailway]
                                          As from The Mead
                                          Wantage
28 September 1959   Berkshire

My dear Coolmore,
I've read you in a Batsford book, a thing I thought I'd never do and with delight as I thought I would. It is a good selection and it shows that we have at any rate one good pair of architects, A. and P. Smithson – also R. Tubbs, and whoever it was who designed the low blocks at Churchill Gardens. Walking about in new L[ondon] C[ounty] C[ouncil] estates as I have been doing lately convinces me that the low blocks and the two-storey and single-storey houses are what we really need. I have found no large blocks I have visited either liked or inviting – they are just plot ratio buildings. What you say at the end of your essay on the role of the architect is gloriously put in your purest,

clearest Harrovian prose. And my goodness, it shows what an unenviable profession the art has become. How true it is that siting and town planning in its literal sense are the chief thing now after shapes. Shapes can only be made by artists like Smithson (and R. Erith I fancy and, dare I say it, at times by Vincent Harris). Oh my word, it *is* a good essay.

But why I wrote was to say how glad I was to see a tribute to our gloomy old friend P. Morton Shand. He is in a bad way. Could you not soften his last days by having him made an Hon. F[ellow of the] R[oyal] I[nstitute of] B[ritish] A[rchitects]? We ought somehow to give him a public pat on the back. He knew it all, as you say, long before Pevsner (and so did you and I). But he started it and always saw through the spoofs.

Cheerioh ole man, John B

The Batsford book was *Modern Architecture in Britain* by Trevor Dannatt – with an introduction by John Summerson. Untypical of Batsford, and J.S.'s last significant piece of writing on modern architecture, with some complimentary sentences about P. Morton Shand: 'Scholar, wit and cosmopolitan with an equal flair for vintages in wine and architecture.'

Ralph Tubbs was architect of the Dome of Discovery at the Festival of Britain. The secondary modern school at Hunstanton, Norfolk, is by A. and P. Smithson.

Churchill Gardens was an award-winning LCC estate in Pimlico by Powell and Moya.

P. Morton Shand was indeed in a bad way by this time but JB and J.S.'s attempts to get their old friend honoured by the Royal Institute of British Architects fell on stony ground, as did JB's attempts to get him made a 'Master of Wine'.

To Evelyn Waugh   The Mead
                                                       Wantage
30 October 1959   Berkshire

My dear Evelyn,

I must write to tell you how much I enjoyed every page of the Ronnie Knox book. Why nobody can write so well as you I cannot understand. The *speed* with which your paragraphs go – the neatness of them – the lovely bits of wit, 'Lindsay bided his time' and that kind of thing. Oh, it *is* a pleasure to read such a book. I'm sure R[onnie] A. K[nox] is pleased with it. Poor man, what agonies he must have gone through when he left the C[hurch] of E[ngland] and how bad was the behaviour of the hierarchy towards his translation. As I read the book I thanked God I had been spared the sort of decisions he had to make. *God moves in a mysterious way*. I wonder if you will get an angry letter from, let us say, Archbishop Amigo's old unmarried sister, if there is such a lady. Yet all you say is wholly justified. I was interested to see so much about Maurice Child whom I knew well.

It might interest you to know that the fête at Mells which you mention and which I opened was much helped by Ronnie Knox and Christopher H[ollis] and the Asquiths. R[onnie] K[nox] wrote to me asking me to open it. It must have been one of the last business affairs he attended to. It makes one proud to think I was concerned in it. I remember how very ill he was at that time and what willpower he must have had to summon to come out and be photographed for the local paper, for he could hardly move about. Your book brings out his quiet detailed selflessness.

Penelope has not been able to get the book till today, although it is here, as I pinched it and read it in bed at nights.

I travelled in the train yesterday with Mrs Alec Waugh. Penelope travelled back from the USA with Alec Waugh.

The vicar of Crowcombe [near Combe Florey] is an interesting study – the Reverend Peter Burkett.

Love to Laura.

Yours, John B

E.W.'s *The Life of the Right Reverend Ronald Knox* had just come out.

R. Knox, E.W.'s close friend, was diagnosed as having cancer in January 1957. They went to Torquay together towards the end of June of that year and E.W. offered to write his biography. During July, Knox took to his bed and died in August at his home, the Manor House, Mells, Somerset.

Alec Waugh, the travel writer and novelist, was E.W.'s brother.

To Penelope Betjeman   Moor View
                                                         Edensor
                                                         Bakewell
27 November 1959   Derby

My darling Plymmi,
I hope you are all quite well and ta for yours of yesterday which arrived when I was in London doing the Vic[torian] Soc[iety] Reception in Drapers' Hall with Anne Rosse and Lord Esher.

The Rev[erend] Harry Williams was awfully good last night about 'Death' on the wireless. He said that we were dying all the time and that refusing to die meant you lost your life, as Jesus said. Refusing to see various manifestations – e.g. putting everything away neatly, seizing worldly power, clinging to the past (like I do with Archie), ordering people about, resenting criticism. It simply was a manifestation of not daring to trust yourself to the unknown. We aren't afraid of extinction *really*, because we can't make our flesh creep with the thought of not being born. But we *can* make our flesh creep with the thought of losing power over ourselves and being pushed about by circumstances. This all leads to the need to trust God and to the moment of departure from the body being one of excitement and adventure if one trusts.

Of course I've put it badly which he didn't. Thursdays in Advent at 10.30 p.m. on Home Service. We must listen next week. Then it's Judgement. After that Hell, then Heaven.

I've got to Sezincote in my autobiography and am finding it v[ery] hard to move on to the delight one had at dining with Maurice.

I do look forward to seeing you and hope to come back *Wednesday* night by the 9.50 to Didcot.

Don't fall off any more. Be careful.

Yorz trewely, Tewpie

The Reverend Harry Williams wrote and broadcast in the fifties and sixties on religion. He supplied a need to those who wanted to go further with their Christian faith and understanding than tradition took them. JB and EC embraced his philosophy and Harry became a close friend.

To Woodrow Wyatt   43 Cloth Fair
28 January 1960   London EC1

Dear Woodrow,
How right you were in raising the matter of Euston Great Arch when you did. The bloody British Transport Commission has now come into the open. I am doing a little piece in the *Telegraph* on Monday week. But that immediately gives a political slant, because it appears in that paper, to something that is far more important than politics. I think that there

should be a survey made at the instigation of Parliament of all railway architecture and preservation orders put on those stations, viaducts, bridges and tunnel entrances which are worth preserving. In architectural and historic significance they are obviously equal to ruined castles. As to the lodges at Grosvenor Gate, I fear I was only speaking from memory of what occurred at the stinking old Royal Fine Art Commission when they were mentioned and somebody said that they had been mucked about since [Decimus] Burton's time and it was not really worth fighting a battle for their retention even on another site. I may be wrong.

Yours, with love to Maria, John B

JB first met W.W., then a Labour MP, soon after the war. He recalls, 'I had lovely visits with him to places like Stourhead and often met him later staying at Chatsworth.'

The Euston 'Arch' – in fact, a Greek propylaeum or entrance gate – was the greatest monument of the Railway Age. Designed by Philip Hardwick, it was built at the London terminus of the first trunk railway in the world in 1837. A century later, the London Midland and Scottish Railway proposed its demolition to make way for a new Euston station but the newly created Georgian Group, of which JB was a founder member, persuaded the company that the Arch could be saved by re-erection on the Euston Road. War cancelled these plans and twenty years on, in 1959, the British Transport Commission, mindlessly determined to shed the steam image of British Railways, insisted the Arch must go when the main line was electrified and a new terminus built. The younger Hardwick's Great Hall was probably always doomed, but JB – who thought it 'the noblest thing in London' – and the newly founded Victorian Society, amongst others, argued that the Arch could and should be moved and saved, although none of the authorities involved was prepared to foot the bill.

Decimus Burton (1800–81), the architect, was a leading figure in the Classical Revival. His masterpiece is the Athenæum, London.

To Candida Betjeman   The Mead
                                                              Wantage
31 January 1960   Berkshire

Darling Wibbly Wobbly,
I was ever so pleased, dear, to get your essays in the hobby which has brought me fame. I like the 'I hug my knees' one and the 'teenage desperation' and the 'teenage dream'. My God! What hell one goes through with one's emotions and how hard it is to put them down in words without coming out as commonplace as the words on a greeting card.

I wish I knew about scansion. Both of us know about it instinctively. It is partly a matter of the right number of syllables in the lyric – as in your 'Late Evening in Florence' poem – partly, indeed more, to do with stress. For instance Pope's famous couplet:

> Where thou, great Anna, whom three realms obey
> Doth sometimes counsel take, and sometimes tea*

scans perfectly, but supposing you change round the words of the second line to:

> Doth counsel take sometimes, and sometimes tea.

There are still the right number of syllables and the same sense, but the line does not scan because the stress has been altered. I'm quite certain the only way to write poetry is to say out loud what one has written again and again, changing the words round until they are in the correct order, for stress, sense and rhyme. This sometimes means altering whole verses or the whole scheme of a poem. And while one is doing this, the mood of the poem goes and one is fed up with it, so that one is left with an uncompleted fragment which may never be used, even when the mood crops up again, possibly weeks later. When I look at the poems I wrote when I was your age, I see they are much, *much* worse than yours. So you may easily achieve real fame, if you go on, not spurious fashionableness which is all I have. The question is, will you go on? It is all a matter of practice. I know nothing in the world, not even love, quite so fulfilling as completing a poem to one's satisfaction.

Powlie and his friend Susan May (who seems to me a very nice girl, quiet and comfortable and calm and good and reliable), Johnny Fry and the Hislops [John and Jean] and Dom Harrod are coming to lunch. As usual someone has drunk all the gin and sherry and I must now go out to a pub and buy some. Really that 'teenage dream' has got something. It rings so true in its first joyousness. What was it Wordsworth said? 'Poetry is emotion recollected in tranquillity.' I dare say a lot of it is.

Tons and tons of love, MD.

I go to White Horses tomorrow for a fortnight (i.e. till Feb[ruary] 14th) to complete my long poem.

* Pronounced 'tay' in the eighteenth century.

At seventeen I was churning out reams and reams of appallingly bad poems, which I always sent to JB.

To Martyn Skinner   The Mead
                                                       Wantage
23 February 1960   Berkshire

Dear Martyn,
I shall not soon forget your heart-warming and appreciative letter.
That our paths have been so similar is probably the reason why you
show so deep an understanding of the subject of that blank verse. But
what pleases me most is that you (and John Sparrow) alone know – or at
any rate have expressed – the laborious technique that went to make it
seem effortless and readable and concise at the same time. I knew that I
had done that, but until you wrote I did not realise anyone had
consciously seen that I had made that particular effort. It involved
cutting out a lot of dead stuff. Now that you have written I feel
immensely cheered up, for this awful publicity (much of it well-
meaning) has been getting me down. It is much harder to overcome
riches than poverty and you have done the former and gone on writing
your poetry as you have been called to do and may you long continue to
do so – unless you do, I don't think you'll feel fulfilled, so I know you
will go on despite discouragement.
    I say, Berkhamsted must have been hell and you may have known W.
W. Jacobs in the [Graham] Greene–[Peter] Quennell set and the
Hastings family of the *Architectural Review*. [C. S.] Lewis was my
undoing at Magdalen as well as my own temperament. Thompie [J. M.
Thompson] was a wealth of goodness and I loved him. You were lucky
with him as Tutor. A Happy Christmas and N[ew] Y[ear] to you and
more gratitude than I can well express for your letter.
    Yours, JB

> M.S. had first written to JB a long blank verse eulogy about *Summoned by Bells*, when it
> came out in extracts in the *Sunday Times*, before the book's publication:
>
>> And yours *is* [a masterpiece], judging by the one instalment,
>> And judged by one who's spent his life, like you,
>> Transmuting with creative alchemy
>> The world around him into strokes of ink.
>> To write a poem on a massive scale
>> In these prose times is not an easy task
>> Even without distractions – and success
>> Can be the most insidious of all.
>
> M.S. had been at school at Berkhamsted with Graham Greene, Peter Quennell and
> W. W. Jacobs.
>   J. M. Thompson (see *Volume One*) was tutor of history at Magdalen.

To Harry Jarvis   43 Cloth Fair
25 March 1960   London EC1

My dear Harry,
I was enchanted with your account of the deanery chapter. F[athe]r
Hassett sounds very nice. I wonder if you could swop pulpits with him
with permission of Stephen C. [Ralph Foster]. Yesterday I had a nice
evening with F[athe]r Foxell, sub-dean of the Chapels Royal and rector
of St James Garlickhythe, a silken-voiced, grey silken-haired pluralist,
mod-High. His City church has been locked and unrepaired since the
war but there are faint signs of its being restored – which was why I was
there – and I don't think he relishes the prospect. He asked me if I knew
anyone who wanted any myrrh. He has a lot and does not know what to
do with it. It is presented together with twenty-five gold sovereigns and
incense (not smoking of course) on behalf of the Queen by Yeomen of
the Guard in the Chapel Royal at the Epiphany Mass. He gives the
incense to [Canon] Freddy [Hood] and gets twenty-five pounds in
notes from the bank in return for the sovereigns and these he gives to the
Aged Poor. To my great surprise F[athe]r Foxell was only too pleased
to accompany the architect and me into that public house at the back of
Freddy's church and to which Freddy does not go for the sake of
decorum. The myrrh, by the way, is supplied by Savory and Moore.
    The Minor Prophet is not much good. He has no sense of proportion
and therefore v[ery] little humour. He has no initiative and, poor chap,
through no fault of his own a personality which drives me nearly mad
with irritation so that he is an occasion of sin. I'm lunching with Freddy
on Wednesday and will ask him to find another job for him. I don't
think I can get rid of him until this is done. He would be v[ery] happy in
a sorting office or filling in forms. If Freddy can otherwise employ him,
I will try and get David [Woodger] who would see the point of the silly
life I lead here. The Minor Prophet is very good – really good – and
makes me feel worldly and old in sin. But he is a bore – remarks on the
weather and asks futile questions. Let me have David's address again
(I've lost it) just in case Freddy can employ the M[inor] P[rophet]
elsewhere.
    Feeble is getting v[ery] pale and washed out again. Partly it is
insecurity about me. I love her. But I also love – and very deeply –
Penelope and the kiddiz. If Feeble falls in love elsewhere, I will be able
just to get along. Of course, without her, I would probably write
nothing more except the dreariest hackwork and would get still more

into debt. But I don't really mind about that. I do mind about not hurting Feeble. I'm so glad we are in your prayers.

Feeble and I hope to come to Edensor on April 1st (Friday) until the Wed[nesday] before Easter (13th). So we will see you. As soon as we are out of London we become calmer. I have bought a bicycle for London. It is dangerous but healthy exercise and saves packets in railway fares.

Last Monday Feeble and I were asked to a tiny little dinner party, my dear, just Anne Rosse and the Earl [Michael Rosse] and the Happy Couple. I thought of poor Hugh [Pickles]. I am writing to Hugh to tell him of our impending arrival at Edensor.

Yours, John B

The Reverend H.J. had met JB after the annual cricket dinner in 1947 in Wantage where he lived – he became JB's temporary secretary for a year between 1959 and 1960, and he left to go to Worksop Priory in Nottinghamshire.

The Reverend Ralph Foster was nicknamed 'Stephen C.' after the composer of popular music, Stephen C. Foster.

Canon Freddy Hood was guild vicar of St Mary Aldermary London and a close friend of JB's. He found places of work for men of the church who had fallen by the wayside. 'It gave him a sense of power which he adored,' remembered H.J.

'The Minor Prophet' was an unfrocked cleric who had become the replacement for H.J.

David Woodger was a friend of H.J.'s.

'The Happy Couple' were Princess Margaret and Tony Armstrong-Jones, Anne Rosse's son by her previous marriage.

Hugh Pickles was curate at Wantage.

To Cyril Connolly   The Mead
                                                                Wantage
11 April 1960   Berkshire

My dear Cyril,

I have read many wonderful writings of yours, but none so devastatingly funny and such glorious parody as yesterday's thing in the *Sunday Times* about that American critical bore. Have no sorry feelings about the impermanence of newspaper writing. Your wit must be collected again in a book and the newspapers do at least ensure that such good writing as yours has the wide circulation it deserves. Oh well done, old boy. It *was* good. I have cut it out and kept it and will read it to anyone I meet who hasn't seen it.

Love, John B

C.C. (see *Volume One*), the celebrated literary critic and intellectual figure, was a friend from Oxford days.

He had written a *Sunday Times* review (10 April 1960) of Hugh Kenner's *The Invisible Poet: T. S. Eliot*.

To George Barnes   The Mead
                                                       Wantage
14 April 1960   Berkshire

My dear Commander,
I was asking the nurses at Bart's today about pain, with your letter to me (which moved me greatly) in mind. It seems that very little is known about it. There is no means of measuring it as it is a comparative thing and does all sorts of odd tricks according to one's mind. It is not, however, necessary for you to feel deep despair about your post-op[eration] pain. Like sorrow it goes in waves. First a high wave of it and then it subsides and the next wave is nearly as high but not quite and the next a little less. Only when one is tired, as you are, it subsides far more slowly and being tired, you are less able to stand up to it and it seems worse. Poor Commander. The only good thing about it is that it must be marvellous when it stops. Hold on. *We'll find a job for you – easily.* You are quite a different kettle of fish from poor bat-ears. You must know that.

Also don't feel you've failed at Keele. I know those dons love you there, whatever you may think, and refer to you as 'The Bridge'. And what seems like failure to you, is not so to anyone else. I fancy that you feel that L[ittle] F[riend] [Princess Margaret]'s marriage has taken some of the joy out of all your life there. It's been a whacking success, your work at Keele. What is 'completion'? That it should be constituted a University? I don't think so. It's very easy for me, my dear Commander, to write to you like this from the comparative comfort of my dichotomous life, but I must assure you that you are NOT A FAILURE and that your friends treasure you from Nancy Thomas down to
  Your old and devoted chum, John B
  Love to Anne and Little P[rawls] and B[rendan] K[enneth] B[arnes] and Sue

G.B. had written, 'I think the point about L[ittle] F[riend] and Keele is (1) We both regard her visits (and Francis and Feeble) as the only escape from Keele. They set standards; we feel appreciated; and we live for them. I hope she will continue to come.

But (2) I suspect she may give up in 1962 when her second term of office ends. I could not face Keele without her. And so I feel justified in leaving now, i.e. in the next two years.'

To John Sparrow   Moor View
                                                         Edensor
                                                         Bakewell
8 May 1960   Derby

Darling Spanzbury,

No words of mine can express my indebtedness to you for your criticisms of the epic. Of all the kindnesses friends have done me, this is the greatest. You have given so much time and thought to the lines and have entered so much into the various moods of childhood I have tried to express, that you have given me new heart about the thing. I have been going very carefully into all your strictures and find I nearly always agree with them. For instance, you have been particularly useful when you say 'expand' and that has often called out lines of which I am quite proud. I have, for example, inserted a passage about the shops in Padstow which the poem needed.

I have so far only got to the opening of the Marlborough chapter but have hurriedly glanced through your later criticisms. There are *some* verses in the Marlborough lyric I like, but I too feel it is unsatisfactory. The truth is that though I fell in love with male Peggy Purey-Custs at Marlborough, I never touched them and rarely spoke to them. I did not suffer real *agonies* of love until Oxford days. What I feel the Marlborough chapter needs is a lyric giving the more joyful side of life there, to contrast with the basket – sketching expeditions to villages in the downs in summer, first discovering Swinburne and Oscar Wilde and Aldous Huxley – becoming aware of eighteenth-century country house architecture. These played a larger part than love, I fancy.

As to the Oxford chapter and the conclusion you have come to, [it is] the same conclusion that Goldilegz [Myfanwy Piper], Mr Piper and I arrived at independently. We must leave out the Huxtable[?] incident and stop at Oxford. Goldilegz suggests, and you hint at, a sort of epitome of my emotions on leaving Oxford. This I think the correct conclusion and it should be in blank verse at the end of the cut-off Edward James lyric.

At present the Oxford chapter is the worst and there is a lot to do on it.

You will not be surprised to know that whenever you have written an alternative line or version or word to my own, I have always found yours much better. Jock is coming up this week where I shall be till Monday week and I'm putting to him your idea of letting me loose with the galleys.

Much love, my darling Coleridge, from William Wordsworth

> J.S. (see *Volume One*), a contemporary from Oxford, was one of JB's best friends, and his greatest literary mentor.
>   JB had written (14 April 1960), 'Here is the manuscript of my childhood epic. The provisional title is *Summoned by Bells*, but you may think of another one. I thought of *Lacrimae Rerum*. . . . You knew my parents and you will be able to judge one of the chief things that bothers me about it, and that is: am I too hard on them since they are dead and cannot answer back? I do not think my mother comes out of it very well. Yet I rather like what I have written about her. Oh Lord, what a cad one feels.'
>   Peggy Purey-Cust had been an early childhood sweetheart of JB's during his Highgate days, described in *Summoned by Bells*.
>   'The basket' was a form of schoolboy torture.

To Penelope Betjeman   Hole of Ellel
                                                             Cark-in-Cartmel
21 May 1960   Lancashire

Darling Plymmi,
I still haven't thought of a wedding present for Tory [Dennistoun]. I will telephone you re it on Whit Tuesday.

I love you. Nooni nooni. I fear you may be exhausted by Whit Monday – dainty lunches and teas.

Diana [Cavendish] is a marvellous cook. Camembert ice we've had and water ice made with currant leaves. I'm not generally an ice eater, but these called for second helps. Her sister Sybil, who is married to a Lowish clergyman, is staying.

Those Glasgow slums are still in my mind. The Glasgow Art Gallery which I had only a fleeting glimpse round, has an enormous collection of the best Italian paintings – Bellini, Fra Lippo Lippi, Salvator Rosa, Botticelli – all from the Burrell and the McLellan collections – also the two best Velasquez I've ever seen – Philip IV of Spain and his little daughter. I think it's worth our going to Glasgow one day just to see the pictures. There is also a room full of Whistlers in the University behind the art gallery. 'The Glasgow School of ART' by C. R. MACKINTOSH is also v[ery] funny and in its way rather splendid.

The country round here at Diana's is all like Peter Rabbit and Mrs

Tittlemouse – grey stone walls, farms with round chimney stacks, little green hills and the lake district mountains beyond. Beatrix Potter's house is only a few miles off and we are really in the Lake District. The Fulfords are coming to lunch. Diana has no servants but is entirely wrapped up in cooking, gardening and entertaining her friends. She seems to live an ordered and happy life. She *is* nice, so kind and so clever and so funny. Last night we went to a Jacobean house full of ghosts called Levens. The host Robin Bagot plays the clavichord. Once when [Bagot] was at Whitehaven playing at a concert some miles away, a R[oman] C[atholic] priest visited Levens and found a man playing the clavichord there. He spoke to him but the man did not reply. Sometime later he revisited Levens when Robin Bagot was at home and went ash grey as he recognised that the man he had seen at the clavichord was Robin Bagot.

Nooni nooni nooni nooni nooni nooni nooni nooni

Yorz trewely, Tewpie

JB was staying with Diana Cavendish, a cousin of EC, having been roped in to give a talk in Cartmel to raise funds for its church.

JB's old secretary Tory Dennistoun was just about to marry John Lawrence (later Lord Oaksey), the racing commentator and journalist.

PB was still cooking 'dainty lunches and teas' in King Alfred's Kitchen.

To John O'Dea

June 1960

Oh oft as I'm dinin' in company royal
I see meself still as a son of the soil
A-singin' me songs to the bog-cotton blooms
And a-weavin me verse upon LEINSTER's old looms
In BUCKINGHAM PALACE – when spoutin' me stuff
I journey in mind back to BALLYJAMESDUFF
With a tear and a smile in my eye I can see
The Carltons' wee motor car waitin' for me
Sure and if it won't start need yez all of yez panic
When *himself* is the qualified motor-mechanic?
Right soon we'll be speedin' by chapel and green
To praties and snuff in the little cabeen.

J.O.'D. and his wife Kathleen were friends from JB's Irish days – they had met at Pakenham Hall in the early thirties. JB always called Kathleen 'the Colleen' and John 'the Engineer' and their house in Blackrock, Dublin 'the Little Cabeen'.

J.O.'D. had written to JB making fun of him, after seeing his picture in the newspaper with Princess Margaret. This was JB's reply.

'Praties' are potatoes.

To Siegfried Sassoon   43 Cloth Fair
8 June 1960   London EC1

Dear Siegfried,

Well I never! I *have* enjoyed *Lenten Illuminations*. They are what they say. Moreover they are you at your most close-knit, clear and moving. I like to think, and I hope you will not think me presumptuous, that I have been through similar experiences myself, though they have not led me to Rome. The truth of the Incarnation – the Sacraments – those I came to, sometimes the Sacraments coming first, sometimes the Incarnation – after the manifest aids 'but only for eyes and ears'. These aids to eye and ear were most useful. Luckily for me I have never had to question the validity of the Sacraments. I find that far the biggest problem is whether there is a beneficent God who cares for us and if this is so (and visualising my death-bed daily, I hope and pray and long for this to be so), then the Incarnation and the Sacraments are obviously the truth. I have known so many people whose lives have been one long love affair with God with death as its consummation, that it is their example which encourages me. And now come your illuminations as a further encouragement. I thank you most sincerely for them. Have you ever read Archbishop Temple's *Commentaries on St John's Gospel*? I read them now alongside Teilhard de Chardin, a paragraph a day (Temple I am re-reading). They are an illuminating and strengthening team.

I keep thinking of those things you said about poetry which are *exactly* my own sentiments:

(1) That you were almost led by the nose by sound.

(2) That if you had to choose between the startling word and the one that sounded well, you chose the latter.

(3) That poetry was meant to be said aloud.

I look forward to seeing that work of Ian Davis.

I hope I will be able to come and see you this summer. I am constricted in my movements until August because of having to be here a lot and having a 'deb' daughter in Wantage whose parties and young men deprive me of the car I use.

I much look forward to coming to Heytesbury and will let you know when I am free and see whether you can receive me when I am free. There's nothing like a nice long literary talk such as we had at Old Christopher [Sykes]'s. It sets me up for days afterwards and I found myself driving back on the downs with poetry singing in my head.

Yours ever, John B

S.S. had sent JB *Lenten Illuminations* which was published in 1958 in an edition of two thousand copies by the Downside Review, Downside Abbey, Bath. They were poems of a religious nature.

Pierre Teilhard de Chardin (1881–1955) was a French Jesuit philosopher, best known for his evolutionary theory which blended science and theology.

To Penelope Betjeman   Moor View
                                           Edensor
                                           Bakewell
23 June 1960   Derby

My darling Plymmi,
I miss you and love you and all the time think about you. I keep thinking how awful our situation would be if it were what that of Anne and the Commander is now. The night before last, Anne heard from the doctor that the Commander had either a week to live or he *might* go on living for about six months. There they both are in that arid Manchester suburb with wonderful flower beds and chain stores and buses and no friends near except T[revor] H[uddleston]. We have now organised relays of people who will stay here and go over to Manchester to keep the Commander company when Anne needs time off and vice versa. The Commander was too ill to see me yesterday. They had drugged him the night before after the shock of the announcement. If the Commander is well enough to be moved to Keele to die, I will at Anne's request move there later next week. If he dies within the next few days, things may be different. This address will find me anyhow.

You are such a brave little thing, you do not mind dying. The Commander who is gallantry itself in the face of great pain is still, I suspect, not one to welcome death nor is Anne, that splendid Cambridge atheist.

Yours, Tewpie

To Anthony Barnes   The Mead
                                                      Wantage
1 August 1960   Berkshire

My dear Little Prawls,
When I saw the Commander last week I was so impressed by him and
so consoled by his courage, dignity and affection that I wanted to write
and tell you. I suppose that facing having to die sooner than one expects
is a matter of adjusting one's mind to the suddenly altered conditions.
The Commander has been given time to make the adjustment and has,
of course, made it. I think we can really put that down to the prayers of
nuns and of his friends and the splendid, calm ministrations of Father
T[revor] H[uddleston]. When I saw the Commander it was towards
the end of the day and his boyhood chum Michael Ramsey had just visited
him to their joint satisfaction. The Commander told me he did not fear
death. What he did object to was all his food tasting like coal and not being
able to concentrate for long. As M[ichael] R[amsey] pointed out to Lady
Prawls, the Commander has rallied at an unfortunate stage. Were he
weaker, it would have been less irksome for him. As you know, I've
always felt very near to the Commander as he has, I like to think, the same
fears as I have (or rather used to have them) and probably the same
temptations. He told me how immensely grateful he was for having made
his confession and wished that I had urged him to make it in the past. I
have never been so impressed by someone so seriously ill before – and I've
done a lot of sick visiting in recent years. Instead of my being of any use to
him, he was of unforgettable use to *me*. He really was like visiting a
cathedral – holy and good and awe-inspiring. He spoke with great
pleasure of you, 'He's a splendid boy – a good boy' and of Sue, and Lady
P[rawls] had been delighted by Sue's visit.

I really don't think we need worry about the Commander – rather for
ourselves because we will miss him so much.

Another marvellous miracle that has occurred has been the way Lady
Prawls has adjusted herself. When Feeble and I first visited her among
those Manchester municipal flower beds, we were truly concerned
about the strain she was under and her near despair. The last two visits
have shown her quite changed, no longer strained and of course of
ineffable use and solace to the Commander which pleases them both.
Though she would *never* admit it, she is greatly reconciled to the idea of
a benevolent creator and the effectiveness of the Sacraments – though
she calls them 'magic', she admits they work.

I expect this testing time has been a severe strain on your faith. And always, the Management, in a most maddening way, leaves one loopholes for doubt and despair. But hold on. And take it from me, my dear Little Prawls, the Commander has done more for my faith than anyone by his tranquillity and goodness. So has Lady P[rawls]. So have you. God bless you all and Sue and B[rendan] K[enneth] B[arnes].

You are in my thoughts and I hope to pay another visit towards the end of the month.

Love, John B

JB had written to Anne Barnes (7 July 1960), 'If you get moments of being low, remember that moments of strength do come. . . . I am so glad Rev[erend] T[revor] H[uddleston] anointed the Commander – that was what I was hoping would happen. It always works.'

George Barnes died a month later and JB wrote consolingly to A.B. about 'the apparent cruelty of the Management in taking the Commander away from us so painfully.' He arranged a Requiem Mass for him at St Mary Aldermary in London.

To John Murray   Treen
                                                                    Trebetherick
                                                                    Wadebridge
15 November 1960   Cornwall

Dear Jock,
Please will you send me a dozen copies of *S[ummoned] by B[ells]* down here. I must send one to George Seferis and have I sent one to Noel Coward? Please send wrapping paper too.

How about this for the menu?

> How sweet the bells of Clerkenwell
>   Are ringing loud and wild
> Across that gaslit warehouse where
>   The Murray stocks are piled.
> The nobs may come from Albemarle,
>   The Major and Sir John,
> It is Fleet Ditch which makes them rich
>   And the warehouse thereupon.

I think the Sharp poem v[ery] good and as it is visual as well as personal I think it would [be] marvellous in the Cornhill illustrated, say, with four indoostrial photographs. I see it as a poetry-cum-picture feature of Durham. Tom Sharp could get you the photographs. There are good ones in the *Shell Guide to Durham and N[orth]umberland* – but better have been taken since.

    Yours, John B

> JB's verse autobiography, *Summoned by Bells*, was just about to be published.
>
>   George Seferiades, the Greek Ambassador in London, wrote under the pen name 'Seferis'.
>
>   The verse was written in praise of the Murray warehouse at 65 Clerkenwell Road where JB had been to sign copies of *Summoned by Bells*. He very much enjoyed going down there and used to go quite often when he published a new book, to sign copies. It was very old-fashioned and looked like something straight out of Dickens. The staff adored his visits and he got on very well with them.
>
>   Tom Sharp (1901–78) had written the *Shell Guide to Northumberland* for JB in 1937. He was a town and country planning consultant and architect.

To William Plomer   43 Cloth Fair
5 December 1960   London EC1

My dear William,
The last sentence of your kind review of my verse autobiog[raphy] has saved me from a nervous breakdown brought on by persecution mania. I really thought the verse not bad and complete in itself and it was much worked on. Fuck Wain and the prig in *The Times* who was probably Griggers [Geoffrey Grigson]. I've gone away to escape further blows. The floods must be good in those flat market gardens round you – almost up to the wirescape.

    Love, John B

> *Summoned by Bells* received decidedly mediocre reviews. The unsigned *Times* review read (1 December 1960), 'What Mr Betjeman has brought off is not the *Prelude* of today, but a lightweight version of *Sinister Street*.'
>
>   W.P.'s review in the *Daily Telegraph* (3 December 1960) read, 'In this poem his humanity, his precision in detail, his powers of enjoyment, and the playful wit that never quite hides his seriousness are all to be found in plenty. It will increase the admiration and affection he has won by being himself and exploring a familiar world in a new way. But it may annoy literary prigs who find popularity unforgivable.' It certainly did.
>
>   John Wain's review in the *Observer* (27 November 1960) was entitled 'A Substitute for Poetry'. He wrote, 'In some quarters the high sales of Betjeman's volumes are taken to indicate a "revival of poetry". I cannot be so optimistic.'

To David Cecil

Moor View
Edensor
Bakewell
Derbyshire

6 December 1960

My dear David,
Your kind letter is just what I need, so given to persecution mania and self-pity as I am. Your goodness in writing it will be chalked up to you in heaven. Poor Elizabeth and I are reading *Said or Sung* by Austin Farrer. My! It *is* a good book. I attended a faculty case in Southwark Diocesan Court last week and suddenly realised that ecclesiastical law was a beautiful enclosed world and that Garth Moore, the Chancellor of it, was a man of genius and dignity whose merit none but those who attend his courts would know. He declared that pyxes hanging from ciboria were legal in a most polished and learned judgement. This new writing paper keeps me artistic. Love to Rachel and the kiddiz and yourself.
    Gratefully I am yours, John B

The Reverend E. Garth Moore, a fellow of Corpus Christi College, Cambridge, was a leading ecclesiastical lawyer, rector of St Mary Abchurch and chancellor of several dioceses.
    A pyx is a vessel in which the Host is kept after consecration.
    A ciborium is a vessel closely resembling a chalice in which the Host is deposited.

Five:

Betjeman, I bet your racket brings you in a pretty packet

===

1961 to 1963

Betjeman, I bet your racket brings you in a pretty packet
Raising the old lecture curtain, writing titbits here and there.
But, by Jove, your hair is thinner, since you came to us in Pinner,
And you're fatter now, I'm certain. What you need is country air.

'Reproof Deserved *or* After the Lecture'

JB always believed anything that was said against him in print. And if anything good was said he thought that the reviewer was only trying to be nice. He became duly paranoid about the criticisms of *Summoned by Bells*, but was touched by a letter which Noël Coward wrote on New Year's Day in 1961: 'I have already read *Summoned by Bells* twice and I am haunted by it, there is great tenderness in it, great beauty. . . . The smell of the city and the south London tube! *the reek* of the Solignum in Cornwall; all the scenes in Cornwall soaked me in nostalgia, so much of my childhood was spent there. There is no part of the book that does not give me pleasure, but I suppose I really like the school and the suburban part best. . . . We had one brief meeting but I feel so strongly that we are old friends.'[1]

Old friends surfaced from the past. Ralph Adams, JB's childhood playmate from Trebetherick days, wrote, 'How odd it was that everything was smaller at Greenaway and how the Tamarisk tree was no longer there.'[2] He wrote about the huge number of boats at Rock and also to tell JB that Vasey, his brother, had died, but the rest of the childhood group of 'Ralph, Vasey, Biddy, John and I' of his poem 'Trebetherick' were still tottering on.

My brother and I, although we still treated Cornwall as a necessary part of our lives, had flown the nest. I was in London, my brother was in his last year at Oxford where he was reading geography. He played the tenor saxophone in a band called 'the Ambassadors' and occasionally with a group called 'the Transatlantics' who played off-beat music. He knew then that his future life would always be centred around music. On leaving Oxford, he joined a band that toured the American force bases in France for nearly a year. He then went to the Berklee Music School in Boston, Massachusetts, to study jazz arranging and composition.

I went to Ireland in the New Year of 1961 and JB gave me a list of what to see in Dublin, with short descriptions and dates – Merrion Square, the Customs House, the Marino Casino, Henrietta Street, Mountjoy Square, St George's Church (those are all exteriors), and (interiors) the Rotunda Hospital Chapel, the Students' Hospital of the National University, Trinity College Library, City Hall and Parliament House. 'I hope you see Powerscourt including waterfall and monkey puzzle font, and Glendalough highly romantic – St Patrick's Cathedral is nice. Isn't all Ireland like an aquatint?'[3] I wrote notes on everything and couldn't wait to tell him what I thought when I returned.

I think the reason JB was my best friend and why I found his company better than anyone else's was because he was such a good listener – he never talked about himself and he always laughed so much at my stories. We shared everything. My mother felt the same way and relied on his judgement and praise. She had written a diary about her riding tour of Spain in the autumn of 1960 and had just gone to the Convent of Goodings in the Downs above Wantage in order to type up her account of the journey. He wrote to her, 'Don't let your typing of it let the freshness which it has at the present, be lost, what makes it so readable at present is the sense of adventure in it. One wants to know where you are going to next and how the horse will behave and what the roads will be like and what the people in the next village will be like. . . . I am proud of my little Plimmy. . . . I KNOW YOUR DIARY IS A WORK OF GENIUS.'[4]

In April 1961 Derek Stanford wrote a book about JB published by Neville Spearman called *John Betjeman, A Study*. 'I am amazed at the trouble you have gone to in reading so many of my works,' JB wrote. 'Its publication will naturally be the cause of a series of attacks on us both, no matter. We have written from our minds and hearts.'[5] William Plomer wrote in the *Guardian*, 'One of the penalties he (JB) has to pay for his success is the annoyance it often causes. This sometimes results in peevish or patronising comment, some of which may be envious. Instead of appreciating him for what he is and what he has done, some critical voices blame him for not being somebody else or doing something else. Does it matter if he is not another Yeats or another Eliot? Or if he finds poetry in the prosaic? Or if his poetic technique is not wholly of his own invention? . . . But Mr Stanford's musings about the poet and his work throw little or no new light on either.'[6]

The poet Philip Larkin also championed JB's poetry and they formed a mutual admiration society. Having praised *Collected Poems*, Larkin went on to write an article called 'Betjeman en Bloc' in *Listen* a year later, in which he defended the fact that JB had been untouched by the modern poetic revolution. Larkin, unfashionably for the time, decried those whom he called 'the loonies' – Ted Hughes, Robert Lowell and Thom Gunn – and eulogized instead and in public the merits of the plain-speaking poets like Thomas Hardy, Edward Thomas and JB. He later wrote that during this century English poetry had clearly 'gone off on a loop-line that took it away from the general reader. . . . The strong connection between poetry and the reading public that had been forged by Kipling, Housman, Brooke and *Omar Khayyám* was destroyed as a result. It is arguable that Betjeman was the writer who knocked over the "No Road Through to Real Life" signs that this tradition had erected, and who restored direct intelligible communication to poetry.'[7]

In consequence, Larkin's work, like JB's, was referred to by the modernists as commonplace and old-fashioned because it was instantly intelligible. This was exactly why JB loved it. He used to read Larkin's poem 'The Whitsun Weddings' aloud so often that I got to know it by heart. JB felt an affinity towards Larkin which he had never felt quite so keenly for his close friends Eliot, Auden, Blunden or Plomer. I think he was also flattered that a younger and clearly brilliant poet should like his work.

Although they had scratched each other's backs in public for almost three years, JB and Larkin did not in fact meet until the spring of 1961, shortly after the latter had suddenly collapsed unconscious and been rushed to hospital. JB immediately went to visit Larkin in hospital and offered to pay the specialist's fees or any other expenses. It was an odd place for their first meeting. Larkin later wrote to his friend Maeve Brennan (18 April 1961) that JB was 'much gentler and quieter than I expected'.[8] Some years later, after JB and Elizabeth had been to a small party at the Garrick Club to celebrate the publication of Larkin's *High Windows*, JB wrote to Charles Monteith of Faber and Faber about him (5 June 1974), 'It is a privilege to be on the same planet with him.'[9]

JB was unable to concentrate on poetry, however. 'They seem to think I am a government department,' he said when he was wading through his morning's mail. The image of JB as a preserver was becoming as well known as JB the poet, but it was more open to misunderstanding for it just wasn't true that he wanted to preserve everything. He often told me he wanted to pull down the whole of Shaftesbury Avenue and the Charing Cross Road and 'that bit pretending to be France between Buckingham Palace and Westminster Abbey'. People continued to write from all over the country, but he took care to be selective with his backing. He became vice-president of the Association for the Restoration of Imber, for instance, and wrote to them in 1961, 'Success to your campaign, the War Office has littered England with huts now useless and empty and has not taken them away. It, with other service departments, has laid waste acres of remote England and that it should still retain them is a scandal, now that so little of what we knew of England is left. God save Imber, fight on Wiltshire and rolling Downs forever.'[10] Spike Milligan, with whom he sat on the committee of the Finchley Society, wrote to him suggesting a combined effort of all preservation societies to form one major group. Sir Albert Richardson was already trying to join together the Ancient Monuments Society and the Society for the Protection of Ancient Buildings, but Spike thought that *all* the relevant societies should be merged. 'My worry is,' he wrote, 'that Sir Albert is an old man, whereas to fight these bureaucratic bastards one needs the courage and energy of an Horatio, so we can gently infiltrate behind him I think, if it would help. Anyhow, I suggest you write and offer your services or help or whatever you have spare time for.'[11] Spare time was thin on the ground – JB was writing to the Bishop of Reading about All Souls, South Ascot; to Solly Zuckerman about the local Exchange Building in Birmingham (eventually demolished in 1965): 'The city wants to pull it down, could the Zoo use it?'[12] He attended public meetings all over the country in places as far afield as Kelso, where he praised the democratic way in which the local preservation societies' views were listened to by the local council, and he went to talk in Dorset about James Paine the architect to raise money for Wardour Castle Chapel. Camilla Sykes (to whom JB had briefly been engaged in 1931), who had begged him to do so, wrote, 'It was angelic of you to come and talk to that strange little gathering. . . . You'll be pleased to hear the results – a thousand pounds' cheque from the Jesuits – I am sure due entirely because Father Coventry was swayed by your speech. Darling Twitchy, I am in the middle of reading your book [*Summoned by Bells*] and it *did* remind me of you. Love, Milla.'[13] Meanwhile the battle to save the Coal Exchange continued, but the angels were not on JB's side.

Despite the increasing piles of rubble in the wake of the inevitable developers' bulldozers, JB continued to write poems, sending any he rated to the *New Yorker* or his new friend Alan Ross who had just taken over the editorship of the *London Magazine* and was the *Observer*'s cricket correspondent. Suitably, 'Cricket Master: An Incident' was the first to fall on Alan's desk. Their friendship flourished. 'I associate him only with pleasure and jokes,' remembered Alan.[14] He wrote to JB (2 March 1961), 'Do you know where the following went to school? Geoffrey Gorer, Robert Kee, Robin Fedden, D. J. Enright, Lawrence Durrell, Bonamy Dobree. Got any more poems?'[15]

Meanwhile JB continued to oversee the new *Shell Guides*, working closely with David Bland at Faber and Faber. He praised Jim Lees-Milne's *Worcestershire* unequivocally: 'We (Mr Piper and I) think your guide frightfully good and the best in the series to date.'[16] As if JB didn't have enough to do, the editor of the *New York Times* wrote haughtily (21 June 1961), 'As you have undoubtedly noticed, the *New York Times* prints a poem daily on its editorial page – a poem previously unpublished. We do not recall that you have submitted any of your work for possible use. We invite you to do so. For reasons of space and format, we prefer to keep the poems short and not too complex in structure. Payment is of course subject to our acceptance.'[17] I very much doubt JB had ever seen an edition of the *New York Times* in his life. He seldom read English newspapers, and then only the obituary notices and the deaths columns.

PB was in Spain, her adventurous spirit burgeoning by the minute, now that I was working in London. King Alfred's Kitchen was sold in June 1961 and JB spent more time away from Wantage, either with Elizabeth at Moor View, or in Cornwall. On the way down there in June 1961, he stayed with Joan Kunzer's relations at Compton Chamberlayne, writing to PB, 'It is indescribably beautiful – an eighteenth-century house in a landscaped garden I should think by Repton, with a huge lake in the pocket of the Downs, and last night in the moonlight we rowed on the lake and saw all the landscape vistas bathed in moonlight and the swans flew over us.'[18] JB wrote in the Berrys' visitors' book, 'The dews of summer night did fall/The moon sweet regent of the sky/Silvered the walls of Compton Hall/And many a beech that grew thereby.' Siegfried Sassoon, who was still very much alive, wrote from Heytesbury House, Wiltshire, 'I shall be alone until the 15th of July, so please come whichever day suits you, I so seldom see anyone I can really converse with.'[19] JB went for a night in July 1961.

In November 1961 he took a bold step and accepted an invitation to go to Australia as a celebrity guest of the British Council. He had long wanted to go. Nevil Shute Norway, his childhood friend from Trebetherick days who had shared lessons with him at Shilla Mill at the back of Polzeath, now lived out there and had written *A Town Like Alice*. He was always pressing JB to come. His friend Kenneth Clark, too, had loved it. 'One reason for going,' JB recalled, 'was the natural desire we all have to escape . . . besides that I was invited for November which was springtime down under. Another reason was that I would not have language difficulties which make the continent of Europe so difficult for one who has had the advantage of a public school education. The overriding reason was to see what it was like.'[20] An official of the British Council in London had asked him to lunch before he went and warned him not to patronise the Australians, which hadn't been his intention anyway. Years later JB told me he had *never* met an Aussie he didn't like.

His trip to Australia was a rip-roaring success. He had already been rehearsing, by signing himself 'Cobber and Pommy' to Norman Williams, the head of the British Council in Melbourne, about his forthcoming arrangements and teasing him about his filing system. When JB finally arrived and met Norman it was as though they were already friends.

JB's programme read like an impossible athletic feat. He gave press conferences, talks and poetry readings, and performed on television and radio. He attended receptions, lunches, teas, drinks and dinners. He visited New South Wales, Queensland, Victoria and Tasmania; he was taken on tours of Sydney, Canberra, Orange, Newcastle, Armidale, Brisbane, Mount Tambourine, Melbourne, Corio, Adelaide and Perth. He stayed with the Governor General in Canberra, the Governor of Tasmania and the Governor of Western Australia and dined with any number of primates and bishops, deans and chancellors.

The official confidential British Council report was eulogistic: 'Because of his unique qualities Mr Betjeman was an ideal visitor for Australia. He aroused in his audiences and acquaintances that pleasant sensation of nostalgia for "Home" which is a feature of the old Australian character. . . . The professorial and academic architects he met were amazed by his knowledge of Australian architectural history, and by the clarity of the canons of taste he applied to Australian buildings. . . . His poetry was a major factor in his popularity in Australia. . . . The agents for Mr Betjeman's publications sold out their stocks of his books during his tour. . . . In Melbourne Mr Betjeman's programme was crowded and rushed. . . . A very successful tour. Press and public alike were convinced of the sincerity of Mr Betjeman's liking for Australia. This visit will remain a yardstick by which Australians will measure the success of other Council visitors. From Regional Representative's point of view Mr Betjeman was delightful company. In spite of his preference for trains and trams as modes of travel and his abhorrence of the telephone, he fell in with whatever arrangements were made for him.'[21] Norman Williams added that it had been the most successful and stimulating British Council visit he had ever been associated with in any country.

It certainly had. Assaults were made on his time by social mountaineers, but Norman defended him well, as did Patsy Zeppel, his assistant and close friend. He became the social catch in Sydney. One well-known Sydney lady, having failed to get him to dinner, dared not admit her failure in the eyes of the city and printed in the paper an account of a dinner she never gave. JB was blissfully unaware. He marvelled at the beauty of Australian girls in the street with their healthy skins and athletic figures. 'Yes,' a girl in ABC make-up said to him as she was 'tarting him up' for a programme, 'we're the longest-legged English-speaking race.' Apart from that, JB also loved the insect and spider life, the architecture, the camaraderie and the jokes and particularly the records of a then unknown comedian, Barry Humphries. He played them in many of the houses he visited – few Australians found him funny – he simply read out the brand names of supermarket goods, very slowly. JB rocked with laughter.

Meanwhile, from Andalusia in Spain, my mother wrote to him in Tasmania. 'Oh, the beauty of it! and the *silence*. Do you know I travelled for four days with my horse and saw only four lorries, one motor bus, ten private cars and eight motor bikes. I counted them. One rides along the mule tracks for mile upon mile, keeping the sun towards one's right and one stops just to drink in the silence. Once I got lost in a gully, but I will tell you all my adventures in detail when we both return home. . . . I long to see you again, and want to live in Wantage *always*: but must have *circa* two months to myself every year to clear my brain and write.'[22]

On JB's return he couldn't tell me enough about Australia. He said that Australia was Wembley and New Zealand (which he had never visited) was probably Wimbledon. He used all their phrases like 'Give us a tinkle', ate almost nothing but avocados 'naked' (with no dressing), and he kept up a correspondence with Patsy Zeppel and Norman Williams. He wrote to Patsy (17 February 1962), 'I saw Brett Whitley – he had a cut lip from a fight about Art with a pom in a pub in Fulham. I am practically entirely Aussie now.' Even a year later he wrote, 'Those six weeks so enriched my life that I have but to see a bit of news about Australia in the paper, or to turn over the pages of any book in the two shelves of Australian books I have now acquired, to feel a longing to go back there which is almost a physical ache.'[23]

Barry Humphries was living in a basement in Notting Hill Gate and acting in *Oliver!* when a friend from Australia sent him a newspaper cutting about JB's visit and his passion for Humphries's records. 'I wrote to him at Cloth Fair, when he got back to England,' remembers Barry, 'and he asked me to lunch. I was *tremendously* excited and arrived much too early and pressed the doorbell. He came downstairs and I remember he greeted me in a way no grown-up had ever greeted me before. We went up to this tiny room – books everywhere and a lot of people. All of them clergymen. I was introduced as a great genius. They looked suitably sceptical. When the time came for me to *prove* this genius which John was raving about, I was a terrible failure, not a *trace* of genius. He sent all his friends to see me at the Establishment, the club in Soho – Osbert Lancaster, John Sparrow and so on, and they didn't think I was at all funny. I remember meeting Maurice Bowra in Oxford and he asked me where I was from. "Australia," I said, and he said, "Oh, Betjeman had a friend from Australia and made us all go and see him at the Establishment – dreadful fellow, long-haired, not a bit funny. Barry Humphries it was." "Never heard of him," I said. John was really trying to promote me when I was unpromotable – difficult and drunk. He just felt this huge *sadness* that although he thought I was funny, I was never going to catch on. Years later, when I finally made it to Drury Lane I was proud to be there, but most proud that he came in his wheelchair, to the Royal Box, to witness that a few other people apart from himself thought I was funny. I think I was more of a vaudeville artist than a satirist, which was the current fashion – I think that's why John liked my act. He loved people like Gracie Fields, and Douglas Byng. I was unfashionable like them.'[24]

In the early sixties, music-hall was fast losing its fight to keep alive. JB wrote to his acquaintance from Magdalen days, Martyn Skinner, who had just moved to Somerset from Oxfordshire (4 May 1962), 'I saw Randolph Sutton (now seventy-four and looking forty) singing 'On Mother Kelly's Doorstep' at the Met[ropolitan] last night and it was so good, it restored my faith in humanity.'[25] Alan Clarkson Rose, JB's friend who ran the touring music-hall show *Twinkle* with a troupe of dancing girls called 'the Rosebuds' wrote to him (28 June 1962), 'You will be sick of the sight of my notepaper, but I thought I would let you know we are nearing the approach of our Exeter season which commences on Tuesday July 10th and I know you are going to let me have the message if possible but in any case I treasure the last letter you wrote me.'[26] JB wrote back, 'Twinkle, Twinkle, Clarkson Rose/Where the Exe's water flows/May your rose buds open there/To the soft Devonian air,'[27] and the show limped on another year.

May 1962 was the saddest landmark in the history of variety – the last performance of the Crazy Gang. JB wrote his poem 'The Crazy Gang' to commemorate the occasion and gave copies of it to 'Monsewer' Eddie Gray, Jimmy Nervo, Jimmy Gold, Teddy Knox, Bud Flanagan, Charles Naughton and Jack Hylton. Alice Stapleford wrote, 'May I on behalf of my dear father Mr Charles Naughton thank you so very much for sending along your poem about the Crazy Gang, we shall all miss them very much – another era gone – it's really very sad. My father asked me to write to you in his stead as at the moment my mother is very seriously ill in hospital and naturally my father is very worried.'[28] It was indeed a huge parting pang; but the television had won the music-hall audiences over: it was cheaper to stay at home.

> On Saturday nights I've seen in plenty
>   At the Bedford, Collins, South London, Met
> And I've laughed and wept since 1920
>   At brilliant talent I can't forget.
>
> But this is *the* Saturday night tremendous,
>   This is the night with the parting pang,
> This is the Saturday night to end us,
>   We say goodbye to the Crazy Gang.[29]

In September 1962, I went to work for the writer Richard Hughes in North Wales. JB wrote to me there, 'Clough Williams Ellis would like to see you and I expect by now you will have seen him. I must say Portmeirion looks an extraordinary and exciting place. I am just discovering Browning rather late in life I know. God bless you and your muse.'[30] (I had written a very bad poem about Richard Hughes and sent it to JB.) In fact I was writing more poems about my future husband, Rupert, with whom I had just fallen in love. By Christmas we were engaged. Angela Grimthorpe, my future mother-in-law, wrote to JB, 'I am very glad that you are so fond of Rupert, to me he is the dearest person. I am devoted to him, he has great qualities, and when he comes into the house, something comes with him of gaiety and affection. I always thought I should not like enough the girl he wanted to marry, but I am quite sure Candida is the right person for him.'[31]

On a boiling hot day in May Rupert and I were married at a nuptial mass in the Church of St Peter and St Paul in Wantage by the suitably High Church Father Schaufelberger. The choir of St Mary's Girls' School sang descants. There was a wedding lunch at Faringdon House, where Rupert and I had first met. The sides of the tent were open to the same beautiful view across the vale which my parents had known and loved since they first came here in their halcyon Uffington days in the early thirties. That evening Michael and Nicole Hornby gave us a wedding dance at their house at Pusey. Nicole, who was very tall and quite alarming, waltzed JB, who was smaller, around the dance floor at great speed. My mother, who had been at school with her, bravely intercepted and put an end to it, insisting that JB would be sick. Michael Hornby remained predictably quiet and calm throughout: 'The perfect gentleman' as JB always called him, 'unlike me, not quite a gentleman in the first place.'

Christopher Sykes, JB's old Oxford pal, who had just finished his biography of Evelyn Waugh, wrote (26 May 1963), 'I saw a picture of your dial in the piper attending the wedding of your daughter like, dressed doubtless in garments formerly owned by a deceased author from over the seas. I have known the Lycett Greens all my life on account of Yorkshire like and think your daughter married into a very nice group of humans.'[32]

1. JB's papers, University of Victoria, British Columbia.
2. JB's papers, University of Victoria.
3. CLG's papers, British Library.
4. PB's papers, Beinecke Library, Yale University.
5. Derek Stanford's papers, Harry Ransom Humanities Research Center, University of Texas.
6. *Guardian* (7 April 1961).
7. Philip Larkin, *Required Writing: Miscellaneous Pieces 1955–1982* (Faber and Faber, 1983).
8. Andrew Motion, *Philip Larkin: A Writer's Life* (Faber and Faber, 1993).
9. Faber and Faber archives.
10. Carbon copy, JB's papers.
11. JB's papers, University of Victoria.
12. Solly Zuckerman's papers, University of East Anglia.
13. JB's papers, University of Victoria.
14. Alan Ross, letter to CLG (1994).
15. JB's papers, University of Victoria.
16. James Lees-Milne's papers, Beinecke Library, Yale University.
17. JB's papers, University of Victoria.
18. PB's papers, Beinecke Library.
19. JB's papers, University of Victoria.

20. 'Aspects of Australia', *Vogue* (February 1962).
21. British Council archives, Melbourne.
22. JB's papers, Beinecke Library, Yale University.
23. Patsy Zeppel's papers.
24. Barry Humphries, CLG interview (1994).
25. Martyn Skinner's papers, Bodleian Library, Oxford.
26. JB's papers, University of Victoria.
27. Carbon copy, JB's papers.
28. JB's papers, University of Victoria.
29. 'The Crazy Gang', *Uncollected Poems* (1982).
30. CLG's papers, British Library.
31. JB's papers, University of Victoria.
32. JB's papers, University of Victoria.

To Edward James   The Mead
                                                     Wantage
31 January 1961   Berkshire

My dear Edward,
I was v[ery] pleased to have your letter in reply to mine from
Derbyshire and I do apologise for this very cheap form of reply. I
realise that if only I lived in Mexican hotels (and thank God I don't) I
would have plenty of flimsy bromo like you write on. I think my poem
is doing fairly well but don't like to ask Jock Murray my publisher. It
has done what I set out to do, been *readable* even if it has not met with
approval. John Murray (Jock) used to be at Magdalen when we were up
and his name was then Grey. He added Murray. Stephen Spender has
your 'Melon' poem at *Encounter*. *Sons and Lovers* is very fine without a
doubt and *Lady C[hatterley]* has some v[ery] good Nott[ingham]s[hire]
descriptions. I like your new poem *but* it is too abstruse for me and will
need re-reading once or twice ere I get the hang of it. Brains have never
been my strong point – only *feelings*. Time is only less alarming than
Eternity. Oh, Extinction! I hope its claims *are* windy. What a very
pretty holly design you have drawn to my letter. Penelope and our
kiddiz are very well. I hope that you are by now out of your deadlock
with the Bank of Mexico. I have just lunched with Ben Bonas, Michael
Dugdale, Philip Harding, Jack James and Jock Murray (Grey). Do you
recall any of them? They all knew you at Oxford.
   Yours, John B

E.J. (see *Volume One*), was at Oxford with JB, whose first book of poems *(Mount Zion)* he
published in 1929.
   By now he was living in a hotel in Mexico. He wrote five- to ten-thousand-word
letters to JB on a regular basis, sometimes sending him chapters of novels he was writing.
   Bromo was a brand of lavatory paper, superior to Bronco.
   He had sent his poem 'To a Melon' to John Murray, mistaking him for the editor of the
London Magazine, who was in fact Alan Ross. It was, however, passed on to Stephen
Spender, who was the editor of *Encounter*.

To Joan Zuckerman   Moor View
                                                        Edensor

23 January 1961   Bakewell

My dear Joan,

I have seldom spent fuller or happier hours than I did in dear Brum
under your and Solly's roof. It is hard, looking back at them, to say
which were the best. The claret and food of course come very high.
That claret at lunch, the [19]49 of a dim but superlative chateau, with
the sweet Climens after, on Sunday. The Lafittes on Saturday. The
visit to Aston Webb and Ingress Bell after the Barbour (or is it Barber?),
the Van Dyke, the Rubens landscape, Archbishop Robinson, the
Gainsborough wagon, the Degas, the Murillo Cana of Galilee and the
battledore and shuttlecock in that non-smoking very Brum hall, the
company of the Bishop and Miss Edith Pitt at dinner. The listening
to Heathcoat Amory at that party after. The good night's rest. The
sung mass in the broad Brum chancel of St James and seeing poor weak
white washed-out gentle Elizabeth on her knees. Mr Shortt and
that marvellous Boulton plate in the jewellers' quarter on a silent
Sunday morning. There was a pair of tripod candlesticks there of such

beauty (one hundred and fifty
pounds the pair) that I don't think
even the pictures in the Barber or
the art gallery outsoared them
for sheer aesthetic thrill. The
conversation with Mr Hobbis
with his memories of Norman
Shaw and Collcutt – he really
should be induced to write
down his recollections
and architectural opinions –

and the sight of Arthur Chamberlain. The visit to the Bishop and
his family and then that tour of the Pre-Raph[aelite]s with you and
Mary Woodall and Lady G[ladwyn] – I say, *what* a feast of joy! How
glad I am that I have the use of my ears, limbs and eyes. Long may they
remain with me. Long may the trains run through that cutting at the
bottom of your garden as the wintry sun shines on Mrs Bullshit's
façade. Oft may I return to Brum and see you again and listen to you
and Solly and talk a lot myself. This writing paper and letterhead were
chosen by Feeble herself at Matlock and as you see it makes my

handwriting very art nouveau and Cadbury garden city in style. My love to you both and deep thanks.

Love from John B

> J.Z. was married to Solly Z., the scientist and zoologist who at this time was professor of anatomy at the University of Birmingham. JB and EC had stayed the night of 21 January with the Zuckermans for the Jewellers' Association dinner at which he spoke.
>
> The Barber Institute of Fine Arts is Birmingham University's art gallery. Mary Woodall was the gallery curator.
>
> Boulton was an eighteenth-century goldsmith.
>
> EC's new letterhead had an art nouveau typeface.

To Woodrow Wyatt   The Victorian Society
                                               55 Great Ormond Street
18 February 1961   London WC1

Dear Woodrow,
Through the kindness of the Society of Antiquaries a meeting is to be held in their rooms in Burlington House, Piccadilly, on Friday March 3rd, at three p.m., to discuss the future of the Coal Exchange.

The temporary reprieve given to this notable building by the Court of Common Council on February 2nd and endorsed by the Minister of Housing and Local Government in the following week provides an opportunity for a full and constructive discussion.

We are inviting members of the Corporation of London, the London County Council, the government departments concerned, and representatives of societies who might find an immediate use for the building or who are interested in the building on the grounds of its architectural quality. Provision will be made for expression of every view, and we are confident that exchange of opinion and information will be fruitful to all. If you can possibly spare the time to come your attendance will be invaluable.

Sir Mortimer Wheeler has kindly assented to act as our firm and fair chairman.

For God's sake come and speak. We must save this building. What is really behind its destruction is a speculator who has his eye on the rest of the island site on which it stands.

Yours sincerely, John Betjeman

> The Coal Exchange was a most remarkable building of 1847–49 designed by James Bunning, Architect to the City of London. The Italianate exterior enclosed an

extraordinary decorated and domed rotunda constructed entirely of cast-iron. In 1958 the Corporation of London decided to redevelop its site and widen Lower Thames Street. In 1960 the Victorian Society submitted three schemes to the government showing how the road could be widened without destroying the Coal Exchange and demolition was deferred. In 1962 the Minister of Housing released the City Corporation from its undertaking to defer demolition and, despite protests and appeals, a majority at the Court of Common Council voted for the extinction of Bunning's masterpiece. The site remained empty for many years.

To John Piper   The Mead
                                                   Wantage
28 May 1961   Berkshire

Dear Mr Piper,
Just a line, ole man, to say how marvellous I think those blue-black stoodies of 'alifax are. They are an inspiration and will send me round Sheffield and Leeds with fresh eyes. I'll let you have some notes in about a fortnight.

Clarissa [Piper] and I had a v[ery] nice journey here and now this house is all youth, youth, youth – swimming up stream like Jap fishes.

Love to Goldilegz. My! she is beautiful. How extraordinary it is that you can interpret both Venice, Rome, Sheffield, Halifax and Ventnor and La France, all so freshly and differently. You show no sign of declining powers, but you gather force.

Cheerioh ole man, John B

The Mead was full of fifteen of my friends who were staying for a moonlight picnic organised by PB, including J.P.'s daughter Clarissa.

To Deborah Devonshire   43 Cloth Fair
6 July 1961   London EC1

Dearest Debo,
Oh! What a jolly time that royal party was. I laughed so much at Tony's imitations that the base of my skull ached. I hear from Feeble that the shots T[ony] took of the water are marvellous. Now the task is to get him not to make too long a film of it. He thinks it can be twenty minutes, I think five is enough. Feeble and I had a v[ery] pleasant journey to London and paused at Ashby St Legers, the ancestral home of Lord Wimborne in whose village inn Feeble drank beer. Her

grown-up dinner party on Tuesday night was *quite* a success. She looks
much better for all those freckles
she caught in Rotherham and for
not going to that brute René for
her hair. I hope Andrew progresses.
I have sent him a note. Ta ever so,
old girl, for a skumptious time.
    Love, John B

Princess Margaret, Tony Armstrong-Jones, EC and Katherine Mersey had just stayed
at Chatsworth. During the weekend Tony Armstrong-Jones made a home movie of JB
going round the great garden water works at Chatsworth, starting at the spring on the
hill above and ending at the cascade below. It was later shown to the Bakewell Women's
Institute.

To Candida Betjeman   43 Cloth Fair
19 July 1961   London EC1

Darling Wibz,
I'm so sorry I lost my temper so badly with you this morning. Oh
breakfast! Oh train catching! Oh nerves! Do be sure that underneath I
love you very much.
    Lots of love, MD

To Ronald Liddiard   The Mead
                                          Wantage
4 September 1961   Berkshire

Dear Ron,
Don't bother to reply to this. It is just to tell you how deeply sorry I am
for you all over the death of your splendid father. He was a real friend of
many years from the days when I used to have 'Berkshire Specials' with
him (gin and ginger wine) at Baulking when I was first married. He and
Mrs Betjeman were great friends too and I often heard her speak of him
and his good remarks when they were hunting with the Old Berkshire.

I think a sudden death was the kindest for him. He knew how to live, thoroughly enjoyed life, gave happiness and friendship and laughter to all who knew him and it would never have done for him to have been ill for months and wasted slowly away in pain. It is for you all who are left behind that I feel so sad. He would not wish you to be. Do tell your stepmother that and tell it to yourself too. He expects you to miss him yet. But he knew that the only cure for his loss is work and you have, thank God, that nice wife of yours and your children to console you. Also, if there's any truth in our Christian faith – and the older I grow the more certain I become that there is despite the, to us, inexplicable behaviour of the Almighty – you'll see him again. He hasn't gone. He's gone on.

Yours ever, John Betjeman

R.L. (see *Volume One*) had served in the XZ Observer Corps with JB in Uffington during the war. His parents were Kit and Cyril and farmed at Baulking Green near Uffington when JB and PB lived at Garrards Farm.

To Jock Murray   The Mead
                                                    Wantage
24 September 1961   Berkshire

My dear Jock,
This may arrive in time to remind you of what we were speaking of on the telephone today.

Penelope is very clever, a good clear writer with a wide knowledge of art and architecture and can speak German, Frog, Eyetie and a bit of Spanish. The children are grown up and *must* find themselves jobs. She has found someone who may buy King Alf's Caff and who at any rate will manage it for her. Now, as I tell her, is her time to begin life. She is not domestic and though I love her more than anyone else in the world, I honestly don't see her devoting her days to looking after me. She is far too active and independent for that sort of thing. She is young enough to do much still.

She has now taken up Spain. If you can commission her either to revise [Richard] Ford and/or [George Edmund] Street or to write an article and let you have a report on how to make one of Ford and/or Street and pay her a commission, say fifty pounds, in advance out of my earnings but without letting her know this, it will be an immense spur to her. She will feel she is believed in and be happy and reinvigorated. You will also get something well worth having whether you publish it or not. But the point is, Penelope's confidence must be established by a *cash offer* and that I am counting on you to make, using my cash but not mentioning my name. It will set her up no end and she needs setting up. This is all apart from Feeble. It is Penelope in her own right as a person and v[ery] important just now for her *amour propre* and I also firmly believe that she is a much better writer than I am and with a clearer brain.

Yours, John B

In late September 1961 PB went to Spain, borrowed a horse from the Duke of Wellington and set out from his estate at La Torre, near Granada. J.M. published her book *Two Middle-Aged Ladies in Andalusia* (herself and her horse) in 1963.
    Richard Ford (1796–1858) had written Murray's *Handbook for Travellers in Spain*.
    George Edmund Street (1824–81), the architect, had written *An Account of Gothic Architecture in Spain*.

To Penelope Betjeman   On the G[reat] W[estern] R[ailway]
25 October 1961   Twyford to Paddington

My darling Plymmi,
Oi aowp yew and Mary [Dunn] and
Haime [Parlade] ad a noice
toime on yer orses.

I keep imagining you as much the tiniest person on the expedition accompanied by Spanish villains and always wearing that round hat you wore at the airport when I saw you off.

I was one of a deputation to the Prime Minister yesterday about Euston Arch. Coolmore [John Summerson] put our case and we were led by Sir Charles Wheeler PRA, and Michael Rosse and Robert Furneaux Jordan also made speeches. We were received politely and our case was put with great skill and backed up by pictures.

I stayed last night with Goldilegz and Mr Piper. Major Dent and his missus and the Reyntiens came to dinner. We talked of you in Spain.

Mrs Folky wrote to say Marco had been ill but was now well again and she is v[ery] fond of him.

I gave Wibz lunch yesterday near her place of work. She loves her job but finds it v[ery] tiring getting back to the Lurots at night, though she likes it. It is scorching here now but will be colder in England.

Nooni nooni.

Write that book. You are a wonderful writer, I really mean it. Write as though you were writing in one of your letters.

Yorz trewely, Tewpie

PB met up with Haime Parlade in Andalusia. Mary Dunn was staying with him.
  The fate of the Euston Arch was sealed by the Prime Minister, Harold Macmillan, who cynically decided not to intervene after this deputation had pleaded with him. The offer by the demolition contractor, Valori, to number the stones so the Arch could be re-erected was rebuffed. Demolition began at the end of 1961.

To Penelope Betjeman   c/o British Council
                                          18 Greenoaks Avenue
                                          Edgecliff
                                          Sydney
4 November 1961   N[ew] S[outh] W[ales]

My darling Plymmi,
I write this at six in the morning in bed as there is really no other time of peace. Even so I found Sydney very invigorating and unbelievably beautiful. The Aussies are very kind and *clever*. Although there are things about the life here that remind me of our miseries of Cincinnati, the place is really much more English and therefore familiar. Sydney is a series of bays mostly tree-bordered and really v[ery] vast and grand like Plymouth Sound going on for miles and with Trebetherick bungalows in gardens full of flowers, jacaranda trees, and tamarisks

and HUGE CENTIPEDES and very loud-mouthed birds. The older houses, of which there are hundreds, are charming with rich cast-iron work and there are rows and rows of them.

You expect cobbers with slouch hats and rifles to come out on to the verandahs and fire guns at kangaroos. The colours of the flowers are amazing. The sea is a series of lakes all over the town. The C[hurch] of E[ngland] is very Low, the R[oman] C[atholic] is very Irish indeed and both dominate the city with their respective cathedrals. The Aussies are not materialistic, it seems to me, though a lot of big business is causing hideous slabs to arise on some charming suburbs. I am never left alone, as I suspected would be the case, but by just treating myself as a parcel, I get along all right. The Brit[ish] Council man Norman Williams is v[ery] kind and protective and looks v[ery] like the Commander. Today I go to Canberra, then to Orange, then back here then to BRISBANE, ADELAIDE, MELBOURNE, HOBART and PERTH but those British Council addresses I gave you will find me and this HQ one is best of all. How I do long to be with you, however much you may not long to get off your horse and leave Spain. Nooni nooni.

Yorz trewely, Tewpie

JB had just left for Australia where he spent six weeks 'jabbering away for the British Council'.

To Penelope Betjeman   c/o British Council
                                                 18 Greenoaks Avenue
                                                 Edgecliff
                                                 Sydney
7 November 1961   N[ew] S[outh] W[ales]

My darling Plymmi,
I won't send you p[ost]c[ard]s as they cost a shilling each to buy and
two and threepence to send by air to get to you in time. So I'll write it all
in [letter]cards.

I'm *loving* Aussieland. This is a glorious time to be here, late spring
with the most violent-coloured trees and flowers and always, here in
Sydney, glimpses of the sea and ships. The jacaranda trees are out,
bright purple flowers, no leaves, and as big as sycamores. Then there
are weird palm-like plants with flowers like exotic birds – cockatoos.
Yesterday I went to a small inland town called ORANGE in N[ew]
S[outh] W[ales] – which was, of course, like Polzeath laid out on a grid
system but here and there surviving three charming old colonial houses
with ironwork verandahs on two floors – and thought to when they first
found gold where there were derelict mines, hawthorn hedges and a
varied farm or two all in the style of old Cornwall – this is because the
Cornish were pioneers to the gold fields in about 1840 which here is as
old as Stonehenge. It is odd that the relativeness of time makes anything
Victorian here seem mediaeval and everything Georgian prehistoric.
The gravestones of old prospectors, just like Georgian headstones in
English churchyards, are just put anywhere beside the road on the old
properties and have the awesomeness of Avebury. The country I went
to was like the downs and full of horses and the people were all
Plymmi-type people and I have an idea you would be very happy here.
But it is a most expensive place to live in owing to inflation. On Friday I
set off on a slow journey to Brisbane and then Melbourne and Adelaide
(for retreat), Hobart, Perth and then, God be praised, home. But it is a
wonderful tour. I only hope Spain is being as good for you as
Aussieland is for me – if I don't crack.
    Nooni nooni nooni.
    Yorz, Tewpie

To Candida Betjeman Newcastle
11 November 1961 N[ew] S[outh] W[ales]

Darling Wibz,
Here I am in a v[ery] British club, 1920s Georgian with an Aussie
accent, and portraits of Churchill and the Queen everywhere.
   Last night I was given a couple of lovely long centipedes in a jar but
alas they have died in the night.
   The British Council man (Norman Williams) and I were also given a
huge iguana, all black and yellow, which had been shot that afternoon.
It was about six feet long. But N. Williams
thought it would go bad, so we put it
into a very smart 'yute' (the
Australian for utility van)
which was parked
outside the club.

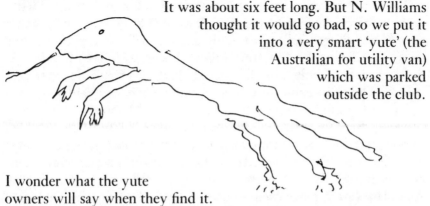

I wonder what the yute
owners will say when they find it.
   Aussie architecture is very good indeed – at least the Victorian is and
of course it seems like mediaeval in this country, where all is so new
except the face of the earth and its weird animals and wonderful flowers
and beetles and spiders and butterflies.
   The modern suburbs are as hideous as their American counterpart
and make even Slough seem beautiful.
   Lots of love, MD

To Penelope Betjeman British Council
  9/67 Queen's Road
  Melbourne sc2
18 November 1961 Victoria

Moi darlin' Plymmi,
I had the most wonderful letter I have ever had from you today from
Inferno. It was so graphic and thrilling, I felt I was there with you. It

only took seven days to reach me as it is dated the 11th – not much slower than the post from London to Wantage. I read out the non-nooni parts of your letter to the Brit[ish] Council people in Sydney and they said you must be a marvellous writer. I said you were. I do hope you do a book. Your letter gives a picture of conditions I should scarcely have believed possible, in those trog caves. It's odd that I should travel thousands of miles to find Golders Green by the sea and you should go only a few hundred and find yourself back centuries. The oddest thing about Aussieland is the way the moon's quarter is the wrong way round and the bath water whirls away from the bath in the opposite direction to that which it does in England.

The birds are most amazingly noisy and one sounds exactly like a whip being cracked which old Patrick would like very much. Another sounds like church bells. Parrots fly about and finches with vivid red backs and triangular blue butterflies. There are a lot of queers in Sydney. I have only just discovered them – interior decorators of course. Their favourite adjectives are 'interesting' and 'fabulous'.

I go to Canberra tomorrow, then on to Melbourne, thence to Geelong, then Hobart, then Perth, then home. I'll write to you from each capital. How *very* happy I was to have your *wonderful* letter. I hope you did not get ill from the bad conditions. I am very happy as everyone here is full of art and poetry and music and very kind and *good*. Aeroplanes are as much used as buses – they are by far the best means of transport. The Aussies drive cars abominably badly. Nooni nooni, I do love you so much.

Yorz trewely, Tewpie

I arrive London Airport Dec[ember] 9th at 11.10 a.m. but I bet it's late.

PB was writing long, graphic letters from Spain about her intrepid trip.

To Penelope Betjeman   c/o British Council
                                                9/67 Queen's Road
                                                Melbourne SC2
23 November 1961 and 24 November 1961   Victoria

My darling Plymmi,
The time of my whirlwind Aussie tour is now nearing its close. I stayed yesterday and the day before with the Governor General himself at

Canberra (Lord De L'Isle and Dudley, VC). I got some idea of the sort of luxury you must have been brought up in in India which is why you can stand troglodyte caves now.

Canberra, as I told you, is like Welwyn set down in a basin of the hills round the city. Melbourne where I am now is, in its old parts, like Paris if none of the homes were more than two or three storeys high. It spreads out into bungalows, the older types very pretty with lacelike ironwork verandahs and charming wooden fences to the gardens, all of different patterns.

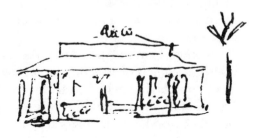

There are trees everywhere in the broad streets of Melbourne, but alas a tremendous amount of the most hideous and out-of-scale contemp[orary] I have ever seen, so that most often it is mindless[?], half-baked sky scrapers. I am staying in Trinity College, Melbourne University. It is High and there is a daily mass very well attended. I have a nice room. I remember you every day at mass and hope you are not falling off your horse. Gerry [Gerald Wellesley] is now on the high seas bound for Canberra with Rupert Gunnis. They are going to stay with the De L'Isles.

In Adelaide I'll be staying at a R[oman] C[atholic] College called Aquinas before going into a two-day retreat with the Kelham Fathers. So I ought to be *very* holy when I come back.

The joy and wonder of Aussieland is a never-ending delight to me, despite rain and cold these past few days. Loelia Westminster is doing a similar tour to mine, but we've not been able to meet though we've talked on the telephone. With Vivien Leigh and Moura Lympany the pianist.

Aussieland's *much* nicer than America. The people are not boring.

Nooni nooni. I'm longing to see you and to hear about what you have written in your diary. You are the best letter writer in the world without a doubt. If your diary is anything like your letters, they should capture the English-speaking world by storm.

I love you very much.

Yorz trewely, Tewpie

Rupert Gunnis was a historian of English sculpture.

To Candida Betjeman

26 November 1961

Geelong Grammar School
Corio
Victoria

Darling Wibbly Wobbly,

I hope you have not gone under with the pressure of London life and that I shall see you again on this earth.

The more I am in Aussieland, the more I love it, especially the big suburb, so much of it is on the sea's edge. Games are always called 'sport' and playing fields are always 'ovals' whatever their shape.

Some of the modern architecture is very good indeed. Most of it is the most cliché-ridden contemp[orary]. But in Melbourne I saw the Music Bowl which is a huge aluminium half-tent covering an arena carved out of a grass hill and an Olympic pool made of a hinged girder series with their hinges in the ground and held taut by the roof and supported by steel guy ropes at the side.

I also saw a square bungalow whose interior contained a circle of glass wall surrounding an open courtyard full of bamboos and roofed with vines. It is warm and bright weather and you never would believe the colour of flowers and butterflies and lizards. Painting is very good and so is the poetry. In fact it is like what England must have been in the reign of the first Elizabeth. This is not to say that some of it is not hideously ugly – sky signs, hoardings, breakfast packets, motels etc.

I stayed last night with the Garnetts whom you met when you dined that night with me at Marlborough. They send you their affectionate remembrance. I come back on Dec[ember] 9th arriving at London Airport at about 11.10 (*D[eo] V[olente]*). I long to hear what sort of a job or jobs you have had and how you are.

Lots of love, MD

PS They talk here about giving one a 'tingle' on the telephone. Second helpings are called returns.

To Harry Jarvis   St Michael's House
                                                            Crafters
3 December 1961   South Australia

My dear Harry,
This is my fifth week in Aussieland and I leave alas on Wednesday for
the Old Country. It is baking hot here with butterflies as large as
autumn leaves flapping about, lizards and snakes, ostriches[?], whip
birds and bell birds in the gum trees, mimosa (called wattle) of every
colour and brilliant flowers of cactus and iris and hills rather like the
downs and dark forests and huge lakes and cities that look a bit like
Slough going on for miles, but somehow much nicer because their
streets are so broad and treelined. I don't think I have enjoyed myself so
much in my life. This is because of the scenery *and* the people. The
Aussies are very church-going and, except in Sydney, which is v[ery]
Low, they are High. The young go to church. I think having nature so
near and one's bath water running away the other way round and the
stars so different and the daylight so brilliant and the place all so vast in
the interior and much of it unexplored, a sense of proportion comes
back even in the mechanised cities. Here I am at the end of a two-day
retreat at this v[ery] comfortable Kelham place, three thousand feet up
looking over Adelaide from gum trees to the Southern Ocean. I have
often thought of you. If you receive a 'call' to Aussieland, take it, my
dear boy. It is a sympathetic country – for a time at any rate. It is
incomparably more fun than America and the art and poetry are
vigorous and very good. A Happy Christmas and love to old Hugh
[Pickles] whom I hope to see on my return. There is plenty of what is
called 'crickut' here for him. I really wish I lived here. It's odd that I
send you Christmas wishes on a bright spring evening.
    Love, John B

Kelham is a High Church Anglican theological college.

To Norman Williams   43 Cloth Fair
5 February 1962   London EC1

My dear Norm,
Ta for your SYD/361/61/10 which must be getting quite thick now.
Yours was dated Jan[uary] 31st. I have had a gracious letter from Sir
Paul [Sinker] which gives me the opportunity of giving him a tinkle
which I will do shortly.
 I'm glad the ABC owe me all that money. I thought they did.
 I had Barry Humphries and his nice golden-haired Kiwi wife to
lunch last week. He came up to all expectations: was a cultivated young
man with long hair and large eyes and a very profound knowledge of the
poets and artists of the nineties and owns some Conder paintings. He
and his wife are C[hurch] of E[ngland]. He hopes to come back to
Aussieland in about six weeks after two years in *Oliver!* – (which is not
all that good, despite its boy appeal) – have proved enough for him. In
Aussieland he will do a one-man show. He was at Melbourne Grammar
before going to Melbourne University and at the last place gave the first
Dadaist exhibition in the Southern hemisphere (1952). One of his
exhibits was a large pair of army boots filled with custard with a note
underneath saying 'Pus in Boots'.
 I hope all works out well with the programme for Tazzie [Tasmania]
and the ABC. No hurry: I am quite happy.
 Love to Patsy and Meg. Cheerioh and all the best, Jack

 N.W. was head of the British Council in Australia.
  JB had just had a 'thank you' letter for his Australian visit from Sir Paul Sinker, the
 Director General of the British Council.
  The Australian Broadcasting Corporation owed JB fees for his Guest of Honour
 broadcasts during his tour.
  JB had first heard Barry Humphries's records at the British Council offices in Sydney
 with N.W. 'I played them over to myself dozens of times.'
  JB alternated his spelling of 'tingle' and 'tinkle' but pronounced it the latter way.

To Penelope Betjeman   On the train to Manchester
9 February 1962

My darling Plymmie,
Many happy returns of St Valentine's day. I will send your prezzie on
Monday but knowing how bad the post to Wantage is, you won't get it
till you come back from Goodings on Friday.

I thought the weekly *Queen* a v[ery] good effort indeed and there must be a lot of hard work in that spending money part which Wibz writes. I wonder if she also writes the philosophising at the top of the article.

I shall escape the beats [beatniks], I'm ashamed to say, by accepting an offer to go to Bignor Park, Sussex (Edward Mersey) with Jock and Diana Murrrrray to bring about liaison between their Joanna's husband Richard Bigham [later Mersey] and Peter Mills re films. So I'll be there Sunday night and travel down from Manch[ester] some time tomorrow.

What most excites me is your diary. I know you get annoyed with me when I keep urging you to complete it. I think the book is as good as written. I think the introductory chapters should just be about:

(1) Why you thought of going to Spain and what sort of thing you expected to see and

(2) What essential equipment, mental and physical, is needed.
The first should be personal, the second practical. Neither need be long. In fact *don't worry about length*. I know how the mind rejects what I can easily do but don't want to do, and invents difficulties for itself.

See you Friday when I come down with Chris[topher Hollis] to Frome.

Yorz trewely, Tewpie

PS I have just had that photograph of you framed and it stands on my dressing table in this dreary cell and it is so much the spirit of you with all your attendant animals, that it makes me want to cry. The only things missing in it are trails of catechists like those children Giles draws.

I was working on the column 'Spending Money' on *Queen* magazine which had just gone weekly.

'The beats' were my friends, Mark Palmer, Penny Cuthbertson and Martin Wilkinson.

Bignor Park was a white stuccoed box by Henry Harrison and home of the Mersey family.

Diana Murray had had a French governess in her youth, and never lost her French pronunciation of r's.

JB wrote a letter of introduction to Peter Mills of Random Films for Richard Bigham, which resulted in him making several films for Random with such titles as *The Lubrication of Roller Bearings* and *Coastal Macadam*, which made JB laugh. His favourite title was *Boto-gas*.

PB had gone to a convent called Goodings in the Downs to write up her Spanish diary.

To Deborah Devonshire   43 Cloth Fair
24 February 1962   London EC1

My dear Debo,
I must write to tell you and Andrew how sad I feel for you about the devastation at Chatsworth. I mean the loss of loved trees and stretches of landscape really is like the death of prized and highly regarded relations. You deserve prayer and support. Take heart from this, however – it is possible that when the fairies have spirited away the poor felled trunks and broken bushes and fences, vistas may be revealed of unsuspected beauty and you will be able to go round with a landscape gardener's eye and create something for the next century which could never have been provided, had the storm not occurred. The eye of an Eric Savill or a Lanning Roper might be useful.

Lots of love and sympathy from John B

There had been a devastating gale on 31 January.
Eric Savill and Lanning Roper were both celebrated landscape gardeners.

To Edward Ardizzone   50 Albermarle Street
12 March 1962   London W1

Dear Ardizzone,
No words of mine can express my delight with your drawings for my verse. They *are* the verse – they are better than the verse. You have completely caught the spirit of Delaunay-Belleville Highgate and you have also caught the vastness of the melancholy sea shore. It *was* good of you to go to West Hill and see it all as I saw it. Like all your illustrations there is a glorious absence of flatness – one can go on walking on the hills and down the lanes and round the corners.

The cover is a TRIUMPH of colour and design and would be ruined by anything but your own handwritten lettering.

God bless you and thousands of thanks.

Yours, John Betjeman

E. A. had been an official war artist like Paul Nash and was one of the greatest book illustrators of the twentieth century. He had illustrated *A Ring of Bells*, a selection of JB's poems for the young made by Helen Slade which came out in 1962.

Delaunay-Belleville was one of the first makes of motor car.

To the Society of Authors   43 Cloth Fair
22 March 1962   London EC1

Dear Sir,

I would be grateful for your legal advice on my position with regard to the *Shell Guides*. I started these on my own initiative in 1933 when I wrote the first in the series to Cornwall and devised the make-up myself. Since then they have been appearing fairly regularly each year except for the war years. They are subsidised by Shell Mex and BP and have been published since the war by Fabers who are also looking into their legal position in view of what has happened.

The Guides have largely been a labour of love for their authors and editor and I now have as co-editor with me my friend John Piper the artist.

Earlier this year I was approached by Mr George Rainbird of a firm of impresarios called Rainbird Maclean to edit a *Shell Guide* to the whole of Britain which he was also intending to issue in separate County form with maps, a colour plate, photographs and topographical information at one shilling per copy to be called 'Shell Guides' and published by him and sold in garages and I suppose bookshops. He has persuaded the Shell people to finance the venture.

The guides looked to me in format so like our own in a cheaper version that I declined his offer. The text, he said, 'would be written by experts in our office'. I told him that I regarded the series as piratical and would ask your advice and ask the publishers to take legal advice too. It is not just that he is using the name 'Shell Guides' (he has already done this in coloured advertisements to Counties appearing in periodicals and without reference to the Faber series of *Shell Guides*) but also that the *Shell Guides* themselves as they increase in number on Faber's lists help to sell each other. They represent twenty years of work and have been a pleasure to edit. They now sell at I think fifteen shillings.

Have I any legal claim to restrain Mr Rainbird from using the title 'Shell Guides' and from producing a cheaper version of our own series?

Yours sincerely, John Betjeman

> The S. of A. replied that there were two options for legal proceedings – the first, Infringement of Copyright and the second, 'Passing Off'. In the event Fabers proceeded with the second option.

To John Summerson   The Mead
                                                    Wantage
13 April 1962   Berkshire

My dear Coolmore,

> God moves in a mysterious way
>   His wonders to perform
> When E. M. Barry is the sea
>   And Coolmore calms the storm.

Hope you enjoyed Germany. Is there anything as good there as Horbury Hunt in Australia? I doubt it. I look forward to coming to Eton Villas when you return.

I remember telling an Anglican nun – who was dying of cancer and so excited at the idea of meeting Christ she said it was like 'packing up one's books at the end of term' – that I found it difficult to believe Christ was God at all, most of the time. She said, 'Oh that's nothing. It's just testing one's faith. What is really worrying is if you think the Church of England is not the true Church. I had those doubts once.' So it doesn't matter being agnostical as most of us are and as I know I am a lot of the time. It's the heart that matters and E. M. Barry will welcome you at the Heavenly Gates with a bearded smile. I wonder if he thinks St Saviours is a good building?

Yours, JB

> J.S., who lived at Eton Villas, London NW3, had written (10 April 1962), 'They have made me Church Warden of St Saviour's (E. M. Barry (1857) – his first and worst church). I never thought this could happen; it is very worrying. It was a choice between two sorts of *guilt* viz:
>   A) Guilt at being an agnostical sepulchral Old Harrovian (you know) Church Warden, or:

B) Guilt every time I looked out of windows and saw the poor old church dying because nobody would do a hand's turn etc.'

To Maria Aitken   43 Cloth Fair
17 May 1962   London EC1

Dear Maria,
Your letter is so glorious a temptation that I must succumb to it. But you know how tightly scheduled is every day of a school term. I hope to visit Sherborne somewhere between the 25th and the morning of the 29th this month.

With a very nice Old Harrovian called Jonathan Stedall and his secretary, Miss Diana Gray, I am making a reconnaissance of the town for a series of films on towns in the West Country which I am making for the commercial television. We thought of Sherborne as a school and abbey town with good streets and what looks good on television is plenty of detail, carved stone and wood and why not some young feet running down the polished floors of school passages?

When I know more definitely on what day I am coming – and I'm afraid it won't be possible to give you more than a day's notice – we will see whether the school authorities will allow me to chatter to some of the lovely girls in the evening.

Yours sincerely, John Betjeman

> M.A., the actress and granddaughter of Lord Rugby (formerly Sir John Maffey) to whom JB had been Press Attaché in Ireland during the war, was then in the sixth form at Sherborne School. She had invited JB to talk to the school's Literary Society and she wrote to him (undated), 'I promise to provide an intelligent audience, with a liberal sprinkling of Joan Hunter Dunns. . . . Miss Reader-Harris, who is, incidentally, the most beautiful headmistress in England, would give you an excellent dinner and put you up for the night.' She later wrote to her mother in June 1962, 'He was of course, an enormous success, and totally disarmed everyone. Not only the girls, who were all enchanted by him, but even the most astringent of the spinsters on the staff. No-one else could have chatted away like that, with nothing planned, and achieved the same effect. I adored it, and am completely enslaved by him.'
>
> JB had dinner with Dame Diana Reader-Harris beforehand and because he was cold he wore her fur coat to deliver his lecture to the assembled schoolgirls.
>
> Jonathan Stedall was a young director/producer for Television Wales and West. He had recently met JB and together they were making a series of quarter-hour films called *Wales and the West*.

To Rupert Croft-Cooke   The Mead
                                                     Wantage
8 June 1962   Berkshire

Dear Rupert,
I did indeed know Bosie [Lord Alfred Douglas] well and he [was]
always kind to me and full of fun and very good company. Do you
remember how good a raconteur he was – those stories about his father?
That high voice and the way he wore a soft felt hat turned up in front
and down behind and was always having to run out, after about four
p.m. when he was in Brighton to buy the *Brighton Argus*, to see if one of
his doubles had come off? I am glad you are writing a book about him. I
first came across him in 1923 when I wrote him a fan letter from
Marlborough when I was a schoolboy and had just discovered the
poetry of the nineties. He replied at once to tell me he was just out of
prison whither he had been sent for that libel on Winston Churchill and
was going to Belgium with his mother to recover from prison food. We
carried on a long correspondence about how to write sonnets and who
was a good poet and who was not (have you a copy of the telegram he
sent to Yeats on Nov[ember] 24th 1936?) but I have not any of the
letters as my parents were so shocked at my writing to him [that] they
confiscated them and I never saw them again.
      I did not meet Bosie in person until about 1930 and then, ironically
enough, through a shooting friend of my father, Sir Frederick
O'Connor. I remember telling Bosie the sad tale of my not being
allowed to write to him any more and how my father deplored my
[?illegible] and told me to be an open-air man. My copy of Bosie's
Collected Poems is inscribed by Bosie with the phrase, 'Get out into the
open air.'
      I had many letters from him which I sent to Fran Morgan and after
his death they went to someone else and I have never seen them since,
so I have to rely on memory of him only.
      I remember how my friend John Edward Bowle who runs [the]
History VIth in Westminster [School] got me to ask Bosie up from
Brighton to see the Westminster Boys perform *The Importance of Being
Earnest* and to come to a little party at John Edward's flat in Chester
Square after the performance. I think Angus Wilson was one of the
performers. Anyhow it was a long time before the boys arrived and
John Edward had disappeared. When the boys did appear I went to
look for John Edward who had finished off a bottle of champagne on his

own and staggered up to [Bosie to] meet his [hero], exclaimed 'Angel Face!' and fell flat on the floor. 'Poor fellow, he's ill,' said Bosie and showed no resentment and talked to the boys and discussed their play and Wilde as a playwright – he always preferred Wilde's plays to his poems. Bosie had the most beautiful manners. I hope you will mention them. He had a voice very like Monty [Compton] Mackenzie's and sometimes when I am listening to Monty it is like hearing Bosie again – the same gift for narration and the same way of pronouncing words.

He used to motor over from Brighton with Frederick O'Connor and stay with Penelope and me when we were first married at Uffington. I remember I often went to lunch and dine with him and his wife Olive in the various flats she inhabited. They got on very well and he was very fond of her and was always so pleased to come and see her. She was a most amusing person – quite as witty as Bosie.

I think you will find Bosie's sister Edith Fox-Pitt is still alive. I went to see her when I visited Bosie at 35 4th Ave[nue] [Hove] and had tea with him and her and their mother.

This is a very dull letter about a vastly entertaining man who gave one a sense of holiday and exaltation whenever one was in his company.

If there are specific questions you want to ask, do let me [have] them, they may prompt my memory.

Yours, John B

By the way, don't forget his passionate love of Shakespeare and how he knew yards of Shakespeare by heart and his love of Scottish border ballads.

R.C.-C., the novelist and playwright, had met JB with Patrick Kinross. He was researching his biography of Lord Alfred Douglas. *Bosie* came out in 1963. JB later wrote to R.C.-C. (20 June 1962), 'The telegram to Yeats went thus: "W. B. Yeats, Abbey Theatre, Dublin. Your omission of my name from the absurdly named *Oxford Book of Modern Verse* is typical of the attitude of the minor poet to the major one. Had Thomas Moore been editing such a book he would have omitted Keats and Shelley. Incidentally why drag in Oxford? Why not Shoneen Irish? Alfred Douglas." It was sent from Brighton and he had printed slips of it to send round to friends. I have one pasted in my edition of his collected poems.'

Bosie married Olive Custance, the daughter of Colonel F. H. Custance, in 1902 (she died in 1944). After about ten years of marriage, they lived in separate houses but still got on well and continued to see each other regularly.

To Deirdre Connolly   [As from] 43 Cloth Fair
25 July 1962   London EC1

My Dear dre,
There is a man opposite me in the carriage where I am writing this and
he has one of those secret smiles on his face which means, I am sure,
that as soon as I stop writing this letter he will lean forward and engage
me in conversation.

All in my mind's eye I see the warm contrasting colours of Bushy
Lodge's rooms, the yellow blind and the purple passage to the view
from Cyril's room and the drawing room of those elms and willows
blowing in the wind and the downs beyond them and the knowledge
that beyond the downs is the sea. It is all ineffably nicer than Berkshire
and the house is bigger and better than Garrards Farm, Uffington ever
was, tell Cyril. It is so nice to see you and him so happy and that nice,
quiet, clever and pretty Cressida shedding sunshine on the carpets and
walls and Cyril at the top of his form.

(If Cressida looks sad
in this picture, it is
because of the artist's
pen slipping. She is not
a sad person.)

Tell Cyril to get an agent so as to fill his cup of bliss to as near
overflowing as it ever can be for such anxious types as he and I are. It
was a most rejuvenating experience staying with you both. I have not
been at the above address long enough, nor to the Mead Wantage yet, to
look out a few objects for that envelope Cyril flatteringly requested.

Well, bung hoski old girl, as Victoria [Zinovieff]'s husband would no
doubt say and ta ever so for a *skumptious* time. I really did enjoy myself
immensely.

Love to you all three, John B

D.C. was married to Cyril C. They rented Bushy, a farm on the Firle estate in Sussex
from 1958 to 1968 and JB and EC used to visit it often. They also went over to Bushy
when staying in Alan and Jennifer Ross's house, near Hassocks, nearby, under the
downs behind Brighton.
   Cressida was Cyril and D.C.'s daughter.
   Victoria Zinovieff (née Heber-Percy) is Jennifer Ross's daughter by her previous
marriage to Robert Heber-Percy.

To Siegfried Sassoon   43 Cloth Fair
26 July 1962   London EC1

Dear Siegfried,
What a joy to have your reaction to that cultivated old lady. The house
was v[ery] good, decayed country-house style – things very well worn
but none of them damp and a suggestion that if personal taste could
have triumphed over the eighteenth century it would have been for
Walter Crane, and brown and olive greens and brick reds and
Elizabethan-style furniture and Edmund J. Sullivan illustrations – in
fact Bedford Park and Norman Shaw – and VERY NICE TOO.

I look forward to my interview with you on your ninetieth birthday.
I'll ask you to tell me what you remember of Gordon and Horatio
Bottomley, Norman and Alfred and Tom Douglas, Norman Gale and
Norman Shaw, Christabel Aberconway and Lascelles Abercrombie. It
should be most *interesting* and we could play recordings of the work and
talk of all these people on the gramophone.

I v[ery] much look forward to coming to see you. I would like to come
over from Wantage via motor car. I'll be there for several days after
August 10th. Any chance of your being able to spare some time from
the cricket pitch, so that I could come and see you? Someone told me
that Edmund B[lunden], that great poet and golden character, was
staying with you. Where is he now? I'd like to see him ere he leaves
these shores.

Yours, John B

S.S. had written (19 July 1962), 'I have just listened – second time – to Gunby Hall.
Would you be kind and let me know the publisher of her reminiscences. The whole thing
moved me very much – in all ways evocative of the civilised world she has outlined, and
which even I had a share in.'

JB had interviewed Lady Montgomery-Massingberd, on the occasion of her ninetieth
birthday, in the BBC radio series *As I Remember*. She was the widow of Field Marshal Sir
Archibald M.-M., and lived at Gunby Hall near Spilsby in Lincolnshire. Her mother,
Mrs Massingberd, was a famous feminist, who preferred male attire, lived with a lady
companion in Bournemouth and was the first woman county councillor. During the
interview Lady M.-M. had banged on about her cousin Ralph Vaughan Williams, 'hey
nonny no' music and forgotten amateur musicians of the pre–1914 era. Thanks to early
elocution lessons she had come across very well. She was not an admirer of JB's poetry
and called it doggerel. He had hardly got a word in edgeways and none of the crew, nor
he, were offered any tea.

Her 'reminiscences' remain unpublished.

S.S. continued, 'Will you visit *me* on my ninetieth birthday? "Yes", I'll say, "Gilbert
and Sullivan often came to our house when I was a child; and so did Waring and
Gillow." I wonder what's become of Waring since he gave us all the slip?'

To Candida Betjeman   The Mead
                                                         Wantage
4 September 1962   Berkshire

Darling Wibz,
How varied a time of sea spray, rain, sun and adventure, emotional and
otherwise, you seem to be having on the Merioneth Strand.

I do know Clough Williams-Ellis. He is a great man and he really
invented the campaign against hoardings and litter and bungaloid
growths when he wrote a book called *England and the Octopus* in the
twenties. His wife Amabel wrote a very good book on poetry for
kiddiz. Clough is an architect and designed Portmeirion and among the
objects to be seen there – I've never been there myself – is the charming
Batty Langley Gothick Colonnade from Arnos Castle in Bristol which
he rescued from destruction and brought to Portmeirion. I have written
to Clough and told him you are at Diccon's. Give Diccon my affections
and also his wife and kiddiz, horses, ponies, seaweed and salt marshes.

I've got a sore throat. I hope it's not chicken pox caught from
Susannah Piper. I can't remember whether I've had it.

There was a v[ery] good arty crafty architect up where you are (head
office at Bangor) called North. Ask Clough about his work. I miss
Powlie who is now chugging over the Atlantic in a steam boat and I miss
you and hope you are as happy as your own temperaments will allow.

Lots of love, MD

> For six months, I worked for JB's friend the writer Richard ('Diccon') Hughes, who
> wrote *High Wind in Jamaica* and *In Hazard*. He lived the other side of the estuary from
> fabled Portmeirion near Portmadoc in North Wales. Portmeirion is an artificially
> created village combining reclaimed buildings with new ones designed by Clough
> Williams-Ellis. From across the water it resembles an Italian fishing port.
>
> Herbert Luck North (1871–1941) built simple, roughcast houses, excellent examples
> of the domestic architecture associated with men like Voysey, using local materials.
>
> PSGB was going to the USA to enrol with the Berklee School of Music in Boston.

To Brian Johnson   Treen
                                                         Trebetherick
23 September 1962   Wadebridge

Dear Mr Johnson,
I have now read the *History of the S[omerset] and D[orset Railway]*. As you
probably gathered from it, the line from Evercreech to Highbridge was

opened in 1854 and extended to Burnham in 1858. It was the Somerset
Central Line which merged with the Dorset Central to become the S
and D. When Queen Square (now Green Park) Bath opened in 1870,
where the head offices of the S and D were, the line from Bath to
Bournemouth became the main line and the poor old Evercreech–
Highbridge line became a branch. It was originally broad gauge as the
old Somerset Central was friendly with G[reat] W[estern] R[ailway]
which was already at Highbridge. The GWR station at Highbridge is
an original Bristol and Exeter line station of the 1840s, nearly twenty
years older than the S and D and that fascinating cross line to Burnham
was a concession made by the GWR to the S and D; part of the battle
for the Broad Gauge of the line to Burnham was broad gauge. The
station at Burnham was not called Burnham on Sea until 1923. The S
and D hoped that Highbridge would be its cargo port for S[outh] Wales
and Burnham its passenger and *light* cargo port. All these hopes died
when the S and D concentrated on linking Bournemouth with
Birmingham and the Midlands via Bath. I don't think any of this is
filmic but it is certainly interesting historically. What we looked at at
Highbridge and Burnham was blasted hopes – as you said, 'The Sad
Road to the Sea' – a sad road for goods as well as passengers.

So we should think of that 1.15 we caught from Evercreech in
September 1962 as the last effort to link the south coast of England with
the Welsh collieries, an effort which started over a century ago. This
gives you a good visual excuse for goods sequences, for this original part
of what became the S and D, was intended to be every bit as important
as, say, the London Tilbury and Southend or the London and
Blackwall or the L[ondon] and N[orth] W[estern] to your own
Liverpool and Holyhead. And no doubt the S and D directors thought,
when they built their stations alone on Sedgemoor – Shapwick, Bason
Bridge and the like – that there would grow up around them thriving
communities as there have grown up around the stations on non-
important main lines – hence that 'Railway Hotel' we saw outside one
of the stations on the south side of the line and the S and D Hotel at
Burnham. Highbridge was to be another Cardiff. But it failed. The
standard gauge of what became the main line of the S and D and the
traffic from the Midlands did in the Highbridge and S[outh] Wales
experiment.

What became of the freight? All that was to go by sea across to Wales
and come from Wales to Somerset and the south coast is a ghost among
those empty trucks at Highbridge Harbour. Even the engine works, to
be another Crewe or Swindon, are a ghost. Three small tank engines

(one is figure 28 in the Barrie and Clinker's booklet) were the only engines built there, but there must have been many buckets of Prussian blue paint and white paint and much gold leaf and many rich transfers for the coats of arms of the splendid S and D line, which I can just remember.

What became of the passengers? The paddle steamers failed (figure 3 in Barrie and Clinker) like the extension beyond Burnham station to the jetty which is no longer there – I remember you noticed the gradient mark right at the end of the line pointing only a few feet to the buffers. And now the swell hotel 'the Queens' contains Birmingham people who come by car, not by S and D, and probably no Cardiff people at all.

Having regard to these grandiose plans, I fancy we should introduce the film with a series of stills (captions I think you call them) of S and D engines, steamships, posters and timetables, and ending on the façade and interior of Bath Green Park so as to give one a chance of telling the S and D story. The only decent bit of writing in Barrie and Clinker is on page 28:

> Under-engined trains crawled hesitantly up the gruelling Mendip grades [and here we might have some shots in still form of trains on the more obviously picturesque parts of the line around Shepton] and went bucketing down the reverse slopes at hell-for-leather speeds to make up time, with the rattletrap coaches cavorting on the primitive, ill-ballasted track. . . . Long delays and complex shunts were the order of the day at the crossing stations, between which trains moved spasmodically on the telegraphed instructions of a functionary known as 'the Crossing Agent', who from his office in Bath endeavoured to play a nightmare game of blind man's chess – with an odd piece or two inexplicably missing ('left Evercreech Village two hours ago, not yet showed up at Shepton').

And then from the grandeur of Green Park we could switch suddenly to live contrast in the country at Evercreech Junction and follow the line from there to Burnham with the end you had in view.

Quite how you are going to mix goods and passenger along this enchanting track I do not know. A lot will depend on what sort of shots you have and which have the most visual appeal. Personally, I think they could be intermixed and there would be no harm in using the passenger train as the main theme and stopping, where there are goods shots, and putting them in.

Though the Evercreech–Highbridge line was started with such high hopes, we don't want to give the impression that it is now a useless anomaly. It occurs to me while writing this, that before we set off in the train from Evercreech you might care to show the line from the point of view of a motorist – the stations like Shapwick seemingly so lonely and pointless in their flat waste when seen from the road (and incidentally miles from the villages after which they were named), so that when we come to travel on the line it has obvious use and significance and seems quite different. I remember how amazed I was to see Shapwick station when motoring over Sedgemoor a few months ago and how different it seemed when we travelled through it on Friday.

Anyhow this is how I see the order of the film:

> History and Posters of S and D
> Evercreech and Country Stations Goods and Passenger Stuff
> Highbridge Works
> Highbridge Harbour and Crossing of GWR thereto
> Burnham Station
> Burnham End of Line and Short

I hope you will be able to read all this. It is partly to remind me as much as you of what I saw and to thank you for so pleasant a time. It will also remind me, when the time comes for commentary, of my impressions. You had Burnham impressions down on the tape. Best wishes to you and to all my Bristol BBC friends.

Yours, John Betjeman
I return the books herewith. JB.

> B.J. seems to have been working for the BBC in Bristol at that time and was involved with JB's film which was eventually broadcast on 21 February 1964.

To Cecil Roberts   The Mead
                                                                Wantage
21 December 1962   Berkshire

Dear Cecil,
You certainly write marvellous letters. I was enraptured by your description of the Ecumenical Council. I stayed with the *Archbishop of Canterbury* in Canterbury a week or two ago. He is a very kind, wise and good man. I asked him if he thought that council would make English R[oman] C[atholic]s any friendlier to us Church people. He said he didn't think it mattered much whether it did or not but that the

R[oman] C[atholic] Church would make *itself* more attractive to outsiders as a result of the council. He said the chief trouble with the C[hurch] of E[ngland] was the alarming increase of bigoted fundamentalists in it, who ought really to become Strict Baptists or some such extreme nonconformist sect. I don't like to think of you spending an Hotel Christmas – even in Rome – best wishes for the New Year. My address in London is 43 Cloth Fair, EC1. (Telephone: Monarch 1698). God bless you.

Yours aye, Iain MacBetjeman

The Archbishop of Canterbury was then the saintly and eccentric Michael Ramsey.

To Audrey Lees   The Athenæum

                                       Pall Mall

9 January 1963   London SW1

My dear Audrey,
The club from which I am writing is wrong *socially* and not in keeping with the engagement. As you see, I have got hold of a bit of its paper which the members use for writing overseas and as this is going across the river to Putney, I thought you would understand. It was sweet of you to write. He's a very nice, *quiet young man* who calls me 'sir' and makes me feel my nails are dirty – which they generally are – and he has a lot of humour. I can't make out why they want to wait six months before marrying. But I never like to enquire.

The pipes at Cliff Bank have burst, Rene [Lightfoot] tells me, and Joc wasn't allowed down because of the chaos. I bet Chris is in a state. I'll write to her. Tell Gawain F. that if only he came and saw me a bit more he would have more to tell you when you and he talk about me. Give him my love. He'll never admit it, but he is a Preraphaelite at heart.

Love to Old Lees. I'd very much like to come to Malbrook again. I must arrange an O[ld] D[raconians] (females) luncheon at 43 Cloth Fair soon for you and we'll get Lord Bridges to give old Lees an extra half hour on to his lunch hour so that he can come too.

Candida is in Switzerland with the young man (and *I expect*, others) and I'll give her your love when she returns next week.

Love, John B

A.L. (née Lynam) met JB when they were both seven in Trebetherick where her parents Hum and May had their holiday house Cliff Bank. She was the sister of Joc Lynam,

headmaster of the Dragon School, Oxford and lived in Malbrook Road, Richmond.
    The quiet young man was Rupert Lycett Green to whom I had just become engaged.
Irene Lightfoot looked after Treen for JB and EC.
    'Old Lees' was JB's name for A.L.'s husband Stanley, who was a civil servant. Lord
Bridges, about whom JB had a bee in his bonnet, had been Permanent Secretary to the
Treasury.

To Gerard Irvine   43 Cloth Fair
16 January 1963   London EC1

Dear Gerard,
I think the article on the Master [Ninian Comper] brilliant. He did not
work from the Priory until about 1938 when his office in an orchard at
Knights Hill, West Norwood was demolished for council flats. He
always called his office there 'the Studio' because he thought architecture was an art, not a profession, and that was why he kept out of the
R[oyal] I[nstitute of] B[ritish] A[rchitects]. I think somewhere you
should stress his remarkable sense of proportion, that is to say, knowing
the right size of window for wall and tracery for window and leading for
tracery, and in the same way how his wooden furnishings were
proportioned to his buildings. Ought there to be something in about his
sense of colour and the famous Comper pink?
    Candida's intended is tall, handsome, quiet, well-dressed and
athletic as his future father-in-law is.
    [John] Brandon-Jones is the man you and Brian Thomas should see
about that Exhibition. I wonder if Gordon Russell has any of the
Gimson, Barnsley and Romney Green work.
    Love, John B

        G.I. (see *Volume One*), Church of England priest and friend of JB's since the thirties,
    shared a passion for the architect Ninian Comper. His interest in Comper had been
    ignited by JB and the article was for the *Church Observer*.
        The architect John Brandon-Jones had worked for C. Cowles Voysey, son of C. A.
    Voysey.
        Gimson, Barnsley and Romney Green were craftsmen in furniture design.

To Norman Williams and Patsy Zeppel   43 Cloth Fair
February 1963   London EC1

    Dear Cobber Norm, Dear Patsy Z, I write
    Here from this snowbound Berkshire slope to say
    I should have sent you Christmas Cards. I know
    How in the Commonwealth these small things count,
    These little thoughts that forge the loving chain
    Which binds the gum tree to the English oak
    And William Butterfield to Horbury Hunt.
    But then I didn't. Why? Because to get
    A Christmas card to Aussie land in time
    For sunbaked Christmas dawn at Mon Repos
    Was far too difficult to calculate
    For one unmathematical like me.
    Your sweet reminder of my erringness
    Brings back the King's Cross fountain to my mind
    As many coloured as electric lights
    Reflected in its bristles after dark.
    Once more at Mascot I am touching down,
    There's Patsy with the British Council car
    And soon we'll climb the heights to Paddington
    Soon catch the stretch of sea at Double Bay
    Tea at the Wentworth, drinks in Adams' Bar
    And oysters at that place upon the shore
    Then on by nature strips to Mon Repos.
    Think not, old cobbers, you are out of mind
    Though out of sight. Day after day I long
    For sun girt, sunkissed, surfing Aussie land
    Would even dare the waves on Bondi Beach
    And risk my life once more for just a sight
    Of Greenoaks Avenue and Patsy's bath
    To stretch my nerves in while the office work
    Continues all around me. 'Oh come back!'
    The wattle and the wallabies cry out.
    And soon, please God, I will. These limping lines
    Are poor return for your so gracious ones.
    And give my love to poor old Christopher
    The cricket maniac from Somerset
    Who loves his drop of drink. Send love all round
    To Daniel Thomas, Morton Herman, Ken –
    Neth Slessor, Stewarts, and Prof Wilkinson
    The artists architects and poets who

Gave back to me my lost self-confidence;
There isn't room to mention all of them
The paper's running out – I'll write again
And until then my love from Pommy land
To Patsy, Norm and their enormous staff.
From Jan Trebetjeman, the Cornish Clot.

After JB's first visit for the British Council in 1962, he sent this late Christmas verse on an air-letter 'as a thank-you to his British Council friends in Australia', N.W. and his secretary and friend P.Z.
   Mon Repos was JB's nickname for the house rented by the British Council for its representative in Vaucluse. King's Cross Fountain resembles a dandelion and its jets, bristles. Nature strips are grassy verges often planted with trees which separate kerbs from footpaths in Australian suburbs. Greenoaks Avenue in Darling Point was where the Sydney offices of the British Council were. 'Poor old Christopher' refers to Christopher Hollis. Daniel Thomas was then curator of Australian paintings at the Art Gallery of New South Wales. Morton Herman is an architectural writer, Kenneth Slessor a poet, Douglas Stewart a poet and playwright and Professor Wilkinson a distinguished architect.

To Jonathan Stedall   The Head Master's
20 March 1963   Harrow

Dear Jonathan,
You were remembered with affection by the Headmaster, Sidney Patterson and Mr Treasure whom I met last night at the dinner before the L[ad]y Bourchier Reading.
   Feeble tells me of your Steiner ideas of teaching. My dear Jonathan, do what you want to do and what you feel is your vocation. If it's teaching then do it. Only you can know. It really is this difficult business of discovering how best one can go on in one's search for God, whether by instructing others or making films or writing, or producing or weaving or home carpentry – it doesn't really matter so long as it helps in the search for who made us. Don't hurry.
   See you Friday at T[elevision] W[ales and the] W[est] at 2.30.
   Yours, John B

J.S., the young director/producer for Television Wales and the West, with whom JB had been working, was undecided about changing careers.
   Sidney Patterson and Geoffrey Treasure were masters at Harrow, consecutively housemaster of the Grove. JB had been that year's celebrity judge at the school's annual Lady Bourchier Reading Prize.

To Mollie Baring   Treen
                                                            Trebetherick
                                                            Wadebridge
1 April 1963   Cornwall

Darling Mollie,
Here on the morn of All Fools' Day and safely out of the regions of
practical jokery, I write to say how relieved I was to see you looking less
ill than I expected and earnestly do hope you are still getting better.
You can buy huge sea urchins in South Cornwall now which look
exactly like Penelope's head. They are in beautiful colours and it is only
a matter of painting the face on to have Penelope in the room, only
quieter of course as they do not speak very much or walk about as they
are hollow.

The shower and downstairs loo here don't work owing to bursts and
nothing has been done to repair it beyond a huge hole being gashed in
the wall. Daffodils, violets and primroses are out and yesterday was
boiling hot and sunny and I took a lot of photographs of old Cornish
manor houses.

Love to Dezzie, Peter (the racing jockey), Nigel and Arne and to *you*.
Love, John

> JB had been to visit M.B. who was in the Acland nursing home recovering after an
> operation.

To James Lees-Milne   Treen
                                                            Trebetherick
                                                            Wadebridge
3 April 1963   Cornwall

My dear Jim,
I'm here till Monday revising my *Shell Guide to Cornwall*. I don't know
when Shell will let us do a new guide to Somerset. I will ask. But not, I
fancy, for a year or two. John K[enworthy]-B[rowne] would be just the
right sort of author.

As to Lord B[ridges] and the Royal Fine Art Commission. Lord B,
being a Civil Servant, thinks only architects know about architecture,
only sculptors about sculpture and so on. Consequently he has stuffed
the RFAC with *practising* architects who were the bugbear of his

predecessor David Crawford. They are only interested in new buildings and not what is to be destroyed to make way for them, and don't know all different parts of England. Laymen should preponderate – people like you and Christopher Hussey and little Mark Girouard and topographers of that sort – also men like Thomas Sharp who care for more than statistics and have an eye for landscape and shape and feel of a place. It is the Royal Fine Art Commission, not the Royal Fine Architecture Commission which Lord B has made it. I'm glad to see there is a formidable and growing body of opinion which thinks the RFAC is becoming 'jobs for the boys'. This is not to say that the architects on the RFAC are not delightful and honourable people. Their position is invidious.

Love to Alvilde and Kitty Farrer and Alfred Waterhouse and Glenarthur and Sir George Arthur.

Bung ho, ole man. Back next week in London and Wantage.

John B

John Kenworthy-Browne was a friend of J.L.-M.'s who worked at Christie's and for the National Trust. The Somerset guide never came off.

Lord Bridges, the retired senior civil servant, was Chairman of the Royal Fine Art Commission on which JB served. He was the son of the poet Robert Bridges and first cousin once removed of J.L.-M.'s wife Alvilde. He was well equipped with degrees but lacking in aesthetic sense and should probably not have been made the Commission's Chairman. He became a standing joke in JB's correspondence with J.L.-M.

Kitty Farrer was Lord Bridges's wife whom JB did not know.

Lord Bridges's mother was the daughter of Alfred Waterhouse, the famous Victorian architect.

Lord Glenarthur and Sir George Arthur were distant relations of J.L.-M.'s.

To Deborah Devonshire   The Mead
                                                                     Wantage
28 May 1963   Berkshire

Dearest Debo,

I must write to tell you how sad I am for you on the death of that great woman your mother. I know what a lot she meant to you and I put down so many of the things I love about you – from your kind cleverness, sure taste and loyalty and warmth, down to such details as using that health crystal salt – to an inheritance from her. It is fearfully difficult when one is deeply sad inside from a loss like that of one's mother, to look about for things to be thankful for so as to get

consolation. There are, however, a few. You have probably thought
of them already – how close you and your mother were is one of them.
You need have no remorse as I did when my mother died for not having
cared for her enough. Another is that her loss only strengthens that
glorious relationship you have by letter with Nancy, Diana, Miss Pam
and Party Member [Jessica] whom I love, or is she Party no more? Also
those three absolutely spiffing kiddiz Emma, Stoker [Peregrine] and
Sophie all there together with Andrew. And lastly old girl, I have an
idea that there *is* personal survival and that the Christian religion is true
– it will be very annoying if it is not – and because it's true, death is only
parting for a bit, not final separation. And of course she'll expect you to
miss her but she'll not want you to be desperately unhappy. I'll
remember you all in my prayers.

   Much love from John B

   Sydney Redesdale (née Bowles) had outlived her husband who had died in 1958. Her six
   daughters, Nancy, Pamela, Diana, Unity (who had been a friend of Adolf Hitler),
   Jessica (sometime Communist) and Deborah, bore the family name of Mitford.

To James Lees-Milne   The Mead
                                                        Wantage
6 June 1963   Berkshire

My dear Jim,
I have just finished reading your *Worc[ester]s[hire]*: and let me, dear boy,
say at once how *splendid* it is. It will make the best Shell Guide we've
ever done. There is so much affection and delicious grumpiness in it. I
know how hard it is to compress a place into two sentences or three and
how long it takes to do so. You have achieved it everywhere. Every
sentence shows eye, heart and brain and stands for a personal visit. You
must have lost thousands of pounds writing this book and I feel it is a
great act of kindness and generosity on your part to have done it. Ta
ever so.

   Two or three details. It might be worth putting under St Michael's
College, Tenbury, that it is by H. Woodyer, Butterfield's pupil, in his
own strange spidery Gothic and that every day in school term-time
Evensong is sung by a superb choir to varied music.

   Is Malvern Link in Worc[ester]s[hire]? I'm not sure, but if it is, I
think you should mention Comper's superb Perp[endicular] chapel
(1898) for the Convent of the Holy Name (Anglican) and Walter

Tapper's very stately Church of the Ascension there – a blend of Bodley and Temple Moore.

My goodness, ole man, that *Worc[ester]s[hire]* book is good and makes life worth living. Now we must assemble good photographs.

Love to Alvilde.

Bung ho, your affectionate cousin, Edward Bridges
pp John B
I thought your notice of Sydney Lady R[edesdale] SUPERB, in *The Times*.

> J.L.-M. did not lose thousands writing the *Shell Guide to Worcestershire* for he lived at Alderley in Gloucestershire and found it easy to visit Worcestershire, his native county, which JB always described as a pancake burnt at one end – the Northern industrial end.
> J.L.-M. had written an appreciation of the late Lady Redesdale for *The Times*.

To Candida and Rupert Lycett Green   The Mead
                                                                  Wantage
15 June (Trinity Sunday) 1963   Berkshire

Darling Wibz and Rupert,

Well, it don't arf sound nice down there at Cimbrone's villa now the sun has come out and by the time you get this it'll no doubt be swell in Sicily too. Your descriptions of the fireworks across the bay and the sound coming later and Rupert reading Kipling's *Jungle* stories conjures up much happiness. I expect you feel, like I do, that when one is enjoying something a lot one is too full to put it down in verse and that can only be done in recollection. 43 C[loth] F[air] is being 'modernised' downstairs by a consulting engineer who is turning the ground floor into his offices. The noise is dreadful and the result will be like an advertising agency including the stairs up to my hovel.

Old Patrick [Kinross] lunched with us and brought the news that you and Rupert had had bad weather which he had learned from David Erskine.

> Airlie Gardens! Airlie Gardens!
> Oh the pleasant sight to see
> The Water Tower from Airlie Gardens
> Where my love climbed up to me.

I should think his Italian wear is something terrific. Mummy is much looking forward to sleeping on the lawn when the house is being dismantled for damp proofing.

People keep coming up to me in the market place and [they] congratulate me on the wedding as though I had been married that day myself. The truth is, of course, that the love and looks of the pair of you made it so wonderful a day in the annals of Wantage, together with your and Mummy's organising, not least that huge ruled card of house parties.

Powlie went back yesterday. He seemed very happy and had enjoyed himself in Cornwall and taken Lynam [Thomas] to a Mormon meeting at St Austell where they both testified. It sounds a nice, simple, *homely* religion of good people and really suited to Powlie and an anchor for him in the chaotic ugliness of USA.

Tomorrow I go to Clough [Williams Ellis]'s eightieth birthday dinner in the House of Commons. By Jove, I did like Anglesey and Plas Newydd and old Diccon [Richard Hughes] and his missus dined [with us] and Sachie and Georgia Sitwell and we put it all right, I think, about forgetting to invite them. I can see what you mean about Italy reminding you of Portmeirion. But is it *quite* so flimsy? I v[ery] much like Clough's house and garden. He is a master with Welsh stone.

Lots of love, MD

What's Sicily like? Different from Italy?

RLG and I were married in May and had gone to his stepfather Ralph Grimthorpe's Villa Cimbrone at Ravello in Italy for our honeymoon.

Airlie Gardens was the street in London where we were going to live on our return from our trip around the world. JB's lines were based on Charles Kingsley's poem:

Airly Beacon, Airly Beacon,
Oh the pleasant sight to see
Shires and towns from Airly Beacon
While my love climb'd up to me.

PSGB had become a Mormon while in the USA.
JB had been to stay with Henry and Shirley Anglesey at Plas Newydd.

Six:

The mellowing bells exultant sound

1963 to 1966

The yellowing elm shows yet some green,
  The mellowing bells exultant sound:
Never have light and colour been
  So prodigally thrown around;
And in the bells the promise tells
  Of greater light where Love is found.

'Autumn 1964'

My mother had always wanted to adhere to the Hindu philosophy which prescribed that once your children had married and gone out into the world, you were then free to lead a spiritual life with few worldly possessions. Although she did not follow this literally, she got pretty near to it. My brother was in America, and Rupert and I had driven off around the world for a year, so she planned a long journey to India which would take her away for an autumn and a winter. The Mead was let and a new pattern began for JB's life. From that moment on, until the end of his life, the number of his letters to my mother and hers back to him, mushroomed. It was almost as though they were in the same room together: when in fact they were often at opposite ends of the earth.

She wrote from Calcutta, 'I am writing out a piece about Indian Christians from St Thomas onwards for you and Billa which I will send when completed. I am just off to see St Thomas's Mount, traditional place of his martyrdom. His tomb is in a R[oman] C[atholic] Cathedral here but his bones were removed to Odessa in Turkey in the fourth century. Then to Chios and finally to Ortona in Italy.'[1]

In 1965 my mother decided to write a book about the Kulu Valley in Northern India. She had fallen in love with the place. She wrote from Simla on her way there, 'I can only say that I intend to be VERY SELfish for what life remains to me and do what I WANT to do (what *would* Mrs Folky [Sybil Harton] say?). To entertain only real chums and to go out v[ery] little and to WRITE and do research because I am really a Pevsner by nature. Yes, I am certainly VERY lucky to have so much to occupy me.'² JB replied from Trebetherick, 'I watch the paper anxiously to see whether the Chinks have invaded Simla. . . . I remembered you at St Endellion Mass this morning in bright sunlight on low granite arches. . . . The nights are cold, the light is caressing and beautiful on Bray Hill. There are rather too many cocktail parties, even for me. Archie is in and asks you to investigate the Visigothic art which he says is buried in the Kulu Valley and was put there by the Furlowes of the Manx.'³

If JB felt close in spirit to my mother, he was saddened by the distance he felt between himself and my brother. JB wrote to him (22 May 1965), 'It may well be that in your heart of hearts you would rather go on living the rest of your life there [USA] and that you don't like to hurt Mummy and me by telling us. Well, you won't hurt us. If you like the idea of becoming an American citizen, then the Harvard degree is an obvious step and I'll help. If, on the other hand, in your heart of hearts you hope eventually to return to teach in England . . . one thing besides the rather low pay teachers get here, that may be putting you off coming back, is the feeling that you have not yet justified yourself and that you are a failure. You are *not a failure*. You are facing a decision. Failures who take to the bottle are those who are unable to decide what to do, and who feel, as a consequence, useless and unwanted. You have decided to teach. What you have not decided is whether it is to be in America or England. . . . All I want to give you is self-confidence (which I never had myself for long stretches) and I know it only comes from earning one's living. . . . Much love, Dadz.'⁴ (My brother did choose to stay in America and become an American citizen.)

With JB in London and my mother spending more and more time in India, they decided, for economy reasons, to divide the Mead in half. It was an eminently divisible house. The Victorian villa tacked on to the front was let to a tidy middle-aged lady with a terrier, and the rambling farmhouse at the back became a new home during the intermittent periods my parents were there together. JB wrote to Rupert and me on my mother's birthday, St Valentine's Day, 1965, 'This is the first letter to be written in my new library. No carpet on the floor and the smell of new paint and the light is so unexpectedly bright after the old library that my books look more moth-eaten and dog-eared than ever – in fact it looks like a rather second-rate, second-hand bookshop in Hull with only the unsaleable items left on the shelves.'⁵ We had been down the weekend before rehanging pictures, moving furniture and shortening curtains. The Mead was altogether different to how we had found it when we first came in 1951. Always short of cash, my parents had sold the two fields either side of the short drive, and their buyers had quickly got planning permission for two new houses, which were soon surrounded by municipal shrubs. But the fields down to the brook and looking over to the church were still untouched and remain so to this day. Miss Molly Butler across the orchard in the grand yellow-brick villa had died in 1963. Her sister Miss Edmée's hand, ever wobblier, penned her hundredth letter to JB (1 June 1964): 'Dear Mr Betjeman, I wonder if you have heard anything from the Wantage Urban District Council? The Notice of Planning Appeal enquiry – it's about the noise – I can't go to the meeting and wonder if you can?.'[6]

In April 1964 JB and I went to the Watts Gallery at Compton in Surrey at the invitation of the curator, his old school friend from Marlborough, Wilfrid Blunt. He wrote (24 April 1964), 'We have just had it cheered up thanks to a thousand pounds from the Pilgrim Trust.'[7] It was a glorious sunny day – the art nouveau chapel like a rich jewel, and the utterly eccentric gallery and its surroundings were perfection – and then I drove JB back through winding Surrey lanes and into South London. I brought him back to Rupert's and my brand new home in Chepstow Villas, Notting Hill Gate. Elizabeth came to supper and from then onwards she was part of the Lycett Green family. What my Dad called 'the Management' (God) seemed to offer its blessing, for my mother and Elizabeth didn't meet. It seemed easier that they didn't. I certainly never thought twice about the situation. Like JB, Elizabeth was a listener and easy to get on with. When in London, JB spent his days at Cloth Fair and his evenings with her. The arrangement worked well and ninety-nine per cent of the friends of all three accepted it.

Without the constant travelling between Wantage and London throughout the winter months, JB's domestic life was less tiring than it had been. His working life, however, was stepping up. By now he was president or vice-president of over seventy societies and associations. Yet the flood of requests for support from almshouses, theatre groups, invalid funds and preservation societies was unending. 'The trouble is,' he said, 'these days everyone is typecast. I have been typecast as a silly old codger who wants to keep old buildings – in fact all I care about is good buildings. I'm an aesthete who loves the variety of English landscape.'[8] His image had been created. There was no escape. Michael Balfour, a director at Hutchinsons, who had taken him out to lunch, wrote (17 April 1964), 'The dark, crinkly-haired taxi-driver opened his hatch after I dropped you in Soho and said, "Wasn't that

John Betjeman, sir?" I said, "Yes." He closed his hatch again. Going
up Great Titchfield Street he opened it again and said, "Well, I belong
to the National Trust." '[9]

JB was now famous. Edmund Blunden wrote to him (20 September),
'Recently I went to a dentist who treated me most sympathetically and
when I asked what I was to pay, he was chiefly concerned to have an
autographed scrap of John Betjeman. His name is Miles Healey, of 59
Harley Street; there I leave it but should you give him his wish you
would give me mine too.'[10] Within a week JB wrote back, 'I have sent
off to your dentist a new harvest hymn I have written . . . but I can't be
bothered to type it all out because it's not good enough for someone as
good as you.'[11]

Alan Clarkson Rose wrote from the Pier Pavilion in Worthing, after
JB had written him a condolence letter about the death of his wife (2
October), 'As you say, ours was a perfect partnership in life and work
for forty-six years. Bless her dear heart, she had her little prides –
delightful little snob prides – and one of them was that John Betjeman
liked us, liked the show, and had written the preface to my book: only
about three months ago she was telling the doctors in the Llandudno
hospital about the book.'[12]

Little did Clarkson Rose know that one of the proudest moments of
JB's life was being asked that same year to the annual dinner of the
Grand Order of Water Rats – a great show-business accolade and far
greater for him than a command from Pamela Berry, the social hostess
who terrified him. She wrote, 'We would be so pleased if you were free
to come and dine here on November 25 *in any clothes*, I literally mean
any. Ted Heath is coming and the Bishop of somewhere.'[13] But JB was
practically always able to enjoy himself, because he had that extraordinary gift of making the most boring people scintillating.

Of his friends who were definitely *not* boring and whose company he
loved were Ian Fleming, author of the James Bond books, and his wife
Anne. A few months before Ian died, JB wrote him a fan letter to which
he replied (10 December 1963), 'A thousand thanks, my dear John, for,
I think the most unexpected and charming letter I have ever had. But as
Annie said when she delightedly read me the letter, "Tell him that he's
the person that created a world." And of course this is true and at that a
world that will outlive by centuries the rather grimy vulgarities of my
friend James Bond. As you know I have collected all your first
editions. . . . But to turn to your exhortations, I must warn you that I
am seriously running out of puff and my inventive streak is very nearly
worked out. However, since you tell me that I must, I will try to keep

going for one or two books more.'[14] Elizabeth and JB saw much of Ann after Ian's death. 'You and Phoeble are awfully good about it,' she wrote, 'and invariably raise my spirits.'[15]

Ogden Nash wrote to JB (26 November 1963), 'I cannot leave without sending you my warmest thanks for the truly glorious two hours you so generously devoted to me, from the opening whisky on through the Charterhouse visit. It made a happy ending to a frustrated and ignominious trip. I am still tottery and all in by the end of the afternoon with all the vigour of a new-born mouse, which last thought prompts me to submit the following horrific pun for your disapproval:

> 'A handsome young rodent from Bashan
> As a lifeguard became a sensation.
> All the lady mice waved
> And screamed to be saved
> By his mouse-to-mouse resuscitation.'[16]

Anthony Blond, the publisher, told me, 'John rang me and said did I want to go with him and Ogden Nash in the underground to Cockfosters and then to Charterhouse Square. *Why* didn't I go? But later that month I took him to Burton Constable and the Mayor of Hull insisted on an impromptu civic reception. The journey back in an aeroplane with the pilot pointing out aged airstrips from the war and your father even older churches and their particularities was the funniest ever.'[17]

In 1964 Karen Lancaster wrote from a nursing home in Bath, 'My heart attack was a very tiny one, they say. Very, very frightening. However I have felt perfectly well ever since and pretty bored here. . . . *Douglas Cleverdon must be mad* to put you and Osbert together on a prog[ramme]. After what happened last time twenty-five years ago.'[18] (JB and Osbert had got the giggles so badly on air that the director of programmes almost sacked Cleverdon for allowing them to be on together.) Karen died soon afterwards, casting a shadow over the Henley-on-Thames life which the Lancasters and the Pipers had created. But now that the Mead was less of a home than it used to be, JB still found solace at the Pipers' farmhouse Fawley Bottom. Later in 1964 he wrote an introduction to a series of John Piper's church lithographs. 'You and I have visited a large number of these churches separately or together over the years,' wrote John Piper (6 October 1964). 'This is a retrospect of some of these churches and a retrospect of the lithographic art as I have tried to understand and comprehend it over the same long period. . . . It would be easier if we could write it as

a dialogue in ten minutes and if you could come here one day.'[19] JB
obliged and John Piper later wrote (2 November), 'The intro is *very good
indeed* and I am delighted with it. Thank you very much and also E.
Cavendish for typing it so beautifully. Osbert seems in good order, and
went to dine last night with Peter Fleming. Hope we will see you soon.
Nice lot of folks here.'[20]

By 1965 trouble was looming at Fabers over the *Shell Guides* which JB
and John Piper had collaborated on so successfully. There had already
been a row over Jim Lees-Milne's mention of the desecration of the city
of Worcester in *Worcestershire* and JB was experiencing increasing
interference in the editing of the guides. He wasted whole days writing
long heartfelt letters setting out endless details of past injustices. In the
end, after thirty glorious years of joint editorship, John Piper wrote to
David Bland of Fabers (22 February 1966), 'I find the present system is
really not working. The public I believe would prefer the county guides
to be more larky, with more old engravings and line drawings, and
maybe quotations and humorous drawings – more like they were when
they first started. I feel to some extent responsible for the present,
possibly over-serious, style. . . . We (JB and I) were told we must
produce two new guides a year. . . . I find the cutting down on pages,
when there is fine material, and the general uncertainty quite
intolerable. A guide should be as long – within reason – as it seems to
the editors it ought to be.'[21]

But JB's spirit was flagging. He knew full well that John Piper was
putting in far more work than he was and in 1967, he picked a quarrel
with Shell when they insisted on the withdrawal of a defamatory
reference to the Norwich Union Society Building in Northampton
which Juliet Smith had made in her *Northamptonshire*. JB resigned and
John Piper assumed sole editorship. There was no ill feeling: 'As one
gets older,' JB wrote to John Piper, 'one can't work so fast, one's ideas
run out.'[22]

JB was always happiest writing poetry, but the older he got, the more
difficult it became: 'Poetry to me is the putting down of moments of
ecstasy or depression that occur to me, in as short a way as possible.'
But JB's poetry wasn't enough to subsist on. He was supporting my
mother and the Mead and, every weekday in London, if he was not
being taken out, he was more often than not taking others out to lunch.
To live on his income, for he never had capital, he *had* to take on more
television work to feel financially secure.

This was the turning point. From the mid-sixties onwards JB
concentrated more on making films than on anything else. His

television career boomed. In 1962 he had met the young director Jonathan Stedall, an old Harrovian, and with him proceeded to make several films for a series called *Wales and the West*. That year, they made films in Devizes, Sherborne, Crewkerne, Chippenham, Swindon, Sidmouth and Bath, in 1963 in Marlborough, Weston-super-Mare, Clevedon and Malmesbury, and over the ensuing years made many more including *Summoned by Bells* and *Time with Betjeman*. 'He loved "telly" at a time when television was still regarded with a certain amount of snobbish disdain,' remembered Tristram Powell, the director and son of Anthony and Violet. 'His love of craftsmanship in architecture and the arts meant that he had a feeling for the technique and skills that went into the making of documentary films – photography, use of sound, the writing of narration, the way scenes could be cut together, all fascinated him, as did the characters of the people who found themselves working together on his films. He would send me fan letters about programmes that I'd made. Most people don't, so his generosity and praise was a big boost.'[23]

But it was with Kenneth Savidge that JB made the most films, almost forty in all. 'I had met JB when he was doing religious radio talks for Martin Wilson, for whom I worked. I graduated to television in the late fifties and was then in charge of religious programming in BBC Bristol. John and I made a series called the *ABC of Churches* which involved filming twenty-six churches all through the sixties.

'John knew the craft of television *well* but at the same time he didn't take it too seriously; he was extremely good with everyone in the crew. He was always sneaking off to the pub with them. I remember losing him completely in the village of Eddington – *eventually* I found him an hour later in the pub with the drivers. I remember there was a yuppie and his bird in there and John said, "I bet they'll order ten Seniors and a Babycham." And they did. Once when we were filming at Parkstone in Bournemouth, John brought Archie to this hotel we were staying in. While we were out filming, the chambermaid removed him from the mantelpiece and put him in the bottom of the wardrobe. JB gave her five pounds never to come near the room again.

'There was nowhere John loved more than a cutting room. "Give me a cutting room and the film and I'm happy," he'd say. He would whiz film backwards and forwards on the Steinbeck for hours and hours. We had such fun with the outside broadcast crew, sometimes there were as many as twenty of us. John named the van in which the video tape recordings were done "the cinema". In the end, it was known as "Ray's Cinema". Ray Burgess was the sound recordist. It's still called Ray's

Cinema to this day. . . . He delighted in the different clerics we met all round the country. We filmed in churches from Aldbourne to Blisland and from Yaverland in the Isle of Wight to Zennor in Cornwall. At Inglesham on the upper reaches of the Thames above Lechlade, JB arrived down the infant Thames in a punt propelled by the willowy son of the incumbent, who was called Father Thomas. Father Thomas was very modern and said immediately, "Call me Padre" and then he said, 'I bet you don't do this for nothing." John and I doubled up laughing afterwards and "Call me Padre," then became a stock description of a certain sort of cleric. I remember he asked a Dorset "Call me Padre" if he could film his church by G.E. Street. "You can come if you want to, but I do not see what *possible* interest my church could be to your viewers." But the point was, that John with his clear grasp of the technique of television could put over his *enthusiasm* and the ability to make people *think*.'[24]

Above all, JB loved the regional attitude of BBC Bristol. He had worked there for over thirty years. By the early sixties, the independence of BBC regions was already being undermined and JB was prophetic when he told Ken, 'The way the BBC is going, it will soon all become accountants and journalists.'

 1. JB's papers, Beinecke Library, Yale University.
 2. JB's papers, Beinecke Library.
 3. PB's papers, Beinecke Library, Yale University.
 4. PSGB's papers.
 5. CLG's papers, British Library.
 6. JB's papers, University of Victoria, British Columbia.
 7. JB's papers, University of Victoria.
 8. JB interview, *Picture Post* (July 1964).
 9. JB's papers, University of Victoria.
10. JB's papers, University of Victoria.
11. Edmund Blunden's papers, Harry Ransom Humanities Research Center, University of Texas.
12. JB's papers, University of Victoria.
13. JB's papers, University of Victoria.
14. JB's papers, University of Victoria.
15. JB's papers, University of Victoria.
16. JB's papers, University of Victoria.
17. Anthony Blond, letter to CLG (1994).
18. JB's papers, University of Victoria.
19. JB's papers, University of Victoria.
20. JB's papers, University of Victoria.
21. Carbon copy of John Piper's letter, JB's papers, University of Victoria.

22. John Piper's papers.
23. Tristram Powell, CLG interview (1994).
24. Kenneth Savidge, CLG interview (1994).

To Rupert Hart-Davis   43 Cloth Fair
20 August 1963   London EC1

Dear Rupert,
I am looking forward to hearing from you about Harold [Hobson]'s finances and don't at all mind going all out to help by writing to David Astor if need be.

Your own predicament strikes a double blow, for you, like Harold, have done so much for so many literary gents including yours truly, have been such a wonderful publisher and producer of good-looking books, such a champion of causes, all on top of being so excellent and scholarly and READABLE a biographer. But you, unlike Harold, have many dependent on you and get this bloody Jugoslav financier doing you down. As you say it's not the cash that matters but the dependants – also to the English world of letters, the loss of a great publisher and enthusiast and a non-Leavis-Lewis-Wain-ite. Will you read Browning's thing which goes, 'Fear death? to feel the fog in my throat . . . .'? (I can't remember where it is or in which poem – but it goes on, 'One fight more, the last and the lost. . . .') We MUST WIN. I don't really think people like Lord Bridges and financial Jug[oslav]s triumph finally – in the end you will triumph. Hold on.
    Yours, John B

> Harold Hobson, the fabled theatre critic, was down on his luck. Hobson worked for the *Sunday Times*. JB's offer to write to David Astor, editor of the *Observer*, displays how seldom he read the papers.
>   The financier was William Jovanovich, a US citizen from Montenegro, head of the American firm Harcourt Brace which had bought out R.H.-D. and then let him down.
>   Browning's poem is called 'Prospice'.

To Harry Jarvis   43 Cloth Fair
13 October 1963   London EC1

My dear Harry,
Your letter was most helpful and kind. I'm sure somehow things will come out all right. Your prayers and intentions are very valuable to me,

as you of all people know the situation. I feel an intense desire for
solitude and *comfort* (i.e. *not* Cowley) but one's desires should not, I
fear, be catered for. I live hour to hour. Candida and Rupert go away
again for a year on Wednesday. We can't let the Mead but it is at last
tidy and clean. I've not seen old Hugh [Pickles] but gather from
F[athe]r J[ohn] S[chaufelberger] he's getting on all right. How's the
Smasher? Give her my deep love. How can one find out whether one's
really queer? By 'pre-marital intercourse'? What an awful phrase! By
self-analysis? Impossible. By Faith? I don't know. The last seems most
likely but best of all is the test of good old physical and mental desire in
not quite equal halves, the balance being on physical and gradually
growing even with the years. Few people get that happy balance and
it's not their fault they don't. It's circ[umstance]s. God bless you in
whatever you do.

   I've written a Harvest Hymn. I may have told it you.

'We spray the fields and scatter
   The poisons on the ground
So that no wicked flowers
   Can on our farms be found
We love whatever helps us
   To line our purse with pence
The twenty-four-hour broiler house
   And neat electric fence
All concrete barns around us
   All Jaguars in the yard
The deep freeze and the telly lounge
   Are ours – from working hard.

   I go to Cornwall on Thursday.
   Love, JB

JB had written to H.J. about his feelings of guilt over EC and PB. H.J. had replied (29
September 1963), 'As promised I offered the Mass for you today and commended you to
the Almighty. . . . I do offer a quick one for you every day but this was a bit more
special. I *do* sympathise with you and wish that there were something that I could say, or
better still do, that would be of the slightest use or help. Sometimes one gets caught in a
lot of circ[umstance]s which are completely outside one's control and have no easy
solution (even if they have a solution at all) except death. All that one can do is face each
moment and leave it to God and try not to feel too guilty and frightful about it. God
knows exactly *how* guilty one is and bearing that sort of pain is all part of the working out
of the Incarnation in the individual life. Ghastly and hell it can be, but then the Cross
(part of the Incarnation) was ghastly and hell too.'
   In October 1963, RLG and I set off to drive round the world in a Land-Rover and did
not return until the following summer.
   The Smasher, as JB called Jean Cunliffe, was H.J.'s intended.

To T.S. Eliot   Treen
                                                           Trebetherick
                                                           Wadebridge
18 October 1963   Cornwall

Dear Tom,
Here I am until November 4th and there's your nice letter of a week ago
unanswered till now because I've been in London for only one day. I
rang up Elizabeth and she's thrilled at the idea of us dining with you
both ere Nov[ember] 30th. She's coming down here with her Mum and
will be *here* Monday so let's fix a date *after* Nov[ember] 4th and *before*
Nov[ember] 30th. Send me or her a line here. I've been staying at St
Michael's College, Tenbury, Worc[ester]s[hire]. I can't recommend it
too highly for a visit. There it is founded in 1853 by Sir Frederick
Gore-Ouseley in Gothic buildings, also 1853 by H[enry] Woodyer, a
Lancing under the Clee hills and a daily Matins and Evensong and
anthem from a large choir of resident boys and men – an amazing and
unknown and beautiful C[hurch] of E[ngland] outpost.
    Yours, John B

> T.S.E. (see *Volume One*), who had been JB's teacher at Highgate School in 1916, worked
> for the publishers Fabers. He and JB had long been admirers of each other's poetry.
>   Jim Lees-Milne, describing St Michael's College in the *Shell Guide to Worcestershire*,
> wrote, 'On the edge of a wide common is a stately group of stone buildings consisting of a
> choir school and chapel joined by cloisters . . . in spidery Gothic 1856.' In the college is a
> famous music library collected by Sir Frederick Gore-Ouseley.

To Harry Jarvis   43 Cloth Fair
16 November 1963   London EC1

Dear Harry,
I am so sorry to be so long answering yours of the 4th inst. Only excuse
was that I put it off as it is a *pleasure* writing to you and other letters are
the product of *guilt* not pleasure. I've been away in Bristol and at the
Mead. We've let it, I think, through Feeble's sister Anne to an interior
decorator, my dear, called Tom Parr (late of Hicks and Parr and now
Colefax's) who will be an excellent tenant and wants the house from
Dec[ember] 8th till end of July. It seems that Penelope left instructions
that she wouldn't mind if someone wanted the house until [the] end of
July, with her solicitor. So she obviously intends staying longer in

India than May – unless she wants to stay with the Barings or in a Convent in order to write.

Of course now P[enelope] is away the strain with Feeble is less great, if not the guilt, and Feeble is wonderfully well and becoming Robust instead of Feeble and Toughness instead of Weakness. We haven't been oop north and I wish I had noted that bit in your letter about the 14th invitation or I would have replied sooner and said I couldn't come. I go to Linc[oln]s[hire] (Louth) at end of month and St Peter's Barnsley on Dec[ember] 3rd to open an exhibition of Temple Moore's work and then Wales. Any chance of seeing you at F[athe]r Phillip's at St Peter's in Barnsley on Dec[ember] 3rd? I'll be staying the night of the 2nd with Kenneth Young at 21 Shaw Lane, Headingley, Leeds. He's editor of the Y[orkshire] P[ost] and I'm God-daddy to one of his kiddiz.

Miss Molly Butler has died.

Old Hugh [Pickles] is settling down well, I hear. If you read a brilliant and v[ery] funny novel called *The Path of Dalliance* by Auberon Waugh (Evelyn's son), you'll see why English R[oman] C[atholic]s make it impossible for us and for the spread of the Catholic Faith in England. I absolutely agree with you about fucking about with Methodists, though – another waste of time. No, the C[hurch] of E[ngland] is the Catholic Church, tempting though it is to think it isn't – and English Romanism is sectarian. It's very odd. Perhaps I'm prejudiced owing to being married to a convert. Do you get a sense, then, of not being a priest? You most certainly are and a wonderful one. I met two charming and handsome friends of yours called Machin of the Dragon School and Westminster who acted as chauffeurs to me at the Mead last weekend.

My love to the Smasher, Jean. That was funny the way you never told me she was lovely to look at and I was expecting just a musical schoolmistress.

Feeble sends her love, so do I.

John B

Hugh Pickles had become vicar of Blewbury.
The Machin boys came from Worksop.

To John Sutro   43 Cloth Fair
26 November 1963   London EC1

My dear John,
I take up my art pen from Bedford Park to thank you for the delicious
treat of yesterday's luncheon at the Garrick. I was ever an Arts and
Crafts worker who delighted in penmanship and I would dearly like to
see penned those immortal lines you recited on the Ward case. They
must not be hidden only in your memory. Pen them and send them out
to us who were there. We will guard the secret if there's libel. Well, ta
ever so, old man. It was a joy to see Harold [Acton] and to meet B[inkie]
Beaumont. Oh it was all joy.
  Bung-ho-ski from John B

> J.S. (see *Volume One*), the film-maker and Oxford friend of JB's, had given a lunch in the
> small private dining room at the Garrick Club to amuse the historian and aesthete
> Harold Acton (see *Volume One*) on his yearly visit to London.
>   'Binkie' Beaumont was at the time London's most successful and influential theatrical
> manager.
>   J.S.'s 'immortal lines' were about the sad suicide of Dr Stephen Ward (whom JB knew
> and liked) who had been involved in the major political scandal surrounding John
> Profumo and his affair with the beautiful call girl, Christine Keeler. The verse, written
> in August 1963, began:
>
>> HIC JACET VIR FAMOSUS STEPHEN WARD
>> By our Society ruined and abhorred . . . .
>> FIAT JUSTITIA RUAT LEX
>> With WARD we bury the delights of sex . . . .
>> This hypocritical and false campaign
>> Ended one Saturday in heavy rain
>> When saying farewell to all the lies and cant
>> 'BARBITURI VOS SALUTANT' . . . .
>
> The Latin lines read:
>
>> Here lies a famous man Stephen Ward . . .
>> Let justice be done, to hell with the law.
>
> In the last line J.S. has adapted the classic line:
>> Morituri salutant [Those who are about to die salute you]
> to refer to Stephen Ward's overdose of barbiturates.

To Tom Driberg   43 Cloth Fair
27 November 1963   London EC1

Dear Thomas,
I must write to you about the Foreign Office. As the power of
Parliament declines, civil servants increase and it is natural that they
should want to expand. But with improvement in communication I
shouldn't have thought it was necessary for thousands of them to be
opposite Downing Street. The Gilbert Scott building is not wholly his
work. It is very much by Sir Matthew Digby Wyatt and the carvings
(by H. H. Armstead (see [the] D[ictionary of] N[ational] B[iography])
in the spandrels of the arches on the Whitehall front are really splendid.
Also it is well proportioned to the eighteenth-century buildings in
Whitehall and on the Park side. If the civil servants must find new egg
boxes for themselves, then it would be far more sensible to pull down
the hideous Leeming and Leeming 1880 Admiralty building and to
blow up the citadel west of it, or to rebuild the War Office or that
dreary building where the Treasury and Ministry of Defence and
Housing and Local Government hang out at the Parliament Square end
of Whitehall. If Whitehall is to be rebuilt then it should be expanded on
the principles by which we expand any historic piece of architecture,
which is the gradual growth of centuries, that is to say, by keeping the
best bits of the old and getting rid of the second-rate. The sequence of
buildings from the Admiralty to and including the Foreign Office on
the west side of Whitehall is really splendid. It is London's equivalent
of St Mark's Square and represents government before it was
controlled by the civil service. That is to say, it is a series of grand and
less grand private houses like Dover House with its Henry Holland
screen (now the Scottish Office), the First Lord's house by S.P.
Cockerell, 10 Downing Street and Kent's Old Treasury building and
Horse Guards. Then comes what might be called the mid-Victorian
clubland phase of government, when Parliament was a club and the
Foreign Office looks like a splendid Pall Mall clubhouse. At the
beginning of this century and the end of the last, we get the Civil
Service phase, tedious official architecture mostly the result of
competitions, like the Admiralty, the War Office and the new
government offices on Parliament Square. I feel that the preservation of
all except these last mentioned is more important really than whether or
not there is a competition for a new Foreign Office. Clearly at the back
of the whole thing is strife between permanent civil servants. The all-

powerful Treasury and Cabinet offices and Ministry of Defence, Housing and L[ocal] G[overnment] will not leave the dull Brydon building, the Admiralty is a law to itself and so, I expect, is the War Office and the weak and obstinate permanent secretary of the Ministry of Works, an old Bradfieldian called Sir Edward Muir, has pushed Mr Rippon into saying he will pull down the Foreign Office.

I do hope, Thomas, that you will be able to get the amenity people on both sides to press for a reconsideration of the architecture of Whitehall as a whole, instead of having one of its best bits of architecture sacrificed to inter-departmental strife. I'll be at the BBC in Bristol tomorrow and back here at lunchtime on Saturday and then back on Wednesday and Thursday next week. Don't bother to answer, but if you can act, old boy, oh, for goodness sake do so.

Yours, John B

> While Britain was gripped by the Profumo Affair, the architect Sir Leslie Martin was busy preparing a comprehensive plan for the redevelopment of the Whitehall area which involved the removal of every post-Georgian government building to make way for efficient new office blocks for civil servants. First for the chop was Gilbert Scott's Foreign Office (including the old India Office by Matthew Digby Wyatt). It was built after the 'Battle of the Styles' of the 1850s, which Geoffrey Rippon, Minister of Public Buildings & Works, considered sufficient justification to announce in November 1963 that, 'I have therefore decided to demolish the existing building.' Also threatened was Norman Shaw's New Scotland Yard. The Victorian Society fought against these proposals and all the buildings – including the Edwardian Baroque building facing Parliament Square by the Scot J. M. Brydon – were eventually saved by a change in public opinion reinforced by bureaucratic inertia. (The state rooms in the Foreign Office have now been immaculately restored.)

To Juliet Smith   43 Cloth Fair
5 December 1963   London EC1

Dear Juliit,
I am so glad to hear from Fabers that the Shell people approve the idea of a guide to Northa[mpton]s[hire]. If you don't mind the idea, I think it would be best if you send, let us say, half a dozen entries to me in your own time so that I can give you any advice and encouragement if you need them.

The value of the *Shell Guides* is to tell people what places are really like now and it doesn't matter a bit if the descriptions grow out of date in twenty years. The *Shell Guides* are a record of what England is now and a candid personal opinion of each parish and town.

It is no good trying to write a comprehensive impersonal catalogue. That is being done already in Pevsner's *Buildings of England*, and does not tell you what the place is really like, i.e. whether it is strung with poles and wires, overshadowed by factories or ruined army huts, whether it is suburban or a real village, nor whether it is a place of weekend hide-outs and carriage-lamp folk with wrought-iron front gates by the local smith. Nor do guide books tell you whether there are trees in the village, nor what sort if they are remarkable for size and planting.

It would be possible to write a full guide book to every parish in Northa[mpton]s[hire] without leaving your house, for there are the standard reference works like *Kelly's Directory*, which is far the most useful book and if you haven't got a *Kelly's Northa[mpton]s[hire]*, I'll try to get my copy from the Mead, which is now let. There are also antiquarian histories like the *Victoria County History* which is over-factual and all about ancient families and ruins. Then there is the *Little Guide* which is generally written by an antiquarian clergyman interested in dates and squinches and pillar piscinas, and from which you would think the only building in a place is the old church and there are also local histories and records of single parishes and deaneries. I have often been infuriated by reading a long entry in a *Little Guide* or in *Kelly* or *Pevsner* about a church, from which one would gather it was so full of antiquities it was like Westminster Abbey, yet when you get there you find the churchyard has been mown and planted with standard roses and the eighteenth-century headstones either broken up or leant like playing cards against the walls, and when you get inside you find the plaster has been scraped off the walls by the Victorians who also laid shiny new tiles on the floor, filled windows with green and pink glass and re-pewed everything in pitch pine with oak for the chancel, so that although all the features described may be there, you can hardly notice them for modern accretions. And probably more prominent than any wall monument will be the switch box to the electric lights and the leads to huge surgical basins fixed as flood lights on to the mediaeval roof.

No, don't bother too much about dates and styles beyond mentioning whether a church is mediaeval or Georgian or Victorian and do the same for houses. Pick out the ones you like and these may often be groups of farm buildings, and for adjectives, avoid dead ones like 'fine', 'ancient', 'magnificent', and instead use words describing shape and colour, tall, fat, thin, square, pink, brown, red, mottled with moss etc. And don't be frightened of saying a place is hideous if you think it.

Besides *Kelly* and possibly The *Little Guide*, the place indexes of

Colvin's *Dictionary of English Architects 1660–1840* and Rupert Gunnis's *Dictionary of British Sculptors* are sometimes useful and show one something one might otherwise miss. But really it is the eye and the heart that are the surest guides.

Dear Juliit and dear Emma [Cavendish], if you are going to do this work with her, don't be frightened, like what you like and say so, make jokes when you feel like it and visit every parish in the county which will take ages. It is useful too in the towns, such as Northampton and Banbury, to visit the suburban churches because they are always in an unexpected part of the town where there may be rows of grand villas or arid new building estates which conjure up another world from the Northamptons of Plumpton.

It is fearfully difficult work writing these equivalents of condensed description which are really landscape and townscape telegrams. I met my co-editor, Mr Piper, by chance in the street while I was taking a breather from writing this letter and he told me to tell you to take a look at Norman Scarfe's *Shell Guide to Suffolk* as a model of condensed writing. It brings in people as well as places.

Finally, some more practical advice – you need one-inch ordnance maps and, if possible, a companion to read them and it is wise to write your descriptions on the spot, or you will find yourselves clogged with places. Prefaces and essays and things can follow when the gazetteer part is done. If you take photographs and if the weather is good, do take them. If there is something you want photographed, let me have a note of it. There is no hurry as Fabers will have told you and you will find it a long job, but I honestly think it is worth doing. Northa[mpton]s[hire] with its wonderful building stones, churches and houses, is about the best county in England for guide book writing as it is so varied and so undeservedly neglected.

Love, John

J.S. (now Townsend) is the daughter of Freddie Birkenhead, JB's literary adviser and friend who wrote the introduction to his *Collected Poems*. Her mother Sheila was my Aunt Patricia Chetwode's sister, and PSGB and I stayed at the Birkenheads' house at Charlton, Northamptonshire, nearly every holidays. I always pronounced Juliet *Juliit*, and envied her cleverness.

Her *Shell Guide to Northamptonshire* came out in 1968.

Freddie Birkenhead had written to JB (29 November 1963), 'I must send a line to thank you most sincerely for your friendly interest in Juliet. It is wonderful news that she may really have a chance of doing the Northants *Shell Guide*. I am delighted about this because I am so anxious that she should have a literary career, and this is a wonderful start. I am sure that she will do the job well, as she is a born writer, and tremendously keen. Also, in my opinion, Northamptonshire although considered rather dim contains as many beautiful churches and country houses and historic interest as any county in England.'

To Mollie and Desmond Baring   Plas Newydd
                                                              Llanfairpwll
21 December 1963   Isle of Anglesey

Dear Mollie and Dez,
Here I am – for a christening but *not asked for Christmas*. I thought it
would be too sad to be around the Wantage area then with the Mead
shut up, so I'm going to stay at Wotton under Edge with my chum Jim
Lees-Milne and his missus. Jim has written a *Shell Guide to Worcestershire*
which is rightly so rude about the frightful things done in the name of
progress to the city and villages, that the Shell people are turning nasty
and won't publish it unless I can get him to alter the text. I'm on his
side.

Love to Arne who must be in East London now, a sort of Florence
Nightingale. Love to Peter. Love to Nigel. Love to Ben [Warner] and
your mother. Love to the Augur. Let's hope we'll meet soon. The
Mead is let till the end of JULY. I've had some v[ery] funny letters from
Penelope and Wibz who've met in 'Injer'.

Harpy Chrieesmuss, John B

> JB was staying with PB's cousin Henry Anglesey, who was married to Shirley, daughter
> of the novelist Charles Morgan.
>   As PB, RLG and I were in India, M.B. had asked JB for Christmas. As a family we
> had traditionally always joined up with the Barings at Ardington House for a meal at
> Christmas and for racing at Kempton on Boxing Day, but on this occasion JB went to
> stay with the Lees-Milnes.
>   M.B.'s father was the bookmaker Ben Warner.
>   'The Augur' was Sam Long who wrote for *Sporting Life*.

To Elizabeth Bowen   Treen
                                                             Trebetherick
                                                             Wadebridge
25 February 1964   Cornwall

Dear Elizabeth,
Do you remember the novels of Norah Hoult? – *Time, Gentlemen, Please!*
is the one I most recall – a sort of Sylvia Townsend Warner type of
writer with rather more bite, and Anglo-Irish or Irish. Well, it seems
she is in a bad way financially and left England to retire to her native
Ireland and live in a cottage which she thought would be cheaper. It

isn't. Her doctor and an American friend have testified to her not having enough to eat and we want to get her a civil list pension. The fact that she's Irish doesn't seem to matter as her books are published in England and usually about England. We aren't telling her we're trying to get her a pension but we know she won't reject it if it's offered but will willingly receive it.

Would you be willing to send a letter through the Prime Minister's Secretary to be addressed 'Dear Prime Minister' saying she is a good novelist and a writer of distinction? If you could, coming from an Anglo-Irish writer of GREAT DISTINCTION, NAY GENIUS, such as yourself, it will carry a lot of weight. Don't bother to reply to me but if you do write about Norah Hoult send the letter to Colin Somerford, 41 Upper Park Road, NW3, who is arranging things. I am in Cornwall till next Sunday, then horrible old London. Penelope is in India till May.

Love, John B

> JB knew E.B. (see *Volume One*), the distinguished and prolific novelist and short-story writer, through one of her lovers, Sean O'Faolain, the editor of the *Bell* whom JB had been close to when in Ireland.
> Norah Hoult also wrote *Farewell*, *Happy Fields*, and *Two Girls in the Big Smoke*.
> JB was acting on behalf of the Royal Literary Fund. Their papers remain confidential for fifty years.

To Harry Jarvis   Treen
                                                              Trebetherick
                                                               Wadebridge
25 February 1964   Cornwall

My dear Harry,
Well, I must say that is v[ery] interesting about St Crispin's Hospital, Durton [Malawi]. You have long wanted to be a hospital chaplain. I think it *is* worth applying *in order to find out about it*. I would hesitate to accept before finding out. I have an idea that you would need a lot of faith – i.e. to go on believing God does work, even when the patient thinks he is a poached egg and has to sit on toast all day, and still more faith when the person *seems* quite reasonable but isn't. There's no doubt that love is far more effective than medicine, mental or physical. It will be a constant giving. You may find some saints more obvious, I expect, among the staff than the patients and some of these may be devout atheists.

Feeble's throat is a little better. St Blaise will be invoked. I am down in Cornwall till next Sunday when I return via other parts of Cornwall and Somerset to London.

You will also know, if you do decide one way or the other, how much you and the smashing Jean need each other for life.

Oh, how difficult life is. At the time of writing I wish I were dead.
Love, John B

The United Society of Propagation of the Gospel had suggested that H.J. go out as a missionary to Southern Africa. He did not take up the offer.

To Wilhelmine Harrod   43 Cloth Fair
3 March 1964   London EC1

Darling Billa,
You know how much you attract me physically as well as spiritually so it is lovely to get a long letter from you. Lord H[ampton] has only the electric, alas, but it is the same sort of house otherwise as yours. He is an FRIBA. I have entered June 6th and 7th in my diary but won't know for certain if I'm free then because of a huge West Country Telly programme lasting an hour. Reading verse is easiest. So let's say yes provisionally (till about May when my programme of movements is clearer), if that's okay by you. I believe I'm due to the other Old Rectory, Holt, somewhere very near that date. I have to be so vague, darling, because of *cash*. The more my royalties diminish the more I have to do telly. I can hardly write at all nowadays. I enclose entertaining letter from Penelope and Candida, which please return. I would love to come to your Norfolk Holt again and spout for the dear old C[hurch] of E[ngland].

Love to Roy H and D[ominick] and kisses to you by the thousand. What we want is love not unity – love first and unity in God's good time – but I'm speaking theologically now of course and trying to drive your Harrod curves from my imagination.
Love, John B

W.H. (née Cresswell, see *Volume One*), to whom JB was momentarily engaged in 1933, was married to Roy H. and was an old friend of the family. She had written the *Shell Guide to Norfolk* in 1957 and was a leading light as the saviour of Norfolk's historic churches. (She founded the Norfolk Churches Trust in 1970.)

W.H. lived at the Old Rectory, Holt, in Norfolk and JB had discovered, to his delight, that Lord Hampton lived at the Old Rectory, Holt, in Worcestershire. Thereafter, he was always trying to discover similarities between the two houses. W.H.'s house had been on gas only when they arrived.

JB had been to read poetry in Salthouse Church, Norfolk, in aid of local churches.
At the time, he was making a television series called *Discovering Britain*.
Roy H.'s economics theory was known as 'the Harrod Curve'.

To Gilbert Nelson   43 Cloth Fair
10 March 1964   London EC1

Dear Mr Nelson,

I must thank you for your charming letter about the old S[omerset] and D[orset]. I envy you living at Bude. I have twice lately been to that town by the London and South-Western and, so far as I can see, the brute Beeching has not yet deprived us of our lines down there and if he does, I don't see how the narrow roads are going to cope with the summer traffic. I never go to Cornwall in the summer now but I love it in the winter and at this time of the year. When you and your corgi set off for the cliffs, remember me to the Atlantic rollers and the long stretch of sand to the canal and every station between you and Halwill Junction.

Yours sincerely, John Betjeman

G.N., unknown to JB, had written to congratulate him on his recent television programme about the Somerset and Dorset Railway. He wrote (22 February 1964), 'I am nearly seventy-six years of age and still remain a boy as regards trains. I have my own GWR Model Railway which is insured for two hundred and fifty pounds and this was built by my son and myself thirty years ago and Dr Beeching cannot touch it. . . . I would like you to give me a call as I would like to show you my lay-out and have a chat about railways in general. When one had been in touch with you through reading and TV and radio one feels that they know you and I hope you will not think me presuming in saying this.'

Richard Beeching was Chairman of the British Railways Board (1963–5) during which time he did a great deal to change, and some would say to ruin, the face of Britain's travel network by closing down thousands of miles of railway line. He was a *bête noir* of JB's.

To Unknown   43 Cloth Fair
12 March 1964   London EC1

Dear Sir,

It was very kind of you to write, but I can't give you inspiration, only advice. It is this. Read the poets you enjoy and always read the poetry before the criticism and even read the biography of a poet before you read the criticism. And anyhow, write about what you really feel and

see and think until you have got the words in what you think is the final
order and be sure that your poem has form, that is to say a shape. Poems
don't have to be long to be good. Personally I prefer the traditional
rhymes and rhythms because unless you know about them I don't see
how you know what 'free' verse is. Then, when you have written a
poem, put it away for a day or two and have a look and see what you
think of it and change it if need be, and go on and on at this and always
be true to yourself and not what you think people think you ought to
be true to, and you will have a deep inner content, even if none of
your poems are published. When you have written one, send it
to a magazine, not to me, as I am at the wrong end of the line and of
life.

   Yours sincerely, John Betjeman

To John Piper   43 Cloth Fair
4 April 1964   London EC1

Dear Mr Piper,
Let me put down in Sweet Italian hand what I said through rosy lips.
Your exhibition was a wonderful, thrilling revelation of your consistent
and deep genius. It made me realise, if I had ever doubted it, that you
are a great man. Fuck the critics. They're jealous of recognition. You
have saved much of England by your pictures of arshytekture and
landscape. What is more you have increased our vision. Things look
like pictures by Mr Piper and look better for having been seen by him.
How different from Dr Pevsner. And this does not take into account
the wondrous abstracts and glass and best of all, the CHURCHES YOU
ARE DOING NOW.
   Bung ho, John B

         J.P. had a retrospective exhibition at the Marlborough Galleries in London in March.
            Later that year a suite of his lithographs called 'A Retrospect of Churches' was
         exhibited at the Marlborough Galleries, and JB wrote a four-page introduction to it.

To Raymond Erith   43 Cloth Fair
2 May 1964   London EC1

Dear Raymond,
I went up to White Stone Pond on a fine evening early this week, to see
Jack Straw's Castle. It is a gem. It looks as though it has always been
there – a Middlesex castellated boat house, come to rest on a hill top.
And yet it doesn't look at all pastiche either. I went into the bars but it
was just on closing time so I couldn't get out into the gardens at the back
nor the upstairs rooms. I shall visit it again. And this is to say how glad I
am it is there and how good an architect you are and how I'm glad
you're a R[oyal] A[cademician]. Don't reply – see you at that bloody
Commission – not May but June.
    Yours, John B

> R.E., the architect, was already much admired by JB. He was on the Royal Fine Art
> Commission with him from 1960 to 1973. In JB's address at R.E.'s Memorial Service on
> 15 January 1973 at St Mary's Church on Paddington Green – one of his great restoration
> jobs – he alluded to the weather-boarded public house with machicolated parapet, Jack
> Straw's Castle in Hampstead, another of R.E.'s jobs, as 'a true Middlesex building
> without, and a delight in its upstairs rooms with their views over the Constable country
> of Hampstead Heath'.

To James Lees-Milne   43 Cloth Fair
6 May 1964   London EC1

Dear Jim,
I go to Cornwall tomorrow and your telephone is out of order, so I am
not able to do more than type my sorrow that I was away on Clifton
Downs with Randolph Sutton when you called at the College Close
Hotel – a very good hotel, by the way. I did not get back from filming
until too late on Monday night and yesterday to ring you. Shell seem to
have capitulated over the guide, but I don't see any point in printing
word for word what I said they had cut out and which received such
enormous publicity. I would prefer instead to say exactly the same
thing in different words so that those who do recall the publicity will
see that Shell *have* interfered with the text, yet we have been able to
convey exactly the same meaning. This controversy has been of the
greatest help for we are now going to be able, I hope, to safeguard
ourselves against future interference, to secure royalties and advance as

well as expenses for authors, in fact, to have no more dealings with Shell at all, but only with Fabers. I expect Fabers will be sending you revised proofs. I have a set here with their comments and you can send for it if you want it for reference. Love to Alvilde. Bung ho, old man.
    John B

An enormous row blew up over J.L.-M.'s introduction to the city of Worcester in his *Shell Guide to Worcestershire*. He said it had been sacked five times in its history, by Romans, Danes, Saxons, Welsh and Roundheads but never so disastrously as by the present mayor and corporation. Shell complained that people wouldn't go to Worcester as a result and hence wouldn't buy their petrol. The row leaked into the local press and JB was ready to resign over his conviction that the truth should be told. In the end J.L.-M.'s text was only mildly tempered and now reads, 'So much of the old city has been cleared away to make way for car parks and commercial development. . . that the visitor may have the impression that there has been yet another invasion.'
    Earlier in the year JB had written to J.L.-M., 'My row with Shell over your guide and my own to Cornwall has now reached proportions which force me to leave off editing them and I only hope Mr Piper will back me.'

To Penelope Betjeman   43 Cloth Fair
9 June 1964   London EC1

My darling Plymmi,
I was ever so pleased to have your two letters, one a continuation about the horrible thunderstorm you experienced in Simla and the other about your trek on horseback among the jeep-infested Himalayas. I had not realised that [the] whole world, even India, was in the devil's grip of the internal combustion engine. I do hope you don't get run over by a lorry on those narrow tracks. Be very careful.
    If they knighted Sri Romesh he would be Sir Sri Romesh like my typing errors. Mrs Folky [Sybil Harton]'s letter was fascinating and reminds me I must write to her, as she has written me a few little digs to which I have not had time to reply. Powlie's semester report has arrived and says he is Beta plus. He is in the inestimable position of knowing his limitations. Mr Snell will let me have what sort of saving there would be if you stayed till October but I should say that whatever it is you should consult your own wishes first and that getting your writing of the book done in the best circ[umstance]s should be the deciding factor.
    You will find that each week you may change in your views as to how long to stay – whatever Snell says and I will inform you as soon as I hear from him. I have warned Lee to expect a tin trunk. The Mead seems to be well cared for by the Parrs so far as I have heard and has become,

Wibz tells me, a fashionable rendezvous – even Sydney Herbert and his alarming wife go there now!

What has surprised me in myself very much is that I don't feel chained to my library as I thought I would be and with the prospect of either an extension of Barretts or a housing estate in the next field to the Mead, it makes me think you may want to sell for either building land or industrial development. I think we need a smaller place. Like you, I have shed much of the need for possessions but know you will want your pony and field for it to graze – and a smaller house. My income is down a lot and this is not because I do less work but because writing is less well paid than manual work today and I am not really very good at either. Curreys say that eighty pounds a month all in is the most I can afford for the Mead. Perhaps they and Mr Benson can work something out. I think Mr Benson seems a very good and reliable man. Anyhow, I remember how a gipsy told you at a fête at Faringdon, I think, years ago that we would never be rich but that we would not starve or be very poor. After all the poverty you must be seeing in India, I expect there is a lot to be thankful for. Nehru was obviously a wonderful man (an Old Harrovian) and you will be able to see the papers on your return. Wibz had her snap in the *Daily Express* as an expectant mother. She is now mad on cooking and being a housewife and has forsworn literature it seems. I am away a lot at the moment and have hardly seen her. I go to Hull today for much of next week (the White House Hotel, Hull) for Telly and then to Truro for more Telly and I have to be in Ha[mp]s[hire] and Sussex and Truro all on Telly. I have got a more efficient agent now who may well be able to help you. I love hearing from you and very much love you but want you to do what you feel suits you best about your book.

You are truly gifted and you don't know you are. Spansbury [John Sparrow] and Maurice [Bowra] have always realised this. I am so busy, I am quite happy and as I said, without you the pull of Wantage is nought and I do not need my books there . . . anyhow many of the best are now in a basement here.

Nooni nooni.

Yorz trewely, Tewpie

> In a later letter to PB, JB wrote, 'In the Royal Station Hotel, Hull, I was favoured in the middle of the night after I woke up from a nightmare about you and me being in someone else's house when we should not be there and I tried to run away and take you with me but you refused to budge and I heard the people coming back and ran for a train and couldn't run fast enough to catch it; anyhow after this dream I really did, before I went to sleep again, get a faint warm bath feeling of the Love of God and however bad one was it didn't matter, he loved one.'

To Bryan Moyne   43 Cloth Fair
6 July 1964   London EC1

Dear Bryan,
I am typing this as you can see, because my handwriting has got so bad
through journalism and I like to think my typing has a look of
handicraft which we both so much admire – work of each for weal of all
– as William Morris used to say, when I went to his socialist lectures in
Bedford Park. Harold Acton is sixty this week. I have told Sir Kaye
that the best thing for him to do is to write to Lord Elveden making
specific proposals. Your letter to me is really helpful for the light it
throws on the situation – the usual victory of chartered accountants
with their unaesthetic outlook over what is personal and humane. Why
you are so wise and good is because you have always been a poet and
minded about what really matters and understood as your poems show
lachrymas rerum – I have put tears into the accusative.
    Bung ho, old man, John B

> B.M. and JB and other friends were involved in trying to get an honour for Harold
> Acton. He received a CBE in 1965 and was knighted in 1974.

To Evelyn Waugh   Royal Hotel
September 1964   Hull

My dear Evelyn,
I must now take up my Pentel pen (made in Japan) to thank you most
warmly for *A Little Learning*, every page of which I have read. Most of
the book I read at a sitting, so great is your gift of narrative. Let me
single out for praise in particular two sections, the first is that which
deals with Hampstead and Arthur Waugh and Rev[erend] Basil
Bourchier. Of distinctly lower class socially than you myself and living
in Highgate and three years your junior, I can safely say I have ne'er
read so good and poetical a description of the de-countrifying of
Middlesex and the joys of the Heath, particularly the fair in the Vale of
Health to which I too used to be taken. Arthur Waugh comes out as a
very much nicer version of what I am myself minus the cricket which
has always bored me to tears. My landlord here in the City of London,
Paul Paget, is enchanted with your description of his Great-Aunt, Miss
Hoare who wore, he tells me, a collar and cuffs and tie. Oh, green and

mauve! Oh, votes for women! Oh, Dame Henrietta Barnett! Oh, Voysey in Platts Lane and Baillie Scott, Barry Parker, Raymond Unwin and then, daringly Georgian Lutyens, up there in the garden suburb!

The other section I like so much is Lancing. How lovably ridiculous appears Hot Lunch Molson, then *Preters*, how characteristic an aesthete of the pre-*Antic Hay* vintage is Francis Crease, a sort of Rook Leigh to your Gyles Isham. Though you don't realise it, your portrait of Roxburgh is of a wonderful schoolmaster who cannot really have been a man of heart so much as of brain. I think he gave you up not because of your going over to Rome but because you turned out not to be queer. We all like to belong to gangs – you seem to have done throughout your early life in this book – and his gang was the queer one, of the dedicated non-practising sort. It was his religion. Old Chris Hollis is delighted with what you've written of him. He is seeing me here this evening. I was very delighted with the Cruttwell picture and I hope that the next Vol[ume] will have more of those full-length portraits such as you have done of Crease and Roxburgh and Arthur Waugh. It is your writing more than the index which matters in your matchless Roxburgh-formed prose. Through them you give the times. I was very flattered to see your Crease-inspired calligraphy on the brown paper parcel for Penelope and me. This day I hand over the book to her, having kept it from her while I read it. She is now back from eleven months in 'Injer' and starting to write a book about it.

Bung ho, ole man, and ta ever so and God bless the work,
John B

A *Little Learning* was the first (and, in the event, only) volume of an autobiography. It was published in instalments in the *Sunday Times*.

Arthur W. was E.W.'s father and a director of the publishers Chapman and Hall.

C. F. A. Voysey, Baillie Scott, Barry Parker and Raymond Unwin (who were partners), and Edwin Lutyens were all innovative Edwardian architects who worked in Hampstead Garden Suburb.

E.W. was at school at Lancing College, Sussex.

'Hot Lunch' Molson was sometimes called 'Preters' due to his habit of answering questions, 'Preternaturally so.' He was Hugh Molson, later Lord Molson, the Conservative MP.

Christopher Hollis was a mutual Somerset friend.

C.R.M.F. Cruttwell (1887–1941) was Waugh's history tutor and the Principal of Hertford College, Oxford. Waugh elevated him to a mythic enemy.

To Marcus Morris   43 Cloth Fair
3 September 1964   London EC1

Dear Marcus,
Turn this subject over in your kind heart and mind. My old friend
Mervyn Stockwood, Bishop of Southwark, with whom we lunched at
the now defunct Coltman's near here, has a sister Jane Stockwood,
whose good work you probably know. He is very worried about her
and the enclosed letter he sends to me does not say what he told me
personally – which is that he thinks that she sometimes does not earn
enough money to have enough to eat. She did what so many of us in this
ruthless world of journalism do, changed over to a new job because
more money was offered and then found it folded up on her.
    Well, anyhow all I can do is to put the facts to you and hope you will
bear her in mind.
    I wish we could meet and have a laugh and some drink. I've joined
Aspinall's in Berkeley Square where the food is marvellous and would
like to take you there.
    Yours ever, John Betjeman

> The Reverend M.M., founder and editor of the comics *Eagle*, *Swift*, *Girl* and *Robin*, was
> by this time managing director of the National Magazine Company Ltd. He employed
> Jane Stockwood later that autumn.
>   JB had first met Mervyn Stockwood, Bishop of Southwark, when working in Bristol
> at the beginning of the war when he stayed at All Saints, Clifton. He had often been on
> holiday with him and frequently dined at the Bishop's House, Southwark.
>   JB much admired John Fowler's work in restoring the Claremont Club (Aspinall's) to
> its original eighteenth-century glory under the auspices of John Aspinall. He would go
> in just to gaze at the staircase, and was eventually made an honorary member.

To John Osborne   43 Cloth Fair
10 September 1964   London EC1

My dear old Top,
Here, in the calm of the morning, I affirm what I said last night to you –
that is a tremendous play. The best thing you – yes, even you – have
ever written. Apart from the sentiments in the diatribe – which I
heartily endorse – it is the most heart-rending and tender study of every
man who is not atrophied. We want to avoid giving pain and we want to
be left in peace. Love makes us restless and we resist it. I felt

increasingly that the play was about *me* and that is what all the great
playwrights and poets can do for their watchers and readers.

Oh, my dear boy, I can't exactly *thank* you for such an agonising
self-analysis. I can only reverence the power and generosity in you
which makes you write such a shattering and releasing piece. Once
more my warmest congratulations on a mighty achievement – oh, hell,
what words are there to express myself? I feel as though I am writing to
the elements.

Love from Bill Maitland-Betjeman

> J.O. was one of the most successful and respected playwrights since the Second World
> War. His plays include *Look Back in Anger* and *The Entertainer*. JB, who became a great
> friend of his in the early sixties and often had him to stay at Treen, had just been to the
> first night of *Inadmissible Evidence* at the Royal Court Theatre: the central character is
> Bill Maitland, a middle-aged solicitor.

To Cecil Roberts   43 Cloth Fair
10 September 1964   London EC1

Dear Cecil,

I am typing this myself, because my handwriting has got so bad, no one
can read it now there are biros. I loved your letter, but was sad to read of
your long time in London clinics. If only I had known, I could have
come to see you. I enjoy visiting the sick, because it always makes me
thankful I am not ill myself. I am glad you now sound well enough to
enjoy the obviously glorious pleasures of that Saracenic castle.

What you tell me about [Reverend] Hanbury sounds fascinating. I
don't think it can be in the county of Nottingham, because it is not in
Pevsner, not that he is very accurate. I suppose it is in Leicester, but I
must go there. The churches I do on Telly have to be in the western
region of the BBC, and it is, alas, outside the area, but that does not
prevent me going to see it. I think it is marvellous of you to have written
another novel. There was one burgeoning in you when last we met,
after that long period in which you thought you would never write
again. I am in such a period myself, but I find television programmes of
buildings fascinating work and do not get the opportunities of making
as many as I would like. I don't think Telly is an art, but it is good
illustrated journalism and the more one can show people good buildings
while they are still a captive audience (and I don't think colour
supplements are going to wean them away from Telly) the more there is

an opportunity to make people use their eyes so that they reject the flashy modernistic with which this country is afflicted. It is all one can do.

Best wishes for continued good health and happiness, dear mentor and friend.

Yours ever, John Betjeman

> JB was making a series for the BBC Western Region called *The ABC of Churches* with Kenneth Savidge as producer which took place from 1960 until 1968. C.R. often suggested churches to feature.
>   C.R. had been in and out of clinics for two months with a duodenal ulcer. He had written to JB about an eighteenth-century vicar, Hanbury, who started French horticulture in the village of Church Langton (in Leicestershire) and had organised a vast performance of Haydn's *The Creation*.

To T.S. Eliot   43 Cloth Fair
5 October 1964   London EC1

Dear Tom,

Well of course, it really ought to be supported. I suppose if it were in Sussex or Kent it would be quite an ordinary Norman country church, but there in East Ham, it is an amazing phenomenon. It is much prettier inside than that exterior photograph would lead you to believe.

It would be lovely to see you both again, ere you move to the West Indies and I will put matters in hand so that we may meet, via Elizabeth.

Yours ever, John B

> St Mary's Church at Little Ilford, which T.S.E. had written to JB about, was small and, according to Pevsner, 'not impressive, though lovable'.

To Harry Jarvis   43 Cloth Fair
21 November 1964   London EC1

My dear Harry,

Fancy your referring to Southwell as a *village!*

I think you are right to go to Basford. Oh, I'm so glad you and the Smasher are to marry. I *love* that girl more and more the more I think about her. That is v[ery] good news about the vestments. Wear them at once. Alas on Dec[ember] 3rd and 4th I'll be in Yorkshire staying, my dear, with the ARCHBISHOP OF YORK in his PALACE. Why? Because I've got caught up into giving a free talk to some f-ing Society.

Mervyn S[tockwood] told me that last Sunday he confirmed a girl with golden hair down to her shoulders, 'Defend O Lord . . . grant her. . ., ' and when he'd done it the Vicar whispered, 'It's a boy,' and it was. The Curate thought it might not be valid but Mervyn said that God knew about the sex.

I've had a v[ery] funny letter from Harry Williams who says about a letter in *The Times* this week on making priests learn business methods, 'Will you join my new sect – THE FIRST CHURCH OF CHRIST TYPIST? The altar will be replaced by a metal filing cabinet; and we shan't begin services with a psalm or hymn, but by my proposing and you, I hope, seconding a motion that the Deity be praised. If the motion is carried by the congregation we shall consult a computer at the back of the church about the odds of there being a God at all. Would you ask Lord Bridges to be our first Archbishop? Leslie Paul can be an assistant curate.'

My love to the Smasher. Keep in touch. God will bless you both at Basford and gently heighten the parishioners when you have made friends among them.

Yours ever, John B

> Throughout November H.J. and JB had corresponded about H.J.'s decision on whether or not to become Vicar of St Augustine's, New Basford, near Nottingham. He was currently vicar choral (singing curate) at Southwell Minster. JB suggested H.J. go into retreat about it. 'My own feeling is,' he wrote (7 November 1964), 'that you might . . . regret *not* having taken the job.' H.J. took the post and remained there for twenty-seven years. He married Jean Cunliffe, who was from Worksop, at Southwell Minster in April 1965 and JB came to the wedding.
>
> H.J. had been discouraged from wearing vestments but he'd bought some in London and defied the advice. He was determined to make St Augustine's High Church.

To Martyn Skinner   43 Cloth Fair
7 December 1964   London EC1

Dear Martyn,

I make a hasty reply to your letter just before catching the train to Cambridge. My feeling is that at all costs, i.e. at your expense, the book should be published as a whole volume and C[hapman] and H[all] are better than no publishers, though we must remember they are not poetry publishers. Whether it is thirty shillings or forty-five shillings is, I think, up to them to decide, with the advice of their travellers. How

many copies will the libraries take, for instance? This a major matter in
the sale of cloth-bound books today. I will certainly write something to
go on the wrapper because I so firmly believe in the poem and I think
other people like Austin Farrer and Kenneth Young should be brought
in to write something. Last week I was staying with Kenneth Young in
Leeds and he is, as you know, a great admirer of your *Arthur* poems
and, indeed, of all your poems. We talked of them and by great good
fortune his friend William Holden of Heinemann was staying there
too. Holden is interested in private press books and Kenneth and I told
him he ought to consider publishing *Arthur* as a whole. Thus the idea is
in his mind and, if you have another copy of the manuscript, together
with the previously published volumes, I will send it and them to him
so that we can get C[hapman] and H[all]'s figures vetted and possibly a
better format and publisher. The train awaits.

   Yours, JB

> In March 1964, M.S. had sent JB the manuscript of the last part of *The Return of Arthur*,
> his long poem. Three parts of it had been separately published already in 1951, 1955 and
> 1959, but M.S. was having trouble getting the last part published. JB wrote back
> praising it (10 March 1964) and then set about helping him out. He wrote to Gillon
> Aitken at Chapman and Hall (6 September 1964), 'There are stanzas in every canto of
> such ravishing beauty and others of such memorable satire that I don't like to think of it
> not seeing the light of day as the whole book it ought to be. . . . Martyn Skinner is shy,
> remote and modest.'
>   *The Return of Arthur* was published in full by Chapman and Hall in 1966.

To Stephen Spender   43 Cloth Fair
13 December 1964   London EC1

My dear Stephen,
How MEMORABLE they are, those poems of yours and MEMORABILITY
is one of *the* qualities of poetry. The right words in the right order and
they are that. As I read through them in that very handsome Random
House selection (much less formidable looking than Faber poetry
printing) I was fascinated to find how I remembered nearly all of them
and how many famous lines there were which are part of the language.
Simon Stewart tells me he always uses that poem 'Rough' (one of my
favourites) as a test poem for reactions at Haberdashers for young boys.
Those who feel with the poet become brilliant. Those who think the
poem describes the nastiness of other classes or poverty are just
average. Thank you so much for sending me the book and writing in it.

'To My Daughter' is a SUPERB one – in fact that latest lot is all even more impressive than the earlier. Keep it up, old top. Happy Christmas to you both.
Love, John B

> Though JB and S.S. the poet had been slightly wary of each other when they were young, their friendship had burgeoned and their mutual admiration was by now established.
>
> Haberdashers' Aske's is a North London school.
>
> S.S.'s *Selected Poems* came out in 1965.

To John O'Dea   The Mead
                                                                    Wantage
1965   Berkshire

Believe me, Idolatry ne'er shall invade
That splendid parabola's sanctified shade
Which shall rise in the turf-smoke forbidding and dark
As it did o'er the childhood of Austin O'Clarke
For now that the POPE is becoming I.C.
With vernacular masses and Wilson to tea
The Ecumenist leap is so light o'er the wall
The Black Church's pinnacles never need fall
Its stones will proclaim in the loudest of hymns
'McQUAID is *at* last in communion with SIMMS.'

To the Cailín [Colleen], the Eigenheer [Engineer] and Hazel ó [from] Sean Ó Betjemán

The church referred to is the Black Church, officially St Mary's Chapel of Ease, just off Parnell Square, one of the most astonishing churches in Dublin. It became a tea shelter for traffic wardens and is now occupied by MGM Financial Services.

Austin Clarke (1896–1974), the poet, spent his childhood in its shadow and his autobiography (1960) was called *Twice Around the Black Church*.

I.C. means Irish Catholic.

Wilson refers to Harold Wilson, the Prime Minister, who was a Methodist.

John Charles McQuaid was Roman Catholic Archbishop of Dublin.

George Otto Simms was Church of Ireland Archbishop of Dublin and later of Armagh.

To Stephen Spender   43 Cloth Fair
12 January 1965   London EC1

Dear Stephen,

I am *tremendously* impressed by your autobiographical pronoun poem. It is direct, moving and beautiful. It also *shews* (notice the spelling) what a high-minded boy you were. What makes what your poem says so impressive – apart from its form which is v[ery] good and original – is that you were mature and serious when most boys were still sadistic bullies or hopeless masochists. It really is awfully good. I'm keeping it.

   Love, John B

S.S., grateful for JB's 'encouraging and – more than that – sweet and kind letter' (of 13 December) and remembering that JB had sent him the first section of *Summoned by Bells*, had written, 'I would like you to have this off-print – a draft of the opening sections of a long poem about us in our time.'

S.S's long poem 'Pronouns in this Time' was first published in the *London Magazine* in May 1963. Part III begins:

> Supposing I should take
> Out of the playground, one
> Of the cocksure players, here
> Prove to him he was I.
> Templar, whose bayonet glance
> Through all my self-defences
> Nails me in the playground
> Each day to my cowardice . . .

To G.B. Stern   The Mead
                                                        Wantage
14 February 1965   Berkshire

My dear Peter,
I owe you a huge debt of gratitude for that essay you wrote on my verse.
I told you so at the time. It is the most perceptive and understanding of
anything written on my poems and characters. I write to thank you
again now because I am in process of moving my library from the front
of this house to its back, as this house is now too big and expensive for us
and we're dividing it into two. During the move your book was taken
up by me again and I was so enthralled by what you wrote that I
knocked off physical book-lifting for an hour and felt set up enough by
what you wrote, to continue carrying books until ten o'clock on Friday
night. I enclose a little present for you because I think the Jack Yeats
pictures are so pretty. I want to see you when I return from Cornwall
on about March 12th whither I go next week to *do nothing*. I hope you
aren't doing nothing. You are too good a writer to do nothing – though a
little doing nothing is useful for recharging the batteries.
    Love from John B

    JB was alluding to G.B.'s essay in the *Sphere* (see letter of 22 August 1954).

To John Hadfield   43 Cloth Fair
10 March 1965   London EC1

Dear Hadfield,
Do call it 'The End of the Century' and not 'The Turn of the Century'.
'Turn' is a misnomer used by broadcasters. The century is a wheel if
you use the word 'turn', its turn obviously refers to the middle of the
century. The year's turn is not winter, but the middle of the year. The
turn of Fortune's wheel can't mean the end of its rotation.
    I very much like the idea of choosing from ten to fourteen poems
from the sort of poets you mention. We must include [John] Davidson
and John Gray, old Bosie [Alfred] Douglas, Edmund John, perhaps
[Laurence] Binyon and Charles Dalmon? I shall deliberately make it
rather queer and dated and not include the well-known nineties writers
such as Yeats and Hardy. This I could explain in opening sentences.
How wise you are to stay near Ipswich. I am thinking of leaving

London for good. I am very grateful to you for asking me to do something that, for once, I shall really enjoy.

Yours ever, John Betjeman

> JB wrote the preface to and made the selection of what was eventually called 'Poems of the Nineties', a section of *The Saturday Book Number 25* which came out for Christmas of that year. J. H. was its editor.
>   JB wrote (18 May 1965) that his selection was overlong: 'I have already gone through an agony of weeding out. I leave you to make the final selection. . . . I think that "The Acolyte" by Edmund John, who knew Norman Douglas, is a marvellous period piece, but I realise it is very long. I should be sorry to lose it.'

To John Arlott   43 Cloth Fair
26 March 1965   London EC1

My dear John,
You mistake my influence which is negligible, but I know what I mean and I so agree about the disruption of little country towns by blind, statistic-minded do-gooders that I must do all I can to get to you. On the other hand, I must get back on the same night, as I have a very early, extremely important meeting on the same subject the next morning. So far as I can see, the only possible trains are the 4.35 ex Waterloo arriving Winchester 5.48, which would give me a little time to have a look round the town, and I would have to catch the 8.32 back from Alresford, if that were possible, as the 10.03 from that station doesn't get back until 11.46 and I am very hard pressed. If I find, as is all too unlikely, that I really can't manage it, I will ring you up on Monday and send you instead a letter along lines we could discuss on the telephone. It was lovely seeing you and Valerie and that large-eyed Robert and drinking that delicious claret and burgundy. Keep heart. Don't exercise the will too much and share your sadness with others. It helps.

Yours, John B

> J.A. (see *Volume One*), the BBC's 'Voice of Cricket', who lived at the Old Sun, Alresford, Hampshire, had asked JB to attend an Alresford planning meeting on 30 March. He had written (23 March 1965), 'I must say that I believe your very presence would make the planners stop and think – and wonder whether they can, in fact, get away with all these small town changes by default or, at least, without any real stir.'
>   JB went, catching the 4.35 from Waterloo.
>   J.A. had never really got over the death of his son James in a sports car in 1962. 'The love does not fade; nor the sharpness of seeing and hearing him,' JB wrote (12 March 1965).

To Evelyn Waugh   Treen
                                                       Trebetherick
                                                       Wadebridge
11 April 1965   Cornwall

Dear Evelyn,
The thanks are to *you*, not to me. The furniture was left to me by old E.
R. B. Graham (a keen Old Westminster) because I loved the house. He
hoped I would take on the house. I could not afford to do so even had I
wanted to live in London. The dilapidations to the Ilchester Estate, run
by some smooth operators, would have amounted to about twenty-two
thousand pounds which is all my capital. If I couldn't take on the lease's
remainder he wanted me to preserve the furniture as a collection.
Penelope and I have no room for it at Wantage, had P[enelope] been
keen on it which she isn't. When vandals got into Burges's Tower
House and smashed such a lot and the bastard agents refused to let it, in
the hope that it would decay and they could erect flats on the site, I got
the V[ictoria] and A[lbert] Museum] to house the furniture temporarily. God knows what the agents will do about the Tower House, but
now at last you have the furniture as a collection and like it and that is
what E. R. B. Graham and his old wife would have wanted. *If* the
agents are thwarted in their attempts to destroy the house and sell the
site and *if* they find tenants who admire Burges and the house, then you
might will it back to the Tower House unless 'Bron wants it.
    I write this all in Cornwall and under the influence of gin. Do you
really think I deserve wine? If so, I'll never say no. Delivery at
Wantage. But really I don't deserve it. The furniture was a *gift* to me.
Except in lawyer's fees to those bastards, I am a beneficiary.
    Bung ho, ole top, John B

> JB had always loved the Tower House, Melbury Road, Kensington, built by William
> Burges (1827–81) for himself. He had become friends of its owners the Grahams when
> researching a film on Victorian architecture and they in their turn had taken a great shine
> to him. In March 1962, E.R.B. Graham's widow died and left JB the remaining two
> years of the lease on the Tower House, and some Burges furniture. On the expiration of
> the lease, JB would have been liable for ten thousand pounds' worth of dilapidations – 'I
> have children, my dear Coolmore,' he wrote to John Summerson (4 April 1962), 'and a
> wife, and a deep love of Burges, and the agents may well ruin me.' In the event, he had
> great difficulty in sub-letting the house which remained empty, but great pleasure in
> giving the furniture to E.W. to go with the Burges wash-stand he had given him some
> years before (see letter dated 26 December 1953). The Tower House is still standing.

To Mark Ogilvie-Grant   '43 Clorthe Fairye'
2 May 1965

Dear Mark,
Well, old man, that *was* a lovely card to get from you. Young Bridges
was once keen on a Secretary of mine called then Jill Menzies – high
cheek-bones, freckles, sulky lips, grey-green eyes, floppy hair, schoolboy appeal. Do tell dear George S[churhoff] that I would have hated to
be Poet Laureate – too inhibiting. One would feel one was being
watched by people with knives in their hands. Give us a tinkle, old
man, if you're coming to England. I would like to come to Greece when
I can get my financial affairs straightened out so that I can have time off
to do an enjoyable thing like visiting my old Athenian chum. There are
a lot of empty Georgian country houses going for nothing in Shetland.
    Bung hoski, John (I hear Dorothea Russell has died.)

> M.O.-G. (see *Volume One*) was an old Oxford friend with whom JB kept in touch
> although he had long lived in Athens.
>   George Schurhoff, whom JB called 'Sarcophogus', was also a friend from Oxford.
>   Dorothea Russell was the mother of JB's sometime fiancée Camilla Russell (see *Volume
> One*) whom both loved to hate.

To Peter Crookston   43 Cloth Fair
12 May 1965   London EC1

Dear Mr Crookston,
Of course I don't mind dear Joan [Hunter Dunn] being photographed.
How could I? She is the only one who might object and I think it would
do her a lot of good in herself to appear in your handsome supplement.
Lord Snowdon will do her splendidly. He will see the point.
    I shall be up in London next week but dashing about a lot, so here is
how I came to write about her, if you can't get hold of me. At the
beginning of the war I was employed in the films division in the
Ministry of Information. The raid that went on then drew us together
in the evenings. I don't say by 'us' that I mean Joan and me, but all of us
at 'Mini' in those days, especially when we had to wait between raids
before bicycling home. Mini was mostly pale green intellectuals like
yours truly and Joan Hunter Dunn was quite different from the rest of
us. She was employed by London University. She was second-in-

command of the catering department, under Mrs Bruce, and she wore a white coat and had a clean, clinical, motherly look, which excited hundreds of us. She had bright cheeks, clear sun-burned skin, darting brown eyes, a shock of dark curls and a happy smile. Her figure was a dream of strength and beauty. When the bombs fell, she bound up our wounds unperturbed. When they didn't fall, which was most of the time, she raised our morales without ever lowering her morals. When I first saw her I said to my friends Osbert Lancaster and Reginald Ross-Williamson, 'I bet that girl is a doctor's daughter and comes from Aldershot.' When I got to know her I found I was right and it is my only experience of poetic prescience. I wrote the verses in the character of a subaltern in Aldershot, but they were really my own imaginings about her. When I showed her the poem, she told me she lived at Farnborough, Hampshire, but I considered that near enough to Aldershot to count. Her father was a very distinguished doctor and she had an uncle who was a bishop. Cyril Connolly kindly printed the poem in *Horizon* and I had to ask her permission for this to be done, which she agreed. Her name in the last line I had printed in capital letters in Cyril's magazine, but when I had again to ask her to be allowed to print the verses in a book of my poems, she asked me not to have her name in capital letters. Of course I obeyed. She was one of the most cheerful, sweet and gentle girls I ever knew. I have not seen her from those days to this, though we have corresponded. You had better consult her about what I have written, if you think she might object. Oh goodness, I wish you had seen her striding about the Ministry. The spirit of Surrey girlhood, and a pine-scented paradise.

Yours sincerely, John Betjeman

P.C. was the editor of the *Sunday Times* magazine.
    Tony Snowdon remembers, 'She (J.H.D.) was very jolly, handsome and still played tennis – I photographed her on the court in shorts. . . . She had a very good, strong, friendly and welcoming face.'

To James Lees-Milne   Treen
3 June 1965   Trebetherick

Dear Jim,
R[OYAL] F[INE] A[RT] C[OMMISSION]
    You are quite right, but how uproot the present practising architects? I don't see how it can be done, as appointments are all made by

Lord Bridges via the Treasury on the advice of God knows who – the Hon. God [Samuel], an ex FRIBA. I have discussed it with Wagner (Garter, my dear) without divulging to him as I did to you, the lengths to which I had gone. He didn't think much of Lord B and suggested we sought Sir Somebody Helsby's advice. From all I have heard of Helsby he is even worse than Lord B and is marked as his successor. No, what we want is a BUFFER between the public and the Civil Servants and Local Authorities. It should be Parliament, which is, alas, non-visual and political, and it will therefore have to be a Commission as the only alternative. To get the appointments of the RFAC put right will take at least five years, probably ten, and by then all we cherish will have gone. If the Civil Service gets to hear of this idea it will take it over and we will be no better off. The idea will be taken over by one Ministry and used as a pawn in a battle with another.

KIDDERMINSTER
I went there this winter. It is A1. The Minster, apart from rich glass by O'Connor, has a War Memorial Chapel at the n[orth]-e[ast] corner by Sir Giles G. Scott which is his best work – delicate Bodley-ish perp[endicular] with glass and fittings to match. The streets up to the Minster are all eighteenth-century, v[ery] grand and *doomed* as is the tenth century canal, basin and arch over entrance to it, the 1801 Methodist Chapel with oval gallery and high pews upholstered in leather. I've written to the Hon. God – but some hope. What will Lord Llewelyn-Davies think of it and Freddy Gibberd and Sir Basil [Spence]? They haven't time to go and look.

Love to Alvilde, back next week.

Bung ho, ole man, John B

J.L.-M. had written (30 May 1965), 'Ever since I last saw you I have been thinking over what you told me. I am sure you would not be wise to set up a rival body to the Fine Art Commission. Even if you succeeded, would you not be duplicating the activities and complicating things? It would be like having the S[ociety for the] P[rotection of] A[ncient] B[uildings] and the Ancient Buildings Committee, which deal with exactly the same issues, and merely confuse the public. I believe that you, with your influence and contacts with high places, would do better to purge the existing Commission. Lord Bloody Bridges KG can't go on for long now. You could give him a helping hand out and then see that the constitution of the Commission is reformed. . . . The longer I live the more sure I am that in a highly artificial society, you must have controls. *Laissez-faire* is out. An advisory body is nugatory. It is a waste of time serving on it. Controlled power is essential in order to prevent mischief. . . . I should like to see a newly constituted Fine Arts Commission, purged of professional architects, civil servants and town planners, and composed of amateur aesthetes like you, Peter F[leetwood]-Hesketh, Hugh [Grafton] and me.'

Godfrey Samuel was the secretary of the RFAC for twenty-one years.
Sir Anthony Wagner, Garter Principal King of Arms, was the leading expert on heraldry and genealogy.
Sir Laurence Helsby, GCB, another very senior civil servant, did not in fact succeed Lord Bridges; Colin Anderson did.
The architects Richard Llewelyn-Davies, Frederick Gibberd and Basil Spence served on the Commission.
The original of this letter has some splodges on it, beside which is written, 'Angostura spilt here.'

To Deirdre Connolly   Treen
                                         Trebetherick
                                         Wadebridge
4 June 1965   Cornwall

Dearest Deirdre,
Your letter has been forwarded here in Cornwall to a paradise of bird song, sea smells and sun on flowers. I can't do June 13th Sunday, alas, as old Philip Harding, a friend of Marlborough days, is coming for a long-delayed weekend and to Wantage and I've said I will be there. Philip Harding, Cyril will recall, is the brother of the late Archie Harding. 'Everything he touches turns to ashes,' as his sister-in-law once said to me, and now he edits those extraordinary supplements thrown away with *The Times*. If I went up to London on Sunday to Uncle Tom [T. S. Eliot]'s programme, it would sadden his brief weekend as he likes a gossip and is so sad I can't desert him. Feeble has been taking VITAMINS and is suddenly very vigorous but still pale as death.
    Love to you both, John B

Archie Harding had been in the glamorous Oxford set with Harold Acton. Philip was quieter and sadder and often stayed at the Mead.
    Following the death of T.S. Eliot in April, *A Homage to T.S. Eliot* was staged at the Globe Theatre on 13 June.

To E. M. Forster   43 Cloth Fair
27 June 1965   London EC1

Dear Mr Forster,
Your kind letter about 'Narcissus' has made my day. I think the composing of it came from reading Harry Williams' *The True Wilderness*

which suddenly makes it possible to write openly about 'guilt'. Praise
from you, a man of few words and all those thoughtful, is praise indeed.
Oh, thank you and thank you.

Yours sincerely, John Betjeman

> E.M.F., the writer, had written from King's College, Cambridge (23 June 1965), 'I want
> to send you this line of thanks for the wonderful poem you call "Narcissus". I don't
> know what it ought to be called, perhaps because I don't know anything like it in
> literature. I don't know which I admire most – the pervading emotion or the progressive
> construction. I thank you most warmly.'
>
> JB's poem 'Narcissus' had just appeared in the *London Magazine* (it later came out, in
> 1966, in *High and Low*).

To Laura Waugh   Alan Ross Limited
                                                     30 Thurloe Place
17 July 1965   London sw7

My dear Laura,
I write from leafy Sussex and not from the business address of my host
to thank you and Evelyn for my delicious remote and restful stay at
Combe Florey. Every moment of it was excitement for the eye, the ear
and the palate. I keep thinking of Cadogan Cowper, that travel series,
the drawing room carpet and the bears climbing up that tree in my
bathroom. I love the bowered world in which you and Evelyn live there
on the red sandstone. If ever you venture as far as Poole whither I went
after that Unitarian Chapel, do have a look at Compton Acres,
Parkstone. There amid rhododendrons are a series of gardens of such
unexampled and elaborate hideousness (admission two and six, open all
the year round) in Japanese, ancient Roman, olde English and Italian
styles that Evelyn will want to put pen to paper again, and that
wonderful gift he has for bringing out the startling and alarming and
funny in the trivial will be spurred into renewed activity. Indeed, the
dark and thoughtful beauty of all at Combe Florey made the excursion
out into the world all the more exciting for me. My love to Evelyn and
very many thanks indeed. Your cousin and Evelyn's niece Jennifer
sends her love.

Love from John B

> L.W. was married to Evelyn W.
>
> JB was filming the eighteenth-century Unitarian Chapel (with an asymmetrical
> Norman Shaw turret) in Mary Street in Taunton, Somerset on Tuesday 13th for *The
> ABC of Churches*, and arrived at Combe Florey nearby just before dinner.

The 'travel series' was Evelyn W.'s pair of *Pleasures of Travel* with pictures by Edward Joy (and Richard Eurich).

The garden of Compton Acres on Canford Cliffs between Poole and Bournemouth was laid out in 1919 – in seven different arrangements.

To Patrick Kinross   Fort Arun Hotel
                                                        Douglas
29 August 1965   I.O.M.

My dear Pa'rick,

I saw the Baroness in Edina last week with your uncle, her brother. We had tea. The Wemysses too, my dear. All in Ann Street. The Baroness was in fine form. She says the sound library at Bolton is not so good as the London one she used to use.

This should not be so. I also saw Ursula [Dallmeyer] and her Colonel husband. I liked your piece on Enterprise Neptune today. I've given my remaining Cornish fields to the N[ational] T[rust]. Back at the end of the week. There's a picture of you on the stairs in Ann Street and a photograph of David Balfour which has, at a distance, quite a look of you.

Bung ho, old top, JB

Penelope's in India till mid Oct[ober].

Ann Street, Edinburgh, was where the Kinrosses had a house.

Ursula Dallmeyer was P.K.'s sister.

Enterprise Neptune, the National Trust's safeguarding of Britain's coastline, had just been instigated.

To Deborah Devonshire   43 Cloth Fair
5 September 1965   London EC1

Dearest Debo,

What is the Heart of Industrial England?   CHESTERFIELD

The Gateway to the Dukeries?   WORKSOP

The Capital of the Peak?   CHAPEL EN LE FRITH

The Town of Personality?   ASHBY DE LA ZOUCH

The Mother of the Midlands?   LICHFIELD

Those are accredited, town clerk approved names on boards at the approach to the places. But:

Who is the Tart of the Peak?   BAKEWELL
What is the Milton Abbas of the Midlands?   EDENSOR
The Venice of the Limestone fissures?   MATLOCK

I had [to] turn my mind to these things so as to avoid being too
electrically minded. What I really wanted to do was to thank you for the
wonderful Marlene [Dietrich] Evening. I shall never forget her
consummate skill and the nonchalant way she works us up to a frenzy.
The Isle of Man was terrific – for beauty, fair weather, paler trees,
ilexes, grapes, gardens, mountains, remote beaches, swamps,
Georgian country houses, butterflies, sheep and sunlight. Now I'm
back in bloody old London.

   Elizabeth Cavendish, that very great Lady in Waiting, sends her love
to you both as does yours with love, JB

To Miss Hargreaves   43 Cloth Fair
3 October 1965   London EC1

Dear Miss Hargreaves,
I spent a most enjoyable Saturday last week here in the City of London
reading the forty-nine poems you sent me. They were all of a very high
level. There were twenty-nine different poets and they really were
poets. Farming obviously breeds poetry. You tell me there were
hundreds of entries and that I saw the selection your office had made. It
was an awful job deciding which six of these twenty-nine poets should
have the prize. I have eventually chosen:

1.'Requiem for Tom'	Brenda Brunt
2.'Harvest Interlude'	Mrs Coleman
3.'Farm Cats'	D. M. Frayne
4.'Underwood'	John Garfitt
5. Tater Woman's Song	K. Tarrant
6.'April Day'	M. Tyndale-Biscoe

These are all in alphabetical order and I think that is how you should
publish them. Never ask me to judge a poetry competition again. It is
agonising selecting which is best out of so much that is good. You ought
to publish the whole selection you sent to me in a book.

   Yours sincerely, John Betjeman

JB received piles of letters each week from unknown correspondents, asking for his
opinion or advice. He always took trouble with his replies.

To Cyril Connolly   In the train
2 December 1965   Plymouth to York

My dear Cyril,
I can't tell you how impressed I am by your book. The standards are so interesting and I think right – what has made the change and how, not, 'Is it "first rate"?' That is what makes me so proud to be included because, of course, I was unconscious of what you see in what I did, and what I now see I did as a result of your book. Your summaries of the books are MASTERLY – of course I've only read a tithe of the books you mention, but if anything would inspire me to read those I haven't read, your book would. You know, it's worth your having stuck to criticism and weekly journalism as you have, just because of this book. Without the painful training journalism is, you would never have been able to write so concisely and clearly and *readably*. But behind all that, there's your calm, uncompromising honest judgement. Oh, you dear old thing. Oh, I do thank you for the gift of the book and its delicious inscription – and Rictus may well be justified, but what does it matter – *you* think otherwise and that's what pleases.
    Yours with love, JB

> *The Modern Movement* was a book consisting of a list of all the books (with short summaries) that interested and influenced writers of the Modern Movement. As a result of its publication a special exhibition of the books was put on soon afterwards at the University of Texas in Austin, USA and C.C. was invited to attend.
>   The word 'Rictus' means a grin. This is presumably a reference to the inscription C.C. had written.

To Diana Cooper   43 Cloth Fair
12 December 1965   London EC1

Dear Diana,
There's a little restaurant at the back of this place in the City where I live which isn't bad. I would v[ery] much like to know whether you could face having luncheon with me there one day, meeting first in my rooms. And then I would like to ask to meet you, one or two of the Paddington set (e.g. Old Patrick [Kinross] or Judy [Montagu] or the Berkeleys [Lennox and Freda] or Adrian [Daintrey]) or, if it would be more exciting for you and less *local*, someone from another set. Will you be in your Paddington set after Christmas? Name a day and say what

sort of a character you would like to meet and also if I am likely to be
able to make up, and I will search around. Left? Right? Theological?
Theatrical? Artistic? Literary? There are so many people who long to
meet you, it won't be difficult to find someone.

I've asked Ava Lady W[averley] (a relation of that mighty architect
G. F. Bodley) to London at this place next Thursday and she will be
able to report to you whether it's up to your standards. I've so oft
enjoyed delicious luncheons with you in your house, I'm a bit nervous
about my own low standards of hospitality.

Happy Christmas.

Love from John Betjeman

> D.C., the widow of Duff Cooper, lived in Warwick Avenue and was the mainstay of
> what JB called 'the Paddington set'. A famous hostess, she had begun to take JB up in the
> late fifties and often asked him to her parties.

To Cecil Beaton   The Mead
                                                     Wantage
26 December 1965   Berkshire
Boxing Day

Dear Cecil,

You sent me months ago a beautiful and evocative series of coloured and
uncoloured pictures and I never wrote to thank you, and then poor,
quiet, good, pale Elizabeth Cav[endish] showed me such a nice letter
you had sent her in which you said you had the shingles. My word, I *am*
sorry for you. Wait patiently. It will go. But oh, the exasperation of the
waiting. May the Broadchalke bells ring out a bright New Year for you.
The sheer beauty of your sets for *My Fair Lady* have inspired me to send
you this letter in my best MGM-ish hand and with it my affection and
good wishes. We've had a fairly peaceful Christmas here in Wantage.

Love, John B

ART-LETTERER

> C.B. had borrowed JB's bound collection of an Edwardian magazine about art and
> artefacts, the *Studio*, as a source of inspiration for his designs for the film of *My Fair Lady*.

To Duncan Fallowell   43 Cloth Fair
30 December 1965   London EC1

Dear Mr Fallowell,
My secretary showed me your kind letter while I was in London today
for a few hours *en route* from Exeter to the North, and I felt I must write
and say how sorry I am I haven't the time at the moment to see you and
have that interview you suggest. The trouble is, you see, that no-one
can live by poetry, if my verse is really poetry and I am never quite
sure, and so I make my living showing off on the television and rushing
about writing articles commissioned by inexorable editors. I never
seem to be able to make firm dates far ahead. If you are at St Paul's
School and living in Wokingham, presumably you are a boarder. I
don't know whether you can ever get away during the day or early
evening at about 5.30 or 6 p.m., but if you can give me a choice of dates
in the middle of the week during the next three weeks before I migrate,
I will try and arrange a meeting. You will find me tired and
disappointing.
    Yours sincerely, John Betjeman

> D.F., the writer and journalist, was at St Paul's School, Hammersmith, and
> subsequently Magdalen College, Oxford.
>   D.F. did meet JB and a correspondence began which lasted through D.F.'s school and
> university days. 'How gorgeously flattering that such a person could be remotely
> interested in any of one's doings,' D.F. recalls.

To Harry Jarvis   43 Cloth Fair
5 January 1966   London EC1

My dear Harry,
I am honoured that you should think of me as a possible godfather.
Before you finally conclude the offer, think over this, however. I am
nearly sixty, I'll probably be dead in ten years, is a godfather any good
who will die before he can benefit the child? Of course if it's confirmed
nice and young, I'll be able to fulfil my duties *(D[eo] V[olente])* in time
instead of having to do so in Eternity. Eternity-Light. No offence taken
if you re-consider the offer. Gerard Irvine tells me that the drug
psychotherapists use now, called LSD, takes you back by stages, first
ears and eyes are sharpened, then the edges of things wobble, then you
go back to the womb and draw up your knees, then you inhabit past

civilisations (e.g. Aztecs and Egyptians), then you feel what being an amoeba was like when all the earth was water and then there is blinding light – God. The same experience as the mystics in the last stage. Won't the Smasher look wonderful as a mother. Oh, I do love her. I wish I could go back and return as a child. What a peculiar idea. Harry W[illiams] has written a wonderful piece which he gave at Cuddesdon to ordinands. It points out that doing springs from being and being is primary and being baptised makes us one with Christ. 'If, as I believe, a sense of muddle and meaninglessness is fairly widespread among the clergy, it is largely due to total neglect of our vocation, what we have been given, to be. Inevitably, therefore, we feel without roots. When doing is divorced from a deep understanding of that fact, no wonder we feel like men who have played every card in the pack and never taken a trick.' I'll ask him if I can send it on to you as it should be v[ery] encouraging to you there in Nottingham. He has sent me the typescript of it.

Penelope had a motor accident in London at night driving alone a fortnight ago and had her head cut, her teeth knocked out, a rib broken and woke up in a dismal hospital near Kensal Green but is at last out and back at the Mead but still a bit tottery. Needless to say she was brave and uncomplaining and when she came to insisted that I shouldn't be told till the morning. Candida turned up trumps and was v[ery] useful to her after her days in hospital.

Love to you both, JB

Feeble v[ery] well and pale and sends love. Lee [Sturgeon]'s got a v[ery] nice looking young man.

> JB did in fact become godfather to H.J.'s daughter Rebekah.
> Cuddesdon is a theological college near Oxford.
> Lee Sturgeon was JB's secretary.

To Edward Hornby   43 Cloth Fair
5 February 1966   London EC1

My dear Edward,
I realise I must use a fair Bedford Park hand when writing to you and so I am making my first letter of the day to you to thank you for (and now what about a little change of texture before going on with the ink?) that delicious dinner this week. I enjoyed food, wine and company, watches, clocks and rings and calligraphy with equal intoxication.

David Keir was most interesting about W. H. Smith and Son, Thelma Cazalet-Keir encouraging about broadcasting and Norah Smallwood fascinating on publishing, Feeble was as usual putting in low-spoken remarks showing she did not miss a trick and there were you the perfect host at the head. Ah, what a good evening it was. We saw Peggy [Thomas] on Thurs[day] and Diana Cooper that night fresh from her robbery. Lee my sec[retar]y and the glorious Martin [Jay] are v[ery] excited about your invitation to them.

    Yours, John B

E.H., the brother of JB's Berkshire neighbour Michael, and JB's stockbroker Anthony, had met JB with the Lynam Thomases in Trebetherick. A collector of puzzle rings, watches and clocks, and a master at the *Times* crossword, his letters to JB were always written in a perfect calligraphic hand.
    David Keir, the author, was writing the history of W.H. Smith, of which Michael H. and his father were and had been, respectively, chairman.
    Diana Cooper had been tied up by a burglar in her house in Warwick Avenue and had made the headlines.
    Lee Sturgeon was walking out with Martin Jay.

To Martyn Skinner   43 Cloth Fair
9 March 1966   London EC1

Dear Martyn,
Of course it should have been under one roof from the start. It is immensely enhanced in this final form. I have been spending hours under its shelter. What interests me very much is your increasing skill – rather like Crabbe's with the heroic couplet, his latest is his best – with the stanzas, you can make them do anything. You are above everything a descriptive poet of scenery and feelings. Your character sketches are secondary to these qualities. But what comes out now is the final swoop of the grand construction. Oh, I am glad to see it as I hoped it would look. You will get few reviews and those you will get will be angry from the Wains and Alvarezes as they won't have time to read and grasp it, being professional reviewers and ungenerous by nature, at least Wain is. But never mind. Thing is the book – complete. It is a great work and a triumph.

    Yours, JB

The Return of Arthur, the entire 'Arthur' poems, had just been published in one volume by Chapman and Hall.
    In M.S.'s published correspondence with R. C. Hutchinson, *Two Men of Letters:*

Martyn Skinner and R. C. Hutchinson, edited by Rupert Hart-Davis, he indicates that he
recognised that JB was less wholeheartedly enthusiastic about his verse than the above
courteous letter suggests.

John Wain and Al Alvarez, both Modern Movement poets, were reviewers of poetry
at that time.

To Duncan Fallowell   The Athenæum
13 April 1966   Pall Mall SW1

Dear Duncan,
I was v[ery] pleased to have *Folio* and your letter. Surely *Folio* is very
high standard – much better than those everlasting accounts of house
matches – and plenty of local wit in it, too, and satire. Of course it is
well known that Paulines [boys at St Paul's] are very clever. I was
charmed and flattered by your article about Cloth Fair and my constant
chatter therein. What a lot you noticed in a short time and how well you
have put it together. I feel unworthy of the attention you gave me – but
proud to have commanded it – what on earth does that mean? It must
come from exhaustion of a meeting of the Royal Fine Art Commission
and sitting in this comical club waiting for the licensing hours to allow
me a drink.

I am v[ery] interested to hear of your nineties' anthology. Don't
hurry over making it and don't be bamboozled by a printer into having
to pay for it, or by a publisher into consenting to publish only on the
condition that I write an introduction. The anthology must stand on its
own merits and I'm sure it will. Start while you have the enthusiasm –
now's the moment – but my word, it is agony selecting and cutting out
former favourites in place of new ones. Then we can see, when it's all to
your satisfaction collected together, whether it really needs an
introduction except your own, or even that.

Yours, John Betjeman

D.F.'s interview with JB had appeared in the St Paul's school magazine, *Folio*.

To John Piper

43 Cloth Fair
London EC1
& The Mead
April 1966
Wantage

Dear Mr Piper,
How is your sciatica? Goldilegz, whom I saw on Thurs[day], said it was still bad. It is hell, I know, having had lumbago, a less acute form of sciatica, and it leaves one so *tired*, my dear. Penelope has a woman who treads on her somewhere near Harrods whom she is anxious to recommend to you. She will give you a tinkle.

I have long wanted to write to thank you for the *intense* pleasure your beautiful and deeply loving portrait of Goldilegz gives me. I don't know when I have had a more generous present and have to tell you that here in the City it DOMINATES THE ROOM. I have put it *on* the chimneypiece as it looks best there and it is very much in the same position as it was in the Bum. What is so very surprising is that you are so good a portrait artist when you put your brush to it.

SHELL GUIDES
Linc[oln]s[hire] is certainly the customers' money's worth. The juxta-position of Skeggie [Skegness] and mediaeval stained glass at Gidney makes a brilliant opening. Perhaps the most beautiful pages are FISHTOFT where the cut (a white gap in my copy I'm looking at) does not matter. That idea of a whole plate across to one or two columns of the right- (or left-) hand side is a v[ery] good innovation of Edward [Piper]'s. Harlaxton is a revelation. In a re-issue I think pages 152 to 153 could go after page 91 so that all Lincoln was together. Louth is superbly displayed. The inking is v[ery] good throughout (except on end papers). *It is far the best of the Shell Guides* so far and the text is really good too. We have got Pevsner on the run.

E. T. Long writes to ask me when the *Dorset Guide* is coming out. He also tells me he is editing a new edition of Arthur Mee's *King's England*. That, I expect, is why he wants to know. Well, we need fear no rivalry there. He can't write and he can't see and he is a mediaevalist-Georgian of the dullest sort.

Am off to Tallyllyn with John Smith on Monday, then Devon and Cornwall [illegible] till after Whitsun. Bung ho, old top. Con-grat[ulation]s on Linc[oln]s[hire]. Thanks, oh thanks, for Goldilegz to whom my love. I like to think of her reading this out to you in that bedroom while you remain as silent as Osbert and Karen used to be in the mornings when they read the papers in bed.

I've got something else fearfully funny to tell you but I can't remember what it is. The enclosed card is for the sole surviving Cubitt, an old lady and a Communist who lives in Clevedon. If I can I'll go.

Love, JB

The portrait was a full-length nude of a recumbent Myfanwy.
   'The Bum' was their nickname for Fawley Bottom, the Pipers' house.
   J.P. did most of the photographs for the *Shell Guide to Lincolnshire*, written by Jack Yates and Henry Thorold, and edited by JB and J.P.
   John Smith, who had been on various architectural committees, had founded the Landmark Trust with his own money in 1965 when he had been exasperated by the destruction of Thomas Telford's house on the Shropshire Union Canal, despite his campaigns to save it. The Trust saved buildings which slipped through the net of other conservation charities. John Smith used to lie down in front of bulldozers to stop canal cottages being pulled down. JB and he visited the Tallyllyn Railway in North Wales which was rescued by their mutual friend L. T. C. Rolt.

To William Plomer   Treen
                                             Trebetherick
                                             Wadebridge
[postmarked 1 May 1966]   Cornwall

My dear William,
I came back from Sicily – wild irises, Greek temples, shepherds and sheep bells and at Syracuse Cathedral the first mass of Easter when the gong-like bells rung out and the lights suddenly filled that Greek doric temple of Athene with Christian walls between the columns and all in honey-coloured stone like the wine – I suddenly realised what I saw with my eyes and heard – that BC and AD become one with the Resurrection and it didn't matter whether one was R[oman] C[atholic] or C[hurch] of E[ngland]. As I said, I came back from Sicily and gathered letters that had piled up while I was away and among them found the *truly marvellous* script introduced by E. Blishen whom I don't know, about my work. I have felt, ever since reading it the day before yesterday, more set up than ever in my life. And you, my dear William, the most perceptive and kind of all those excellent people, have made life worth living again. Oh, thank you and thank Ross and Ida. George Turner has had a heart attack. I told a nice man from Rediffusion called Hughes that I'd like you to read one of your poems for a popular poetry programme. Bung ho, old top.

Love to Rustington and you, John B

JB had been to Sicily with EC and Harry Williams, their close friend and spiritual mentor.

Edward Blishen, the broadcaster, had made a programme for the BBC World Service featuring JB for which he had interviewed Philip Larkin, Peter Porter, W.P. and Osbert Lancaster who described how he and JB were going round Liberty's and had seen some elephants made of leather which made the two *roar* with laughter. A crowd formed round them and the manager asked them to leave.

Blishen met JB about a year later in the Duty Office of the BBC and remembers exchanging memories with him of reading Hans Christian Andersen as children. Both Blishen and JB felt that they had been left with an ineradicable streak of melancholy as a result.

JB referred to Treen, after Plomer's bungalow in Rustington, Sussex, as 'my Rossida'.

He seldom wrote to W. P. without making some reference to Rossida.

Seven:

Awed strangers in a foreign land

1966 to 1969

The railway crossed the river Dee
　　Where Mary called the cattle home,
The wide marsh widened into sea,
　　The wide sea whitened into foam.
The green Welsh hills came steeply down
To many a cara-circled town –
　　Prestatyn, Rhyl – till here were we,
As mountains rose on either hand,
Awed strangers in a foreign land.
　　　　　　'A Ballad of the Investiture 1969'

'When I think how few of our friends have fulfilled their first promise
or how little one has oneself done from first hopes, your achievement in
poetry stands up solid and splendid and encouraging and defiant,'
wrote Maurice Bowra (29 October 1966) after he had just received his
copy of *High and Low*, JB's new collection of poems. 'The old boy
[Ernest Betjemann] must be pleased – he was after all an artist, and the
worms won't have taken that from him. Your poetry is of course
entirely your own (though you owe a bit to old Tom Hardy), but it is
also the poetry of our times. It is these small corners of towns and
villages, of the countryside and the suburbs that we have left to us out of
the vast nature that was once there. Silly for us to go Wordsworthing
about and you are the guide to secrets around the corner, which we
should all have missed if you had not spotted them and given them just
the right shape that keeps them real. This is all very pompous, but I
hope you won't mind. I have always loved your poetry, and it means a
great deal to me. I am now old enough to be able to say so.'[1]

In June 1967 Philip Larkin wrote and asked JB to come to Hull for a
year. His desire to escape 'the clutches of Michael Berry and the BBC'
was strong and to have a lot of laughs and expeditions would have been
his idea of bliss, but earning his living had to come first and he would
have been weighed down with guilt about missing his many London
jobs on various committees. 'While I have it in me to earn by journalism
(e.g. telly and the *Weekend Telegraph*) I probably ought to go on and will
have guilt if I don't,'[2] he replied. However, he complained, 'Oh God,

Oh God! let me off the hook,' and despite being at the pinnacle of his success he found there were penalties to be paid. 'The worst thing is the letters,' he said. 'About thirty arrive every morning and they've all got to be answered. It's been bad for the last ten years but in the last two or three it's becoming hell. The post varies according to how much one has been showing off. It's really bad after a television series when people think they know you – temporary notoriety. The BBC could filter the letters but they don't. ITV are better. The new book of poems doesn't make much difference to the pestering. . . . But the most tiresome and constant letters are invitations to lecture to schools, technical colleges, societies and Women's Institutes. They automatically believe you have time and they never send stamped addressed envelopes. People send me poems and articles which have been rejected by *Punch*. . . . I answer letters in the mornings otherwise they would never get done. Here I am at sixty, working even slower than in the past. We do television, if we don't no one will buy our books. But wanting to write is like wanting to pray and not having the time. . . . It gets harder as you get older – and there is no solution to the latter problem. You can go away to Cornwall, then they discover you and you have to go somewhere else. There just seem to be so many more literate people in the country, with more money to spend on stamps. It's insoluble – except by death.'³

His post was not all awful – his old flame Margaret Wintringham, who had been watching his series of BBC films, *Betjeman at Random*, wrote, 'But WHAT a pleasure to hear you speaking poetry, I shouldn't think there is anyone alive who does it better. I don't know whether seeing adds anything, perhaps so – but I shut my eyes and concentrate on the words!'⁴ During these last years of the sixties JB made an inordinate number of films, probably over fifty. Apart from *The ABC of Churches*, he made six films about London in the *Betjeman's London* series; as well as *The Picture Theatre* about the architecture of early cinemas. He also took part in a series called *Pride of Place* with Arthur Negus the antiques expert, which involved visiting houses like Frampton Court in Gloucestershire and Saltram in Devon and describing the architecture. He travelled to the Holy Land to make the film *Journey to Bethlehem*. He made films for a BBC series called *Contrasts*, the first of which was called *From Marble Arch to Edgware* and began with JB at the top of Marble Arch itself, looking through a little window up the Edgware Road, and ended in farming country in rural Middlesex.

His next film was *Tennyson: A Beginning and an End*. Julian Jebb, the director, wrote in his diary (Monday, 14 August 1969), 'John is very cheerful and immediately takes out maps and guides from the large broken-down raffia shopping bag which he always carries with him. After he has rested at our hotel we start on our walk to Farringford [Tennyson's house], which is now a hotel and where we have arranged to dine. We are in the country at once going through tree-lined lanes; the sun is setting. We are already looking for suitable location set ups for shooting. . . . I say, "It's beautiful." And so it was. Soon we came to a crumbling farmhouse with an entrance topped by two stone balls. . . . John talked about Tennyson's extreme short sight and how he used to leap into ditches when he was on one of his six-mile walks to examine flowers and lichen at a quarter of an inch distance. . . . We have a fantasy about a new series of guide books John will edit called *Betjeman's Dim Counties*. Clackmannanshire, Renfrew and Bedford will launch the series.' On 9 September he wrote, "What we've got to show is how funny Tennyson was. And how nice. We'd have liked him more than Byron," John says. On John's last day we have a celebration dinner. John and I do a parody of *Woman's Hour*. Box cameras flash and the best from the Whitehart cellars is produced. We talk about the excitements of filming and all the crew agree that it is among the five chief pleasures in life.'[5]

JB was brimming with ideas for films and could think of little else. The BBC approached him about filming England from a helicopter, a completely innovative idea. He suggested using the helicopter as though it were God; tracing prehistoric tracks along the tops of the chalk downs; looking down on the swamps that the Saxons tamed and drained; seeing the winding lanes criss-crossing counties like Devon, some of them Saxon boundaries. All this could show how much transport had changed England.

Meanwhile JB never lost his appetite for seeing new films himself. He had developed a love for them as film critic on the *Evening Standard* in the early thirties. I'll never forget how much he loved *If. . .*, Lindsay Anderson's film about a boys' public school which came out in December 1968. He went to an afternoon performance and enjoyed it so much he sat through and watched it again. He then wrote immediately to Anderson, whom he'd never met. Anderson replied (26 January 1969), 'Your letter gave me – and David Sherwin who wrote *If . . .*, to whom I showed it – great pleasure and that warm glow one experiences when one can feel one's work has made an intimate and personal impression. The film is such a peculiar medium: so susceptible to handling of the greatest subjectivity, so able to give reality to the most poetic imaginings, *such a wonderful medium of communication* – yet through the economics of it, and our whole woeful organisation of society so fettered [and] perverted, misunderstood at every turn.'[6]

With JB's fame, particularly through his films, came a certain anger in some circumstances if people did not listen to what he said. He was at an age when some of his friends who had gone into politics were in powerful positions. Tom Driberg and he had long fought for various bits of England together, but he had other allies in Woodrow Wyatt and Wayland Kennet. By the end of the sixties, JB was a 'friend' or member of no less than two hundred associations and societies all over the country.

Meanwhile his work on the Diocesan Advisory Committees continued, taking him and John Piper on visits to familiar Oxfordshire churches, which they loved. At Blewbury the best headstones had been ranged round the edges like a series of jagged teeth in order to facilitate the mowing. JB made a plea for the churchyard to be put back as it was. He wrote in his report (29 April 1969), 'Unfortunately, some of the best eighteenth-century headstones and early nineteenth-century ones were removed from their original positions and arranged in straight rows. . . . It is definitely a churchyard and could never become a park, with rambler roses and birdbaths and short grass, which would be quite out of character. I sympathise with the desire of the people who want to keep the village tidy but it would be out of keeping with the spirit of the village churchyard and a liberty with the history of the village to remove any but broken stones or ones with no decoration on them whatsoever.'[7] He told the indomitable Mrs Dance, the secretary of the Society for the Protection for Ancient Buildings, about the granite gateposts at Worthyvale near Camelford in Cornwall, where the farmer could not afford to re-erect one which had just been knocked down by a lorry. His work in small corners of far-flung counties was untiring. He made a conscious decision to use all the powers that were given to him through his fame.

By chance, fame brought him one of the most important and fruitful friendships of his life. Far from the limelight and completely un-connected to his other worlds, it came at a time when he most needed quietude. On the night of 6 November 1967 he met Mary Wilson, the wife of the Prime Minister Harold Wilson. 'Garrett Drogheda had asked Harold and me to go to the opera,' Mary remembered. 'When I saw the guest list with John's name on it, I was very excited, because I had never met him. I had the seating plan changed for dinner in the interval, so that I could sit next to him. We established a rapport straight away and both wrote to each other the following day. Our letters crossed. From then onwards we met regularly right until the end of his life. We both loved quoting poetry to each other and we both liked the same sort of things. Sometimes we'd meet in St James's Park, sometimes I'd go to his house or more often he'd drop in on me at Number 10 on his way to or from a meeting.'[8] JB found the lift at Number 10 very erotic. It was lined with red suede and always took a very long time to reach its destinations. He told Mary how he imagined all the things that had happened in it.

When JB and Mary met, usually around teatime, he was often exhausted from a day which might have involved filming or sitting through a long meeting. 'He would sit down and say, "Read to me darling." Sometimes he'd actually fall asleep but not often. One afternoon he said, "Why don't you try 'Maud'," and I read the whole of Tennyson's "Maud" in one go. We greatly enjoyed it. Another day I read the whole of "Enoch Arden", but he didn't like that quite so well. His poetry tastes were so simple – he didn't really enjoy something if it was inexplicable. I once read him a poem of mine and he said, "Yes darling, but what does it *mean*?" He used to advise me to read Swinburne when I was having trouble with my poetry. He wasn't very keen on Longfellow and used to parody him a lot and talk in Hiawatha metre that made us laugh – he had such an *infectious* laugh. We were once walking from the House of Lords along the Embankment past the Henry Moore statue and I said, "John, come and look at this building." It was covered in turrets and balconies and towers. Of course John knew all about it and how it was designed by these two brothers and he described an imaginary conversation between them – "Well, that bit looks a bit plain, let's put another balcony on it," and we were craning our necks upwards and laughing. The policeman who walked by took us to be drunk and disorderly. It was John's *enthusiasm* for life that was so wonderful. He was never much interested in politics – when I talked about someone who'd been to dinner he'd say, "Is he Left, darling?" '

From the outset, JB's rapport with Mary had a lot to do with her understanding of his melancholy side. 'I once saw him on the television long before I ever met him,' she recalls, 'and he was talking about human frailties, and I thought then that I'd like him because he *understood* and wasn't afraid to talk about anxieties. I always knew when he was worried about something – he had this habit of putting his hand to his mouth and biting his knuckles.' I don't think JB ever knew he did this, but his very close friends must have noticed it. 'When I knew he was worried I would always read to him – it seemed to calm him down.'

Mary's loyal and completely private friendship was to remain a gentle support which he knew he could always turn to. 'I never wanted to mix in with his other life,' she remembered. 'He once took me to dinner with John Osborne and Jill Bennett, but it didn't work – I preferred to see him on his own.'

Meanwhile, literary and society hostesses, friends and neighbours, clamoured for JB's and Elizabeth's company. 'Well my dears, we did enjoy that social and political evening, *drunk with power I am as a result*,'[9] he wrote to Osbert Lancaster and Anne, his second wife (7 November 1968). He helped Iris Tree have her poem 'The Marsh Picnic' printed by his favourite printer, Will Carter, of the Rampant Lions Press. To Deirdre Connolly he wrote, after a weekend in Sussex, 'You were glorious to look at and glorious to talk to. You are perfect at making an old man like me comfortable. I adore you and Cyril and Cressida. Cyril's generosity over those gorgeous wines we had, particularly that magnum of claret, overwhelms me. Poor Elizabeth and I had a very happy and unalarming journey back.'[10] He and Elizabeth often stayed with Ann Fleming's sister Laura and her husband Michael Canfield. 'Fond thoughts of Hertfordshire House bowered in roses, dowered with glorious views into beechy Bucks, showered with the generosity of your and Michael's hospitality, powered with your vital and marvellous personality . . . flowered with delphiniums and sweet peas, towered with urns and birds and balconies,'[11] he wrote.

JB never got carried away by grandeur and he never forsook a soul from his past. He was concerned about his old Oxford friend Lionel Perry who lived in Ireland and was suffering from pleurisy, and kept in weekly touch with 'Cracky' William Wicklow about the former's progress. Cracky wrote (7 February 1968), 'I have had a card and letter from old Li and he really seems to be on the mend. I discovered the Mosquito [Patrick Kinross] had a Dugdale aunt, Una, who went to jail as a suffragette (so did her husband) and wrote a book about marriage called *Love and Honour But Not Obey*.'[12] Later he wrote (March), 'Old Li was delighted to hear from you. I honestly think he is better, and as soon as he is able to move we will go to fetch him. You always were v[ery] kind about writing to sick people. I hope your own health is good? Mrs Trelease was always convinced that you were "very delicate". Do you remember how you always had her butter ration and could only eat the breast of the chicken?'[13] Mrs Trelease was housekeeper to 'Colonel' Kolkhorst at Yarnton and Cracky William's missives, which he always wrote on a series of six or seven picture postcards of Irish scenes, often recalled those old days.

JB offered support to another close friend, the Reverend Harry Williams, who was at the same time in a vulnerable and, in his words, 'het-up' state over his decision to become a monk and to join the Community of the Resurrection at Mirfield in Yorkshire in the spring of 1969. Harry went to stay at Trebetherick. 'The atmosphere at Trebetherick with the company of Elizabeth and John soon put me once again on an even keel. After a week when I was fully stabilised, I felt at dinner that something was in the air. I was right. It fell upon me like an avalanche while after dinner we were sitting round the fire. Elizabeth told me straight out that she thought I was making the most catastrophic mistake in going to Mirfield and said she was going to spend the evening telling me why . . . . I prepared for the worst.' As he was a gregarious character and a popular social figure, Elizabeth could not envisage his being happy in an order where the luxuries of life were pared down to the minimum. 'John's face, meanwhile, was a mixture of concern, anxiety, amusement and reassurance. He remained silent . . . [and then he suddenly said,] "I suppose you reach a state where a *petit beurre* tastes delicious."[14] (In the event Harry went ahead with his decision to become a monk.)

JB had the perennial ability to enliven potentially serious or even staid situations. Tristram Powell remembered, 'One weekend, in the late sixties, he promised me tea and anchovy toast in the RAC Club. I was expecting a quiet time. When I arrived he said we were going to have a swim in the pool before tea. He had hired a baggy black bathing costume, which he had pulled up so high round his waist that his private parts, or part of them, had slipped out. He didn't notice because he was concentrating on two old club-men, who were doing vigorous exercises at opposite ends of the pool, swinging their arms in a bizarre, geriatric manner, making John laugh a lot as he bobbed about in the water.'[15]

Although my mother had been in India for long spells during the latter half of the sixties, she remained close to JB. The longer she was away, the more he wrote. 'I had a horrid dream last night that you had hidden yourself in a cupboard and refused to have me back, I was very offended. So your letter was very reassuring,'[16] JB wrote. On the increasing number of grandchildren that I was bearing he showered love. By the time of the birth of our third daughter Endellion, JB's shambling figure in the corridors of St Mary's Hospital, Paddington, was a familiar sight. 'Wibbily, wobbily, wib,' he wrote on the present he left by my bed only hours after her birth. 'With love to blessed Endellion from Mad Dadz.'

1. JB's papers, University of Victoria, British Columbia.
2. Philip Larkin's papers, Beinecke Library, Yale University.
3. 'Penalties of Success', *The Author* (Spring 1967, VolumeLXXVIII, Number 1).
4. JB's papers, University of Victoria.
5. *A Dedicated Fan: Julian Jebb 1934–84*, ed. Tristram and Georgia Powell (Peralta Press, 1993).
6. JB's papers, University of Victoria.
7. Carbon copy of Diocesan Advisory Committee report, JB's papers, University of Victoria.
8. Mary Wilson, CLG interview (1994).
9. Osbert Lancaster's papers, Lincoln College, Oxford.
10. Cyril Connolly's papers, Tulsa University.
11. Laura Duchess of Marlborough's papers, Hugo Vickers's archives.
12. JB's papers, University of Victoria.
13. JB's papers, University of Victoria.
14. Harry Williams, *Someday I'll Find You* (Mitchell Beazley, 1982).
15. Tristram Powell, CLG interview (1994).
16. PB's papers, Beinecke Library, Yale University.

To Lionel Esher   43 Cloth Fair
17 May 1966   London EC1

My dear Lionel,
I don't know how experienced you are with film scripts, but I can assure you they do not give the impression that the film gives. They are even further removed from the medium than is a play text from the play when it is acted. Dear old Godfrey told me today that he had let you have a copy of a telly comedy I wrote called *Pity About the Abbey*, the theme of which was mine, but the love interest of which was added by a professional telly scriptwriter. I didn't reprove him when he told me this, because I regarded him and you as a friend, but, as a matter of fact, a television film script is the private property of the corporation and the author and the BBC let Godfrey have the script as a personal favour to me. I did not expect it to be handed round, least of all to Lord Bridges, who has not exactly got a visual mind. Now, why I am annoyed about this is that the film was a very serious argument disguised as a comedy, against developers of an unscrupulous sort, and civil servants who keep big things dark from the public and who have tame architects. It was a blow in favour of preservation societies and a strong uncompromised equivalent of the Royal Fine Art Commission. Though I don't expect many of the Commissioners have television sets (I haven't one myself), had they seen the play, I should have expected to have had letters of congratulations and thanks. As it is, I gather from others, but not from Godfrey, that there is a general impression in the Commission that I have behaved in an ungentlemanly fashion. I am so thunder-struck by this that I must ask you to let me have your reactions.
    Yours, John B

L.E. (formerly Brett), the architect, served on the Royal Fine Art Commission from 1951–69.
    JB had written an hour-long play for BBC Television (together with Stuart Farrar who had written in the love interest) about selling Westminster Abbey to Texas to make way for traffic improvements and offices. It was transmitted in July 1965 and again in 1966 as the *Wednesday Play*.
    L.E. wrote (20 May 1966), 'Godfrey [Samuel] asked me privately to look at your script because he was in some doubt as to whether he ought to show it to Lord Bridges

(who had asked to see it). I of course said he should try not to, as it was obvious it would hurt the old man's feelings. As for the Commission as a whole, since you ask me, I'd say that I am all for the Commission, like any other official body, being made fun of, but not by one of its members, even though of course I know and sympathize with what you wanted to put over.'

To Philip Larkin   43 Cloth Fair
25 May 1966   London EC1

My dear Philip,
I'm so sorry you were telephoned to by my chum Geoffrey Hughes of Rediffusion about televising you reading your poems. A most un-nerving and amazing experience – not reading your poems, but being rung up by Telly. They always do ring up. Geoffrey, a sensitive and really nice man, should have known better.

I've been asked to do four programmes, half an hour each, just reading poetry of the past to see whether we can make people interested in it. So I'm doing it as a sort of variety *artiste*, trying to keep people interested. I'm using Cowper, Tennyson, Burns, Rev[erend] R. H. Barham, Dowson, Vachel Lindsay etc. stories and lyrics intermingled. The only modern poet I had in mind was you – 'Take One Home for the Kiddiz', 'Toads Revisited' and 'A Study of Reading Habits' – these last three in that order to end the whole series. Can I have permission to read them? I would *far sooner* you read them because you read so well and your melancholy voice is exactly suited to them. They are spellbinding and SO ARE YOU. Or who else could read them if you can't? We can't have each programme all my voice. We've got Charles Tennyson doing some Tennyson, a Scot [David Grant] reading Burns and a Manxman [Llew Gardner] reading bits of that under-rated man T. E. Brown. (Those are the only other *artistes* save me, one in each programme.)
    Yours, John B

    PS If you *can* do it almost any date would do.

> P.L., the poet, had read and liked JB's poetry while at Oxford and praised *Collected Poems* in the *Guardian* when it first came out in 1958, but did not meet him until 1961.
>   The series of four programmes was called *Betjeman at Random* and included readings by P.L., Sir Charles Tennyson, Llew Gardner and David Grant. It was screened in August of that year.

To John Summerson   43 Cloth Fair
14 June 1966   London EC1

My dear Coolmore,
I have just finished Arnold Lunn's *The Harrovians*, 1913, and am now
reading his *Loose Ends*, 1919, and both are jolly good about our old
school. *The Harrovians* was a pioneer show-up of public school life,
earlier than *The Loom of Youth*. Its author, like Victor Pasmore, Cecil
Beaton, Terence Rattigan, you and Alexander of Tunis is still with us.
I have written him (Lunn) a fan letter.

Have you come to admire, as K[enneth] Clark and I have, some of the
work of Sir [George] Gilbert [Scott], including St Pancras station,
which is to be pulled down? Would you be prepared to write an
appreciative article on it? You count and I don't. It is no good my
writing about Sir Gilbert and St Pancras in particular, because I have
been so denigrated by Karl Marx [James Richards], and the Professor-
Doktor [Pevsner] as a lightweight wax fruit merchant, I will not carry
the necessary guns. K[enneth] can't do it, as he is overworked, though
his spirit is willing. Now will you?
     Bung ho, old top, John B

> Arnold Lunn, the fabled British skier who invented the slalom, was an Old Harrovian.
>   Despite having been at Marlborough himself, JB had always favoured Harrow School
> above all others, partly for its impressive list of old boys, partly for its suburban location
> and partly for its old school songs, particuarly 'Ducker'. He often wore a Harrow School
> straw hat and talked about 'my old school'.
>   Sir George Gilbert Scott (1811–78) built the Midland Grand Hotel, St Pancras,
> (1868–74) with four hundred bedrooms for the Midland Railway Company. It cost over
> £400,000.
>   In 1966 British Railways announced that it intended to combine King's Cross and St
> Pancras stations by demolishing all of the former and most of the latter terminus. But,
> owing to the scandalous destruction of the Euston Arch four years before, public
> opinion was now aroused and the Victorian Society, with JB as vice-chairman,
> vigorously and successfully opposed this plan. British Railways were thwarted by the
> listing at Grade I in 1967 of both the stupendous St Pancras train shed and Gilbert
> Scott's magnificent Midland Grand Hotel; King's Cross had once been the more
> admired for its apparently 'functional' simplicity but now, JB was pleased to find,
> Scott's once despised Victorian Gothic was increasingly admired. Both stations still
> stand, and both are in use.
>   J.S. replied (15 June 1966), 'St Pancras Station – i.e. hotel. No, I just couldn't put any
> heart into the idea of preserving it. I have been looking at it very carefully these last few
> weeks, trying to identify to what extent Sir Gilbert used up his Foreign Office details
> (you know the story). Every time I look at the building I'm consumed with admiration in
> the cleverness of the detail and every time I leave it I wonder why as a whole it is so
> nauseating. I think Sir Gilbert put his finger on it when he said, "For my part I think it is
> *too* good for its purpose." What he really meant was that a vast quantity of expensive
> detail had been squandered on a composition which is inherently weak. Emmet said that

compared with K[ing]'s Cross it was "a piece of vulgar art manufacture" and I think he was right – and Emmet was a middle-pointed man. I shall hate to see all that gorgeous detail being hacked down but I really don't think one could go to a Minister and say this is a great piece of architecture, a great national monument.'

To Penelope Betjeman

15 June 1966

43, Cloth Fair,
London, E.C.1.
Monarch 1698.

Moi darling Plymmi' Oi naow see that yew

& Ben an crriitin' the book & oi'm

intresss to notis that that darn animal

criiti's with his LEFT paw. Oi awope

'e is not disturbin yew in yer work

at the book tew mooch.

yors vvy trewdly
T. OTOIV.

This facsimile letter is a good example of the peculiar language in which JB and PB always wrote to each other. It reads:

My darling Plymmi,
I now see that you *and Ben* are writing the book and I'm interested to notice that that dim animal writes with his LEFT paw. I hope he is not disturbing you in your work at the book too much.
Yorz very trewly, Tewpie

PB was working on her book about the Kulu Valley, for John Murray. Her dog Ben was a border terrier.

To Siegfried Sassoon 43 Cloth Fair
17 June 1966 London EC1

Dear Siegfried,
I'm so glad you are over that operation. I know quite a lot of people who have been *rejuvenated* by it. It is most important not to get up too soon. So stay in bed for a bit in the Heytesbury hermitage. Hospital life has a monastic order about it which I enjoy – the regular times for meals and cups of tea and dressing of wounds after operations. One is quite sorry to leave. Ah, but Heytesbury! Hope I get a chance in August to come down and see you there. You are our mightiest poet and you've gone on being better and different all the time. I read 'The General' on the telly, and hope you'll tell your agent to claim a fee from Rediffusion. It's very interesting, but it has much less wordiness about it than other war poets of the [19]14 war. You are such a masterly craftsman as well as so beautiful a poet.
    Yours ever, John B

S.S. had had a prostate operation and had written from a nursing home in Bath (15 June 1966), 'The best mental holiday I'd had in years. . . . Enjoying extreme popularity with the wee nurses who thought me a cheery old card. I'm now glorying in the majestic silence of this place in the comfort of my own bed. . . . I wish Wantage was nearer, you'd love this place, which is a poem.'
    Heytesbury House, Wiltshire, is a great early nineteenth-century mansion in huge downs just above the Wylye Valley and now has a busy road slicing its park.

To Edith Garratt 43 Cloth Fair
10 July 1966 London EC1

My dear Edith,
I'm so grateful for your helpful letter. I've changed that first stanza as a result of your and Tom Driberg's efforts to:

> The flag that hung half-mast today
> Seems animate with being
> As if it knew for whom it flew
> And will no more be seeing.

I don't think 'will' matters in the last stanza as the flag goes on. I had in a stanza after that one about the flag seeing him walking to the club house and I'll have a try on the page proofs, though I rather like the *Times* bit. Will be down in October. Hope you and Oliver are well and that Oliver is doing more water-colours. I'm glad I won't be there in August and I expect you both feel the same.
    Love, John B

> E.G. and her husband Oliver owned a house called Boskenna opposite Treen in Trebetherick, and kept an eye on the latter in JB's absence.
>   JB had sent his poem 'The Hon. Sec.', about the St Enodoc Golf Club secretary, to E.G. for her to check.

To Anthony Barnes   The Mead
                                                       Wantage
10 July 1966   Berkshire

My dear Little Prawls,
I wrote to Lady Prawls to say would she mind my printing those verses on the Commander which I wrote, in a forthcoming slim vol[ume]. I also wrote to ask her if the rumour was true that you had left Schweppshire for Covent Garden, my dear. She said yes to both. As you know, I *adore* opera and am a balletomane so you will, of course, often be seeing me there. But just in case you don't, I apply to you too. Do you think the reference to the name 'Commander' and to his life in Keele and Kent too intimate for a book of verse? Personally, I don't think that they need be explained or changed or deleted. If they are incomprehensible, so much the worse for the sensibility of the reader and so much the more his bad luck for never having known the Commander. But if you think otherwise, I will omit the poem. Lady P[rawls] said I was the best judge of this. But she asked me to ask you and I think you are as good if not better a judge on this matter. Love to my god-kiddi Brendan and to Sue and to B[rendan]'s brother and to you.
    Love from John B

A.B. and his mother were happy for JB's poem 'The Commander' to appear in *High and Low*. Stanzas 4 to 6 read:

> I remembered our shared delight in architecture and nature
> As bicycling we went
> By saffron-spotted palings to crumbling box-pewed churches
> Down hazel lanes in Kent.
>
> I remembered on winter evenings, with wine and the family round you,
> Your reading Dickens aloud
> And the laughs we used to have at your gift for administration,
> For you were never proud.
>
> Sky and sun and the sea! the greatness of things was in you
> And thus you refrained your soul.
> Let others fuss over academical detail,
> *You* saw people whole. . . .

A.B. had been working for Schweppes.

To Penelope Betjeman

22 August 1966

Villa Pianetti Nuovi
Casteleone di Suasa
Ancona

My darling Plymmi,
I am very surprised I like abroad so much. This place is a paradise of olive grass, little hills, oaks to your head all over the place among the farms and little walled towns and shrines of our lady and smells of sage.

It is eighteenth-century pale brick and looks over towards Urbino. There is a little disused chapel in the garden for my daily devotions. Oxen yolked pass below the villa and [along] a white road carrying widows' grapes and spinach. It is a constantly changing undergraduate reading party with married couples arriving now and then and going on to some other place. Senigallia is the market town. It is very beautiful with a sixteenth-century chapel full of Barroccios. No English tourists seem to go there. It is obviously old-fashioned. Simon S[tuart] has a car and so have the undergraduates. Servants look after the house which is well supplied with baths and *toilets* and, thank God, no telephone. We lunch in and go out to dinner and have mussels and local wine and pellegrino. I at last feel rested and uncoiled after that spate of telly and thankful no one knows me or sees me. Harry W[illiams] has written a long treatise on Evil while here and Simon Stuart is writing a book on education but all I am up to yet is reading Agatha Christie. I can't even read Pater.

Wherever I go I keep seeing your nut.

Sometimes it is cut up in slices which makes me very sad.

A married lady staying here has an Archie which goes with her everywhere, is v[ery] like Archie but smaller. He is called Teddy. I feel the lack of Italian v[ery] much and wish you were here. I must close now as this is the longest consecutive bit of writing I've done since I've been here as I was too tired even to read Agatha for the first twenty-four hours.

I much prefer this part to Calabria. There seem to be no posts in or out, no letter boxes, so you won't get any more from me except my constant thought and love sent over the ocean to Liverpool. The Town Hall at Liverpool is a splendid Adam. The Walker Art Gallery and St George's Hall are worth seeing. Love to all the catechists.

Yorz trewely, Tewpie

JB and EC stayed in Italy in Simon Stuart's villa with some of the Church of England Ramblers, including Harry Williams.

To Candida Lycett Green   American Colony Hotel
11 November 1966   Jerusalem
Armistice Day

Darling Wibz,
Your letter is the nicest and kindest that any father could have from any daughter. I'm so glad the critics didn't kill me.

I cannot recommend Jerusalem too highly. But this hotel is *the* place – old-fashioned, huge bedrooms, flowers and endless servants and quiet and run by Anglicised Americans.

Now this is the very *odd* thing about Jerusalem which makes me so glad I came. It really does make you aware that Christ (whether he was God is for the moment irrelevant) lived and walked here. There the devotion of centuries, despite raids by Persians, Romans, Moslems and modern computers, make one see that Christ was God i.e. Man and God in one. And that is brought about by the churches here (Eastern Orthodox, Coptic, Syrian, Latin and the dear old C[hurch] of E[ngland]) all sucking honey from the rose of Jerusalem like bees. I am most surprised at how I love this city. But come at this time of year, not in pilgrim time. God bless you. Your letter has made me full of euphoria and I think the poster idea a very good one. We'll discuss it when we meet. I'm no good. Just fashionable. But very happy. Lots of love and to Rupert and Lucy and the ex-maggot.
MD

> JB was making the BBC Television film *Journey to Bethlehem* which was screened at Christmas. It was the story of his first visit to the Holy Land. His journey started at Jerusalem where he visited many early churches, to Bethlehem and the Garden of Gethsemane, and he also visited an Arab refugee camp.
>
> His new book of poems *High and Low* had just come out.
>
> I had written to JB with the idea of having his poems printed on posters and put in the underground or sold in gift shops.
>
> Lucy was RLG's and my first child, and Imogen our second whom JB referred to firstly as 'the maggot' and then as 'the ex-maggot'. Later he raved about her beauty.

To Duncan Fallowell   43 Cloth Fair
29 November 1966   London EC1

Dear Duncan,
I was laid low with 'flu for six days after the excitement of Jordan. Nobody had told me how beautiful the place was and how hot it was

going to be. The colours of the desert were just like they are in Holman
Hunt's *Scapegoat*. Then the old city was full of smells and holiness and
hadn't got much architecture. It bristled with character. I was much
encouraged by Copts, Syrians, Armenians and Orthodox. They
seemed as old as the hills. It was quite possible to think of incarnate God
walking about in the country there. I was glad in a way to escape from
all the reviews and then the 'flu spared me the rest. I am glad you liked
Maurice Bowra's *Memories*. I read them while I had 'flu and enjoyed
every word. Nothing escapes the old boy and he is as good value to meet
as he is to read. Your [A. L.] Rowse poem is splendid. He is a very
strange character. I enjoyed his *Cornish Childhood*.
   Yours, John Betjeman

   Maurice Bowra's *Memories* (1898–1939), published in 1966, had just come out.

To Mr Percival   43 Cloth Fair
9 January 1967   London EC1

Dear Mr Percival,
I am absolutely amazed to think it's thirty years since *Slough* was
published. As a matter of fact, it's longer ago still that it was written. I
should think I wrote it just after I was sent down from Oxford and
when I was a private school master for one hilarious term at Thorpe
House, Oval Way, Gerrard's Cross, Buck[ingham]s[hire]. That was, I
think, in about 1928. Mr and Mrs Noble, the headmaster and his wife,
used to drive my colleague Mr Saunders and me through the leafy lanes
of beechy Buck[ingham]s[hire] when work was over. I remember we
used very much to hope we would get back in time for Mr Saunders and
me to have a drink at the inn by Chalfont St Peter Church. But on these
expeditions, we used to see Slough, and what shocked me about it in
those days was the Trading Estate as it was called, and it was about that
and not the town that the verses were written.
   Since then, of course, the equivalent of the Trading Estate has
appeared all over England and most of the home counties are like
Gerrard's Cross, but in those days there was a lot of real country which
we used to drive through and I fancy that I saw, in the Trading Estate,
which was such a sharp contrast with real country, the menace of things
to come. One used to see the flash fronts of the factories on the main
road with the administrative blocks looking on to regular lines of

commercial flower beds and one thought of the whirring noise and impersonality of the factory behind these blocks.

There was also the additional information, which I think is true, which I was given, and that was that the Slough Trading Estate was built on some of the most valuable agricultural land in England and that it came into existence simply because in the 1914 war it was the most convenient distance from which some General or Ministry could dump disused army lorries from London. The town of Slough was not, when those verses were written, such a congestion as it is now and I was most certainly not thinking of it but of the Trading Estate, which was also called Slough, you remember, and which had originated in a dump that now stretches practically from Reading to London. Indeed, I think you will find that the verses were written before that charming stucco hotel, seventeenth century, I should think, in origin was taken down at the crossroads and replaced by a sham Georgian one in red brick. The chain stores were only then just beginning to deface the High Street, but already the world of 'executives' with little moustaches, smooth cars and smooth manners and ruthless methods was planted in my mind along the fronts of those Trading Estate factories. I hope this letter will help you and I thank you very much for yours to me.

Yours sincerely, John Betjeman

To Jonathan Stedall   Treen
       Trebetherick
25 January 1967   Wadebridge

My dear Jonathan,

> Marcus Stedall's house is shuttered
> And the waves are mountains high.
> Cry of gull and seamew uttered
> Vainly as the wind roars by.
> Safe in Somerset or Surrey
> Marcus Stedall counts his chips
> While down here the breakers hurry
> Smoothing slate and smashing ships
> Here where cliff and spume are meeting
> Watch the coarse sea-spinach grow
> That it makes delicious eating
> Marcus Stedall doesn't know.

I must say there have been tremendous seas – just like in documentary –
this week, Feeble has been looking at them open-mouthed.

Those lectures look v[ery] interesting. Let's meet after or before one of
them (not Feb[ruary] 7th as I have to be in Kennington). F[eeble] sends
her love. Back next Monday.

   Love to you all down there.

   Love, JB

      Marcus S. was J.S.'s second cousin and owner of 'Brock', one of the cliff-top houses at
      Trebetherick. He and his brother Oliver, who ran the family building and engineering
      merchants' business, were both at Marlborough with JB.

9a Kingsley Amis.

9b Mollie Baring.

9c George Barnes.

9d Cecil Beaton.

10a Maurice Bowra.

10b David Cecil.

10c Cyril Connolly.

10d Deborah Devonshire.

11a Tom Driberg.

11b Mark Girouard.

11c Wilhelmine 'Billa' Harrod.

11d Harry Jarvis.

12a Patrick Kinross.

12b Osbert Lancaster.

12c Philip Larkin.

12d James Lees-Milne.

13a Joan Leigh Fermor.

13b Compton Mackenzie.

13c 'Freckly' Jill Menzies.

13d John 'Jock' Murray.

14a John Osborne.

14b John Piper.

14c Alan Pryce-Jones.

14d Siegfried Sassoon.

15a Martyn Skinner.

15b John Sparrow.

15c Stephen Spender.

15d Jonathan Stedall.

16a G. B. 'Peter' Sterne.

16b John Summerson.

16c Evelyn Waugh.

16d Mary Wilson.

To Duncan Fallowell   The Mead
                                                         Wantage
3 February 1967   Berkshire

Dear Duncan,

I was glad to get your gloomy letter and I understand the gloom, but
envy you the energy which makes you put it down so attractively and
well. I have half a bottle of whisky before me but no clay pipe as I've
given up smoking and the restraint has driven me to the drink faster
than ever.

Last night I went, for the first time for twenty years, to Magdalen. I
had to listen to the choir there at Evensong in order to write some Irish
prose as a prelude to a recording of the choir on the BBC. In the crisp
night it was beautiful. I parked my car in a place where it said, 'Private.
Pass holders only,' and walked by paths I had not walked for forty years
to the cloisters and then to the candlelit chapel where the singing – I am
unmusical – seemed first class. What surprised me was how Magdalen,
though it may be Gothic in style, *feels* Georgian especially the chapel
with its pre-Pugin but still sophisticated House-of-Lords furnishing.
No one spoke to me, except the verger who was a scout in my day and
recognised me, so I was unable to tell anyone what a brilliant fellow was
coming up from St Paul's next autumn. I will look about for a job for
you. I have a friend (a very old man) called Canon C. B. Mortlock who
occupies such a lot of positions I call him the Pluralist to his face and he
doesn't mind. He is a Canon of Chichester with a house in the Close,
'Urbanus' in the *Church Times*, Ecclesiastical Correspondent to the
Daily Telegraph, Ballet correspondent to *Punch* and Rector of thirteen
City churches with a palace in Foster Lane next to his HQ, St Vedast's.
He is Anglo-Catholic and very quiet and you wouldn't think he could
do all these things. He was in the 1914 war. Well he told me last week he
wanted *temporary* help, so I told him about you and I've this day written
to him and given him your address. Keep in touch and let me know if
nothing turns up and I will try elsewhere. But Man Proposes and Mrs
Gamp Disposes.
    Yours, JB

Charles Bernard Mortlock, who was on the committee of the Victorian Society with JB,
was in fact quite ill by this time. (He died, on 31 October 1967, at the age of seventy-
nine.) He was in fact dramatic and ballet critic to the *Daily Telegraph*, *Punch* and the
Church Times.

D.F. had asked JB's opinion about what to do between leaving St Paul's and going up to Magdalen.

Mrs (Sarah) Gamp was the drunken nurse in Dickens's novel *Martin Chuzzlewit*.

To the Secretary of the Athenæum   43 Cloth Fair
3 February 1967   London EC1

Dear Mr Secretary,
Your letter to me of last year following my protest about the ugly new lighting in the entrance hall and the trivial wallpapering of the Great Room on the first floor put me in a dichotomy. You will remember that you said that the lighting couldn't be altered as it had just been put in and that my letter would be 'borne in mind'. Alas, that phrase – a Committee-like civil servant's – means nothing will be done and my letter is now in the waste-paper basket.

I must tell you, and I hope you will tell the Committee, that I have had to weigh up in my mind my regard for the splendid club servants and my many friends among the members against the deep disquiet at the affront to Decimus Burton and T. E. Collcutt which the present lighting and decoration are. I fear I must resign. I am sending a copy of this letter to my friend Sir John Summerson. The Athenæum is indeed a club for intellectuals, but not for aesthetes like
    Yours faithfully, John Betjeman

JB had been elected to the Athenæum in 1948. He had written to Harry Jarvis (5 December 1966), 'I'm going to leave this place, they've done it up like a Trust House and though it is in its way a super-sophisticated joke to do such a thing, I find myself getting too simple for such jokes. I shall try and join the RAC instead.' JB indeed joined the RAC Club that year.

To John Sparrow   43 Cloth Fair
[?April] 1967   London EC1

DEAREST SPANZBURY
I AM
WRITING THIS
LINE UPON LINE
TO TRY TO
EXPRESS TO YOU

IN THE SUBTLE WAY YOU
WORKED OUT IN THAT BRILLIANT
BOOK YOU GAVE TO PENELOPE VALENTINE HESTER
CHETWODE
MY ADORATION
OF
YOUR ART & PERSON
&
HEART & SUITS
AND TO THANK YOU FOR SUNDAY'S GLORIOUS
LUNCHEON WHICH PENELOPE ENJOYED
TO THE FULL
AS DID YOUR
LIFE-LONG FRIEND
& ADORER
JB

J.S. had given PB his new book *Controversial Essays*, a collection of his reviews and essays in periodicals.

To Jonathan Stedall

24 April 1967

The Mead
Wantage
Berkshire

My dear Jonathan,
Your letter of nineteen days ago from Treen, which reached me on my return last week with the C[hurch] of E[ngland] Ramblers from Spain, gave me unmitigated pleasure. First it gave me pleasure that you enjoyed Treen despite the OIL that must have come along with its stink and destruction. Next that Dede found it peaceful. Next that you saw all my friends the neighbours including that smashing Aussie Joan Oakley. But best of all was the news, dear Jonathan, that you were going to come back to the BBC. Mind you, I don't think you would have been certain of where your vocation lay had you not gone to the Steiner School. It gives one proportion to go into 'retreat' which that was and retreat clarifies. I knew, as soon as I saw that orphanage film and indeed that Ludwig film and the Cothill film – I knew you had the real genius. I knew it as a matter of fact long before when we were making those Telly-Welly [Television Wales and West] films. You can

handle people and you can also film them. Not one in a million can do both those things and you *are* one in a million. One usually has to do what one doesn't want to do in order to do what one wants to do. I daresay the BBC won't be perfection – but, my goodness, I'm glad to think you're there or rather that you will be there – both for my own sake and for yours. Most producers are pretty rough stuff except for you.

The C[hurch] of E[ngland] Ramblers had a lovely time in Spain – green grass, wisteria, arum lilies in flower, oysters, prawns, good local wine and wall-flower-stuffed cliffs of Baroque in Santiago and those same Atlantic rollers on the shore above near Corunna. We saw twenty-seven things that *thrilled* us all – not bad in fourteen days. See you soon. Feeble's got a job as location advisor for *The Charge of the Light Brigade* and is v[ery] excited. Love to you all down there on that Sussex height.

Love, JB

[Ann] Benbow has gone into Brompton Hospital – she's been looking ill and God knows yet what's wrong with her.

In March 1967 the oil tanker the *Torrey Canyon* was wrecked off Land's End. The pollution which resulted was described by the Under Secretary to the Navy as 'the greatest peace-time menace to Britain's shores'.

Dede is J.S.'s sister.

J.S. made the 'orphanage film' as part of a six-part series called *World of a Child* about a convent which looked after abandoned children. The Cothill film about a prep-school boy was part of the same series.

Ann Benbow was JB's secretary at the time.

To Francis Turner   The Mead
                                                       Wantage
24 April 1967   Berkshire

Dear Francis,

I came back from Spain last week to learn the sad news of George's death. I feel the very nasty gap it leaves in our lives and it makes me want to write to *The Times* (though Robert Birley's, the only notice I saw, was rather good) to say how much he meant to us. Then I thought better still write you and to his surviving sisters. The addresses of them I will have to ask you to send me when you have a moment. You and George were so close, Chichester must seem empty – despite the Dean and his Cathedral – without him. The only matter I should think on which you and George didn't agree was that on which I agree with you

– Gidney. George was the first breath of civilised life I encountered at Marlborough – those white rooms and the oval-framed portrait of your mother, the leather-bound edition of Pope and the conversation he used to lead us on with, never putting himself first. I should say that Louis MacNeice, Anthony Blunt, Philip Harding, John Edward Bowle, and Arthur Elton and me – and for all I know the film-star James Mason – owe more to George than we do to our parents even. This is because at an impressionable time of our lives in a tough community he and Clifford Canning made us aware that being good at games was not all. What was so marvellous about him was that he kept up with us afterwards. I have some delightful letters from him full of short wise bits of perception and plenty of jokes too – though they were more spoken than written.

 Yours, John Betjeman

> F.T. was Canon of Chichester. His brother George T. had been an inspiring master to JB at Marlborough College. Although F.T.'s tendency to smoke in bed in his eighties put paid to many of his papers and his brother's which were left to him, this letter survived.
>
> A.R. Gidney had been the classics master, whom JB had loathed.
>
> Clifford Canning was another master at Marlborough.

To Dan MacNabb   43 Cloth Fair
3 June 1967   London EC1

Dear Dan MacNabb,
That is a very kind and heartening letter you wrote to me on May 30th. If I *were* offered the P[oet] L[aureateship], I would accept it. It would be arrogant not to. But I know with an inner conviction I won't be. I'm too 'unreliable' and eccentric. It is splendid to hear you have finished one creative labour and gone on to another. While the energy's there use it. It is the meaning of the word 'inspiration', I think. It certainly comes from outside, the desire to create.

 Glad you liked that programme. Bruce Beeby the actor (an Australian) was the reader with me. Write to Hallam Tennyson who produced us, about your poetry. He is a good man and a good straight producer, honest and sensitive.

 Yours, John B

> D.MacN., the poet, had written to JB about one of the poetry programmes he had made for the BBC with the producer Hallam Tennyson.
>
> John Masefield, the Poet Laureate, had just died. C. Day-Lewis was appointed as his successor in 1968.

To Osbert Lancaster   The Mead
                                                              Wantage
4 June 1967   Berkshire

Dear old top,
Now that I've a free moment, I write to say I read your book at two
sittings, *entranced* (Burges has one 's' by the way, the only error the
Thomas Edward Neil *wise one* spotted). Yes, entranced. It suffered by
being given in extracts in the *S[unday] T[imes]*. The effect of the whole is
powerful and that effect is double. One you may not have noticed
because it is you. It is written by a very good, kind man who is the soul
of honour. It is wholly without malice though it takes a liberty with
facts, I'm *glad* to say, to give the right impression of a situation e.g. the
exploding home-made wine. But the second effect is one of overwhelming beauty and tenderness in the descriptive passage on the I[sle]
of W[ight] as I mentioned in my last letter to you, the approaching war,
and Fleet Street, Oxford rooms, St Ronan's and even Charterhouse.
And then of course I adore that convoluted prose you write. A bit of
Max [Beerbohm] and Gibbon mixed with your own conversation.
Perhaps the most brilliant bit is the contrast between the approach to
the psychic of Clare and your mother-in-law. I had no idea Sir Austin
[Harris] was such an unconscious comic. You have immortalised him
even though often he immortalised himself. I hope you will go on
writing memoirs or topography or history. It is those slow winging
flights of descriptive prose, whether of people or places, that is as good
and individual as your drawing. I know. I've been a reviewer for years.
You are readable – a very RARE gift. Love to Anne, Clare, Max
[Hastings] and Cara and Willie and Doggers* and Aldworth and Eaton
Square and God bless you.
    John B
    *Dauglish not Counsell

> *With an Eye to the Future*, the second part of O.L.'s autobiography (published by
> Murrays), had just been serialised in the *Sunday Times* before publication. (The first half
> was called *All Done from Memory*, 1963.)
>   'The exploding of the home-made wine' refers to PB's recipe written in the *Daily
> Express* which had specified the wrong ingredients and caused explosions of marrows all
> over England.
>   Sir Austin Harris (1870–1958), vice-chairman of Lloyds Bank and an art collector,
> was the father of O.L.'s first wife Karen. He had a habit of turning off lights whether or
> not there was anyone in the room.
>   O.L. had married Anne Scott-James, the gardening writer and journalist, earlier that
> year. She had previously been married to Macdonald Hastings.

To Robert Graves 43 Cloth Fair
20 June 1967 London EC1

Dear and best of poets,
That was a *splendid* address you gave on Masefield today – affectionate,
humorous, fair, personal and loyal. I had to write and thank you for it
and of course I don't expect a reply – writing letters is hell. I got your
address from the Soc[iety] of Authors.
    Yours, John Betjeman

> R.G. had given the address at the Poet Laureate John Masefield's memorial service at
> Westminster Abbey, during which an urn of his ashes was interred in Poets' Corner.

To Peter W. Mills 43 Cloth Fair
7 September 1967 London EC1

Dear Peter,
I am so sorry I cannot come with you to see Mr Beloe tomorrow. I have
to go down to Spelthorne to write an appeal for the home for drug
addicts that the Wantage Sisters run there. If I had not put off my visit
once already I would have come with you but I could not put them off a
second time.
    Please would you explain this to Mr Beloe as I am very excited about
the film and am anxious to know his views on how we ought to change it
to fit in with what he and the Archbishop would like.
    You will be able to tell him that we had thought of doing the film in
terms of people connected with the Cathedral, in their houses and in the
Cathedral and precincts. For instance, we would have a verger to tell us
about visitors, and which he thinks is his own favourite part of the
Cathedral; the clerk of the works and a mason, and if there is one – I
hope there is – someone who deals with the stained glass so that we can
compare the glass at Canterbury with the other great glass of
Christendom at Chartres and Bourges; we would need either the
architect and surveyor to the fabric or a canon interested in architecture
to show his favourite parts of the Cathedral or those that interest him
most; we would want a choirboy leaving where he lives to go and sing in
the choir; we would want a cleaner of floors; we would want someone
connected with the Registry or one of the bookshops; and probably we
would need someone from King's School and Kent University. Then

we would move to the clergy and see the dean and (as a lead to the Archbishop who would be the climax of the film), a Kentish church whether it be in Canterbury itself or in the diocese, and as far away as Croydon, where the Archbishop is the bishop of the diocese and therefore in touch with the vicar or rector.

This should lead to the Archbishop as the chief bishop of all Anglican churches throughout the world, and if presentable film exists of the church in America, Africa or India so much the better. I had hoped that it would have been possible to have had the Archbishop tell us about St Augustine's College, but its function has now, I believe, changed.

You, Peter, will be able to point out to Mr Beloe that our suggestion of doing this film in terms of people is not going to be a series of interviews, i.e. 'How long have you been here, Mr Dean, and do you like it?' but as it were catching people on their way to, or in the course of, their work, and the film will work up to what is the object of a cathedral, which is a service where all the senses are engaged in worship (I suppose we will have to rule out incense!) but we could stress the Sacraments, and show that Canterbury Cathedral is the mother church of Anglican dioceses throughout the world, that it is Catholic and reformed, High, broad and Low, liberal and the truth. All these last remarks are not filmable, but they must be implicit. So they will be if the people we show are as fond of Canterbury and the church as I know they are, with aid from the authorities you will be able to find who is filmic and interested. I don't think the film need be very Christmassy, the church goes on despite Christmas, and it will remind people of the fact.

Yours, John B

Tales of Canterbury, produced by P.M. for ITV, was transmitted on Christmas Day 1967.

To James Lees-Milne   Paddington Set w9
21 September 1967

My dear old boy,
I haven't seen your book on St Peter's but here I am at Adrian [Daintrey]'s with Lennox and Freda [Berkeley] and they tell me you are v[ery] depressed at no reviews. Just two maxims as an old literary gent:

(1) Illustrated books are not reviewed until Christmas by the literary editors who pinch them because they can sell them to Clark-Hall for half published price and yours will be regarded as an illustrated book.
(2) Reviews don't count. Publishers' travellers are the only people who really sell a book.

But this brings me to the final point and that is if the book is good – and written by you, old top, it is bound to be – it doesn't matter about reviews. Slowly it will sell. And even if it doesn't, there's something written, worth reading, in boards and there for as long as print or paper last.

Love to Alvilde. Lord Bridges is a defeated man. I'll tell you both when we meet.

Love, John B

Fuck the Americans. They're just smart. If you get good notices from them, then you may really lose self-confidence.

J.L.-M.'s book about St Peter's in Rome had just come out.

To Jonathan Stedall   Treen
                                                            Trebetherick
                                                            Wadebridge
28 September 1967   Cornwall

My dear Jonathan,
I'm just down here with Feeble (who has a nasty cough) clearing up before the lets come in. Last night I woke up with a strong sense that I must urge you to do a film of I didn't quite know what, perhaps it was a cathedral, or a loony bin or Barts [St Bartholomew's] or Charterhouse or a local council but anyhow it was a communal sort of life which only you can show. And now this morning comes your letter. I was about to write to you, so strong was the urge, to say that films and drama and bringing people out on them was your vocation. But you may have found out otherwise.

As to March 18th till April 9th, I've rung up Button, Menheniott and Mutton Estate Agents, Wadebridge, Cornwall (sufficient address) and booked the place in your name but you'd better confirm it in writing. Five people maximum because of the cess pit and drain capacity, no doggies except male dogs because of Feeble's garden. You'll have to

deal through Button, M[enheniott] and M[utton] as the place is
certainly in their hands in the 'season' and they would take umbrage if I
did a private deal. I love to think of you down here and Dede and the
kiddiz and David [Stedall] and the divine vegetarian [Mary Rose
Stedall] and Mr and Mrs [Cecil] Harwood, but not all at once because
of drains, as I said. Feeble is very, very quiet and has lost her voice.

Love to you all, John B

> JB let Treen for much of the year through the Wadebridge estate agents Button,
> Menheniott and Mutton.
>   J.S. was still undecided about whether to return to the BBC or become a Steiner
> teacher. He had asked if he could stay at Treen with his sister and friends.
>   Cecil Harwood was a pioneer Steiner teacher and a close friend of JB's erstwhile tutor
> at Oxford, C. S. Lewis.

To Terence de Vere White   43 Cloth Fair
1 November 1967   London EC1

Dear Terence,
It was mighty kind of you to give me so good a luncheon as you did at
dear distinguished Boodle's yesterday. St Margaret smiled down at us.
It was very wet and alarming at the top of Marble Arch to which we
climbed and there were little rooms inside the arch lit by gas *and* electric
so that if one went out, the other was there to come to the rescue. I don't
think Television is anything but a minor art – except now and then
when immediacy, as at Churchill's funeral, gives it an extra dimension
– but I think it is delightful team work. And so is filming and the key
person is an editor (provided the material to edit is good) and film *is* an
art. It *can* be the poetry of today. I'm so glad your daughter is a fellow
editor. Tell her to get her card. I'll be here all Friday (Canterbury
tomorrow) so if you're free ring and we'll eat.

Yours, JB

> JB kept up with his friend the writer T. de V.W. (see *Volume One*) from Dublin days.
>   After lunching with him, JB went on to make a film for the series *Contrasts* called
> *Marble Arch to Edgware* which was screened in 1968 and directed by Julian Jebb.
>   JB was a staunch member of the National Union of Journalists.

To Mary Wilson

Treen
Trebetherick
Wadebridge
Cornwall

12 November 1967

Dear Mrs Wilson,
Oh, I do like the two poems, particularly the carol 'How sweet and clear. . . .' It is simple, sincere, direct and strikes at the heart. Although all the words are much used and the pictures in it are familiar, it is *fresh* and touching. Because you *are* a poet. I like the lines:

> To watch her baby lying in the hay
> *And think about the wonder of his birth.*

There's a lot in that line I've underlined. It's like praying. The *Weekend Telegraph* is getting more than it deserves and you ought to get them to cough up to a charity you favour. Wed[nesday], four p.m., Nov[ember] 22nd would suit me splendidly. I hope it suits you. I like 'After the Bomb' but the deliberate break in the rhythm at 'And he laughed' was a clever idea. But I like the carol better. It is so *good* like you are, really good. I much look forward to the 22nd and if that doesn't suit, will keep the 27th free. The 28th is less easy as I have to give away some prizes in Wandsworth and the prospect will hang over me like a cloud as I have to address a live audience. I don't mind cameras.
    Yours sincerely, John Betjeman

> JB had met M.W., the wife of Harold W. the Prime Minister, at the opera, where they were guests of JB's old friend Garrett Drogheda who was chairman of the Royal Opera House, Covent Garden. She wrote to him (10 November 1967), 'I did so enjoy meeting you and it would be delightful if you could come to tea and a proper talk. . . . I enclose the carol and I am also sending a copy of "After the Bomb".'

To Cyril Connolly
17 November 1967

43 Cloth Fair
London EC1

My dear Cyril,
I cannot thank you enough for that beautiful Edward Thomas. He reads better than ever on Japan paper and so handsomely bound. Also he is of a consistently high standard and brings back my early intense delight in country scenery which this bright autumn weather down in

Cornwall intensifies. In fact I almost feel young again and I have you to thank. The more I think of it, the more sure I am that you should move into a seaside town and that the provincial town with schools, concerts, theatre, films and large enough to escape bores and small enough to find silence and country, is the right way of life left for us. Eastbourne for ever. Freddie Hood, Hugh Casson and Woodrow Wyatt were at its college. Love to Deirdre and Cressida.

    Love, John B

> Edward Thomas, the poet (1878–1917), was highly rated by JB.
>   C.C., Deirdre C. and their daughter Cressida had been looking for somewhere to live since their rented farmhouse Bushey Lodge on the Firle estate in Sussex had been reclaimed. They moved to a large Edwardian house in Eastbourne. Deirdre C. remembers, 'JB loved it because it had the sea at one end of the street and the downs at the other.'

To Mary Wilson   43 Cloth Fair
20 November 1967   London EC1

Dear Mrs Wilson,
I *did* enjoy our talk. It was noble of you to see me at a time of stress like that must have been.

    I long for our dinner at eight at the Garrick on Monday Dec[ember] 4th. It is very nice of you to come. I've asked my publisher to send you *Summoned by Bells* because the first chapter (but you need not read *any* of it) expresses a love of Hampstead and Highgate which I think we share.

    Again with my thanks and affection for all the same things we like.

    Yours very sincerely, John Betjeman

> The 'time of stress' referred to the furore caused by the devaluation of sterling. The day before, Harold Wilson had told the public, 'The pound in your pocket has not been devalued.'
>   M.W. wrote (27 November 1967), 'Could I, without appearing to be rude about your handwriting, ask if you could possibly address your letters to me in a fair, round hand, because the messengers mistook Mrs for Mr. Consequently your letter went downstairs and was opened by Philistine hands. . . . I was so pleased by *Summoned by Bells* and took it down to Chequers to read. I particularly like the part about Oxford.'

To Christopher Fry   43 Cloth Fair
30 November 1967   London EC1

Dear Christopher Fry,
This letter needs no reply. It is just to tell you how deeply I sympathise
with you over your burglary. Pictures and books are like old and
trusted friends and to lose them is to lose part of oneself. Still worse
than [the] vandalism and malice of the burglary, [it] destroys one's faith
in human nature and goodness.
    Hold on.
    Yours sincerely, John Betjeman

> C.F. the dramatist, an exact contemporary of JB's, wrote many plays including *The
> Lady's Not for Burning*, *Venus Observed* and *A Phoenix Too Frequent*.
>   C.F. recalled that he had always hoped to know JB better but had simply met him
> fleetingly on various social occasions.

To William Wicklow   Alderley Grange
                                                         Wotton-Under-Edge
2 December 1967   Gloucestershire

My dear Crax,
I am staying in a very nice house with very nice *writing paper* and it
belongs to your and my old friend Jim Lees-Milne who sends you his
love. I saw Nevill Coghill yesterday evening. He has retired to the
Severn Vale and is what Maurice [Bowra] calls 'on skates', with many
young friends whom he sees in London and has to stay. He lives with
his BARONET brother. Jim L-M's cousin is LORD GLENARTHUR, the
last one ran a male brothel in Lisbon. Jim's wife Alvilde is Lord
Bridges's cousin. Lord Bridges's wife is Lord Farrer's daughter. Both, I
am sorry to say, are first creations. Penelope is going to New York on
Jan[uary] 2nd to see her son Paul (and mine) who never writes and
teaches music in a N[ew] Y[ork] suburb full of Puerto Ricans. I *think* he
is happy. As you can imagine she is very full of preparations.
    Love to Eleanor. How is Katie?
    All the best, John B

> W.W., one of JB's closest friends from Oxford, had long lived in his native Ireland but
> kept in constant touch. Hardly any of his letters survive. JB and he carried on a running

joke about obscure members of the aristocracy and over the years the explosions of
laughter brought on by each other never diminished.

Nevill Coghill (1889–1980, see *Volume One*), by now retired from being an English
professor at Merton College, Oxford, had been a touchstone of JB's.

In 1959 W.W. had married Eleanor Butler; Katie was his sister.

To Patsy Zeppel   43 Cloth Fair
  December 1967   London EC1

Dear Patsy,
How sweet of you to write to me. Norm would have laughed. I would
rather be a very obscure drunk Irish Peer of the Act of Union in 1800,
but we can't have everything we want, can we? I would have replied to
your letter much sooner had I not wanted to write at length and to type,
which I do slowly in order that I might be a bit clearer. I am sure you all
miss Norm very much. Lord Euston and I went together to the
Investiture of the Prince of Wales yesterday, I don't know how I got
asked, but he got asked because he is something to do with the Royal
Household. A lot of the way up in the train we talked of Norm. He was
very alike both in appearance and in his sudden fits of rage and in his
funny stories against himself, to someone we both knew very well
called Sir George Barnes, who was once Head of Television. I hope
Norm was not miserable, frightened or what hospitals call 'uncomfortable' in his last illness. I have never met Mrs Norm so I could not write
to her. Yes, indeed, I remember Hugh Paget, I think he will be just
what you want, calm, kind and efficient.

  Hold on, much love, John B
  Love to Double Bay and Paddington and the North Shore

P.Z. worked with Norman Williams of the British Council in Australia and had met JB
on his tour in 1961. She had written to tell him of Norman Williams's death in
November.

Hugh Euston, who succeeded his father as the Duke of Grafton in 1970, is known as
the 'Duke of Conservation'. He first met JB in the early fifties on the committee of the
Society for the Preservation of Ancient Buildings, of which he was vice-chairman and
chairman for forty years. He recalls, 'I had done a lecture tour for the British Council in
Australia only a year after JB. Norman Williams was delightful and Fortune and I stayed
with him in Sydney. He introduced us to all the arty world in Sydney which was really
very interesting. Of course he adored JB and my task was made really quite easy because
I merely had to mention his name at the beginning of a lecture to have everyone on my
side.'

Hugh Euston's wife Fortune was at the time Mistress of the Robes to the Queen.

To Mary Wilson   43 Cloth Fair
3 December 1967   London EC1

Dear Mary,
Oh dear. Never again the Garrick. What a gauntlet of eyes. I never
thought it would be like that as I very rarely go there in the evenings.
Due apologies.

I send as a peace offering a little present of old favourites (and how
good some of them are) such as 'The Private of the Buffs' which you
mentioned.

I feel sure it would be wiser to meet at tea-time in future at Number
10 or where you will.

Love to Sir Cloudisley. Yours, John B

> M.W.'s thank-you letter crossed (5 December 1967), 'Thank you for last night. I so
> much enjoyed it! We didn't really have a great deal of time to talk about poetry. I adore
> quoting and listening to quotations, particularly if I recognise them, and can cap them! –
> but we certainly had a hilarious evening. We should always be able to say, "Do you
> remember that night we dined at the Garrick?" '
>
> Admiral Sir Clowdisley Shovell (sometimes spelt Cloudesley) was the captain of the
> *Association* which foundered in Scilly along with three other ships of the British line in
> 1707. (The wreck is still being dredged today.) M.W. wrote a poem about it called 'The
> Treasure'. JB and M.W. had just seen the monument to Sir C. in Westminster Abbey.

To Candida and Rupert Lycett Green   43 Cloth Fair
27 December 1967   London EC1

DARLING WIBZ AND RUPERT,

THAT EYE which came among
the exquisite books of verse and
other treasures of my stocking tells
me, with a premonition of guilt,
that I have a lot of Christmas letters to write. But the first must come to
you for a HEAVENLY CHRISTMAS. TA EVER SO. I LOVE THE KIDDIZ and
that is saying a good deal as I am not by nature a kiddi-lover. Lucy's
gleaming, humorous eye and sweet looks, and Imo's glorious beauty
which is already beginning to blaze out. They are both personalities
and I love them both. I was very, very happy and I loved our smart
entertainment and our Midnight Mass afterwards and Lucy up at the

altar in that black fur at Tony Bridge's Ch[rist]ch[urch] Lancaster Gate and the candlelit party and Psycho Park next day and the Jig Saw. In fact I'm very sorry to be back here at the galley. Luncheon with Miss Leroy was as guilt-giving as I thought it would be and I did not dare to suggest I should go elsewhere.

Rupert told Mummy and me that sixteen people slave away for him at Blades. He is very clever and modest and in order to give him a sense of uplift I have asked some of his friends to sign this letter of thanks to you both and best wishes for the New Year.

Hector Powe, X his mark
Burton of Taste
Gloria
Cecil Gee
To Rupert all the best!
Mr Fish
Henry Hepworth
Jack Anderson and Hilary Shepherd
Stephen Michael
Michael Stephen
John Michael
Michael John

JB and PB spent Christmas with RLG and me at our house in Chepstow Villas, London WII. We went to midnight mass at Christchurch, Lancaster Gate.

Miss Leroy was JB's literary agent. She worked for David Higham Associates with whom he was unhappy (he did not break with her until March 1969).

RLG's tailoring business Blades was now well established. JB's spoof signatures played with the names of the current big names in the rag trade.

To Mary Wilson   43 Cloth Fair
3 January 1968   London EC1

My dear Mary,
Never have I heard of such success on Telly as your sweet self's. I was in the train between Salisbury and Basingstoke so could not see it. *I must see a replay of it.* Niceness and goodness always come across. I posted two people, close friends of mine and each different, to watch and give me a report. They were unanimous in praise and the one I thought most likely to be critical said [that] everything you said was sensible. Oh, I do long for a walk in St James's Park and, if wet, in the

cloisters of the Abbey. Have you written any more poems? Bring them. I've written one and I've got the beginning of another. Let me know when you have a free afternoon.

I can't do the 10th.

Love, John B

M.W. wrote the next day, 'I'll meet you on the bridge in the middle of the park at three p.m.'

To Mary Wilson   43 Cloth Fair
5 January 1968   London EC1

My dear Mary,

> I will be on the bridge at St James's
> When the clocks are striking three
> And if the rain is falling
> I will telephone up to thee
> Till then accept all love from
> Henry Wadsworth B.

Please look out some completed poems for me to see and praise. That bit of one you produced from your bag was deeply moving and has haunted me. It was very good indeed. Here's my latest complete effort. A bit pale, I know.

Love, John

M.W. wrote after their meeting (10 January 1968), 'I did enjoy our jaunt yesterday – particularly when we went through that dark door into the Abbey and saw the cribs and all the candles. I found our conversation very comforting and such a pleasure to talk about poetry:

> We came through the gloomy door
> From the cloisters wet with snow,
> To the Abbey lit high with candles,
> And the Baby asleep below.'

To Mary Wilson   43 Cloth Fair
11 January 1968   London EC1

My dear Mary,
I am very grateful to you for three things:

1) Returning my diary. I am sunk without it. There's only one date
in it I remembered in my head, 3.30, Pall Mall RAC Club, January
24th. All the rest I had forgotten.
2) Lending me this script which I return. It is interviewing at its best.
Cliff Michelmore is gentle and coaxing. You are gentle and explicit.
Even without seeing you, it makes good reading. It also brings out a
lot of things you have said to me. For instance, I hope you will have
better news of your brother. Your tastes are like mine in the Arts –
and I think, though few will admit it, like most people's. You
probably like Tennyson because his poetry is three quarters huge
skies like East Anglia of your childhood. Do look at *In Memoriam*, the
descriptive bits. I must say all this script makes me long to be talking
to you again. My poor wife Penelope has written to me to say our son
Paul takes very little notice of her and she consoles herself by doing
what the Americans call *ree*search in libraries. It also brings out what
I knew all along and that is that you are very clever and a strong
character.
3) The third thing I want to thank you for is existing. That letter
reflected shortly and perfectly, like a poem, the high spots of our
walk. I am as certain as I am of stars in the sky that there is a lot of
good poetry already written by you and more to be written.
Somehow you must be given self-confidence about it. Good poets
are always shy of criticism or even of showing their poetry, for if it is
good it is part of themselves, a newborn vulnerable baby when first
written and a worn old bore years later but still part of one. Don't
feel you must write letters (I have got into the habit. It gets one off
the dread act of creation – poetry writing) first? Put them second. I
believe in you and so does your family and so do thousands of people.
Thank you, dear Mary, and go on being kind to the bald old
journalist who signs himself
Yours with love, John

Cliff Michelmore, the television personality, had interviewed M.W. on *Time With
Michelmore*.

To Elsie Avril   43 Cloth Fair
15 January 1968   London EC1

Dear Elsie,

> You so young and I with hair
> Both of us now lined with care
> All the airs that you have played
> All the verses I have made –
> What are things like joy and truth?
> I think we faintly know in youth
> Now the bloom has left the rose
> Maybe only Archie knows.

I am delighted to have your letter and five a.m. poem. This is my nine
a.m. reply. I go to Cornwall tomorrow (Treen, Trebetherick,
Wadebridge – Kathleen Roseveare's cottage as was) till Sunday week to
recover from having done too much badly in too little time. Love to
Q[ueenie]. Let's meet in Feb[ruary] all of us and the heavenly
Majorcas.
    Love, John

> E.A. and her sister Queenie were cousins of JB through his mother Bess. They never
> married, and lived together in Montagu Square, near Marble Arch.
>   E.A. often stayed at Trebetherick in the 1910s and 1920s with the family. She had
> sent JB a photograph taken around 1913 of her looking out of a window and JB clutching
> a young 'Archie' (Archibald Ormsby-Gore), his beloved teddy bear. In April that year
> Duncan Andrews, the American collector of Betjemaniana, approached E.A. and
> offered her one hundred pounds for the photograph. He had seen it in *John Betjeman: a*
> *study* by Derek Stanford (published by Neville Spearman Ltd) which came out in 1961.
> She refused.

To Lionel Perry   43 Cloth Fair
8 February 1968   London EC1

My dear Li,
What a joy to have your letter from Letterkenny. How difficult it must
be cleaning out the lavatories. Crax's latest p[ost]c[ard] (of Cheddar
Gorge) says you are definitely on the mend. Thank God for that. I'll see
Buntin and you yet. Harry Williams, Dean of Trinity Camb[ridge],
Simon Stuart (Castlestuart's brother, my dear, and a cousin of yours, I
suppose) and I are going to Lerwick for a fortnight before Easter on
March 30th. Shetland is very bracing and beauteous. Peenalloppee is

back from N[ew] Y[ork] and didn't like it at all. She says the USA has
sent her very Left. Powlie is teaching music in the equivalent of a
comprehensive in a place called Brentwood on Long Island and
Brentwood is the equivalent of Willesden. He lives alone in a large
house with poison ivy in the garden. He supports himself, just. He will
become an American. It is very sad. P[enelope] painted a gloomy
picture of the USA she saw. It is certainly a different USA from
Captain Bog [Alan Pryce-Jones]'s or Peter Perry's. My old teddy bear
Archie sends you his best wishes. I have become friendly with *Mrs*
Wilson. I don't know him. I met her at the opera, my dear (*Fidelio*) and
she likes to talk about poetry. She is very shy and persecuted but I
strongly suspect has a will of iron and rules the household. I wonder
what old Hugh thought of *her*. He didn't like him. I saw Anthony
Blunt yesterday and didn't speak. He always makes me feel trivial and
shallow. Your handwriting hasn't changed you dear old thing. Mine is
worse. Johnny Craxton – yes, a saintly man and v[ery] kind and a v[ery]
good artist. Derek H[ill] sent me a p[ost]c[ard] about you. I can just
imagine what the County Hospital Letterkenny looks like:

On the outskirts of the town and with 'a sprinkling of light industry'
near it. Men on one side and women on the other. No sex. Tiled
interior. Red-brick and half-timber. I had tea with Shane Leslie in
Brighton and stayed the night at Lancing and sent p[ost]c[ard]s to
Roger [?Fulford] and Thomas Edward Neil [Driberg] MP.
  Bung ho, old top, John B

> JB had befriended L.P., 'the Golden Boy' (see *Volume One*), at Oxford and shared rooms
> with him in Walton Street. Their friendship was constant although he lived at
> Letterkenny in County Donegal, Ireland, from the fifties onward.
>   JB wrote again (20 March 1968), after hearing L.P., who had pleurisy, had had a
> relapse and had decided not to move house after all, 'There's so much to be said for
> familiar shapes of hills and bends of the road and smells and tastes known for years.'

To Mary Wilson   43 Cloth Fair
27 February 1968   London EC1

Dear Mary,

       Part 1

     Yes, it will be bliss
     To go with you by train to Diss.
     Your walking shoes upon your feet
     We'll meet, my sweet, at Liverpool Street.
     That levellers we may be reckon'd
     Perhaps we'd better travel second;
     Or, lest reporters on us burst,
     Perhaps we'd better travel first.
     Above the chimney pots we'll go
     Through Stepney, Stratford-Atte-Bow
     And out to where the Essex marsh
     Is filled with houses new and harsh
     Till, Chelmsford pass'd, the landscape yields
     A momentary glimpse of fields –
     Flint church towers sparkling in the light
     Black barns and weatherboarding white
     Cricket-bat willows silvery green
     And elmy hills with brooks between
     Then malting, salting, staithe and quay
     And somewhere near the grey North Sea
     And further gentle undulations
     And lonelier and less frequent stations
     Till in the dimmest part of all
     The train slows down into a crawl
     And stops in silence. Where is this?
     Dear Mary Wilson, it is Diss.

       Part 2

     May go a bit further but it isn't composed yet.
Love, John

M.W. had been brought up in Diss as the daughter of a Congregational minister and lived there until she was five. JB and she decided to visit the town together to see the house where she was born and had never been back to.

    The poem appeared, with various changes, as 'A Mind's Journey to Diss' in *A Nip in the Air* (1974).

    'Chelmsford' became 'Witham', 'A momentary glimpse of fields' became 'On left and right to widening fields', 'Black barns' became 'Black beams', 'Then malting, salting,

staithe and quay' became 'Maltings and saltings, stack and quay', 'part' became 'place', and the last line became 'Dear Mary Wilson, this is Diss'. A second part was never composed.
    M.W. replied:

> 'Yes, it is perfect bliss
> To go with you by train to Diss!. . . .
> Now, as we stroll beside the Mere
> Reporters suddenly appear.
> You draw a crowd of passers-by
> While I gaze blandly at the sky. . . .
> We reach a teashop, where we find
> The food is good, the waitress kind. . . .
> What day could be more sweet than this,
> Dear John, the day we came to Diss?'

M.W.'s poem was published in *New Poems* with the title 'Reply to the Laureate'. JB gave her permission to print his own poem beside it.

To David Wemyss   43 Cloth Fair
16 April 1968   London EC1

Dear David,
I have just returned from Shetland, where I was for a fortnight, using Lerwick as a base. The Queen's Hotel was very good, and so is Voe House at Voe. I visited all the islands that are inhabited except Burra Isle and Trondra.

    You were the original inspiration of my going to Shetland and everything you told me has stayed in my head. Now I am wanting your advice as how best to stop the Lerwick Town Council destroying the remaining old parts of the town. The new housing development might be worse but it would be far more sensible to repair the old buildings in the narrow lanes. There is also a tendency for the local council to replace the old paving stones across the streets with cement or concrete square blocks, all of the same colour and size. And in the new housing estates they are in squares of red and cream and nothing like the old stone, plenty of which is available. The most serious threat of all is to the charming house Annesbrae at the top of the town, alongside St Columba's. It is dated 1791 and a charming Laird's House, three-storey with two little pavilions either side, a stretch of lawn, and two more cottages further apart on the road, making a subtle composition which has not been improved by a Victorian fence of stone and ironwork between the two lodges, but this at least keeps the building private. It is empty now, owned by the Council, who are said to be going to demolish it for housing. It is in good order and I am wondering whether you could approach anyone in the Scottish Office or on the Royal Fine Art Commission of Scotland, to intercede for Annesbrae and find a use for it. It would make a nice boarding house or institution. Its walled gardens are much needed sheltered open space in this part of the town. I do not like to interfere myself as I am, so to speak, a foreigner. But there must be somebody you know whose word would carry weight up there. There would be quite a lot of opinion in Lerwick in favour of saving Annesbrae, and the remaining pavements and old houses.

Yours, John B

D.W., chairman of the National Trust for Scotland, was responsible for persuading JB to go on his tour of the Scottish islands in 1958. He had visited Shetland with the Church of England Ramblers.

In the event Annesbrae was saved and is now listed. At the time it did in fact belong to the Mowat-Camerons of Garth, but is now owned by Shetland Islands Council as a halfway house for the mentally handicapped.

To Canon Jenner   43 Cloth Fair
19 April 1968   London EC1

Dear Vicar,
This doggerel based on the 'Ballad of Bedford Park' may help for a 1968 greeting:

> The dogs do bark in Bedford Park,
> The Festival to praise.
> There's not a flaw in Norman Shaw;
> The sunflower gardens blaze.
>
> From Turnham Green to Stamford Brook,
> Our gabled houses rise,
> From Queen Anne balconies we look
> Upon a paradise.
>
> Across the *rus in urbe* here
> St Michael's bell will call,
> To this the best and earliest
> Of garden suburbs all.

Yours sincerely, John Betjeman

Canon Jenner was vicar of St Michael's and All Angels (Bedford Park, London W4). He had asked JB to write something as part of the second Bedford Park Festival, to help restore the church and recreate a community spirit.

JB was patron of the Bedford Park Society which was set up in 1963 when its houses were still unlisted. The three hundred and fifty-six houses were listed in 1967. By 1968 the Bedford Park Society was a force to be reckoned with under the agile secretaryship of Tom Greeves.

JB later wrote of the place, 'The pioneer Arts and Crafts garden suburb was Norman Shaw's Bedford Park:

> With red and blue and sagest green
> Were walls and dado dyed,
> Friezes of Morris there were seen
> And oaken wainscot wide.'

'The Ballad of Bedford Park' had appeared in the *St James's Gazette* in 1881 (17 December).

To Osbert Lancaster   43 Cloth Fair
24 April 1968   London EC1

Dear Old Top,

Kenneth Ross, the Vicar of All Saints' Margaret Street, has asked me, as though I were Jean Leroy, whether you would design the dresses for the ladies' choir they are going to have there as part of a mixed choir, now that the resident choir school has been given up. Sir Larry [Olivier] was at the choir school before going to St Edwards. I've lost his letter to me but I enclose a copy of my reply. I felt I ought not entirely to forbid him to write to you, but I am sorry to welcome you back to England with such a troublesome business.

I love the idea of Alpha [Anne Lancaster] dressed as a choirboy in All Saints'. Some of our friends might like it very much too. The Shetlands were a great success, I only hope France was. The Ramblers drank a lot.

Love to Alpha and Clare [Hastings].

Jean Leroy was JB's literary agent.
    O.L. never did design the dresses.
    Clare Hastings was Anne L.'s daughter by her previous marriage and usually named 'Trendy' by JB because of her *outré* clothes.

To Candida Lycett Green   BBC Bristol
20 June 1968

Darling Wibz,
That was a very jolly luncheon at Padd[ington]. V[ery] good news
about January. . . . . [letter damaged] I think one can judge
about what one took hours and days composing – but not about the light
personal stuff which may sometimes be better than what one has
laboured on. I think you need a *minimum* of thirty poems to make a
book. So if you can collect say forty or fifty poems or scraps of poems,
however trivial, however personal and intimate, fleshly, scurrilous or
juvenile and then hand them over to someone who doesn't know the
people or events they are about but who does know about poetry, then
you can decide. Hanbury [John Sparrow] did my verse that service and
so did Freddie Birkenhead. Publishers are not good judges of poetry,
only of selling. I will do it myself if you want me to, but it might be
better to choose a poetical friend you can trust. One's poems are part of
oneself and it is hell to have them criticised except by those whose
judgement one knows is unbiased.
    As to the mechanics of the business, that is easy once the selection is
made. You may also find making the selection spurs you on to write a
few more poems.
    Love to Rupert, Lucy and Imo. Love, MD

> The 'good news' was that I was expecting Endellion Rose Lycett Green, who was born
> on 29 January 1969.
>   My poems were so bad, that to think I ever thought of publishing them fills me
> with embarrassment. The idea went no further.

To the Minister of Housing and Local Government   43 Cloth Fair
22 July 1968   London EC1

Dear Sir,
I wish to write in support of the objectors to the demolition of the
Theatre Royal, Portsmouth. I agree entirely with the summary of the
objections which have been made by Mr B. J. Press.
    In support of the contention that it is a beautiful theatre, I would say
that it is unique also in that its decoration makes reference to the City of
Portsmouth and is one of the most charming small examples of what
may be called 'the architecture of entertainment' to survive in England.

This sort of architecture can never be achieved again, except as a fake, so that it is virtually irreplaceable. Although it has a proscenium arch and there is a fashion at present in the theatre for having a centrally placed stage, as at Chichester, this may only be a temporary fashion. Moreover the present Theatre Royal could be adapted, if need be, to the present fashion, without damage to its charming architecture.

I realise the crippling conditions imposed by the owners of the Kings Theatre, Southsea, on the Theatre Royal, but I think that these may be of a temporary nature. Taking the long view there is every likelihood that television will send people back to live theatre increasingly, partly because of reaction from too much television, and partly because it educates people in dramatic values, so that they become interested in theatre, just as they have become increasingly interested in music.

Yours sincerely, John Betjeman

> Originally built in 1850, the Theatre Royal's last adaptation was by the architect Frank Matcham (1854–1920) in 1900. He was the most successful of the late Victorian and Edwardian theatre architects, who had designed the London Palladium and the Coliseum. JB admired his work so much that in the late seventies he planned to make a film about him, but his health prevented it. The Theatre Royal has remained untouched since 1900 and contains decorations with a nautical theme, many seafaring emblems such as prows between the boxes, dolphins, anchors, mermaids, life belts and shells on the dress circle. It is now at the focal point of the new Portsmouth town centre.

To Antony Snowdon   43 Cloth Fair
2 August 1968   London EC1

Dear Tony,

CLOUDY BRIGHT
When I get to Paddington this evening I will buy the *Amateur Photographer* off the Scotch firm that has taken over Ryman's, and when I get to Wantage, I'll go and see a very boring man I know who loves singing his own praises by showing one his photographic efforts. I will also get one of those wrapped-up instruction books. I think the technique must be that the verse is in a complacent first person, and in the manner of Longfellow, e.g.:

> Tell me not in mournful numbers,
> Life is but an empty dream.
> For the soul is dead that slumbers,
> And things are not what they seem.

Those four lines give time for at least one cut or dissolve, and if you say the verse out loud in a stately manner, you will find it lasts just about ten seconds. Therefore there will have to be about thirty stanzas for a five-minute film, though allowing for pauses, musical effects and titles, probably twenty stanzas is enough. I will write a few specimen verses to see if we think it will work. I think it is a very funny idea. I would like to get in some of those 'subjects' which are set for competitions. Like 'It ringeth through Evensong' and 'In the steps of the Master', and we could have some lovely sunsets. We must end the verse with the film stuck, and some of those numbers and perforations one gets at the end of a film in a camera. It is a very funny idea, and pleasantly removed from politics, religion, student protest and atomic research.

Yours, John B

A.S., the photographer and son of JB's friend Anne Rosse and her former husband R.O. L. Armstrong-Jones, got to know JB when he was courting Princess Margaret, to whom EC was lady-in-waiting.

A.S. and Peter Sellers had lunched with JB at the RAC. (Sellers was not allowed in at first because he wasn't wearing a tie. He put one on *under* his shirt and was stopped for a second time, but said, 'You told me I had to wear a tie and I have.' He was let in.) They spent the whole lunch plotting a film inspired by the instruction on a Kodak film packet, 'Cloudy Bright'. JB was to write it, A.S. to direct it and Sellers to act in it. It was to be very, very boring indeed, about the technique of photography or film-making. It never went beyond this letter.

To Edward Pickering   43 Cloth Fair
26 September 1968   London EC1

Dear Mr Pickering,
I have just completed the location work for the Tennyson film, and we were blessed with fine weather throughout. There will now be about two days' work for me some time late in October, writing commentary for the edited version in those parts of it, which are not sync[hronised]. But possibly this is all too technical.

What I wanted to ask you was whether you knew I was going down to Portsmouth by the 6.50 that evening, when you got out at Haslemere, and I was bound for the Isle of Wight? If you did not know then the coincidence is most extraordinary because of what happened the next day. You will remember that you gave me a very useful essay on Aldworth by Sir Charles [Tennyson], which I was able to make use of, when we filmed the following Friday at Aldworth. But on the next day to that on which I met you, our last shots on the Island after doing Farringford were of Emily Tennyson's tomb in Freshwater Church-yard. The sun shone and the camera was to pan up to the Downs beyond Farringford, after which there was to be a mix into the view from Aldworth. While this was happening I was to read 'June Bracken and Heather' which as you will remember was Tennyson's dedication to Emily of his last book of poems. Twice we couldn't take the shot because of noise, once from hovercraft or some such thing, and the other time from aeroplanes. At the third take there was silence enough, and when I came to the bit about the June blue heaven, all the birds around burst into song, as though it were spring, and the cameraman noticed the startled look on my face.

I ask you the question at the top of the previous paragraph because if our meeting was a true coincidence, it looks as though the Tennysons are watching you and me.

Yours sincerely, John Betjeman

E.P. was the newspaper editor and vice-chairman of Times Newspapers Ltd at the time, and did not know JB. He recalled in the *Tennyson Research Bulletin* (November 1990), 'One night in 1968 I was catching the 6.50 Waterloo/Portsmouth train which took me to my home in Haslemere. I entered a carriage, sat down and found John Betjeman in the opposite seat. Immediately he launched into a sad story of how he was doing a television series on the life of Tennyson; how he was on his way to Farringford (Tennyson's Isle of Wight home) to record part of the series; but how he lacked material for the second part dealing with Aldworth (Tennyson's Haslemere home for the last twenty-five years of his life). By an astonishing coincidence, I had that week received from Sir Charles Tennyson (Tennyson's grandson and biographer) an essay recalling memories of life at Aldworth with his grandfather. I handed a copy of the essay to Betjeman and thought no more of it, until on 26 September 1968, he wrote me the following letter.'

The film was in the BBC *Contrasts* series and was called *Tennyson: A Beginning and an End*. It was directed by Julian Jebb, a personal friend of JB's, who made many arts programmes in the early days of BBC2.

To Patrick Garland   43 Cloth Fair
27 November 1968   London EC1

Mon cher Patrick,
Quelle an addresse comique! Quelle papier exquise! Je go avec Féble et Raymond Leppard et son ami a *Quarante Ans En* demain. Oui s'il vous voulez, the festival, mais the whole idea of it depresse moi somewhat, and I will be afraid of rotten apples or no one at all. Pour moi je prefer poesie morbide et seul.

Au revoir, et mes salutations a monsieur et madame et forêt nouveau et a Edouard couleurs (Hues – Hughes).
Jean B (J. Betjeman)

> P.G., the film and stage director (who worked with JB on various films, including one with Philip Larkin and one about the Victorian diarist Kilvert), had connections with JB's family which went back a long way. P.G.'s grandmother had been great friends with Bess Betjemann and his father Ewart had been asked discreetly to take JB to Paris, in the early twenties, 'to teach me about sex with ladies,' JB later wrote to A. L. Rowse, 'but it failed, because I fell ill.' (In fact JB got flu, and stayed in his hotel room while Ewart had a ball.) Ever after that JB used to write to P.G.'s grandparents in *franglais*, and when he sent them a copy of his poems *A Nip in the Air* he referred to it as *Un Japonais dans l'Air*.
>
> JB also always wrote to P.G. in *franglais*. At the time P.G. was trying to inveigle JB to perform at the Aldeburgh (which JB called 'Alderbugger') Festival.
>
> JB was going to see the play *Forty Years On* by Alan Bennett.
>
> P.G.'s grandparents lived in the New Forest.

To Mary Wilson   Treen
                                                                 Trebetherick
                                                                 Wadebridge
14 January 1969   Cornwall

Personal

My dear Mary,
How strange it was to hear that disembodied voice, much stronger than I had suspected and utterly captivating. I heard it in the room of an American in the Ritz on Wednesday. I WAS FLATTERED TO BE MENTIONED. It has been lovely opening the papers and finding the fickle writers in them, full of praise of you both and you no longer in the background. Also all the photographs of you, except for that in that hateful pseudo-progressive elderly with-it, the *Times*–server – very good. Lady Pam's paper [*Telegraph*] had, I thought the prettiest of all. What only those who've seen you know, is your exquisite colouring.

Now to come to that poem of yours. It is the best I've seen that you have done and that is saying a lot. I cannot fault it. Of course the drive in it comes from the emotion in it. I think you are best as a love poet. It must be maddening that you cannot publish that piece – but I don't see that if you pre-date it and put it back in 1930 at the bottom – many poets do date their poems, you could not publish it. But what really matters is that you have written it.

The greatest inhibitor of writing poetry is the thought of anyone else seeing it. Then one also wants it published. What a fix. But there's no doubt – and that poem shows it – that if we write from the heart, regardless of the public and publishers, we write best. That is what makes John Osborne so good at playwriting. There is a whole play in those stanzas of yours.

We must have a look at Bedford Park, Chiswick. A house with front and back garden that you could probably get for about twenty thousand pounds. They are well-built 1880 and individual and were designed by Norman Shaw and his followers. Bedford Park is the precursor of all the garden suburbs. It is less remote than Hampstead. But it may still be too far.

It rains here without stopping. Trevose Head fog-horn moans, the sea mist is down, the silence is profound. I feel fairly secure.

Congratulations on your poem and on your discs and on yourself.

Those sermons I hope you did not find boring. They are a bit stiff but repay re-reading. Their author arrives in this cot tomorrow. He has had a great influence on Prince Charles who likes him very much. 'Let's all get drunk with Harry the Monk,' is of course about Harry Williams going to Mirfield. Harry is delighted with it. Back on 24th.

Love, John

M.W. had just made an LP called *Mary Wilson Reads Her Selected Poems*, with music by Cyril Stapleton.
     She was not really serious about moving but JB was always looking for houses he thought she would like.
     JB had sent her a collection of sermons by Harry Williams.

To C. Day-Lewis and Jill (Balcon)   43 Cloth Fair
1 March 1969   London EC1

Dear Jill and Cecil,

Long ere this I should have written to thank you for a delicious and happy luncheon on old Croome's Hill o'erlooking Greenwich Park. I went to North Northumberland next day where all was under snow and the great cliffs of Norman Shaw's masterpiece stood like giant molars on the sky – Cragside it's called, untouched 1880 within and without and the first house in the world, except for that of Mrs Swan of Ediswan, to be lit with electric light. I had thoughts of Daniel far away in Kent at Sevenoaks School. Like Tamsin and both of you, he is

goldenly good and sensitive. I wish I knew the answer. We can't avoid
suffering. Perhaps this term will be the worst – the second always is. I
don't think human nature changes – we all agreed on that. There is to be
weighed up in the mind the trouble of being a new boy all over again.
Has he any friend with whom he can laugh and weep at Sevenoaks?
Those alone carry one through. I will go on thinking of him and you all
with affection and gratitude for your existences.

Keep in touch. Love, John B

C.D.-L., who had become Poet Laureate after John Masefield's death, and his wife, the
actress Jill Balcon, had JB to dinner in their house on Croome's Hill on 23 February. 'If
you'd prefer it I'll have tinned grapefruit for you [which JB loved] rather than one of my
exotic confections,' J.D.-L. had written (11 January 1969).

   Cragside was built for the first Lord Armstrong and was in fact the first house in the
world to be lit by hydro-electricity, through a process of cables and underground pipes
devised by Armstrong. He also created forty miles of drives and footpaths and planted
tens of thousands of trees and shrubs.

   Daniel D.-L., who was also to become an actor, eventually ran away from Sevenoaks
School where he was so unhappy. He ran to Bedales where his sister Tamsin was and
eventually had happy schooldays there.

To Edward Mirzoeff   43 Cloth Fair
10 March 1969   London EC1

Dear Eddie,
You ask for a list of places suited to helicopter visitations. I don't quite
know how to treat the subject yet, without boring everyone to death,
but I have an idea we should treat it rather on the lines of Edmund
Gilbert's *Essay on the Holiday Industry and Seaside Towns in England and
Wales*. We should start with the history and end with the threat to our
shrinking unspoiled coast. In fact we should go from the Marine Villa
of George III's reign to the caravan of Elizabeth II's. And first we begin
inland and need a look at the inland spas such as Epsom, Tunbridge
Wells, Harrogate and Cheltenham, where people went to take the
water. Then we need to see Scarborough, of which there are many
coloured aquatints, which started as a mineral spa and happened to be
on the sea. Then came your telephone call.

   We should take the seaside spas chronologically, that is to say the
Georgian ones first and then the Victorian. These are Brighton,
Ramsgate (particularly good, I was there last week), Margate (rather
ruined), Weymouth, Ryde, Dover, Tenby and Torquay, which
represents the transition from Georgian to Victorian. For early

Victorian seaside places you can't beat Ilfracombe and Ventnor. Then
the conifers begin to sprout, the heather attracts, red brick and half
timber come in, roads are broader and tree shaded, and the Queen of
this sort of scenery is Bournemouth and her attendants, Boscombe and
the Chines. I fancy that Clacton and Southport are other Bourne-
mouths, though the first mentioned is probably less high grade socially
than Southport. After that we should show an Edwardian or late
Victorian spa, such as Frinton. I see all this part being rapturously
beautiful and interspersed with advertisements for day trips by rail or
steamer, programmes of concerts on the pier and Winter Gardens, and
posters and the covers of brochures, and of course advertisements for
family hotels and for less family hotels, which have electric lifts and
suites. Then I think we must have the barricaded seaside resorts of the
war. There ought to be some shots of these, and then we might show
the last seaside resort to pick up after the war, which was Folkestone.
And somewhere of course here we must change the key entirely and go
in for escapism. Old sea salts who have never been to sea impressing
cockneys like me at 'the Sloop', St Ives or rowing about in Polperro
harbour. Then we must go out beyond the seaside resorts to the
remaining few miles of unspoiled coast and show caravan sites and with
them we can put appropriate pop music, and we must have chalets and
Butlin's, and then we must go to the untouched bits of coast remaining.
It sounds a very dull end but anyhow this is something to discuss in the
Palm Court of the Ritz on Wednesday at six.

    Yours ever, JB

> E.M., the television producer/director with whom JB was to make some of his greatest
> films, was at the time series editor of the *Bird's Eye View* series – the most expensive series
> the BBC had ever done, pioneering the technique of aerial filming. He wanted the
> commentary to be very personal to counterpoint with the impersonal and often long-
> range pictures.
>   E.M. and JB were about to make *Beside the Seaside* for the series. It was accompanied by
> JB's verse and screened on Christmas Day 1969 and trailed in the *Radio Times*: 'A swooping
> seagull takes its flight From Weymouth to the Isle of Wight From Cornish clifftops wild and
> bare, To crowds at Weston-super-Mare. . . . A scrapbook made at Christmas time Of
> summer joys in film and rhyme.' JB also made *The Englishman's Home* (directed by E.M.)
> and *A Land for All Seasons* (directed by John Bird) in the same series, the commentary of
> which was a miscellany of verse, some of which JB wrote specifically. Film from the whole
> series was culled to produce *A Queen's Realm: A Prospect of England* which was screened as a
> tribute to the Queen in 1977 for the Jubilee. Again the commentary was a collection of verse
> interspersed with JB's own. It was hugely popular and repeated many times.
>   JB later wrote to E.M. (21 April 1969), 'Thank God there's going to be a lot of
> commercial breaks. Bude is a good place for a stretch of sand, and is very handy for
> Hartland. There is also Watergate Bay and Constantine. Oh, don't send me the reviews
> of the other film [*The Englishman's Home*], I only notice the bad ones, and they give me
> terrible persecution mania.'

To Lionel Perry   43 Cloth Fair
11 March 1969   London EC1

My dear Li,
I am dining with the Widow [John Lloyd] tonight at Brooks's, my dear,
as she is in London for 'positively two nights only'. Crax [William
Wicklow] writes to me to say that Eleanor [Wicklow] says she is so
charming she can't understand why she has remained a Widow for so
long. You must be getting quite used to the outlines of the hills from
Letterkenny County H[ospital] and I most earnestly look forward to
the news that you have returned to your loose boxes. I enclose a letter
from Arthur Marshall, an old Oundleian, which may interest you.
Hamish Hamilton was at Rugby. I know one ought not to bother about
such trivial things. I knew most of Arthur's list, but not about Laurence
Irving. Where were Hugh Casson, Freddie Hood and Woodrow
Wyatt? The Answer is on the next sheet*. While at Rugby Hamish
Hamilton was in love with Joc Lynam. Old Philip H[arding] has gone
to retire in furnished rooms in Arundel. He left *The Times* (which is now
not so good even as the *Daily Telegraph*) prematurely as he was
considered too old and *The Times* is out to catch 'students'. I dined on
Sat[urday] in Oxford with Mr Bryson. My word he hasn't half filled his
luxury two-floor flat with masterpieces – Degas, early John, Sickert,
Fantin Latour and a great many male nudes. He has taken to painting
them himself. In Aberdeen the week before last I went to a house in the
suburbs belonging to a recently dead colour printer. The furnishings
were ordinary – pink candlewick bed covers and brown walls – but
there were three Utrillos, two Matisses, three Gaugins, three Derains,
a Cezanne and not one bad picture – many early Welsh period Johns
etc., a Derwent Lees, Sickert of Bath and v[ery] good Lowry. Millions
of quids' worth of stuff all up there in a granite suburb. I think they may
deliberately keep it dark. I got in by a back door. Well, bung ho, old
top. Any social notes I have I will pass on to Letterkenny.
    Bung ho, old man. Love, JB
    * Answer (Eastbourne College)

> Arthur Marshall had sent JB a list of Old Oundleians.
>   John Bryson (see *Volume One*) was one of JB's favourite dons from his Oxford days and
> a member of 'Colonel' Kolkhorst's set.

To Wayland and Elizabeth Kennet   43 Cloth Fair
11 March 1969   London EC1

Dear Wayland and Liz,
What a glorious setting for what a glorious party. [Charles] Barry and
[Augustus Welby] Pugin must be pleased.

Barry   Pugin

   But they got on well together whatever people say and Barry was
quite at home with Gothic viz Highclere. Oh, thank you, thank you,
dear Saviours of what's left of England, dear Liz and Wayland, and
poor Elizabeth and I will be getting in touch with you next month.
   Yours, John B

   W.K., Parliamentary Secretary for the Ministry of Housing and Local Government,
   and his wife E.K. had first met JB in 1956 when their co-written book *Old London
   Churches* was published. Gerard Irvine introduced them.
      They had just entertained JB and EC in the House of Lords.
      Barry and Pugin had collaborated in building the Houses of Parliament. Pugin was
   the most influential nineteenth-century architect in fervent pursuit of the true principles
   of mediaeval art and design. He established the Gothic Revival. Highclere Castle, near
   Newbury, Berkshire, designed by Barry in the 1830s, displays extravagant use of
   Gothic as well as moorish and rococo styles.

To Mary Wilson   The Mead
                                                     Wantage
6 April 1969   Berkshire

Personal

My dear Mary,
I think you must have had a Happy Easter, all of you, if the weather
was as beautiful as it has been here. On Good Friday I was at Morton
Hadley near Barnet and the sun on the white palings and the ponds on

the common and the woods and on the flint of the church and the umber-brown red old brick walls and the old houses of all sizes made it all look as though Charles Lamb and Leigh Hunt and Keats were alive and looking at it too.

I lost in my attempt to ward off too many articles to satisfy the man at the *D[aily] Telegraph Magazine*. I will have to go to Cornwall and write for most of May.

A dear old Australian I know called Ian Mais, who was literary critic of the *Melbourne Age* and has now retired, told me a very nice story about the Prime Minister which will please you. He said that when he was in Melbourne (or was it Sydney? I can't remember which) he got up early and avoided the press reporters who eventually ran him to earth in an arcade where he was buying presents to bring back to you and your sons.

My two granddaughters are here, but away on an egg hunt so that there is blessed quiet and I can write to you. This brings me to the most important part of what I have to say – collect *all* your poems, the ones you are ashamed of and have never published, the incomplete ones, the ones you have published. Then look at them and see if they will make a book *without* illustrations. Poetry does not need illustrations. It is better and truer and shorter than photography can ever be. Only great painters equal it. So if R[obert] Lusty wants you to write for his Scilly book – don't turn it down, but decline to put your poems in it. The Cloudesley Shovel poem will not be enhanced by photographs. Photographs will look *ordinary* beside it and too like journalism. Instead, if you like the photographs, write some prose to go with them. I shall never forget that preface to the Scilly book, one of the two you wrote. Prose can accompany photographs and you might do a real service to Scilly if the photographs are good. It would be hard to beat Gibson, though, at photography.

I do hope you can read this. See you at the Garrick on the 25th at eight p.m. by which time I hope the oil painting will be framed. When I rang up last week it was not yet finished. Frames take months.

Love, John

Oh would I were by the waves and rocks and sapphire sea.

In spring 1969 Robert Lusty, head of Hutchinson's, wrote to M.W. suggesting that he publish a selection of her poems. He came to tea at Number 10 and M.W. agreed to go ahead.

To Valerie Eliot   43 Cloth Fair
10 April 1969   London EC1

Dear Valerie,
I must address you by your Christian name because it was by that I
called you when we met with Tom, and I should be honoured to be
called by mine by you.

I have read these poems and of course they are old-fashioned,
particularly when she comes to personalising the months, as she does in
some of them, but they are skilled, condensed and deeply felt. I am not
surprised at the judgement of the O[xford] U[niversity] P[ress],
because a line like: 'Nor rain, nor dew can slake the gusty drought,' in
'Sorrow, Sit Down', an otherwise so good poem, is too literary and yet
it can't be changed. 'A Retort', which you mentioned, gains tremendously when you realise the circumstances in which it was written.

I think it matters a lot to people who write poetry that they should
appear in print, even if it be only a poem or two. I therefore suggest that
as a first step, you send the present collection, using your own name,
because you are yourself a splendid introduction, to someone like Jock
Murray, who edits the *Cornhill*, and to whoever edits the *Poetry Review*,
because that magazine is much better than it used to be, and to Howard
Sargent of *Outposts*, whose address I've lost.

Then when some of them have appeared, and let us hope they will, I
think it is worth having a collection of not more than thirty poems
printed by someone with a private press, and who is himself a good
enough printer for people to collect his books, simply because they are
printed by him, I mean someone like Will Carter of the Rampant Lions
Press, Cambridge. I think you'd find it would cost about one hundred
and fifty pounds or maybe twice that figure if you use boards to print
them, and you'd probably get your money back, provided you keep the
edition limited to not more than two hundred, but really dear old Faber
and Gwyer could advise you on the costing side.

I often think of Tom and I can imagine how much you miss him. I
only hope my advice to you over these poems is as good as his would be.
I know that Elizabeth Cavendish much wants you to dine with her, and
she has your secret telephone number. I will tell her I have heard from
you.

Yours very sincerely, John B.

V.E., a director of the publishers Faber and Faber, is T.S. Eliot's widow.

V.E. had written (7 April 1969), asking JB for advice about publishing Miss Lascelles's poems. They were later published by the Rampant Lions Press in a finely printed edition.

Eight:
The last year's leaves are on the beech

1969 to 1972

The last year's leaves are on the beech;
    The twigs are black; the cold is dry;
To deeps beyond the deepest reach
    The Easter bells enlarge the sky.

                                    'Loneliness'

On the occasion of JB's knighthood in the Queen's Birthday Honours
List in June 1969, Desmond Baring gave him a magnum of Château
Margaux claret. 'Ta ever so, you dear worried-looking old thing,'
wrote JB (28 June), 'and if you can find a day when you and Mollie can
dine I will save it for that occasion. We ought to be in fine form by the
end of the meal. You will be very quiet indeed. Oh, a Margaux! It never
lets one down.'[1] The reaction of JB's friends to his honour was a cause
for general celebration and he received over a thousand letters. Angus
Wilson wrote, 'That your *Herald* review set my books on the right road
would alone suffice – but seriously, it is the greatest pleasure to me as to
thousands and thousands of others who have attended your adolescent
dances, your beach cricket, and wept with you at the Café Royal and
the Cadogan Hotel. Long years of rhododendrons and pony clubs to
you.'[2] From Wokingham in Berkshire he received an illegibly signed
letter (1 July): 'You have earned the respect and affection of tens of
millions of people, many of whom I have heard referring to you as
familiarly as though they were personally known to you. I therefore
feel that a knighthood could have the effect of creating a gulf and the
appropriate honour which should have been conferred upon you
should have been an O[rder of] M[erit] or a C[ompanion of]
H[onour].'[3] Nancy Mitford wrote from Versailles in France (14 June),
'If I had accepted your invitation – "Since Miss Pam won't marry me I
think you had better" – I should now be a lady. Alas too late.'[4]

    JB's own reaction was more modest. He wrote to Frank Longford (25
June), 'Ever since I heard of it I have been wondering who suggested it
and got it through what sort of committees. . . . I haven't noticed any
change in my status in Wantage or indeed in the City. I still can never

find a taxi when I want one. But I suppose the magic will work when I'm dubbed.'[5] My mother was fairly unaffected by the whole affair on the surface though inwardly also proud. She complained bitterly that the dubbing at Buckingham Palace, which took place on 22 July, was on the same day as the Arab Horse Show at Windsor. In the end she managed to attend both events. For ever afterwards she ticked people off for wrong usage of her name; for, being an Honourable already, she now became The Honourable Lady Betjeman and no-one got it right when corresponding with her. People called her 'Lady Penelope' which made her furious. 'I'm *not* the daughter of an Earl,' she insisted.

If JB was happy on the surface he was inwardly pressured by the accolade. It made him feel that he should be working all the harder. Unknown to him and his doctor, John Allison, he was suffering the first stages of what was later diagnosed as Parkinson's Disease. He was at a low ebb and only to his most intimate friends did he let on quite how low he was. He told Mary Wilson that he was in a well of depression and from Trebetherick he wrote, 'All the old folk are dying. Tregeriatric is what Trebetherick should be called.'[6] My mother well knew JB's periods of deep depression. She did not, however, approve of the Valium which was being prescribed to him and believed steadfastly in alternative medicine and a healthy 'Hay diet', both of which she had supported from the beginning of the sixties onwards. She argued with JB about his treatment but in fact there was nothing he loved better than slipping away into the comfort of chemical euphoria. Barry Humphries remembers, 'He was certainly aware of the curative powers of human laughter, but he used to be so hurt when the London he loved got changed by huge new developments and I think that pain was heightened at the stage he was on Valium. The pain dug deep. I don't think Valium helped him – he had some very dark moments when I was with him, quite close to despair – it's hard to say what the origins were *exactly*.'[7]

My parents' shared life at Wantage was drawing to a close. I know this made JB sad, for he had lived in the Vale of the White Horse or just above it for nearly forty years, and his friendships there were as deep-rooted as the oaks in the hedgerows. But it was my mother who had taken the initiative and decided to travel in India for a long time and to let the Mead meanwhile. JB told his friend Nicole Hornby, 'I remember her father, that alarming but sad man, saying to me when presented with the *fait accompli* of our marriage, "Penelope will always do what she wants to do." '[8] He wrote to Harry Jarvis (1 July 1970), 'I don't think I am kidding myself when I say that Penelope really wants to go to Injer and it is her vocation. Her last typescript is really magnificent, as yet unpublished, and convinced me of that and when she is not in Injer she is wasting her time except for her grandchildren. She likes me but I am not essential to her as they and Injer are.'[9]

In September 1970 my mother left for India with Elizabeth Simpson, Elizabeth Chatwin and Elizabeth Cuthbert and did not return for nearly a year. Her Indian summer was just beginning and for the next decade she travelled there on a yearly basis, sometimes taking tours for different travel agents in order to pay her fare out and sometimes taking her grandchildren. Even the un-let half of the Mead was becoming redundant. JB wrote to his old chum, the archaeologist Stuart Piggott, 'Penelope is having a wonderful time on a horse and accompanied by a young male pencil artist of real talent [John Nankivell]; in the "Himarlyers" in Injah with a Kulu family. . . . I don't think we'll be able to afford to go on living at the Mead on our own.'[10]

'Oh I wish you were here,' my mother wrote in September 1971, 'as you would go quite dippy over this railway with lovely little steam engines pulling the Arctic-blue and white rolling stock and Mr Vaughan of Childrey would be beside himself with delight.'[11] Her letters were often twenty or thirty pages long and read like novellas full of vivid descriptions of various, sometimes hair-raising, adventures. My mother remained close to JB through her letters – it was as though she was talking to him. I know they gave her great comfort to write. She felt safe sharing all the architectural discoveries which she made in the most obscure places in the Indian hills, describing, for instance, how the Kulu temples resembled Scandinavian churches.

Wantage life trickled on. Miss Edmée Butler wrote from the Knoll in June 1971, 'You have both done so much for me for years and given me things and I so often look at things I am using and say, "The Betjemans gave me that." Mr Betjeman rearranged all my books for me. You are all so kind. This is not very well written. I would like to see you at any time when you can spare it.'[12] She died later that year. I know JB was sad. That life in the Vale was now almost out of his reach.

When my mother was abroad he used to visit Rupert and me in Chepstow Villas more. He enjoyed his grandchildren's company but only when they were quiet. (He hated noise, and yelling children were one of his worst nightmares.) He would open his mouth hugely and his eyes would twinkle when he saw them. He always brought stacks of presents. Sometimes we would go on an outing to Battersea Funfair, or St Cuthbert's church in Philbeach Gardens or Kensal Green Cemetery

which the children loved the best. He took us across the top of Tower
Bridge from one end to the other. We were escorted by the Captain of
the Bridge who wore a naval cap. JB was extraordinarily good at
arranging treats and magical mystery tours. We would take off on the
tops of buses to Willesden or the heart of the city or out in the
underground all the way to Ongar and end up by going to see Bruce
Forsyth in cabaret at the Talk of the Town. He made everything feel as
though one was on holiday.

But on these excursions JB was already dragging his feet and I often
had to hold his arm. Afterwards he would go back home to the City
alone and I felt strongly that he should be in Chelsea with Elizabeth and
that the constant journeying between one and the other was wearing
him out. During his last years at Cloth Fair, his secretary Jackie looked
after him attentively. If he was away from London she would write him
news of what was happening: 'Mrs Bennett is dusting the books across
the road at 41, she does so many each day. She has had a cold but it is
much better now. Miss Cundle is about the place and I saw her the
other lunchtime. The most obscene postcard arrived here today for you
from Sarcophagus. Who is he? [George Schurhoff.] The postcard is of
two men holding the other's private parts. When I go to tea I may
casually place it on the table and see what reaction it gets in the
Bartholomew [a café].'[13] JB often had breakfast at Number 41 with
Paul Paget and his new wife Verily Anderson, who liked to look after
JB and trim his hair for him and cut his nails – he had always had the
ability to seem helpless. He often told me he would really like to be in a
wheelchair taking Valium every day. He had a thing about going back
to the pram, and preferably being wheeled about by Myfanwy Piper.

I felt happiest of all when JB was with Elizabeth – she looked after
him in a way that my mother never could. Her comforting cocoon of a
sitting room in Radnor Walk felt utterly safe and, although JB didn't
leave Cloth Fair until 1973, I often wished he had done so sooner. I did
not like to think of him alone in the City when he was in such a wobbly
and often sad state. But most of their life was spent together anyway
and, although she worked as a magistrate in what he always called 'My
Courts' and was often exhausted at the end of the day, she would
always cook him something or have people in to supper. Their social
life ebbed and flowed. Raymond Leppard, Mervyn Stockwood,
Patrick Garland, Peter Shaffer, Jonathan Stedall, Kingsley and
Elizabeth Jane Amis, Harry Williams, Osbert and Anne Lancaster,
Rupert and I, often came to suppers in Radnor Walk.

Still the demands on JB came pouring in – the North Berkshire Bellringers Society invited him to their annual dinner, the Friends of Holy Trinity Bradpole asked him to lunch – but as his doctor John Allison had *ordered* him to take on fewer official commitments, JB cut down on them a little. Seeing friends, however, was deemed healthy, so he stepped up his lunching and dining with old favourites, including such close and easy ones as Douglas and Nest Cleverdon in beautiful Barnsbury Square where JB and Elizabeth often went. JB wrote (20 April 1971), 'I love artistic books, I love you both, I love your children. . . . Poor Feeble Elizabeth and I are planning a little dinner for you both when we return from Cornwall at the end of May.'[14] During the two years following his knighthood, one hundred and seventy lunches or dinners were entered in his diary, many of them with old stalwarts like Cyril Connolly, John Murray, David Cecil, Cecil Beaton, Christopher Hollis, Nicolas Bentley, Peter Quennell, Ann Fleming, John Sutro, Wayland Kennet, Mary Wilson, John Lloyd, Patrick Kinross and Osbert Lancaster, but also with young blades such as David Bailey and Anne Lancaster's son, Max Hastings. Max recalled, 'With his characteristic genius for making others feel good, he signed one of his books, "To my fellow journalist Max," and indeed he several times said to me, "Dear boy, I am just a journalist like you." God knows how he found time to take so much trouble with a host of people like me aged twenty-one: lunch one day before I went to America for a year, followed by a tour of the city views of St Paul's – "None of which you will be able to see any more by the time you come back." Even at that age, I was capable of perceiving the anxiety and melancholy so close to the surface.'[15]

JB was a great champion of the young. If he thought they merited it, he always wrote to the children of his friends on their achievements – to Jonathan Cecil on his acting, to Auberon Waugh on his novels, to Tristram Powell on his films and to Mark Girouard on his books. He encouraged Tristram Powell's wife Virginia to keep on painting when she was on the verge of packing it in.

Meanwhile he kept an eye on his by now large group of struggling acquaintances. Brooke Farrar, the artist, who was in a nursing home, wrote to him every other day saying that the nurses were trying to do away with him by putting too much salt in the cooking. JB tried to sell Brooke's paintings in order to raise enough money to get him removed to a better nursing home. He succeeded in the end in selling some to the art dealer David Bathurst, some to Pamela and Michael Berry and to Ava Lady Waverley (whom he sometimes called Ava Lady 'Quaverley'). He lent one thousand pounds to Tom Driberg in 1969 which he paid back in monthly instalments of twenty pounds. Bronwen Astor wrote to him (7 July 1970) about Bishop Savage of Buckingham's fall from grace owing to his affair with a Bunny Girl. Savage had been particularly kind to the Astor family throughout the Profumo affair. 'Having myself been involved in a similar experience of systematic vilification,' she wrote, 'I can appreciate better than most how cruelly the facts can be distorted by selective presentation. It is imperative that he should have a period of complete rest for two or three months.'[16] JB sent money to the fund which was to allow Savage to seek refuge abroad.

Meanwhile, he gaily flirted with the women he liked. To Mary Wilson he wrote, 'I long to walk beside you in the Army and Navy Stores, under the trees of Vincent Square and round the Abbey to the R[oman] C[atholic] Cathedral.'[17] When Eddie Penning-Rowsell wrote to him (12 March 1972), 'Thirty-nine years ago today I first met Margaret Wintringham in Hyde Park,'[18] JB replied (21 March), 'And to think of Margaret Wintringham's windswept cheeks and stormy grey-blue eyes and petulant suffering lips. . . . Oh, to have been in Hyde Park thirty-nine years ago on 12th March and just have been a few yards ahead.'[19] But among these light moments came a blow which darkened his life. On 1 July 1971 Maurice Bowra died. JB wrote immediately to Joan Leigh Fermor, one of Bowra's closest friends, in Greece. 'I am most touched by your writing to me when you must be so miserable yourself,' she replied. ' Of course life without Maurice will never be the same, something so good and vital and strong has disappeared as well as one's oldest friend and I think of him the whole time.'[20] But JB knew that Maurice Bowra had a firm conviction of the afterlife and told his friends that he hoped to meet him in it. John Sparrow wrote to JB:

> 'Which of the two, when God and Maurice meet,
> Will occupy – you ask – the judgment seat?'
> 'Sure, our old friend – each one of us replies –
> Will justly dominate the Great Assize:
> He'll seize the sceptre and annexe the throne,
> Claim the Almighty's thunder for his own,
> Trump the Last Trump, and the Last Post postpone.'
> Then, if his strong prerogative extends
> To passing sentence on his sinful friends,
> Thus shall we supplicate at Heaven's high bar:
> 'Be merciful! you made us what we are:
> Our jokes, our joys, our hopes, our hatreds too.

> The outrageous things we do, or want to do –
> How much of all of them we owe to you! . . . [21]

Despite his own troubles, JB still had the ability to make the more onerous duties of his life a lot more fun than most people. He fought the battles for his friends with verve and alacrity. Wayland Kennet wrote to him from 100 Bayswater Road asking for his support to stop it being pulled down. Pamela Berry, who had hitherto used him as a social carrot for her dinner parties, begged him to come and stop the proposed Wing airport near her country house at Oving in Buckinghamshire. She wrote (22 February 1970), 'I can't begin to tell you how thrilled we are that you have agreed to come and address us on the subject of the airport menace. It is *so* good and public-spirited of you to do it when you have so many claims on your time and must be run ragged between them all. Everyone is wildly excited about your appearance and we hope to get an enormous amount of money for the cause.'[22] JB and I went to Oving together to attend a large gathering of protestors from all the surrounding villages, and he delivered a parody of one of his favourite poems, Cowper's 'Binsey Poplars':

> The birds are all killed and the flowers are all dead
> And the business man's aeroplane booms overhead
> With chemical sprays we have poisoned the soil
> And the scent in our nostrils is diesel and oil.
>
> The roads are all widened the lanes are all straight
> So that rising executives won't have to wait
> For who'd use a footpath to Quainton or Brill
> When a jet can convey him as far as Brazil.[23]

Lady Pam later wrote (31 March 1971), 'I feel that if we win it will be a great deal due to you and your magnificent and effective propaganda. Also to the fact that you focused public attention on the whole issue a year ago when nobody was in the least bit interested in it.'[24]

Buckinghamshire was easy to reach from London but Wales was a good deal further and when Henry Anglesey asked him to come and give a lecture in Bangor he declined (3 February 1972): 'Get the Widow (John Lloyd) to give a recital of her poems, especially the one about Firewoman Fuchs. Why I can't give a lecture is that I only like talking about architecture and my slides are heavy and cracked and without slides lectures on architecture are useless. I used to be a professional exhibitionist, I am now a professional evader.'[25]

By the end of the sixties JB was getting over three hundred letters a week. His way of life was becoming untenable. He resigned from the

Royal Fine Art Commission at the end of 1970, after eighteen years'
service, although this did not stop him fighting until his last days for
things he cared about. On 17 May 1971, he wrote one of his rare,
pompous but powerful letters to the Minister of the Environment about
the siting of a new hotel in the Avon Gorge at Bristol under Brunel's
great suspension bridge: 'I am a topographical writer, and a poet and
broadcaster, a Royal Commissioner of Historical Monuments, an
architectural adviser to the Greater London Council's Historic
Building Committee, a member of the Committee of the Society for the
Protection of Ancient Buildings and on the Council of the Georgian
Group and Vice-Chairman of the Victorian Society. I am on the
Council for the Care of Churches and a trustee of the Historic Churches
Preservation Trust. Until this year I was a member of the Royal Fine
Art Commission. I am a Companion of Literature and an Honorary
Associate of the Royal Institute of British Architects. I consider a hotel
on the proposed site in the Avon Gorge utterly unsuitable.'[26] It
worked; they never built it.

On the whole though, JB was becoming disillusioned about his fight
to save England's 'indeterminate beauty'. The early seventies saw a
high point in the desecration of London. Piecemeal development was
going on everywhere, little corners were constantly being lost to
monolithic slabs. The developers seemed to be winning. He wrote his
poem 'Young Executives', full of the new business jargon which he so
hated, and it was published in the *Sunday Express* in May 1971. He wrote
to his friend John Junor, the editor, about this 'blistering little
piece . . . . I thought it might amuse you as we see so many of the type
who use those meaningless words like "actually", "essentially",
"basically" and "viable".'[27] He knew no other way of getting at the
people he thought were ruining England.

He often felt trapped. I knew the look so well – the arms in the air, the
exasperated, 'Oh God, Oh God' when he saw the pile of letters in the
morning. I saw in his eyes the longing to get away. This was one of the
many reasons he liked making films. He loved crew life and staying in
hotels in dim seaside resorts. Eddie Mirzoeff was a series editor for the
Bird's Eye View series which pioneered the technique of aerial
photography shot, as it was, entirely from a helicopter. JB wrote the
commentary for three of the thirteen programmes. When the camera
showed the grandeur of Castle Howard from the air, JB's voice was
heard speaking these lines:

Stay traveller! With no irreverent haste
Approach the mansion of a man of taste.
Hail Castle Howard! Hail Vanbrugh's noble dome
Where Yorkshire in her splendour rivals Rome!

Here the proud footman to the butler bows
But kisses Lucy when she milks the cows.
Here the proud butler on the steward waits
But shares his mistress at the castle gates.[28]

JB's very first helicopter flight had been a traumatic event. He had never been in a helicopter before and Eddie found that the communication system was not working with the result that they could not talk to each other about the area they were flying over. At one point the pilot, a Polish veteran of the Second World War, wrote them a note saying that he was uncertain of their location and that JB might attempt to identify a church. JB took out his cheque-book, the only paper to hand, and wrote back, 'Please can we go home now.' On landing JB was taken to Oxford station and given a double brandy which eventually brought him back to life again.

He also appeared on a host of chat shows and television panel games, which he referred to as 'money for jam'. David Attenborough remembers, 'I produced this new series called *Where on Earth?* based on photographs of exotic scenes which the contestants were supposed to identify from details of architecture, natural history, local dress etc. It wasn't a huge success but your father did enliven the proceedings considerably. We showed a photograph of burning ghats in Benares, all temples, turrets, burning pyres and naked people washing themselves in the Ganges. After the rest of the team, including Peter Fleming, had quite unaccountably failed to identify this most obvious scene, your father, after a moment of bafflement, responded triumphantly, "Got it – the Thames just above Maidenhead!" '[29]

With every new appearance and every new film came waves of further requests. Duncan Grant, the painter, wrote, 'I should love to have a film made showing Vanessa [Bell]'s pictures. Would you do the interview? If so that would be marvellous.'[30] In the event he didn't and the ultimate escape, which enabled him to forget about the mountains of letters and the encroaching new villas being built around the Mead, was his visit to Australia for three months to make three half-hour films on Tasmania, Queensland and Brisbane. He wrote to his old friend Patsy Zeppel at the British Council (27 August 1971), 'I am happy to say that I am coming to dear old Aussieland and for three months setting out by air to Sydney from London on September 14th. With my friends Julian Jebb and Margaret McCall as producers and Elizabeth Cavendish as personal assistant, we are jointly employed by the BBC.'[31] JB was still in love with Australia a decade after his first visit. Just as he used racing language when dining in Lambourn and talked about 'going over the sticks', so he slipped into Aussie and talked about having 'a fun time in Brizzy'. What he always mentioned and what excited him were the 'arachnidal joys' – in other words the size of the spiders. Julian Jebb was forced to direct the filming of a tarantula during one of the films. It sat above the lavatory in what JB referred to in Aussie speak as 'the smallest room in the house'.

This second trip to Australia was not as successful as his first, partly because Julian Jebb was unhappy in love which caused a lot of tension, and partly because of the punishing programme. This must have exacerbated JB's increasing symptoms of Parkinson's Disease, but he nevertheless managed to enjoy it. He often told me he would like to settle in Surrey with the blue hills in the distance and the laburnum in the driveway. He felt this same cosy familiarity in Australia which he had never felt in any other foreign country.

Back in England, home in the form of the Mead was melting from the screen. Early in 1972 my mother wrote, 'Buckell and Ballard are coming tomorrow morning to measure up the Mead. VERY SAD IN SOME WAYS, but I am sure it IS the wisest thing to do before I get too old and mind moving much more.'[32] I was desperate for my mother to buy a cottage locally so that she could keep in touch with all her old ties but she made a typically brave and independent decision to look for a house in the country she had always loved, the Welsh borders, and which she connected with distant childhood holidays with her mother. She wrote to JB (12 April 1972), 'So far we have had two offers for the Mead, one from a developer of forty-two thousand, and one from Christopher Chetwode [her nephew, who worked for Knight, Frank and Rutley] for forty thousand, who also wants to develop it! . . . None of the nice people have been round a second time or made an offer but there is still just a month to go before auction. I am going to stay with Mark Palmer, now no longer Sir Galahad but wants to be a horse dealer in the Duke's country, and Penny Cuthbertson in Montgomery for the night and to look around for a house.'[33] My mother's fiercely pioneering spirit, and her insatiable desire for discovery and journeying, never waned. She identified with travellers, and loved my friend Mark Palmer because he had travelled England for three years in a horse-drawn caravan. She liked sleeping under the stars if it was warm enough and gathering wood for her fire with a horse and cart when it was cold. The older she got, the more she did this. It was completely the reverse of what JB craved – the glowing fire, the cosy room, the cup of tea, the hot buttered toast which Elizabeth could always provide.

1. Desmond Baring's papers.
2. JB's papers, University of Victoria, British Columbia.
3. JB's papers, University of Victoria.
4. JB's papers, University of Victoria.
5. Frank Longford's papers.
6. Mary Wilson's papers.
7. Barry Humphries, CLG interview (1994).
8. Nicole Hornby's papers.
9. Harry Jarvis's papers.
10. Stuart Piggott's papers.
11. JB's papers, Beinecke Library, Yale University.
12. JB's papers, University of Victoria.
13. JB's papers, University of Victoria.
14. Douglas and Nest Cleverdon's papers.
15. Max Hastings, letter to CLG (1994).
16. JB's papers, University of Victoria.
17. Mary Wilson's papers.
18. JB's papers, University of Victoria.
19. Edward Penning-Rowsell's papers.
20. Joan Leigh Fermor's papers.
21. JB's papers, University of Victoria.
22. JB's papers, University of Victoria.
23. Simon Elliot's papers.
24. JB's papers, University of Victoria.
25. Henry Anglesey's papers.
26. Carbon copy, JB's papers, University of Victoria.
27. Carbon copy, JB's papers, University of Victoria.
28. 'The Englishman's Home' (1969), *Bird's Eye View* television series, BBC archives.
29. David Attenborough, letter to CLG (1992).
30. JB's papers, University of Victoria.
31. Patsy Zeppel's papers.
32. JB's papers, Beinecke Library.
33. JB's papers, Beinecke Library.

To David Attenborough   43 Cloth Fair
20 June 1969   London EC1

Personal

Dear David,
It was a joy to get your letter. Telly gives me joy. I like it because it is
team work. I like all the technical terms – 'brakes', 'save that ten, Jack',
'I want a pup over there with a barn door on it'. That you, the head of
my house of happiness, higher even than Stephen Hearst of the Palace
of Arts, Richmond Way, should have written – my cup runs over. Oh,
those merry days when you shared that little bedsitter with Paul
Johnson in Lime Grove. Oh, my happy memories of your mother and
father and the latter's superb photographs – Hurrah and thank you
again.
    Yours, John B

> D.A., the natural history broadcaster and traveller, recalled, 'I had first met him in 1949
> when he came to stay with my parents in Leicester (see *Volume One*). My father then was
> Principal of the struggling University College.'
>   D.A. had written to congratulate JB on his knighthood in the Birthday Honours List.

To Pamela Jackson   The Mead
                                                       Wantage
22 June 1969   Berkshire

Dear Miss Pam,
How sweet of you to write. The sight of your writing makes me long to
be folded in your strong arms. The letter I had from Nancy was lovely
too. I have replied to her on ordinary writing paper and put a lot of
Manx stamps (which are legal here) on the envelope. I shall be
interested to know, when next I see one of you, which got there first. I
am v[ery] sorry Nancy has been operated on. But what could be nicer

than to have you as a convalescent nurse. I would enjoy that very much.
I would like to be spoonfed by you. Nancy is obviously recovering
well, for her letter to me is in her wonderfully funny style and has a joke
a line. I wonder whoever ARTOIS was to have a rue. A Frog I suppose.
Darling Miss Pam, ta for writing. May [Allende] has written as I've
told Nancy.

  Lots of love, John B

> JB had been in love with P.J. (née Mitford, see *Volume One*), sister to Nancy, Diana,
> Unity, Jessica and Deborah, when she was working as farm manager to Diana's then
> husband Bryan Guinness (later Moyne) at Biddesden in the early thirties. She continued
> farming throughout her life and always owned a farm in Gloucestershire, but at this
> point was living in Grüningen in Switzerland.
>   Nancy, who lived in the rue d'Artois in Paris, had just had a malignant tumour
> removed from her liver.
>   May Allende had been the parlourmaid at Biddesden.

To Nancy Mitford   43 Cloth Fair
22 June 1969   London EC1

Dearest Nancy,
It is nice to think of those triangular eyes of yours reading this.

                                                           I hope
this letter will speed you to recovery from the operation which Miss
Pam said you had had. I had a letter from May Allende but, of course,
couldn't read it. I hope you can read this. Do you still see Lord Moyne?
it said. Indeed I do. And talking of honours what I would really like
would be to be the heir of a very dim Irish peer – Molesworth or
Ventry, instead of a non-gentleman as I am. But we can't have all we
want, can we? If you haven't seen it, I enclose a v[ery] nice piece about
Mark [Ogilvie-Grant] from the *Horticultural Society Journal*. I saw him
in Guy's. He was far from distressed, thanks to the excellence of
modern drugs. I suppose they will send this to you from England even
if it isn't on AIRMAIL paper. I will send one to Miss Pam on airmail
paper and we'll see which gets there first.

  Much love and ta ever so. Cheerioh-ski, John B

> N.M. (see *Volume One*), the writer, who now lived in Paris, was JB's old friend from the
> thirties.
>   Mark Ogilvie-Grant died later that year.

To Alan Pryce-Jones   43 Cloth Fair
27 June 1969   London EC1

Dear Bog,
What a joy to hear from you. I feel a bit of a fraud – alternately vain and
coy. Newport, the Widow [John Lloyd] tells me, is a not v[ery] good
address. He sent me a postcard showing views of four Welsh passes and
wrote, 'These are being made at you.' But your Newport is a different
one and I know it is a v[ery] good address. Oh, I would like to see you
again. Give me a ring on your return. Here's the secret London
telephone number: 606–8483. In Wantage we are in the book – 2150.
    Love to your birds and love to you, dear Bog, from all at Simpson
Road, Bletchley, the Duke of York's HQ and 53 Church Street.
    Your old chum, JB

> A.P.-J. was living (and still does) in Newport, Rhode Island, USA, not the Newport in
> Wales near where John Lloyd lived.
>   Simpson Road was a former abode of A.P.-J.'s.
>   'The Duke of York's HQ' was the nickname for his parents' Chelsea house near JB's
> teenage home, 53 [Old] Church Street, Chelsea.

To Mary Wilson   43 Cloth Fair
27 June 1969   London EC1

My dear Mary,
My word! Weren't you both fine on the Telly! Well done! Irresistible.
An exceedingly well-produced (Geoffrey Hughes) programme, well-
interviewed (David F[rost]), well-performed (both of you). I'm so glad
you mentioned the poems. To me it was as though you were talking to
me. No wonder Robert Lusty wants to publish. It must be obvious to
anyone watching that you have it in you to write poems and to be
serious about your power, and modest. I v[ery] much liked the change
of moods too. On the stairs you were that vivacious person who rushes
about at the parties seeing everyone is catered for.
    I *may* be landing a job editing a sort of gazetteer of the UK which may
free [me] from the hateful *Daily Telegraph Magazine*. I am to do what
will, pray God, be my last article for it, today or tomorrow.
    As to that queer poem, I am going to try to change the crime – I can't
do it to the Armed Forces, the only other crime which comes in the act,
because then it will too obviously be Oliver Ford. I think I shall hint

more at the crime. The point is that it should be an unacceptable crime. There aren't many.

I've also thought of doing one on someone who has been given so many months to live by his doctor. His own reaction. The reactions of persons who know him or know what he knows, e.g. the inward struggles they have – ambition, fear, shyness, love – ending with his own last moments. I regard the first thing as a practice for it.

I do envy you in Scilly. Now as to the poems by you – for the first few days you will be too stunned with relief and joy to be home in Scilly to write anything. Then you'll find peace returning and the powers will assemble. Re-write old pieces. I think old things are often *improved* by re-writing. Keep the old pieces too. I'll look at both if you'll let me, and choose, if you are in doubt. And finish incomplete ones. And keep everything – even what you don't dare publish.

I see you in my mind's eye in trousers and shirt in a dinghy on the emerald water, and making tea in the new shed on a methylated spirit stove because the electricity has failed in the bungalow. Swim out to Bryher and bring me a piece of bladder wrack.

Love, John

M.W.'s letter crossed with this. She was having misgivings about having her poems published as a book. She wrote (24 June 1969), 'All of a sudden I am filled with dreadful doubts. I've just read a review of the *Wives of Westminster* exhibition in an obscure anarchist newspaper and although it pours scorn on everyone's efforts it was particularly vitriolic about mine. It said that the only good thing about "The Treasure" is that it's well-printed, and that it's doggerel.'

The 'queer poem' is 'Shattered Image' which came out in *A Nip in the Air*. (It is seven pages long and in blank verse.) Oliver Ford was a Berkshire neighbour of JB's.

M.W. and Harold W. had a holiday home on St Mary's in the Scilly Isles which they went to every summer.

To Patrick Kinross   43 Cloth Fair
6 July 1969   London EC1

Dear Pa'rick,
Ta ever so. Of all the letters I have had, I really think yours is the most gratifying. It is a most funny sensation getting these letters. It's something like being dead with *The Times* not being allowed to say anything bitchy in your obituary. But you and I have known each other so long, we know what we've suffered and therefore your memories of Ernie and Bess and the Baroness and Evelyn – by the way Sarcophagus has written me a letter about the spoliation of Blandford or threatened

spoliation as though I am a gov[ernmen]t officer and could call the vandals off – and Hollom IV and Hollom V and George Greaves and Crax are a tonic to me. It will be fun to see Capt'n Bog and his bride on Wed[nesday] evening.

Cheeriohski and love to the Paddington set. Yours, JB

Hollom IV and Hollom V were two brothers whom JB had taught at Heddon Court.

To Mary Wilson   Queen's Hotel
15 July 1969   Lerwick

My dear Mary,
Would that I were in this remote town's hotel with Bergen in Norway the nearest railway station and the warm North Sea lapping below my bedroom window – but I am in Cloth Fair as usual. That was a very fetching flowing number you wore for the Liberian President when you and the P[rime] M[inister] stood in front of that Georgian-style chimney-piece yesterday. What will you wear for the Finns? Pale blue I suggest, to show up the purple depths of your eyes.

I am slowly reading through that Christopher Ricks edition of Tennyson. It is fascinating to see how good A[lfred] T[ennyson]'s judgement was. Those that were really not worth reprinting he invariably left out. I see that in next week's *T[imes] L[iterary] S[upplement]* or maybe this week's, Ricks will be telling us what he has found in Trinity Library which has at last lifted the ban. There is apparently a lot about the origins of 'Maud'.

I had a very enjoyable evening with Raymond Leppard last night. He told me that the film of *King Alfred* (for which he did the music) was awful. He didn't think his music for it good either. He told me that Ben Britten was quite hard and ruthless underneath but undoubtedly a genius. He said that Walton was as great a genius and much nicer man.

I am loving this heat. You must be looking virginal and cool in it. I saw a bit of an eye operation yesterday at Moorfields. My word, it was alarming. What precision. What a tiny threshold of thunderingly awful pain. I couldn't go on looking.

See you. Love, John

Raymond Leppard, the conductor, helped JB with some of his musical choices for his *Desert Island Discs* in 1975.

To Joan Leigh Fermor

The Mead
Wantage
18 July 1969   Berkshire

Darling Joanie,
It was nice to see that country-house, relief-nib handwriting of yours
even though on Greek paper. I saw Paddy [Leigh Fermor] at Patrick
[Kinross]'s. We met the Captain [Alan Pryce-Jones]'s new bride. She
seemed to me to rule the roost, but I think the Captain will escape. I
can't tell just from our dinner party what she was like – whether there's
any love there. I have an idea the Captain is very kind and very weak.
*I would very much like to have far closer contact and of a physical nature, with
you.* But then, as you know, in letters especially letters to Abroad, one
gets very indiscreet. I went and filmed
the Ritz in colour lately. I thought
of you. I wish I had realised I could
have spoken then. Look at me now,
fat, bald and finished and knighted like
Sir Henry Newbolt (v[ery] good) and
Sir William Watson (less good) and
Sir John Squire.
    Paddy was very blithe* at Patrick's
and I like to think of you both, which
I do happily and pleasantly enviously.

    Penelope has a very strong bout of hippomania at the moment and
seems to have lain down her pen. She talks of going to Injer next year in
the autumn. What she talks of she does. It is very nice to think of how
annoyed and amazed Sir P and Sir B would have been. If there is an
after life we'll be able to find out – that is to say if there's personal
survival and I think there is but I don't think we'll be bothered by such
interesting things as that. Poor E[lizabeth] C[avendish] is v[ery] well
and white and effete and quiet. Darling Joanie, ta ever so for writing.
Hope you'll forgive my bad handwriting.
    Love, John
    *BLITHE in case you can't read it and get worried.

    Alan Pryce-Jones had married Mrs Mary Jean Kempner Thorne in 1968. She died later
    in 1969.

To Margaret Ann Elton   The Mead
                                                    Wantage
20 July 1969   Berkshire

My dear Margaret Ann,
I read every word of your pier article. It is splendid and informative. I
read it in the G[reat] W[estern] down to here. By a coincidence the
sadist who edits the *Daily Telegraph Mag[azine]*, which is my only
regular means of support, asked me for an article on piers. Your account
of Clevedon bears out a truth. They were originally just extensions of
quays. The first place to use them for recreation was Margate *c.* 1800.
[?illegible] pier was [illegible] with a band at the end for spectators to
listen to. Seaside music was an inheritance from inland spas like Bath.
All piers till about 1870 were for landing steamers – paddle steamers
usually. Then when they became as much promenades as landing
stages, theatres and halls were built at the ends of them, but this was not
until the nineties. Your description of the opening of Clevedon Pier is
poetry – poetry can be prose when in a master hand like yours. I was
transfixed by it. It's nice, too, that something so good is hidden in a
local paper. All the best things are a bit hidden. You are all genius.
Arthur is an inspiration to us all. The Bicks [illegible] of Tennyson is
SUPERB. Love to Julia. Love to Arthur and Rebecca. Love to Charles
and Graham Elton. Tell him to try something classic and grim and
Low*. By Lowness we come to love Highness. I love PEERS
(hereditary, of course, not life Peers) as well as Piers.
    LOVE TO EVE.
    Love, John B
    *Marylebone Parish Church.

M.A.E. was the wife of the pioneer of documentary film, Arthur E. (see *Volume One*),
who had been at Marlborough with JB and a close friend ever since.
    Their home Clevedon Court where Tennyson had often stayed, was near the seaside
town whose pier, built in the late 1860s and the most graceful of all, JB had always loved.
M.A.E. had written a centenary history of Clevedon Pier for the *Clevedon Mercury*. Two
spans collapsed under testing in 1970, following which Arthur E. started the Clevedon
Piers Trust and raised over seventy thousand pounds. He died in 1973. A public inquiry
was held in 1980 and the local District Council's decision to demolish was rejected. JB,
who was too ill to attend, sent a tape-recorded statement about the pier's importance.
    JB supported the founding of the National Piers Society in 1979 and gave the
inaugural speech at its launch in the Connaught Rooms in London.

To Henry d'Avigdor Goldsmid   43 Cloth Fair
29 July 1969   London EC1

Dear Harry,
It was worth having lived to have had so enjoyable an evening as
Monday night – everyone on top of their form, Captain Pryce-Jones
talking about racing do you think? John H[islop], Mr Piper discussing
art with old Patrick [Kinross], Maurice [Bowra] booming away, Roy
[Harrod] merry, Osbert observing, through those huge round eyes,
Ran [Antrim] and Thomas Edward Neil Driberg veering between
amenities and gossip, Christopher S[ykes] I could not see enough to
notice whether he was more in with Mr Piper and old Patrick or with
Ran and old Patrick, Jock [Murray] smiling peacefully among those
distinguished authors at the other end, Cyril [Connolly] and Peter
[Fleetwood-Hesketh] talking a lot – again what about, I wonder,
Byron? Pope? Shakespeare? John Hanbury Angus Sparrow in that
sweet suit from the Winchester School Tailors, just not having an
argument with Maurice across us – and us.
    Oh, thank you very much, Harry. I feel undeserving. That
Margaux! That Montrachet! The Taylor's '45. Even gloomy old Jack
James was cheerful. Ta once more. Love to Rosie and Chloe. What a
pity the Colonel [Kolkhorst] and Toby [Strutt] couldn't come. Who
put that bit in the *Evening Standard*? Not
    Yours gratefully and for ever, John B

H.d'A.G., a generous Oxford friend of JB's with whom he often stayed at his house
Somerhill in Kent, had given a banquet at White's Club to celebrate JB's knighthood on
28 July. There were drinks at John Murray's beforehand. JB helped compile the guest
list and the following people came:
    His Oxford friends (see *Volume One*): Christopher Sykes, Peter Fleetwood-Hesketh
who had illustrated JB's *Ghastly Good Taste* in 1933, John Summerson, John 'Widow'
Lloyd, William 'Cracky' Wicklow, John Bryson, Lionel Perry, Philip Harding,
Christopher Hollis, Michael Dugdale, John Edward Bowle, John Murray, Alan Pryce-
Jones, Jack James, Patrick Kinross, Osbert Lancaster, Maurice Bowra, Cyril Connolly
and John Sparrow; John Hislop, the racehorse breeder, a friend and neighbour of JB's in
the country; Randal Antrim, Chairman of the National Trust; Robert Heber-Percy (see
Volume One); Hugh Cruddas, a war hero and Robert's companion; Godfrey Samuel;
Alan Ross, Gerard Irvine and Freddie Birkenhead.

To Paul Paget   43 Cloth Fair
4 August 1969   London EC1

Dear Paul,
What a glorious crowded visit.
Here is a picture of poor white
washed-out quiet Elizabeth looking
at a Norfolk water lily midst the
reeds and the rest of us. The journey
back was quiet and comfortable.
We dined at the Great Eastern and
had some Beaujolais. I had a bath
when I got home, cut my finger-
and toe-nails and slept like a log.
Miss Cundle told me she got back
at 11.30. All seemed to have enjoyed
themselves. None could have done
so as much as yours ever and
gratefully,
    John B

> JB and EC had been to stay with P.P. at Templewood, his self-designed Palladian villa
> in Norfolk, which he used at weekends and later retired to.
>   Miss Cundle was P.P.'s housekeeper in both Cloth Fair and Norfolk.

To Joan Leigh Fermor   43 Cloth Fair
20 September 1969   London EC1

Darling Joanie,
Oh, I did enjoy myself in Kardamyli. Of course that big room, as I've
written to Paddy, is one of *the* rooms of the world. It is the thought in
everything you look at which delights me about the house(s). In that

way Paddy is like Butterfield. In proportion and use of garden as part of the architecture, he is like [Edwin] Lutyens and [Gertrude] Jekyll – and all the time he is himself. I've never seen you so beautiful, not even when with eyes as big as your cheeks and downy soft and straight, you stood in the Ritz. I've *written* to Jock a long letter giving him news of George ['Seferis'] and telling him also about the house – how it is really a book of Paddy's and more lasting. Give my love to Graham [Eyres-Monsell]. I hope poor white washed-out quiet and effete Feeble and I will be seeing you ere you go and Graham. I can't thank you enough for your kindness in my straits of pain and piles. I'm well again from them. Andrew has had his veins operated upon in Westminster Hospital, very painful. He will be able to swim and dash about a lot more when he comes out. Poor Eliz[abeth] and her mother and I went to *Much Ado* last night. It is really very good – enthralling in fact. I don't think I've ever seen it before and certainly never seen it properly acted. Hope to see Pinero's *Magistrate* on Monday. My love to you and Graham and to Trephane and all Ogles.

    Love, John

> JB and EC had been to stay with Patrick and J.L.F. (née Eyres-Monsell, see *Volume One*) at their house overlooking the sea just outside Kardamyli in the Mani at the foot of mainland Greece. Richard Beer, the painter, had also stayed. Patrick L.F. had built on a large room to work, sit and eat in. JB wrote to him, 'What is so marvellous about it is the use of light – day light or evening light and electric light. It changes and is perfect in each. It is something to do with proportion and you have an instinctive sense of it.'
>
>   The architect William Butterfield (1814–1900) was one of JB's favourites and built Keble College, Oxford.
>
>   Graham Eyres-Monsell was J.L.F.'s brother, a friend of JB, known as 'Groundsel'.

To Wayland Kennet   43 Cloth Fair
19 September 1969   London EC1

Dear Wayland,
Greece was enchanting as scenery and as siting for temples, but the atmosphere of not being able to speak freely was markedly noticeable. Even I noticed it. I don't think it could ever be like that in Italy. I don't think it was even like that under Mussolini. I look back with love to the shores of your lake, and to the walk up to the echoing wine vaults. In Greece I got fever and then a stoppage and then piles, the well-known complaint of journalists. The nastiest man I ever met in my life was the Chief Reception Clerk at the Grande Bretagne in Athens, never go there.

This letter is really written about a serious matter your Ministry has done much to preserve, that notable Greek-Italianate and Early-English manufacturer's suburb of Broomhill in Sheffield, and I have even written a poem about Broomhill. Indeed, if you haven't got my last book of verse, I'm sending it to you and you can give it to Roy Worskett if you and Liz have it. On page 28 you will find a description of Broomhill. Surely the dull, out-of-scale and unimaginative block is unthinkable on the site indicated in the cutting enclosed with Colonel Haythornthwaite's letter to me.

Love to Liz. Bung ho, old top. Yours, John B

> JB and EC had been to stay with W.K. and Elizabeth at their house Vigna Grande on Lake Bracciano, north of Rome.
>
> The proposed development at Broomhill, which JB later referred to as 'that frightful bit of withitry' was to be built on the site of a disused chapel.
>
> Roy Worskett was an architect who worked in the Ministry of Housing and Local Development, and the author of *The Character of Towns*.
>
> Colonel Haythornthwaite was general secretary of the Council for the Preservation of Rural England in the fifties and sixties.

To Ashley Barker   Trebetherick
11 October 1969   Cornwall

Dear Ashley,

I return from Cornwall next Thursday, but the enclosed, forwarded to me by that splendid actress Jill Bennett, seems to me urgent.

I seem to remember either you or our dauntless and clever chairman (for whom I enclose a copy of this letter to you) telling me that the 'developers' who had bought the Lyric site were trying to get out of re-erecting that attractive Frank Matcham interior. From the enclosed letter from the General Administrator of the Lyric, it looks as though the 'developers' are carrying out this threat by making the theatre impossibly expensive for the Lyric.

I have told Bob Swain I have written to you and that I've sent his letter to you. I also enclose my letter to him.

> Fight on Fight on for Matcham
> And his sumptuous designs
> Down with the mean 'developer'
> And his pseudo modern lines.

Yours, John B

A.B. of the Historic Buildings Department of the Greater London Council became a staunch ally of JB's.

JB had been warned about the danger to the Lyric theatre, Hammersmith, by Jill Bennett who was married to his friend the playwright John Osborne.

The Lyric was dismantled and re-erected in the belly of a modern building.

To Patrick Leigh Fermor   43 Cloth Fair
16 October 1969   London EC1

Dear Paddy,

Those poems are *marvellous* – particularly the London one. It reads very well to oneself as well as out loud – a *double* and true test. Of course the Eddie [Sackville-West] one is terribly funny. It is funnier than the Maurice one. I think *I* will try the London one and the Christmas lines on Alan Ross. Let me know if you think not. I'll wait. I've been reading the George Seferis in Rex Warner translation. Having been to Greece one gets the true beauty a hundredfold. The 'Bernard of 19' meter comes out like Hopkins. That book *The Waters of Marah* which Osbert lent me about the Greek Orthodox church made me love the C of G (Church of Greece) more than ever. Ever since I left I've been trying to put down Kardamyli in a verse letter in couplets to the Vicar of Edensor, but I can't do it. If I do, I'll send it to you. Joanie is immortal and so *beautiful*. I'm writing a fan letter to George S[eferis]. I've chucked the *D[aily] Telegraph* and dropped two and a half thousand pounds per annum plus five hundred expenses. And has it been worth it? My God, yes. It's freedom. Newspaper men are shit. Stay in the Aegean and build and write poems in prose or verse form.

Feeble sends her love. Penelope is sold on Norway. Love to your sister. Love, John B

JB had met P.L.F. in the early fifties and in the 1954 summer edition of the *Cornhill* P.L.F. wrote a poem 'In Honour of Mr John Betjeman' which began:

Eagle-borne spread of the Authorised Version
Beadles and Bell-ropes, pulpits and pews,
Sandwiches spread for a new excursion
And *Patum Peperium* under the yews.

To David Cecil
16 December 1969

43 Cloth Fair
London EC1

Dear David,

I have now finished *Visionary and Dreamer*. (The trick of underlining the title of a book I got from Lord Alfred Douglas.) I hasten to say that it is the best book even you have written and that is saying much for I have read them all. The essay on [Samuel] Palmer (how proud I am to be quoted in it) *exactly* hit off my mood and has left me exalted and happy. I will explain a reason – Harry Williams told me that since he has become a monk at Mirfield his thoughts on the Resurrection have been shaping into book form. He told me that when one is lowest that is when one is nearest to being raised up. Reading your Palmer essay and P[almer]'s talk of Blake, I can see that the Resurrection is going on all the time and death is the Crucifixion which is also going on all the time in us and when hymns tell about 'Christ within me' etc. it means death and resurrection in us. Palmer, having had that vision as a youth at Shoreham and in his last days on earth, seems also to have had that sense of resurrection glory which hangs round landscapes and etchings. It is an unbelievably wonderful bit of writing that essay of yours. B[urne]-J[ones] is the more human and humorous and less dotty man and *far the sadder*. Oh, what a book! Oh, thank you for it. Love to Rachel and Laura (and Angelo [Hornak] whom I liked on sight) and don't you think Rachel and Laura look a bit like Georgina B-J and Margaret B-J?

Yours, John B

> *Visionary and Dreamer: Two Poetic Painters Samuel Palmer and Edward Burne-Jones* had just come out.
> Laura C. married Angelo Hornak.

To Simon Jenkins
31 December 1969

43 Cloth Fair
London EC1

Dear Simon,

I greatly admired your Strand article. It will be fun if you do some public interiors in a street like the Strand. Australia House, which is rather heavy Marshall Mackenzie outside, is an Edwardian Baroque extravaganza within of Australian marbles and gold and ironwork which rivals the Ritz in splendour. And I can't tell you how greatly I

admired yesterday's article by you about the future of London. I had a
nice letter from Ann Riches. I hope you will collect your articles into a
book, and get an artist like John Nankivell, with an eye for a building
regardless of date, to illustrate it. I think that block of you is delightful
shorthand. Keep in touch, you know the address. Let's go and eat again
somewhere with the delightful Ann. I wonder what it would be like in
Debenham's Restaurant or the Army and Navy, we might go when the
sales are over, or we could try Waterloo Station, the Surrey Room.
    Yours, John B

> S.J., the journalist and architectural writer, and JB had formed a mutual admiration
> society, S.J. was at the time writing campaigning articles against the desecration of
> London in his 'Living in London' column in the *Evening Standard* (of which he became
> editor in 1977). JB had written to him and they had started going on walks round London
> together. Once they bumped into Osbert Lancaster in the Aldwych. 'I'll never forget
> that day, I stood in wonderment watching these two elderly men pointing up all the
> time.'
>   S.J.'s collection of articles and writings was published as *A City at Risk* (1969) and later
> *The Selling of Mary Davies* came out in 1993.

To John Osborne   43 Cloth Fair
22 January 1970   London EC1

Dear John,
I am very sorry you have got gout, on the other hand it's considered a
very aristocratic disease.
    I don't think it is all a mistake to do this anthology for BBC2. Railway
Timetables, yes particularly an old Bradshaw, I have one here. I have
an idea that there are some very poetical lines in the wording of old-
fashioned advertisements like Owbridges Lung Tonic, and then there
are the rhyming advertisements which are really like nursery rhymes –
they come as a boon and a blessing to men, the Pickwick, the Owl and
the Waverley pen, and those Bravington rhymes about rings. They
have the advantage of not needing tunes. On the other hand lots of good
poetry is overshadowed by its tune. Far the best hymn writer was Isaac
Watts; the latest edition [of *Hymns] A[ncient] and M[odern]* has got good
stuff by him and of course the *English Hymnal*, [with] Percy Dearmer's
socialist inclusions, has good stuff, like Ebenezer Elliott's 'God Save
the People'. As for the prayer book it is matchless. I shall be at Feeble's
over this Saturday and Sunday, so give us a tingle. Love to Jill
[Bennett]. I heard from someone who really knows about that kind of

thing that her play is breathtakingly good. So was a comedy by Shaw called *A Village Wooing*, which I saw last night.

Love, John B

J.O., whom JB had recently befriended, had written (21 January 1970). 'I am supposed to be doing an "Anthology" Programme for BBC2. . . . I don't want to pick your brains exactly but there are certain areas in which you could be uniquely helpful. . . . What I want to do is to try and avoid the usual solemn-voiced recitals of Keats, Wordsworth and so on, but explore the common references that nearly everyone has access to, however ordinary or commonplace they might seen to be. We all know the poetry of Railway Timetables and no one has taught us this better than you.'

To James Lees-Milne   43 Cloth Fair
29 January 1970   London EC1

Dear Jim,

Forgive my typing, old boy. I have had a most interesting thing, a sort of mental disintegration, which meant I lost my balance, couldn't keep my temper, telephone bell sounded like a dagger in my heart, and my lack of self-confidence was such that I couldn't write a letter, let alone an article, and felt I would never write a book or a poem again. Feeble insisted on my going to a GP and I have been given a lot of pills, and am all the happier from them. I think a book called *Don't Come to Britain* is a very good idea, or one might make it purely sarcastic, and a sort of parody of the British Travel Association. Years ago O. G. S. Crawford compiled such a book called *Bloody Old Britain*, but no-one would publish it.

I think the thing to do is to go on a package tour to Rumania, and meanwhile through my friend, John Satterthwaite, Rector of St Dunstan in the West and liaison man with the Rumanian church, fix ourselves with visits under church auspices there; once we have reached the country on the package tour.

All the best, old man, and love to the Dame. Feeble is *very* quiet at the moment.

Yours, John B

The disorders which JB was experiencing were later diagnosed as Parkinson's Disease.
  J.L.-M. didn't pursue his idea for a book on Britain about which he had written to JB, nor did he go to Rumania.
  Alvilde L.-M. used to live near Versailles, in Jouy en Josas, and Nancy Mitford always referred to her as the 'Dame de Jouy'. This became her lifelong nickname.

To Hubert de Cronin Hastings   43 Cloth Fair
16 February 1970   London EC1

My dear Obscurity,
That's a very nice electric typewriter you've got. It will be very nice to
receive the *Archie [Architectual Review]*. For years I have had to pretend
I'd just read it at the Royal Fine Arts Council, to people like Lionel
[Esher] and Jim [Richards] and the Doctor [Pevsner]. Every page a
surprise. Your motto has been mine and it has made some very
surprising things happen. I am sorry A. E. D[oyle] is not alive, and I
often think of Mr Chatterton. His favourite architect was Collcutt – I
used to think such an idea ridiculous, now I'm not sure that I don't see
Collcutt through Frederick Chatterton's eyes. Penelope is going to
Injer again and for a year in September. If you want anything written
about the photographs she'll be pleased to oblige.
   Jaggers

> JB considered H.de C.H. (see *Volume One*) the greatest editor of all time. He had been his
> boss and mentor on the *Architectural Review* in the early thirties and had edited it from
> 1927 to 1973. He had taught JB the importance of layout and art direction and they were
> always joking together. He had written (10 February 1970), 'I have just discovered
> thirty or forty years late that you get no free copy of the *Architectural Review*, a thing
> which every past member of the paper gets – whether he wants it or not. The *Archie* is so
> bad that I can't believe you will even open it. Nevertheless, duty must be done, and its
> second-hand value will be enormous if you ever have any place to lock it away.'
>   A. E. Doyle and Frederick Chatterton were colleagues on the *Archie Rev* (as JB called
> it).
>   Thomas Edward Collcutt (1840–1924) built the Imperial Institute, Kensington and
> the River Front extension of the Savoy Hotel and the Wigmore Hall.
>   H.de C.H. always called JB 'Jaggers'.

To Mary Wilson   43 Cloth Fair
1 March 1970   London EC1

My dear Mary,

> Alas on Tuesday next I can't
> Attend I fear on Willi Brandt
> Although to see you too I pant
> I still can't meet with Willi Brandt
> For what has gripped me by the collar
> Is Greed for the eternal dollar

> Although I've ruined my imago
> I fly today to dread Chicago.

Love, John

I hope my sec[retary] will have sent the office's number. The doctor says I'm quite okay to go now and I'm filled with Valium and Tryptizol.

> Willi Brandt, the leading Social Democratic politician and at this time Chancellor of West Germany, was a well-respected international statesman. He was awarded the Nobel Prize for Peace a year later.

To Mary Wilson

20 March 1970   Trebetherick till Monday evening

My dear Mary,

Don't take my suggestions for the preface too literally, I may be quite wrong. It might be better to have no preface at all. Yet I do like the idea that you who are much loved, should express your pleasure in the difficulties of writing poetry and how alarming it is but necessary to publish.

I think 'dying lamps' is better than 'flickering' as it is dramatic. But *do* they die: Ask a miner. Maybe they just go on 'flickering' indifferently while death is all around – in which case flickering may be better. Not much help I fear. Technical ignorance. Glad you like Durham and its Dean.

Elizabeth Cavendish and her mother have been staying here and yesterday EC and I went to see Tresco Gardens. Her mother couldn't face the early start though she wouldn't have minded the helicopter. At the Penzance Heliport, a tall handsome blue-eyed hero spoke to me – *John Hamilton*! He said did the Dorrien Smiths know I was coming over. I said no, it had been a last minute decision. I used to know the first Mrs D[orrien] S[mith] before she married. Well, he rang up and came in the helicopter with us. It was fine and sunny and the sea 'a peacock's neck in hue' and the Land's End and the islands were at their best. The characterful bus driver pointed out your house to the bus load but I did not have time to take in more than its splendid elevated position. John Hamilton then talked to us both a lot about his business of jewellery and he is now making scent and how Tom Dorrien Smith lets him stay on the island. Then when we were about halfway across to Tresco, he talked [of] you and said he believed I knew you and he said how fond he was of you and how you were one of the most perfect women he had ever met and how sympathetic, with all of which I agreed. Then we walked up the granite quay and through the gate after we had crossed that mysterious football pitch and there was that high shorn avenue up to Neptune and the peacocks in full splendour two thirds of the way up. The camellias are out, the scented heathers and the bushes that smell of curry and Eliz[abeth] who knows all about shrubs and flowers was in heaven at all this sunlit beauty and so was I. She told me she thought that John Hamilton was one of the happiest and most fulfilled men she had ever met. The D[orrien] S[mith]s gave us lunch and I felt like royalty. But the man who stays in my mind is J[ohn] H[amilton]. He is a sort of redeemer for Tresco. Eliz[abeth] thinks he probably redeems Commander D[orrien] S[mith]. On the way back at New Grimsby [we] met Mrs Hamilton who was, E[lizabeth] thought, a splendid person and as nice as J[ohn] H[amilton]. So did I. We had lent J[ohn] H[amilton] a basket for some things he was carrying and she was returning it. On the boat with us going back were the retiring Manager of Tresco and his wife. The wife told E[lizabeth] that it had been very difficult and you had to be so careful of the temperaments of the people on the island of Tresco. I gather he had been sacked and was pleased to go to the mainland. Neither E[lizabeth] nor I thought they were the quality of the Hamiltons. I should think the Commander is an autocrat and has a 'Happy Valley' quality of Kenya, but I can see the Commander must have suffered a lot from his first wife who was one of those people who never grow up and go on looking about eighteen. It was for me a marvellous day and everywhere I thought of you and almost saw your ghost on the shore and down by the quay and in the little lanes back to the airport. I couldn't imagine you in Tresco Gardens. But I saw you going across to Bryher. God! it was wonderful. It must keep you all sane and brave as you seem to have it as a hide-out. But I wouldn't like to live there for ever – certainly not on Tresco. Personalities are too strong. Like the Irish, the Cornish say what they think you want to hear, not what they mean. You're right to have another bower even if it's Number 10. Do forgive my handwriting – it is arthritic, I think!

Love, John

John Hamilton was a soldier and artist who painted many pictures of Second World War battles. He was a great friend of the Wilson family and had a studio on Tresco and later at St Mary's.

Tom Dorrien Smith leased Tresco from the Crown. (His son Robert succeeded him.)

To Joan Kunzer   Treen
                                                        Trebetherick
                                                        Wadebridge
[?May] 1970   Cornwall

Dear old girl,
Ron [Hubble] told me:
(1) how paper is made on rollers in paper mills in India
(2) how cement is mixed
(3) how cement is tested
(4) the difference between Babui Income Tax procedures and
Healy's.
(5) He also told me about a sum of money, forty-five pounds, to be
precise, which he had placed on deposit at the bank to await the
financial year by which time interest was due on it. He told me how
he omitted to declare the amount to the authorities, which had asked
him about it through his accountants.
I go to Norfolk next week till May 19th after which what do you say
to lunch?
Feeble sends her love, so do I. Love to Simon, grandkiddies and to
Carolyn and her spouse, John B

> J.K. and JB ofted vied with each other for the most boring bits of information they had
> been told about, at length, by a mutual friend Ron Hubble who lived in Trebetherick.
> 'Ron used to send us into hysterics. John used to ring me up and say, "I've got *terribly*
> interesting news about Ron's accounts".'
>   Simon and Carolyn were J.K.'s children.

To Mary Wilson   43 Cloth Fair
4 May 1970   London EC1

Personal

My dear Mary,
Re your telephone conversation of today, if you will excuse business
phraseology, my thoughts are these:
1) Whether there is an election or not, the politically minded will say
it is electioneering or cashing in on success or failure.
2) Whether you publish now or then, there will be the envious to
blame you and pick you to pieces and impute wrong motives.

3) All [that] people like you and I remember is the blame, and injustice, never the praise. That is how we are made. It can't be helped.

4) As to Bob Lusty's getting the *S[unday] T[imes]* to take six, that is good and leave it to him to know when to let the *S[unday] T[imes]* publish, it depends on when he decides to publish the book.

5) The *S[unday] T[imes]* will take six that have not appeared before.

6) You will go through agony. You will be parodied, misconstrued, patronised. You would not be a poet if you did not thus suffer.

7) You will have the consolation of seeing yourself in boards and well printed and produced. That makes up for everything, election or no election, harsh criticism or lavish praise or utter neglect.

8) Don't bother about reviews. It's the travellers who sell books and word of mouth.

Love, John

M.W. was feeling nervous about the timing of Hutchinson's proposed publication of her book of poems.

To Mary Wilson   43 Cloth Fair
4 June 1970   London EC1

My dear Mary,

The courage and calm you both must need, and obviously have, amazes me. Yet when I think of how dull most people's lives are, it seems to me to be worth having the ups and downs to avoid monotony.

I went and saw a very funny film last night called *Cactus Flower* wtih Ingrid Bergman in it. It was a constant laugh like those William Powell/Myrna Loy films used to be. I went with my Tory friends the Lancasters! I have bought a pamphlet and a good one on racialism published by the Mother's Union. It is naturally against it.

Tomorrow I go to Scotland for this Conference on Preservation. I will have to get up at eight a.m. I return to London Monday morning. Candida is reporting the World Cup in Mexico from the woman's angle for the *E[vening] Standard*. It seems quite good stuff. I went to the 'open day' in her stead, to the kindergarten where my eldest granddaughter Lucy goes. It made me realise I prefer the dotage of senile decay, to infancy.

I have been slowly reading all R. L. Stevenson's poems. It is amazing how much Rupert Brooke owes to him. I hope some poems come out of you from the next few weeks of electioneering. They will be moments recollected in tranquility.

This book on Oxford you lent me is of untold value to me as I go today to Batsford's to look through the photographs of old Oxford they have collected and I must take care not to duplicate. Thank Robin and my beloved Joy for giving you the book.

I'll keep on thinking of you. Take plenty of drugs to keep you calm.
Love from John

> A general election was just about to be held.
>   Robin and Joy were M.W.'s son and daughter-in-law.

To Mary Wilson   43 Cloth Fair
19 June 1970   London EC1

Private and Confidential

My dear Mary,
I have your OXFORD ILLUSTRATED book and I'd better keep it here till you tell me where to send it. I can imagine your mixed feelings. Relief or depression. Through them both the only thing that matters is *affection*. Hundreds have it for you both. I'm one of them. I'm so glad you've got the poems coming out. I have no doubt that they will do well – none whatever. I think now is the moment to go on writing more. There's a very beautiful poem of Hardy's called 'The Rejected Member's Wife'. Wait and you will feel the affection for you surging back, for both of you. And all the time, on top of it all, there's poetry. I go to HULL on Monday but will be back here on Tuesday. Please count on me when you want me. I hope to go to Cornwall on June 27th for ten days. Isn't it a relief that waves still break, estuaries fill up and flowers bloom and the steady friends who are inanimate remain. I'll be gassing away against WING airport in Oving tomorrow.
Love, John

> Labour lost the election and Edward Heath became Prime Minister.
>   'There was dismay at Hutchinson's when we lost the election,' recalls M.W., 'but Robert Lusty was still determined to publish.'
>   JB refers to his visit to Buckinghamshire to speak against the proposed Wing airport.

To Wayland Kennet   43 Cloth Fair
19 June 1970   London EC1

Dear Wayland,
It will be awful without you at Housing. Do you think they will make
Sir Keith Joseph, the developer's moll, Minister of Housing once
more? If they do, we might as well all shut up shop. I enclose a letter
from John Schofield, which is only one of the many tributes to you that
arrive here.
    Love to all, John B

> Peter Walker, not Keith Joseph, became Minister of Housing with the Conservative
> Government.

To Mary Wilson   43 Cloth Fair
19 July 1970   London EC1

My dear Mary,
I was a little troubled for you when we met today. I know that great
tiredness, but mine can never have been as great as yours. I think the
unity you have as a family will keep you going. In the long run this
counts even more than the poems – thank God for Giles, *Joy* and Robin
and the Leader of the Opposition. The colour telly at the Garrick was
too purple. But I didn't like the idea of the L[eader] of the O[pposition]
finding me in your bedroom! You must get one of those little V[incent]
Square houses. They are real London and you don't need something
big. You want a garden and a ground floor and human scale. Enter in
your diary TUESDAY 28th July you and/or Giles and/or [the] L[eader]
of [the] O[pposition] or you alone Garrick, eight p.m. I think the cover
is SMASHING.
    It was sweet of you to come to tea with me. You seemed happier and
more relaxed. Long may you be so. And we did have some laughs with
and at Hardy.
    Love, John
    Telephone to me. I daren't do so to you.

> M.W. recalls, 'We laughed and shuddered at "The Work Box" by Hardy in which a
> village joiner and undertaker gives a work box to his wife and says the rest of the wood
> went to make a coffin for a young man who, the poem hints, had been his wife's lover.'
>   Giles was M.W.'s second son.
>   Following his defeat, JB reverted to calling Harold W. 'Leader of the Opposition'.

To Ken Savidge   43 Cloth Fair
August 1970   London EC1

Dear Ken,

I was enchanted with your letter and its news of the Church in Pakistan. The Rev[erend] Simon Delves-Broughton must come from the same family as produced Rhoda Broughton, the Victorian novelist. They are what is called 'well-connected'. I have not yet had prostate trouble, but I notice that it is afflicting many of my friends, including the Widow [John] Lloyd, who was eighteen times Mayor of Montgomery, a town of seven hundred inhabitants. She was always very acid and amusing. I am glad to say she has recovered. As my friend Crax [William Wicklow] said in a postcard to me, 'The world would be such a sugary place without the Widow.'

I have only once been down to the late Western Region since you left. It was the same and not the same. I hear from Peter West from time to time.

His lovely sister Ursula lives near us in Berkshire. Penelope is going to India for eleven months in mid-September. I will give her your address. She is learning Hindi, and has already written one book about the Temples and tribal life in the Kulu Valley and English settlers. I read it in typescript and thought it magnificent, it almost made me want to go and brave the East myself, except that I couldn't stand the discomfort of those Guest House huts in the mountains. Poor Elizabeth has been doing a three-week course in Criminology in Cambridge. Her Little Friend [Princess Margaret] asked us to dinner last night. I have a very sore throat this morning.

I am sure it is rather nice out there. I am sure that the pace is slower. Keep in touch with
Yours ever, John B

K.S., the television producer, had met JB when he worked for the religious broadcasting unit of the Bristol BBC series *The Faith in the West*. He had gone on to make twenty-six films called *The ABC of Churches* with JB from 1960 to 1968. He was at this time working for the BBC in East Pakistan.

Peter West was the head of engineering in the West Region. He owned a white open-topped Rolls.

To Harry Jarvis   43 Cloth Fair
15 September 1970   London EC1

Dear Harry,
I am staggered that you have passed your driving test. I am glad to say
that I got my licence before such tests were necessary. I think a *pneu*
school is a frightfully good idea, of course I will give all references, and
if I have got any money will try to help out a bit.

Penelope leaves for India today for a year, and she has let the Mead
for that time to some American Jewish psychologists. The husband is
working at the Warneford [Hospital] and the children seem rather nice.
She has let the place for fifteen guineas a week, so it won't bring any
profit because of the rates and the upkeep of hedges. But I won't have to
pay the telephone bills or the heat and light or the motor car unless I
take it over myself. She is going with three people called Elizabeth,
whose surnames are Simpson, Cuthbert and Chatwyn, and she is taking
John Nankivell to do some drawings. It is costing the earth, but let us
hope it will repay at any rate part of itself.

I like to think of Jean [Jarvis] in that trouser suit of gold, which is
bound to be duller than the sheen of her hair. I've moved my books into
two rooms at Seely and Paget, I am having to pay rent for the rooms,
but if this flat is extended it will mean that my library is no longer
divided. I expect I shall stay as divided as ever.

Love to my god-kiddie and her brother David and to glorious golden
enticing Jean. I saw old Hugh [Pickles] looking very battered from his
latest motoring accident, of course the cricket always makes him over-
excited during the summer.

Yours, John

Paul Paget, JB's landlord, had made space for JB's books at 41 Cloth Fair, his own house.

To Mary Wilson   Treen
                                                       Trebetherick
                                                       Wadebridge
7 October 1970   Cornwall

My dear Mary,

It was a joy to hear you on the telephone yesterday. It will be a joy to see you at 5.30 p.m. at 14 Vincent Sq[uare] on Tuesday October 13th. I'll be in Ealing BBC studios looking at rushes of the Isle of Man from noon onwards. I'll deposit my luggage off the night train at Cloth Fair that morning early-ish.

I am in a strange state of mental constipation and cannot think of the poem I want to write. I *did* think of it and it has gone. At last, today, having got rid of guests and locals and written the day's letters I am still blank and stale. *Ora pro nobis*, my muse and me.

I do hope this pen is better to read than the biro. It is a gift given me by Judi Dench. Now I can repeat I am very stale and without inspiration. Not even a line or a mood have come. We'll read some poetry at 14. I have been reading with increasing admiration the *Fo'c'sle Yarns* of T. E. Brown. He really is somebody. Stories in dialect sounds unattractive, for me they are marvellous. Perhaps it is because I know the Isle of Man.

I have been having a lot of nightmares of the usual terror of loneliness and loss of love. Dreams go by opposites, one hopes. I also dreamed I saw Edward Hornby who stays down here with me, playing rugger in a game of soccer and I felt embarrassed for him. He is very correct in all his ways (and very nice).

I do hope your fellow author in number 14 is *enjoying* writing. I dread it myself.

Oh, I am glad your poems have done so well. Now for some more. Keep it up. Don't feel because you have done well now, you can't do it again. Of course you can.

Love, John

M.W.'s *Selected Poems* had come out (22 September 1970).
   Harold W., the 'fellow author', had just started writing his book *The Governance of Britain*.

To Candida and Rupert Lycett Green   43 Cloth Fair
22 October 1970   London EC1

Darling Wibz and Rupert,
I must thank you and Rupert for sacrificing yourselves, your kiddiz and
your house to that reprint of an old book of mine this week. I liked the
curious admixture of booksellers and Fortune Euston and Pe'ter
Fle'it!wood-Hésketh. I cannot write down his curious enunciation.
Considering he is forty years older than when he made the original
drawing it is amazing that he has changed so little. Paul Paget says he
should be called 'He' as a counterpart to Rider Haggard's 'She'. His
drawing is wonderfully witty. But all this is really to wish you both
well in the USA and to say how sorry I was not to be able to say
goodbye. The Sharpes' little party, including ENDELLION Sharpe, was
very happy indeed and musical though I'm not musical. We raised
about six hundred pounds, Anne Feversham tells me, that night at
Newburgh when I showed off and people had to pay to see. I am always
sad for people in the USA and I hope you are not unhappy. I've heard
nothing more from Mummy. If you see Powlie send my love. The only
addresses I have are c/o CHAZANOV Apmt 5A W103 NYC 10025 and at
certain but unknown days Riverdale High School. If he seems in need I
think I ought to cough something up (via you if need be). I am inclined
to be of the opinion he now likes the USA and will settle down there
until I am dead. It must be awful to bear my name in England as he
must always be being asked about whether he's my son. It is the curse
(one of many) of having an unusual name. But in the USA I am
unknown and he can escape. The only sums I can let him have are so
small they are unlikely to be of much use.
    Lots of love and many many thanks, MD

Ghastly Good Taste, which was originally published by Chapman and Hall in 1933, was
reprinted by JB's friend the publisher Anthony Blond with additional comments by JB
and further drawings by Peter Fleetwood-Hesketh on a nine-foot-long pull-out section.
    RLG had opened a branch of Blades in New York.
    JB had read poetry in aid of the Distressed Gentlefolk's Association at Newburgh
Priory, Yorkshire, under the auspices of my brother's godmother Anne Feversham.
    PSGB was by now teaching music at Columbia University, New York City.

To Richard Bramall   43 Cloth Fair
26 October 1970   London EC1

Dear Mr Bramall,
I hang on to my faith by my eyelids, a lot of the time I think it is all rot.
The most positive thing I can say is that I would prefer it to be true, that
is to say, the Incarnation and the Resurrection. If you think our readers
would like so weak a testament as mine, they are welcome to it, but not
until January. My agent is Graham Watson, Curtis Brown Ltd, 13
King Street, London WC2.
    Yours sincerely, John Betjeman

> R.B. was programme director of ATV and had written to JB about a new series he was
> making, *The Christian Commitment of Public Figures*: 'I should be delighted if you could
> find time to appear and tell us what your undoubted faith has meant to you.' The
> programme went out to the Midland Region in March 1971.

To Mollie and Desmond Baring   43 Cloth Fair
21 December 1970   London EC1

Darling Mollie and Dezzie,
I had a v[ery] good time indeed with all that drink, company and
religion. What good fun the Todhunters are and what a genius Arne is
with kiddiz. That carol service was vastly moving despite Mrs
Whitehouse and her husband the vicar. I think I have had more laughs
in your house with you all than I have had even at the Mead and it was
lovely to renew them. I live from day to day very warily. The train I
went back in was UNHEATED but I went to dine with Tony Richardson
and with warm arms, a blonde whose name I never got received me on a
sofa after dinner and though there was, I'm sorry to say, no sex in it,
there was such a revival of heat in my body that I recovered from the
train. I also had whisky.
    To you all a very happy Christmas. Let's have a Baring Banquet at
the Hungry Horse, St Andrew's Hill, EC4 opposite Blackfriars
underground station. I suggest Jan[uary] 14th Thursday. You and
Dezzie and any kiddiz that can come. The food is the next best thing to
what Coltman's was.
    Love, John

JB had been to a carol service at Ardington near Wantage followed by dinner with M.B. and D.B.

Michael and Caroline Todhunter had bought our old house, the Old Rectory, Farnborough.

JB had met Tony Richardson, the film director, with John Osborne.

To John Edward Bowle   43 Cloth Fair
16 March 1971   London EC1

My dear John Edward,

I have taken to typewriting and as you can see I have got quite good at it. I go to Cornwall on Thursday and am only back in London for today and tomorrow. Penelope returns from Injer on October 20th and I may be in Australia from September 20th until mid-November. Penelope is wildly happy in Injer and I have had some funny letters from her which outwitted the postal strike, and I may say I adored the postal strike. I don't think we will be able to get hold of Penelope until about a month from now as she is on a pony somewhere between Delhi and the Kulu Valley, but I know she will be as delighted and honoured as I am at the though of your book being dedicated to us. Such a thing happening makes me feel more of a fraud than ever, because you really know what you are talking about and I only talk.

I feel very much for you about your mother, and all one's life, whoever one is, is a constant adjustment to changing circumstances, and of course the older we get the harder it is to adjust. I suppose the only thing to do is to do what you do, a daily visit, ordeal though it be. I think when one gets very old, one day is more or less the same as another, and one's world contracts until it becomes little more than the table next to the bed and the pattern on the wallpaper. People matter much more, kind hands and arms, and there is nothing for it but to go on. I have recently had strange experiences which make it look as though Providence looks after us in an oblique and weird way. It will look after you and your mother, the difficulty is to trust it. If it doesn't sound too pi, 'underneath are the everlasting arms'. I return to London in April and shall have to move out of this house for a couple of years while it is pulled down and enlarged, after being rebuilt to look like what it looks like now. This address will find me as I shall be next door, but in less convenient quarters.

Yours ever, John B

J.E.B. (see *Volume One*), the historian, had been at Marlborough with JB. They had
remained friends, with occasional frosty intervals, ever since. J.E.B. was interminably
long-winded and took himself very seriously. His academic career as an historian failed
to prosper, but he wrote several good and successful general books. JB and PB were ever
generous to him. He remained single and spent much time at the Mead.

To Robert Aickman   43 Cloth Fair
31 March 1971   London EC1

Dear Robert,
The two great things about the Waterways campaign are that you
founded it when it seemed hopeless as a cause, and that it was a success.
As to your methods of bringing this about, I am ignorant. Clearly no-
one financed you, did you finance yourself? Whence was the money?
You cannot have done it entirely on drive. Who besides Alan Herbert
and John Smith were your chief allies? What first put it into your mind
to run the campaign? Why did you like canals and not, let us say,
churches or eschatology? What influence did your uncle, or was he
your father, the architect W. A. Aickman, have on your decision to
champion canals? How old are you? What do you regard as the
significant and insignificant parts of your education from childhood
until today? If you think you can bear to bring yourself to answer these
questions I will write one of the hundreds of worthless forewords I
everlastingly seem to be writing, and I would have something which
would interest posterity to say. You are one of our great men and have
always kept yourself hidden, and if you would rather it like that, so it
had better remain. Whichever way you want it, foreword by me or not,
the selection must be yours and probably some remarks from you on
the principles on which the selection was made.
    Yours sincerely, John Betjeman

R.A. was the founder and vice-president of the Inland Waterways Association. JB had
been a member of the IWA since its foundation in 1955 and often attended meetings and
dinners.
    R.A. wrote several collections of ghost stories and his autobiographical account of the
IWA, *The River Runs Uphill*, was published posthumously in 1986. JB was presumably
writing a foreword for a promotional book to help the cause, which was to save and
restore the canal system.

To T. A. Robertson   Treen
                                                            Trebetherick
                                                            Wadebridge
3 April 1971   Cornwall

Dear 'Vagaland',
I well remember my visit to you in Greenwill and I cannot tell you how
pleased and proud I am to have your beautiful poem in the *New
Shetlander*. So much did it bring back the scene you described, and so
much does it recall Shetland, that I did not need the glossary you kindly
sent, not even for 'froadin' (foaming)! I could hear every word and the
poem is so graphic that any local words explain themselves. In fact the
third stanza is as terrific as the scene must have been. It is a joy to me to
know a real poet such as you are, and to think that you have
remembered me by sending on 'Da Wastern Waves'.

I was in Orkney since I saw you last, but not for long enough. Just
like Shetland, each island has a strong personality. St Magnus's
Cathedral and Mellestrane House and the stones at Staines were great
subjects but what equals Fetlar, Papa Stour and the Church at Westing,
and the stones there? I hope I may live long enough to see Shetland
again and again. Through your poem I see it as though I were there.

All the best to Dr Manser. Yours truly, John Betjeman

On a visit to the Shetlands in December 1970 JB had visited the poet T.A.R, pen-name
'Vagaland', at his house 'Greenwill', through the auspices of the editor of the *Shetland
News*, Dr Manser. He liked T.A.R's poetry written in the local dialect and after the
latter's death helped to organize the poems being recorded on cassettes.

To Coral Howells   43 Cloth Fair
20 April 1971   London EC1

Dear Mrs Howells,
The tram is a number 7 and it was brown when it was L[ondon]
C[ounty] C[ouncil]. I can just remember the horse trams which were
open on top and I longed to clutch one of those bobbles that hung
temptingly near from the plane trees.

Hampstead Heath then had buttercups and daisies and dandelions in
the grass at the Parliament Hill Fields end. Daniel's was a kind of
Selfridge's and it was from the corner of Prince of Wales's Road, or
very near that corner. There was a cinema higher up on the same side

and there I saw my first film, very early animated pictures, it was called the 'Electric Palace'. Then a grander cinema was built between Daniel's and Prince of Wales's Road. My father who was deaf very much liked going to silent films here and took me with him. The Bon Marché was an old-fashioned draper's shop with about three fronts north of the cinema, and opposite Kentish Town underground station was a Penny Bazaar and next to that was Zwanziger which always smelt of baking bread. Here too was the tram stop for the last stage of the route north. Then there was an antique dealer and picture framer called Yewlett and a public house. My father visited the former but not the latter.

Then there were some late-Georgian brick houses with steps up to their front doors, then the always-locked parish church of Kentish Town (that was the one I referred to in the poem). It was rebuilt in Norman style in 1843 by J. H. Hakewill and seems to have no dedication. It was very Low. Then there was Maple's warehouse always rather grim, then some squalid shops and a grocer's shop called Waile's which was very old-fashioned. Then came Highgate Road station with a smell of steam and very rare trains which ran, I think, to Southend from a terminus at Gospel Oak. Then there were some rather grander shops with a definite feeling of suburbia; Young the chemist on the corner, Young had a collie dog; Pedder the oil and colourman; and French for provisions; the Gordon House, grim behind its high grey walls. I remember thinking how beautiful the new bits of Metroland Villas were in the newly built Glenhurst Avenue, and my father telling me they were awful. Then there were the red-brick gloom of Lissenden Gardens and Parliament Hill Mansions. I was born at 52 but moved to West Hill as a baby so cannot recall the flats. Where the school is now there were trees, but they were not part of Parliament Hill Fields.

I could go on like this for ever, but I must stop or I shall arrive at 31 West Hill. It was very countrified. My greatest thrill was to walk with my father down a place in Kentish Town called Faulkner's Lane. I then thought it was a slum, but now realise it was charming Middlesex Cottages. It was a little village south of the Great Eastern [Railway] and on the east side of Kentish Town Road. I remember going with my mother to visit a 'poor family' in Anglers' Lake, Kentish Town. The only toys the children had to play with were pieces of wood from a bundle of kindling.

Yours sincerely, John B

C.H., a local historian, was writing about Highgate and the district and had written to JB asking him for his reminiscences.

To Judith Scott   43 Cloth Fair
30 April 1971   London EC1

Darling Judith,
Words cannot enough express my sadness at your leaving the Council.
You *are* the Council. You continued what Dr Eeles began and as he
would have wished, you made it greater. It was fitting, in a way, that
the crowning earthly reward of your devoted work should be that *at*
most the Council will have more of a say in Church affairs. But what
makes you, darling Judith, so superb is that you are a leader *and* so
tactful and kind with all sorts of recalcitrant people and that you are
unafraid of blustering bullies and one can be tactless to you and have a
laugh and be sure of a loyal friend. I hope you are not so badly ill that we
won't see you. I shall miss our letters and writing 'Darling Judith' and
ending 'love and kisses'. I should like to continue doing that as long as
possible. I think Peter Burman is a *splendid* fellow – twinkling with
humour and likely to get a good team around him. But oh, how I'll miss
you. No answer needed. This is a Collins.
      With love and kisses from John B

PS This is you.

J.S. (see *Volume One*) had worked for the Council for the Care of Churches since she
started as Dr Eeles' assistant. JB had long had a flirty correspondence with her over
church matters. 'I was *very* fond of him,' J.S. remembers.
      A Collins is a coterie word for a thank-you letter, deriving from the obsequious
behaviour of Mr Collins in Jane Austen's novel *Pride and Prejudice*.
      Peter Burman took over her post as Secretary.

To Mary Wilson

Treen
Trebetherick
Wadebridge
[May 1971]   Cornwall

ON A PAINTING BY JULIUS OLSSON RA

    Over what Bridge-parties that luscious sea
       Has sparkled in its frame of bronzed gold
       Since waves of foaming opalescence roll'd
    One warm spring morning, back in 'twenty-three
    All through the day, from breakfast-time till tea,
       When Julius Olsson, feeling rather cold,
       Packed up his easel and, contented, stroll'd
    Back to St Ives, its fisherfolk and quay!

    Over what bridge-parties, cloch-hat, low waist –
       Has look'd that seascape, once so highly-prized,
       From Lenygon-green walks, until, despised –
    'It isn't art. It's only just a knack' –
       It fell from grace. Now, in a change of taste,
    See Julius Olsson, slowly strolling back.

John Betjeman 1971

My dear Mary,
What about this? I've just made it up. I got the picture from a dealer in Falmouth, Peter Jackson. It's not as big as yours and it's bright sunlight and in a very 1920s frame of 'dull gold'.

What have you made up lately? What was the USA like? I only saw your back in the photograph I saw in the paper. Your hair was very recognisable. I come back to London late on May 20th by way of Iron Gorge which I must defend against an hotel by Maxwell Joseph which would ruin that 'romantic gorge which slanted'. The kind architects are paid witnesses. Paid witnesses in these enquiries should not be allowed.

    Love, John

Since I wrote this you have telephoned – thought transference. I also dreamed of you last night and that you were gloomy and needed cheering. I also dreamed I was looking at Surrey churches and that an incense-laden procession went by and you were mystified by it. I look forward to hearing you nine a.m. Friday week, if not before.

In 1969 JB had bought a seascape of the Cornish coast in oils by Julius Olsson and given it to M.W. for Easter. He had just bought another for himself.

JB also sent this poem to Tom Driberg who had criticised the rhythm in the octet: 'I knew there was something odd about it and you have found it you clever old thing.' The final version with its changed first two lines, which was first printed in the *London Magazine* before it appeared in *A Nip in the Air*, read:

> Over what bridge-tours has that luscious sea
> Shone sparkling from its frame of bronzèd gold.

To Margaret Breadmore   43 Cloth Fair
6 May 1971   London EC1

Dear Mrs Breadmore,
Without seeing your cottage I couldn't possibly date it and even then I should have to refer to the local council for the name of the builder. I am not an expert on these matters, and I would suggest that your friend goes to the local council offices and makes enquiries as to who was building in the area at about the time you think your cottage was built. It is very difficult to trace these facts and I would not set too much store on your friend being able to find out much.
    Yours sincerely, John Betjeman

M.B. had never met JB but, assuming him to be a government department, had written from Brightwalton in Berkshire, 'I wondered if you would let me know how *old* my cottage is.'

To Mary Adams   43 Cloth Fair
21 May 1971   London EC1

Dear Mary,
I am typing this myself, and that is why here and there there may be a mistake or two, but my handwriting has got too insultingly bad for any friends to receive it. I so well remember coming to the Ally Pally [Alexandra Palace] and you giving me my first job in telly, and I suppose that man on the blackboard which was one of my drawings, was there to show you the boring sort of antiquary who looks at fonts and can't see the wood for the trees, and I think those extraordinary objects by which I am surrounded are there to show that guide-books ought to be about significant objects like weather vanes, whatever their dates. It's the most happy memory for me, my darling Directress, for I

remember too, how one used to look out from your room on to that pathetic little garden, surrounded by hurdles which Mr Middleton had made; and was I with you that day when we walked into the depths of the Palace, and found ourselves in a huge theatre, and Gracie Fields rehearsing to an empty house? I wish I saw you many more times than I do and I am very glad you are nearby in Camden Square. This is where I am, and I would like to take you out to lunch, almost any time after Whitsun. My number is 606–8483 and it is X-directory, because I am so vain.

Love, JB

M.A. (see *Volume One*), the television producer, who had produced *How to Make a Guidebook* in 1937, had sent JB a photograph of himself when advertising his first television programme 'with love and happy recollections of old days'. At the time, JB had sent M.A. a drawing of himself in the same pose (see *Volume One*, letter dated 14 September 1937).

To Rosie d'Avigdor Goldsmid　　　　　　　43 Cloth Fair
14 June 1971　　　　　　　　　　　　London EC1

My dear Rosie,
You are a wonderful hostess, a beautiful girl and restful and understanding to yours truly. I shall never forget those two sunlit days of unexampled glory. Also it's nice, for a change, to be with people one hasn't met before and to find them *all* refreshing. Of course I *had* met Teacher, but hadn't got to know him. He is a wonder. He is so understanding and humorous and well-read and *kind*. I ask no more of a son-in-law for my lovely Chloe, who is so smashing to look at I still go at the knees when I see her and long for the twining sinuosity of her long arms.

That blue-eyed and contented person in the pram is joyful fruit of the Teacher loins, cooing under the spreading cedar above the sylvan weald and wearing that jockey cap. Derry Moore drove Feeble and Susan Cecil and me back in no time. I fancy the Bedfords lost their way for they did not seem to overtake us in that huge and wonderful Rolls. I greatly enjoyed myself and this ecstatic letter is proof. I'll be sending under separate cover *Real People* which got packed in my things by mistake. I've got a sonnet that may entertain Harry and you which I'll enclose with it.

Love and thousands of thanks, John B

R.d'A.G. was married to JB's friend Harry. He had just been to stay with them at Somerhill in the Weald of Kent.

James Teacher was married to R.d'A.G.'s daughter Chloe.

To Mary Wilson   43 Cloth Fair
25 June 1971   London EC1

Dear Mary,

Don't think when you read this that you are seeing things, it is simply that I am switching over from biro to pencil which I find softer and more reliable.

Further to our telephone conversation you must remember these points:

1) Old fashioned 'withits' who regard rhyme and rhythm as fetters and out of date, don't know the rules you and I set ourselves of ear and metre or stress. So these judgements technically are worthless. It is as though an abstract artist who had never mastered perspective or drawing, accused a representational artist of being no more than a colour photographer.

2) I'm sure you are good. And if you want convincing proof of it, it is that you so resent ignorant criticism like what you quote. By 'doggerel' these silly idiots mean lines that rhyme and scan.

3) The literary world is malicious and personal. I suffer under [Geoffrey] Grigson and his like and even under people who pretend to be friends (e.g. John Piper and his wife) who feel, one knows, that one is 'trivial' and not 'important'. One of the agonies of publishing poetry is that you get such attacks. I remember telling you as much. I had fearful lambastings until 1939 for any book of poems I produced. I will get them again. They will never forgive a knighthood just as they can't forgive *you* for being the P[rime] M[inister]'s wife. That does not really affect whether one is born to be a poet or not. What does affect it is not having the courage to go on and face the ridicule. I believe in you and I say go on.

Love, John

M.W. recalls, 'I did have a bad review which talked about "doggerel".'

To Richard Ingrams   43 Cloth Fair
2 July 1971   London EC1

Dear Old Pressdram,
If you can run to the cash, please send Lewis Morley down to Exeter,
and ask him to stand in Southernhaye and look at the back of the GPO
building as seen from there, in contrast with the few remaining
Georgian houses in Southernhaye. It will make a nice little picture. I
don't think I have ever seen worse modern buildings than there are in
Exeter, and there would be lots of themes for his lens to which I could
add words of highfalutin' praise.
     An Exeter friend of mine told me that a councillor said to him, 'We
would like to get rid of those old cobbles in front of your house, and run
a smooth road straight through to Southernhaye from the High Street.'
My friend said, 'And why don't you take down that old building over
there, Alderman, it would make a useful car park?' The Alderman
replied without a smile, 'Oh no, we couldn't take that down, it's the
Cathedral and it brings a lot of trade to the City.' I like the look of my
stuff in the latest number. Ta ever so.
     Yours ever, Betj.

> R.I., who was the founding editor of *Private Eye*, had first met JB when I took him to the
> Mead in 1962 when we were rehearsing a revue together for the Edinburgh Festival.
> (Many of us who had acted in the revue stuck together afterwards and in 1963 *Private Eye*
> was born in a basement room. I sent subscription forms to all JB's and PB's friends. John
> Piper was the very first official subscriber to the magazine. JB soon followed suit.) JB
> began to call R.I. 'Pressdram' which was the name of *Private Eye*'s publishers.
>   Lewis (Fred) Morley was a fashionable sixties Australian photographer, with a studio
> in Greek Street near the offices of *Private Eye*. He was famous for his nude photograph of
> Christine Keeler astride an office chair. JB started and wrote the 'Nooks and Corners'
> column for *Private Eye* beginning with issue 246 (21 May 1971).

To Kenneth and Jane Clark   43 Cloth Fair
11 July 1971   London EC1

Dear K[enneth] and Jane,
The adorable Kelli [Clark] with whom and Annie Fleming and John
Hanbury Angus Sparrow I attended Maurice's funeral as a non-
Wadham intruder, the adorable Kelli, as I was saying, thought you
would like an account of it all. I was very glad to hear from her that you
are over your operation. Operations are almost bearable during the

process, but afterwards one is a complete wreck and thinks one is never going to pick up. *It takes months.* Do not come to the memorial service on Sat[urday] and *do not bother to answer this letter which is sent purely for info.*

We lunched with Spanzbury [John Sparrow] in All Souls. We walked in burning heat to Wadham Chapel and there was the coffin in the full chapel and on it pink sprays of flowers. Except for some Bowra ladies we never met, all was Wadham. The service was bleakly C[hurch] of E[ngland] as Maurice would wish. I found myself next to the Rev[erend] F.G. Brabant who was Chaplain when Maurice was Dean and a great friend of Maurice always. He became a missionary in Africa and told me Maurice wrote to him out there more than anyone else had done.

At the memorial service Isaiah [Berlin] is preaching it seems. A very good idea. I expect he knows that Maurice had a lively sense of personal survival and of the next life – 'Much looking forward to it,' he often said to me, 'I'll see Brother Tom (Adrian Bishop) and old friends. Of course I won't see important people. You won't see Dr Norwood (my headmaster at Marlborough) but those you had pleasure with.' He was very reverent. I remember years ago going to look over the Cowley Fathers' place with him and we came to an altar where the Blessed Sacrament was exposed and he called out alarmed and said, 'It's like an open wound.' All this knowledge of him made his funeral not depressing but remote. Maurice is quite all right. That stentorian voice which is with us for life on earth as a memory, is, I like to think, at a terrific gathering of old friends and a joined appreciation of all the things he shared enjoyment in and with such heightened appreciation. It's that or nothing. I hope the former. Faith, Hope and Charity – for the faint-hearted such as yours truly, the greatest of these is Hope. The sadness is for us – you and Jane and Kelli, Joan [Leigh Fermor], Paddy [Leigh Fermor], Penelope (to whom I have written the news, she is in the *Himarlyer* until Oct[ober] 20th), Isaiah and Spanzbury and hundreds of people to whom he was probably as important as he is to us.

Annie and I in sweltering heat walked round to Holywell Cemetery where his mortal remains were laid. Near there, Walter Pater, Warden Wells and Kenneth Graham and Sir Herbert Warren. We were too late for the committal. Never mind. He is not dead. He had a lot more of Christ in him than most. This letter sounds like a sermon. That is another reason for your not answering it but sinking back into peaceful convalescence and much love to Jane. The last letter sent on to me from Penelope, started 'Dear Jane and K' and then that was crossed out and it went on to me about Kulu carving in wooden temples.

Love, John B

Maurice Bowra (see *Volume One*), JB's friend and mentor, had died on 2 July at the age of seventy-three. He was warden of Wadham College, Oxford, for thirty years and the ablest vice-chancellor and administrator of his time. He was the funniest and wittiest of men. At the memorial service in St Mary's Church on 17 July, Isaiah Berlin said of Maurice B., 'He was, in his prime, the most discussed Oxford personality since Jowett, and in every way no less remarkable and no less memorable.'

JB wrote to Berlin, who wrote back (2 August 1971), 'I cannot get used to the idea that Maurice will not ring me tomorrow morning or especially when I'm surrounded by grave colleagues and his inimitable voice will say, "I have a piece of news, no I cannot telephone in half an hour. Hertford is going to elect . . ." etc.'

To Bevis Hillier   43 Cloth Fair
27 July 1971   London EC1

Dear Bevis,

Far from leaving me implacably unchanged, your *Expo* book has enlarged my vision. I had already been thinking about having a colour photograph taken of the Hoover factory, and am now determined to have it done. I think your introductory paragraphs superb writing about sunlit Sunningdale and the twenties. One feels you were alive in them. But what is so enjoyable about this book is that its illustrations are so intriguing, that instead of being repulsed or superior, one feels at one with the world. I used to know Charles Boyton, he was a friend of my father, and I think I can probably provide a few objects suitable for you, as my father's firm in the Pentonville Road carried out a lot of work in silver and onyx and that kind of thing, for these anonymous artists. I should think my father's friend, Philip Asprey, who is still alive, could supply you with a good many names of designers. I would love to see you and Andrew again before I sail for Aussie. If you are free after 22nd August and before September 14th. September 2nd is no good.

Yours sincerely, John B(etjeman)

B.H., eventually JB's official biographer, had been asked by his friend Andrew Graham, who had worked in the British Embassy in Paris, which two people he would *most* like to meet. 'I named JB and Lady Diana Cooper. So Graham asked us all to lunch at Pensioners' Court, the Charterhouse, London. We all got on. I had just organised the big summer exhibition, *Art Deco*, at the Minneapolis Institute of Arts, USA.'

To Mary Wilson   43 Cloth Fair
September 1971   London EC1

My dear Mary,
I long to see you. I've written this reverie for my next book if I ever get
another out. It applies to all of us, not writers only, who have 'done
well':

> I made hay while the sun shone:
>   My work sold.
> Now if the harvest be over
>   And the world cold,
> Give me the strength to be grateful
>   As I lose hold.

'Losing hold' – I remember my father-in-law clutching my hand on his
deathbed and saying, 'I'm going.'

How was Scilly? Osbert Lancaster and Ann S[cott] J[ames] *loved*
Tresco. I've been with the C[hurch] of E[ngland] Ramblers to France
and Barcelona and *hideous* Andorra.

I have you down as coming *here* at 4.30 p.m. on Thursday 9th. I hope
this suits you. I go to Aussie on the 14th.

Love to Giles. Love to you and the Leader and my dear Joy. One day
I'll meet Robin I suppose. You I must see often and often. Love, JB

To Candida Lycett Green   145 Elizabeth Street
                                                       Sydney
29 September 1971   Australia

Darling Wibz,
I am gradually thawing and getting less dotty. We are all four very
happy because Australian wine is so good. So is Australian architecture
right through to Moderne and real contemp[orary]. I am ravished by it
and you will be. The hotels are awful. The one at Bendigo smelt of cats
and my pillow smelt of pipe smoke. The motels, though they are all 'do
it yourself', are good. Rupert's white hat and suits are v[ery] good. So
far it has been v[ery] cold in Melbourne and Tazzie [Tasmania] and this
suits me. Brizzie [Brisbane] will be sweltering. I've brought a lovely
rubber centipede. I often think of poor fallen Lucy and hope she is
okay. I won't get any letters till Saturday next as they are being

forwarded by the BBC from Brisbane. Fisher is a rum cove. Still, write care of him. Julian [Jebb] is our life and soul, Eliz[abeth] organises us all and supports me when I lose my balance (physically) and Margaret McCall is highly efficient and kind and calm. We all get on v[ery] well and drink a lot. I hope our films will startle the world. I wish you were with us. You would laugh. Have seen a lot of Barry [Humphries] and his two wives. Start filming in N[orth] Queensland among snakes and scorpions next week. We often talk of you and wonder what you would say and how much you would be embarrassed by us.

Lots of love to you and Rupert and L[ucy], I[mogen] and D[ell]. Love, MD

JB, EC (as his official personal assistant) and Margaret McCall the producer (who had produced *Time with Betjeman* in 1970), went to Sydney, Australia on 14 September 1971 to make a series of films.

Lucy LG had fallen out of a tree.

JB had written to John Drummond, who was responsible for setting up the films (26 October 1970), 'I like the idea of doing an Australian film or films. . . . They could be a revelation over here and I daresay in Australia too, of the superlatively good eighteenth- and nineteenth-century architecture and planning and layout of suburbs to be found in that country. I'd also like some marsupials ambling about, and horned lizards walking up garden fences. . . . Subjects I should like to do are: 1) the architecture of Horbury Hunt, e.g. Newcastle and Grafton and Armadale Cathedrals; 2) the City of Brisbane and along with it some Drysdale-looking country town; 3) Sydney's Georgian and later architecture; 4) Ballarat, a town I have never visited but which I am told has splendid relics of its golden days. The possibilities are so immense, I don't really know where to start. The Botanic Gardens at Melbourne are worth a film to themselves, along with the Mint and the Governor's house. The railways of Australia, the steamers to Manley, unvisited places like Zeehan in Tasmania, with its empty Opera House and cyclamen-scented ruined streets. The marvellous paintings of Australia done by Tom Roberts, Conder, Streeton and the Boyds. Drysdale desert scenes. It is too beautiful for words. The Australians take it for granted and we don't know about it.'

The four-part series which Julian Jebb directed was a collaboration between the BBC and ABC and was called *Betjeman in Australia*. He had arrived ahead of JB and EC and was ecstatic about the country. *The Land of the Golden Fleece*, *Pomp and Circumstance*, *Landmarks*, and *Tasmania: Still Partly Unexplored* were first screened in 1972.

To Candida Lycett Green   A[ustralian] B[roadcasting] C[orporation]
                          145–149 Elizabeth Street
                          Sydney
9 October 1971   Australia

Darling Wibz,

Hope you can read this, don't try too hard. Julian [Jebb] and Eliz[abeth] and Margaret McCall and I have a lot of laughs. We are now in a sort of Montego Bay of N[orth] Queensland, palms and sand and coloured fish and snakes and wallabies and kookaburras and koala bears and endless beer and Aussie wine – fatal at midday. The heat is unbearable, [illegible], the houses are like Trebetherick if it had tin roofs and every garden is bright with jacaranda, bougainvillaea, camellia, magnolia, pear and eucalyptus. Red, purple and pink prevail over here. The sea is grey and polluted-looking and huge things called sting wasps with tentacles as long as cricket pitches kill the surf bathers. They are worse than funnel-web spiders and [illegible words] spiders. The order of good architecture of [the] nineteenth century is banks, post offices, custom houses and government buildings, the churches, and there is nothing else in the way of country houses to compare with ours. Tazzie is better for houses. It is primarily an urban place with people wandering away from the vast desert and sheep and wild animals outside. The abo[rigine]s are silent, dignified and quite numerous but they see with their ears and they are alert to sounds but not to sights. Love to Rupert and the kiddiz and Jean and all chums.

Lots of love, MD

To Candida Lycett Green   Brisbane
                                                            Queensland
14 October 1971   Australia

My darling Wibz,
Hope all is okay. I have huge mosquito bites. We've been doing a lot of filming in tropic islands off Cairns and Townsville.
I saw a cassowary. Horned head. Black beak.
Huge eyes. Black and blue feathers. Ten foot high.
Terrifying. Julian talks to the Aussie crew in Aussie.
They don't seem to mind and think he's married.

Saw a spider four inches long in a private house 'toilet' (a v[ery] dainty toilet) and filmed it.
God knows whether these films will ever have any shape or mean anything. Eliz[abeth] is invaluable in keeping me calm and covering over the unfortunate impressions we make and the offence we give to Governors and authorities. It is hellish expensive in Sydney, less so in Q[ueens]land.

Hope the kiddiz and Rupert are okay. Tell Rupert the Aussies are very dressy indeed but Bangkok (Thailand) is the place for shirts and ties and suits. I'll write from Sydney when I've found my letters.

Tons of love, MD

To Candida Lycett Green   GPO Box 487
                                                   Sydney
17 October 1971   Australia

My darling Wibz,
Oh, I *did* enjoy your letter about the K[enneth] Clark event. After the trials and mosquitoes of Q[ueens]land, I am feeling better and less full of self-pity. I saw Reggie Ross-Williamson's widow Eileen last night. Her flat here has the best Pipers ever – a Church in North[ampton]-s[hire] and a Welsh mountain, really great – as you [?know] the R[oss]-W[illiamses] were great friends of Osbert and Kareen [Lancaster] and the Pipers and Reggie succeeded me as [Press] Attaché in Dublin. Mummy left Powlie in Eileen's charge when P[owlie] was four. He said at breakfast, 'Pass the shugger, you silly boogger.' 'I don't think that's a very nice word to use, Powlie.' 'Yes, it is. It's the loovliest word there is and God looves it.' The Irish always get their U's that way round: 'shugger' for 'sugar' and 'boos' for 'bus'.

Today I've got to film an ultra-modern house with glass walls in a jungle suburb. All the pictures are mobiles and so are the kiddiz' toys. You can't tell one from t'other. I *think* I can make myself like it. On Sunday next we film the State Cinema here in full colour – it is Mexican-Jacobean with a picture gallery and a monkish parlour and melodious organ – tiptop 1927. On Oct[ober] 28th we fly to Melbourne.

Julian [Jebb] is v[ery] funny. We are too busy to drink. The Aussie men are v[ery] nice indeed and v[ery] funny and young and take Julian in their stride as one of them. They regard me as dotty and professional (I hope). N[ew] S[outh] W[ales] is *twice* as expensive even as Britain. But I think it is a country I could live and die in. Seton Gordon (do you remember him – ninety-ish on the Scottish islands cruise?) lives in Queensland with his daughter and I have been in touch. St Kilda and N[orth] Queensland – a long hop.

Love to Rupert, the kiddiz and Jean. A v[ery] funny p[ost]c[ard]
from you came from Julian. Mummy should be back late Oct[ober].
My love to her. I'll write to her at the Mead from Melbourne.
  Tons of love, MD

> Kenneth and Jane Clark had been to dinner with Rupert and me at Chepstow Villas and
> Jane had got very drunk and fallen over.

To Mary Wilson   Sydney
17 October 1971

My dear Mary,
I was so happy to get your letter. It cheered me and made me miss you
and our quiet talks and laughs very much.
  We have moved into a flat overlooking Sydney harbour. Very
beautiful but very hot and noisy kiddiz on the same floor. Queensland
was TERRIFIC. How very good Alan Moorehead is on Captain Cook in
the Pacific with *Fatal Impact*, The Whites should never have come here.
There's not such a thing as progress. Better a trodden path from hut to
hut and the rattlesnake bites cured by a witch-doctor.
  If I were young, I *think* I would settle out here. People are all so nice
to each other. I can't get over it. I'm not of any consequence here and
they're nice to me too even though I'm a 'Pom'. Queensland is
particularly uncompetitive and peaceful. Not so quiet as Sydney.
Kenneth Slessor is a good poet. Just died, alas. It's local of course, as
much good poetry is. I don't think that matters. I have a feeling you
may be putting pen to poetry again. Don't bother about publication or
publishers. Write for yourself and those who love you and to hell with
the rest.
  I haven't seen an English paper since I arrived and know nothing of
elections. The papers here hardly mention English affairs. Mostly it's
the USA, Japan and China and still more they're sport. That blasted
Melbourne Cup next week and we'll leave Melbourne for it.
  Hope Giles is okay. Kiss Joy for me. Shake hands with Leader and
much love to you.
  Love, JB

To Mary Wilson   Port Arthur
10 November 1971   Tasmania

My dear Mary,
In an odd way this terrifying Tasman Peninsula is like Cornwall –
gorse, lilies, and the difference is the glorious gum trees brown in the
rich greenness.
    The latent sadism in the human race: Port Arthur is the Belsen and
Buchenwald of the 1830s – the English this time, but most unusually,
the Irish doing the floggings and tortures. *For the Term of His Natural Life*
by Marcus Clarke is a melodramatic classic about the prison life here
and on Norfolk Island. Tourism has contributed its little offering –
where men were flogged to death, and others turned cannibal, you can
buy little model prisons as keyrings. It is horrible. We are filming it,
and it's not for me to turn moralist but I *hate* the place and Tazzie
generally – brutal in the South, [?smug] in the North. The cheap
labour of the convicts produced some good architecture (Georgian). I
return (D[eo] V[olente]) by about November 30th and shall ring you
up. I see a little about the Leader in the paper (to whom best wishes) but
more news about the bloody IRA.
    I think it is worth coming to Tasmania for its natural beauty and the
flowers and sandstone and long white surfy waves and tree-clad points
and peninsulas. Forgive my handwriting. Over-work or some paralysis
of the hands seems to have done it in. Too much dictating in the past.
    I long to ring you up which I will do on my return. One is a wreck for
a day or two after these long flights. Andrew Lang wrote one or two
good poems.
    Much love, dear Mary, John

To James and Alvilde Lees-Milne   Treen
                                                                   Trebetherick
12 December 1971   Wadebridge

My dear Jim and Alvilde,

THE ARTHURS OF UPPER CANADA

I found myself making a film about them in Tazzie [Tasmania]. I am
proud I know their relations. Of course in Tazzie, Governor Arthur is

made out the wickedest man who ever lived. He certainly did authorise the abo[rigine] hunt so that there are no aborigines left in Tasmania though there are some in Aussie land. He came to bring order to the Penal Settlement, and Port Arthur which we've filmed is named after him. What had happened was that the garrison at Hobart – which was meant to have the recidivist prisoners sent from N[ew] S[outh] W[ales] – had grown slack, and no-one's life was safe in Tasmania. So Arthur was sent to bring order back and founded Port Arthur on a remote peninsula unreachable and guarded by wild dogs, and many a felon was lashed to death in what might have been (for those days) a model penal settlement. Arthur brought *order* to Tazzie but was recalled to Upper Canada. Is there a life of him? It would be worth writing. I think he may be much maligned. No portraits are sold of him to tourists. He is a mystery. So is Butterfield. I think the [Paul] Thompson book good in its thorough way. But why 'High Victorian' for Mid-Victorian?

At Port Arthur Feeble saw a spiny-backed anteater but I did not stop to stroke it. She was disappointed, Alvilde, by the Aussie flowers.

ARTHUR FOR EVER!

God bless the Arthurs and Upper Canada! Give them back their baronetcy.

Bungho'ski, John B

> J.L-M.'s aunt was married to an Arthur.
> Paul Thompson's book was on Butterfield.

To Edith and Oliver Garratt   43 Cloth Fair
31 December 1971   London EC1

BACK FROM AUSTRALIA

Cocooned in Time, at this inhuman height
The packaged food tasting of flavoured clay,
We never seem to catch the running day
But travel on in Everlasting Night
With all the sad accoutrements of flight:
Lotions and essences in neat array
And yet another plastic cup and tray.
'Thank you *so* much. Oh no, I'm quite all right.'

Back home in Cornwall, under crimson skies
At lowest tide line where the empty shore
Reflects a sailing cloud in sea-wet sand,
In mid-December quiet I realise
How trivial were the [illegible], the space and roar,
How great the sky is looked at from the land.

For Edith and Oliver, 31 December 1971

Happy New Year. Back in Feb[ruary].

'Back from Australia' was published in *A Nip in the Air* with radical changes.
The second line read, '. . . tastes neutrally of clay'; the fifth, 'With all the chic
accoutrements. . . ';
and the last six lines:

> At home in Cornwall, hurrying autumn skies
> Leave Bray Hill barren, Stepper jutting bare,
> And hold the moon above the sea-wet sand
> The very last of late September dies
> In frosty silence and the hills declare
> How vast the sky is, looked at from the land.

To Harry Jarvis   43 Cloth Fair
8 February 1972   London EC1

Dear Harry,
Ta ever so for your sympathy about my crucifixion, which indeed it
was. I only wish I'd been paid for it, but no, there is no justice. Just wait
a moment while I go and get myself a drink. I have a lot of interesting
things to tell you. Penelope, persuaded by her lawyer and the
accountant, has decided to sell the Mead, while she is 'sound', and to go
away for three months each year. It is impossible to let so large a place
or to keep the vandals out, or pay for the upkeep out of income. She is
thinking about Herefordshire. I am going through trying times about
accommodation here, as they are going to raise my rent, and God
knows to what extent. It is amazing to me that you have been all those
years at dear old New Basford, and now they are crowned with the
Chaplaincy. You are becoming like Canon Mortlock, the mighty late
lamented Pluralist. I had a very nice letter from the Mediterranean
coast somewhere, from Bishop Savage, enclosing his annotated copy of
The Hymmal Companion, presented to him by Father Dodgson Sykes. I
have much to tell you and long to see you. Feeble is very, very weak and
ineffective, and constantly in 'my courts' and in 'my lampshade class'

far too little. I am going to Cornwall from Feb[ruary] 15th to 28th. So if
you come later or earlier, preferably later, so much the better. Harry's
True Resurrection is terrific consolation to
    Yours truly whatever the Theologians say.
    And love to the Smashing Jean and my adorable godchild and her
bro[ther] David and to you.
    John B

> 'The crucifixion' probably refers to some bad publicity.
>   H.J. had become Chaplain to Basford Hospital – which at that time specialised in the
> care of geriatrics and terminal cancer patients.
>   Gordon Savage was Bishop of Buckingham during the early sixties when he
> befriended one of the Astor family during the Christine Keeler and John Profumo affair.
> He then became Bishop of Southwell but had to resign because the press hounded him
> about an affair with a Bunny Girl. They went to live in Tenerife and had a child. He was
> a delightful man and very kind to H.J. and JB.
>   Elizabeth was a magistrate and on her working days JB referred to her being in 'my
> courts'.

To Charles Monteith   43 Cloth Fair
17 February 1972   London EC1

My dear Charles,
A friend and I over the last few months have read out loud to each other
the entire poetical works of W. E. Henley and have marked the poems
according to merit. Apart from the three well-known anthology pieces,
'England my England', 'Margaritae Sorori' and 'Invictus', there are
about twenty pieces worth printing. The Hospital poems are the best
section. I think unless they are reprinted Henley will be forgotten. So
too will some other poets who have never been seen to any extent
because they were not in the recognised Oxford, Macmillan and
Routledge editions – I mean such men as Lionel Johnson, Isaac Watts
and Lewis Stevenson, as I prefer to call R[obert] L[ouis] S[tevenson],
and John Gay. Then there are poets who wrote such a hell of a lot,
much of it bad, that they deserve a selection. I think of Southey,
Longfellow, and for all I know Ralph Waldo Emerson. I feel that there
is a public need for paper-bound bookstall poetry, printed in large type
and not more than thirty poems at a time and two pages of biography. I
don't know whether it is so with you, but I find it with a lot of people I
meet, that they want poets now rather than anthologies. I have always
wanted this. In order to make poetry readable it must be well printed
and well leaded. The Penguin books are too dreary in paper and inking.

The last really good things were those Augustan poets which Benn published in the late twenties. David Cecil and I would like to do this series, if it would help you to come to a conclusion. I would like to see the typography by Will and Sebastian Carter or their like. I would like to start off with Henley and if you give me the word I will send you the marked copies [which] my friend Mrs Geddes and I have read. *Virtute, Studio, Ludis*. It is a pity Henley was such a brute to Oscar [Wilde].

    Yours, John Betjeman

> C.M., the well-known editor at Faber and Faber, had commissioned JB to edit Henley's poems for one of a proposed series of volumes called *A Choice of* . . ., which was to include selections from many English poets. W. E. Henley (1849–1903) was by now a forgotten poet who wrote much patriotic verse such as 'For England's Sake': 'Ever the faith endures, England, my England: Take and break us, we are yours, England my own.' Mary Wilson and JB had trawled the poems of Henley for the selection, which was never published. JB was also helped by Margie Geddes, a close friend whose brother he had known since his schoolmastering days.

To Philip Larkin   43 Cloth Fair
21 March 1972   London EC1

Dear Philip,
You don't know what joy the latest lot of poems of yours have brought down on the old aesthete who signs the bottom of this letter. Perhaps the most beautiful is 'Livings', the most alarming 'Posterity' and the most memorable to yours truly 'To the Sea'. They are all like you, sparing, uplifting, searing and not a word wasted. You are a clever old thing and I only hope I can do them justice with my fruity voice in some astringent hall which Patrick [Garland] chooses from among the auditoria of the metropolis. Meanwhile may the Humber slide safely between its banks and curl round at Spern Head to meet the open sea and look back in its last gasp as it meets the source at the University which has the pleasure of you as its librarian. The 'Common Room' piece is a winner.

    Yours, John B

> P.L. had sent some of his unpublished poems to JB including 'Livings' (written October to December 1971), 'To the Sea' (written in October 1969) and 'Posterity' (written in 1968) which later came out in his volume of poems *High Windows* (1974).
>   Patrick Garland was planning to direct a reading of Larkin's poetry by JB and Michael Hordern at the Royal Court Theatre for Alan Bennett's BBC television series *On the Margin*.

To Constance and Stephen Lycett Green   43 Cloth Fair
June 1972   London EC1

Dear Con and Stephen,
How proud and happy am I to have the Lycett Green family connected
with me e'en though I am only in it by marriage of my daughter to
Rupert. Long may the sun lighten those yellowing oaks, spreading
sycamores and copper beeches. Long may the waders cheep on the
wide shore and the pines add darkness to the many-coloured fore-
ground to its plain as viewed from J. J. Stevenson's MASTERPIECE, for
such it is. And why this highfalutin' and illegible prose? Because I am
still under the spell of Ken Hill. It is even more beautiful than Candida
had said and I am glad I saw it in such brilliant light. I felt really happy
and welcomed and I have returned to London *refreshed*, contented in
body and mind. You are the most thoughtful and generous of hosts.
Lady S[trickland] said Billa [Harrod] would be furious that I hadn't let
her know I was staying at Ken Hill. I said it was no business of Billa's as
I was miles away from Holt. We had a harmonious and swift journey
back through spacious CHATTERIS and lots of country like this in

HUNTINGDONSHIRE humming with aeroplanes and we all had tea and
cakes at GUMSTER [Godmanchester]
and sat by the WINDING OUSE in
the sunlight. I still see in my mind's
eye the elegant profile of those
chimney stacks by J. J. Stevenson
and his theme was re-echoed in
the mouldings in my bedroom.

The children behaved
v[ery] well on the
journey home and
were congratulated
by their pa and ma.
They will miss
Edward [Lycett
Green] and we all
of us miss Ken Hill and I renew my thanks. I long to meet you both
again.

    Yours, John B

> JB had been to stay at Ken Hill, Snettisham, Norfolk with Rupert's first cousin S.L.G.
> and his wife Constance. The spectacular house built by the Lycett Greens as a glorified
> shooting lodge, conveniently near Edward VII at Sandringham, was designed by J. J.
> Stevenson, with especially commissioned furniture and paintings of the time. Stephen
> L. G. recalls, 'We all went for a visit to the beach. It was dead low tide and about a
> quarter of a mile of black wash mud separated us from low water. Your father insisted on
> walking across it to the sea, where he fell down. Rupert raced across the mud to pick him
> up. On Sunday, he was insistent on going to church. We rigged him out in an old coat of
> mine, which hung down to his ankles, crowned by an old shooting cap. He refused to be
> taken by car. The congregation rapidly identified him and Barbara Strickland carried
> him off to the Old Hall and brought him back here for his lunch.'
>   Billa Harrod, Barbara Strickland's daughter, had been brought up at the Old Hall at
> Snettisham and had been an early girlfriend of Stephen L.G.'s.

To John Murray
8 June 1972

43 Cloth Fair
London EC1

Dear Jock,

I *v[ery]* much *like* the layout and photographs in the *R[ai]l[wa]y Station*
book. I dread the notices of it and of the *Architecture* book. I ought to
give both books to John Edward Bowle, 24 Woodstock Close, Oxford.
Will you do so? Charge to me of course. I return to London Sunday.

    I wonder where P[enelope] and I will land? It will be odd not living in
Berkshire any more. I will miss Wantage, but not the expense.
P[enelope] seems less tied to places than I am. Yet I would not be in
Berkshire without her being with me. It would seem empty. She does
not lack personality!

    I have written to John G[ay] to congratulate him on *R[ai]l[wa]y
Stations.*

Anne and Osbert must be given my book at my expense. Very many
cheers for your kindness and forbearance with
Yours, John B

London's Historic Railway Stations, with photographs by John Gay, which came out later
that year, and also *A Pictorial History of English Architecture*, were both compilations of
JB's *Weekend Telegraph* articles. They were well received by the press.

To Colonel G. A. L. Chetwynd-Talbot   43 Cloth Fair
13 June 1972   London EC1

Dear Colonel Chetwynd-Talbot,
I have been asked by my friend Terence Stamp to supply you with a
reference for him. I can assure you that he is honourable, quiet, sober
and a keen vegetarian. In addition to this he is honest, good company
and entertaining as well as a most distinguished actor.
    Yours sincerely, John Betjeman

G.C.-T. was the secretary of Albany, Piccadilly, an exclusive collection of apartments.
Getting on to the list for a 'set' of rooms there is more difficult than entering Fort Knox.
Terence Stamp's application was successful and he still lives there.

To John Edward Bowle   43 Cloth Fair
4 July 1972   London EC1

Dear John Edward,
I am typing this because my writing has collapsed, and I can only do my
signature. I am told it is a form of nervous prostration, but I must say I
feel very calm. You are very generous about my books, you always are,
and I am most grateful. But the last two are really newspaper articles
dished up by the publishers to look like complete books. The *Railway
Stations* one I enjoyed writing, the other one was a heavy task, and it
made me appreciate still more your own skill in being both informative
and readable. Most of all it made me appreciate how balanced your
work is.
    This is the first day on which the Tibetans enter into ownership of
the Mead. Our furniture and household effects are with the Barings at
Ardington House. Penelope's papers and books and photographs are at
All Souls under care of Hanbury [John Sparrow] and my books are

here. Penelope goes to India in January for six months to make a film
with Jonathan Stedall. We are looking for a smaller cottage and
Penelope has her eye on one in Herefordshire, but there is no water.
Something will turn up, it always does. We don't want more than three
bedrooms, sitting room, dining room and kitchen, hot water and quiet.
I find I am more distressed at leaving Berkshire than I thought I was
going to be. For I had a long apprenticeship of estrangement in
Penelope's absence.

   Yours, John B

> PB sold the Mead to a Tibetan family whom she deemed suitable as safeguarders of rural
> Wantage. She turned down several higher offers.
>   PB's film *One Pair of Eyes*, directed by Jonathan Stedall, was screened in 1973.

To Mary Wilson
19 July 1972

   On Leaving Wantage, July 1972

   I like the way these old brick garden walls
   Unevenly run down to Letcombe Brook.
   I like the mist of green about the elms
   In early April. More intensely green
   The duck weed undulates; a mud-grey trout
   Hovers and darts away at my approach.
      From rumpled beds on far-off new estates,
   From houses over shops along the square,
   From red-brick villas somewhat further out,
   Ringers arrive, converging on the tower.
      Third Sunday after Easter. Public ways
   Reek faintly yet of last night's fish and chips,
   The plumes of smoke from various chimney pots
   Denote the death of last week's *Sunday Press*,
   While this week's waits on many a step and sill
   Unopened, folded, supplements and all.
      Suddenly on the unsuspecting air
   The bells clash out. It seems a miracle
   That leaf and flower should never even stir
   In such great waves of mediaeval sound;
   They ripple over roofs to fields and farms
   So that 'the fellowship of Christ's religion'
   Is roused to breakfast, church or sleep again.

> From this wide vale, where all our married lives
> We two have lived, we now are whirled away
> Momently clinging to the things we knew –
> Friends, foot-paths, hedges, houses, animals –
> Till, borne along like twigs and bits of straw
> We disappear below the sliding stream.

For Mary.
   Love from John

The poem was published in *A Nip in the Air*.
   In the fourth line, 'In early April' became 'In earliest leaftime'; in the thirteenth line, 'various' became 'upright'; and in the last line 'disappear' became 'sink' and 'of time' was added after 'stream'.

Nine:
Clear air, wide skies

1972 to 1976

Fetlar is waiting. At its little quay
   Green seaweed stirs and ripples on the swell.
   The lone sham castle looks across at Yell,
And from the mainland hilltops you can see
Over to westward, glimmering distantly,
   The cliffs of Foula as the clouds dispel.
   Clear air, wide skies, crunch underfoot of shell –
The Viking kingdom waits what is to be.

                            'Shetland 1973'

'Oddly enough I really did not mind leaving the Mead at all,' my mother wrote to JB from India (10 August 1971). 'As Mrs Folky [Sybil Harton] said, "It has outlived its purpose," and as such a nice young family has succeeded us, *I feel it is all to the good* as it is essentially a family home and should have children, ponies and perhaps yaks running about.'[1] (The Tibetan family who had bought the house and whom my mother deemed perfect new owners promptly sold it on for a large profit). Meanwhile, the furniture went into store at the Barings' house in Ardington and my mother went to stay in Portugal with Michael and Nicole Hornby. It was an odd time. Neither of my parents was settled anywhere. JB wrote to my mother, 'I feel very lost without any news of you or of Wibz or of Paul.'[2] He took refuge at Treen in Cornwall with Elizabeth, surrounded by his Trebetherick friends.

    On 10 October 1972 JB received a telephone call from Buckingham Palace and the next day the *Daily Telegraph* reported, 'Sir John Betjeman, 66, author, poet and formidable enemy of developers, was yesterday appointed Poet Laureate in succession to Cecil Day-Lewis who died in May aged 68.' The press and television descended on Treen. While he was still in his dressing-gown, he told them, 'I don't think I am any good and if I thought I was any good I wouldn't be any good. I don't watch much television, except for *Coronation Street* and Alf Garnett who is outrageous but I am going to watch myself tonight on television. We are going to have a grand celebration with all my childhood friends at the home of Mrs David, the widow of the Bishop of Liverpool who was formerly Headmaster of Rugby. She has a colour television set.'

Philip Larkin wrote in the *Sunday Telegraph*, 'In a sense Betjeman was Poet Laureate already: he outsells the rest (without being required reading in the Universities), and his audience overflows the poetry reading public to take in the Housman-*Omar Khayyám* belt, people who, so to speak, like a rattling good poem. In this he is like Kipling, and if Betjeman had not been appointed the two of them would have gone down the ages as the two unofficial Poets Laureate of the twentieth century. Lucky old England to have him.'[3]

The letters, nearly six thousand of them, flooded in. To many JB replied, 'I consider myself very lucky in having caught the public attention with poetry. *It is luck* and pride comes before a fall.'[4] 'Dear Mr Betcheman,' wrote Richard Finch, signing himself 'a secret Cockney admirer', in a congratulatory letter, 'I doubt if you will recall me by my name, I spent a night at your house in Wantage after taking you to Salisbury in General Grand's car in 1954. I was then gardener/chauffeur for the latter. I am now back living in the East End, not by choice, and you will be surprised that I am a natural born Spiritual Healer and have many successes to date. Please don't misunderstand me, I am not advertising.'[5] Letters came from bell-ringers, hermits and would-be poets. Helen Arlington, the Buddhist Poet Laureate, wrote from America, 'May your reign in this role be an inspiration for contemporary poets around the world, Mudita (Sanskrit for the joy of others).' 'At least you'll not be Austin-tatious,' wrote Henry Anglesey. 'Shirley and I have enjoyed our breakfast more than usual. We have read aloud to one another your "Press". Has *any* poet ever had a better one?' Scores of would-be poets wrote, like Marguerite Allan: 'I am a war widow of seventy, I am glad to see you have become Laureate. I have written thirty poems and I am just trying to get them known and published. I have sent them off to the *Lady*. I hope you can help me, I am having to sell my house here in Romney Marsh. I wish I could join you in Cornwall.' Poems were sent from far and wide. Jack Barlow of the BBC wrote:

> 'The dust motes in the light beam show him still
> Against the ghostly slope of White Horse Hill . . .
> Our Jovial John, Our Betch British,
> Our Portly Poet, Our Laureate Skittish.'

Harold Acton wrote from Florence, 'This report has given me the greatest pleasure in a blank and barren period. Heartiest congratulations! I rejoice to think that your muse will be refreshed and invigorated by such an honour.' 'Blow up the trumpet in the new moon and thank you for winning my bet,' read Basil Blackwell's telegram. A Mr Budd wrote from Hampshire, 'Long may you prosper in your love and interest in old things. I am a butler here at Breamore, where there is much old around us but due to two fires, one in 1656 and another in 1850, much was lost, but the new must grow old again.' The Marlburian Club sent a poem:

> 'Our dear Sir John now summoned by a regal bell
> To celebrate and fight the cause you love so well,
> To hound and harry those who, wilful, desecrate
> Our land; our son, we praise you, POET LAUREATE.'

Chris Williams, a nine-year-old from Monmouth Boys' Prep School, wrote, 'We are looking out for some of your poems on cricket as we have two teams at school. I am in the first XI. Last year some boys wrote some quite good poetry but it was not as good as yours.' Cyril Cusack, the actor and friend from Dublin days, sent a telegram, 'About time too, your people knew that forests walked and fishes flew. Hearty congratulations.' But among the waves of pleasure, pride and honour came dreaded truths. Arthur Eden FRIBA wrote from Harpenden, 'I don't know whether I ought to congratulate you or commiserate with you on your appointment as Poet Laureate. After all it's not like being made a Lord – you've got a job to do, and not an easy one at that, writing odes "On Entering the Common Market" or laments for "The Demise of Queen Anne's Mansions".'

After the euphoria the gloom took hold. There is no doubt that the onerous task JB thought he had taken on, made him physically ill. He and my mother, Rupert and I had all spent the Christmas of 1972 together with John and Tory Oaksey in their Wiltshire farmhouse. We certainly never stopped laughing but my mother, who had not seen JB for a bit, voiced her unhappiness to me about his health. It worried her so much that she immediately wrote to Elizabeth, 'I am writing to you to see if we cannot work something out for John whereby we take it in turns to look after him? He was in a really bad state at Christmas, worse than I have ever known him and really pathetic with his loss of balance, etc. . . . . I spoke to Jackie [JB's secretary] who for the first time opened her heart to me. I have naturally avoided discussing John's condition before and she said she had to give in her notice as she could not take it any longer. . . . I expect you are having an equally trying time? I never thought it would really help his condition to become Poet Laureate: twenty years ago, yes, had Masefield died sooner, but now that he has reached the age of retirement it means that he can NEVER retire and relax completely, but must always have this yoke about his neck. And the correspondence it has involved him in has been enough to finish off anybody. I fear it is going to take at least a year to get the new wing built on to this tiny cottage. I am having a sound-proof bedroom built for him with a writing table in it so that he won't rave about the occasional cars which go by! But until that is ready I do not suppose he will come down much, as with his loss of balance trouble he finds the stairs very difficult to negotiate. But I can always come up to London now he has got the ground floor of number 43 and look after him there. . . . Naturally I was jealous when he first got fond of you, many years ago now. But over the years I have realised that from HIS point of view at any rate it has been a wonderful thing for him, as you are literary and I am not really, and you have provided the sort of companionship he needs and never really gets from me. I simply cannot get him to slow down now, can you? I mean I suggested, and Jock Murray thought it an excellent idea, that when he reached retiring age he should put a notice in the papers saying he could no longer afford a secretary and could therefore answer no more letters except from personal friends. Correspondence is KILLING him. And he should give up all, or nearly all, committee work so that he can have more time to relax and read. But WHO CAN MAKE HIM?? He has recently gone on to the board of governors of the King Edward's School in Oxford. WHY? Why give himself one more completely unnecessary chore at his age? Is there NO-ONE who can persuade him to cut down to what really interests him and to hell with the rest? Obviously he LOVES his television films and will enjoy going on with them for as long as his health lets him, but so much of his public work really could be given up now that he has reached sixty-five.'[6] Elizabeth replied, saying how touched she was at such a generous and nice letter and commiserated with my mother about her concern over JB. She suggested that my mother get in touch with his doctor, John Allison, who had told Elizabeth that JB had a prematurely early failing of his leg muscles which was not at that stage thought to be a disease. He had already told JB off for working too hard and had ordered him to rest each day. Nonetheless my mother was worried about going to India again lest JB's condition should worsen. But Elizabeth gently suggested she should and said that she could cope. JB wrote to my mother in India in February 1973, 'I am quite all right, do not worry about me. E[lizabeth] has bought a house in her street and I have given notice for 43. I have severely cut down my work and have got a part-time secretary called Mrs Mountain.'[7]

In April JB moved to 29 Radnor Walk, which Elizabeth had bought and let to him. It was a few doors down from her own house at number 19. In May, Paul Paget his erstwhile landlord wrote, 'Following your move from Cloth Fair several of what we believe are your possessions seem to have been found in various temporary resting places. 1. Your CBE citation. 2. A Great Western Railway level crossing sign. 3. A book of plates of Burges's Tower House. 4. A scrapbook compiled by a Victorian architect. 5. A book on Danish houses (in Danish). 6. A book on art nouveau, in German. 7. A photograph of Cork Cathedral. 8. A number of appointments diaries. . . . Possibly some are unwanted and if you tell us we can throw them away with a clear conscience.'[8]

JB told his friends that he had been driven out of the City by the noise of 'Arctic' lorries at dawn. This was true in a way but he also needed looking after. Not unnaturally, the gossip columnist William Hickey of the *Daily Express* had a field day. Though JB and Elizabeth had been constant companions since the early fifties, and all the press knew, their privacy had been respected until now – an almost unprecedented privilege. In the end the *Express* could no longer hold out and printed a story under the headline, 'Old friend Lady Elizabeth comforts Betjeman'.[9] JB wrote to my mother, 'I did not like all that probing and prying in the *Express*, I felt very sorry for you, what business is it of theirs, fuck them. It is absolutely lovely here in London in August because the dog messes on the pavement dry up much quicker. I laugh a lot when I think about your labour camp but what the *Sunday Express* *ought* to have said was that you are a very distinguished Indologist in your own right which is what you have always wanted to be and it has only recently been broken to me by John Allison, my doctor, and by Elizabeth that I had to be moved here last year because I was not fit to be left alone in the City with no-one else in the house. I am really very much better now but will never be able to walk fast and far or keep up with the grandkiddiz. But you will be doing that as you are a much better person in all respects than yours truly.'[10]

My mother replied to his letter from New House (which JB always called 'Little Redoubt' just as he always referred to Hay-on-Wye as 'Kulu-on-Wye'), 'You need not worry AT ALL. I am blissfully happy up here in the LR.'[11] She was busy creating a new house where she could have her grandchildren to stay, preferably one at a time so that she could give them her complete attention. She taught them all to ride and took them for fifteen-mile treks across the mountains on woolly Welsh ponies which she had broken in herself. 'It is simply beautiful up here,' she told JB. 'It is like a much lovelier part of the Downs than

Farnborough.' JB replied, 'I love you very much though I am quite happy in my little Bijou Chelsea slum.'[12]

Despite the doctor's orders, JB did not ease off on his work. Guilt drove him along as always. The Laureateship had been created in 1670 and had then involved receiving 'two hundred pounds and also a butt or pipe of the best yearly canary'. The salary had varied over the years and the payment by drink fell into abeyance. JB asked for the gift of wine to be reinstated and subsequently received an annual present of wine from the Queen's wine merchant in addition to a token stipend of two hundred and fifty pounds. Apart from this the job brought nothing but extra work and an enormous feeling that something was expected of him which he couldn't produce. He was utterly uninspired by pomp and circumstance, and although he was extremely fond of his friends Princess Margaret and the Queen Mother, he found it hard to write poems about Royal occasions. He was inspired by the notion of following in the footsteps of the greatest of his poetic heroes, Alfred Tennyson, but as for what went with this accolade, it was the stuff of nightmares. The first poem he was expected to write was about Princess Anne's wedding. For him, it was like getting blood out of a stone, and the series of verses that were to follow were hardly a poem. He sent his offering to Patrick Plunket, the Queen's private secretary, telling him that 'the lines were composed last night on the Pullman from Manchester to London after four double Scotches slowly consumed . . . Perhaps in the cold light of tomorrow they will seem unworthy. . . . I have kept horses out of them and I would like to think they are not too much like a Christmas card verse.'[13]

On 27 October 1973, during a wake following W. H. Auden's memorial service in Oxford, JB told Philip Larkin that he wanted to pack in the Laureateship. He became so worried about it that in the end his doctor decided to take action. He rang up Rennie Maudslay, an old patient of his, who was Keeper of the Privy Purse and asked him to ask the Queen to speak to JB. She confirmed to him that it was indeed not a *duty* to write something every time there was a Royal occasion. But somehow the *public* expected it of him – and it was the public to whom JB felt he owed something. After all, it was they who had supported him over the years. 'I think you should write a poem in lament for the Arrow,' wrote George Behrend from Jersey. 'I am preparing for a centenary book on the Wagons-Lits.'[14] Though he managed to avoid such far-fetched requests, JB did in fact write several more poems on more heartfelt themes.

He was inspired to write 'The Mistress' by a woman he had seen

across the aisle from him during a church service. After moving to
Radnor Walk JB and Elizabeth worshipped regularly at the Grosvenor
Chapel in South Audley Street where the priest in charge was the
Reverend John Gaskell. He remembered, 'John and Elizabeth always
sat on the left-hand side and John would gaze round at various members
of the congregation to whom he gave nicknames. There was "the
Parrot", a lady with a beaky nose and feather hat; "Venetia", who had
a creamy complexion and black hair; and "the Mistress", a regular
worshipper who John never spoke to but always admired.'[15] She was in
fact a well-known beauty writer called Joan Price, married to the
Grosvenor Chapel Sidesman, Michael Constantinidis. JB's poem about
her, 'The Mistress', was published in the *Daily Express*:

> Isn't she lovely, the mistress,
> With her wide apart grey green eyes.
> And her drooping lips and when she smiles
> The glance of amused surprise . . .

JB wrote in the *Express*, 'She was the most beautiful creature; she had a
slightly sad expression, and I didn't even know her name – but it was
probably all the better for that . . . I like there to be a mystery between
me and my beloved, and I don't think there was anything wrong with
looking at her in church. I don't think there's anything wrong with
loving the beauty of the human figure whether it's in the church or in
the street. I'm not in sympathy with people who think that anything to
do with physical good looks is not being profound or deep, or who think
it's wicked to think about what people look like when they go to church:
as if you couldn't really love someone unless she was a State Registered
Nurse.'[16] In their next issue, *Private Eye* published a riposte by 'the
Poet Laureate Sir John Thribb':

> Lovely lady in the pew,
> Goodness, what a scorcher – phew!
> What I wouldn't give to do
> Unmentionable things to you.
>
> If old God is still up there
> I'm sure he wouldn't really care.
> I'm sure he'd say, 'A little lech
> Never really harmed old Betj.'[17]

Composing his official poems, of which he wrote only a few, continued
to be a nightmare. Lyman Andrews, reviewing *A Nip in the Air*, JB's

new collection of poetry, wrote, 'The best of his writing has always been concerned with man's foibles. . . . with what is sometimes private, sometimes poignant in our existence. . . . I can't help feeling the poet is constricted by the Poet Laureate.'[18] JB was easily wounded and could not, like my mother, rise above hostile criticism. She wrote to him after a particularly nasty review, 'You have fulfilled your vocation far more fully than the great majority of people. You have given your best involving a tremendous amount of hard work. GOD DOES NOT EXPECT ANY MORE OF ANYONE. You will go on serving Him till your dying day and whether silly critics say you are a major or a minor poet does not matter at all. Archie says you are suffering from pride and I think he is quite right.'[19]

Gone were the days when he had found it easy to write poetry. He replied to a Mr Ellman, a would-be poet and fan, 'I was much enamoured of Alfred Lord Tennyson's sonnets when a boy at Marlborough and still have many of them by heart. In those happy Uffington days it was always quite easy to make up a correct Petrarchan sonnet straight out of one's head retaining the rhyming scheme a,b,b,a; a,b,b,a; c,d,e; c,d,e. Wystan [Auden] certainly could do it.'[20] JB never lost his memory. He could spout other people's poetry till the cows came home. (Barry Humphries remembers several years on, when JB was ill and silent for long periods, 'We were sitting at supper in Radnor Walk with Elizabeth and someone said, "Is Kipling *really* any good?" "By jove, yes!" JB suddenly said and then proceeded to recite the whole of "Gunga Din". He never faltered. He was word perfect.')

JB had dedicated *A Nip in the Air* to his three granddaughters, Lucy, Imogen and Endellion. In 1973 we moved from Chepstow Villas to Blacklands in Wiltshire and so saw less of him. Instead of two or three times a week, I now only saw him on a fortnightly visit to London. He came to stay, sometimes when my mother was staying as well and always for Christmas. Those were the happiest times. His grand-children put on quite an elaborate show of sketches and songs which, as they got older, became gradually more sophisticated. JB wrote after the first Wiltshire Christmas (30 December), 'I can't forget Delli's rapturous, thrilling singing in the hall. The spreading meadow and limestone on one side, the hump of downland on the other. . . . Your well-organised work greatly impressed the lazy, self-pitying, fat, bald, old reprobate who signs himself your old dad.'[21]

The Uffington and Wantage roots were gradually being pulled up but JB still kept up with Mollie and Desmond Baring as though nothing had changed. Peter Baring, their eldest son, married a girl from the nearby village of Fernham in the heart of Old Berks hunting country. JB wrote (25 July 1973), 'What a marvellous wedding. A swansong of the Berkshire Penelope and I knew when we first married and lived in Uffington. . . . I am v[ery] glad that Peter is married to that golden Adams girl. It keeps everything Old Berks.'[22]

JB's England had always been divided into hundreds of areas, each with a fiercely different regional character. That is why he minded so much about the dilution of that rich diversity through the standardised building materials being used on new developments all over the land. 'Old Berks' country could still hold its own, as could Southend-on-Sea with its cockle stalls, which never lost its air of frivolity or its East End holiday atmosphere. JB came to love visiting Southend, sometimes by boat but mostly on the train from Fenchurch Street station. 'I am one of the millions who have used Southend Pier as the nearest place to London for real sea air, recreation and complete change of scene,' he wrote to *The Times* (20 February 1974). 'It is easy to reach by train from London. In winter or summer the pier is a delight, with its tramway, once a toast-rack type, running for a mile and a third into a wide prospect of sea and sky. There is all the advantage at the end of the pier of being right out to sea and no feeling of seasickness.'[23] The future of the pier was at that time uncertain.

JB had by this time given up his major committee work, but his crusades on behalf of threatened buildings or areas of England from Crewe to Carlisle continued. One of his hardest fought was for Holy Trinity, Sloane Street, the Arts and Crafts church by J. D. Sedding which in 1974 was due to be demolished by the rector, the landlord and the churchwarden. He started a publicity campaign against this and asked Gavin Stamp to help by illustrating a booklet, *A Plea for Holy Trinity Sloane Street*, for which JB wrote the slogan:

> Bishop, archdeacon, rector, wardens, mayor
> Guardians of Chelsea's noblest house of prayer
> You who your church's vastness so deplore
> 'Should we not sell and give it to the poor?'
> Recall, despite your practical suggestion
> Which the disciple was who asked that question.

There seemed to be no machinery to stop a diocesan bishop from demolishing a church, whatever outside objections might be raised. 'We are told that Holy Trinity, Sloane Street, is going to cost two hundred thousand pounds to put in working condition. . . . It would be worth having this investigated,'[24] he wrote in longhand to the

Minister of the Environment (23 May 1974). There was skulduggery afoot, but the battle was won. Holy Trinity still stands.

JB began to attract like-minded successors to his role as saviour of an indefinable, uncategorisable England. He was not a 'conservationist' nor a setter-in-aspic of just any *old* building; he cherished the feeling of places. Simon Jenkins, the journalist, understood that, and their mutual admiration grew into a close friendship. They would go on endless walks around London together but when JB insisted they go to Heathrow Simon was reluctant. 'The expedition to discover the ancient villages of Heathrow had been hatched some weeks before over an execrable lunch at the Great Eastern Hotel. Betjeman loved eating in unfashionable places, provided only that the wine was good. . . . [He] seemed to relax when surrounded by anonymous businessmen, people who might recognise him but would never accost him. They were besuited and conventional. If they had secrets they kept them in safe places. He shared the comfort they took in faded hotels and familiar food under baroque ceilings. He was delighted when the restaurant at Charing Cross was named after him – though dismayed when they changed the ancient menu. At this time he was still a walker. Our journeys had taken me to Metroland, to Southwark, to Southend and round a portion of the North Circular Road. None possessed so little apparent promise as the lost villages of Heathrow. Yet Betjeman portrayed them as the ultimate antidote to airport blues.'

They went to Harmondsworth where JB had taken me many years before to see one of the wonders of the world. There, within earshot of the fierce roar and only a mile from the main runway, is the greatest timber and tiled barn in all England. When Simon and JB visited it it was still a working farm. They had to climb under a rotten locked door and get up through bales of hay stacked against them. Simon saw through JB's apparent helplessness. 'Betjeman, who declares his incapacity when it suits him, can also display an astonishing agility. He enters the barn like a gymnast. He burrows up through the hay with delight, gasping and cheering as the interior emerges through the gloom. "Oh look, oh look." Vast oak columns rear up from the stone base towards the roof – "Purlins, trusses, collars, wind braces, aisle ties, wall plates." The technical terms pour forth with attendant superlatives. He proudly carries the incriminating hay on his clothes for the rest of the day. He gazes down at it in the car and encants, "Harmondsworth hay, Harmondsworth hay".'[25]

JB may have found official patriotic verse hard to write but he continued, in films, to celebrate the England he loved. He was becoming a past master in the art. He had long harboured the desire to make a film about the beauties of suburbia. Back in 1971 he had persuaded his director, Eddie Mirzoeff, but had to seduce the comptroller of the BBC, Robin Scott. 'It is a rich theme and could be full of praise and stimulation. Most people are suburban and won't admit it. What trim gardens we could show, what shopping arcades, front halls, churches, schools and human-scale paths and bicycle tracks and open spaces. I see it as a thanksgiving for traffic-free privacy throughout Britain – but not Southern Ireland, which isn't surburban, as is yours gratefully and ever, John Betjeman.'[26]

Scott was won over and work began on a film originally called 'Joys of Urban Living'. It appeared under the title of *Metroland* in 1973 and was hailed as JB's greatest film – 'All team-work,' he said, 'all team-work.' He wrote to the comptroller Robin Scott again (20 March 1973), 'I would like in a year's time, if I am still alive, to follow up *Metroland* with another film about people, their architectural surroundings, individuality and eccentricity. I have talked to Eddie Mirzoeff and Edward Roberts, those masters of production and editing, and they have talked to that genius of a cameraman, John McGlashan, who, like me, is very High Church. We would all like to work together again, and have thought it would be fun to make a film of that dim and under-appreciated institution, the Church of England, in the form of a celebration of it.'[27] The resulting film, *A Passion for Churches*, was made with the same team.

JB stayed with Billa Harrod, his old chum and the leading spirit in the campaign to save Norfolk churches, and wrote to her, 'What fun Norfolk is being and who is making it shine for us all? You.'[28] To Mary Wilson he wrote (26 May 1974):

> 'I have been given a silken tongue
> To praise the towers where bells are hung
> The flinty stoned East Anglian towers
> Sparkling with sunlight after showers.'[29]

By the mid-seventies JB was an enormous celebrity. I remember him suggesting, as a way of getting away from all the traffic and pressure, that he would like to be the stationmaster at Blake Hall on the Ongar branch of the underground's Central Line, where there was a lovely wooden Saxon church and he would be able to walk over the fields in springtime to Ongar, where 'Twinkle Twinkle Little Star' was originally written.

On his second go at *Desert Island Discs*, JB chose champagne as his luxury and 'Ducker' sung by the Harrow School Choir as his favourite song. He also chose 'Max at the Met' by Max Miller, 'Let's Do it' sung by Ella Fitzgerald, Douglas Byng singing 'Flora MacDonald' and some classical music by Handel and Bach which he had definitely not chosen himself but which his friend the conductor Raymond Leppard had suggested. He also chose his favourite hymn at that particular moment which was 'There is a Land of Pure Delight' by Isaac Watts. 'I should like the hymn to be sung at my funeral. All the verses are terrific, particularly the last two,'[30] he wrote to Roy Plomley, the programme presenter (5 March 1975).

I am surprised he didn't choose the signature tune of *Coronation Street*, which had become part of his life. He seldom missed an episode. 'Wasn't it awful Albert Tatlock getting beaten up by those soccer fans,'[31] he wrote to me. We conversed weekly about the goings-on. 'It's better than Dickens,' he told Richard Ingrams. Jean Alexander, the actress who played Hilda Ogden, wrote and asked him to visit the cast in Manchester. Tony Warren, creator of the series, remembers, 'John and Elizabeth arrived in the Ducal Daimler from Chatsworth. John was in seventh heaven and didn't want to leave; he talked to everyone. The only way I could get him to go was to take him to see St Peter's, Swinton, a church by Street that he didn't know – when he got there he said, "Tony, you've brought me to heaven twice in one day." '[32]

I think it was the cosy provincialism of *Coronation Street* which JB so loved. He felt relaxed and happy in its world. He had felt that same degree of warmth for Australia and was already curious about Canada, which he thought might provide the same atmosphere. At the end of May 1975 he went there. Under the auspices of the Macdonald Stuart Foundation, John Julius Norwich had organized a seminar on High Victorianism and secured a fee of two thousand pounds for JB. Hugh Casson, Asa Briggs and Elizabeth went too. They flew first class and during the flight JB lost his braces. They were nowhere to be found, neither in the loo nor under his seat. When the party was met at Toronto airport by Jack Jamieson of the Baptist McMaster University, JB's trousers fell down and Jamieson took off his own belt and lent it to JB. The trip was an enormous success. John Julius remembers, 'John was surrounded by scores of admiring teenagers the whole time we were there – he *never* stopped signing his books they brought him, always something different, *"Le maple leaf toujours"* and such like.'[33]

After the seminar they travelled on a train through the Rockies to Vancouver. JB sat in the observation car and discovered the joys of rye whisky. Larry Ryan, who was a member of the Canadian Victorian

Society, remembers taking him to see a large Victorian house on the shores of Lake Simcoe, and stopping on the way to admire a Sharon temple built by a Quaker group called the Children of Peace. 'John simply loved it and we were very late for lunch with Connie Matthews who was in her eighties. We were also quite drunk because we had been drinking rye from ten o'clock in the morning onwards. John said, when I dropped him and Elizabeth off at their hotel, "What a wonderful day it's been – to think that Scotch made it all possible." '[34]

On his return to England, JB wrote a verse to the publisher Carson Kilpatrick (senior) and his family with whom he had stayed on Vesta Drive, Toronto – he was head of the publishing house where JB's Canadian editions were produced:

> *Rye-on-the-Rocks For Ever*
>
> Carson and Anne Kilpatrick
> Are beautiful children to me:
> Carson is strong and his hair is long
> And his eyes are as blue as the sea.
>
> Anne has a peach complexion
> And beautiful curves and hips;
> When she looks in her brother's direction
> There's a secret smile on her lips.
>
> For they serve at their parents' parties
> Where the men have a healthy tan,
> And the eye runs off where the heart is
> To fall at the feet of Anne.
>
> I look through the leaded window
> Over the neat mown grass,
> As a small wind moves in the garden
> And the stately Cadillacs pass.
>
> Oh, rye-on-the-rocks for ever!
> And I'm glad that I'm still alive
> While Carson and Anne Kilpatrick
> Are living on Vesta Drive.[35]

All through the seventies old friends were fading fast and, being the articulate celebrity that he was, JB was asked to speak or to read the lesson at many of their memorial services: for Noël Coward in June 1973, for Edmund Blunden in March 1974, for Raymond Erith in January 1974, and for Freddie Hood in February 1975. In October 1974 he unveiled the memorial to W. H. Auden in Westminster

Abbey. JB's sadness welled up. He wrote to my mother in a state of great distress (6 November), 'Cyril [Connolly] is dying very fast. I went to see him today. Liver and no hope. Joanie and his new girl called Sheila, and Deirdre, take it in turns to watch by his bed. He sent you his love: "Give my love to Penelope." I am very proud of how much you are loved by our friends.'[36] Deirdre Levi, who was then married to Cyril, remembers, 'John was simply wonderful – he arranged Cyril's memorial service in St Clement's. I talked to him on the telephone daily about it. He was angelic.'[37]

The blows came thick and fast. Patrick Kinross wrote to JB (13 January 1975), 'I went down to the Yeo after Cyril's memorial wake. The house is empty. I think the GLC should put up a blue plaque to say, "Cyril lived there," leaving space for your name too, and mine when it comes.'[38] Patrick died a year later. 'Cracky' William Wicklow wrote, 'One never thought of him being ill. He was so full of vitality.'[39] JB gave the address at Patrick's funeral at St Mary's Church on Paddington Green. They had been friends for over fifty years. 'For all of us here, Patrick was chiefly a friend and the mainstay of our happiness. At his table I met friends I've known for the rest of my life. . . . He listened with the same patience with which he listened to me over fifty years ago when I was a young man complaining about lack of sympathy. He supplied the sympathy, he entered into one's enthusiasms with a tolerant smile. . . . I am thankful to have known him so long and so well.'[40]

Charles Osborne, who worked for the Arts Council and met JB in the seventies, remembered in the summer of 1976, 'Once, in his publisher Jock Murray's office, whither we had, for some reason, ventured after a lunch together, JB introduced me to a man we found there, a tall, ravaged-looking individual wearing a cloth cap. "Charles," said JB, "I want you to meet John Huston." We shook hands, and Huston began to talk in his strange American-Irish accent of the most recent film he had directed. Had I seen it? I had, and began to discuss it enthusiastic-ally. After a minute or two, JB got a fit of the giggles, which also infected Jock Murray. Only Huston kept a grave face, as he and I continued to talk about Hollywood. But when JB collapsed into an armchair, helpless with laughter, John Huston's face began to crease as well, and he confessed to me that his name was not John Huston, whom he somewhat resembled, but Tom Driberg.'[41] Tom Driberg died later that year.

JB had now been told he had Parkinson's Disease. He described the feeling of 'being unable to move your limbs at all or at least with difficulty: being unable to cross a room, let alone a street without "freezing"; being always terrified lest you fall. These are made far worse and more terrible by the fact that whilst our bodies fail us our minds remain alert and we are aware of our deterioration.'[42] And so by his seventieth birthday he was pretty wobbly. When we walked together he lent hard on my arm; sometimes I needed someone on the other side of him to help hold him up. He arrived at Blacklands for his seventieth birthday party leaning on my mother's arm and was surprised by the people Rupert and I had gathered together: the Pipers, Osbert Lancaster, Robert Heber-Percy, Mary Dunn, Mollie and Desmond Baring, John and Tory Oaksey, Richard and Mary Ingrams, and various of their and our offspring. Christopher Simon Sykes, the nephew of his old friend, came and took pictures but the film never came out – except for one shot of Osbert and JB laughing hugely with their mouths wide open. 'What an amazing evening it was. I felt transported into the next Life,' he wrote to Robert Heber-Percy. 'The loyalty of old friends was rock-like in its security for one so insecure and such a fake as I am.'[43]

1. JB's papers, Beinecke Library, Yale University.
2. PB's papers, Beinecke Library, Yale University.
3. Philip Larkin, 'Lucky Old England's Poet', *Sunday Telegraph* (15 October 1972).
4. Carbon copy, JB's papers, University of Victoria, British Columbia.
5. This letter of congratulation, and eleven following, all in JB's papers, University of Victoria.
6. EC's papers.
7. PB's papers, Beinecke Library.
8. JB's papers, University of Victoria.
9. *Daily Express* (21 August 1974).
10. PB's papers, Beinecke Library.
11. JB's papers, Beinecke Library.
12. PB's papers, Beinecke Library.
13. Carbon copy, JB's papers, University of Victoria.
14. JB's papers, University of Victoria.
15. The Reverend John Gaskell, CLG interview (1995).
16. *Sunday Express* (13 May 1973).
17. *Private Eye* (25 May 1973).
18. *Sunday Times* (24 November 1974).
19. JB's papers, Beinecke Library.
20. Carbon copy, JB's papers, University of Victoria.
21. CLG's papers, Beinecke Library, Yale University.
22. Mollie Baring's papers.
23. Carbon copy, JB's papers, University of Victoria.
24. Carbon copy, Gavin Stamp's papers.
25. Simon Jenkins, *The Selling of Mary Davies* (John Murray 1993).

26. BBC archives, Caversham, Reading.
27. BBC archives.
28. Wilhelmine Harrod's papers.
29. Mary Wilson's papers.
30. BBC archives.
31. CLG's papers, Beinecke Library.
32. Tony Warren, CLG interview (1995).
33. John Julius Norwich, CLG interview (1994).
34. Larry Ryan, CLG interview (1994).
35. David Cobb's papers.
36. PB's papers, Beinecke Library.
37. Letter to CLG from Deirdre Levi (May 1994).
38. JB's papers, Beinecke Library.
39. JB's papers, Beinecke Library.
40. Carbon copy, JB's papers, Beinecke Library.
41. Charles Osborne, *Giving It Away* (Secker and Warburg, 1986).
42. Parkinson's Disease Society book.
43. Robert Heber-Percy's papers.

To Harry Jarvis　　　　　　　　　　　43 Cloth Fair
13 August 1972　　　　　　　　　　　London EC1

Dear Harry,
Ta ever so for yorz of Aug[ust] 8th. P[enelope] is in Norfolk with the
dogs and old Billa Harrod. Her horses are in various local stables. She is
very happy. She accepts and goes on. I don't but I was so little at
Wantage [that] although I miss it much I ought to survive. I miss
Penelope who, I feel, has gone for ever.

　　　　　　　　　　　　　　　　　　　　　　But I hope not.
She goes to Injer in Jan[uary]. I would like to give my god-kiddi a
prezzie (i.e. five pounds). Cash or an object? Let me know which. Oh,
how I love the Smasher [Jean Jarvis] when I think of her naughty looks
and gold hair and peach-like skin. I dread the day when I cease to
delight in the human body; contours and emanations.

　　Penelope goes to Norfolk, Wilts[hire] (Malmesbury), Wilton,
Heref[ord]s[hire] in that order. I go to Cornwall in Oct[ober] for a
fortnight. Until then I'm here. When coming to London alone or all let
me know.

　　Yours, John B

To Tom Driberg　　　　　　　　　　　　　Treen
　　　　　　　　　　　　　　　　　　　Trebetherick
　　　　　　　　　　　　　　　　　　　Wadebridge
4 October 1972　　　　　　　　　　　　　Cornwall

My dear Thomas,
You will be glad to know that on Saturday last I preached about you
and Roger Fulford and Evelyn [Waugh] at LANCING in the Great Hall
to a crowded audience of the Friends of Lancing Chapel of whom I am

one. I said that you corrected all my verse for me, were a very good poet yourself and as well as left-wing *Very High*. I told the story of you, Evelyn and the altar cloth; they pretended they had not heard it, so it went down very well. I also mentioned Hot Lunch [Lord Molson]'s good work and said you all said you owed most to Roxburgh. Gerard [Irvine] was in the audience. Now you are a neighbour to Cloth Fair I do not see you. Barbican is so hideous I avoid it, as I do that Lord Mayor Howard of Glendure, Clackmannanshire and Church Demolishers Ltd. Back October 22nd. Give us a tinkle. You ought to be a peer so as to oppose developers.

Bung hoski, John B

Sandy Baird has died at Exeter. I preached his funeral oration in St Leonard's Church, Exeter (Low).

Ta for your *LUVLY* p[ost]c[ard]s of modern abroad. Is it better than ours?

JB's friend Henry Thorold, who taught at Lancing College, Sussex, had asked JB to speak. T.D., Fulford and Waugh were old boys.

   T.D. wrote in *Ruling Passions* (posthumously published 1977) his side of Waugh's story: 'I had better record here that his account, in *A Little Learning*, of an incident in chapel, when he and I, both sacristans, were getting the high altar ready for a festival, is inaccurate. He says that he indicated to me that he had ceased to believe in God. He did no such thing. When I was fussing about the proper hang of the linen cloth, he merely said, "Nonsense! If it's good enough for me it's good enough for God." This may be mildly blasphemous: it is not a proclamation of atheism.'

   T.D. had moved to a flat in the Barbican.

   In 1975 T.D. was created Baron Bradwell, of Bradwell-juxta-Mare, Essex.

To Philip Larkin

                            Treen
                            Trebetherick
                          Wadebridge

17 October 1972   Cornwall

Dear Philip,

You are a kind old thing writing so sensibly *and* sympathetically about me [in] the *S[unday] T[imes]*. However low I feel in future after this spate of publicity, I will be able to turn to the wise words of Philip whom I regard as our best living poet. You were the one I wanted for the job – not that I was consulted – and failing you, Charles Causley. There may be others. I never thought it would be offered to an old show-off who signs himself

   Your and Monica's admiring chum, John B

JB was made Poet Laureate on Tuesday 10 October.

P.L. had written after the death of John Masefield to Judy Egerton (17 May 1967), who suggested him as Laureate, 'No, Betjeman for Laureate, it would *do* more for poetry than all the Arts Council grants put together.'

Charles Causley, the poet, who lives in his native Cornwall, was much admired by JB. Monica Jones was P.L.'s companion and a lecturer at Leicester University.

To Audrey Lees   Treen
Trebetherick
Wadebridge
17 October 1972   Cornwall

My dear Audrey,
The Right Acting Magistrate E[lizabeth] C[avendish] and I are just getting ready to go to Rea and Joan. Rea Heckle has had trouble with his dentures. We are sure to hear about them. Then after drinks with Joan [Oakley] and Rea, we dine with Peggy and Lynam [Thomas] and Joan Larkworthy [Kunzer]. I hope Old Lees is getting better of his cataract. It takes time I'm told. Tell Old Lees that James Lees-Milne is 'a good man and true' for his list. He used to be architectural adviser to the Nat[ional] Trust and was at Magd[alen], Oxon with me. My love to those kiddiz of yours and Lees, especially that lovely great girl who went to America or was it Canada. I think all my life I was looking for you but Old Lees found you. Jock [Lynam] is very happy – not that he was ever depressed, but he's vigorous and marvellous whenever I see him. Does Old Lees still cook? Robert Bridges is a relation of yours through the Waterhouses. Back in London Thursday next, alas.
Love, John B

JB had known A.L. since he was seven and enjoyed reminiscing with her about Trebetherick. There had been a long gap while A.L. was a nurse at Paddington Green and he was at Oxford but years later when he moved to Cloth Fair they resumed their friendship.

To John Sparrow   43 Cloth Fair
27 October 1972   London EC1

Darling Spansbury,
I'm getting like Penelope and typing everything. She loved it with you and has now gone to Portugal, and it is very quiet here. Your goodness

to her and me over housing her possessions in time of crisis such as there was over this move, I would like to repay with the gift of my all to you, and by that I mean 'all', if you will accept it in the sense it is meant. I have been right through the poems of [William Ernest] Henley for Charles Monteith; Henley deserves a reprint because he was a rather splendid buccaneer with a real eye for a picture, with a love for Whistler's *Nocturnes* and Millet's engraving, and a friend of course of [Charles] Nicholson and Keene. Two excellent sorts of poetry. The hospital poems written in Edinburgh when he was under [Joseph] Lister and the Whistlerish poems which are muted river landscape. Things like 'The Song of the Sword' are painful to me and so is 'England My England', but I don't think he can be ignored and I like the idea of selecting him for a Faber and Gwyer paperback.

See you soon. Bung ho and thank you more than I can say for your encouraging letter and loyal friendship.

Love, John

To Pierce Synnott   Padua
30 November 1972   Italia

My dear Pierce,
Thank you for your Latin poem and inscription. BRILLIANT of course, but here where Livy laboured and Tasso delivered Jerusalem, I am still enough of a scholar to translate the Latin until I see Spanzbury [John Sparrow] in All Souls back in England to which I soon return to post this piece of GARAMOND type. Indeed it is nice to think of Ernie [Betjemann] up there by the throne and Bess [Betjemann] on the other side of it, and [illegible] behind it and Brother Tom [Eliot] and Maurice

17a Before a television quiz show, early 1960s.

17b JB taking a break from filming with the antiques expert Arthur Negas at Frampton Court, Gloucestershire.

18a JB in the model village
at Weston-super-Mare, 1963,
filming *Wales and the West*.

18b Mary and Harold Wilson
in the mid-sixties.

18c Lunch at Faringdon House, 1965.
(*Left to right*) John Sparrow, JB, Hester Knight.

19a JB with Osbert Lancaster at his seventieth
birthday party, Blacklands, 1976.

19b JB and PB at New House, near Hay-on-Wye, 1978.

20a PB during one of her many sojourns in India, mid-seventies.

20b Treen, Trebetherick, showing kitchen and bedroom extension on the right by John Brandon Jones, who had worked in the offices of the architect C. A. Voysey.

21 JB reading proofs of Gavin Stamp's book *Temples of Power* at 29 Radnor Walk, September 1979.

22a JB and EC with Tony Warren, the creator of *Coronation Street*, during their visit to Manchester in 1975 to meet the cast.

22b JB, wearing Diaghilev, with CLG at Blacklands, 1977.

22c JB with his grandson David LG at Blacklands, 1978.

23a JB and Barry Humphries at 29 Radnor Walk, 1982.

23b JB and Harry Williams at 29 Radnor Walk, 1982.

23c JB with Myfanwy and John Piper and Jonathan Stedall (*wheeling chair*), filming *Time with Betjeman*, 1982.

24 JB on the cliff above Daymer Bay, Trebetherick, 1970.

[Bowra] joining in. Meanwhile down here John Hastings, James and Matthew Ponsonby shine with you and me [at] the centre. That nice nephew of yours [Jasper Synnott] who lived in Melbourne [and] on whom I called then, hailed me the other day in London and I have lost his name and address. Kindly give his organisation mine when next you are in the mood and call on me yourself when next in London. Yours was the first country house in which I stayed (excepting that of Ernie's friend Sir Henry Webb in South Wales) and since then how many pairs of linen sheets have received my lustful limbs in what fine mansions. Oh thank you, dear old thing, for your kind and scholarly appreciation of

Yours, Seán ó Betjemán

P.S. (see *Volume One*), one of JB's oldest Oxford friends, with whom JB had often stayed at his house Furness in Co. Kildare, Ireland, had got a double first at Oxford and wrote in Latin with ease. He had written to JB in Latin.

JB and EC were staying in Padua with Raymond Leppard, who was conducting there. EC remembers that when walking under the arcades, Raymond had noticed JB's shuffling and said, 'You must get John to a doctor.'

The Garamond type refers to the 'Thank you, oh thank you' which JB had had printed to acknowledge the hundreds of letters he received on the Laureateship.

To Margaret Ann Elton   43 Cloth Fair
5 January 1973   London EC1

Darling Margaret Ann,
I constantly think of you and Julia and (my handwriting has gone for a Burton) Charles and Rebecca over the death of Arthur, my oldest and dearest friend. I can faintly imagine your own sense of loss and I can do and will pray for him and you all. I am having him mentioned in the RIPs at the Grosvenor Chapel on Sunday next. He is being mentioned at mass all this week, F[athe]r Gaskell told me today. I think Arthur was a truly great man: patient, perceptive, encouraging and kind and A GENIUS. He had an eye for a building, a picture and a machine *and* a person. His certain judgement set one up. He was an invigorator too. It is maddening for all of us that he has been snatched out of time. We'll certainly see him again, we who loved him. I did a piece for the *N[orth] S[omerset] M[ercury]* about him. Quite inadequate. Words don't work. I've written to Eve and to Julia as the next two I know best, besides yourself, of the family. I'm confined to the house by wobbly knees but hope to be about the week after next. Love and keep in touch with me.

I will be in London for some weeks. You must have a life of Arthur written with *plenty of illustration*. Fight on. *Ora Pro Nobis. He's* all right.
   Love, John B

Arthur E., JB's old Marlburian friend, had just died.

To Edward Heath   43 Cloth Fair
26 January 1973   London EC1

Dear Prime Minister,
Stephen Dykes Bower is going to give up his work as Surveyor of the Fabric of Westminster Abbey in April, when he reaches the age of seventy. He cleaned the stone there and brought colour and light into the building. At Bury St Edmunds he built what I consider our finest modern Cathedral, for he added to the east end of what was a parish church, choir and transepts so harmoniously and subtly, that Bury Cathedral is a glory even of East Anglia. His restoration work and his original churchwork is well known. I would particularly cite the beautiful organ case he built for Norwich Cathedral and the restoration and new work which he did there. He is modest, self-effacing, shy and when need be, deeply and dryly humorous. He is one of the great men of architecture alive today, and I think that others would agree with me, that he deserves recognition. I feel sure that the Dean and Chapter of Westminster would support me, and *all* architects who are versed in the tradition of English architecture as opposed to copiers of continental styles and various forms of with-itry.
   Yours sincerely, John Betjeman

Stephen Dykes Bower died in 1994: his obituaries commented on the lack of recognition, i.e. a knighthood, in spite of influential lobbying.

To Joan Leigh Fermor   43 Cloth Fair
February 1973   London EC1

Darling Joanie,
O worship the Lord in the beauty of holiness. Who wrote that? We heard it the other day in Jerusalem Chapel. My sec[retary] has left in very high dudgeon and I am up the spout with self-pity – therefore your

letter about my verse was balm to me. The P[oet] L[aureate] business
was no joke. I put on weight and drank more and more and got so testy
that I was insupportable. Paddy [Leigh Fermor] is a glorious writer.
I am re-reading *Mani*. Wherever you open it it is good. Cecil B[eaton]
is writing a history of photography including Bassano and Lenare.
He ought to put in you and Barbara Ker Seymer. Saw Diana Cooper
last night. Clear in the brain and brave in the body and wonderful.
But there is no one so attractive and beautiful as dichotomic myopic
Joanie.

Penelope is in Injer filming with the BBC having just taken a Swan
tour round the Himarlyer as she calls it. Love to Paddy. Love to Greece
and the sea and that place in the garden where you see the peacock-blue
waters of the Aegean and love, dear Joanie, to you again and again.

John B

> JB's secretary of three years, Jackie, had left, partly because she was not happy about
> moving from Cloth Fair which JB was just about to do and partly because she was fed up
> with 'the thousands of demanding letters from dud poets and self-pitying pests' which
> had to be answered.
> Patrick L.F.'s book *Mani* was published by Murrays in 1958.

To Cecil Beaton   43 Cloth Fair
13 February 1973   London EC1

Dear Cecil,
Forgive my typing this, but my handwriting has become an insult to
recipients.

Re: National Trust and pictures in houses. I think John Pope-Hennessy
would be wise, short and sensible with his advice. I think I will write to
him and ask him whether he thinks it worth you, him and me writing to
The Times or whether it could be done more effectively through a
Government Department, and if so which.

I enclose a book of poems that I seem to have had a long time. I
thought you might like the work of Studio Hugo, Cheltenham. He is
very much my type (of photographer).

When I finished our delightful conversation and I went to bed, I
thought of a whole sequence of photographers who were first class in
their way, whom I came across in the early thirties when I was on the
Architectural Review and later when editing the *Shell Guides*. They were
the photographers of things rather than people (Maurice Beck by the

way was an engineer primarily). Batsfords in the persons of Sam Carr and Brian Batsford would know of the very fine topographical and ecclesiastical photographs there were. They bought the copyright of Brian Clayton, who used to go about in knee-breeches and an old Marlburian tie, photographing the churches of the West Country and the houses. He is long dead and lived in Ross-on-Wye. There were also such men as F. H. Crossley, whose photographs adorned the early Batsford books and were sharp in detail, and ideal for half-tone reproduction.

On the *Archie Review* Jim Richards, Sir James as he now is, would know of the photographers we used there besides Dell and Wainwright, whom I mentioned. But there were very good local photographers who did postcards, such as Judges, Gibson and Sons of Penzance. (A book has just come out published by David and Charles of their photographs of Scilly.)

Frith of Reigate and Valentines of Dundee and that man whose name I've forgotten who worked at Gloucester. They would all have considered themselves photographers and artists first, and postcard manufacturers second. The Gordon Fraser cards are their successors.

The people whom I've known personally who take good photographs are Penelope (particularly of India), Joan Eyres-Monsell [Leigh Fermor], Paddy Rossmore, and Lewis Morley who is now in Australia. There must be many others, an obvious one is Mr Piper and I expect his son Edward.

Bung ho, old top. Yours 'till the cows come home, John B
I am thrilled at the idea of your book.

> C.B.'s *The Magic Image: The Genius of Photography from 1839 to the Present Day*, written with Gail Buckland, was published by Weidenfeld in 1975.

To Penelope Betjeman   43 Cloth Fair
18 March 1973   London EC1

My darling Plymmie,
I'm very happy to hear of Jonathan [Stedall]'s red Japanese nose. I'm very sorry to leave 43 but Elizabeth has bought number 29 Radnor Walk and it will be more convenient and cheaper. The new Jackie is turning out very well and efficient. You are a very sweet little thing and I love you v[ery] much and miss you.

Your nut is a very funny shape, with
that point at the top and your hair
parted above the fringe.

I very much like to think of the
amethyst Nepalese pendant I am
giving you. I suppose you will
wear it at Baptist receptions.

I fear your college [missionary school] may be General and not Strict
and Particular. Was Carey the great Baptist missionary to Injer Strict
or General? I can get by without Jackie. I have now a part-time
sec[retary], rather *soignée* and with two sons at Uppingham, called Mrs
Mountain. Your personality is very strong and I do miss you. I'm not
going to miss Cloth Fair, the noise is awful by night as well as day –
[Chelsea] couldn't be so bad as EC1.

I would say I have a sore throat at present and am staying put till I am
rid of it. I continue my exercises however each day. I hope Jonathan has
turned up, he is a wonderful producer and knows what he wants and
has lovely manners (Harrow).

Wibz and Rupert you will be surprised to hear have gone to
Switzerland for ten days.

Yours truly, Tewpie

> PB had gone to India in January where she was making a film with Jonathan Stedall. She
> was very concerned over JB's welfare and state of health.
>   JB had given notice to the Landmark Trust who now owned Cloth Fair.
>   PB had a habit of buying her own birthday and Christmas presents, usually books,
> and then telling the would-be donors what they were giving her.

To Penelope Betjeman   43 Cloth Fair
24 March 1973   London EC1

My darling Plymmie,

I hope as how you haven't fallen off a rock with illness. In my mind's
eye I picture you both swimming in a lake in Kulu. The man with red
hair and a red nose is Jonathan [Stedall].

I am getting very windy about the move to 29 Radnor Walk (that is its
number) as all you say about Cloth Fair is true. The views from the
house are beautiful, the rooms are beautiful and so are the books. I write
this on a Saturday and feel very sad. BUT I have to admit that friends
matter more than views and that here I am just a public view and at
Radnor Walk there are friends near in all directions and my books. I *can*
move now. I may not be able to in a year or two.

I can't understand what you and Jonathan mean about my English
Architecture book. I will have to ask Jock. Nooni, nooni, I miss you. I
don't miss Wantage a bit. Nooni. Nooni.

Yours truly, Tewpie
When do you return?

To Penelope Betjeman
30 March 1973

43 Cloth Fair
London EC1

My darling Plymmie,

How's your hat? I now see you and
Jonathan in my mind's eye looking
out of a temple at the far Afghan snow.
I notice that in this drawing Jonathan has
got quite priest-like and you have gone
statuesque like Mrs Woad [Lady Chetwode].

E[lizabeth] had a fascinating letter from Jonathan saying you were much respected out there and loved and how Simla had a quality of the old British Raj.

The little house, number 29 Radnor Walk, is going ahead fast. The rooms are going to be plain, the stairs only Willow and white dado below them. *There are two rooms at the top for beds*. Though it is smaller to look at than 43, the rooms are deeper. I wish I liked Chelsea better as a district. The City though has got very drab with that awful new Barbican.

Eddie Mirzoeff and I are thinking of doing a film on the Diocese of Southwark as it has real country on the Surrey border (rather more real than Berks[hire]) and slums in Bermondsey and miles of middling houses and many characters and a worker-priest system.

I expect while I am writing this you and Jonathan are meditating upon the stars.

I think you are a dear little thing. Wibz came this morning to look at 29 and said the rooms need only be white because I had such a lot of pictures. Quite true. Willow on stairs only. Love to Jonathan. Much love from
Yours truly, Tewpie
Wibz brought Lucy and Delly to see 29 who rushed about noticing inessentials just as children do. We have unearthed your letters stored away by Jackie and posted them yesterday. Not many.

'Willow' refers to the William Morris wallpaper pattern, which JB had always loved and had in all his houses from Garrards Farm onwards.

To Kingsley Amis   43 Cloth Fair
5 April 1973   London EC1

Dear Kingers,
A bloody good review, I thought, in *The Times* this morning. I enjoyed
every word of the book, including the extremely complicated end, but
top for me is the chapter called 'Moments of Delight'. I think it would
be very nice if you were to write a school story. No one has done it
properly for years. What is so wonderful about your writing about
Peter Furneaux, old boy, is that you've entered completely into the
unshockable practical mind of Peter and his friend, Reg. That's the
way to do it. It's the way Dean Farrar did it in *Eric* and in *St Winifred's*.
If you just substitute what really happened, which was quick, practical
sex for drinking whisky, you have got the guilt and doom-ridden life
that I lived as a boarder in the early twenties, and that you probably
partly lived as a day-boy, and which may also have been lived by
Martin [Amis]. It's a wonderful book and your style is so vigorous,
your observation is so sharp, and your narrative power so strong and
economical, it is an honour to know you, old top.
     Lots of love to [Elizabeth] Jane [Howard], Sargy [Mann] and all at
Gin-and-Lemons, John B

> K.A. first came across JB's *Ghastly Good Taste* at school in 1936, began to read his poetry
> and was particularly won over by 'Croydon'. In 1941 or 1942 he saw JB at the English
> Society in Oxford talking about Tennyson, but it wasn't until the mid-sixties that they
> met and became friends.
>   K.A.'s detective story *The Riverside Villas Murder* had just come out.
>   K.A. and his wife, the novelist Elizabeth Jane Howard, lived at Lemmons in Hadley,
> Hertfordshire, where JB often stayed. He usually wrote to Elizabeth Jane as Avril, Lady
> Netherthorpe, the fictitious wife of a Lord Netherthorpe who lived near Hadley.
>   Sargy Mann is a painter from whom JB bought several landscapes.

To Penelope Betjeman   29 Radnor Walk
27 April 1973   London SW3

My darling Plymmie,
I am now very nearly in 29 Radnor Walk, SW3 4BP, [Tel.] 352–5081 to
give it its full titles. This is my first letter from it. The long delay is due
to the horrors of moving. The new place is very tiny but very cheerful
and much easier to reach than the City. Wibz has been very helpful and
so has E[lizabeth]. I am going to Cornwall while the workers are in on

toilets and other luxuries like shelves. There is no garden. That will have to be at Kulu-on-Wye. I am longing to hear how all the religious maniacs got on in Kulu. I bet it will be a good film, all sorts of editing always occurs. The cans get lost. Yards of film fall down precipices. All the best shots have a 'hair in the gate'. Ask Jonathan about hair in gates and French flags and brutes. No word from Paul. I've told him my new address and phone numbers. I feel very tired and upset at the move. Possessions are a curse. I have to preach at Noël Coward's memorial service. I never knew him well and I haven't read him much. I can't get out of it. It is a bad dream. There is an actual bedroom for you in the new house. Not as nice as the book cave but cosy.

Love to all.

Yours truly, Tewpie

'Kulu-on-Wye' was how JB referred to Hay-on-Wye where PB had found a house. The 'book cave' was where PB slept at Cloth Fair.

To Patrick Cullinan   29 Radnor Walk
13 August 1973   London sw3

My dear Patrick,

You can't imagine what pleasure your letter and book gave me. They are sad and beautiful poems, and I have read and re-read them. I am going to send on my copy to William Plomer who is a South African and friend of mine. How I miss the Colonel and Toby. The Colonel with his hair parted in the middle and those old clothes and too many dogs and Toby who was said to be what the Colonel was like when no one else was there. I have never laughed so much. And what about your Magdalen lunch when we put the concrete gnome in the garden? I hope you get a few laughs at Machadodorp. Is it all tin huts or is it by Sir Herbert Baker? Candida has three daughters and lives in Wilts[shire] with her nice husband. Powlie teaches music at Riverside High School, New York, and never writes. Penelope is exactly the same and wedded to horses and has moved to Herefordshire, lovely quiet rolling country of red earth and oak trees. I am here in Chelsea where the river is awful but I have my books. Please write again and write more poems and send them to

Yours affectionately, John B

P.C.'s book of poems entitled *The Horizon Forty Miles Away* had just been published.
William Plomer never received the book because he died before JB could send it to him.

JB was referring to P.C.'s time as an undergraduate at Magdalen College, Oxford, in
the late forties. By this time P.C. had been back in his native South Africa for over
twenty years. He farmed in the mountains of the Eastern Transvaal but continued to
write poetry.

To Mary Wilson   Treen
                                                          Trebetherick
                                                           Wadebridge
5 October 1973   Cornwall

Dear Mary,
I saw one or two photographs of you looking second fiddle to the
Leader, which is of course quite right except for Woman's Lib. I wish I
had been to Blackpool, I am sure I would like it. I was very taken with
Southport and Lanc[a]s[hire] generally especially LIVERPOOL.

Very sad about old Wystan [Auden], a close friend of mine from
Oxford days. We always kept in touch. I loved his schoolmasterish
ways. I liked hearing him laying down the law on poetry. He was right
and not really arrogant at all. And he was a most kind and generous man
and a loyal friend. William Plomer is another great personal loss. I think
there is a lot to be said for prayers for the dead. If they are alive in one's
mind they will go on living, as [Thomas] Hood's 'Sonnet to Death'.

Oh God, the Royal poem!! Send the H[oly] G[host] to help me over
that fence. So far no sign: Watch and pray. Ring up from Scillonia. I
leave October 21st.
    Love, JB

M.W. and Harold W. had been at the Labour Party Conference.

W.H. Auden (see *Volume One*), the poet, had died on 28 September. He had been a
close friend of JB's from Oxford days and had long lived in the USA. He was responsible
for getting JB's poems published there and wrote a eulogizing preface to the selection
Slick But Not Streamlined published in 1947.

William Plomer had died on 21 September.

Thomas Hood's (1799–1845) poem was called 'The Death Bed':

> Of our very hopes belied our fears
> Our fears our hopes belied –
> We thought her dying when she slept
> And sleeping when she died!

JB was due to write a poem for 14 November 1973 on the occasion of the wedding of
Princess Anne to Captain Mark Phillips.

To Frank Muir   29 Radnor Walk
11 November 1973   London sw3

Dear Frank,
I have very much enjoyed your Muir/Norden volume. It's the sort of
humour I like. It warms instead of chills. It is brief and it could only be
you (your part that is) and I can hear you saying it. I find the funniest
and most ingenious of all the one about the restaurant at the top of the
post office tower. Now I know. I was never intending to visit it
anyhow.
     You are a gallant and encouraging captain on that delightfully
imaginative game. I think it is so good because you and Patrick
C[ampbell] are imaginative and good people.
     Very many thanks once more from your doddering old friend and
ally, John B
     I say, Fiona and Joyce [Hopkirk], they would have been a nice pair
with whom to go on a tour of the Lake District under canvas. Oh,
what fun it was and what a happy and to-be-treasured souvenir is
your and D[enis] N[orden]'s book.

> F.M., the humorist, writer and broadcaster, was the captain of JB's team on an episode
> of the BBC television programme *Call my Bluff*. Denis Norden and he had co-written *You
> Can't Have Your Kayak and Heat It* which had just been published.
>   Fiona was an ex-model 'who looked rather like an SS Colonel in drag,' remembered
> F.M., and Joyce Hopkirk, a woman's magazine editor.

To Hugh Casson   29 Radnor Walk
10 January 1974   London sw3

Dear Hugh,
I think that George Whitby's addition to [E. W.] Mountford's Old
Bailey is a marvellous piece of street architecture. In fact the whole of
that side of Old Bailey is a happy combination of styles pulled together
by George Whitby's grim fortress of the law which recalls George
Dance junior's Newgate.
     One bright and frosty day at about noon last year I came up in a taxi
from County Hall to Waterloo bridge. I was with Osbert Lancaster.
Suddenly I gasped at a beautiful view of a snow-white tower and a
lesser tower north of it. They framed St Paul's Cathedral. They were as

you know by now the new National Theatre. Externally, and externally is what matters, for us on the pavements, I think the new National Theatre is magnificent as a conception beside the Thames. It looks like a sketch by Rembrandt or rather ascribed to Rembrandt which I once saw of the Thames South Bank. And what about Lord Ferrers, old boy? Wouldn't he be worth a sketch?

Yours, John Betjeman

H.C., the architect and artist, had sat on the RFAC since 1960 with JB and was a close friend, who shared his passion for architecture. He published several illustrated books on Cambridge, Oxford and London, for the latter of which JB made some suggestions. H.C. illustrated *Summoned by Bells* which came out in 1989.

The Old Bailey was built (1900–07) by Edward W. Mountford in the neo-English baroque style. The east wing was extended in 1967–69 by George Whitby (1916–73), who had been in partnership with Donald McMorran (1904–65), in a plain segment-arched style. JB wrote 'In Memory of George Whitby, Architect' which was delivered at his memorial service at St Mary Woolnoth, 29 March 1973.

The National Theatre was designed by Denys Lasdun.

To Mark Girouard   29 Radnor Walk
15 January 1974   London SW3

My Darling Little Godson,
I felt very proud of my little godson when I saw that he had for THE SECOND TIME won the gold medallion of the RIBA*. My, how I did like your sister Theresa whom I met. I think I told her about my being your godfather. Dick must be very happy and consoled with his so glorious children and daughter-in-law to whom my love. Do go and look at Raymond E[rith]'s restoration of St Mary's Church, the pretty Polly Perkins of Paddington Green (J. Plaw 1788). He has numbered the stockbricks and set up a few tombstones stacked against it, and then the steeple bellcote, slate roof, [illegible], porches and box pews. Ah, it is an aquatint come to Paddington's Middlesex Hillock.

Love to you both, JB
*RIBA Journal 12 1974

JB always pretended, as a joke, that he was godfather to M.G., son of his old friends Dick and Blanche G.

M.G. never won the RIBA gold medal but he did win the Alice Davis Hitchcock medallion given by the Society of Architectural Historians.

'Pretty Polly Perkins of Paddington Green' is a music-hall song.

To Ian Fletcher   29 Radnor Walk
18 January 1974   London sw3

Dear Mr Fletcher,
I am so glad you have undertaken to edit a 'Nineties Anthology' and will include Olive Custance. She was most amusing and very fond of Bosie [Lord Alfred Douglas] though they lived apart. 'Olive loved changing houses,' he used to say. She had a cottage in Bembridge which was known locally as 'Safe Haven' after a stormy passage. She was very fond of Byron and knew everything about him. Her appeal when young to Bosie must have been that of a tomboy. I remember her telling me about walking with her father, Colonel Custance, who so greatly objected to Bosie, down a street in the back of Cromer where some bungalows had been built on Custance land. Her father, who was immensely tall, leaned down and looked in through the windows of a bungalow and said, 'Good Lord, do you mean to say people actually live in these things?'
    I think Bosie and Olive were very fond of each other. I remember he was very distressed at her death and sought the consolations of his much-loved Roman Catholic Church.
    If you go to the Tate Landscape Exhibition shutting on February 23rd, there is a magnificent oil painting by Hofland of the house and park at White Knights.
    I've just sent to Dr Krishnamurti pages of chit-chat about nineties people. Olive's great friend was Stuart Ellis whom I met in one of her houses. I'm very pleased to have the Dolben book. It is a revelation. You are very kind to
    Yours sincerely, John Betjeman

> I.F., a professor at Reading University, had been asked to edit an issue of the *Francis Thompson Society Journal* devoted to unedited letters and poems of Olive Custance, the writer, who married Lord Alfred Douglas in 1902.

To Alastair Service   29 Radnor Walk
19 January 1974   London sw3

Dear Alastair,
Forgive long delay. Windsor station should most certainly not be menaced. I am sure I must go to Canada before I die. John Julius

[Norwich] speaks so highly of it. What bothers me is not speaking French. I will be in Norfolk much of the next two months filming but the Empire calls me more than anywhere today. Australia I now prefer to Watford or Bath or anywhere else. I think Canada has probably equal appeal. I would like to travel by train there and reach the country by steam-ship. Perhaps John Julius will be able to effect this.

Love to the Magistrate and congratulations on the work you do for Belcher and Joass and Mewes and Davis. I wish I had been at Fettes under the shadow of Bryce. As it is I was at Harrow in all but fact. Once again love to the Magistrate and kindly give a tingle here when you are free for luncheon. I can't manage those February dates, 8th or 9th.

Yours ever, John B

> On meeting A.S., the writer, architectural historian and one-time head of the Family Planning Association, JB had insisted that he send his essay on Edwardian Baroque to Nikolaus Pevsner. It was then published in the *Architectural Review*. JB introduced A.S. to Pevsner whom JB by this time had come to like and recognise.
>
> JB helped A.S. get *Edwardian Architecture and Its Origins* commissioned, which was published by the Architectural Press in 1975.
>
> Windsor station (by Sir William Tite, 1850) was under threat of demolition.
> A.S.'s wife Louisa was Canadian and a magistrate.
> Fettes College, Edinburgh, is by the Victorian architect David Bryce.

To Edward Mirzoeff   29 Radnor Walk
24 January 1974   London sw3

Dear Eddie,
I am still reeling with delight at the soaring majesty of Norfolk and our tour there with Jane Whitworth. I put down here some preliminary thoughts only.

I think the obvious is the best and that the film should be our earthly pilgrimage expressed in the sacraments and psalms of the C[hurch] of E[ngland] to which most people belong even though they may have forgotten. It will stir memories. Phrases from the *Book of Common Prayer*, especially the General Thanksgiving, that Norwich invention – the psalms and hymns *A[ncient] and M[odern]* will wander through the script, much of which should be spoken by someone with a Norfolk accent, and a *strong* Norfolk accent. All the time what we look at must be Norfolk and that may help to imply the remoteness of this separate country which Norfolk is, miles from London and miles even from Cambridge and the Midlands.

Having now read most of Colin Stephenson's *Walsingham Way*, I realise we cannot ignore it. The pilgrimage was of European fame before the Reformation and though I don't much like relic worship myself, things do get an extra quality when they have been revered for centuries by thousands. They are something like the monarchy. That well at Walsingham and the water that is sprinkled from it (we might even sprinkle over the lens of the camera to surprise and bless our readers!) are a nice incident on life's journey. I like to think there is illimitable light all round us waiting to press into our lives if we will let it. We come from it trailing clouds of glory, we go into it after death and we see it portrayed in the Resurrection. But one thing we must avoid is solemnity and conscious do-goodery and taking ourselves too seriously. The film must be natural and life-like and full of jokes like Chaucer and some of those carved bosses and bench-ends we saw. All round us are fields and trees and the toil through the seasons. These are shown in glass and wood and stone in the churches. They are going on all round us in the towns whether it's selling second-hand books in Reepham or second-hand cars in the industrial suburbs of Norwich or sitting in a field of turnips having lunch as we saw those two ladies doing at Booton. The C[hurch] of E[ngland] will be taken for granted and Norfolk will be taken as the whole world but what we show must, so far as possible, be essentially Norfolk – gossip in ringing chambers before the bells are rung up or during a pause in the ringing. Tower after tower we will see as we go down unfenced roads, the most dominant things in the landscape now that windmills have disappeared and the towers which gave England the name of the 'Ringing Isle'.

We see them first at the birth of the film which is the hard struggle up the shingle from Cley beach, with a few pulled-up boats and some bits of rusty machinery and then the Saltings where the vegetation is grey and strange and muddy, Crabbe-like ponds abide. And we look up from them to the tower and beacon-tower of Blakeney or maybe the stretch of Horsey Mere and the sand dunes on the seaward side of it or the view of King's Lynn shown in Billa [Harrod]'s *Guide*. All will show, without words being necessary for emphasis, that Norfolk is a fleet of churches on undulating pasture, meadow and breck. We begin church with Baptism in the font at Trunch or we need only film that font and its soaring cover and the pouring of the water or immersion of the baby can be somewhere else. Then we have Sunday School and all over Norfolk in glass and wood and stone are school scenes, the beating of bottoms as in the porch at Cley or in the Cathedral and Bible lessons painted on walls and carved on stalls. Then we can have Confirmation and a Bishop's hand and the words and flaxen or reddish Norfolk hair on boy or girl or adult. Then we must have a village wedding, the coming out from the cottage and all the finery and ribbons on the hired car and illegal confetti and the relations in the pews. That unrestored church at Walsingham or South Creek would be a place for that. The Market Place which is an essential part in the daily life scenes in our film could be that fair Billa mentioned which is held annually outside Worstead, a wonderful Norfolk church and village and this could introduce us to a totter through the traffic-less lanes of Norwich City with a church round every corner and [George John] Skipper's art nouveau shopping arcade as well, and Norwich cattle market and fish being bought from the trawlers in a harbour and carried home straight to the cottages and houses without being sent to Grimsby. And now the keepers of the house tremble and the grinders cease and mourners go about the streets and that will bring us to a village funeral, the motor hearse and professional undertaker. All this is under wide sky in the sound of waves on shingle and bells in church-towers, single bells in dim churches. A ring of ten from big ones and from there we go to the singing angels in Norfolk mediaeval glass as at Bale and Warham-St-Mary. Up and up to the roof at Cawston and down for light relief to those Victorian ladies waiting to go to heaven and queuing in the stained-glass at Booton. And then more feathered angels in glass and wood. Then out into clouds and sky and from that the gold rays of the Resurrection gush to Lady Harrod (Wilhelmine and called Billa by me) and to Paul Paget.

With best wishes for a Happy Christmas and New Year to you, the missus and the kiddiz.

Yours for aye, Iain MacBetje

E.M. and JB had been on a reconnaisance with the BBC researcher Jane Whitworth before making the television film *A Passion for Churches*.

To Penelope Betjeman   29 Radnor Walk
31 January 1974   London sw3

My darling Plymmie,
Magda is typing this so that you may be able to read it. I thought the film was wonderful. Indeed it was awe-inspiring and seemed to flow naturally. It had an audience in Elizabeth's house of the following:

Cecil Beaton, Elizabeth, her sister Anne [Tree], Barney Platts-Mills, (a very good film director who made a film about children called *Bronco Bullfrog*), Barney's wife Marion and yours truly. We were all held spellbound by it and did not go on eating but pushed away our chairs to watch the television, and Elizabeth said your love of India came right through and it made Anne long to go back there herself. They all said that it made them very fond of you as a person for your delight in what you were looking at. I think it is the best thing Jonathan [Stedall] has done and I am sending him and John McGlashan notes of congratulation. By the arrangement of Providence it came just when we all feel in need of the uncomplicated life it showed. Believe me when I say I am

   Very truly yours, Tewpie

> Magda Rogers was JB's new secretary.
>   PB had made the film *A Passion for India* in the series *One Pair of Eyes* in Kulu in April 1973.
>   John McGlashan was the cameraman who worked on the film *Summoned by Bells*. JB loved him and used to call him 'the Bishop'. He was in fact a lay bishop in the Liberal Catholic Church.

To Wilhelmine Harrod   On the G[reat] W[estern] R[ailway]
15 February 1974   to Henley

Darling Billa,
You have no idea how much we all (Eddie [Mirzoeff], Jane and I) enjoyed our visit. Eddie is still waiting tremulously to be asked again.

   Your kindest action to me in our long and loving friendship was to speak to me so kindly and clearly of Penelope. I love her. *But I cannot live with her for long without quarrelling*. I sensed her anguish when we went to the cinema last night with Emily [Villiers-Stuart]. I cannot bear to hurt her. She kissed me on the cheek when she got out of the taxi last night and I went back to Radnor Walk.

   You said being loved is a great burden. I have lived so long apart from Penelope, that Elizabeth now loves me more than anyone else in the world. I cannot hurt *her* either, any more than I can Penelope. I depend on Elizabeth for food for my body and mind. She is v[ery] much part of me too.

   Both P[enelope] and E[lizabeth] feel threatened. Fear steps in and with it hatred and anger. It is difficult. I *think* Penelope would be wounded if we separated, though she says that is what she wants to do.

I don't want to, but may have to because she will precipitate it in rage at Eliz[abeth] and all Cavendishes. I can understand her rage and misery. She won't believe how much I love her. I think she needs to be given her rights and dignity. She is okay at Kulu-on-Wye and insecure in London with me in the enemy's camp. I must buy, if it ruins me, a camp for her in London where she can entertain her friends with me.

In all this awful storm of misery, the one thing I cling to is my love for Penelope *and* for Elizabeth who has given up marriage and a family life with her own children, out of love for me.

I think, but am not sure, that P[enelope] is more defenceless than E[lizabeth] and must therefore be propped up by a London base as well as Kulu-on-Wye. Radnor Walk would never do. It is too near the enemy, though P[enelope] has tried to be friendly with Eliz[abeth].

Ora pro nobis and God bless you (and Roy) for your goodness to
Yours with love, John B
Don't bother to answer this odd b[read] and b[utter] letter. It is written in the G[reat] W[estern] R[ailway] on the way to the Pipers in Henley – hence the vile handwriting.

> JB and Eddie Mirzoeff had stayed at the Old Rectory in Holt with W.H. while doing research for their film *A Passion for Churches*.

To John Murray   29 Radnor Walk
18 February 1974   London sw3

Dear Jock,
I agree to the changes in the 'Investiture Ballad' which I return. As to your suggested changes, I know Watford is in Hertfordshire. Perhaps 'Through Watford safe in leafy Herts' might be better but I don't mind 'then' instead of 'on' in that line and really I prefer the line as it is as Watford stops and trees begin.

I think all we need for the notes to the first stanza is that the names are of friends and acquaintances at Cambridge and only note that Harry [Williams] is, as your note says, now a monk at Mirfield and was at the time Dean of Trinity College, Cambridge. I rather doubt whether it's necessary to put note 5. I don't want the poem to sound too much like Debrett, much as I revere that volume.

If you're going to have 'thread' instead of 'sense' in stanza 5, I suppose you ought to have 'holds' or 'stills' but it sounds to me weak and like cotton, what about 'a mounting tension stilling all'. I much prefer 'lifted' to 'carry' for the next stanza. Many thanks.

As for 'George Whitby', I must go through it at my leisure and you must send me your version of 'Aldershot Crematorium'. I have lost everything and am very unhappy.

Yours ever, John B

PS The order is excellent. It's 'Dilton Marsh Halt' not 'Hall'.

> Five years before, after a visit to Cambridge, the Prince of Wales had asked JB to write a poem. The second stanza of 'A Ballad of the Investiture 1969' hence reads:
>
>> Then, sir, you said what shook me through
>>> So that my courage almost fails:
>> 'I want a poem out of you
>>> On my Investiture in Wales.'
>> Leaving, you slightly raised your hand –
>>> 'And that,' you said, 'is a command.'
>> For years I wondered what to do
>>> And now, at last, I've thought it better
>> To write a kind of rhyming letter.
>
> The ballad was published in *A Nip in the Air*, and ended up with the following changes to the original sent to the Prince of Wales (4 January 1974).
>
> The sixth line of the third stanza was left as 'Through Watford on to leafy Herts'.
>
> The only footnote made was to explain Harry Williams. 'Elizabeth' (Cavendish) remained unexplained as did the Prince of Wales's Cambridge friends (William) 'Hastings-Bass' and 'Edward' Woods, the younger son of the Dean of Windsor, Robin.
>
> The seventh line of the fifth stanza became 'A mounting tension stilling all'.
>
> In the fifth line of the sixth stanza the word 'carry' became 'lifted'.
>
> 'In Memory of George Whitby, Architect', 'Aldershot Crematorium' and 'Dilton Marsh Halt' all came out in *A Nip in the Air*.

To Mary Wilson   Treen
                                                        Trebetherick
                                                        Wadebridge
26 February 1974   Cornwall

My dear Mary,

I thought of you on the 23rd in Univ[ersity] Chapel. I hope the service was some sort of consolation. I think that services are a help – a bit. I have just read in a booklet by Quoist[?] that we are seeds planted here and become roots of Eternity on earth but Eternity is when we blossom and flower. I hope I have got it right. If I have then you will know John W[ebster] more fully after death. Certainly time is a dreadful pit to be landed in. Struggle out. All who love you are with you. This isn't an invitation to suicide. It is to say we are all little bits of immortality –

little bits of 'God' as I heard Mary Hughes say in [a] Westminster [illegible] Meeting forty years ago. Two days of wonderful sun, whilst high tides have made way for damp today.

All the best to you all in Lord N[orth] Street. The Leader's energy is amazing and courageous.

Love from your effete friend, John B

M. W.'s friend John Webster, who had played the organ at her and Harold's wedding, had died. JB met him when they all three went to the Festival Hall to hear a cycle of M.W.'s poems sung by James Bowman, the counter-tenor. M.W. wrote a poem about John Webster which was included in *New Poems* (1980).

Harold W. had just been returned to power, having formed a minority government.

To Denis Forman   29 Radnor Walk
4 April 1974   London sw3

Dear Denis,

I might have known that your Helen [de Moulpied] would have taken a Min[istry] of Inf[ormation] Arts Council view of *Coronation Street*. Tell her that what I love in it is that it never plays a false note. The sets are perfect, the interiors both as to colour and furniture are true to life. Those awful browns and oranges and greens and I love the things displayed for sale in that corner shop. I think it is brilliantly written and faultlessly acted. I get very concerned about the characters. I can imagine what a fiasco *The Importance of Being Earnest* is going to be so inexpertly rendered. Somebody pointed out to me how clever it was of a good actor to act as a bad actor as Jerry Booth does in *The Importance*. The call of that music before *Coronation Street* is to me like a call to prayer for a Muslim. Do tell the cast and the designer of the sets and the producers how much I admire their humour and fidelity.

Yours sincerely, John Betjeman

D.F., Chairman of Granada Television, and married to Helen de Moulpied, had written to JB (29 March 1974), 'I felicitate you on your devotion to *Coronation Street*, which you mentioned in the BBC programme *Nationwide*. What good taste you have – so many silly and superior people like to run it down (and most of them have never seen it).' He had signed himself 'Mendicant for Coronation Street'.

To Edward and Prudence Maufe   29 Radnor Walk
17 April 1974   London sw3

Dear Edward and Prudence,
Don't bother to answer this letter for it is in the nature of a Collins to
thank you for your church of St Thomas, Hanwell. I went there for the
first [time] yesterday having just visited the old village parish church
(started Gothic by Scott in his youth 1841) and charming cottages. I
was with my friend Rev[eren]d Harry Williams CR who was once
Dean of Trinity Cambridge and tutor to Prince Charles. We travelled
in brilliant evening sunlight down the road to Brentford and there, on
the right, was your noble brick tower of St Thomas. We pulled up, and
magnetised by the proportion and nobility of the exterior, braved the
traffic, found the church locked but the vicar, a charming man called
Sharp, was having tea in your neat vicarage and took us in. He did it
most cunningly and dramatically, for we came in at the s[outh] e[ast]
corner and he switched on the lights so that we suddenly saw the whole
mysterious length of the vaulted south aisle. Then he made us walk to
the w[est] and see the whole church. It is TERRIFIC: all done with scale:
the decoration is beautifully subordinated and subtle, as is the skin of
brick-work on the outside with its bands of red with purple. The
chancel is so grand that it has accommodated that huge reredos from St
Thomas's. I see a lot of Guildford in the church. I loved the font, the
[Moira] Forsyth glass and the statue of Our Lady given by Prudence
and safe in its niche in the Lady Chapel.

As we stood on the vicarage lawn and in the fading sunset light saw
the great bulk of the church and n[orth] chapel and tall campanile, we
realised we were in the presence of a masterpiece. I shall always
remember it. I was proud to be able to tell the vicar that I had had a
delicious luncheon with you both last autumn.

It is good to know that while we are all here, that glorious, simple
noble and original church is still rising over its red suburb and lifting up
the hearts of thousands.

Thank you, thank you.

Yours ever, John Betjeman

E.M., the architect, married to Prudence, was a tall, handsome and courteous man who
lived in a Sussex farmhouse with off-white walls, limed oak furniture, Eric Gill
sculptures and giant-leaved zimmer lindens. His most famous building was Guildford
Cathedral. Maufe's obituary read, 'His work is not likely to appeal to the present
generation of architects because it was essentially traditional and restrained.' JB had

grown to admire his work and had met him on the RFAC in 1953.

JB had recommended to both John Summerson and Arthur Bryant that they visit St Thomas's Hanwell which was built in 1934 as a precursor to E.M.'s Guildford Cathedral. E.M. said later that he used it to try out some of his ideas for the latter which was begun in 1936.

The reredos was by Cecil Hare and came from St Thomas's Portman Square, whose demolition provided funds for the building.

To Penelope Betjeman   29 Radnor Walk
24 April 1974   London sw3

My darlin Plymmi,
I am ever so sorry to hear of your broken arms. I suppose one gets brittler with age. I hope it does not hurt very much. Went with Billa [Harrod], little Osbert Lancaster and Henry's kiddiz to an incense-laden mass at S[outh] Creake yesterday which we filmed.

Have just talked to Rupert and Wibz who may come to see you while I am in Cornwall. Raymond Leppard is coming to Cornwall. He will fit in v[ery] well to Trebetherick. The horse above looks very like Archie. I wonder if it is related to him.

I will write you when I'm in Cornwall. Filming was (as you will know) very fatiguing so I can barely keep awake.

Nooni nooni. Yorz trewly, Tewpie

PB had fallen off her Arab horse, Sidi Habismilk, just below Urishay near her house at Michaelchurch. He had shied at a dog and jumped over a sheep hurdle.

The film of the mass at S. Creake was not used.

To Wilhelmine Harrod   29 Radnor Walk
21 May 1974   London sw3

Darling Billa,

Well, I hope I haven't let the old C[hurch] of E[ngland] down. I certainly enjoyed the filming but right at the end in the churchyard of that touchingly beautiful Hales I could not remember my lines owing to exhaustion. These are they:

> Baptism, marriage, death,
> Saxon, Norman and Gothic
> There it stands
> Alone in the Norfolk wild flowers,
> It has weathered the storms.
> A steadfast and lasting witness
> To the Faith
> To the Church of England.

I don't think any of them can object to that.

As Eddie M[irzoeff] was saying, we couldn't have made the film without you. All the really good things were your knowledge and suggestions. My writing now is very like Bosie's but less legible. I had a heavenly letter from Puffin[?].

Love to Roy [Harrod] and Dom [Harrod] and Henry [Harrod] and all and Father and Gregory and Arthur [Illegible]. Love will find a way. So with lots [to] both, JB

W.H. had helped with the planning and research of *A Passion for Churches*. Having founded the Norfolk Churches Trust in 1970, she knew and loved a large proportion of the county's 659 churches, and co-wrote the *Shell Guide to Norfolk* (1957), arranged by JB.

The Norman church of St Margaret, Hales, has a round tower and good doorways. Inside are early fifteenth-century paintings of St Christopher and St James.

To Jill Day-Lewis (Balcon)   29 Radnor Walk
28 May 1974   London sw3

Dearest Jill,
I am so sorry I did not see you ere I left with the Birkenheads [Freddie
and Sheila] to congratulate you on the SUPERB reading of Cecil's poems.
The Gallant Captain was taking notes all the time. What can they have
been about? It was so good a performance that you and Gary [Watson]
gave that I would like to think there was some permanent record of it.
You both ought to do it on a disc. The variety was great and the timing
perfect. I think Cecil was supervising it. The effect was magic and the
greatness and gentleness and un-flashiness of his poetry came out. You
must have noticed how entranced all of the audience were. Thank you
dear Jill and thank Gary and love to Dan and Tamsin. I loved that last
poem and I'm sure they did.
    Much love, JB

> Jill Balcon had performed at a Memorial Reading for her late husband Cecil D.-L. given
> at the Royal Society of Literature, together with Gary Watson.
>   The 'Gallant Captain' was Antony Brett-James, Head of the Department of War
> Studies and International Affairs at the Royal Military Academy at Sandhurst, a
> linguist, military historian and setter of *Mastermind* questions. He came to all the D.L.'s
> poetry proms and Jill remembers JB, on seeing him, exclaiming, 'There's the gallant
> Captain; now I feel SAFE,' and Antony blushed with pleasure. Jill and he later lived
> together.

To James Mitchell   29 Radnor Walk
6 June 1974   London sw3

My dear James,
I agree with what you say in your letter but I'm not going to sign it
because I am in an invidious position with regard to Ireland. For a
whole year during the War I was Press Attaché to what was then called
the United Kingdom Representative (Sir John Maffey, later Lord
Rugby). I learned a lot about the strange tribal nature of Ireland then.
The problem is insoluble. Before the Civil Rights campaign in
Northern Ireland, in fact in the exact year before, the Protestant (i.e.
Presbyterian) demonstrations in Derry were becoming light-hearted
folklore and you would find harmony and laughter on both sides.
Because of some inexplicable tribal division, nothing to do with

politics, all the amity of after the War has gone. The Northern Ireland Presbyterians (their motto is 'Ardens sed virens') can be as bitterly opposed to Britain as the wildest people in the South. But bitterest of all are Northern Ireland R[oman] C[atholic]s. The people on whom you can rely for sound judgement in Ireland are the Jesuits, probably most of the Professors at Maynooth and certainly the Church of Ireland, which is really the C[hurch] of E[ngland] and consists of landowners like the Donoughmores and which bred all the most effective revolutionaries in Ireland e.g. Robert Emmet, Swift, Parnell, Lord Edward FitzGerald, Wolfe Tone, Henry Grattan. If Grattan's parliament had survived there would never have been all this division and misery. The Archbishop of Armagh, who is Primate of the Church of Ireland (George Simms), would be the person to consult and because of all this I don't feel I can put in my oar. I would ask George Simms first, and if you'd like me to do that I will do so and if he says I can sign the letter then I will. He knows I haven't his knowledge.

Yours ever, John Betjeman

J.M. and Richard Holme had written a letter to *The Times* (30 May 1974) advocating a time limit on the presence of British Troops in Northern Ireland. The response had been immense and they were now seeking to gain many more signatures to the letter and take a half page advertisement in *The Times*.

To Mary Wilson   Treen
                                                                    Trebetherick
                                                                    Wadebridge
June 1974   Cornwall

My dear Mary,
I very much enjoyed the Beating of the Retreat and the cordiality of the Leader whom I feel I can now call Harold. It was a beautiful note to end London on and, I feel, my worldly career from down here in Cornwall. Proofs of my poems have arrived and I think them so bad ('Mary Wilson at Diss' is a *bit* better than some) that I don't think I ever ought to have been made Poet Laureate. I read like a rhyming Marie Corelli. The hot smell of Nivea Cream on Brummy [Birmingham] limbs tanning in glorious June weather here, is more potent than thyme. The sea pinks are just over.

I DO HOPE YOU CAN READ THIS. PERHAPS I HAD BETTER STICK TO CAP[ITAL]S. THE SEA PINKS ARE JUST OVER, AS I SAID IN LONGHAND,

THE ELDERS ARE CREAMY GREEN, THE SEA IS EMERALD WITH PURPLE
SHADOWS. LITTLE MARK GIROUARD AND HIS WIFE ARE COMING TO
STAY. HE WRITES BETTER ON ARCHITECTURE THAN ANY. THE BLACK-
BIRDS ARE IN FULL SONG AND THE THRUSHES. A GOSHAWK HAS BEEN
SEEN HERE. I AM SELECTING HENLEY'S POEMS SO BOMBASTIC AND
FRANK BRANGWYN-Y. GILES WAS IN GOOD FORM ON THE WAY TO THE
BUS WHICH TURNED INTO A TAXI IN WHITEHALL. I AM GOING TO BUY A
BLACK BERET AND DARK SPEX SO AS TO FRIGHTEN THE TOURISTS.

THAT BOOK OF A. L. ROWSE AND YOURS TRULY ON OLD CORNWALL
NEEDS BETTER AND BIGGER PHOTOGRAPHS.

I HOPE YOU COMPLETE YOUR NEXT TWO POEMS. I AM PICKING UP THE
BITS OF MYSELF SO AS NOT TO WRITE.

Love from Ian Hall but love from JB

> The Beating of the Retreat is an annual military display at Horse Guards, Whitehall.
>   JB's latest collection of poems, *A Nip in the Air*, was at proof stage. 'Mary Wilson at
> Diss' was published in it as 'A Mind's Journey to Diss'.
>   Ian Hall was an organist known to M.W. and JB.

To Mollie Baring   Blacklands House
                                                      Calne
5 August 1974   Wiltshire

Darling Mollie,
I am writing this on the terrace in the sun looking south to the downs at
Wibz's new abode. Rupert is working the motor mower, the children
rush about; only the Downs and expensive-looking horses are still. It
will make the most beautiful house and garden and has affinities with
Ardington. The Heck [Hester Knight] and Ag [Catherine Clan-
william] of here are Frances Eliot and her husband [Charlie
Shelburne].

I wanted to write to you anyhow to say how sad I was to learn of your
father's death. He was an angel of a man. Always pleased to see one and
he loved you all and lived a full and happy life. He did know how to
enjoy himself and make those round him happy and confident. You and
your mother must miss Ben terribly. I talked to Nigel on the telephone
last week – I was drinking champagne! – and he told me Ben was not a
long time ill. Thank God for that. And thank God for such a good and
happy life as his and for you his daughter and all of you at Ardington,

slaving away in that forgotten garden.
   Love to Dezzie and all and to your mother. Love, John B

> RLG and I had just moved to Blacklands, near Calne in Wiltshire beside the river
> Marden, a large Georgian house which was in a bad state of repair, having been gutted
> by fire on its top two floors. It had had a lot of money lavished on it and the grounds in
> the late nineteenth century and none since.
>   'Heck' Knight had been a near neighbour during JB's days at Wantage. JB always
> talked of her coupled with her sister's name 'Ag[atha]'. JB equated their social standing
> in the neighbourhood with that of our new neighbours Frances and Charlie Shelburne
> who lived at Bowood near Calne.
>   M.B.'s father, Ben Warner, had just died. A remarkable character, he had started as a
> baker's boy and began to take bets from people he delivered bread to. He ended up as a
> successful and respected bookmaker owning his own racehorses. He never left his native
> Newbury. M.B. was his only child.

To Candida Lycett Green   29 Radnor Walk
6 August 1974   London sw3

Darling Wibz,
Ta ever so for a glorious sunlit idle stay in the Wiltshire summer.

Ta for the view from the brick-walled garden
On to the downland over the Marden
Ta for the monotone, evenly-flowing
Of Rupert's football and Rupert's mowing.
Ta to Lucy for bringing a chair
That I might bask in the Wiltshire air
Ta for Imo I never will find
One so gentle, and loving and kind
Ta to Delli whose eyes so round
Go rolling about with never a sound
And over it all the long day through
Ta oh wonderful Wibz to you.

Love, MD

To Mary Wilson   29 Radnor Walk
21 August 1974   London sw3

My dear Mary,
I am typing this myself and if there are any mistakes you must
understand. And not mind when I sometimes type the same words

twice. I am hoping that the sounds of the sea and the scent of the breeze
and the huge silence at night and the winds and storms when they get
up put all back into perspective so that you are the happy person you are
and it's funny to think of you reading this in Scilly.

I have been having a terrible time in the newspapers – mis-
represented, lied about, often with the best intentions, and made so
nervous I hardly dare put pen to paper. Perhaps it would be rather a
good thing if paper runs out. Have you got that excellent book John
Arlott did called *Island Camera*? Please write to me when you are in the
mood but feel no obligations. Guilt is the death of art. Amen.

Love, John

I dreamed last night I was a liberal MP from S[outh] Lancashire in
the *farming* interest and went and played with TRAMS at the back of
the H[ouse] of C[ommons] with the Leader. What can it symbolize?
All the best to Giles and all.

  Last week I took Ava Lady Waverley to Peterborough to the
cathedral by train. I think she is very fond of you.

To the Manager, Great Eastern Hotel   29 Radnor Walk
13 September 1974   London SW3

Dear Sir,
I went into the Great Eastern yesterday at lunchtime and I had not been
there for more than a year. I was very sad to hear from the Head Waiter
and his second-in-command and the wine waiter that Mr Stokes had
died. They each came to me with the news for they all regretted him
deeply as I do. I can imagine how sad you must feel without him and I
told them that in losing him I felt I had lost a friend. There is some
consolation in the thought of his having so well spent his life and having
endeared himself to so many. He was the right man for the right job and
that does not often happen. Please accept my condolences and
sympathy. My long absence from the Great Eastern was because I left
the City and came to live in Chelsea which is not so nice.

  John Betjeman

> Arthur Stokes had worked at the Great Eastern Hotel, Liverpool Street, London, for
> many years. An imposing and well-respected figure, he was head waiter in the main
> dining room and had a good rapport with regular customers such as JB.

To David Astor   29 Radnor Walk
17 September 1974   London sw3

Dear David,
I am either extreme Left, extreme Right or extreme Liberal. I am non-
political and I like keeping quiet on the subject of politics. Sorry not to
be able to contribute. I wish we were all in Cornwall and walking along
at low tide from Daymer to Rock whatever the weather.
    John Betjeman

> D.A., who edited the *Observer* and had a house in Trebetherick, had written for a feature
> he was planning to ask JB to say which way he would vote in the forthcoming elections.

To Mrs Noonan   29 Radnor Walk
26 September 1974   London sw3

Dear Mrs Noonan,
I did meet a lady on a wet day in Dungarvan when she was staying in
Helvick and I was in Dublin. I was driving on to a house (on the
Blackwater River) which has now, I believe, been destroyed. The name
Moira McCavendish was as fortuitous as Greta Hellstrom. They are
there for their euphony and for their faces and figures in the memory of
    Yours sincerely, John Betjeman

> Mrs N. had written to JB asking him about the reality of various events and people in his
> poetry. The poems from which the questions arise are 'The Irish Unionist's Farewell to
> Greta Hellstrom in 1922', in which the line 'through Dungarvan in the rain' occurs, and
> 'A Lament for Moira McCavendish'.

To Mary Clive   29 Radnor Walk
3 October 1974   London sw3

Dearest Mary,
That was the most rewarding visit I have had to Penelope since she first
went to Injer. We really came together and I feel what you said to me
sometime ago is quite true – she is really happy so long as she can see a
grandchild now and then. I see her as Queen of Ewyas which is Nepal
with Wales as China and Whitfield as Injer's New Delhi and I think she

will run her kingdom of hip[pie]s and devotees of Buddha long after we have left the earth. I felt very near to her and as fond as ever and so, I think, did she. This does not argue the necessity for physical propinquity. You have been a rock of our salvation. So has wonderful Eliz[abeth] Cavendish.

Thank God for you and George [Clive], the most selfless of hosts – Oh God, that I mistook a claret for burgundy – and your goodness to your undeserving but ever affectionate chum, JB

> JB and PB had been to stay at Whitfield in Herefordshire with their old friend M.C. (née Pakenham, see *Volume One*) and her son George.
>   Whitfield, a bow-fronted red-brick eighteenth-century house, set in a ravishing park of ancient trees, was a comfortable haven which PB often visited either for Sunday lunch or to stay the night. When at New House, PB acted as a catalyst to soul-searching mystics who abounded around Hay-on-Wye. 'Mike the Meadow' did her grass cutting, for instance, and her kitchen was seldom a lonely place.

To Penelope Betjeman   Treen
                                                             Trebetherick
                                                             Wadebridge
6 December 1974   Cornwall

My darling Plymmi,
I am badly on the lose (not drink and sex. I am now twelve stone eleven pounds) but on the lose-looz. I keep losing things which is why I have had to come to Cornwall and keep my weight down.

Here are two Jain Temples and you are waiting to go inside them. You are in an ecstasy. The dots are insects.

Yorz very trewely and with loove to all Clives and Whitfield, Tewpie

To Bruce Shand   29 Radnor Walk
30 December 1974   London SW3

My dear Major,
The message on the enclosed Christmas card reminds me of my passion
for sulky, freckled, wide-eyed Mary Shand swinging her satchel as she
walked reluctantly from school over the Bath pavements, lucky stones
to have been trodden by her gymshoes. My son-in-law Rupert Lycett
Green has given me as a Christmas present a book called *Worrals Goes
East* by Captain W. E. Johns. Flight Officer Jan Worralson ('Worrals'
to her comrades in the WRAF) and her friend Flight Officer Betty
Lovell (otherwise 'Frecks') outwit the Arabs. Rupert found it in
Hovingham, and pencilled on the half-title in a neat hand which could
be the governess but might be the glorious owner herself, 'K. Worsley'.
This made my Christmas.

But what I'm really writing about is that the halves of extra dry J and
B Epernay which I bought with my annual twenty-nine pounds as Poet
Laureate, are so good as a morning pick-me-up that I would like to buy
some more. Let us say three dozen half-bottles to last me till Easter and
with my own money. Can you tell the splendid Mr Jameson of this
whim of mine? It is much the best champagne I have bought for the
price but I have a fear that stocks are limited and that it may be a royal
prerogative.

Yours ever, John B

> B.S., the soldier and writer, had been abandoned as a child by his lothario father P.
> Morton S., and only met him again in later life. Mary S. was the daughter of P. Morton
> S.'s fourth wife Sybil (née Sissons) with her previous husband who was a naval officer
> called John Ambrose Steel. She was a small child at the time of their marriage, and was
> brought up with Elspeth Shand and was elected to be called Shand – though was no
> blood relative.
>
> Captain W.E. Johns (1893–1968) was also the author of the series of eighty books for
> boys about Biggles.
>
> JB's passion for the Duchess of Kent (née K. Worsley)'s looks was a well-known fact
> among our family. Although he had barely met her and she remained blissfully unaware
> of his feelings, he often spoke of her in trembling tones and when he heard that RLG had
> been brought up in her neighbourhood in Yorkshire, and had been to the same children's
> parties, he was tremendously excited.
>
> JB received an annual wine allowance from the Queen. Geoffrey Jameson was Clerk
> of the Royal Cellars and ran the wine firm of Justerini and Brooks.

To Craig Brown   29 Radnor Walk
30 December 1974   London SW3

Dear Craig,

>   I can't come
>   It's me 'plates of meat'
>   I'm bad at walking
>   And worse at talking.

Yours sincerely, John Betjamin

> C.B., the writer, had written from Eton where he was a pupil, asking JB to speak to a
> school society.

To Peter Quennell   29 Radnor Walk
21 January 1975   London SW3

Dear Peter,
There are one or two observations I would like to make on *The Marble
Foot*. The first and the chief is that you are a very good poet as I have
long known. I own a copy of your poems and remember them in
Georgian Poetry. It makes your writing quite different from anyone
else's. There is that sudden moment when you recall a line from
Traherne and there are deeply-felt moments such as your first glimpse
of Rouen and these become poetry. But then there is something else I
want to put down in black and white and that is that you have never
written ill. Everything you write, commissioned or spontaneous, is
clear and elegant and memorable. You have a beautiful dandified
detached manner of writing which makes you compulsive reading to
anyone who takes up one of your books. Also you are very funny and
can look back and laugh at yourself. I find the most hilarious moments
in this book are those describing Crabtrees and the discomfort and the
cold coming up through the floor-boards and the garden where nothing
would grow and the noisy plumbing and constantly flushing lavatory. I
don't think anyone since H. G. Wells has written so vividly of the silent
middle classes or lower middle classes as M[arjorie] and C. H. B.
[Quennell] seem to have wanted to describe themselves. These early
chapters are an essential foil to the grand life of country houses and
hostesses and seductive women which carried on until you were sent

down for that 'foolish escapade' at Skindles. I have no doubt that you will be able to go on until the war and describe your life as a series of adventures in which you are usually the innocent victim of a predator. The book is so compelling that I would like it to go on until you die. What happens in it and told in your delightfully off-hand way, punctuated with sudden punchlines, doesn't matter much. I hope there will be some illustrations of C. H. B.'s work and of M[arjorie] and her work. All over the world their works are known and it's nice to read of how they got written with you and your brother and sister lying about at the feet of author and authoress. Barry the architect of the H[ouses] of P[arliament] was just the same. He liked to work at his drawing board with his children playing about round his feet. M[arjorie] and C. H. B. at their twin desks in their living room seem to have been very like Barry. I think you should just go on writing the book as you are doing now and stop when you are bored. Your readers never will be.

Yours, John Betjeman.

P.Q. (see *Volume One*) was an old friend of JB and PB who had often stayed at Garrards Farm in the early thirties. He was a poet, biographer, author, critic and one time editor of the *Cornhill Magazine* (1944–1951). At this time he edited *History Today*. *The Marble Foot* was the first volume of his autobiography.

In February 1976 P.Q. wrote to JB, 'Do you remember that, when you kindly agreed to look through my autobiography, you sent me a very generous letter on the subject, which you said that I might show my publishers? I have now changed publishers – Collins instead of Sir Geo[rge] Weid[enfeld], thank God! They, too, have seen the letter; and I find that in the *blurb* they have just produced, they have quoted three sentences.'

Marjorie and C. H. B. Quennell (the architect), writers on social history for children, were P.Q.'s parents.

To Auberon Waugh   29 Radnor Walk
13 February 1975   London sw3

Dear Bron,

I very much enjoyed yesterday's luncheon, so did my friend Harry Williams. We talked about it all the way back in that luxurious car to this place. It was very kind of you to ask me. I was silent and pre-occupied. This was because, I now realize, there was welling up in me a desire to let the cat out of the bag about an enormous land deal being made by British Railways over the sites of Liverpool Street and Broad Street Stations. It will mean goodbye to the Great Eastern Hotel with its dome of many-coloured glass, to the Abercorn Rooms and the

Masonic Temples; to that glorious elevated walk across from Bishops-
gate; through the Miss Hook of Holland part of the station and on to
those interlacing Gothic arches of the original Great Eastern. It will
mean goodbye to Broad Street echoing and forgotten and to those
Lombardic stairs that climb up its southern side to the North London
Railway war memorial. Instead the whole area will be covered by
offices. We know what they'll look like and under the offices there will
be, amid fumes and the tannoy system, some platform for trains to East
Anglia. It will be the new Euston only much worse, if that were
possible, and much higher of course because the buggers will feel fully
justified in being higher than the Stock Exchange or the appalling new
Barbican. Much ridicule will be poured on preservation-mad nostalgics
such as yours truly, for admiring this 'essentially second-rate' collection of buildings, and for not seeing the glorious smooth-running future
the financiers see for their new slabs. I think that there has been some
pretty smart land dealing and I can't find out about it but you can
through your brilliant staff.

Fight on for the right and thousands of thanks,
Yours ever, John B

A.W., Evelyn's son, and JB were great friends – they had formed a mutual admiration
society.
  Liverpool Street, the terminus of the Great Eastern Railway, was chaotic and had few
friends other than JB, who called it 'the most picturesque and interesting of the London
termini' and addressed the AGM of the Victorian Society in the Great Eastern Hotel in
1974. The following year British Railways unveiled plans to rebuild Liverpool Street
Station and to remove its high-level neighbour, Broad Street Station, the City terminus
of the North London Railway, altogether as part of a commercial redevelopment. The
reasons for this were ostensibly concerned with efficiency and rationalisation but in
truth were merely financial. These plans were vigorously opposed by the Victorian
Society and others, and a lengthy public inquiry was held in 1976–77. When the verdict
was announced two years later, the fine Gothic western train shed of 1873–75 at
Liverpool Street was reprieved, along with the Great Eastern Hotel (with its Masonic
Temples, beloved by JB), but poor Broad Street – 'saddest of all London stations' – was
doomed. Liverpool Street has since been partly rebuilt and partly preserved as part of
the Broadgate office development, but its magic has gone.

To Hugh Linstead   29 Radnor Walk
5 March 1975   London SW3

Dear Sir Hugh,
I have thought of a four-line stanza which might look quite nice under
that splendid photograph you sent me of the Windmill:

When shall we hear across the windy common
  Over loud voices and the barking dogs,
Your notes again, old Surrey working-woman,
  Sweeping your sails round, and clacking with your cogs?

I hope this is enough. I don't expect you will ever get the machinery into working order, not even if you sell the wholemeal loaves of Wimbledon ground corn at five pounds an ounce.
  Yours ever, John Betjeman

> H.L., Chairman of Macarthys Pharmaceuticals, had been MP for Putney for over twenty years and wrote to JB as a member of the Wimbledon and Putney Commons Conservators asking for help to raise money for the windmill on Wimbledon Common. 'What a splendid stanza!' wrote H.L. (6 March 1975). 'If ever we grind our own corn there will be a monthly packet for you in perpetuity!'

To Edward Carpenter   29 Radnor Walk
20 May 1975   London SW3

Dear Edward,
Henry James (though I have always preferred M. R. James) – I am fully aware that he is a king among writers. Unique and grand. Why isn't there a shrine to him in St John's Cathedral New York? Or Rye parish church, Kent? He lived in Rye and loved it. Of course he is a writer of international stature and I am sounding a bit pompous. Do you think it can be the cares of Office?
  Yours ever, John B

> E.C., the Dean of Westminster Abbey, wrote to JB about a request which had been made to commemorate Henry James (1843–1916), the novelist and native New Yorker who became a British subject in 1915. He had lived in Lamb House, Rye, since the end of the nineteenth century. The Dean made an informal enquiry as to the status and durability of James (JB was all the more approachable for he was on the Architectural Advisory Panel) as to whether James was worthy of Abbey commemoration.
>
>   Although JB wore Henry James's morning suit which had been left to him, he never much cared for his writing.
>
>   A stone in Poets' Corner, Westminster Abbey, commemorating Henry James, was unveiled on 17 June 1976.
>
>   M. R. James (1862–1936), provost of Eton, wrote several volumes of ghost stories including 'Oh, Whistle, and I'll Come to You, My Lad'.

To Rupert Lycett Green   The Royal Automobile Club
21 May 1975   Pall Mall SW1

My dear Rupert,
This is one of the only places you can find INK and a DIPPING PEN.
Hence this lovely handwritten letter to say how pleased I am to have a
grandson called David Lycett Green. May he join the Navy or the RAC
and take up art and craftwork.

I met the Governor of Wandsworth in Grosvenor Chapel on Sunday
and asked about Tom. He said he was now in the Scrubs. I said I hoped
he would be safe from the other prisoners. He said there was a sudden
wave of violence over the country. Love to Wibz, Lucy, Imo and Delli
and you.

I go to Cornwall till Oct[ober] 21st on Sunday.

In the sure and certain life of a speedy resurrection

I am, your tasteless unathletic father-in-law, John

> David Petroc, our first son, was called after RLG's father who was in the Navy.
> Tom was a handsome mutual friend who was doing time for fraud.

To Tom Driberg   29 Radnor Walk
22 May 1975   London SW3

> Nothing can hide the pleasure that I feel
> Who here salute you, Thomas Edward Neil,
> On this your seventieth birthday. Can it be
> That of the sons of Lancing you are he
> Who Roxburgh's standard into Fleet Street bore
> Further than Fulford, Molson, Evelyn Waugh
> Dudley Carew and others? Yes it can
> Gulielmus Hickeyus née Dragoman,
> Christ Church and Church of England, who would guess
> That you would ever write for the *Express*
> A Presbyterian journal with a tone
> More puritan and moral than your own?
> Testy at breakfast, difficult at tea
> But in the evening oh how free, how free!
> True poet, honest aesthete, loyal friend
> Kindly be with me 'till my sticky end.

T.D. was taught by J. F. Roxburgh at Lancing, who he described as 'a dandy and a sceptic with a sonorous voice'.

Roger Fulford, Hugh Molson, Evelyn Waugh and Dudley Carew were fellow Lancing old boys.

T.D. had been Gulielmus Hickeyus or William Hickey of the *Daily Express*.

To Penelope Betjeman   29 Radnor Walk
1 December 1975   London sw3

My darling Plymmi,
What fun it was at the L[ittle] R[edoubt]. So warm and comfortable, as well as beautiful. I shall never forget our drive through all that Augustus John, J. D. Innes and Derwent Lees country to Barmouth and Lady Chetwynd's 1870-ish fantasy palace of tiles and iron and coloured marbles and steep gables. I liked her a lot and will find out from little Mark Girouard who was the architect.

I love you as much as I ever did and this visit was like old times. I saw a very good telly last night on hell. It was a film. It said hell is now and is separation from God. Quite true.

Gerard [Irvine] and I are catching the 12.15 on Sat[urday] arriving at 1.58. Wibz will meet us. I will return on Sunday.

The train from Newport took four hours. It was diverted through *Westbury* and Hungerford to Reading. A very interesting route but the train was unheated.

John N[ankivell] has given me beautiful drawing of an eighteenth-century cathedral interior. Injer I think. I look forward to seeing you on Saturday next at the font.

Yorz trewely, Tewpie
If you are snowed up
then we'll meet at Christmas.

JB wrote to Mark Girouard (12 December 1975), 'I am however, concerned about a truly splendid and quite untouched seaside château designed in Gothic and ascribed to Pugin. It is called Tyn-Y-Coed, Arthog. I'm glad to say it is owned by a Dowager Peeress who loves it from the noble entrance hall with free-standing stone staircase to the flowered lavatory bowls in the rambling passages cut into the dripping Welsh cliffs. I saw it with Penelope and her friend Jenny Houston of the Hereford Tourist Board a fortnight ago. The house is in a bad way and could be saved. If you have seen it can you send corroborative evidence to me here which I can forward to the Historic Buildings Commission.' (The house, built in the 1870s for David Davies by no known architect, was not listed until 1979, despite its dazzling interior with marble staircase and fireplaces.)

Gerard Irvine came to Blacklands to christen David LG.

John Nankivell was the artist who often accompanied PB to India to draw temples.

To Lucy Lycett Green   Letterhead of
[January] 1976   *The Industrial Exhibition for 1851*

My dear Lucy,
It seems wicked of me to write on so lovely and genuine a piece of Victorian writing paper as this, but I thought you would like it. The Crystal Palace was built in Hyde Park in 1851 and taken down later and rebuilt in South London and burned down about fifty years ago. I remember it well. They had firework displays in front of it.

Much love from Grandpapa

JB wrote constantly to his grandchildren as soon as they were old enough to take things in.

To Endellion Lycett Green   29 Radnor Walk
27 January 1976   London sw3

Darling Delli,
Many happy returns of the day. A present will arrive this week for you with love

Grandpapa

Christmas 1975

Catch the hour and make it last
Christmas Day is going fast
Loud and clearly Delli sings
A carol to her King of Kings.

I can hear her where I'm standing
Halfway up upon the landing
Halfway up and in between
Different sorts of Wiltshire scene
On one side chalk the other cheese
The house looks out on each of these.

JB's grandchildren always staged a Christmas show and in 1975 the audience sat on the wide first-floor landing while Delli, among others, sang from the half landing of the second-floor stairs.

To Harry Jarvis   29 Radnor Walk
17 March 1976   London SW3

Dear Harry,
Phoeble is very much enjoying the political crisis and if only we ran out of water or the country were invaded by Russia, Penelope would be very happy on her mountain-top. I have a very strong feeling that this earth is going to crack beneath me and I will sink into fire through mattresses of chicken-wire, telephone cables and sewage pipes which compose the ground under our feet in Radnor. On Monday night the whole of it was bathed in an ominous violet pink light.
    Yours in the sure and certain hope of a speedy Resurrection, John B

JB's poem 'Chelsea 1977' describes the street bathed 'in winter sunset pink,' and later continues:

> The earth beneath my feet is hardly soil
> But outstretched chicken-netting coil on coil.

JB had often told me about his vivid imaginings which, in retrospect, I believe were caused by the drugs prescribed for him at the time.

To Mary Wilson   29 Radnor Walk
18 March 1976   London SW3

My dear Mary,
How strange that I should have read into your photographed face, a look of resignation. It must be relief to have the headlights and searchlights switched elsewhere. Selfishly I am glad as we shall have

more time for verse and you will have more time for Scilly. A taxi man
said to me, 'He's all right – he can go to the Sicilies.'

You've both done so well for so long you deserve a rest and some
LAUGHTER. I go to Gloucester and Hereford on Tuesday and
Thursday and Cornwall on 27th: Any chance of Tea next week *except*
Tue[sday] or Wed[nesday]?

God bless you all, Love John

Harold W. had resigned as Prime Minister, to be succeeded by James Callaghan.

To Bevis Hillier   29 Radnor Walk
25 March 1976   London sw3

Dear Bevis,
Forgive Magda [Rogers]'s typing but I can't *write* at all. I'm very sorry
you're giving up the *Connoisseur* because it really is a good journal. One
only wants money to get rid of anxiety. It has no other purpose. Are
you in a terrible state of angst?

By all means write my life. It's kind of you to undertake so dull a job.
You writing, Jock publishing should assure a modest sale in the
circulating libraries among the older folk.

Give us a tingle when you come back from Los Angeles. I am very
fond of the Reverend Marcus Morris, a good and lonely man.

Love, John B

B.H. had just resigned as editor of the *Connoisseur*.
Young Betjeman, the first part of B.H.'s biography of JB, was published in 1988 by
Murrays.

To Sophy Bridgewater   29 Radnor Walk
21 April 1976   London sw3

Dear Sophy,
I did like your letter. I hope you like the postcards I enclose of Chelsea
as it was even before I was a kiddi. I think I prefer the Rawlinson Road
and Northmoor Road and Gees Florist shop and St Philip and St James
bulging over the brick gables of North Oxford. Your letter cheered me

up on a Monday morning when I was feeling lonely and afraid. Afraid of what? Nothing I suppose. My love to you and all in your house.
   Love, John B

S.B., who was twelve years old, had written a fan letter to JB. She lived at 8 Rawlinson Road in North Oxford, a favourite street in a favourite area of JB's.

To Endellion Lycett Green   29 Radnor Walk
30 April 1976   London sw3

Very dear Delli,
You asked for a letter from me and here it is. You have got a lot more hair now and so I have done
a new drawing of you.
Here it is.

   Here is a little book for Easter that I bought in Romania. A very pretty country, full of coloured churches. I am off to Cusop to stay with Grandma Elope. Give the other two little books to Lucy and Imo.
   Love to you all, Grandpapa

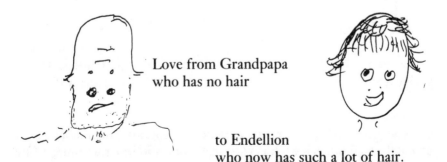

Love from Grandpapa
who has no hair

to Endellion
who now has such a lot of hair.

ELG had a regular correspondence with JB until he was too ill to write. 'We drew
pictures for each other, Grandpapa depicting me as an egg-headed sort of person with a
wide-open mouth,' she recalls.

   My children all called PB 'Gramelope' which was a shortened and scrambled version
of Grandmama Penelope.

To John Murray   29 Radnor Walk
5 May 1976   London SW3

Dear Jock,
Thank you for the enormous cheque. I shall be away until the end of
June in Cornwall filming. Magda [Rogers] will be in charge here. I
spent four days on Penelope's mountain-top and in her garden was a
golden river of daffodils running to the edge of the garden with blue air
beyond. It started cold but grew warmer. I think she is very happy. She
refuses to have a car but she will have to have one and this will help
towards buying it. Jenny Houston, the Hereford lady in the tourist
office there, is a good friend to Penelope and full of humour and
firmness. Penelope goes to India in October taking John Nankivell.
Romania was like England in 1450 when you got off the main road and
the tourist tracks. The churches passing belief in mysterious beauty.
No sign of restoration of an insensitive kind. The Romanian impressionists are as good as the Australian equivalent. I now sign myself,
   Yours, Ivan Betjescu

   JB had been travelling around Romania from 11 to 19 April with EC, Jonathan Stedall
   and John McGlashan on a final recce for Jonathan's film *The Long Search* (with Ron Eyre)
   about the Orthodox Church in Romania.

To Mary Wilson   Treen
                                                           Trebetherick
                                                           Wadebridge
5 May 1976   Cornwall

My dear Mary,
I was delighted with your *Guardian* article. It sounds more like a written
article than an interview. It is very well done and heart warming. The
'Christmas Eve' by Cecil [Day Lewis] is very touching and like him.
His death is a loss to literature. Ted Heath appointed me P[oet]

L[aureate]. In Wadebridge two days ago I bought Pam Ayres's book of poems. They are honest good country stories, some warm and funny, like jokes at a Farmers' dinner. All well told. Some good last lines to others. My heart warms to her humour and directness but it is the kind of verse you and I could make up as we walked along a street or lane or sat at tea. The Lays of Ancient Rome style. But sometimes funny and good. Not Burns or Housman. Forgive poor handwriting. I can only use one eye at present.

Never has it looked lovelier down here. There was a huge sea the day before yesterday. But alas it blows down no hoardings or beach huts.

All the best to Sir H[arold]. I'm glad you're doing another book of poetry. My God, I shall have to do a Pam Ayres about the Queen.

All the best to Giles too. See you [for] tea at 29 [Radnor Walk]. Return on Wednesday June 9th.

Love, John

M.W.'s *New Poems* was published in 1980.
Pam Ayres's recitations of her humorous verse were at that time popular on radio and television.

To Elizabeth Ponsonby   29 Radnor Walk
6 May 1976   London sw3

Dear Bess,
No gentleman, as Matthew would have been quick to notice, but slow to point out, would type a letter to a friend. But I have just got double vision which will right itself but which makes it impossible for me to write straight lines in long-hand. I had to say how sad I am for you and your family with the loss of Matthew. I thought *The Times* yesterday was very good about him. It brought back his shrewdness, humour and loyalty. I see him in my mind's eye in that little room shaped like a mutton chop in Oriel Street when he was an undergraduate. I was very pleased to see you both after your Suffolk days and I'm absolutely delighted that Tom [Ponsonby] is Chairman of the GLC. He has the great humorous calm of Matthew and things won't go wrong with him in charge.

I shall always remember Matthew while I am alive on earth and it makes me happy to think of him in all that Surrey quiet and in his happy family life, with you and your children. No need to reply. I've

written this because I wanted to write it and I shall write to Tom too,
I have done so.

Love, John B

E.P. was the recent widow of Matthew P., who had been at Balliol College, Oxford, when JB was at Magdalen. He often used to visit him and Bess at their family house, Shulbrede Priory, near Haslemere in Surrey, in his later years. 'He was one of a few old friends who could reduce my father to a helpless shoulder-heaving silent laughter which we loved to see,' remembered Kate Russell.

Tom Ponsonby, chairman of the London Tourist Board, succeeded to Matthew's peerage as Lord Ponsonby of Shulbrede.

To Edward Bawden   29 Radnor Walk
8 May 1976   London SW3

My dear Edward,
My word, it was fun. It was what the Academy ought to be and
probably was before the prigs cold-shouldered it. I loved the company
of Lady Nicholls who was so full of life, warmth, humour and
acuteness. She must send a brilliant ray through Saffron Walden, and
certainly when Elizabeth and I went upstairs to see your exhibits, we
were irradiated by the Grecian landscapes and indeed all your exhibits.
I don't think there's the slightest doubt that your eye has enhanced the
vision of everyone who has seen your pictures. You are never the same
but your pictures are always recognizably Edward Bawden's and
though I used originally to think of you along with Eric Ravilious and
John Nash and even Paul [Nash], I now see you as strong, strange and
yourself. Oh, good old Art, there's nothing like it. How it leads one on
and never lets one down. I am greatly indebted to Osbert Lancaster,
Jim Richards and Mr Piper for originally praising you to me. It was a
lovely luncheon and the crowds were too thick for me to find you to say
goodbye.

Yours ever, JB

E.B. (1903–89), the painter and illustrator who studied at the Royal College of Art under Paul Nash, was a friend of Eric Ravilious and an official war artist. He lived at Great Bardfield in Essex for many years. He had just had an exhibition at the Fine Art Society in Bond Street, London, one of JB's favourite galleries, which he never passed without looking in.

To Candida Lycett Green   29 Radnor Walk
14 June 1976   London SW3

Darling Wibz,
I keep thinking about your garden and how good and spacious it is and
how beautiful you have made the house and what a poor sort of father I
am to you and the worst grandfather to those four different and
delightful people. Magda is typing this because I have given up writing
by hand and am off to see Pat Trevor-Roper about my eyes. Jonathan
[Stedall] has been filming with me today in burning heat at Gerrards
Cross. Some people like lumps of meat hot and red with over-
indulgence were lunching at the horrible Greyhound Inn, Chalfont St
Peter. And would not budge up so as to let us have seats when we came
in from filming. Do have a look at the Master's Garden, Marlborough
College. He is Roger Ellis and his wife Margaret is as remarkable as he.
We sang Harrow songs outside his front porch at the finish of our
filming there. Also do see Dr Hallbart, his brother was a famous
headmaster of Clifton who died young. He has bought for an immense
sum the bit of land behind Treen and below Mrs Oakley's. Jonathan
tells me he is coming to stay with you on Saturday. He does not drink
spirits but he likes wine.
    Love to Rupert and them all, MD
    Old Patrick [Kinross]'s funeral was very sad. Diccon [Richard]
Hughes's Memorial Service was on the same day and drew greater
crowds to St Martin's-in–the-Fields. I am glad I am still alive.

> JB wrote to John Edward Bowle (2 July 1976), 'I took your advice and went to Pat
> Trevor-Roper who is very good indeed, meticulous, careful and kind. He has given me
> two new pairs of specs, one for reading and one for walking. He says my eyes will get
> better and they are already a bit better. I'm very grateful to my eyes and my sense of
> touch and above all my taste-buds. Life is real, life is earnest/Two things stand alone/
> Silence in another's trouble/Self-pity in one's own.'
>   He wrote to PB, 'You will remember the limerick:
>
> > There was a young man at the Copa
> > Who made a most terrible faux-pas
> > He abstracted a sailor
> > From Desmond Shawe-Taylor
> > And found it was Pat Trevor-Roper.
>
>
>
> 'Don't forget to wear your pearls for washing up. Much love, Tewpie.'

JB had been filming *Summoned by Bells* for the BBC, directed by Jonathan Stedall – it was screened later that year.

Roger Ellis was formerly an assistant master at Harrow.

Patrick Kinross had died on 4 June.

To Penelope Betjeman   29 Radnor Walk
28 June 1976   London SW3

My darling Plymmi,
I think you will be in favour of this protest against motorcars on the Ridgeway. Archie is very much against it too, as it impedes his archaeological research. I cannot go to the Public Inquiry. It is too hot.

Yours, Tewpie

How is Ben?

JB had sent PB a brochure about the Ridgeway, Europe's oldest road, beside which they had lived most of their married lives. It once stretched from Devon to the Wash, but today is most in evidence between Goring and Streatley and the Pewsey Vale. In 1974 there had been an aerial survey followed by a ground survey in 1975 which resulted in Oxfordshire County Council's attempting to make a Traffic Restriction Order on the stretch of Ridgeway between Woolstone Hill and Sparsholt Firs. There was both objection and support and a public inquiry followed. The upshot of the inquiry was that the Traffic Restriction Order should *not* be made. Controversy continues to this day.

To Endellion Lycett Green   29 Radnor Walk
3 July 1976   London sw3

Dear En  ion,

 ed your poems. The one about the

was true and cheerful. The one about the was true and sad.

Both were BEAUTIFUL. If always write when in the

 and say what you feel and think you will go on

being a poet. Let's have lots more flower 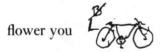 ems. One for every

flower you

Lots of love from Grandpapa

> The letter reads, 'Dear Endellion, I loved your poems. The one about the dandelion was true and cheerful. The one about the bluebell was true and sad. Both were BEAUTIFUL. If you always write when in the mood and say what you feel and think you will go on being a poet. Let's have lots more flower poems. One for every flower you like.'

To Tom Driberg   29 Radnor Walk
21 July 1976   London sw3

My dear Thomas,
I had a very nice luncheon with Jock yesterday. I think I've sent you the
hymn I've written for the Jubilee. It is definitely written as a hymn and
not as a poem and Malcolm Williamson cheered me by saying that the
words were the sort he wanted as they left him the gaps he needed.

Two sayings worth recording for your *Oxford Dictionary*: one is from
the late Lord Quickswood, 'Old age is the outpatients' department of
Purgatory.' Another more cheering one said to me by your peer Harry
d'Avigdor Goldsmid, 'Good news rarely comes in a brown envelope.'
I shall be here all August.

Yours in the sure and certain hope of a speedy Resurrection,
John B

> Malcolm Williamson, the composer and pianist and Master of the Queen's Music, wrote
> music to accompany JB's hymn written in his official capacity of Poet Laureate.
> T.D. was collecting funny phrases for a proposed dictionary, which came to nothing.
> Hugh Cecil (Quickswood) (1869–1956), son of the 3rd Marquess of Salisbury, was
> the Conservative MP for Greenwich 1895–1906, and for Oxford University 1910–37.

To Anthony Blunt   29 Radnor Walk
13 August 1976   London sw3

Dear Anthony,
Early this year I did a tour of Romania with friends in the BBC who
were filming the Orthodox Church.

I thought the Romanians could startle the Western world with an
exhibition of their religious painting done on glass by monks and then
in quite another room their excellent Impressionist painters like
Andreescu (Anderson) and Grigorescu (Grigson). If you think the idea
worth following I will write to Hugh Casson quoting your name and
you may have other and better suggestions. I thought the initiative
should come from this side of the Iron Curtain. Do you know what is
the correct method of approach to Romania? If I have your backing I
shall feel more confident.

Yours ever, John B

A.B. was at this time Surveyor of the Queen's Pictures and one of the most respected art historians in the country. It later transpired that he had been a KGB agent.

His brother Wilfrid B. wrote in his autobiography *Slow on the Feather* of A.B.'s 'close friendship in early days with JB later falling apart because he felt that John, who had the makings of a scholar, elected – as Anthony saw it – to prostitute his talents by popularising what he could have directed into serious study. Even Kenneth Clark – whose arrogance, admittedly, always jarred – seemed to him not to have made full use of his potential, and I recall Anthony quoting, with obvious relish, a line from a parody about the Clarks that was at one time current: "Jane and Sir K in all around I see." '

A.B. replied to JB's letter (20 November 1976), 'I wish I knew more about Romanian art – but I fear I can't give you much moral support, because I don't know their glass paintings, and I suspect – perhaps wrongly – that their Impressionist paintings would (like the Hungarian Impressionists) be regarded here as "provincial".'

To Penelope Betjeman   29 Radnor Walk
8 September 1976   London SW3

My darling Plymmi,

I have read and re-read with increasing pleasure your letter to me of Aug[ust] 31st. It makes me feel slightly less inadequate than I usually do. I can't help feeling that it's a marvellous bit of *luck* my poems should be liked, and sell. I quite agree with you about them. The funny ones are a nuisance but I suppose there must be first steps on into *lachrymae rerum*. I find I am getting to like Indians. When Jonathan and I were filming *S[ummoned] by B[ells]* in Oxford, Jonathan and the crew stayed in a really terrible hotel called the Eastgate run by some very bad Birmingham chain of hotels. There was no service and there were huge bills. So we took to eating in the Indian restaurant off the Turl where the food was good, the attention excellent and the management friendly. For our last meal they insisted on our having dinner on the house. In London people are beginning to recognize how polite and clever the Indians are. You have been right all along. Just as you were ahead of everyone in noticing Greek Revival in Injer and Government houses – you and Lord Curzon. It was really an awful experience making *S[ummoned] by B[ells]* with Jonathan because I had to go back to the very earliest places I can remember and see Ernie's grave in Highgate Cemetery and a passport photograph of Bess and remember nursery things. It was like being the bath water and running down with it as part of the London drains. And then suddenly the BBC girded its loins and started a sort of fiesta so that I find myself not myself but a public figure and quite inhuman. I greatly look forward to September 20th when I shall arrive at Calne and see you all. Wibz comes to luncheon tomorrow. Not a bleep from Paul who is still hung up in his subconscious but I think greatly benefited from your painful visit. Wibz is bringing Lucy who goes to school at Hatherop, the next day. Why we are all here on earth seems to me a matter of speculation. Elizabeth has looked after me marvellously daily. For I am really very infirm and difficult and bad sighted. I went through hell with Malcolm Graham last week and have three more visits ahead. It's very nice of you to like my sad poems.

Yorz trewly lovingly and sadly, JB

> JB and PB went to the great dentist Malcolm Graham in Beaumont Street, Oxford, on a regular basis. He would stand on his head while waiting for the local anaesthetic to work.

To John Sparrow   29 Radnor Walk
8 September 1976   London SW3

Darling Hanbury,
I was entranced by what Penelope has called your loyal piece about me on the wireless. I listened to it, preening myself like an old queen and scarcely believing it was true. All the same you've said it and you would never tell an untruth and you have always been a friend. Crax [William Wicklow] in a letter to me called Mr Bryson a true friend and so he was. Very different from C. S. Lewis. There are several All Souls matters I look forward to talking about with you, not concerning myself but other Fellows. You will be a great loss to them. You are their friend whatever their foibles. I sound rather as though I were writing for posterity. Not at all. It is simply that I am dictating this from an armchair after a glass of champagne. I think the following poets are worthy of appearing in Faber paperbacks selected by you and me – T. E. Brown, W. E. Henley, Thomas Hood, Arthur Symons, Isaac Watts, Charles Wesley, Edmund Blunden, Edward Thomas, Charles Tennyson Turner. Turn these over in your mind for I am greatly looking forward to coming to All Souls with Penelope in October. I cannot gather what date except that it will have to be before October 7th when I go to Cornwall. Is this going to be possible? I feel over-exposed and as though I were walking about waving my private parts at the multitude, who will soon cut them off.

Yours in the sure and certain hope of a speedy Resurrection, John B

J.S. had taken part in a Radio 3 programme on 28 August (JB's birthday), called *Betjeman at Seventy*. J.S., who had known JB for more than fifty years, talked about the life and verse of his old friend: 'Well, looking back, I can only say that if anyone had told me fifty years ago at Oxford that my undergraduate friend, that exuberant, irreverent, mocking, light-hearted, mischievous elf, would be transformed into a pillar of the Establishment – an Honorary Doctor of his old University, a Companion of Literature, a Knight Bachelor, Poet Laureate – I would simply have laughed him to scorn. I have used the word "transformed"; but the miracle is that John Betjeman has achieved all this without any transformation – and of course without any pretence and without any compromise on his part: he has simply been recognised for what he is, and what he has been from his earliest youth – on the surface, yes, amusing, eccentric, an enemy of pomposity and smug conventionality, a gay, delightful figure; but at the same time a serious man, a man with a shrewd and penetrating mind, and above all with a passion for architecture and for nature, a concern for our "whole over-populated island", a fellow-feeling for his fellow men, and a genius for expressing those feelings in intricate, appealing, and memorable verbal patterns.'

Fabers' planned poetry anthologies in their series *A Choice of . . .* ran into economic difficulties and were abandoned.

JB revered John Bryson and always referred to him as 'a real don'.

Ten:

Sunday silence

===

1976 to 1979

Snow falls in the buffet of Aldersgate station,
　　Soot hangs in the tunnel in clouds of steam.
City of London! before the next desecration
　　Let your steepled forest of churches be my theme.

Sunday silence! with every street a dead street,
　　Alley and courtyard empty and cobbled mews,
Till 'tingle tang' the bell of St Mildred's Bread Street
　　Summoned the sermon taster to high box pews.
　　　　'Monody on the Death of Aldersgate Street Station'

'I often wish I was back in those days when we used to go in the river from Lechlade and when Gerald was alive,' JB wrote to my mother (7 December) 1976 in India. 'I miss you and those days. Achievement is nothing. Love is everything. I don't give you enough but I do often think about you, with deep love. I love you deeply and calmly. Now you are fulfilled by the Little Redoubt and its millions of friends and animals. Benjamin Britten has died so there will be deep sadness at Fawley Bum. Jane Clark has died. I think K[enneth] is all right because his kiddies rally round. This has been two months of death and something like three months of road drills. I am very much looking forward to seeing you again.'[1] PB replied a month later (9 January 1977), oblivious to Chelsea drills, 'We are at the Kambala – the buffalo races – and cannot get away because a huge lorry (which brought some of the buffalos) is blocking our way so I have sat down in the shade to write to you.' She then went on to write a twenty-seven page letter about the buffalo races.[2]

JB was mellowing. 'I was terribly arrogant as a young man,' he wrote. 'I regret very much having attacked certain people at that time, particularly people in architecture who were probably only trying to do their best. I see now that anybody who is true to his own ideas is probably all right. I would say that the companionship of my friends has been the most important thing in my life. . . . Sometimes I have known such deep depression that I wouldn't mind something running me over.'[3]

Throughout 1976 the obligation to compose a Jubilee Hymn had hung over JB like a black cloud and made him ill with worry. Despite my mother's prayers to the Holy Ghost, the lines which JB submitted were clearly uninspired. He wrote to her, 'The commonplace verses I have written for the Jubilee have pleased the Master of the Music, an Aussie, and been passed by the Queen. They are not at all good, just like a Christmas card. But they have to be comprehensible to the TUC and natives of Africa. They are that and that's all there is to be said for them.'⁴ The Queen was said to be well content and sent her warm thanks, but it seemed that she was the only one and there was mockery to follow. Nicholas Fairbairn attacked the Jubilee hymn in the press and as a result a few hundred letters came winging in from fans telling JB not to worry. Mary Coleman wrote from Vancouver, British Columbia (8 February 1977), 'It grieves me that you have been attacked. As the daughter of an Anglican clergyman and widow of a bishop, also as a poet for fifty of my fifty-eight years, I know that the writing of hymns is a specialised and difficult art. I have been a Betjeman admirer for years, and to hear you accused of banality now is a blow. Of course you are not the first Poet Laureate to be attacked thus and probably you will not be the last.'⁵ Mr Waller, the managing director of the Birmingham and Midland Canal Carrying Company Limited, wrote from Birmingham (9 February), 'Lest you feel downhearted by the ill-mannered criticisms of it, I feel bound to say that I like the hymn you have written in connection with the Queen's Jubilee.'⁶ Matthew W. Jones wrote to him, 'I hope you are not feeling too bad despite all the afflictions that seemed to have been rained down on you.'⁷ To which JB replied (21 February), 'I was enchanted to have your kind letter. As Prince Philip said in a letter to me, "Please don't forget that criticism is much easier than creation and the persecution of individuals has always been the pleasure of thick-headed bullies since time immemorial." '⁸

The Laureateship seemed to be a ticket to nowhere but anxiety and depression. Complications arose. Should he remain as chairman of a committee to select the Winners of the Whitbread Literary Awards? He seemed to be in constant correspondence with Sir Rennie Maudslay, Keeper of the Privy Purse. 'I committed a lapse of taste last month,' he wrote (22 January) 'and I will not be surprised if I am dismissed from my honorable office. A respectable and literary pop group called the Barrow Poets wanted me to recite some of my verse to music. This I did and was pleased with what little of the result I heard. However, the publicity of the pop world is so appalling that I was not prepared for it. They called the pop record "Betjeman's Banana Blush". . . . They've had a teeshirt made for me to wear which I refuse to do. It had on it in white letters this frightful title. Well I have made my confession now, Reverend Father. It is up to you to give me my penance, counsel and absolution if you can."[9] Rennie Maudslay replied (4 March), 'I can echo the admonition from *Hamlet*, Act III, Scene IV, "O shame, where is thy blush," but as this is your first offence, I am prepared to offer you a more gentle reproach from *Henry V*, Act V, Scene II, "Put off your maiden blushes." '[10]

The need to reply to the hundreds of letters JB received after his Jubilee hymn drove him to write again to Sir Rennie (13 March), 'It is undeniable that the number of letters I have received has increased considerably over the past few years and the majority of my correspondents unfortunately do not enclose stamped addressed envelopes but nevertheless anticipate a reply, and I do feel that part of my job as Poet Laureate is to take the trouble to respond to these letters if members of the public have taken the trouble to write to me. In addition I am invited to speak at numerous functions; all this time of course involves me in considerable expenditure to cover postage, stationery and secretarial expenses. I estimate this to be approximately one hundred and fifty pounds a month.'[11]

JB's payment as Poet Laureate was slightly increased. In 1977 he was paid with fourteen bottles of Sancerre Clos de Beaujeu 1973 as well as champagne which he loved. If anyone arrived to see him at around ten or eleven in the morning he would open a half-bottle. During this period I visited him in Radnor Walk almost weekly. Sometimes we'd have lunch in San Quintino, the Italian restaurant down the street where he would order mussels if they were in season. He told me he loved them because they tasted like 'all the drains of Europe'.

I looked forward to seeing JB as I would to seeing a best friend. I could make him *laugh* so easily. But as his illness wore on, I felt his energy steadily winding down and his enthusiasm for ambitious expeditions waning. He was still the person I most sought to please. It was his praise I needed. When I wrote articles I wanted him to say he liked them. When John Bryson, to whom JB had always looked up in the same way, died on 20 August 1976, JB wrote to Ann Thwaite, 'With the death today of my old friend . . . I feel the last reader for whom I am writing has disappeared.'[12] Bryson was one of those Oxford dons JB had always sought to please. He had visited him often over their fifty-year acquaintance and his praise meant more to JB than that of most others.

Nonetheless JB was still able to light up a room full of people. During these later years I could detect when he was forcing it, but he was such a brilliant actor, few others knew. He worked magic with all Rupert's and my friends – he had always been in love with showbusiness and he struck up immediate friendships with the actors Kenneth Cranham and Terence Stamp whom he took to art exhibitions and on architectural tours of the City. He also got on like a house on fire with our next-door neighbour, the poet Christopher Logue.

He needed Elizabeth more and more. She looked after him better than anyone else could have done. My mother openly admitted she had no patience with invalids – she was frustrated even by the length of time it took JB to cross a room or get out of a car. She was always longing to get on with something else. Elizabeth was the opposite and her patience knew no end. The ambience at Elizabeth's house – the armchair (which he called the 'green hell' because it was so difficult to get out of) where he sat was just as cosy as could be. He felt safe, happy and, most importantly, unthreatened.

JB so easily felt threatened. He appeared on the *Parkinson* programme in 1977, together with one of his heroines, Gracie Fields, and although there was a jollity in his air and the audience laughed at almost everything he said, I could detect a fear in his eyes. He told me afterwards it had been one of the most frightening experiences of his life. He was terrified that he was going to be asked difficult questions. He had always said he was a fraud and I know now that he genuinely meant it. All his life he had thought he might be 'found out'. He dreaded anyone asking 'difficult' questions about the 'meaning' of his poetry. He thought he was expected to give lots of quotations in foreign languages, because that was how the Bright Young Things of the day wanted poets to be.

On 24 January 1978, Peter Parker, the then chairman of British Rail, gave a speech at the opening ceremony of the Betjeman Restaurant in the Charing Cross Hotel: 'We are here to celebrate Sir John Betjeman and this magnificent room which he himself has described as one of the finest appointed and best proportioned Victorian hotel dining rooms in London. . . . The room is named in honour of Sir John Betjeman, Poet Laureate, Railwayman Extraordinary – and one of our greatest and toughest customers. . . . Sir John has been at his most relentless in reminding railways of the treasures that we have in trust from our history. Indeed British Rail and Sir John have wrestled with what I call the riddle of the railways: the riddle of reconciliation of those two sometimes contrary imperatives.' (JB had in fact campaigned five years earlier for British Railways to have a subsidy towards the maintenance of their train sheds, offices, viaducts, and tunnel entrances and station buildings. He had said, 'If landowners, clergymen and country house owners are entitled to an endowment on architectural grounds, so too are British Railways.') Peter Parker went on, 'Henceforth and I hope for hundreds of years to come, it will be the Betjeman Room because his spirit has taken possession of the place. His particular vision, his eyes, have opened ours to the confidence and glories of the Victorian and Edwardian times. And so, may people who come here be wise in his poetry and his work, and be refreshed. Certainly for railways, the qualities of his works, their elegance and accessibility and permanence, these qualities ring bells for us.'[13]

JB wrote to Peter Parker (25 January) that it had been one of the happiest evenings of his life. He and Elizabeth had been on a tour which started at six o'clock that evening from Victoria where they boarded an inspection saloon and went by way of Grosvenor Bridge, Elephant and Castle, Blackfriars, Cannon Street to Charing Cross, which JB described as a Venetian tour through the south of London. 'Sometimes the moon was on our left and sometimes on our right. We did not mind, as we were gliding through Heaven with lights sparkling in the tidal Thames and various inhuman chunks of Colonel Seifert glittering in the dark. Jill [Parker] brought us all together and seemed to be the gondolier though the driver at each change seemed to know the route as if he had walked it. What is the capital of England? When I think of it in terms of good architecture, I think it is Liverpool, but last night London became the capital again, particularly when we stepped into the station entrance of Edward Middleton Barry's masterpiece the Charing Cross Hotel. . . . I feel uplifted, fulfilled, contented but not, I hope, complacent about last evening for which I cannot thank you and British Rail enough.'[14]

JB was still performing for the sake of the public. If shaky on his feet, he was not shaky on his film commentary and together with Ken Savidge made *Betjeman's Belfast* and *Betjeman's Dublin*. He wrote to Ken (9 August 1977), 'Of all the things we have done together, I think *Belfast* is the best. Well proportioned, right timing and plenty of jokes.' He was also pleased with the *Dublin* film and suggested to Ken that they should give a party for the London showing. 'Can you arrange this? I will pay. I think I owe this to the great and neglected race, the Anglo-Irish and to the Church of Ireland.'[15] He wrote to my mother (6 October 1978), 'I have just completed the commentary on a film on Dublin. Just as you were influenced by Woad and Mrs Woad, I find my love of Ireland all stems from Ernie reading Goldsmith's "Deserted Village" to me. It is still my favourite poem. The melancholy of Ireland and the ruined mansions prevail in its melifluous couplets.'[16]

JB confided in me that he had been very upset by another story in a gossip column about him and Elizabeth. Though no one questioned the fact that he and Elizabeth were asked everywhere together, he was still hurt that my mother should be described as 'eccentric and always abroad'. He told me that she was worth twenty of him and he minded that her great achievements as a travel writer and Indologist had not been given a second thought. He said he felt both humiliated and shameful.

What uplifted him greatly during those late seventies was my brother's relationship with a beautiful American girl, Linda Shelton, whom he loved. It somehow brought my brother and JB together after all those years of separation. He had always regretted not being closer to him. He seemed to have lost touch when my brother went to Eton and the intimacy he had shared with Paul as a child was never recaptured. Through Linda everything changed. They began writing to each other and he and Linda came over for a long visit in the summer of 1977. In May 1979 my mother and JB received a telegram: 'Linda and I are getting married on Saturday May 19th at the Advent Lutheran Church on 93rd Street and Broadway New York. Please be there in spirit although we do not expect you there in body. Paul and Linda.'[17] They were to have three children, Thomas, Timothy and Lily.

Gradually JB stopped feeling quite so pressured as he had done at the beginning of his Laureateship. He sank back on to his laurels and began to enjoy life without quite such a disproportionately large dollop of guilt. Harry Williams often stayed at Radnor Walk on his visits from Mirfield and kept the jokes going. JB's social life slowed down to a more leisurely pace and he saw only his closest friends such as the Lancasters. He and Elizabeth stayed with Michael Astor on the island of Jura, and often for weekends near Plumpton in Sussex with Bruce and Rosalind Shand. 'I think of that graceful ilex and the shaven lawn and the rolling scenery beyond,' he wrote to Rosalind, ' I recall how much it reminds me of Tennyson's home and garden at Somersby, North Lincs, and I see in my mind's eye you and the Major and the kiddies at just such a party next summer outside the Laines. And can you beat it?'[18] To Joan Kunzer, his 'earliest girl chum', he wrote (25 September 1978), 'I will come up to Beaconsfield for your birthday and would like to give you lunch at the most ostentatious and swagger place you can find – for I am both those now.'[19]

John Piper, who was illustrating a collection of JB's church poems for John Murray, wrote to him (8 June 1978), 'You are right. It is boring to be made to return to one's old stuff all the time, and to be made to take an interest in it. But you are also right in saying that Jock knows what the standard porkers want and he treats all his authors (and illustrators) alike. Including such divergent types as K[enneth] Clark and Dervla Murphy. So I am pegging away at St Barnabas and Chisle-hampton. . . . Goldilegz is probably getting out of plaster this afternoon. It is a wrist, and she did it playing table tennis with me. I often think of playing table tennis with Etchells at Edstone, that health food place we all went to, and drinking illicit sherry in the Shakespeare Theatre at Stratford.'[20]

In early 1978 Roy Harrod died. 'Poor old thing,' Billa confided to JB. 'At the moment I can only think of him sad in those last years and still more the last months and weeks. I hope that soon I shall be able to think of the way he used to be. *Real* friends are so comforting, especially ones like you who really loved Roy. It is horribly sad.'[21] But when Cracky William Wicklow died soon afterwards, a huge chasm opened in JB's life. 'I like to think he is having a good laugh about us and now with any luck meeting the Colonel [Kolkhorst] and Maurice [Bowra] and Toby [Strutt],' he wrote to Lionel Perry (13 March). 'The only thing the death of friends makes bearable is the thought of seeing them again. Apart from theories about time and space and eternity, what are we all here for if not for laughter and to see each other again? Harry Williams, the well-known and wholly *sympathetic* Cambridge theologian who is staying here at Radnor Walk, said that everyone will be a bit nicer in the hereafter. Talking of that sort of thing, I asked Harry why we would all be a bit nicer in the next life and he said, "Because we would all have learnt so much in this." '[22]

On a dreary March morning in 1978, I was driving home from London to Wiltshire and had just turned off the motorway when I heard on the radio that JB had been rushed into the Royal Brompton Hospital with a heart attack. My own heart came up into my mouth and I continued round the roundabout in the rain and sped at over a hundred miles an hour back to London. I kept him alive in my mind. I could do nothing but say the Lord's Prayer constantly. As I drove up the Fulham Road I saw thirty or forty press men outside the Royal Brompton Hospital. It was raining even harder. I still kept JB alive in my head. I did not ask them any questions. I parked the car and walked into the hospital with my head down and eyes on the ground. I didn't ask the porter if my father was dead. I still kept him alive. I asked what ward he was in and went up to the fourth floor saying the Lord's Prayer all the way up in the lift. He was alive. I sat by his bed and held his hand. He had the softest hands I have ever felt on a man, and when I looked back, I realised it was because he had never done a stroke of manual work in his life.

1. PB's papers, Beinecke Library, Yale University.
2. JB's papers, Beinecke Library, Yale University.
3. 'The Lonely Laureate', unidentified article.
4. PB's papers.
5. JB's papers, University of Victoria, British Columbia.
6. JB's papers, University of Victoria.
7. JB's papers, University of Victoria.
8. Carbon copy, JB's papers, University of Victoria.
9. Carbon copy, JB's papers, University of Victoria.
10. JB's papers, University of Victoria.
11. Carbon copy, JB's papers, University of Victoria.
12. Ann Thwaite's papers.
13. Bernard Kaukus's papers.
14. Peter Parker's papers.
15. Kenneth Savidge's papers.
16. PB's papers.
17. JB's papers, University of Victoria.
18. Bruce Shand's papers.
19. Joan Kunzer's papers.
20. JB's papers, University of Victoria.
21. JB's papers, University of Victoria.
22. Lionel Perry's papers.

To Alan Pryce-Jones   29 Radnor Walk
10 September 1976   London sw3

My dear Bog,
Ta ever so for yours of September 1st. Jim Knapp-Fisher has died, so
have Christopher Wood, John Bryson and Colonel Kolkhorst. The
Widow [John Lloyd], Crax [William Wicklow] and you and I remain
with the Reverend Colin Gill, on earth. Freddie Hood has gone. On the
other hand Osbert L[ancaster] is still with us. I hope Paul [PSGB] is
but I don't know his address nor whether my letters, which are few and
friendly, ever reach him. You and I can still see Groundsel [Graham
Eyres-Monsell], Paddy and Joanie [Leigh Fermor]. I am beginning to
understand that hymn 'Oh happy band of pilgrims'. Newport would
be nice next year but you over here would be best of all. I don't miss C.
S. Lewis and I feel I am going down the bath-waste into the drains of
London but have only to think of Bertram Grosvenor Goodhue to
struggle to life again.
    Love, JB

Jim Knapp-Fisher (see *Volume One*) was JB's friend who owned Sidgwick and Jackson
and for whom he edited the *Watergate Classics*.
    Christopher Wood had been a friend from the early thirties.
    The Reverend Colin Gill was a High Anglican priest.
    Bertram Grosvenor Goodhue was an American architect, designer of Nebraska State
Capitol.

To Ena Driberg   29 Radnor Walk
1 October 1976   London sw3

My dear Ena,
I can't make myself legible if I use a pen, hence the typewriter in reply
to your kind letter of September 13th. Yesterday I had the melancholy

duty of going with the lawyer, an extremely nice man, John Underwood of Winckworth and Pemberton, to choose two pictures and twelve books left me in Thomas Edward Neil [Driberg]'s will. Joan Rayner accompanied me. I did not often go to that flat of his. Only someone as eccentric and individual as Thomas Edward Neil would choose to live in such a frightful, lonely, hideous bit of housing. I always told him how awful it was but he didn't seem to notice it. I collected an Edward Lear of an Italian tree, a drawing of the old portico at Euston and a Nonsuch Milton. I find Milton very heavy-going and thought he might be easier in that beautiful edition Tom had. All the time I felt I was taking things from you and I asked the lawyer but he said he didn't think you were unprovided for.

I would very much like to come and see you when I get back from Cornwall at the beginning of November. I hope you are not forbidden alcohol. I know that place the Swillett. I once sat in its inn with a film crew when we were filming *Metroland* for the BBC. I shall very much enjoy coming there and will take the Metropolitan from Baker Street and a taxi from Chorley Wood Station. I can understand how you miss Thomas Edward Neil. I find myself constantly thinking of the old thing and his crotchetiness and his tremendous integrity and humility and, lucky old thing, faith. I think Faith is rather like an ear for music, a gift kindly supplied by the Management. Mine is very weak and I only hope I shall be able to face the advance of old age with the courage and goodness you show. Arthritis is a fearful thing and doctors are very poor about dealing with pain.

Don't bother to reply to this. It is to tell you that I shall be coming to see you when back from Cornwall and that I am with you in spirit.

Love, John B

Tom D. (made Lord Bradwell in 1975) died suddenly getting out of a taxi on 12 August. He had been sure that he wouldn't live very long. His autobiography *Ruling Passions* was not published until after his death because two of his fellow peers in the House of Lords had read it and advised against it. He was determined not to modify his crusading exposition and defence of homosexuality.

In 1951 he had married Mrs Ena Mary Binfield. E.D., who had refused the title, really loved him and was prepared to occupy the back quarters of Bradwell Lodge, leaving the grand front rooms exclusively for Tom D.'s promiscuous carryings on. She was too crippled with arthritis to come to the funeral but asked that 'The Red Flag' be played.

To Lucy Lycett Green   Treen
                                                         Trebetherick
                                                         Wadebridge
12 October 1976   Cornwall

My very dear Lucy,
I was so glad to get your torchlight letter from Hatherop. You write a
much clearer neater hand than I do. I hope you can read this.

I am down in Cornwall and I enclose some photographs taken long
ago before so many houses were built so they are of historic interest.

I am very glad to hear David can walk four steps. I think it is very
clever of all of us to stand upright and not fall down again. Do you
remember when you so kindly hauled me out of that deep chair in the
garden? I do and was very grateful.

I WRITE SO ILLEGIBLY, WILL HAVE TO END IN CAPITAL LETTERS.
REMEMBER ME TO THE MISSES MELANIE ACROYD AND ANNIE
UPTON.

BY THE TIME YOU GET THIS GRANDMAMA ELOPE WILL BE ON HER
WAY TO INDIA. LIFE WILL BE SAD FOR ALL HER HORSES AND YOU AND
ME WITHOUT HER.

MUCH LOVE FROM GRANDPAPA

To Penelope Betjeman   29 Radnor Walk
2 November 1976   London SW3

My darling Plymmi,
I hope [Alfred] Wuerfel was a nice man and scholarly. Did he have a
moustache? I have had a letter from Delli. She is very keen on
gardening and asked me how big my garden was (a back yard with one
cotoneaster and a bit of someone's vine).

I went through such hell at Malcolm Graham's last week. Injections
in the gums from three o'clock 'till 6.15. No taxi back to the station and
unceasing pain since so I have decided to make the next visit when he
takes the stitches out, my last. It really is too difficult for me to travel to
and from London. I shall have to go to a nearer dentist.

I wish we lived at Southend-on-Sea. It is a beautiful bracing place
with leafy public gardens and flimsy Georgian villas. It is also very
unfashionable. But it is useless for horses. The views across the

Thames Estuary are skyscapes like Turner and they change all the time. I wouldn't mind dying there. I believe you can buy a house for very little. But then I could never live there because in my infirm old age I have almost to be wet-nursed. London provides that unattractive service. Duncan Andrews has been here but I have missed him. This must all sound very remote out there among the tsetse flies and the shouts from the Bazaar. Hanbury [John Sparrow] never ceases to correct the words I have written to go with Malcolm Williamson's Jubilee music. W[illiamson] says the words as they are suit him better than later, and to me slightly better, versions. I don't think any of the words are any good, to tell you the truth, and they will be a signal like a down flag for all my enemies on *The Times* to rush in with ridicule. Oh, for Southend and eternity.

Yorz v[ery] truly, Tewpie

Alfred Wuerfel was a German scholar friend of PB's who lived in New Delhi and with whom she often stayed.

At this time one of JB's favourite pursuits was to take me and the children and groups of friends on journeys from Fenchurch Street Station to Southend. We would walk down the street to the sea front and cockle stalls, and to the pier (the longest in Britain) from where a small train took us two miles out into the Thames Estuary with liners passing in the distance. At the pier's end there was a restaurant (now closed) owned by the corporation, where JB became a regular customer.

JB wrote to John Summerson (10 November 1976), 'Each villa has a view of the sea. Sky and sea at Southend are a constant Turner exhibition, changing hourly. The air is like wine, the Veronica is wind-slashed.'

The American Duncan Andrews had formed a large collection of JB's first editions and manuscripts. PB later left all her letters from JB to him.

To Simon Jenkins   29 Radnor Walk
9 November 1976   London sw3

Dear Simon,
I should have written long before this to thank you for our Southend trip. From the first glance at that overgrown cemetery in Tower Hamlets to the last sunset rays over the spreading estuary. I should have said much more at that little ceremony in the Westcliff Hotel. I should have said that the Pier is really the making of Southend's landscape. By its immense length the Pier draws the sea towards the visitors, even when the tide is right out. It also unites sky and sea. It *is* Southend. It will kill the town to destroy it, and make the town to put it back into repair with a nice spidery, flimsy folly to gather shore and sky

together. Robert Buchanan would have liked this, so might have Swinburne whom he so harshly attacked. You do a great local public work by keeping the *Standard* a local paper and not just nothing.

Yours ever with great gratidue, JB

S.J. recalls, 'We gave JB lunch at the Westcliff Hotel with the leaders of the Council, at which he made a short speech in praise of the glories of Southend. They were totally amazed – and not a little flattered. Since he made the same speech to a mother with a screaming child on the station platform earlier in the day, he had had some practice. She thought he was completely mad.'

To Paul Betjeman   29 Radnor Walk
12 November 1976   London sw3

Dearest Paul,
We are all scattered. Mummy in India till March, Wibz in North Wilts[hire], yours truly here. The Mead is unrecognizable and surrounded by dark evergreens and facing south. I tried to find Marco's grave but could not. The present owners are an Oxford don and his parents. Wantage has a fearful Civic Centre in glass. The square remains. Farnborough is far less changed. So is London. I would like to come over to see you when I can fix it on some sort of mercy return fare if such exists and stay two nights in New York. Would this suit you? If it doesn't I shall take no answer as meaning it doesn't. I'd far sooner hear whether you were happy or not and fulfilled, than bother you with my presence. I would far sooner ring you up than write but am not sure of the number. If you fix a time I would like to book a call over Christmas.

Have you ever heard of a composer, an Australian, called Malcolm Williamson? I have written some terrible words for a Jubilee hymn to suit his music. I felt I was poaching on your territory. Archie is very well and quite unchanged except for a new muzzle which rather suits him. His eyes are as deeply dismal as ever. Phyllida Gili, daughter of Reynolds Stone, has adapted my drawings for Jock to publish as a kiddiz book. Everyone talks about prices except

Your absent but affectionate father, JB

JB's book *Archie and the Strict Baptists* came out in 1977. He had written the book in the mid-forties for PSGB and me and copied it out into a Rowney's sketch-book. He then illustrated it beautifully with his own water-colours but Jock Murray thought it would not reproduce well. Phyllida Gili was employed to echo JB's paintings.

To Penelope Betjeman   29 Radnor Walk
6 and 14 December 1976   London sw3

Darling Plymmi,
I hope this reaches you in Bombay and that the Taj Mahal is an insect-
free hotel. In Borneo, the vicar of St Barnabas, Pimlico, who is a
Norwegian, told me, centipedes that sting *at both ends* hang over the
electric light switches. They are not insects as you and I know but just
as dangerous. I am glad to say a tower block at the World's End,
Chelsea has been invaded by red ants, so perhaps nature will triumph
over barbarism.

I stayed a night with Spansbury [John Sparrow] and Widow [John]
Lloyd for John Bryson's memorial service where I preached to
Christopher Hill and many first-class brains. John Edward [Bowle]
was not in the congregation. I don't think he thought highly of Mr
Bryson's brain.

Spansbury is getting very worried about moving from his comfortable lodgings and living in Iffley. He much looks forward to your
return to England. I think he is far lonelier than I realized. I stayed at
Blacklands the other day for one night and was very comfortable and
happy. I don't seem to have heard anything from you lately and I like to
think that it means you and the PPM [Sheldon Nash] are measuring
temples and putting them on to tape. Archie much dislikes publicity. I
am having Duncan Andrews to lunch and have asked Rosie Kerr to
meet him. I thought the RAC a better venue than the Athenæum. I
don't think Rosie's ever seen it and, as it's very American, Duncan
A[ndrews] will feel at home. *I do hope you are not ill.* I am not. I feel
secure while you are alive. Kindly do not predecease me.

Yorz trewly, Tewpie

Yew are much noicer than oi am.

PS There are you and the PPM in the Himalayas having LOST A
TEMPLE.

A very happy Christmas.

> John Bryson's memorial service took place on 27 November 1976. JB had loved and
> admired him. John had been a fellow of Balliol College since 1940. After the service JB
> had lunched with his relations at Balliol and written to the Master, Christopher Hill (29
> November 1976), 'I must also thank you for letting me preach in that splendid
> Butterfield chapel. I am so sophisticated now that I can also enjoy the A. S. G. Butler
> panelling and the Ted Heath organ case. But of course best of all is the seventeenth-
> century glass and that superb late-mediaeval east window. Norman Shaw said that
> stained glass should really be splodges of colour like a Turkey carpet. He was quite right.
> Butterfield knew this too. I wish we didn't have to die.'
>   John Sparrow had been Warden of All Souls College and lived in the elegant warden's
> lodgings on the High for twenty-five years. On his retirement he moved to Beechwood
> House in Iffley, also owned by All Souls, but he was no longer at the heart of things.
>   The 'PPM' stood for 'Paper Plate Manufacturer' and was PB's name for the American
> millionaire Sheldon Nash, who had made his money from them. He so enjoyed her
> group tours that he paid her to take him round India privately.

To Harry Williams   29 Radnor Walk
19 January 1977   London SW3

My dear Harry,
Feeble had tears in her eyes of delight when she saw your book and its
dedication at breakfast on her table yesterday. I dried my own in order
to thank you as I do now via Magda. I am going to get a typewriter with
big letters such as are used by the Royal Family in order that I can see to
read what I have written.

I went to see a Persian doctor yesterday who specializes in nervous
diseases and I shall be going into hospital in Denmark Hill while he

experiments for a fortnight. I look forward to that as I will be able to find out, while there, what I am. You couldn't have chosen a fairer or better title. It's going to make Denmark Hill glow with glory for me.

You are much missed here. Dusty [Albert Miller] and Magda are in the room. I hope one day I will see that familiar bag in the hall here and those towels hanging up in the bathroom. There's a marvellous piece to which Feeble drew my attention by Hilary Beasley in this month's *C[ommunity of the] R[esurrection Review]*. I have just opened an exhibition called *Off the Rails* consisting of excellent photographs of railway architecture, the terrible destruction of it done by BR. It is at the RIBA, Heinz Gallery in Portman Square. I have already started your book but am keeping it as a *bonne bouche* for King's College Hospital, Denmark Hill where I hope to arrive very shortly.

Love and thanks, JB

H.W., EC's close friend and a spiritual touchstone of JB's, had dedicated his book *Becoming What I Am* (Darton, Longman and Todd) to JB and EC. He often stayed at Radnor Walk with JB. He wrote (11 January 1977), 'The publishers offered to present you with a morocco-bound copy at a special luncheon to which (of course) five or six reviewers would be invited. I refused this as I thought it would be a bore for you and also an attempt to make you into a publicity stunt. . . . It isn't a book at all really, but it is more positive and less critical than most of what I write.'

Doctor Zilkha was the Persian doctor who specialized in treating Parkinson's Disease.

Albert Miller, invariably known as 'Dusty', was the owner of Frank Hollins Bookshop at 45 Cloth Fair, two doors away from JB's flat. He sorted through all JB's papers, catalogued his books and later handled the sale of the major part of JB's archive to the University of Victoria, British Columbia.

Hilary Beasley was a priest at Mirfield.

To Simon Hornby   King's College Hospital
1 February 1977   Denmark Hill

Dear Simon,
Everything here is W. H. Smith, and W. A. Pite who designed the Chapel here, at King's College Hospital, was a bit of a genius in a Lutyens way. I wonder if your grandfather did the lettering in the chapel. I was sorry not to be in Portugal Street, whose chapel the one here replaces. I hope you like being a retail Director but isn't wholesale more refined than retail? I hope to be out of hospital by Saturday but mustn't rush about afterwards.

Love to Kneecoal [Nicole], Michael and Sheran [Hornby] and Charlie [Hornby], and the long, long line of the Downs so missing here on Denmark Hill.

S.H., elder son of Michael and Nicole, brother of Charlie and married to Sharon (née Cazalet), was at the time retail director of W.H. Smith (he went on to become chairman). He had written to JB offering to send him *Wilt* by Tom Sharpe to read in hospital.

King's College Hospital was the largest work of William Alfred Pite (1860–1949). It was built (1905–14) on the pavilion plan in accordance with the precepts of Florence Nightingale. The original chapel at Portugal Street was attached to King's College Hospital when it was on its original Strand site.

C. H. St J. Hornby (1867–1946), an early director of the firm and S.H.'s grandfather, had commissioned Eric Gill to design a special typeface for W.H. Smith. Gill also did lettering in King's College Hospital, one of W.H. Smith and Sons' early benefactions.

To Endellion Lycett Green   29 Radnor Walk
21 July 1977   London SW1

Darling Delli,

That was a very nice long letter you sent to me and so in return I am going to tell you a long, quite true story which happened to me and I wonder what you can make of it.

When Gramelope and I were first married, we lived in a farmhouse in Uffington, Berkshire in the Vale of the White Horse. We lived there because it was the furthest place from London I could find which you could leave and get back to in a day. Fares were low, it was lovely getting beyond Reading in the train from London into what was true country. In Uffington people still talked with Berkshire accents like Pam Ayres on the television. A lot of them were called Ayres and must have been her relations. Uffington had its own railway station then lit with oil lamps. It was a junction for Faringdon and a little train left on a single line from Uffington station through fields to a terminus some way out of the town of Faringdon. Many people from Uffington had never been to London. Swindon was the other big town near us.

I used to get up at about seven in the morning and Gramelope would drive our car to Uffington or Challow Station (both of them are now shut) and there at about 7.30 I would catch a slow train to Didcot and then a fast one to London. I was working on the *Evening Standard* newspaper in those days writing about new films. We used to be shown the films in the morning and I would have to write about them in the afternoon and then catch the train home. It was always a bit of a rush. The slowest part of the journey was the underground railway from Paddington to Farringdon Street, the nearest underground station to the *Evening Standard* office.

I remember how glad I used to be in the evenings to get back to Berkshire. The further we were from London, the quieter everything grew. Gramelope had a white Arab horse called Moti and she used to meet me at Uffington oil-lit station and we were very happy to be in real country and alone.

One morning I was travelling down on the Inner Circle underground from Paddington to Farringdon Street when the train did a very unusual thing. It waited for a long time at King's Cross station. My father, your great-grandfather, had a factory, founded in 1820, on the Pentonville Road (it is still there and now owned by the Medici Society). King's Cross underground was the nearest station. I remember thinking as the train waited at King's Cross, 'Shall I go out and see my father?' A voice inside me seemed to say, 'Yes, do go and see him. It won't take you long and you won't be too late for the film.' The train went on waiting but I felt too lazy at that time of the morning to bother to get out and take a tram up the hill. Then we went on and with other film writers I saw an American musical film called *George White's Scandals*.

When I got back to Uffington that evening the telephone rang. It was my father's managing clerk, Mr H. V. Andrew, and he told me that my father had died that morning while talking to him. He was recalling a date. Do you think my father was trying to get through to me? Do you think he knew he was going to die so swiftly? I don't know. All I can tell you is that it happened and Gramelope will remember it.

She offered me a strawberry that we had grown in our garden at Uffington when I heard the news and I remember being too upset to want to eat it. This is the longest letter I have written to you and it is in return for yours to me. It is the only ghostly experience I had which can be witnessed.

I enclose a silver Maria Theresa dollar. These are specially made at the Mint for Arab countries which will use no other currency.

Love from Grandpapa

To Keith Miller   29 Radnor Walk
12 September 1977   London SW3

Dear Keith,
I still can't use a pen legibly, that is why Magda is typing this. I was very sorry not to be at your father's funeral. One thing a day is all I can

do at present. He was a very dear friend and I shall miss him terribly so that I have a faint idea of what you must be suffering. What I used to enjoy was talking about books to him. We used to laugh our heads off about the sort of second-hand books that would never sell and could always be found in second-hand shops – odd volumes of Scott, Motley's *Dutch Republic* and Barber's *Isle of Wight*. He had a marvellous knowledge, the real tutors of literature are not the universities but second-hand book dealers. Dusty's tolerance was as marvellous as his wide range of knowledge. Those chess books make me laugh when I think of them. Was there ever such company as he was? Never. It was a joy his coming on Wednesdays and looking round my books which were mostly bought from him. I can see why you are studying psychology. Dusty was the ideal psychologist, putting up with people's eccentricities and laughing with them. How I shall miss his chuckle and then his saying, 'Oh, that reminds me' and producing some coveted book which he knew I wanted.

I am so glad you are on earth to remind me of him and if you want references written or strings pulled leave it to his old friend,

Yours ever, John B

K.M. was the son of JB's bookseller friend Albert 'Dusty' Miller, who had just died.

To Angela Grimthorpe   29 Radnor Walk
7 November 1977   London SW3

My dear Angela,
I am writing to you out of the blue, *and expecting no reply*. November is a depressing month and one needs cheering. I got from Rupert your address in Ampleforth. My greatest and oldest friend from childhood was a monk there, Dom Richard Wright, now, alas, dead. He and I used to double up with laughter whenever we met, which was daily in school holidays.

I am very grateful to you for the existence of Rupert, the rock of my family life, and of Penelope's and Candida's. Our son Paul appeared this summer with a smashingly pretty, and humorous girl from Missouri. They lightened life and warmed the cockles of my heart. They stayed at Blacklands. I am very fond of you and wish I saw more of you. Life has its compensations and you are one of them. I hope we will meet ere long and have a gossip and a drink. I wrote this out in longhand – the whole letter I mean, not the part about the drink – and then realised I would have to have it typed as it is illegible. It was the first handwritten letter I had written for months and I had better not try again. I enclose it. This has been typed by Elizabeth East, my *very* pretty secretary.

> A.G., RLG's mother (whose second marriage was to Ralph G.), had been in hospital with cancer.
> PSGB had brought Linda Shelton with him to England and they subsequently married in New York in May 1979.
> JB's turnover of secretaries continued fast and furious.

To Penelope Betjeman   29 Radnor Walk
3 December 1977   London SW3

My darling Plymmi,
Nov[ember] 27th 1977 was *the* day of my life at 11.45 onwards when you very kindly came along to the 1662 service in Hereford Cathedral and SHARED IT with me. I have never felt so happy and fulfilled. Ta ever so to you (to Mrs Folky too and Janey) but to you chiefly with your nut and eyes and straight hair. The happiness still steals over me like radiant heat. I very much like talking to you on the telephone. It is like those daily letters Woad and Mrs Woad wrote to each other. I wonder if we could work out some way by which you could make regular calls to me at stated times. It may be too difficult. We could discuss it at Blacklands. The benefits of no telephone are very great for you. I *have* to have the bloody [thing].

> This was the first time JB and PB had worshipped together in the spirit of ecumenism at a Church of England service (apart from at weddings and funerals) since 1947, when PB became a Roman Catholic. She was a great one for keeping the rules of her church and it wasn't until the late sixties that the post-Vatican II regulations became generally accepted and it became all right for Roman Catholics to attend Anglican services. JB, however, chose not to attend Roman Catholic services, partly as a result of his 'anti-popery' obsession fired by the hurt of PB's 'defection' to Rome.
> When PB's father, Field Marshal Lord Chetwode was away from his wife on army duty, he wrote to her daily.

To Lucy Lycett Green   29 Radnor Walk
1978   London sw3

Dear Lucy,
Your lovely letter with a gazelle arrived today. Thank you so much for
it. I had a letter from Delli the other day and have only just replied.
Yesterday Elizabeth East told me on the telephone she is going to get
married, I think next month, to a nice man I have met called Graham
Boal. I have always called him Old Boal but really he is quite young,
though he will seem old to you. I think Cranborne Chase School must
be pretty good. I know the stairs which lead up to it inside are good,
very delicate and beautiful, though anything associated with school is
poor after home. Gramelope and I and Billa Harrod had luncheon this
week in the Charing Cross Hotel, not a fashionable place, where a
restaurant has been named after me. There is a lift to it, which is just as
well as my walking gets worse and worse. Your handwriting is very
nice. I have two friends, Billy Henderson, a painter, and Frank Tait, a
doctor, who live in a house, or rather a cottage, called Jays at Tisbury.
When last I stayed with them you had not arrived at your school. My
old bear, Archie, must be the oldest bear in use. I fell out of bed this
morning, and found myself talking to him when I was on the floor. I
send you nothing in return but my love.
    Love from Grandpapa

> LLG had written from Hatherop School saying that she was learning nothing and that
> we were wasting our money paying the fees. We removed her to Cranborne Chase
> School at Wardour Castle (by James Paine, 1770–76) whose swooping double staircase is
> one of the greatest in all England.
>   Dr Frank Tait, the psychiatrist, was also a neighbour of JB's in Radnor Walk, and a
> great friend of his and EC's.

To Imogen Lycett Green   29 Radnor Walk
23 January 1978   London sw3

My dear Imo,
This letter is being typed by Elizabeth East. Her father is a Colonel.
    They are opening a restaurant in the Charing Cross Hotel, London,
tomorrow named after me. What a funny thing to do. I hope it will not
drive custom away. It would be rather nice to go there when you come
to London next. As it is, it is lovely to hear from you for I love you very

much and I hope your hair is still the same colour and that your eyes
have not changed colour.

Years ago I was joint editor of an anthology of poetry for children and
there is a funny joke opposite the title page. The illustrations are
puzzles to us all. I like some of the poems more than others but I don't
know whether anyone ever bought the book. This edition looks rather
moth-eaten but it is because it has been asleep on my shelves here at 29
for a long time.

I am like a child.

Lots of love, Grandpapa

[PS] Elizabeth East is a qualified nannie.

To Philip Larkin   29 Radnor Walk
3 February 1978   London sw3

Dear Philip,

Last night at 19, Oxford Road, sw15, I met a boy aged twelve destined
for Harrow, where *I think* I was at school, who had written a poem of
such beauty I have had it typed out for you. Wherever I go I carry
'Aubade' about and read it out. It improves with every reading. It
probes everywhere. I read it to my friend, Mervyn Stockwood, Bishop
of Southwark, who really understood it and said the only answer is that
Now is more important than past or future. I think this boy feels that.
He is the great-grandson of Dana Gibson, the American artist.

I saw Elizabeth Jane [Howard] yesterday in a restaurant. I am so
grateful to you and Kingers [Kingsley Amis] for going on existing,
knowing the terrors of life. You encourage your old friend. With love to
Monica, and from Elizabeth and don't bother to reply. Writing letters
is hell. Writing poetry such as yours is much more important.

Yours, JB

> Some days my thoughts are just cocoons,
> All dull and grey and blind,
> They hang from dripping branches in the
> Grey wood of my mind.
> And other days they drift and shine,
> Such free and flying things;
> I find the Gold dust in my hair
> Left by their brushing wings.

EC remembers that it was later discovered that the twelve-year-old's poem was a fake, and not by him at all.

PL's poem 'Aubade' first appeared on 29 November 1977 in the *Times Literary Supplement*. It was just up JB's street – deeply gloomy:

> I work all day, and get half-drunk at night.
> Waking at four to soundless dark, I stare.
> In time the curtain-edges will grow light.
> Till then I see what's really always there:
> Unresting death, a whole day nearer now,
> Making all thought impossible but how
> And where and when I shall myself die.
> Arid interrogation: yet the dread
> Of dying, and being dead,
> Flashes afresh to hold and horrify.

To Lionel Perry   29 Radnor Walk
8 February 1978   London SW3

My dear Li,

I have to type because I have eye trouble. Thank God for your postcard of one of those fearful gods Penelope is now looking at in Injer. I very much hope Crax [William Wicklow] was in no pain and, as you say, drifting away and happy. Life will seem pointless without the old boy though Widow [John Lloyd] is still alive and Wyndham [Ketton-Cremer]. I suppose Crax is the greatest and grandest man we shall ever know and, oh my God, the laughs he has given us all. I should think that Cecil must have been the obscurest heir one could wish for. I much loved his little sister, Katie. Oh, thank you so much for writing.

There is a bit of consolation which comes to me in a sermon preached by the chaplain of the Dragon School at Joc Lynam's funeral last week. He said that Joc believed that the soul is immortal. And that having shed the physical body, it enters the spiritual dimension and returns to its maker. It tells us that not only is the soul immortal but that the soul retains its identity. I will still be me, you will still be you. It tells us that loves and friendships forged on this earthly place will be deepened and renewed:

> I trace the rainbow through the rain
> And feel that promise is not vain
> That morn shall cheerless be.

All the best, John B

'Cracky' William Wicklow had died on the day JB wrote this letter. Cecil Aymar
Forward-Howard, who succeeded him as Earl of Wicklow, was his cousin.
    L.P. later wrote a full account of Crax's death and JB replied (9 April 1978), 'Crax was
a saint, the only *certain* one we knew. Saints don't die. As long as I think of him and what
he would say, he is with us. He is with me now as I write to you, perhaps he is keeping
me legible.'

To Archie Polkinghorne   29 Radnor Walk
22 February 1978   London sw3

Dear Archie,
Mr Sharpe telephoned yesterday to say that the big elm tree at Treen
had fallen and that you very kindly came to the rescue. I think trees are
more important in Trebetherick than houses. In fact they are essential.
Cornish elms (*ulmus cornubiensis*) in particular. I would like to see a little
spinney of Cornish elms and ash and sycamore across the back garden
of Treen and the bottom garden of St Enodoc Cottage and continued on
the other side of the road where the earthworks are, which at present
look rather like a war memorial.
    I have offered to present the owners of the land with these trees and
they have kindly agreed to let them be planted. The next step is to get
the job done. I think we want as tall saplings as possible. I would like to
see them before I die and to know that this little bit of the lane will still
be Cornish. Would you be able to do this for me and if you can't let me
know.
    All best wishes to you and Mrs Polkinghorne.
    Yours sincerely, JB

        A.P. was the local builder who had worked for JB at Treen.
        Adrian Sharpe was a neighbour who lived down the lane from Treen.

To Jemima Brown   29 Radnor Walk
6 March 1978   London sw3

Dear Jemima,
Will you please tell Ted how very grateful I am to him for his letter.
I am pleased to think he may be going along to the Uffington Strict
Baptists. The Baker's Arms was always very quiet and old-fashioned.

I remember Tom Weaver in the village wanted to paint a sign for it which would have been a lady with very large arms dipped in a barrel or tub.

I very much liked Uffington Church when I lived there.

Yours sincerely, John Betjeman

Jemima B., then six, lived in the Baker's Arms at Uffington and had written as from her bear about JB's book *Archie and the Strict Baptists*.

To Penelope Betjeman   29 Radnor Walk
29 April 1978[?]   London sw3

My Darling Plymmi,
A terrible thing happened last week.
Archie's head came apart from his
body, worn through at the neck.
But the old thing's face and
personality were the same.
E[lizabeth] did an emergency
operation which has given him
a goitre so that he looks rather

like the Michelin man. His personality is the same and he is easier to carry about. It sounds to me as though you have had a very tiring time, if you have lost a stone. I hope I will recognize you and hear about the trip from other passengers. I will be back from Derbyshire on 2nd June having been to Cornwall previously.

Believe me and with much love,

Yorz trewly, Tewpie

To Jonathan Stedall   29 Radnor Walk
18 May 1978   London sw3

My dear Jonathan,
My mind is full of that Newton Abbot man Frank Matcham, the best theatre designer of the lot. Having seen the Buxton Opera House in Viennese Baroque, the Victoria Palace, the Coliseum and the Moss Empires and knowing of the Grand at Blackpool and his work in the North Country, I know we are on to a winning subject of great beauty

and not just nostalgia. Bill Cotton and Dick Cawston will know all about that subtle change from the pubs to the clubs, from variety to revue and the theatres that go with them. This is a framework for a winning fifty-minuter. But the interiors of the theatres, the pros[cenium] arches, boxes and safety curtains are all part of it as well as the houses in the suburbs and 'Coronation Streets' from which the audiences came.

Let us not forget that down here in Trebetherick at Mrs Bone's is Carroll Gibbons's own piano which he used for the Savoy Orpheans and it's in tune, so is (though he cannot sing),

Yours ever, JB

> JB had developed a passion for the great theatre architect Frank Matcham (see letter to Minister of Housing and Local Government, 22 July 1968) and was determined to make a film about him. He had already written to J.S. about the shape of the film he envisaged and was fascinated by how Matcham's childhood by the River Exe in Devon could have turned his mind to theatres. What was he like? Where did he meet his wife Elfie? He built over a hundred Palaces and Empires in the UK: 'From the banks of the Exe to a box in the Palladium, what a poem the whole story is, waiting to be written.'
> Matcham's pupils W. G. R. Sprague (1865–1933) and Bertie Crewe (d. 1937) went on to build over a hundred more theatres together and apart. John Summerson insinuated that they were in a vulgar set. 'Sprague seems a decent enough fellow,' wrote Summerson to JB (undated), 'but Bertie Crewe seems to have got himself into trouble. It's Gertie this and Florrie that and have you seen the show?'
> JB later wrote to Ashley Barker (7 September 1978) that it was the class basis that explained the absence of information about Frank.
> In the end, JB became too ill to continue with the film.
> Dick Cawston was head of the Documentary Department at the BBC and Bill Cotton controller for BBC1.
> The Savoy Orpheans were a light music orchestra.

To Mollie Baring   29 Radnor Walk
14 June 1978   London sw3

Darling Mollie,
What fun that was with you and Dezzie [Desmond Baring] and Peter [Baring] and his missus [Rose]. You will be interested to hear that Elizabeth East found Dezzie's eyes very attractive. Freckly Jill was attractive but in a more sensual way than is Elizabeth East. Thank God for sex.

Oswin [Bateman-Brown] seems twenty years younger as is not
Yours with love and gratitude, John B

> Oswin Bateman-Brown was an interior designer, and Berkshire neighbour.

To Kingsley Amis   29 Radnor Walk
26 June 1978   London sw3

My dear Kingers,
Susie [Allison] is typing this very fast and calmly. I wanted to write
very fast and excitedly about *Ending Up*, which I have returned to her
with your heartfelt inscription. It is a book to make one want to cut
one's throat before getting old. It is your best. Marigold is particularly
awful. Do you think everyone's like that four? I suppose most of them
are.

I wrote to Peter Parker about the filthy meat at the Charing Cross
Hotel and said you and Elizabeth Jane were with me. We will never go
there again.

What I really want to say is how much I admire the *New Oxford Book of
Light Verse*. It's proper light verse, and it makes one see how good Praed
and Calverley are and always were. A fellow I think rather good is
Douglas Byng. You can get him on a record. He's still alive in Brighton.
Your 'Helbatrawss' is a masterpiece of dialect; more ought to be
written in that dialect before Cockney disappears. Old Philip [Larkin]
never fails, does he? You were a nest of singing birds at St John's. I am
very proud of the Alan Bennett. You are a clever old thing to have
composed an anthology which is readable all through and right on the
mark. Wystan Auden's *Light Verse* was too heavy.

Bung ho, old top, and love to [Elizabeth] Jane, John B

> Susie Allison was the widow of John, JB's former doctor. She also helped K.A. with his
> letters.
>   JB found K.A.'s satirical study of old age, *Ending Up*, rockingly funny and
> recommended it to all and sundry.
>   Peter Parker was chairman of the British Rail Board at the time. (His wife Jill was JB's
> G.P.)
>   K.A. had edited the anthology *New Oxford Book of Light Verse* which came out the same
> year.
>   'The Alan Bennett' refers to a television series the latter had made which included an
> appreciation of JB's verse.

To Williams Brothers, Builders   29 Radnor Walk
14 July 1978   London SW3

Dear Sirs,
Could you please tell me for how many more days the noisy machine
you installed for a building on the King's Road corner of this residential
street is to continue? Could you tell me whether anything can be done
to put it out of earshot of the houses here? It does start very early in the
morning and work becomes impossible.
    Yours faithfully, John Betjeman
    cc W. Bell Esq, GLC

> The Fulham building firm, W. Bros of Dawes Road, wrote a letter of apology and the
> noise subsided ten days later.

To Kingsley Amis   29 Radnor Walk
11 August 1978   London SW3

My dear Kingsley,
That was astonishingly good of you, old boy, to stand me luncheon in
that posh Charing Cross Hotel. I enjoyed every minute of our time
together and have just bought *The Works of Sir Lewis Morris*. He is no
good at all. Absolutely none. I hoped he might have a line or two. Now
the person who really *is* good is you, old top, whether it is prose or
poetry. You can't help it. I love your jazz poem. What a delightful
surprise it was and how truly learned it is. Old Philip [Larkin] will like
it too.
    Love to [Elizabeth] Jane up there on your Leigh Hunt height.
    Yours ever,
    pp Richard Le Gallienne
    John B

> The manager of the Charing Cross Hotel had mended his ways.
>   Sir Lewis Morris (1833–1907) was a hopelessly bad poet who imitated Tennyson.
>   R. le Gallienne (1866–1947) was a nineties poet.
>   K.A., Elizabeth Jane, JB and EC lunched together often. The latter remembers, 'I
> once took John to lunch at the Tate where he loved the dry Martinis. He was in a
> wheelchair then and as I pushed him between the tables while people stared he said, in a
> joke voice, "Look at that disgusting old man in a chair. They shouldn't let them out
> when they're like that!" '

To Gavin Stamp   29 Radnor Walk
16 August 1978   London sw3

Dear Gavin,
I am very pleased with your letter and carried a catalogue to Penelope at
Kulu-on-Wye. In time she will look at it but not until her grand-
children have left.

I think, as I have just said to Brother Boyd Harte, Electricity was an
inspiration. Perhaps she is best represented on [Charles] Clarke's
headquarters of the Met[ropolitan Railway], where she is grasping a
handful of white faience darts. Clarke is still with us, or was last year,
his Chiltern Court is very good and his Met[ropolitan] stations. He
lives at East Portlemouth where he is known as the Skipper.

A man called George Richards married Elizabeth Scott and has a
deep knowledge of Middle Scott. He used to live in Poole. He would be
worth your meeting. Dickie Scott knew nothing about Middle Scott's
madness and I don't like to mention it to him when we meet at [the]
F[oreign] A[rchitectural] B[ook] S[ociety]. [Ninian] Comper thought
Middle Scott's history of English architecture, before the reformation,
the best book on architecture written. Comper modelled himself on
Middle Scott, even more than on his old master Bodley. St Agnes was a
dream of beauty, that wretched little man Covell never restored it but
put up his own mingy little substitute. St Mark's at Leamington is still
all right, though very Low. Wasn't Peach something to do with the
Dryad Handicrafts and Leicester and Ernest Gimson? I long to see
your book, I doubt if there is much I can add by way of introduction.
I am so glad that the tables are turning away from the prigs and old-
fashioned with-its.

May St Alphege pray for us.
Yours, John B

G.S., the architectural writer, and Glynn Boyd Harte, the artist, had collaborated on
Temples of Power, a limited edition book on the electric power stations of London (Cygnet
Press 1979). JB's introduction began, 'Electricity is the daintiest handmaid of Science.'
At the launch in the National Liberal Club, JB ceremonially cut a cake in the shape of
Battersea Power Station – pink icing with solid marzipan chimneys.

The headquarters of the Metropolitan Railway Station (1912) were designed by
Charles W. Clarke, the Metropolitan Railway's own architect, whom JB used to call the
'Clarckitect'.

Elizabeth Scott won the competition for the Shakespeare Memorial Theatre at
Stratford-on-Avon in 1928. She was descended from Sir Gilbert's brother Samuel King
Scott. 'Middle Scott' was poor, mad George Gilbert Scott junior (1839–97), Sir
Gilbert's eldest son. Middle Scott's book of 1881 was called *An Essay on the History of*

English Church Architecture Prior to the Separation from the Roman Obedience. His masterpiece was St Agnes', Kennington, in south London.

The Foreign Architectural Book Society, to which JB belonged, survives as an architectural dining club.

Charles Stanley Peach (1858–1934) had surveyed a railway across the Rocky Mountains before becoming an enthusiast for electricity. He also designed the Wimbledon Stadium (1920–21) in reinforced concrete.

G.S. lived in the clergy house of St Alphege's, Southwark.

To Laurence Udall   29 Radnor Walk
7 September 1978   London sw3

Dear Mr Udall,
The picture of the stables dominates my room here. I have altered the second stanza a little so as to increase the effect of ancient peace which is in it. Osbert Lancaster saw it and was much impressed – your picture I mean, not the poem. It may well be impossible to reproduce it satisfactorily, colour printing is so unreliable. So is photography. My publisher, John Murray, is away for two weeks at least, and I would like to consult him first about methods of reproduction.

Best wishes to your Elizabeth and Susan and Bobbie [Udall].
Yours sincerely, John Betjeman

To Laurence Udall – Artist

He has painted the noise of the fountain
    In that classical stable square
And the sound of the hooves of horses
    Once exercising there.

In this golden ironstone cloister
    With its plaster vaulting white
The descendant of Roister Doister
    Has reflected the Derbyshire light.

L.U., the painter, first met JB outside the post office in Edensor and asked him if he would come to his house in the village to sign his copy of *Summoned by Bells*. L.U. later gave JB a painting he had admired on that first visit. He remembers, 'From then on he visited us at home on many occasions over the next ten years with continuing encouragement and welcome commissions from him and the Dowager Duchess of Devonshire.' In 1977 L.U. was commissioned to paint a view of Edensor by JB and in 1978 a picture of the stables at Chatsworth, about which JB wrote the verse, with the idea that the two should be reproduced together as a postcard. Jock Murray did not think it a practical idea. In its earlier version the second and fourth lines of the second stanza had read:

With its vaulting of plaster white
Has caught the Derbyshire light.

To Penelope Betjeman   29 Radnor Walk
25 September 1978   London sw3

My darling Plymmi,
Susie Allison is typing this for me. I am very much better if I do very little each day. Your journey sounds to have been hellish by Air Injer. I think Heathrow is the saddest place in England. Next time you come, you must come and see Chelsea Hospital. I can manage the walk. Wibz is expecting on October 23rd at the Lindo Wing in Paddington, St Mary's. What a different place from that general hospital where you looked like a sad balloon after your accident. I had a very cheerful postcard from Angela [Grimthorpe] from Vezelay. So sorry to be so late answering. I get into panics and can do nothing and then I do too much. I go to Cornwall on October 6th till the end of the month, keeping my fingers crossed for you and Wibz and Rupert. I have just re-read Goldsmith's *Deserted Village* which influenced me more than any other English poem. Ernie [Betjemann] used to read it to me almost daily when I was six or seven. I still think it is one of the best English poems and gave me a longing for Ireland from which I have never really recovered. I am most surprised at that passion for Ireland induced by Ernie of all people.
    Very truly yours, Tewpie

> PB was returning from Delhi.
>   John LG was born 23 October 1978, named after JB.
>   The eighteenth-century poet Oliver Goldsmith's *The Deserted Village*, published in 1770, caused a political furore at the time. During the latter half of the eighteenth century many estate owners were pulling down old villages and building new model ones at some distance away. Though some villagers welcomed the changes and the new cottages in exchange for their old hovels, others were unhappy. Goldsmith recalled the old pastoral idyll, 'Sweet Auburn, loveliest village of the plain.'
>   Ernie, JB's father, had always read poetry to him as a child.

To Candida Lycett Green   29 Radnor Walk
6 October 1978   London sw3

Darling Wibz,
I long to hear more of your front-garden film. Chalkwell-on-Sea is a great place for front gardens. It is the classy part of Southend. I'd like to be there at cocktail time.

I have written to Linda [Shelton] and to Mummy – the enclosed letter from the latter is very funny about the monkey.

I wish I were as extroverted as I am not. I am only happy as are you when doing what I know I can do and that is writing commentaries for films.

It always cheers me up to think of your garden; the new roof on the stables; the new baby in the womb; the waterfalls; the line of down; the market place at Devizes; Rupert and my old bear Archie and Lucy, Imo and Delli and David on whom Jonathan Stedall dotes.

Harry [Jarvis] has gone to Southend for the day – lucky old thing.

Jake's Thing by Kingsley Amis is gloriously depressing – 'Jake washed down his Mogadon with some of his second glass of what was supposed to be claret.'

Elizabeth and I have been sent Barry [Humphries]'s new record which is spoken from the grave and gives an account of his funeral and how pluckily Beryl behaved at the party afterwards.

I don't think there will be time to call in on our way down to Cornwall this weekend. We go on Saturday morning – early, returning at the end of the month.

Oh! I am so sorry for your inheriting my temperament. The number at Trebetherick is 2295 – I keep my fingers crossed for October 21st which was your grandfather's birthday.

Much love from Dadz

I wrote and presented *The Front Garden* for BBC 2, made by JB's winning team of Eddie Mirzoeff as director and Ted Roberts as editor. Philip Bonham Carter was the inspired cameraman. It had been JB's idea, that the book I had compiled with the photographer Christopher Simon Sykes would make a good film. It was first screened on Christmas Day 1978.

To Monica Dance   29 Radnor Walk
9 November 1978   London SW3

Dear Mrs Dance,

> Civilisation's sure retreat
> Is fifty-five Great Ormond Street,
> It is from there the troops advance
> Under the flag of Mrs Dance.
> Let foul developers beware,
> She looks at them with glassy stare

> And though she makes them freeze with fright
> She manages to be polite.

This is composed straight on to the typewriter as a result of that truly wonderful soirée in the Institute of Directors.

As the Duke [of Grafton] said to me, you had never revealed, until then, your sustained powers of oratory. You were marvellous, both as Secretary and Mother and Nurse, to all those delightful girls, who flitted so fearlessly and helpfully about the well-worn rooms of number 55.

I like the feel that in the background there is always reliable Mr Dance. You have kept the S[ociety for the] P[rotection of] A[ncient] B[uildings] voluntary, friendly, and in the tradition of our founder and of that great character you referred to as 'Bertie Powys'.

I don't consider these lines quoted above as a poem, they are an impromptu of affection from

Yours ever gratefully, John Betjeman

M.D. had been secretary of the SPAB all through the time JB had served on its committee (1954–77). (JB served on the Council from 1981 until his death.) On her retirement in 1978 M.D. remembers, 'Ill as John was at the time, he came to make his farewell speech to me on behalf of the members – it was a heart-throbbing event which I will never forget and at the end, as he left the Hall of the Institute of Directors where the meeting was held, he said he was going to write and send me a poem. This arrived the next morning.'

The Society for the Protection of Ancient Buildings, situated at 55 Great Ormond Street, was founded by William Morris in 1877.

In 1989 the John Betjeman Memorial Fund was established by the SPAB to honour his memory by promoting the repair of churches and chapels in use in England and Wales.

To Philip Larkin   29 Radnor Walk
23 November 1978   London sw3

Dear Philip,
No need to reply to this. I met Ben Travers at lunch the other day with Bishop Mark Hodson and his wife [Susanna]. Ben Travers asked me who was the Greatest English Poet; naturally I said you were and I sent him one of your volumes. He says in his reply:

> I feel ashamed that in my inability to get on with our present day poets and my consequent wholesale disdain and neglect, I have missed out on Larkin. You have made me read (and re-read as is my wont) all the poems in this collection. His observation and often

quite brilliant flair for giving expression to it are remarkable and treasurable. My only reservation is that he seems obsessed with what the *Times Lit[erary] Sup[plement]* quoted in the backcover blurb described as his 'Sense of Waste'.

This isn't bad from someone who is ninety-two who writes in a clear beautiful hand. Long live *Rookery Nook* and the Aldwych Farces. Love to Monica.
　　Yours, JB

　　Ben Travers (1886–1980), the dramatist and novelist, wrote *Rookery Nook* and many other famous farces.
　　Bishop Mark Hodson, previously Bishop of Hereford, was an assistant Bishop of London with special responsibility for the City of Westminster.

To Edward Mirzoeff 　　　　　　　　　　　　　29 Radnor Walk
10 January 1979 　　　　　　　　　　　　　London sw3

Dear Eddie,
I think the research you have sent me by Cathy Palmer really excellent. It almost reads like a film. I am sure we could make a film, part ghost, part actual site and do the line from beginning to end, but ending in Bath, because Bath Green Park is, as it were, a Cathedral of West Country commerce. Make, let us say, a ten or twenty-minute documentary and I am sure we can hold it together with words and ghosts. Cathy Palmer is a find, but so were you and I when we were young.
　　Yours ever, JB

　　E.M. had sent the research notes by Cathy Palmer on the remains of the Somerset and Dorset Railway. JB and he had thought to make a film on London's railway stations following the publication of JB's book, *London's Historic Railway Stations*, but British Rail wanted to charge a 'feature film facility fee' which was prohibitive. A rural railway was thought to be a cheaper option.

To Candida Lycett Green   29 Radnor Walk
15 January 1979   London sw3

Darling Wibz,
I must write to thank you and Rupert for the happiest Christmas I can
remember for years. What was so nice about it was that it was a family
affair and each of your children is as nice as the other, and each has
strong character. I have never known Mummy so happy nor felt so near
to her. I think she enjoyed the heavy snow on her Welsh mountain-top
as much as you all did St Moritz. Your delightful combined postcard
made me very glad to be in London and Derbyshire, considering how
utterly unsporting I am. I think you are all very tolerant of the futile,
bald old buffer who signs himself with much love and gratitude,
    Love, Dadz
    PS Gerard Irvine is much looking forward to the baptism on 11th
Feb[ruary]. If there is somebody who can give me a lift let me know.

    John LG was baptized at St Peter's Church, Blacklands, by Gerard Irvine. JB and PB
    were both present.

Eleven:

The harvest is over

———

1979 to 1983

I made hay while the sun shone.
  My work sold.
Now, if the harvest is over
  And the world cold,
Give me the bonus of laughter
  As I lose hold.

'The Last Laugh'

After that first heart attack in 1978, Gerard Irvine had rushed over from St Matthew's in Great Peter Street to the Royal Brompton Hospital and given JB the last rites. He recovered surprisingly quickly and the first thing he said to me when he saw me sitting beside his bed was that I was looking particularly 'subfusc' (I was wearing a grey dress which was out of character). Archie sat by the bed as well, on the locker.

Noel Annan wrote from a holiday in India, 'I am so sorry to hear you haven't been well and hope that you are on the road to recovery. You mustn't get into that condition which Maurice used to call "strokes all round the wicket". I can't think of anyone who is loved by so many people who have never met him as you are. I do hope the Muse is still speaking to you. She doesn't seem to be speaking to anyone else, except Philip Larkin.'[1] Philip Larkin meanwhile described JB's face, 'Like most old faces, it has collapsed somewhat, but he is still watchful, the eyes moving from speaker to speaker, faintly apprehensive. When he himself says something, there is a hint of the old nostril lifting in irony, corners of the mouth turning down crookedly; then suddenly comes the uproarious back-of–the-pit-horse-laugh, wide open, all teeth and creases.'[2]

Though the Muse never returned, the laughter kept him going. He was safely cocooned by his friends and by God. Harry Williams helped to reinforce his faith and Sybil Harton, the wife of the Vicar of Baulking, who had never stopped writing to him with her (mostly spiritual) news in the most beautiful script, wrote to him on Christmas morning in 1980, telling him she had just heard his poem 'Christmas' read on the radio. 'John, isn't that WONDERFUL, that flung high into the air over Great Britain is your affirmation of faith (requiring doubt), hope (resting on despair), love, love which is the final resolution of life. It seems to me to be a veritable crowning of your life, for which a great surge of thanksgiving springs from me to you, from Earth to Heaven. It makes me so happy to think of Paul and Linda and that lovely baby Thomas.'[3]

And still JB flirted. He asked his old flame Emily Villiers-Stuart out to lunch 'in a restaurant of your choice, in a district of your choice, be it Peckham or Mayfair!'[4] He told Chloe Teacher, Harry and Rosie d'Avigdor Goldsmid's daughter, who had given him a scarf, that he would rather have *her* wrapped around his neck.

To Kingsley Amis and Elizabeth Jane Howard he reminisced about good martinis they had drunk at the Tate Gallery, about good dinners and about a good weekend he had spent with them. 'I must thank you both for wheeling me about uphill and down through all those varieties of Suffolk. I am still besotted with the county . . . . I suppose it contains in Haverhill some of the ugliest housing in the kingdom.'[5] JB still drank champagne most mornings and still lunched in the San Quintino restaurant with friends like Alan Ross, Osbert Lancaster, John Wells, Richard Ingrams or Bruce Shand, who remembered beginning a joke which was to run and run. 'I told John about a commercial traveller I had overheard on a cross-channel boat returning to England. He was complaining about the French food and drink that he had been obliged to consume. It was with relief that he was able to ask the steward for "a small Allsopp". It made John laugh a lot and after that if ever I asked him what he wanted to drink, he'd say, "I'll have a small Allsopp." '[6]

The conservation letters kept on coming – from champions of the Old Rectory at Wimslow, the windmill at Thaxted, the Ilfracombe Hotel and Royal Seabathing Hospital at Margate, from the Woodstock Town Hall Restoration Committee and the Rye Preservation Society. Scots conservationists wrote begging him to stop the traffic proposals in Old Aberdeen. And so it went on. But by now JB had enthused an army of fellow battlers. He wrote to the indomitable Ivor Bulmer Thomas, who had started Friends of Friendless Churches, 'You are a wonderful old thing, you ought to be a peer and have a Lambeth doctorate.'[7]

'If it hadn't been for you,' wrote Colin Amery, co-author of *The Victorian Buildings of London* (2 February 1981), 'Gavin Stamp and I wouldn't have written this book. It is dedicated to you because you have opened so many eyes to the glories of Victorian architecture. I hope you are well and that your energies remain constant – because there are still plenty of philistines left.'[8]

What made JB different from many other tireless crusaders was that he lacked any form of pomposity. He had a joke correspondence with Gavin Stamp who, after a particularly good lunch, wrote (27 January 1982), 'I was delighted to have the opportunity today to have lunch with you and explain my visionary plans for a new public space between the British Museum and the Victoria Embankment, to be named "Holford Piazza" in honour of England's greatest planner. As one of my aides told you, I have the plans drawn up in 1941 by the late Albert Speer for a thirty-six storey barracks, which incorporate an interdenominational quiet room and worship centre to replace the outmoded structures of St George's, Bloomsbury, and St Mary-le-Strand, which will stand in the new landscaped open space which will afford unobstructed views of Centre Point and the Betjeman Suite of the Charing Cross Hotel. I look forward to your support on the Royal Fine Art Commission in ensuring that London does not lose the finest civic opportunity of the last thousand years. Sir Hugh Casson has prepared some charming perspectives of my scheme, which are sure to win over the public to our side. Yours, Herbert Welch, pp Peter Palumbo.'[9]

My mother wrote (8 January 1982), 'I am sending you a copy of Gavin's lecture in the *Society of Arts Journal* with my introduction which is not much like what I said impromptu but I wrote it especially for the journal and I think it is *rather good*. It is actually entirely *your* philosophy of art history in that the whole point of it is to enthuse other people to want to see what you are writing about. There is now a new school of Kunstgeschichte [art history] Wallahs who call themselves *architectural anthropologists* and the stuff they write is quite unreadable.' My mother was writing from the 'Hereford Himalaya' in the middle of the great snow of the winter of 1982. 'The Hereford Himalaya makes the Indian Himalaya look *pansy*. We are enjoying a really spiffing *blizzard* and the noise sounds just like the sort of O[xford] U[niversity] D[ramatic] S[ociety] play you used to do the noises off of. Wibz rang Clive Greenway this morning to find out if I was okay and she said they cannot get up the drive because of the drifts and the M4 is closed. The drifts here are colossal and I had to dig myself out of the back door to go and feed my pony and now I cannot shut it again so I have had to put a cylinder up against it to stop it blowing wide open.'[10] My mother was in her element in terrible weather conditions. There was nothing she enjoyed more than being cut off and having to fend for herself and it always used to worry JB, not to mention me – she was not on the telephone and her writing paper proudly announced, 'No telephone, thank God.'

In April 1981 JB had gone up to stay at Moor View with Elizabeth. John Piper wrote to him there (3 April) about *Church Poems* which had just come out. 'I am delighted to be part of the *Church Poems* book, and I think Jock has made a pretty decent job of it ("not ridiculous," as Bill Coldstream used to say about a picture he specially admired). We are just back from Manchester. What *wonderful* Victorian buildings in the centre of the city, and how they have wrecked everything outside the centre (and a lot *in*). I thought a lot about George Barnes while there, and Prawls, and his love of Fairfield.'[11] On Easter Sunday morning, JB lingered in bed. Elizabeth remembers telling him to hurry up or they would be late for church, but she soon discovered that he was unable to speak or to move his right arm. He had, in fact, suffered a stroke and was admitted to the Royal Hallamshire Hospital in Sheffield where the brilliant and extraordinarily good-looking neurologist Dr Davies-Jones looked after him. JB stayed there for over a month. God once again intervened and orchestrated the visiting hours between Elizabeth (who was with JB almost daily) and my mother, who travelled from Herefordshire to see him as often as she could.

On that high eleventh floor overlooking the city of Sheffield and its verdant parks, I felt it was time to ask questions of JB. I wanted to assure him that I would look after things should he die. I knew he worried about Elizabeth and I promised that I would always see she was all right and love her. I asked him why he hadn't married her. I never got an answer. I knew that my mother, in her great magnanimity, had offered him a divorce soon after my marriage to Rupert. I knew also that he was desperate to avoid hurting my mother, because he loved her so much. He told me that he loved Elizabeth too. I remember thinking angrily at that point, that he was an archetypal ostrich, and that he *should* be married to Elizabeth. But despite my anger I understood that for him, with his particular penchant for guilt, the situation was as insoluble as it had always been.

'I hope you are doing all the things Nurse Younghusband tells you to do,' Sandy Stone (alias Barry Humphries) wrote from Melbourne (29 May), 'and remember to say the right thing when they put their heads around the screens and ask, Yes or No. Would you like me to send you some Australian crystallised fruit to put with the Callard and Bowser Dessert Nougat in your locker? I'm sending you a few daffs and carnies

as well. At least we heard you were getting better fast at the same time
as we got the news you'd had a bit of a turn, so we hope you're as fit as a
Mallee Bull by now, as toey as a two-year-old, and as happy as a box of
budgies as well. I hope your hozzie smells nice – too often the
combination of chloroform and brussel sprouts and roast potatoes can
be a bit much. Would you like an Airwick for the top of your locker?'[12]
Thelma Barlow, the actress who plays Mavis in *Coronation Street* wrote
'with her most sincere and loving wishes for your gentle recovery. God
bless you.'[13]

Immediately after his stroke JB had forgotten a lot of quite ordinary
words, but because of his huge vocabulary and inimitable use of
language he was always able to get round this. He made a slow and
steady recovery though he preferred being in a wheelchair to having
walking lessons with a physiotherapist. He took communion regularly
on Sunday mornings and was allowed out for tours in the car. We drove
among silver-walled fields on the hills around Sheffield and discovered
churches and villages we had never seen, returning to the hospital in
time for tea. Some mornings he showed no enthusiasm or concentration
for anything but I suspected that it was because he loved being
mollycoddled by the nurses. He would rather be washed by them than
wash himself. And still after three weeks of being in hospital he worried
about Elizabeth and voiced his worries to the nurses. I think he thought
he would die in hospital. Sometimes Elizabeth would sleep in the
hospital to assuage his fears.

Kingsley Amis wrote, 'I hear encouraging reports of steady progress
and shameful cosseting by attractive nurses. Jolly good show . . . .
They say the May rainfall probably won't beat the 1979 record, but it's
been the unsunniest spring I can remember . . . . I'm looking forward
very much to the opening of the Humber bridge (Barbara Castle's bribe
to the local voters, costing some horrible sum like forty million quid and
quite unnecessary). Did you know old Philip (Larkin) had written an
(embarrassing, he said) ode to be set to music by a Hull composer and
sung at the ceremony? He's been praying for years that the bridge
would fall down or never be finished. Of course one so often agrees to
do hateful things if the day of reckoning is far in the future. I can't
imagine what public, celebratory, organ-voiced Larkin will be like.
. . . I went to the Royal Academy, sporting my CBE as may readily be
imagined, and got unluckily tight. I mean I tanked up at the club just a
bit because I thought we might well be given one sherry and then
driven in to the table. Not a bloody bit of it; the whisky flowed like
wine. I grabbed it because now I thought it might be cut off at 7.25; not

a bit of that either. Then there was a lot of wine. All in all I was not the ideal neighbour for Constance Cummings.'[14]

JB left the Hallamshire Hospital and went back to Edensor but returned on a regular basis for physiotherapy. By the middle of July the speech disturbance, the blunting sensation down his right side and the visual loss to his right eye had all resolved themselves. He wrote to Dr Davies-Jones, 'The nerve is doing well, thanks to you and Sheffield. The waters are pleasantly stirred, thanks to you and Thomas the Water. I am much less afraid than I was. God bless us all and endless thanks to you for your ministration in those ecstatic times.'[15] Dr Davies-Jones remembered that throughout his time in hospital JB was patient, equable, but at times rather anxious. 'He was most grateful for everything that was done to him. He had a delightful manner towards everyone, without exception, and we all enjoyed having him around during his stay on Ward NI.'[16]

In July 1981 while he was staying at Moor View Elizabeth wrote in longhand, to JB's dictation, to Edward Adeane, the Private Secretary to the Prince of Wales, 'I am recovering from a stroke and cannot yet write in longhand. However, I have managed to compose the enclosed poem about the forthcoming marriage of Prince Charles and Lady Diana.'[17] It was a brave and moving effort.

Gradually he got back into an extraordinarily gentle routine. In October he took part in a poetry reading at Tamsin Day-Lewis's school in Greenwich. She wrote to him, 'I do hope you enjoyed the poetry reading. I howled with laughter at the poems you read. I only wish that there could have been more time for you to read us some more.'[18]

In 1982 his *Uncollected Poems* were published, many of them gathered over the years of sorting through JB's papers in British Columbia by the librarian Joan Ryan. JB's biographer Bevis Hillier, together with John Murray, whittled them down to twenty-nine. Some of these JB had never intended for publication but he agreed and the slim volume was dedicated to Elizabeth. The reviews were not overwhelmingly good.

There were, however, wonderful reviews for Jonathan Stedall's series of films *Time with Betjeman* which were shown in 1983. 'While making *Time with Betjeman* I sometimes regretted that we hadn't filmed a year or so earlier,' wrote Jonathan Stedall.' It was clear in some scenes that by then JB not only had difficulty with his speech but that he couldn't always hold on to a line of thought. His attention often wandered. But on the whole I think the timing was actually fortuitous in that he was almost totally unselfconscious in front of the camera. The performer in him was largely laid aside. He behaved and responded very much as he did with me when we were alone. By then I had known him for about twenty years.

'For me he was, in a way, like the father I never had – but without the complications. Although I often experienced his highly amusing and entertaining side, I also knew something of the JB who lay behind the performer and the seeming extrovert. And it was this aspect of JB's character that often emerged in *Time with Betjeman* and which I feel was a clue to what he was really like. In the year or so that followed the making of those last programmes, before his death in 1984, he became increasingly silent, not I believe because he was particularly gloomy, nor because he couldn't actually speak. It was as though he became more transparent, more truly what he was in essence – an observer and a listener.

'His silence was essentially a peaceful silence; the anxious frown appeared less and less. On the cliffs he started to talk about eternity – "I think there *is* something beyond death and that it's all the time – eternity is around us all the time." And yet in the next breath he said, "Growing old is the most disillusioning thing we have to go through . . . . Poetry is life, and you can't do without it. It makes life worth living."

'In his garden at Treen, he spoke about silence – "People are afraid of silence." We left space for that silence. It was not a performance for camera. Then, much to JB's amusement the silence was interrupted by a passing lorry – "There goes Mother's Pride!" He certainly never lost his sense of humour. And above all, in that peaceful Cornish garden, it was clear that JB felt "safe".'[19]

Billa Harrod always looked in on JB whenever she came to London. In March 1982 she wrote, 'I *loved* seeing you yesterday; thank God your brain ticks over absolutely okay, that is *really* what matters with chaps like you; but it's a bore about your legs and your *fear*. How can we stop it? You've always had guilt, which is I suppose a sort of fear; you *shouldn't* have it now; you really are the Tops – much more than you can know; you only know the official rather public, Londony side; but *I* know how you are regarded all over England by quite simple people who may, but not necessarily, have seen you on the telly – but they've *heard* of you (not always even *heard* you) and somehow your very extraordinary personality has come across and is now part of folk-lore. I really mean this, and it is no longer, "Oh Mr Betjeman, you would love it, it is so *hideous*" – it is a sort of understanding and a deep affection that you have inspired. You may think this is all BALLS but it *ain't*. *I* know, and *you* can't, how ordinary, quite dim people think of you. Of all the very distinguished friends Roy and I have had, you have far and away the widest circle of followers and admirers. Maurice [Bowra], Isaiah [Berlin], Francis Bacon, Wystan Auden, S[tephen] Spender, etc., etc. all have their esoteric circles, and their fame; but it's *tiny* compared with yours. You have done more good to make people understand the English landscape, the architecture (including, but not exclusively, the formerly despised Victorian), the language, and the atmosphere, than all those others put together. This is *true*. *And*, you have remained the loyallest and most affectionate of all friends. So you, of all people, should not have guilt or fear. If that is what is stopping you walking, I think you could get up and run. Well, that's all for today, but I feel it so strongly that I may say it all again. Very much love darling, I *am* glad you are my friend.'[20]

JB was by now completely confined to a wheelchair. Tristram Powell remembered, 'I took him and Elizabeth to an exhibition of English landscape paintings, from all over the country, pictures that I felt sure John would remember from visits to provincial museums. We took his wheelchair up in the Hayward Gallery's lift for the disabled. The *Time with Betjeman* series had recently been on television. The first to approach him was a beautiful, pale-skinned red-haired girl and as we wheeled him from picture to picture more people, mostly young, came and said how they had enjoyed his programmes. He wasn't able to speak much, but it was a touching last expedition.'[21]

By 1983 he often looked sad and haunted behind his long, clear gaze. He would spend each morning at number 29, sitting at his Swedish-made pine table opposite his gentle secretary, Elizabeth Moore, whom he always called 'Dorinda' and who lived on the other side of the street. The letters still poured in and in a way they anchored him, they gave a structure to his day. His dictated replies got shorter and shorter. Sometimes Elizabeth Moore would write them herself and say that JB was not feeling well and could not do this or that. He told Janet Watts of the *Observer*, 'One must go on protesting, Denmark Hill Station, Southend Pier, the Natural History Museum, Dickens' House at Chatham. . . . They are trying to kill the railways but I think there will be a return to them. This island is thick with them and the more disused ones I see the more I am meant to be discouraged, but where there have been trains there will be trains. I think the age of the railway is only just coming.'

In September 1983 he had another heart attack due to a coronary thrombosis and on 16 October he had another stroke. Elizabeth wrote to Patrick Garland, 'John was doing so well against all the odds, but for some reason he has become very withdrawn and I find it agonizing seeing him look so sad and tormented and being unable to help him at all. He has been unbelievably looked after by two nurses who have been coming mornings and evenings since he had his stroke and are now here all the time and love him. All one can do is just hope and pray it will pass.'[22]

He never really recovered. Elizabeth kept him feeling secure and safe but he never spoke much again. Friends called in to number 19, to read to him, and my mother sometimes saw him at number 29 by diplomatic arrangements with Elizabeth Moore. Prunella Scales came and read his old favourites – Hardy and Tennyson. Gerard Irvine called often to give him communion. Elizabeth's house was cluttered up with plants and pictures and books and piles of her papers and often he would use the ironing board as a surface on which to put the holy sacrament. It acted as a temporary altar. Gerard thinks that the last verse JB ever composed was when he suddenly said after a long silence:

'Of all the things within this house that are by me possessed
I love, oh yes, I love by far, my *ironing* board the best.'[23]

I gained great comfort from going round to see JB and felt safe as well in the warmth and welcome of Elizabeth's sitting room. I would sit and hold JB's hand and read to him. His eyes could still speak.

JB kept up his sojourns in Derbyshire and Cornwall and after a visit in December 1983 to the Hallamshire Hospital, Dr Davies-Jones wrote to Jill Parker, Peter Parker's wife and JB's GP in London (15 December), 'I discussed the position at length with Elizabeth Cavendish and with his nurse and there was no doubt that he was desperately unhappy in hospital, feeling very lonely, and he went out to stay in Chatsworth for a few days with Elizabeth and to be looked after by his nurse, Carole. Carole is doing an excellent job and is caring for him superbly. She has a great rapport with him and she understands what he wants. I told Elizabeth Cavendish that there is no indication to treat him vigorously in any way because I do not think he would be improved, and I cannot see him going on for all that much longer.'[24]

1. JB's papers, University of Victoria, British Columbia.
2. Philip Larkin, review of Patrick Taylor-Martin's *John Betjeman: His Life and Work, Observer* (1983).
3. JB's papers, University of Victoria.
4. Peter Patrick Hemphill's papers.
5. Kingsley Amis's papers, Huntington Library, Pasadena, California.

6. Bruce Shand, CLG interview (1994).
7. Ivor Bulmer Thomas's papers.
8. JB's papers, University of Victoria.
9. JB's papers, University of Victoria.
10. JB's papers, Beinecke Library, Yale University.
11. JB's papers, University of Victoria.
12. JB's papers, University of Victoria.
13. JB's papers, University of Victoria.
14. JB's papers, University of Victoria.
15. Dr Davies-Jones's papers.
16. Dr Davies-Jones, letter to CLG (1994).
17. Prince of Wales's papers.
18. JB's papers, University of Victoria.
19. Jonathan Stedall, letter to CLG (1994).
20. JB's papers, University of Victoria.
21. Tristram Powell, letter to CLG (1994).
22. Patrick Garland's papers.
23. Gerard Irvine, CLG interview (1994).
24. Hallamshire Hospital archives.

To Ralph Bennett   29 Radnor Walk
29 January 1979   London sw3

Dear Mr Chairman,
I am really a tram man, not a bus man, though my heart was always
with the L[ondon] G[eneral] O[mnibus] C[ompany] and the pirate
companies. I ought to tell you that I am now wobbly on my legs and
very bad at standing about and talking to lots of people. So if you decide
to have me under these rather awkward conditions, when I can sit down
much of the time, I should be happy to accept your invitation for March
2nd.
    Please give my best wishes to that great man Michael Robbins and to
the sculpture that hangs around your building at 55 Broadway.
    Yours sincerely, John Betjeman

> R.B. was chairman of London Transport at the time.
>   JB went to the 150th Anniversary celebration of the Shillibeer (Horse) Bus in
> Guildhall Yard on 2 March.
>   Michael Robbins, who had worked for Collins the publishers, had specialised in
> writing on transport. He contributed to *English Parish Churches* when working for Collins
> and helped with arrangements over *Metroland*.
>   55 Broadway is the HQ of London Transport, built (1927–29) by Charles Holden,
> affixed to which are two large groups of sculpture by the top sculptors of the twenties.

To Joan and Patrick Leigh Fermor   29 Radnor Walk
15 February 1979   London sw3

Dearest Joanie and Paddy,
Your ingenious lines in that gloriously complicated metre have cheered
me up a lot. I hear the waves of the Aegean softly lapping against rock,
and I picture Groundsel [Graham Eyres-Monsell] at Dumbleton
striding over his acres. And I long to put into such catching rhyme and
rhythm my memories of Sir Bolton and the Viscountess and the
terrified children. Today London is like Siberia and there's every
chance of Feeble and me being sent to Gothland in the Baltic to look at

the old churches there. What a life you and Joanie have had, and how wisely and well you have spent it, where the orthodox saints look down with olive-shaped eyes from the walls of the basilica and the goats leap from crag to crag and the olives are silvery. Penelope comes to luncheon today and I have ordered chocolate éclairs for her but not for
    Yours with love, John B

P.L.F., who had just swum the Bosphorus, as Byron before him, had sent JB his verse on the subject.
    JB's verse 'Dumbleton Hall', about the Eyres-Monsell family home, appeared in *Uncollected Poems* (1982).

To Maurice and Richard Elliott   29 Radnor Walk
4 April 1979   London sw3

Dear and marvellous Brothers,
I very much enjoyed my Onion Soup and Herrings and the exquisite Claret (Beychevelle) at the Institute of Directors yesterday. I am so sorry I was late by calling at the wrong place and having to feel my way along Pall Mall wearing a red tie and asking for aid to walk. I may have been taken for an IRA man as well as a Communist.
    I am writing to Ashley Barker today about Ally Pally [Alexandra Palace], Greenwich and the Strand, and I will try to fix for us to meet him. It will be my turn to be host.
    Yours sincerely, John Betjeman

JB had met M. and R.E. through their shared interest in transport and had visited the Covent Garden Floral Museum. M.E. recalls, 'We were converting it into the new London Transport Museum and we discussed a project which was still on the drawing board at Crystal Palace – the dream of a lady called Miss Dawn Smith – to restore the BR station (at that time defunct at the head of a branch line) . . . This sparked off the idea of a renaissance of trams somewhere in London. John eagerly started canvassing people and thinking about sites. The venture never came to fruition.'
    JB wrote to Ashley Barker at the Greater London Council (4 April 1979), 'There are two remarkable brothers called Elliott (Richard and Maurice) and they live at Bishop's Stortford and they build buses and trams . . . . We have a scheme for bringing trams back . . . . You are their great hero. The days of electric traction are drawing near. Trams, will we be able to get them back anywhere?'

To Anne Rosse   29 Radnor Walk
6 September 1979   London sw3

Dearest Anne,

I am so glad you sent me that excellent article about Michael by James White. The more I think about it the more I realise how great a man, in his quiet way, Michael was. Quiet and kind and sympathetic. He was the best chairman I ever served under because he was always alert and always polite and with tremendous authority. This is all apart from the fact, which seemed to me very unlikely, that he knew so much about trees. He kept it all dark as he did Womersley, and would smile tolerantly if one spoke about trees or Womersley. And how fond he was of the Mall at Birr and Mr Garvey. I shall always remember him sharing rooms in the High Street at Oxford with Bryan Guinness, whom I thought of as a sort of henchman to Michael.

I think the Parsons family deserves a readable illustrated book; there are excellent writers on architecture today such as little Mark Girouard, the pupil of Billa Harrod and Gavin Stamp and Alistair Service and their great hero is Robert Byron who was always in such a rage and was the friend of the least-known peer in the world, my old friend Cracky William (Wicklow). And who dominates all this and who was the ideal step-father to Tony [Armstrong-Jones]? *As always it was Michael.* I am so glad you married him and that the drawing room at the castle is still there, looking through the Gothick windows to the waterfall while far off stands that curious construction for holding the Earl of Rosse's telescope.

I will certainly come to the Memorial Service on November 15th. I am glad Harold [Acton] was with you. You are a great standby, as he is, to our generation.

Yours not at all pompously and with much love, John B

Michael R. had died on 1 July. JB had first served under his chairmanship on the Advisory Committee for the Recording of Irish Architecture in 1939.

Womersley, Yorkshire, seat of the Harvey-Hawke family, came into the Parsons family, earls of Rosse, through a marriage to the Womersley heiress in 1870. Michael R. inherited the Queen Anne house and four-thousand-acre estate in 1921 and brought up his family there. He was patron of the church of St Martin's there, where his funeral (and A.R.'s in 1993) took place.

Mr Garvey was the agent at Birr Castle, County Offaly, who both looked after and really saved the estate throughout all the difficult years until Michael returned after the Second World War.

Harold Acton was the Rosses' closest friend.

To Penelope Betjeman   29 Radnor Walk
14 May [1980]   London sw3

Darling

Sophie [Paget] types this, I can't be legible for long. I wanted to tell you
how much I enjoyed your seventieth birthday. More, I think, than any
day I can remember. Wibz has inherited your talent and kindness and
gloomy humour. Rupert is a tower of generous strength and the
children are all strong, individual characters. I was very pleased when
David, looking at Archie, said he had a smiley eye. He has. One eye
smiles, the other is gloomy. I find John a comfortable wondering little
character and as for the girls, they are perfection. Delli with her private
life and poetry. Lucy with her care for others and Imo who put her
hand in mine and left it there without saying anything. It was lovely to
be with you, for you really are the source of it all and I am glad to say
that Wibz's brilliant organisation of us all was worthy of Woade.
Whatever happens, and there is always terror in the offing, your
seventieth birthday was *the* day in my life and you were looking just the
same, just as morose and funny as Wibz is in *The Front Garden* which is
repeated on April 11th, BBC 2 at 9.40.
    Believe me when I say that I am yours very trewly, Tewpie

    Sophie Paget, the daughter of PB's cousin Henry Anglesey, worked as a temporary
    secretary for JB.

To Robert Etty   29 Radnor Walk
23 May 1980   London sw3

Dear Mr Etty,
Tennyson would be pleased with his fellow townsmen for carrying on
in the vein of his great satire 'The Northern Farmer New Style'. I think
your parodies of my parody really excellent, particularly those by Paul
Edwards and Karen Webster. You have brightened my working
morning.
    Yours sincerely, John Betjeman
    PS I liked them so much I have taken the liberty of keeping them
along with Tennyson on my shelf.

R.E., the English Teacher at Monks' Dyke High School, Louth, had set his second-year class to write a further verse to JB's 'Harvest Hymn'. One of the pupils went to the library and got JB's address from *Who's Who*. Paul Edwards had written about pesticides that 'make some wildlife sick', and Karen Webster used the phrase 'velvet-padded loos'.

To Penelope Betjeman　　　　　　　　　　29 Radnor Walk
2 July 1980　　　　　　　　　　　　　　　London sw3

My dear Penalloppy,
I have come to the conclusion that I cannot accept an invitation I had to visit Gothland in the Baltic. A beautiful island of flowers and rocks and Hanseatic Romanesque. It would mean foreigners, different food and no protection unless Jonathan [Stedall] came, which he can't at the moment.

I long to see our grandchildren and am very happy they are with you. This disease makes me too tired to do more than one thing a day. No pain is involved and little despondency. I went last week, at Sophie's organisation, to Milton Keynes. It is a new town. It was the poet Cowper's country which I had visited, when a Freshman at Oxford, by steam train. By a miracle of planning all the old villages I remembered were untouched and the new town had lorries running along the routes so that it was comparatively quiet.

I would like to hear from you on the telephone almost any morning after 10.30 when I have got my nerve back. I like talking to you on the telephone. I miss your voice and jokes. I miss you.

Yesterday I met Griggers [Geoffrey Grigson] at a meeting about the Queen's Medal for poetry. He told me there is a very good restaurant in Devizes and I think he said there is one in Calne. It would be worth your ringing him up to find out about them. His present wife Jane [Grigson] writes on cooking. He has got very fat. I am no fatter nor thinner. I wish I could walk and swim, though the magician on Winchmore Hill is pretty good.

Sophie is marvellous and has happy memories of Kulu-on-Wye. I wish I saw more of you. Archie sends you his best wishes, so does Jumbo. Reynolds Stone died mowing his garden, what a nice way to go. I would like to write to all the grandchildren but don't want to give them the guilt of unanswered letters and so I will do nothing at all until I hear from you.

Believe me, yours very trewly, Tewpie
Ta ever so for yesterday's letter.

Geoffrey Grigson (see *Volume One*), the poet, critic and anthologist, had had a long on-off friendship with JB since the thirties.

The 'magician on Winchmore Hill' was a physiotherapist JB visited.

To Mary Wilson   29 Radnor Walk
24 July 1980   London sw3

My dear Mary,
I have been thinking about you a lot lately because of Harold being in St
Mark's and Giles in Tisbury and Robin in Chalfont Road. BUT
grandchildren are a great consolation, I am just finding that out and I
know you love the twins and they you. Scilly is a nice thought and soon
you will all see the sun on the water and smell the salty air and dried
seaweed. Hold on. Best wishes to Harold in hospital; the world, when
he comes out, will be like a re-birth, so it was for me after my short time
in the Brompton. I hope it will produce a poem or two from you all this
tribulation.
      Love, John

Through the late seventies, with JB's increasing unsteadiness, M.W. came to visit him at
Radnor Walk much more often than she had before and their correspondence, which had
been abundant when they were both so busy, became less frequent.

The Wilson family were all temporarily separated. Harold W. had had an operation in
St Mark's Hospital, Giles was in Wiltshire, Robin in Oxford and M.W. in London.

JB had just spent a week in the Brompton Royal Hospital after suffering a mild stroke.

To Penelope Betjeman   29 Radnor Walk
4 September 1980   London sw3

My darling Plymmi,
I was so glad to hear from you; I agree with every word you say about
the films of my verse. To begin with they were too literal; even had
they been good it is no good trying to film the imagination. 'Tiger tiger
burning bright' – how would you film that? Well, you can't. The only
thing you can say in favour of making a film of poems is that you may
capture an audience to listen to poetry who would normally never read
or listen to it unless they were trapped by a telly set. That makes it
worth while, perhaps.

It was very nice of you to write at such length. You agree with Gavin Stamp and I expect Hanbury would too. Wibz and Rupert are in Cornwall and I will be going down there on 20th September. 'Til then I'm here.

Yours trewly, Tewpie. Look forward to hearing from you shortly.

Late Flowering Love, a twenty-minute 'short', was a visual treatment of four poems by JB. The soundtrack was his own reading of the poems to an orchestral accompaniment, but he had no influence over what turned out to be a sad and demeaning visualisation of 'Agricultural Caress', 'Invasion Exercise on the Poultry Farm', 'A Subaltern's Love-Song' and 'Myfanwy'. The cast included Jenny Agutter, John Le Mesurier, Eric Morecambe and Susannah York.

To Mrs Braddell   29 Radnor Walk
24 September 1980   London SW3

Dear Mrs Braddell,
I am so sorry to be unable to cross to Northern Ireland to Lionel [Perry]'s funeral today. Parkinson's Disease, which I have, is painless but impeding and I couldn't cope with the journey.

Thank you so much for letting me know about the arrangements. Lionel was my oldest friend from Oxford. I remember the photographs he had of his brother Patrick and his sister Pamela Penelope. I was looking lately at the only portrait I have seen of Peter Perry his father. It is in Herbert Baker's reminiscences. I don't think I have ever laughed so much as I did with Lionel when we hired a house at Haywards Heath called Briar Lea. We used to call it Brierly Park which gave it a bit of class. Michael Dugdale, that brilliant and neglected man, was of our company. We used to sing hymns to the piano. I don't think I can ever be grateful enough for the friendship of Lionel.

Yours sincerely, John Betjeman

Mrs Braddell was Lionel Perry's cousin and close friend.

To Penelope Betjeman   29 Radnor Walk
16 October 1980   London SW3

My darling

I had a very nice time in Cornwall and feel in very good health and Wibz
is going through the torment of making a film on horse mania. I have
kept away.

I tried to get you on the telephone at Blacklands but got Rupert who
seemed very cheerful. I would like to know where you are and to have
lunch with you when you come to London. Whenever I drive past
Marlborough Road Station I think of our early days and Mr Prewett
and Honor Guinness. I wish I saw more of you and that I wrote every
day as Woad used to do. Osbert has done a beautiful drawing of a
Norfolk church under Billa's instructions.

I have just read Mary Lutyens's life of her father which Jock
[Murray] has published. What a very nice man [Edwin] Lutyens was
and he adored his Emily and what a good architect he was. [Herbert]
Baker is much duller. Shoosmith is mentioned in Mary's book. I would
like to see New Delhi before I die. I am most surprised at myself. I
think it is the Lutyens work that attracts me.

Hoping this reaches you as it leaves me, which is in the pink.
Tewpie

Following the screening of *The Front Garden*, Eddie Mirzoeff had suggested that I make
another film with him which culminated in *The Englishwoman and the Horse*.
A.G. Shoosmith was Lutyens's assistant in New Delhi and the designer of the
Garrison Church there.

To Candida Lycett Green   29 Radnor Walk
17 October 1980   London SW3

Darling Wibz,
This is about the time when you begin to despair about filming and you
feel distrust and fear and that nothing will come out right and you know
what you want to do and you don't think your producer knows his own
mind. All I can say is keep it up and trust Eddie [Mirzoeff], something
will come out quite different from what you expected and from what he

expected. Keep your hair on, it's very difficult, it is the pangs of birth and they *are* worth it in the end.

Love to Rupert and the kiddies, MD

To John Summerson   29 Radnor Walk
12 November 1980   London sw3

My dear Coolmore,
What do you know of Ingress Bell? I am always thinking about him. Did he quarrel with Aston? Did he drink? I remember at an RFAC meeting how affronted Maxwell Ayrton was when I suggested his partner drank. I miss you.

Yours ever, JB

> Said Aston Webb to Ingress Bell
> Our partnership is doing well
> I think it would do better still
> If you had far less time to kill
> 'I do not like aspersions cast on
> My selfless labour for you Aston
> So let it now be Fare you well
> Please make your egress Ingress Bell'

Sir Aston Webb (1849–1930), designer of the Queen Victoria memorial and the Admiralty Arch, was the quintessential Edwardian establishment architect. His career had taken off when he won the competition for the Victoria Law Courts in Birmingham at the beginning of his partnership with Edward Ingress Bell (1836/7–1914). As the mysterious Bell was an older man, perhaps he merely retired after the turn of the century rather than taking to the bottle.

To Endellion Lycett Green   29 Radnor Walk
8 January 1981   London sw3

My dear Delli,
Cadwallader is the name of that crocodile you made for me, he is very happy in Chelsea, he hopes you enjoyed Switzerland. He does not like it himself as he cannot ski because he is the wrong shape, it's very bad luck on reptiles that they cannot ski. Bears are at home in the snow. Love to them all by that waterfall and grotto. Love from Grandpapa

ELG had made a bean-bag crocodile in sewing class.

To Mark Girouard   29 Radnor Walk
22 January 1981   London sw3

Dear Mark,
Of course we can't have this hole-in-corner bargaining about the Hoop
and Grapes. Everything depends on the architect and fuck the
developer. Of course I'll talk on the telly if it will help. My love to
Dorothy and the kiddi and of course to Colville to whom I am greatly
indebted for an introduction to Joe Corvo the foot massage man.
   Love and kisses, John B

> The Hoop and Grapes was an untouched seventeenth-century half-timbered inn in
> Whitechapel High Street. The developers, Haslemere Estates, wanted to gut it and
> demolish the seventeenth-century building adjoining it. The Spitalfields Trust was at
> this time desperately trying to save it and was begging the Minister to call it in. He
> wouldn't and the development and demolition went ahead. JB had helped to found the
> Spitalfields Trust in 1977 when two buildings, numbers 5 and 7 Elder Street, were
> threatened by demolition. He told the press that 'Elder Street would be like a smile with
> two front teeth missing if 5 and 7 were to go.' They were saved.

To Deborah Devonshire   29 Radnor Walk
February 1981   London sw3

For Debo,

> *A Border Ballad*
>
> O come wi me tae Scratchwood
> And wield the woodman's axe
> Tis there we'll clear a bonnie space
> Fro petrol and fro snacks
>
> And mony a fey frae Hertfordshire
> Comes waltzing through the dark
> By way of Brockley Avenue
> And on tae Porter's Park
>
> Iain MacBetjeman

'For some reason (unknown to me) I reminded him of the service station just north of
London called Scratchwood!' recalls D.D.

To Alice Hardy   29 Radnor Walk
2 March 1981   London SW3

Darling PE,
I loved your annual letter. As you know, you are the original of 'In a
Bath Tea Shop', the shortest poem I wrote. I'm so glad to hear of old
friends and so sad for Eileen Malony, I think of her sitting with me in
the little branch line to Iron Acton, she will remember if she is well
enough. I loved her deeply and she was a very good producer, the slave
of the lady who was head of her department. That was the most creative
time of my life, everything was thrilling and the Avon flowed through
Clifton Gorge and under that mighty mosquito of a bridge.
   I wouldn't half mind that book of Teddy Wolfe's, I would buy it on
the strength of your recommendation. I'll ask my accountant if I can
afford the two hundred pounds.
   My affection to Rosemary Colley. Stands Corkagh still under the
grey Dublin sky? While Clondalkin station waits the ghost of a train
down to Kingsbridge. Does Rosemary remember Mrs Madan? 'Wasn't
she decoratin' the church and didn't she fall off the Holy Table?' How
Penelope and I laughed about those dear old Church of Ireland days.
Alas, that things have got so serious. Brian Patten I remember with
delight, give him my affection.
   Darling, you bring sunshine into this neat but dingy room.
   Love, John B

> A.H. first met JB in 1943 when she was married to her first husband Mr Jennings and JB
> was working for the Admiralty in Bath. He was making a broadcast under the auspices
> of Geoffrey Grigson in the Bristol BBC studios: 'I came into the Listening Room in
> order to put him on the air, being the Programme Engineer, now called Studio
> Manageress, and John said "Who's that girl?" And Griggers from a great height said
> "That's your PE." At that time everybody in the BBC and probably elsewhere too was
> bristling with initials, and, coming upon this latest one, John burst into a great chortle of
> enchantment, so infectious that I joined in too, and that's how our friendship started up,
> and how henceforth I was called PE.'
>   JB fell in love with her. They were both away from their families and missing them. 'It
> was all lovely and gorgeous and funny,' remembers A.H. 'We used to go to Bath tea
> shops together. When John wrote "In a Bath Tea Shop" I said to him, "You may be a
> 'thumping crook', but I'm *not* 'an ordinary little woman'." He admitted it was not a
> physical description of us but of a couple we had been watching.' JB wrote to Alice
> (Jennings as she was then), 17 July 1944, 'I've had rather a pang in this heart, sitting here
> at Fortt's having tea, at seeing a girl who is obviously you with rather skinny shoulders
> and J.M. Barrie hair sitting by a gallant RAF boy. He's nuts about her, I can see from his
> eyes. She's got her back to me. I hope it's not you. Because he's not like Jennings. . . .
> My dear thing, just go over that day again – the bicycle, the iron stairs, the sweet on the
> carpet, the constant change of dress, the quiet of Clifton treetops and the U[nion]J[ack]

flag beyond them, shopping, . . . the drunk lunch with Beadle and Co. – then the sleep in that little cell of a bedroom, tea, love – my ruined raped Wendy – the rocks, Teddi Wolfe, the wonderful walk back. Oh heaven! What a height we reached . . . I'm in a hell of a tangle. I love you: I love you: keep your few eyelashes free from blast.'

'In a Bath Teashop' was published in *New Bats in Old Belfries* in 1945:

> 'Let us not speak, for the love we bear one another –
> Let us hold hands and look.'
> She, such a very ordinary little woman;
> He, such a thumping crook;
> But both, for a moment, little lower than the angels
> In the teashop's ingle-nook.

Eileen Malony (see *Volume One*) was the BBC Talks producer and her boss was Mary Semeris, the head of 'Schools Talks' who never gave Eileen her due. Eileen was ill at the time.

Edward Wolfe RA was a great friend of A.H.'s and JB's and they were always going to his studio by the river for drinks made of Metatone, a sort of wartime tonic which tasted quite like Vermouth, and gin stored in milk bottles made illegally by university students. Wolfe, always broke, had made a limited edition of prints illustrating the *Song of Solomon*.

Rosemary Colley, whose sister JB had known in Ireland, was the 'Auntie Rosemary' of *Children's Hour*.

To Wilhelmine Harrod   29 Radnor Walk
4 March 1981   London SW3

Darling Billa,

> She sat dead calm among the wasps
> Hemstitching at her evening gown
> The Norfolk sunlight floated by
> The Dowager Viscountess Downe.

I wonder if I could write anything like that about the forthcoming Norfolk marriage. I am very fond of Ruth Fermoy and I recall that she lives in the Norfolk house of the Baker Baronets who edited *Hymns A[ncient] and M[odern]*. Roy would have been the first to know the real facts, I can only guess at them. I have always preferred a rood screen to the bare altar and darling, you are the rood screen between me and reality. There is that lovely little slope of hill between the Old Rectory and Holt.

Lots of love, John

The 'Viscountess Downe' (née ffolkes) was W.H.'s aunt. On becoming a widow she had returned to her native Norfolk where, there being no male descendants, she had inherited the family estate at Hillington. W.H. and JB had visited her in the fifties and JB had never forgotten her fearlessness with wasps.

The Norfolk marriage was that of the Prince of Wales and Lady Diana Spencer, granddaughter of Ruth Fermoy who lived in various houses in Norfolk.

To David Lycett Green   29 Radnor Walk
25 March 1981   London sw3

Dear David,
I would like to tell you and your brother John why I am so fond of spiders. Flies are the enemy of man: they spread disease, they gave Gramelope malaria in India. Spiders are the enemies of flies and therefore the friends of man: they cannot inflict a serious wound, they can only nip when they are afraid. They are very good mothers, they have eight legs and are wingless and defenceless. They enjoy jokes and if you talk to them they smile. Not all flies are enemies, wasps can be quite friendly if you talk to them and do not make any sudden movement. I knew an old lady who used to put out saucers of jam for the wasps in Norfolk. Old Billa Harrod knew her, so did I.
    Love to your father and mother and the divine sisters and Proper Chetwode of a brother,
    Love from Grandpapa

JB's love of and interest in spiders never wavered, particularly the large barn spiders. He would talk to them and to wasps. He taught PSGB and me to keep stock still in the latter's presence.

To Kingsley Amis   Hallamshire Hospital
3 June 1981   Sheffield

Dear Kingers,
I loved your letter about poetry. What nice stuff it is. This is the town from which Ebenezer Elliott came – or rather Rotherham. There is a statue to him here, he was rather a good nature poet.
    I have never heard of Ashbery. I like the idea of a book of short poems also of a book of long poems, it is the ones in between I can't stand.
    I can't yet write with my right hand.
    Yours ever old top, John Betjeman

Ebenezer Elliott (1781–1849) was known as the 'Corn Law rhymer' because of his satirical poems condemning the bread tax. He was also a master-founder.

After JB's stroke in April 1981 while staying at Edensor in Derbyshire, when he was taken to the Hallamshire Hospital in Sheffield where he stayed for six weeks until he had recovered, he could no longer sign his name. He dictated letters and got his secretary Elizabeth Moore (whom he called 'Dorinda') to sign his name for him.

To Henry Thorold   29 Radnor Walk
22 September 1981   London SW3

My dear Henry,
Last week I took up your *Lincolnshire Guide* thinking of you and our late friend Jack [Yates] and read it as though it were a thriller. Such it proved it be, it is funnier and succincter than any *Shell Guide*. Norton Disney is the funniest entry I know, I wish I had let you know before how much I liked the book.
    Yours ever, John B

H.T., the Lincolnshire squire/parson of Marston Hall, author, and a former master at Lancing College, had written, together with Jack Yates, the *Shell Guide to Lincolnshire* for JB which came out in 1965. H.T. and Yates, the legendary bookseller of Louth, had visited every church in Lincolnshire over a period of three years. The Norton Disney entry reads, 'Lost in the willows of the Brant, and surrounded by woods, this romantic village was once dominated by the castle of the Disney family whose name lives on in the creator of Mickey Mouse, a descendant of a junior branch.'

H.T. recalls that after Jack Yates had suffered a coronary JB said, 'I say, dear boy, I think our own dear friend Jack is rather sad having to give up his bookshop and he gets a bit bored sitting on his bum in Westgate. I think you and he ought to do a *Shell Guide* together. He'll do all the work, of course, but you and he can have some expeditions together in the school holidays.' JB then went to see Jack and said, 'I say, old boy, I think you and Henry ought to do a *Shell Guide* together. He'll do all the work, of course. . . .'

To Rupert Lycett Green   29 Radnor Walk
16 October 1981   London SW3

Dear Rupert,
Your friend Andrew Fraser came in this morning and gave me the welcome news that he had seen your photograph after you had won a race on the Cresta Run, after twenty years' silence. The last time you had competed was as a bachelor twenty years ago, now you were watched by Wibz and your five children. I am proud of you.
    Yours ever, JB

Andrew Fraser (1950–94), the dashing entrepreneur, was a founding partner of the firm Aid Call whose office was in Radnor Walk. He had given JB one of the very first experimental Aid Calls, an alarm button to hang round the neck and press in emergencies, especially for old people falling when alone. JB's alarm rang straight through to the Aid Call office. He began by using it sparingly and ended up pressing it several times a week to summon Andrew or his pretty secretary to come up the street and drink champagne with him. 'I can't open the bottle,' he would say.

To Stephen Spender   29 Radnor Walk
1 December 1981   London SW3

Dear Stephen,
Thursday November 19th was the happiest day of my life, I can hardly believe it has happened.

I often feel myself an interloper who has got in under false pretences; now, with your wonderful generosity, you have established me in my own estimation as quite a good poet, for here you are, the most eminent poet in England, giving me a present of your original poems. What more can a man want. Thank you.
  Yours ever, John B

In 1981 Roger Pringle, founder of the Celandine Press, conceived the idea of celebrating JB's seventy-fifth birthday by commissioning poems in his honour from over twenty poets. The result was *A Garland for the Laureate* published by the Press in an edition of three hundred and fifty copies, with a title-page woodcut by Miriam Macgregor depicting a garland of wild flowers. The poets who contributed were Dannie Abse, Kingsley Amis, Patricia Beer, Alan Brownjohn, Charles Causley, Leonard Clark, Patric Dickinson, Roy Fuller, Ted Hughes, Elizabeth Jennings, Philip Larkin, Edward Lowbury, Norman Nicholson, Alan Ross, A. L. Rowse, Sacheverell Sitwell, Stephen Spender, R. S. Thomas, Anthony Thwaite, John Wain, Ted Walker and Laurence Whistler. It was kept a secret from JB and the book was presented to him as a surprise one morning in November, with many of the poets present, including Philip Larkin and R. S. Thomas, who had arrived at Radnor Walk in a fleet of taxis, accompanied by bottles of champagne and smoked salmon sandwiches.

  JB wrote to Pringle (4 December 1981), 'The wild flowers in the Garland are innocently beautiful and make me think of the Christian names of the nurses who attended me at the Royal Hallamshire.'

To Phyllis Foran   29 Radnor Walk
5 January 1982   London sw3

Dear Phyllis,
I am so pleased with my braces, so is Archie who has no need to wear
them. I much appreciated that barley sugar.
    I am walking quite well but not perfectly yet.
    Happy New Year. Yours ever, John Betjeman

> P.F., a nurse from Mexborough in Yorkshire, recalled (in 1992), 'Lady Elizabeth always
> wrote to engage me when they came up to Moor View or Chatsworth House. I had a
> great affection for Sir John, he was always so kind and grateful whatever you did,
> however small his request. We had many a laugh as we talked to Archie. I had given him
> the braces for Christmas, and took him some barley sugar in hospital, but his favourite
> was Mackintosh's toffee deluxe.'

To Jonathan Stedall   29 Radnor Walk
8 March 1982   London sw3

Dear Jonathan,
I have thought of some objects worth filming, made at my father's little
factory built out over back gardens – 36 to 44 Pentonville Road, N1.
    They are beautiful, and I have been slow to realise this.
    Chiefly I think of an onyx cigarette box covered with vivid pieces of
lapis lazuli. The lid had a lazy hinge of gold enabling it to shut slowly
without cracking the lid. Eric Asprey showed it to me at Asprey's in
Bond Street. He also made very ingenious dressing cases with patent
concealed drawers. His skill as a designer of furniture I have only lately
fished out of my subconscience.
    He was a great man, and because he was deaf I feared him.
    Love to Jackie, John

> J.S. was making *Time with Betjeman*, a series of interviews with and about JB covering all
> his life from early childhood reminiscences to last regrets. It was screened over seven
> weeks starting 13 February 1983.

To Charles Thomson   29 Radnor Walk
17 May 1982   London SW3

Dear Mr Thomson,
I like your poems very much. Who is your favourite poet? At the
moment mine is Cowper but at any minute there may be another.
    I don't know what a poet is but I know you are one.
    Yours sincerely, John Betjeman.

> C.T. had sent JB his poems. He had never met him. 'His response to my poetry was a
> great source of encouragement and one I value very much. For the last five years I have
> been able to make a full-time living from my work as a poet,' he wrote (4 March 1992).

To Laura Hornak   29 Radnor Walk
30 July 1982   London SW3

Dear Laura,
My heart is too full for your loss. They were our oldest friends, your
parents were – that is to say Feeble's and mine. I felt they were so close
together that nothing could sunder them. I am very glad you took on
that agency work because it seemed the work you were destined for,
and your work will help to soften the loss of such a beloved parent as
Rachel.
    When I think of the hospitality your parents showed me and Feeble I
am sure it can never be replaced.
    My love to you and Angelo, John

> L.H. (née Cecil), the literary agent and JB's god-daughter, is the daughter of David
> and Rachel Cecil. Rachel had just died. Angelo H., her husband, had taken many of the
> photographs for JB's *A Pictorial History of English Architecture* (John Murray, 1971)
> designed and produced by George Rainbird.

To Roger Venables   29 Radnor Walk
6 November 1982   London SW3

Dear Mr Venables,
I hasten to reply although you bid me be silent.
    I think old Bosie Douglas was a good poet although he is still

overshadowed by scandal which has left him a period piece. I think that one of the most beautiful poems in the language is Kipling's 'The Way Through the Woods'. It is glorious to hear it read aloud. I try to remember that poem at night.

Thank you for saying such nice things about my poems, anything that boosts my ego is welcome as I lack confidence.

Yours sincerely, John Betjeman

> R.V., the Cornish poet, had corresponded with JB for many years.
> Rudyard Kipling's poem goes:
>
>> They shut the road through the woods
>> Seventy years ago
>> Weather and rain have undone it again,
>> And now you would never know
>> There was once a path through the woods
>> Before they planted the trees,
>> It is underneath the coppice and heath
>> And the thin anemones.
>> Only the keeper sees
>> That, where the ring-dove broods,
>> And the badger roll at ease,
>> There was once a road through the woods.

To Michael Bolan   29 Radnor Walk
18 May 1983   London sw3

Dear Michael Bolan,
Thank you for your letter and for sending me your poems. Poems are private to their writers and time alone will show whether they are good. It is important to say things in as few words as possible and as memorably. Repeat your verses out loud to yourself and then see if you can remember them.

You have my best wishes and they are my best.

Yours sincerely, John Betjeman

Much enjoyed your poem

> M.B., a fan who had never met JB, recalled, 'I'd read in the press that he was not well and had sent him some of my Cornish poems to remind him of Padstow. . . . I treasure this reply.'
> M.B. later published a collection of poems (1985) called *Amphorae*, dedicated to JB.

To Mrs Joan Dyer   29 Radnor Walk
31 May 1983   London sw3

Dear Mrs Dyer,

What a nice letter yours of 15th May was. Letters like yours make life worth living.

> Is life worth living?
> Yes, so long as the spring receives the year
> And hails it with the cuckoo's song.
> (Alfred Austin)

Thank you for taking the trouble to write to me.
  John Betjeman

J.D. of Manchester was a fan who had written saying how much she liked his poetry.

To Pansy Lamb   29 Radnor Walk
23 June 1983   London sw3

Darling Pansy,

It was lovely to hear from you from Rome. I am so glad you like my poetry read aloud, so do I. I think all poetry should be read aloud.

> The calm of Coombe Bissett
> Is tranquil and deep
> Where Ebbel flows soft
> Mid her downlands asleep
> And beauty to me came a-pushing a pram
> In the shape of sweet Pansy Felicia Lamb.

You sound as if you are happy in Rome. I am so glad.
  Love, John

After her husband the painter Henry Lamb died in 1960, JB's old friend the writer P.L. (née Pakenham, see *Volume One*) had eventually moved to Rome. Her early married life was spent at the village of Coombe Bissett in Wiltshire. She recalls, 'I had just written to him to say how much I had enjoyed the cassette of his reading his poems aloud. His reply also contained the first verse of a poem about me written in 1932 – the time when he had a romantic image of me. It is now lost but it was a sort of pastiche of a poem by Campbell. John represents himself as a poor boy standing outside the "doctor's white gate" (Henry had been a doctor in his youth). All I can remember is:

> I too could be arty, I too could get on
> With the Guinnesses, Gertler and Sickert and John.'

To Peter Parker   29 Radnor Walk
27 June 1983   London SW3

Dear Peter,

I can't express my thanks enough to you and to the Board of British Railways for its so generous treatment of me on Friday. It was a memorable day indeed and after it all things an anticlimax.

You could not have devised a more beautiful thing to present me with than the model of the Propylaeum at Euston.

Goodbye with great regret and my warmest good wishes for the future.

Yours ever, John

> P.P., the husband of JB's doctor Jill P., was at that time chairman of BR. On 24 June JB, silent and in a wheelchair, together with his eight-year-old grandson, David, unveiled 'Sir John Betjeman', an electric locomotive, number 86229, at St Pancras Station. Afterwards he was treated to a lunch in the General Manager's Mess at Euston. P.P. gave a short speech and presented JB with a large model of the Euston Arch in a glass dome.
>
> The latter was a sad memorial. JB had gone on fighting for the Arch's re-erection long after its demolition and wrote to the Architectural Department of British Rail (17 December 1970), 'And what excuse can your department give for refusing to re-erect Hardwick's Doric portico when even the demolisher, Mr Valori, offered to number the stones?' No satisfactory answer has ever been given.

To Osbert Lancaster   29 Radnor Walk
4 August 1983   London SW3

Dear Osbert,

I am glad it's your birthday. This is the first time I have expressed my feelings in writing. 'Many Happy Returns' sounds to me so formal but we survive to remember the Colonel and Toby, and Captain Pryce-Jones is still with us. Love to the old girl.

Bung ho, John B

> It was O.L.'s seventy-fifth birthday.

Twelve:

Epilogue

1983 to 1984

In May 1984 JB made his last journey to Trebetherick with Elizabeth and his nurses Carole and Vicky. PB had written to him, 'I wish you would not worry about me. . . . I am very happy and have had a very full and happy life and am now indulging myself by going to India again and I am very relieved to know that you will be well looked after by Elizabeth. . . . Please relax in Cornwall and don't fuss about anything and don't drink any WHISKY. Take Archie with you to keep a restraining eye on you. . . . *Don't* get any guilt at all about your little Plymmie: she loves you and only wants you to relax and not worry.'

I came down to see him at Treen and read the whole of *The Ordeal of Gilbert Pinfold* to him. He was utterly happy in Trebetherick. I could see it in his eyes. He was due to return to London by a special ambulance on 19 May. He must have heard it being arranged. I know that at that point he decided that he wanted to die at Treen.

Elizabeth read to him on the evening of Friday 18 May and Carole attended to him in the night and the early hours of Saturday. He died peacefully at 8.30 a.m. Elizabeth rang me at Blacklands and I rang my mother in Herefordshire. In a way, it was what we all wanted, but at the same time didn't. I went into the garden and picked every single parrot tulip that I had planted the autumn before. There must have been two or three hundred of them. I put them in the back of the car and later that afternoon my mother and I drove down to Cornwall. It felt like coming home. Everything was all right.

Elizabeth later wrote to Billa Harrod, 'I truly think those last months he was more serene and at peace than I have ever known him. No one will ever know how wonderful the two nurses Carole and Vicky were to him and it was so lucky that they were both down in Cornwall. He died on the most beautiful sunny morning with the sun streaming into the room and the French windows open and the lovely smell of the garden everywhere. Carole was holding one of his hands and me the other and Vicky was just gently holding his head and he had old Archie and Jumbo in each arm and Stanley the cat asleep on his tummy. He was completely conscious right up to that last moment. We none of us moved for nearly an hour afterwards and the sense of total peace was something I shall never forget. Then the nice vicar came and said some beautiful prayers and wouldn't even let me move Stanley the cat.'

John Ezard reported in what JB liked to call '*The* Manchester *Guardian*' on 23 May 1984, *Betjeman's rainswept burial among the Cornish dunes*:

It began when a boy from the suburbs was taken by horse and cart on his first holiday to Trebetherick before the First World War. He saw the 'wideness which the larksong gives the sky' and noticed how, as they reached the village by night:

> *The carriage lamp lit up the pennywort*
> *And fennel in the hedges of the lanes.*

It finished yesterday, with pennywort and fennel still flourishing in the hedges, when Sir John Betjeman, Poet Laureate and the Wordsworth of suburbia, was laid to rest by the light of oil lamps and by his own wish in the Norman village church of St Enodoc, the hermit, a place smaller than the smallest side-chapels of the City churches he also came to love.

St Enodoc stands in the heart of the north-western outcrop of Cornwall, around the river Camel estuary. He used to roll its names around his tongue: Polzeath, Chapel Amble, Padstow, Port Isaac, St Issey. The church's spire, hedged by tamarisk shrubs to screen the winds, peeps like a witch's hat from a little valley of grass-covered sand dunes where, Betjeman wrote, 'the silver snake of the estuary curls to sleep in Daymer Bay'.

The trouble for his funeral organisers was that the estuary was wide awake yesterday, blowing a horizontal monsoon and an umbrella-splintering wind. . . . The sand under the thin topsoil of the graveyard was so wet that the two gravediggers were worried that their work might collapse.

But everything came wonderfully right as the hearse drew near the church and the knots of local men and women stood outside throughout the private ceremony, drenched from head to toe.

The undertaker and six pall-bearers drove through the dunes until the track ran out three hundred yards away. Then they got out and bore the coffin very slowly and precisely through the rain up the winding slope to the lych gate, with still more valleys of dunes stretching in the background to the long rollers of the sea.

They carried the coffin not on their shoulders but in old-country fashion, on struts waist high, so that they could use the coffin rests in the middle of the lych gate when they reached it. As they walked the spectacle composed itself into the lines of a nineteenth-century coastal village painting by John Singer Sargent.

Only the closest relatives and friends were able to get into the church. The lessons were from Isaiah and from Ecclesiasticus and the Apocrypha, with its tribute to the modest youthfulness of writers of poetry. . . .

Sir John's widow and close relatives followed the coffin to the grave. Reporters were standing – by agreement with church officers – under the lych gate at the churchyard entrance. But the scale of the place was so intimate and Betjemanesque that as they peered out they made an ashamed discovery. It is possible, even when rainwater is streaming down people's faces, to tell that they are also crying.

I wrote a letter of thanks to John Ezard. This was his reply:

Dear Mrs Lycett Green,
Spending my own childhood holidays at Polzeath in the 1940s helped a little; but what helped much more was your father's own writings on the antiquity and violence of north Cornwall ('the sea wastes all'). As you will know, his name is a very happy one to mention there and elsewhere. The landlord of the Molesworth Arms, Wadebridge, gave me a fire and guest lounge to dry out and write in, refusing to accept money and saying, 'He was well thought of in these parts.' The tobacconist opposite sold me a thirty-five pound reject Waverley pipe for ten pounds. A Bodmin waitress said over breakfast, 'You'll get very wet but he was a good man.' In my home pub in Brentwood, Essex, on the evening after his death, I interrupted a Cup Final conversation on a very mixed table full by asking diffidently of country people and commuters, 'Does everyone know John Betjeman is dead?' and everybody talked about him for ten minutes, knowing him mostly from television but a surprising number from his written poems which turned out to have stimulated one, a young City insurance clerk, into attempting his own verse. A remarkable thing on Cup Final night.

Dramatis Personae

Amis, Sir Kingsley (b. 1922): Novelist and poet. Educated City of London School and St John's College, Oxford. Lectured in Swansea, then Cambridge (1949–63). First popular success, the novel *Lucky Jim* (1954), marked Amis out as one of the generation of young writers of the mid-1950s who challenged the established order. Others in the group included John Osborne and Colin Wilson. Amis's *Collected Poems 1944–79* came out in 1979. His novel *The Old Devils* (1986) won the Booker Prize. Knighted 1990.

Baring, Mollie, née Warner (b. 1912): Educated Endcliffe, Eastbourne and RADA. Daughter of successful racehorse owner, Ben Warner. Happily married to Desmond Baring for fifty-two years, and lives at Ardington House near Wantage. She was a Justice of the Peace for twenty-seven years.

Barnes, Anne (b. 1905): Daughter of Dr Henry Bond, Master of Trinity Hall, Cambridge. Married George Barnes in 1928. The confidante of many of her own and her son's generations.

Barnes, Anthony (b. 1931): Son of George and Anne Barnes. A scholar at Eton and King's College Cambridge. Worked for various companies before becoming Director of the Redundant Churches Fund, from which he retired in 1992. He moved to Norwich and is now Secretary to the North Norfolk Churches Trust.

Barnes, Sir George (1904–60): One of the most eminent BBC figures of the century. Long career, starting in the Talks Department in 1930. Became Head of the BBC's Third Programme in 1946 and finally Director of BBC TV in 1950. In 1956 became Principal of the University of South Staffordshire at Keele. Knighted 1953.

Beaton, Sir Cecil Walter Hardy (1904–80): Photographer and designer. Educated at Harrow and Cambridge. His photographs were exhibited in the National Portrait Gallery in 1968. He designed the costumes for both the New York and London stage productions of *My Fair Lady* as well as its film production and that of *Gigi*. Amongst his many publications are *Cecil Beaton's Fair Lady* (1964), *The Best of Beaton* (1968) and *The Magic Image* (1975).

Bowle, John Edward (1905–88): Historian and writer. Worked with JB on the *Heretick* at Marlborough. Later became a history master at Westminster School. Held many professorships in overseas universities and wrote over a dozen books including *England: A Portrait*, *The Concise Encyclopaedia of World History*, *Henry VIII: A Biography*, *The English Experience*, *Napoleon* and *Charles I: A Biography*.

Bowra, Sir Maurice (1898–1971): Classical scholar and writer. Dean and later Warden of Wadham College Oxford, he was renowned for his wit and humour. Spent his entire life at Oxford (where he took up JB), and became famous for his conversation, influencing a generation of English intellectuals. Published over thirty books. Knighted 1951.

Cavendish, Lady Elizabeth (b. 1926): The daughter of the 10th Duke of Devonshire. Extra Lady-in-Waiting to Princess Margaret since 1951, Justice of the Peace in London since 1961, chairman of the Cancer Research Campaign since 1981. A member of the Advertising Standards Authority between 1981 and 1991 and a lay member of the Disciplinary Committee of the General Council of the Bar since 1983. Chairman of the Board of Visitors for Wandsworth Prison 1970–73. Chairman of North Westminster Magistrates' Court between 1980 and 1983 and of the Inner London Juvenile Courts between 1983 and 1986. Member of the Council for St Christopher's Hospice and the Press Complaints Commission since 1991.

Cecil, Lord David (1902–86): Writer. Educated Eton and Christ Church, Oxford. Fellow of New College, Oxford 1939–69. Goldsmiths' Professor of English Literature 1948–69. President of the Poetry Society. Author of wide range of books on historical and literary subjects including *The Stricken Deer*, *Melbourne*, *Two Quiet Lives*, *Hardy the Novelist* and *Library Looking-glass*.

Clark, Sir Kenneth, later Baron (1903–83): Patron and interpreter of the arts. Educated Winchester and Trinity College, Oxford. Director of the National Gallery 1934–45 and chairman of the Arts Council

1953–60. Books on art inclue *The Nude*, *Landscape into Art*, *The Romantic Rebellion* and *The Gothic Revival*, all published by John Murray. His TV series *Civilization* made him a renowned public figure. Life peer.

Comper, Sir Ninian (1864–1960): The most distinguished pupil of the Victorian architect, George Frederick Bodley. The leading and most original ecclesiastical architect of his time. Refused to become registered which made his knighthood, for which JB pressed relentlessly, difficult to achieve. His principal works included the nave windows, Southwark Cathedral, and Warrior's Chapel at Westminster Cathedral. Knighted 1950.

Connolly, Cyril (1903–74): Literary journalist and intellectual. Educated Eton and Balliol College, Oxford. Wrote for *New Statesman* before Second World War. In 1939, with Stephen Spender, founded *Horizon* magazine which he edited until 1950. Lead reviewer on *Sunday Times* for over twenty years. Among his published books are *The Rock Pool* (a novel), *Enemies of Promise*, *The Unquiet Grave*, *The Condemned Playground*, *Previous Convictions* and *The Evening Colonnade*.

Cullinan, Patrick (b. 1933): Poet, critic and short story writer. Born in South Africa, he was sent to England to be educated at Charterhouse and Magdalen College, Oxford. Returned to South Africa to farm in the Transvaal and in the seventies founded the Bataleur Press for young South African writers. Has published three collections of poetry: *The Horizon Forty Miles Away*, *Today is Not Different* and *The White Hail in the Orchard*.

Devonshire, Deborah, Duchess of, née Mitford (born 1920): Writer and shopkeeper. Youngest daughter of the late 2nd Lord Redesdale. Married Lord Andrew Cavendish in 1941, who became 11th Duke of Devonshire in 1950. Her books include *The House – A Portrait of Chatsworth*, *The Estate – A View from Chatsworth*, *Farm Animals* and *Treasures of Chatsworth*. Her enterprises include the farm shop and other retail outlets at Chatsworth, the breeding of prize-winning Shetland ponies. For many years president and now chairman of the Children's Society in Derbyshire and trustee of the Royal Collections.

Driberg, Tom (Thomas Edward Neil), MP (1905–76): Journalist and politician. At Oxford with JB. Wrote the 'William Hickey' gossip column for the *Daily Express* 1923–43, and subsequently employed by

Reynolds News and the *New Statesman*. A life-long Anglo-Catholic and Socialist, he entered Parliament in 1942, and was chairman of the Labour Party from 1957 to 1958. His homosexual promiscuity (paraded in his posthumous autobiography, *Ruling Passions*) inhibited further promotion in the Commons. Nevertheless in 1975 he was created a Life Peer with the title of Lord Bradwell.

Eliot, Thomas Stearns (1888–1965): Poet, playwright, critic, editor and publisher. Perhaps the most influential poet of the twentieth century. A prolific writer, his most famous works were *The Waste Land*, *The Four Quartets* and *Old Possum's Book of Practical Cats*, and his plays include *The Cocktail Party* and *Murder in the Cathedral*. Order of Merit 1948.

Elton, Sir Arthur, Bt (1906–73): One of the pioneers of documentary film-making. Publisher of the *North Somerset Mercury*, governor of the British Film Institute 1949–50, director of Shell International Petroleum Company in charge of films and television 1957–60 and wrote books on the history of technology. Lived at Clevedon Court, Somerset. Ran a private press in the early twenties.

Fallowell, Duncan (b.1948): Writer. Came to know JB while at St Paul's School; subsequently at Magdalen College, Oxford. Wrote about JB in his *20th Century Characters* (published 1994).

Girouard, Mark (b. 1931). Writer and architectural custodian. *Life in the English Country House* is the best known of his numerous books. Worked on *Country Life*, was Slade Professor of Fine Art, Oxford, 1975–76, chairman of the Spitalfields Historic Buildings Trust 1977–83, and sits or has sat on various commissions and committees. Married Dorothy Dorf, painter, from Chicago, and has one daughter, Blanche. One of JB's three literary executors.

Goodhart-Rendel, H. S. (1887–1959): Musician and architect. Studied music at Cambridge, but practised as an architect from 1910. Professor of Fine Art at Oxford 1933–36 and governor of the Architectural Association and RIBA in the forties. Vice-president of the Royal Academy of Music in the fifties. Wrote on architecture and fine art, particularly English architecture since the Regency.

Hadfield, John Charles Heywood (b. 1907): Author and editor, deputy chairman of the Rainbird Publishing Company. He edited the annual devoted to the arts, the *Saturday Book*, between 1952 and 1973 and frequently persuaded JB to contribute. He also edited *The Shell Guide to England* and *The Shell Book of English Villages*. His book *Love on a Branch Line* has recently been filmed for BBC television.

Harrod, Wilhelmine, née Cresswell (b. 1911): Known as Billa. Married Roy Harrod, the economist, in 1938. He was knighted in 1959. A keen conservationist, she has been involved with the Council for the Protection of Rural England, Oxford Preservation Trust, Historic Churches Preservation Trust and was briefly secretary of the Georgian Group. Wrote *The Shell Guide to Norfolk* (1957). Founded Norfolk Churches Trust in 1970. Awarded OBE 1992.

Hart-Davis, Sir Rupert (b. 1907): Author, editor and publisher. Director of Rupert Hart-Davis publishers. Married (first) Peggy Ashcroft in 1929. Director of Jonathan Cape in the thirties. Edited the letters of Oscar Wilde and the diaries of Siegfried Sassoon. Published six volumes of the Lyttelton Hart-Davis letters. In 1960 published the poems of Charles Tennyson Turner, edited by JB. Knighted 1967.

Humphries, Barry (b. 1934): Music-hall artiste and author. Educated Melbourne Grammar School and University of Melbourne. Theatre shows include *Housewife Superstar* (1976), *A Night with Dame Edna* (1979), *An Evening's Intercourse with Barry Humphries* (1981–82), *Tears Before Bedtime* (1986), *Back with a Vengeance* (1987). His TV series include *The Dame Edna Experience* (1987). Numerous other plays, films and broadcasts. Publications include *Les Patterson's Australia* (1979), *Dame Edna's Bedside Companion* (1982), *My Gorgeous Life: the Autobiography of Dame Edna Everage* (1989). Now married to Lizzie, daughter of Sir Stephen Spender.

Irvine, Gerard, The Reverend Prebendary (b. 1920): Priest of the Church of England. Ordained in 1945, he ministered in various parishes, including St Thomas's Regent Street (where Dorothy L. Sayers was churchwarden) and finally St Matthew's, Westminster. Installed a Prebendary of St Paul's Cathedral 1985.

James, Edward (1907–84): Publisher. Educated Eton and Christ Church, Oxford. Godson of Edward VII and fabulously rich. Published JB's first volume of poetry, *Mount Zion*. Married the actress Tilly Losch and was a notable patron of the Surrealists, especially

Magritte and Dali. Ended his days living in Mexico and designed buildings there.

Jarvis, Wilfrid Harry (b. 1920): Parish priest. Educated King Alfred's School, Wantage and Leeds University. Attended College of the Resurrection, Mirfield, Yorkshire. Ordained a priest in Oxford 1946. Became assistant priest at St Margaret's, North Oxford 1946 and chaplain at Summerfields School, Oxford 1948. In 1965 became vicar of St Augustine's, New Basford until it was pulled down in 1979 and then of St Aidan's, Old Basford until 1993.

Jenkins, Simon David (b. 1943): Editor and journalist. Educated at Mill Hill School and St John's College, Oxford. He has edited both the *London Evening Standard* and *The Times* and still writes a twice-weekly column for *The Times*. He has also written for the *Economist* and the *Sunday Times*. An inveterate lover of London and fighter against mediocre development. His publications include *A City at Risk* (1971), *The Battle for the Falklands* (with Max Hastings 1983), *The Selling of Mary Davies and Other Writings* (1993) and *The Complete Guide to Outer London* (1981).

Kennet, Wayland Hilton Young, 2nd Baron (b. 1923): Writer and politician. Educated at Stowe and Trinity College, Cambridge. Labour Spokesman on Science, Foreign Affairs and the Environment 1971–74. Parliamentary Secretary for Ministry of Housing and Local Government 1966–70. Wrote *Old London Churches* with Elizabeth, his wife, amongst other books and pamphlets.

Kinross, Patrick Balfour, 3rd Baron (1904–76): Author and journalist. Worked in Fleet Street in the thirties on the editorial staff of various newspapers including the *Daily Sketch*, *Weekly Dispatch* and *Evening Standard*. Travelled extensively in Africa and the Middle East. Met JB at Oxford and later served with him as a member of the Georgian Group. Wrote seventeen books including *Society Racket*, *Europa Minor*, *Portrait of Greece*, *Atatürk: the Rebirth of a Nation* and *Portrait of Egypt*.

Lancaster, Sir Osbert (1908–86): Artist, cartoonist and architectural writer. Educated Charterhouse and Lincoln College, Oxford. Best known for his famous series of pocket cartoons in the *Daily Express* through which he became a national institution. He was also one of the most stylish writers of his generation, and wrote light-hearted architectural books. Designed theatre sets for Covent Garden, Sadlers Wells, Glyndebourne etc. Wrote two volumes of autobiography. Married Karen Harris 1933 (died 1964), Anne Scott-James 1967. Knighted 1975.

Larkin, Philip (Arthur) (1922–85): Poet and novelist. Educated King Henry VIII School, Coventry and St John's College, Oxford, where he was a contemporary of Kingsley Amis. Developed a taste for jazz during his time at Oxford which bore fruit in the collection of essays *All What Jazz* in 1970. From 1943 onwards worked in various libraries before eventually becoming Librarian of the Brynmor Jones Library, University of Hull. His *Collected Poems* were published in 1988 by Faber and Faber.

Lees-Milne, James (b. 1908): Author. Educated Eton and Magdalen College, Oxford. On the staff of the National Trust for thirty years until 1966, latterly (1951–66) as their Adviser on Historic Buildings. His book *Roman Mornings* (1956) won him the Heinemann Award in that year. He also wrote *Worcestershire: a Shell Guide* (1964), four volumes of diaries covering the years 1942–49 and *People and Places*, a book about the owners of twelve National Trust houses. In 1994 he published a further volume of diaries *A Mingled Measure (1952–73)*.

Leigh Fermor, Joan, née Eyres-Monsell (b. 1912): Photographer and traveller. Brought up at Dumbleton in Worcestershire. Married John Rayner 1938. Kept company with the travel writer Patrick Leigh Fermor from 1946 onwards and married him in 1968.

Lloyd, John (Davies Knatchbull) (1900–78): Educated Winchester and Trinity College, Oxford. Mayor of Montgomery 1932–38 and 1961–62. Member of the Historic Buildings Council for Wales 1953–75, Ancient Monuments Board for Wales 1954–78. Editor of *Archaeologia Cambrensis*, 1956–69.

Liddiard, Ron (b. 1913): Farmer and writer. In Observer Corps with JB in Uffington during Second World War. In 1971 wrote a book about the racehorse, *Baulking Green*, with a foreword by Lord Oaksey. At present writing his memoirs.

Mackenzie, Sir Compton (1883–1972): Educated St Paul's School and Magdalen College, Oxford. Author of *Whisky Galore* as well as the *Four*

Winds of Love series. Editor of the *Gramophone* 1923–61. His auto-biography *My Life and Times* was published in ten volumes, *Octaves One to Ten*, between 1963 and 1971.

Mirzoeff, Edward (b.1936): Television director, producer and editor. Joined the BBC in 1963 and co-directed the first-ever BBC colour transmission. Directed and produced many film documentaries for the BBC including *Metroland*, *A Passion for Churches* and *The Queen's Realm* with JB. His first major series was *Bird's Eye View* (1969–71), shot entirely from a helicopter. He has been nominated seven times for BAFTA awards and won three.

Mitford, The Hon. Nancy (1904–73): Writer. Eldest daughter of the 2nd Lord Redesdale. Published her first novel in 1931 and continued to write light fiction in the thirties, but didn't make her name until 1945 with *The Pursuit of Love*. Also wrote biography and history. Is well known for her editing of *Noblesse Oblige* which popularized the concept of U and non-U.

Moyne, Bryan Guinness, 2nd Baron (1905–92): Poet, novelist and playwright. Educated Eton and Christ Church, Oxford. Called to Bar 1930. A governor of the National Gallery of Ireland. Wrote many books and published several collections of poetry. Books include *Landscape with Figures* (1934), *A Week by the Sea* (1936), *The Children in the Desert* (1947), *Priscilla and the Prawn* (1960). His plays were *The Fragrant Concubine* and *A Riverside Charade*. Married Diana Mitford 1929 and Elizabeth Nelson 1936.

Murray, John (1909–93): Educated Eton and Magdalen College, Oxford. Universally known as 'Jock', he was in fact John Murray VI in England's oldest dynastic publishing house, founded in 1768. He published JB's *Continual Dew* in 1937 and from then on was JB's main publisher. He became a close personal friend of JB and others of his stable, including Osbert Lancaster, Kenneth Clark, Patrick Leigh Fermor and Freya Stark.

Ormsby Gore, Archibald (b. 1908): Archaeologist. Strict Baptist, and very easily shocked. JB's constant friend and mainstay. Has suffered many operations on his nose and has lived all his life with Jumbo, who hardly ever speaks.

Osborne, John (James) (1929–95): Dramatist and actor. Educated at Belmont College, Devon. His plays *Look Back in Anger* (1956), *The Entertainer* (1957) and *Luther* (1961) established him as one of the 'Angry Young Men' of the fifties and sixties. His outpourings of rage against 'the Establishment' were his strongest theatrical weapon. His work was often known as 'Kitchen Sink Drama' due to its portrayal of working class characters with emphasis on domestic realism.

Perry, Lionel (1905–80): The grandson of a Church of Ireland clergyman and son of J. F. Perry, a Fellow of All Souls College, Oxford. At Magdalen College, Oxford, before being sent down for failing preliminary exams. Volunteered as Air Gunner in the war. Lived in County Donegal, Ireland, from the fifties, looking after his ailing mother.

Piper, John (1903–92): Painter, water-colourist, ceramicist, engraver, printmaker, stage designer, photographer, writer, deviser of firework displays and stained-glass artist. His many church windows include one for the new Coventry Cathedral and the memorial glass in Farnborough for JB. Collaborated on *Shell Guides* and illustrated many of JB's works including *Church Poems*.

Piper, Myfanwy, née Evans (b. 1909): Read English at St Hilda's College, Oxford. In the thirties she edited *Axis*, journal of French and British *avant garde* art and *The Painter's Object*. Married John Piper 1937 and had four children. Author of *Frances Hodgkins* for Penguin Modern Painters series. Wrote the librettos for operas by Benjamin Britten: *The Turn of the Screw*, *Owen Wingrave* and *Death in Venice*, and others for Alan Hoddinott.

Plomer, William (1903–73): Poet. President of the Poetry Society 1968–71. Founded and edited *Voorslag* with Roy Campbell and Laurens Van der Post. On the fringes of the Bloomsbury Group. Literary consultant to Jonathan Cape where he discovered Ian Fleming, creator of James Bond. His collected poems were published in 1960 and he wrote several librettos for Benjamin Britten.

Powell, Anthony (b. 1905): Novelist. Educated Eton and Balliol College, Oxford. His novels include *Afternoon Men*, *From A View to a Death* and the series *A Dance to the Music of Time*. Has written four volumes of memoirs and was a Trustee of the National Portrait Gallery 1962–76.

Married to Lady Violet (née Pakenham). Companion of Honour 1988.

Pryce-Jones, Alan (b. 1908): Author, critic, journalist. Worked on the *London Mercury* 1928–32. Contributed to the *Times Literary Supplement* and was editor from 1948 to 1959. Critic on *New York Herald Tribune* 1963–66. The title of his autobiography, *The Bonus of Laughter*, is taken from a line of JB's poem 'The Last Laugh'.

Roberts, Cecil (Cedric Mornington) (1892–1976): Literary editor of the *Liverpool Post* 1915–18 and editor of the *Nottingham Journal* 1920–25. Won the Kirke White Memorial Prize in 1912 with his first published poem 'The Trent'. In 1965, made an Honorary Freeman of the City of Nottingham. A prolific writer of poems, plays and prose works. His autobiography, *The Growing Boy*, was published in 1967.

Rosse, Anne, Countess of, née Messel (1902–93). Formerly married to Captain Armstrong-Jones, she married JB's friend Michael Rosse in 1935. Was at various times châtelaine of Birr Castle in Ireland, Nymans in Sussex, Womersley in Yorkshire, and most famously of 18 Stafford Terrace, London. The latter inspired her and JB to form the Victorian Society in 1958. She was one of Britain's leading gardeners.

Rosse, Lawrence Michael Harvey Parsons, 6th Earl of (1906–79): Educated Eton and Christ Church, Oxford. Vice-Chancellor of the University of Dublin 1949–65. Trustee of the Historic Churches Preservation Trust 1961–76. President of the Friends of the National Collections of Ireland and Ancient Monuments Society. Chairman of the Georgian Group 1946–68.

Savidge, Kenneth (b. 1927): Television producer. Joined BBC West Region in Bristol in 1951. Later worked in the Middle East, India, Pakistan and Ireland. Produced JB's *ABC of Churches*, *Betjeman's Belfast*, *Betjeman's Dublin* and others.

Sassoon, Siegfried Loraine (1886–1967): Poet. Educated Marlborough and Clare College, Cambridge. A prose writer on country pursuits, as well as more famously a war poet, his semi-autobiographical trilogy *Memoirs of a Fox Hunting Man* (1928), *Memoirs of an Infantry Officer* (1928) and *Sherston's Progress* (1936) relates the life of a lonely boy, whose loves are cricket and hunting and who is brutally matured by life in the trenches of the First World War.

Shand, Philip Morton (1888–1960): Writer. Educated Eton and King's College, Cambridge. Wrote books on food and architecture including *A Book of Food*, *A Book of Wine* and *The Architecture of Pleasure*, and translated *The New Architecture* and *The Bauhaus*. Influential contributor to the *Architectural Review* during the early thirties.

Skinner, Martyn (1906–94): Writer. Winner of the Hawthornden Prize in 1943 and Heinemann Award in 1947. Wrote *The Return of Arthur*, *Letters to Malaya I and II*, *Two Men of Letters* and *Alms for Oblivion*.

Sparrow, John (Hanbury Angus) (1906–92): Barrister, scholar, bibliophile and Warden of All Souls College, Oxford 1952–77. Educated Winchester and New College, Oxford. Double first. Elected Fellow of All Souls 1929, re-elected 1937 and 1946. Called to the Bar 1931. Distinguished military career. Various reviews and essays in periodicals. Publications include *Independent Essays*, *Controversial Essays*, *Sense and Poetry*, *After the Assassination* and *Visible Words*.

Spender, Sir Stephen (Harold), (1909–95): Poet and critic. Brought up in Hampstead and educated at University College School, London and University College, Oxford. His time in Hamburg and Berlin during the years after he left Oxford sharpened his political consciousness particularly due to his mother's German-Jewish ancestors. His autobiography *World Within World* (1951) revealed his links with the Communist Party and it was this and other similar writings which tended to obscure the intensely personal nature of his poetry, for example the elegies for his sister-in-law in *Poems of Dedication* (1947) as well as much of the work in *Collected Poems 1928–53* (1955).

Stedall, Jonathan (b. 1938): Documentary film-maker. Educated Harrow. Made first television films with JB for Television Wales and West in 1962–63. Worked for twenty-seven years with BBC where he made further films with JB: *I. K. Brunel* (1965), *Thank God It's Sunday* (1972), *Summoned by Bells* (1976) and seven-part autobiographical series *Time With Betjeman* (1983). Also directed *A Passion for India* with Penelope Chetwode (Lady Betjeman) in 1974.

Stern, Gladys Bertha (1890–1973): Started writing plays at the age of eight and wrote her first novel at twenty. Also worked at studios in Hollywood and Denham. Amongst her many publications were *The Donkey Shoe* and *The Patience of a Saint*. Also wrote reviews and short stories and was a freelance journalist.

Summerson, Sir John (1904–92): Architect and architectural historian. Lecturer in History of Architecture at Architectural Association 1949–62. Various other lectureships and professorships in the UK and USA. Curator of Sir John Soane's Museum. Wrote on architecture including books on the work of Sir John Soane, Sir Christopher Wren, Inigo Jones and John Nash. Knighted 1958.

Taylor, Geoffrey (1900–56): Born Geoffrey Phibbs, but later took his mother's name. Writer and editor of anthologies, principal works include *English, Scottish and Welsh Landscapes* and *English Love Poems* (both edited with JB), *Insect Life in Britain, Some Nineteenth Century Gardeners, The Emerald Isle* and *The Victorian Flower Garden*.

Waugh, Evelyn (1903–66): Novelist. Educated Lancing and Hertford College, Oxford. Major works include *Decline and Fall, Vile Bodies, A Handful of Dust, Put Out More Flags, Brideshead Revisited, The Loved One* and *Helena* which was dedicated to Penelope Betjeman. Became a Roman Catholic 1930.

Wicklow, William Cecil James Philip John Paul Howard, 8th Earl of, formerly Lord Clonmore (1902–78): A zealous Anglo-Catholic. On leaving Oxford worked at the Magdalen Mission in Somers Town, and was ordained deacon before proceeding to the priesthood. Converted to Roman Catholicism and thereafter lived as a layman. Served in the Second World War as a Captain in the Royal Fusiliers. Succeeded to the Earldom in 1946 and in 1959 married Eleanor Butler, a Senator in the Irish Parliament.

Wilson, Mary, née Baldwin: Married to Harold, Lord Wilson of Rievaulx, the ex-Prime Minister. She was born at Diss, the daughter of a Congregational minister. Spent her childhood in East Anglia and has lived in various parts of the country, including the Lake District and Sussex, where she was at school. Began to write poetry at the age of six, and published *Selected Poems* (1970) and *New Poems* (1980). Has two sons and twin granddaughters, and now lives part of the time in London and part of the time in the Isles of Scilly.

Zuckerman, Solly, Baron (1904–92): Educated South African Collegiate School, University of Cape Town (Liberman Scholar), University College Hospital, London (Goldsmid Exhibitioner). Chief Scientific Officer to HM Government 1964–71. Had been honorary secretary to the Zoological Society of London 1955–77 before becoming the president in 1977. Made Baron Zuckerman of Burnham Thorpe in 1971 (life peer). Published a string of books on scientific themes as well as editing *The Zoological Society of London 1826–1976 and Beyond* (published 1977).

List of nicknames

Arne	Anne Baring
Bess	Mabel Betjemann
Billa	Wilhelmine Harrod
Captain Bog	Alan Pryce-Jones
The Colonel	G. A. Kolkhorst
The Commander	George Barnes
Coolmore	John Summerson
Cracky, Cracky William, Crax	William Wicklow
Feeble, Phoeble	Elizabeth Cavendish
Mrs Folky	Sybil Harton
Goldilegz	Myfanwy Piper
Gramelope(Grandmama Penelope)	Penelope Betjeman (to LG children)
Griggers	Geoffrey Grigson
Groundsell	Graham Eyres-Monsell
Kingers	Kingsley Amis
Kneecoal	Nicole Hornby
Little Friend	Princess Margaret
Little Prawls	Anthony Barnes
MD (Mad Dadz)	JB to CLG
The Mosquito, Pa'rick	Patrick Kinross
Obscurity	Hubert de Cronin Hastings
Old Top	Osbert Lancaster
Mr Pahper, Mr Piper	John Piper
Plymouth, Plymmie	Penelope Betjeman
Powlie	Paul Betjeman
The Sarcophagus	George Schurhoff
Spansbury	John Sparrow
Tewpie	JB to PB
Wibz, Wibbly Wobbly	Candida Lycett Green
The Widow	John Lloyd
Woad	Philip Chetwode
Mrs Woad	Hester Chetwode

Index